MAINE DE BIRAN TO SARTRE

A
HISTORY OF PHILOSOPHY

VOLUME IX
MAINE DE BIRAN TO SARTRE

BY
.FREDERICK COPLESTON, S.J.

Professor Emeritus of Philosophy in the
University of London

SEARCH ● LONDON

PAULIST PRESS ● NEW JERSEY

Published in the United States by
Paulist Press
997 Macarthur Boulevard, Mahwah, N.J. 07430

Published in Great Britain by
Search Press Limited
Wellwood, North Farm Road
Tunbridge Wells, Kent TN2 3DR, England

First published 1975

ISBN (USA) 0–8091–0196–3
ISBN (UK) 0 85532 341 8

Printed and bound in the
United States of America

CONTENTS

CONTENTS

PREFACE

THE seventh and eighth volumes of this work were originally intended to cover nineteenth-century philosophy in Germany and in Great Britain respectively. The seventh volume conforms to this plan, inasmuch as it ends with a treatment of Nietzsche who died in 1900 and whose period of literary activity falls entirely within the nineteenth century. The eighth volume however includes treatments of G. E. Moore, Bertrand Russell and the American philosopher John Dewey. All three were born in the nineteenth century; and both Dewey and Russell had published before the turn of the century. But all were active well on into the twentieth century. Indeed, Russell was still alive when the volume was published and was able to make an appreciative comment in a letter to the author. The present ninth volume carries even further this tendency to go beyond the limits of nineteenth-century thought. It was originally intended to cover French philosophy between the revolution and the death of Henri Bergson. In point of fact it includes a fairly extensive treatment of Jean-Paul Sartre, a briefer outline of some of Merleau-Ponty's ideas and some remarks on the structuralism of Lévi-Strauss.

This extension of the account of French philosophy after the revolution to include a number of thinkers whose literary activity falls within the twentieth century and some of whom at any rate are still alive has meant that I have been unable to fulfil my original plan of including within the present volume treatments of nineteenth-century thought in Italy, Spain and Russia. Reference has been made to one or two Belgian thinkers, such as Joseph Maréchal; but otherwise I have restricted the area to France. Indeed, it is more accurate to say that I have treated of French philosophers than of philosophy in France as a geographical area. For example, Nikolai Berdyaev settled at Paris in 1924 and pursued a vigorous literary activity on French soil. But it seems to me improper to annex him for France. He belongs to the religious tradition in Russian thought. There may indeed be more reason for annexing Berdyaev for French philosophy than there would be for counting Karl Marx as a British philosopher on the ground that he spent his last years in London and worked in the British Museum. At the same time the Russian writers who lived and wrote in exile in France remained Russian thinkers.

If we leave foreign exiles out of account, France is in any case rich in philosophical writers, both professional philosophers and literary figures whose writings can be described as having philosophical significance. Unless however the historian proposes to write a complete comprehensive survey, which would amount to little more than a list of names or require several tomes, he cannot include them all. There are of course philosophers who obviously have to be included in any account of French philosophy since the revolution. Maine de Biran, Auguste Comte and Henri Bergson are examples. It is also clear that discussion of a given movement of thought entails reference to its leading representatives. Whatever may be one's estimate of Victor Cousin's merits as a thinker, it would be absurd to write about eclecticism in France without saying something about its chief representative, especially in view of the position which he occupied for a time in the academic life of his country. Similarly, an account of neo-criticism involves some discussion of Renouvier's thought. Though however there is a considerable number of philosophers whom the historian would rightly be expected to include, either because of their intrinsic interest and their reputation, contemporary or posthumous, or as representatives of a given movement of thought, there are plenty of others among whom he has to make a selection. And any selection is open to criticism on some ground or other. Thus in regard to the present volume some readers may be inclined to think that space has been allotted to cloudy metaphysicians and idealists which might have been more profitably devoted to philosophy of education or to aesthetics, or to a more extended treatment of social philosophy. Again, if a religious thinker such as Teilhard de Chardin is to be given prominence, why is there no mention of Simone Weil, a very different sort of writer, it is true, but one who has been widely read? Further, in view of the fact that the volume includes a treatment not only of nineteenth-century French political thinkers but also of Sartre's version of Marxism, why is nothing said, for example, about Bertrand de Jouvenel and Raymond Aron?

In the cases of some philosophers it may be relevant to point out that reputation and influence in their own country may very well justify their inclusion, in spite of the fact that in a country with a different philosophical tradition they are little known or read. The reader presumably wishes to hear something about thinkers who have enjoyed some prominence in France, even if they are pretty well unknown in England. Indeed, if their names are little known in England, this could be advanced as an excellent reason for including them. The thought of Louis Lavelle, for instance, would doubtless have left G. E. Moore in a state of mystification; and it would hardly have commended itself to J. L. Austin. But this is no more a reason for omitting Lavelle from an account of recent French philosophy than the lack of sympathy which many French philosophers would probably have with J. L. Austin's preoccupation with ordinary language would constitute a valid reason for omitting Austin's name from an account of recent philosophical thought in Great Britain.

At the same time it must be admitted that there are gaps in the present volume. This is partly due of course to considerations of space. But it is only honest to add that it is partly due to the circumstances in which this volume has been written. If one is Principal of a School of the University of London, one's time for reading and research is inevitably very limited. And one has to use for writing such intervals as may occur. I have doubtless tended to write about philosophers of whom I already knew something and have omitted thinkers who might well have been included. This might be considered a very sound reason for postponing completion of the work. As however I have already indicated, I wish to use the time which retirement may put at my disposal for a rather different sort of volume.

Even when one has decided, for good or ill, on the philosophers about whom one intends to write, there may well be problems of classification or labelling. For example, in the present work Jules Lachelier has been considered in the chapter devoted to what is customarily described as the spiritualist movement. Though however there is precedent for doing this, Lachelier's best-known work is a treatise on the foundations of induction; and it might thus be thought more appropriate to put his ideas under the heading of philosophy of science. At the same time he develops his ideas in such a way as to outline a philosophy which would qualify him for classification as an idealist. Again, while Meyerson has been considered in the text as a philosopher of science, his theory of identity might equally well be treated as a speculative philosophy of the idealist type.

Talk about problems of classification may appear to be the expression of a misguided desire to fit all philosophers into neatly labelled pigeon-holes or of a failure to appreciate the complexities of human life and thought. Or it may seem that one has fallen victim to the bewitching influence of language, imagining that one enjoys conceptual mastery over what one has named. The matter is not however quite so simple. For hesitation in regard to labelling may express not so much a passion for pigeon-holing as a real difficulty in deciding which aspect or aspects of a man's thought are to be regarded as the most significant. The question arises of course: significant in what respect? Consider the case of Berkeley in British philosophy. If an historian is intent on tracing the development of classical British empiricism, he is likely to emphasize those aspects of Berkeley's thought which make it plausible to regard it as a link between Locke and Hume. This has been a common enough procedure. If however the historian is more concerned with Berkeley's declared interests and with the bishop's own estimation of the significance of his philosophy, stress will be laid on the metaphysical aspects of Berkeley's thought and on its religious bearing. Similarly, if an historian is concerned with exhibiting a movement of thought leading up to the philosophy of Bergson, he is likely to label as a 'spiritualist' a writer such as Lachelier, whose thought, considered by itself, might well be given a different label. Again, in the present volume Brunschvicg's philosophy has been treated under the general heading of idealism. But if one thought that idealism was undeserving of attention, one might include Brunschvicg among philosophers of science. For he certainly had something to say on the subject.

Classificatory problems might indeed be avoided by treating the development of philosophical thought in terms of problems and themes, as Windelband did, rather than by taking philosophers in succession and treating the thought of each as one block. This procedure might seem to be especially appropriate in the case of French philosophers, who have frequently had wide-ranging interests and have written on a variety of topics. Though however this procedure has much to commend it, it also has disadvantages for the reader who wishes to devote his uninterrupted attention to a particular philosopher but is unable to find his thought considered as a whole. In any case, in this ninth volume I did not wish to change the procedure which has been followed, for good or ill, in the preceding volumes. There will be scope for a different approach in the projected tenth and final volume.

Reference has been made above to cloudy metaphysicians. This remark should not of course be understood as a judgment on French philosophy. The present writer is not indeed quite so impressed as some people seem to be by the common assertion that French thought is conspicuous for its logical structure and clarity. This may apply to Descartes, the foremost French philosopher; and the writers of the Enlightenment were doubtless clear. But some more recent thinkers seem to have done their best to rival the obscure language which we tend to associate with German philosophy since Kant. It is not that they are unable to write clearly. For they often do. But in their professional philosophical writings they seem to prefer to express their ideas in turgid jargon. Sartre is a case in point. And as for the metaphysicians, talk about *l'être* is not necessarily more illuminating than talk about *das Sein*. At the same time it would be quite wrong to imply that French philosophy is predominantly concerned with metaphysical obscurities. A concern with man is a much more conspicuous feature. The first notable philosopher to be treated in this volume, Maine de Biran, approached philosophy by way of psychology; and it was reflection on man's inner life which led him to metaphysics. The last philosopher to be discussed at some length, Jean-Paul Sartre, is a thinker who has concentrated on man as a free agent and whose personal commitment in the social and political area is well known.

Obviously, philosophers can be concerned with man in different ways. Some have focussed their attention on man's spontaneous activity and freedom, as with Maine de Biran and in what is commonly described at the spiritualist movement in French philosophy, while others, such as Le Senne, have emphasized man's recognition of values and his transcending of the empirically given. Other philosophers have dwelt more on the life of thought and on man's reflection on the mind's activity as manifested in history. Brunschvicg is a case in point. These various approaches have tended to broaden out into general interpretations of reality. Ravaisson, for example, started with reflection on habit and ended with a general view of the world, while Bergson reflected on man's experiences of duration and of voluntary activity and developed a religiously oriented philosophy of the universe. In the case of those who concentrated their attention on the mind's self-criticism and its reflection on its own activity, as manifested in various spheres, the resulting general view has tended to be of an idealist type.

With other thinkers the emphasis has been laid on man in society. This can of course take the form of objective and dispassionate inquiry, as in, for example, the sociology of Émile Durkheim or the structuralist anthropology of Lévi-Strauss. Reflection on man in society can also be pursued in a spirit of commitment, with a view to promoting action or change rather than simply with the aim of understanding. This was naturally the case in the aftermath of the revolution. In the first chapter of this volume attention is paid to a group of thinkers who were deeply concerned with the reconstruction of society and who believed that it could not be effected except through the reassertion of certain threatened traditions. In the fourth chapter another group of thinkers are briefly considered who were convinced that while the revolution had overthrown the old régime, its ideals had still to be realized in positive social construction and development. For the matter of that, Auguste Comte, the high priest of positivism, was profoundly concerned with the organization of society, even if he had a rather naïve faith in the perfecting of society through the development of scientific knowledge. At a later period we find a similar spirit of commitment, manifested in a desire to transform society either through Marxist-inspired revolution, as with Sartre, or through the development of a more personalist socialism, as with Emmanuel Mounier.

Such distinguishable lines of thought are not of course all mutually exclusive. They can be found in varying degrees of combination. The thought of Sartre is an obvious example. On the one hand he has laid great emphasis on human freedom and on the individual's choice of his own values and on the way in which the individual gives meaning to his life. On the other hand he has emphasized self-commitment in the social–political sphere and the need for the transformation of society. The effort to combine the two lines of thought, individualistic and social, has led to his attempt to present a version of Marxism which incorporates in itself an existentialist insistence on human freedom. It is no matter for surprise if he has found difficulty in combining his conviction that it is man who both makes history and gives it meaning with the Marxist tendency to depict history as a dialectical and teleological process, or in combining his existentialism, with its 'every man is an island' atmosphere, with a Marxist emphasis on the social group. The point is however that in the thought of Sartre the emphasis on human freedom which was characteristic of the line of thought stemming from Maine de Biran has met the line of thought which lays stress on man in society and regards the French revolution as simply one stage in an unfinished process of social transformation.

To claim that concern with man has been a conspicuous feature of French philosophy is not of course to assert that philosophy in France has been concerned simply with man. Such an assertion would be clearly untrue. If however we compare recent philosophical thought in France with recent British philosophy, it is evident that what Georges-André Malraux has described as 'the human condition' occupies a place in the former which it certainly does not occupy in the latter. And themes which have been treated by, for example, Gabriel Marcel and Vladimir Jankélévitch hardly appear at all in British philosophy. As for social and political thought, British philosophers are accustomed to follow a policy of neutrality which would be clearly unacceptable to a writer such as Sartre. In general, French philosophical thought gives an impression of relevance to man and society which is not given by the recently prevailing line of thought in Great Britain.

Such remarks do not necessarily imply a comparative judgment of value. How one evaluates the situation depends to a great extent on one's concept of the nature and functions of philosophy. Bertrand Russell did not hesitate to commit himself on moral and political issues; but he did not regard the writings in which he did so as belonging to philosophy in a strict sense. If one believes that the philosopher's function is to reflect on the language of morals and politics, and that if he commits himself on substantive issues he does so as a man and a citizen rather than as a philosopher, one will obviously not regard it as a failure or a fault on the part of philosophers if they maintain in their writings a predominantly detached and analytic approach. It is not the intention of the present author to follow Bertrand Russell in endorsing the sustained attack on leading British philosophers which was made by Professor Ernest Gellner in his provocative and amusing, even if exaggeratedly polemical book, *Words and Things*. This does not however alter the fact that there is a difference in philosophical atmosphere, so to speak, between the two countries. In England philosophy has become a highly specialized pursuit, with a great care for clarity and precision of expression and a marked distaste for emotively charged and ambiguous language and for slovenly argumentation. In France there are much closer interconnections between philosophy, literature and art. Obviously, one can find philosophical specialization and what some people regard as ivory-tower philosophy in France as elsewhere. But the area in which philosophy and literature are inter-related seems to be considerably more extended in France than in England. Perhaps the fact that in the French educational system students are introduced to philosophy while still at the lycée has something to do with this. As for political commitment, there are clearly historical and socio-political reasons why, for example, since the second world war there has been a preoccupation with Marxism which is not to be found in England, certainly not to the same extent.

The claim, advanced above, that man has been a conspicuous theme in French philosophy was made with a view to counterbalancing any impression which might be given by the passages in this volume on metaphysicians such as Lavelle and idealists such as Hamelin that philosophy has been predominantly concerned with 'metaphysical obscurities'. Though however man would commonly be considered a more concrete and relevant theme than l'être or das Sein, it must be admitted that talk about man is no guarantee of clarity and precision. In the opinion of the present writer it is much easier to understand Bergson's general view of the world than it is to grasp the meaning of certain more recent French writers on, say, the phenomenology of human consciousness. I am not thinking of Sartre. His jargon is simply irritating. If what he says sometimes seems to be extremely obscure, this is not because what he is saying is unintelligible, but because he has chosen to express in difficult language something which could have been said much more plainly. There are however certain other philosophers whose writing seems to be so impressionistic and vague that the author of this volume saw little prospect of being able to summarize their lines of thought in a manner suitable for presentation in a history of philosophy. One can of course retort, 'so much the worse for histories of philosophy'. This may be fair comment. But it is noticeable that in the case of some philosophers available expositions of their thought are even less illuminating than the original texts. Merleau-Ponty is of course quite right in saying that philosophers should not hesitate to pursue exploratory inquiries which require fresh concepts and expression. To demand that nothing should be said except what can be precisely handled with already available tools would be to demand an abandonment of creative thought and a petrification of philosophy. But this does not alter the fact that what is in process of coming to birth and has not yet acquired shape is hardly apt material for the historian of philosophy.

PART I

FROM THE REVOLUTION TO AUGUSTE COMTE

CHAPTER I

THE TRADITIONALIST REACTION TO THE REVOLUTION

Introductory remarks—De Maistre—De Bonald—Chateaubriand—Lamennais—Traditionalism and the Church.

1. To us the French revolution is an historical event, the causes and development and effects of which can be investigated in a dispassionate manner. At the time judgments were obviously accompanied and often affected by strong feelings. To many people the revolution naturally appeared not only as a national liberation and a regenerating force in French society but also as a movement destined to bring light and freedom to other nations as well. The Terror might of course be deplored, or perhaps excused; but the ideals of the revolution were approved and welcomed as an assertion of human freedom, and sometimes as a long-awaited extension of the religious Reformation into the political and social spheres. Equally naturally however there were others to whom the revolution appeared as a disastrous event which threatened the foundations of society, substituted an anarchic individualism for social stability, was wantonly destructive of the traditions of France and expressed a rejection of the religious basis of morals, education and social cohesion. Obviously, hostility to the revolution could be prompted to a large extent by selfish motives; but so could support of it. And just as idealism could be enlisted on the side of the revolution, so could there be an opposition to the revolutionary spirit which expressed a sincere conviction about its destructive and impious character.

A thought-out opposition to the revolution on the philosophical plane was expressed by the so-called Traditionalists. Both supporters and opponents of the revolution were inclined to regard it as the fruit of the Enlightenment, though they obviously differed sharply in their respective evaluations of and attitudes to the Enlightenment. It is of course easy to dismiss the Traditionalists as reactionaries filled with nostalgia for the past and

I

blind to the movement of history.[1] But however myopic they may have been in certain respects, they were eminent and influential writers and cannot simply be passed over in an account of French thought in the early decades of the nineteenth century.

2. The first writer of whom mention must be made is the famous royalist and ultramontanist Count Joseph de Maistre (1753–1821). Born at Chambéry in Savoy, he studied law at Turin and became a senator of Savoy. When the French invaded his country, he took refuge first in Aosta and then at Lausanne, where he wrote his *Considerations on France* (*Considérations sur la France*, 1796). De Maistre had once had some liberal sympathies; but in this work he made clear his opposition to the revolution and his desire for a restoration of the French monarchy.

In 1802 de Maistre was appointed minister-plenipotentiary of the King of Sardinia to the Russian court at St. Petersburg. He remained in Russia for fourteen years, and it was there that he wrote his *Essay on the Generative Principle of Political Constitutions* (*Essai sur le principe générateur des constitutions politiques*, 1814). He also occupied himself with the composition of his work *On the Pope* (*Du Pape*), which was finished at Turin and published in 1819, and the *Evenings at St. Petersburg* (*Soirées de Saint-Pétersbourg*) which appeared in 1821. His *Examination of the Philosophy of Bacon* (*Examen de la philosophie de Bacon*) was published posthumously in 1836.

In his earlier years de Maistre had been associated with a masonic circle at Lyons which derived some inspiration from the ideas of Louis-Claude de Saint-Martin (1743–1803), who had himself been stimulated by the writings of Jakob Boehme.[2] The circle was opposed to the philosophy of the Enlightenment and turned to metaphysical and mystical doctrines representing a fusion of Christian and Neoplatonist beliefs. And Saint-Martin saw in history the unfolding of divine providence. History was for him a continuous process linked throughout to God, the One.

It is perhaps not unreasonable to discern some echoes at any rate of such ideas in de Maistre's *Considerations on France*. True,

[1] This phrase is ambiguous. If the movement of history means the succession of events, the Traditionalists were obviously not blind to it. If the phrase implies that change and progress (in an evaluative sense) are synonymous terms, this identification presupposes a philosophy of history which cannot be simply taken for granted. It is however doubtless possible to fail to appreciate the fact that the emergence of new forces and ideas exclude the successful restoration and revivification of a previously existing structure.

[2] See Vol. III of this *History*, pp. 270–3.

he is horrified by the revolution, the act of regicide, the attack on the Church and the Terror; but at the same time his concept of history stands in the way of an exclusively negative evaluation of the revolution. He regards Robespierre and the other leaders as scoundrels and criminals, but he also sees them as the unwitting instruments of divine providence. Men 'act at the same time voluntarily and necessarily'.[1] They act as they will to act, but in doing so they further the designs of providence. The leaders of the revolution thought that they were in control of it; but they were instruments to be used and thrown aside, while the revolution itself was God's instrument to punish sin: 'Never had the divinity shown itself so clearly in any human event. If it employs the vilest instruments, it is a case of punishing in order to regenerate.'[2] If the factions involved in the revolution sought to attain the destruction of Christianity and of the monarchy, 'it follows that all their efforts will result only in the exaltation of Christianity and of the monarchy.'[3] For there is a 'secret force'[4] which works in history.

De Maistre's idea of history as exhibiting the operation of divine providence and of individuals as instruments was not in itself a novelty, though he applied it to a very recent event or series of events. The idea is obviously open to objections. Apart from any difficulty in reconciling human freedom with the unfailing realization of the divine purpose, the concept of revolutions and wars as divine punishments gives rise to the reflection that it is by no means only the guilty (or those who may seem to human eyes to be guilty) who suffer from such cataclysms. De Maistre tries however to meet such objections by a theory of the solidarity of the nation, and indeed of the human race, as constituting an organic unity. It is this theory which he opposes to what he regards as the erroneous and pernicious individualism of the Enlightenment.

Political society, de Maistre insists, is certainly not a collection of individuals united through a social compact or contract. Nor can a viable constitution be thought out *a priori* by the human reason in abstraction from national traditions and the institutions which have developed through the centuries. 'One of the great errors of a century which professed all errors was to believe that a political constitution could be written and created *a priori*,

---

[1] *Considérations sur la France* (Brussels, 1838), p. 2.
[2] *Ibid.*, p. 21.   [3] *Ibid.*, p. 127.   [4] *Ibid.*, p. 128.

whereas reason and experience are united in showing that a constitution is a divine work, and that it is precisely what is most fundamental and essentially constitutional in the laws of a nation which could not be written.'[1] If we look at the English constitution, we can see that it is the result of a vast number of contributing factors and circumstances which served as the instruments of providence. A constitution of this kind, which was certainly not constructed in an *a priori* manner, is always allied with religion and takes a monarchic form. It is not surprising therefore if revolutionaries, who wish to establish a constitution by decree, attack both religion and the monarchy.

In general terms de Maistre is violently opposed to the rationalism of the eighteenth century which he sees as treating of abstractions and as disregarding traditions which, in his opinion, exhibit the operation of divine providence. The abstract human being of *les philosophes*, who is not essentially a Frenchman or an Englishman or a member of some other organic unity, is a fiction. So is the State when interpreted as the product of a contract or convention. When de Maistre makes a complimentary remark about an Enlightenment thinker, it is because he regards him as transcending the spirit of *a priori* rationalism. For example, Hume is commended for his attack on the artificiality of the social contract theory. If de Maistre goes back beyond the Enlightenment and attacks Francis Bacon, the reason is that in his view 'modern philosophy is entirely the daughter of Bacon'.[2]

Another rationalist fiction, according to de Maistre, is natural religion, if the term is taken to mean a purely philosophical religion, a deliberate construction of the human reason. In reality belief in God is handed down from a primitive revelation to mankind, Christianity being a fuller revelation. In other words ,there is only one revealed religion; and man can no more construct a religion *a priori* than he can construct a constitution *a priori*. 'The philosophy of the last century, which will form in the eyes of posterity one of the most shameful epochs of the human spirit . . . was in fact nothing but a veritable system of practical atheism.'[3]

According to de Maistre the philosophy of the eighteenth century has found expression in the theory of the sovereignty of

---

[1] *Essai sur le principe générateur des constitutions politiques*, p. IX. The page reference is to the essay as printed in the same volume as the *Considérations sur la France* (Brussels, 1838).

[2] *Examen de la philosophie de Bacon*, II, p. 231 (Paris, 1836).

[3] *Soirées de Saint-Pétersbourg*, p. 258 (Brussels, 1838).

the people and in democracy. The theory of the sovereignty of the people is however groundless, and the fruits of democracy are disorder and anarchy. The remedy for these evils is a return to historically grounded and providentially constituted authority. In the political sphere this means the restoration of the Christian monarchy, while in the religious sphere it means acceptance of the supreme and unique sovereignty of the infallible pope. Human beings are such that government is necessary; and absolute power is the only real alternative to anarchy.[1] 'I have never said that absolute power, in whatever form it may exist in the world, does not involve great inconveniences. On the contrary, I expressly acknowledged the fact, and I have no thought of attenuating these inconveniences. I said only that we find ourselves placed between two abysses.'[2] In actual practice the exercise of absolute power is inevitably restricted by a variety of factors. And in any case political sovereigns are, or ought to be, subject to the jurisdiction of the pope, in the sense that he has the right to judge their actions from the religious and moral points of view.

De Maistre is best known for his ultramontanism and his insistence on papal infallibility a considerable time before this doctrine was defined at the first Vatican Council. This insistence however was by no means acceptable to all those who shared his hostility to the revolution and sympathized with his desire for the restoration of the monarchy. Some of his reflections on political constitutions and the values of tradition were similar to those of Edmund Burke (1729–97). But it is very much as the author of *Du Pape* that he is remembered.

3. A more impressive figure from the philosophical point of view was Louis Gabriel Ambroise, Vicomte de Bonald (1754–1840). A former officer of the royal guard, he was a member of the Constituent Assembly in 1790; but in 1791 he emigrated and lived in poverty. In 1796 he published at Constance his *Theory of Political and Religious Power in Civil Society* (*Théorie du pouvoir politique et religieux dans la société civile*). On his return to France he supported Napoleon, in whom he saw the instrument for the political and religious unification of Europe. But after the restoration he gave his support to the monarchy. In 1800 he published an *Analytical Essay on the Natural Laws of Social Order* (*Essai analytique sur les lois naturelles de l'ordre social*). This was followed

---

[1] De Maistre makes an exception, though with reservations, for England.
[2] *Du Pape*, p. 172 (Brussels, 1838).

in 1802 by *Primitive Legislation* (*La législation primitive*). His other writings include *Philosophical Studies on the Primary Objects of the Moral Sciences* (*Recherches philosophiques sur les premiers objets des connaissances morales*, 1818) and a *Philosophical Demonstration of the Constitutive Principle of Society* (*Démonstration philosophique du principe constitutif de la société*, 1827).

It has sometimes been said that de Bonald rejects all philosophy. The statement however is inaccurate. It is true that he emphasizes the necessity for a religious basis of society, and that he contrasts this necessity with the insufficiency of philosophy as a social foundation. In his view a union between religious and political society is 'as necessary for constituting the civil or social body as simultaneity of *will* and *action* is necessary for constituting the human *ego*',[1] whereas philosophy lacks the authority to dictate laws and impose sanctions. It is also true that he dwells on the succession of conflicting systems and concludes that 'Europe . . . is still awaiting a *philosophy*'.[2] At the same time he shows an evident admiration for some philosophers. He speaks, for instance, of Leibniz as 'perhaps the most comprehensive (*vaste*) genius who has appeared among men'.[3] Further, he distinguishes between the men of ideas or concepts, from Plato onwards, 'who have enlightened the world',[4] and the men of imagination, such as Bayle, Voltaire, Diderot, Condillac, Helvétius and Rousseau, who have led people astray. The description of writers such as Bayle and Diderot as men of imagination may seem odd; but de Bonald is not referring to poetically inclined thinkers. He is referring primarily to those who derive all ideas from sense-experience. When, for example, Condillac talks about 'transformed sensations', the phrase may appeal to the imagination which can picture to itself at will transformations and changes. 'But this transformation, when applied to the operations of the mind, is nothing but a word which is void of meaning; and Condillac himself would have been very embarrassed at having to give it a satisfactory application.'[5]

In general the men of imagination, as de Bonald understands the term, are sensationalists, empiricists and materialists. The men of ideas or concepts are primarily those who believe in innate

---

[1] *Essai analytique*, p. 23 (Paris, 1812). *Oeuvres*, v. p. 10 (Paris, 7 vols., 1854).
[2] *Recherches philosophiques*, I, p. 2, *Oeuvres*, iv, p. 1.
[3] *Essai analytique*, p. 36, *Oeuvres*, v, p. 16.
[4] *Ibid.*, p. 20, *Oeuvres*, v, p. 9.
[5] *Recherches philosophiques*, I, pp. 33–4. *Oeuvres*, iv, p. 16.

ideas and ascribe them to their ultimate source. Thus Plato 'proclaimed *innate ideas* or universal ideas, imprinted in our minds by the supreme intelligence',[1] whereas Aristotle 'humiliated the human intelligence by rejecting innate ideas and by representing ideas as coming to the mind only by the mediation of the senses'.[2] 'The reformer of philosophy in France was Descartes.'[3]

It is indeed true that de Bonald refers to the absence of philosophy among the Jews of Old Testament times and among other vigorous nations, such as the early Romans and the Spartans, and that he concludes from the history of philosophy that philosophers have been unable to find any secure basis for their speculations. He refuses however to admit that we ought therefore to despair of philosophy and reject it altogether. On the contary, we must look for 'an absolutely primitive fact'[4] which can serve as a secure point of departure.

It hardly needs saying that de Bonald was not the first man to look for one secure basis for philosophy. Nor was he the last. It is interesting however to read that he finds his 'primitive fact' in language. Philosophy in general is 'the science of God, of man and of society'.[5] The primitive fact which is being sought must therefore lie at the foundation of man and society. And this is language. It may seem that language cannot be a primitive fact. But according to de Bonald man could not have invented language to express his thoughts, as thought itself, involving general concepts, presupposes language of some kind. In other words, to express his thoughts man must be already a language-using being. Language is required for man to be man. Again, human society presupposes language and could not exist without it.

In looking on symbolic expression as an essential characteristic of man de Bonald is not saying anything which is likely to cause astonishment nowadays, even if there are various puzzling questions which can be asked. He goes on however to argue that man received the gift of language at the same time that he received existence, and that consequently 'there must necessarily have existed, before the human species, a first cause of this marvellous effect (i.e. language), a being superior to man in intelligence, superior to anything that we can know or even imagine, from

[1] *Ibid.*, p. 12. *Oeuvres*, iv, p. 6.   [2] *Ibid.*, p. 13, *Ibid.*
[3] *Ibid.*, p. 35. *Oeuvres*, p. 17.
[4] *Recherches philosophiques*, I, p. 85. *Oeuvres* iv, p. 40.
[5] *Ibid.*, p. 80. *Oeuvres*, p. 37.

whom man has positively received the gift of thought, the gift of the word . . ..'[1] In other words, if, as noticed by Rousseau,[2] man needs speech in order to learn to think but could not have constructed speech unless he could think, he cannot have invented language; and this fact serves as the basis of a proof of God's existence.

There is no need of course to accuse de Bonald of overlooking the multiplicity of languages, nor the fact that we can and do invent linguistic expressions. His contention is that we cannot reasonably depict man as first developing thought and then sitting down, as it were, to invent language to express this thought. For actual thinking already involves symbolic expression, even if no words are uttered aloud.[3] De Bonald certainly makes a good point by refusing to divide thought and language with a hatchet.[4] Whether his account of the relation between thought and language can serve as a basis for a proof of the existence of God is another question. He assumes that while our ideas of particular objects in the world depend on sense-experience, there are certain basic concepts (of God, for instance) and certain fundamental principles or truths which represent a primitive revelation by God to man. As this revelation could not be grasped or appropriated in the first instance without language, and as man cannot himself have invented language, it (language) must be a primitive gift of God to man at his creation. De Bonald is obviously thinking of man as having been directly created by God as a language-using being, whereas we probably think within the framework of an evolutionary theory.

The social philosophy of de Bonald is triadic in the sense that, according to him, 'there are three *persons* in every society.'[5] In the religious society there are God, his ministers and the people whose salvation is the aim of the relation between God and his ministers. In the domestic society or family we have father, mother and the child or children. In political society there are the head of the

---

[1] *Ibid.*, p. 98. *Oeuvres*, p. 46.
[2] Rousseau makes this remark in the first part of his *Discourse on the Origin of Inequality*.
[3] It is arguable that thinking 'to oneself' presupposes language as a social phenomenon.
[4] Some distinction must obviously be made. Otherwise it becomes very difficult to account for our ability to translate. But we might represent the distinction as analogous to Aristotle's distinction between 'form' and 'matter', thought being analogous to 'forms' which do not exist apart from all matter but can inform different matter.
[5] *Législation primitive*, I, p. 134 (Paris, 1817). *Oeuvres*, iii, p. 49.

State (representing power), his officers of various kinds and the people or general body of citizens.

Now if we ask whether in the family power belongs to the father as the result of an agreement or compact, the answer, for de Bonald, must be negative. The power belongs naturally to the father and is derived ultimately from God. Similarly, in political society sovereignty belongs to the monarch, not the people, and it belongs to him by nature. 'The establishment of the public power was neither voluntary nor forced; it was *necessary*, in conformity, that is to say, with the nature of beings in society. And its causes and origins were all natural.'[1] This idea can be applied even in the case of Napoleon. The revolution was both the culmination of a long sickness and an effort made by society to return to order. That someone capable of bringing order out of anarchy should assume power was necessary and therefore natural. Napoleon was the man.

Like de Maistre, de Bonald insists on the unity of power or sovereignty. Sovereignty must be one, independent and definitive or absolute.[2] It must also be lasting, from which premise de Bonald concludes to the need for hereditary monarchy. The peculiar characteristic of his thought however is his theory about the origin of language and of the transmission, by means of language, of a primitive divine revelation which lies at the basis of religious belief, morality and society. It is perhaps none too clear how this theory of the transmission of a primitive revelation squares with de Bonald's enthusiasm for the theory of innate ideas. But presumably he thinks of innate ideas as required for the appropriation of revelation.

4. Both de Maistre and de Bonald were obviously traditionalists in the sense that they upheld the old political and religious traditions of France against the revolutionary spirit. Further, de Bonald in particular was a traditionalist in the technical sense of one who defends the idea of the tradition or handing-on of a primitive revelation. Both men attacked the philosophy of the Enlightenment, though of the two de Maistre was the more sweeping and indiscriminate in his condemnation. In one sense of the word 'rationalism' they were both anti-rationalists. Neither however can properly be said to represent simply irrationalism. For both men offered reasoned defences of their positions and

---

[1] *Démonstration philosophique*, p. 108 (Paris, 1830). *Oeuvres*, iv, p. 448.
[2] Absolute power is distinguished from the tyrannical or arbitrary use of power.

appealed to reason in their attacks on the thought of the eighteenth century.

When however we turn to François-René, Vicomte de Chateaubriand (1768–1848), we find a rather different emphasis. Educated in the philosophy of the Encyclopaedists, Chateaubriand went into exile at the revolution, and it was in London that he wrote his *Historical, Political and Moral Essay on Revolution* (*Essai historique, politique et moral sur les révolutions*, 1797). In this work he accepted the force of the objections brought by eighteenth-century philosophers against Christianity, with its doctrines of providence and immortality, and went on to maintain a cyclic theory of history. In the cycles of history events substantially repeat themselves, though the human beings involved and the circumstances are of course different. It is idle therefore to look on the French revolution as a completely fresh start which will bring permanent gains. It repeats substantially the revolutions of former times. The dogma of progress is an illusion.

Later on Chateaubriand was to say, doubtless rightly, that in spite of his onetime rejection of Christianity he still retained a religious nature. In any case he was drawn to the Christian religion, and in 1802 he published his famous work *The Genius of Christianity* (*Génie du Christianisme*). The subtitle of the work, 'Beauties of the Christian Religion' (*Beautés de la religion chrétienne*), expresses well the spirit of the work, in which the author appeals above all to the aesthetic qualities of Christianity. 'All the other kinds of apologies are exhausted, and perhaps they would even be useless today. Who would now read a theological work? Some pious men who have no need to be convinced, some true Christians who are already persuaded.'[1] In place of some old-style apologetics one ought to try to show that 'the Christian religion is the most poetic, the most human, the most favourable to liberty, to the arts and to letters, of all the religions which ever existed.'[2]

This sounds as though Chateaubriand intended to argue that the Christian religion must be true because it is beautiful, because its beliefs are consoling and because some of the greatest artists and poets have been Christians. And apart from the fact that some minds might not agree about the beauty of Christianity, this point of view lies open to the objection that the aesthetic and consoling qualities of Christianity do not prove its truth. If Dante and

---

[1] *Génie du christianisme*, I, p. 13 (Paris, 1803).   [2] *Ibid.*, p. 12.

Michelangelo were Christians, what does this show, except some-thing about Dante and Michelangelo? If the doctrines of the resurrection and heaven are a source of consolation to many people, does it follow that they are true? It is understandable that Chateaubriand has been accused of irrationalism or of substituting appeals to aesthetic satisfaction for rational argument.

It is true that with Chateaubriand traditional philosophical arguments to show the credibility of the Christian religion are relegated to a completely subordinate position, and that appeal is made chiefly to aesthetic considerations, to sentiment and to reasons of the heart. At the same time we have to remember that he has in mind those opponents of Christianity who argue that Christian doctrine is repellent, that the Christian religion impedes the development of the moral consciousness, that it is inimical to human freedom and anti-cultural, and that, in general, it has a cramping and stifling effect on the human spirit. He makes it clear that he is not writing for 'sophists' who 'are never searching for the truth in good faith',[1] but for those who have been seduced by the sophists into believing that Christianity is, for instance, the enemy of art and literature, and that it is a barbarous and cruel religion, detrimental to human happiness. His work can be regarded as an *argumentum ad hominem* which aims at showing that Christianity is not what these people think that it is.

5. A more interesting figure is Félicité Robert de Lamennais (1782–1854). Born at St. Malo, Lamennais was in youth a follower of Rousseau, though he soon returned to Christian belief. When de Bonald's *Primitive Legislation* appeared in 1802, Lamennais was profoundly impressed by it. In 1809 he published *Reflections on the State of the Church in France during the Eighteenth Century and on its Actual Situation*, in which he made suggestions for the Church's renewal. Ordained a priest at Vannes in 1816, he pub-lished in the following year the first volume of his *Essay on Indifference in Matters of Religion* (*Essai sur l'indifférence en matière de religion*, 1817–23), a work which brought him immediate fame as an apologist for the Christian religion.

In the first volume of this work Lamennais insists that in religion, morals and politics, no doctrines are matters of indif-ference. 'Indifference, considered as a permanent state of soul, is opposed to the nature of man and destructive of his being.'[2] This

---

[1] *Ibid.*, p. 11. The 'sophists' are presumably *les philosophes*.
[2] *Essai sur l'indifférence*, I, p. 37 (Paris, 1823).

thesis is based on the premises that man cannot develop himself as man without religion, that religion is necessary for society, inasmuch as it is in the basis of morals, and that without it society degenerates into a group of persons each of whom is intent on furthering his own particular interests. In other words, Lamennais insists on the social necessity of religion and rejects the belief which spread in the eighteenth century that ethics can stand on its own feet, apart from religion, and that there could be a satisfactory human society without religion. Given this point of view, Lamennais argues that indifference towards religion is disastrous for man. It might of course be maintained that even if indifference in general is undesirable, it does not necessarily follow that all points of traditional religious belief possess social importance and relevance. According to Lamennais however heresy prepares the way for deism, deism for atheism, and atheism for complete indifference. It is therefore a case of a package deal.

It may appear that Lamennais is attaching an exclusively pragmatic value to religion, as though the only justification for religious belief was its social utility. This is not however an adequate account of his attitude. He explicitly rejects the point of view of those who see in religion nothing but a socially and politically useful institution and conclude that it is necessary for the common people. In his opinion the Christian doctrines are not only useful but true. Indeed, they are useful because they are true. This is the reason why, for Lamennais, there is no justification for picking and choosing, for heresy in other words.

The difficulty is to see how Lamennais proposes to show that Christian doctrines are true, in a sense of 'true' which goes beyond a purely pragmatist understanding of the term. For in his opinion our reasoning is so subject to a variety of influences which can operate even 'without our knowing it'[1] that it cannot yield certainty. It is all very well to claim that we can deduce conclusions from self-evidently true axioms or basic principles. The fact of the matter is that what seems self-evidently true to one man may not seem so to another man. In this case we can well understand Lamennais' rejection of any attempt to reduce religion to 'natural' or philosophical religion. But the question remains, how does he propose to exhibit the truth of revealed religion?

The remedy for scepticism, Lamennais maintains, is to trust not one's own private reasoning but the common consent of mankind.

---

[1] *Ibid.*, II, p. 137.

For it is this common consent or *sentiment commun* which is the basis of certitude. Atheism is the fruit of false philosophy and of following one's private judgment. If we look at this history of mankind, we find a spontaneous belief in God, common to all nations.

Passing over the question whether the historical facts are as Lamennais claims them to be, we can note that he would be involved in inconsistency if he meant that most human beings, each by his own reasoning, conclude that there is a God. If, that is to say, the alleged common consent were equivalent to a collection of conclusions arrived at by individuals, Lamennais could be challenged to show that it possessed any greater degree of certainty than that attaching to the result of the individual's process of inference. In point of fact however Lamennais has recourse to a traditionalist theory. For example, we know the meaning of the word 'God' because it belongs to the language which we have learned; and this language is ultimately of divine origin. 'It must be then that the first man who has transmitted them (i.e. certain words or concepts) to us, received them himself from the mouth of the Creator. Thus we find in the infallible word of God the origin of religion and of the tradition which preserves it.'[1]

To say this is to say in effect that it is on authority that we know the truth of religious belief, and that there is in reality only revealed religion. What has been called natural religion is really revealed religion, and it has been commonly accepted because human beings, when unspoiled and not led astray by false reasoning, see that 'man is always obliged to obey the greatest authority which it is possible for him to know'.[2] The common consent of mankind about the existence of God expresses acceptance of a primitive revelation;[3] and belief in the teaching of the Catholic Church expresses acceptance of God's further revelation in and through Christ.

This theory gives rise to a number of awkward questions which cannot however be discussed here. We must pass instead to Lamennais' political attitude. Given his insistence on authority in the religious sphere, one might expect him to emphasize the role of monarchy in the manner of de Maistre and de Bonald. But this is not in fact the case. Lamennais is still a monarchist,

---

[1] *Ibid.*, III, p. 14   [2] *Ibid.*, II, p. 382.
[3] Obviously, on this view it is necessary to interpret polytheism as representing a process of degeneration of an original monotheism.

but he shows a realistic attitude. Thus in his work *On Religion Considered in its Relations with the Political and Civil Order* (*De la religion considérée dans ses rapports avec l'ordre politique et civil*, 1825-6) he remarks that the restored monarchy is 'a venerable souvenir of the past'[1] while France is in reality a democracy. True, 'the democracy of our times . . . rests on the atheist dogma of the primitive and absolute sovereignty of the people.'[2] But Lamennais' reflections on this state of affairs led him in the direction of ultramontanism within the Church rather than to a hankering after absolute monarchy. In contemporary France the Church is tolerated and even supported financially; but this patronage by the State constitutes a great danger to the Church, as it tends to make of the Church a department of the State and to hamper the former's freedom to penetrate and christianize the life of the nation. It is only emphasis on the supreme authority of the pope which can prevent the subordination of the Church to the State and make it clear that the Church has a universal mission. As for the monarchy, Lamennais has misgivings. In his work *On the Progress of the Revolution and of the War against the Church* (*Du progrès de la révolution et de la guerre contre l'église*, 1829) he remarks that 'towards the end of the monarchy human power had become, thanks to Gallicanism, the object of a real idolatry'.[3] Lamennais still thinks of the revolution as dissolving the social order and as the enemy of Christianity; but he has come to believe that the trouble started with the rise of absolute monarchy. It was Louis XIV who 'made despotism the fundamental law of the State'.[4] The French monarchy sapped the life of the Church by subordinating it to the State. And it would be disastrous if in their desire for the apparent security of State patronage and protection the clergy were to acquiesce in a similar subordination to the post-revolutionary and post-Napoleonic State. A clear recognition of papal authority in the Church is required as a safeguard.

In spite of his continued attack on political liberalism and individualism Lamennais had come to believe that liberalism contained a valuable element, 'the invincible desire of freedom which is inherent in the Christian nations which cannot put up with an arbitrary or purely human power'.[5] And the revolution of 1830 convinced him that no reliance could be placed on monarchs

---

[1] *De la religion*, p. 33 (Paris, 1826).   [2] *Ibid.*, p. 95.
[3] *Du progrès de la révolution*, p. 58 (Paris, 1829).   [4] *Ibid.*, p. 7.
[5] *Ibid.*, p. 256.

for the regeneration of society. It was necessary to accept the democratic State as it was, to secure a complete separation of the Church from the State, and, within the Church, to insist on the supreme authority of the infallible pope. In other words, Lamennais combined acceptance of the idea of a democratic and religiously non-affiliated State with insistence on ultramontanism within the Church. He hoped of course that the Church would succeed in christianizing society; but he had come to believe that this end could not be attained unless the Church renounced all State patronage and any privileged status.

In 1830 Lamennais founded the newspaper *Avenir* which stood for the authority and infallibility of the pope, acceptance of the French political system of the time, and separation between Church and State. The paper enjoyed the support of some eminent men, such as the Comte de Montalembert (1810–70) and the famous Dominican preacher Henri-Dominique Lacordaire (1802–61); but the views propounded were by no means acceptable to all Catholics. Lamennais tried to secure the approval of Pope Gregory XVI; but in 1832 the pope issued an encyclical letter (*Mirari vos*) in which he censured indifferentism, liberty of conscience and the doctrine that Church and State should be separated. Lamennais was not named in the letter. While however the pope's condemnation of indifferentism could be taken as an endorsement of Lamennais' early *Essai sur l'indifférence*, the editor of *Avenir* was clearly affected by the encyclical.

In 1834 Lamennais published *Words of a Believer* (*Paroles d'un croyant*) in which he supported all oppressed and suffering peoples and groups and advocated complete freedom of conscience for all. In point of fact he endorsed the ideals of the revolution, liberty, equality and fraternity, as interpreted in a religious setting. The book was censured by Pope Gregory XVI in June 1834 in a letter addressed to the French bishops; but by then Lamennais was pretty well detached from the Church. And two years later, in *Affairs of Rome* (*Affaires de Rome*), he rejected the idea of achieving social order either through monarchs or through the pope. He had become a believer in the sovereignty of the people.

In later writings Lamennais argued that Christianity, in its organized forms, had outlived its usefulness; but he continued to maintain the validity of religion, considered as a development of a divine element in man which unites him with God and with his fellows. In 1840 he published a brochure directed against the government and police and underwent a year's imprisonment as a result. After the 1848 revolution he was elected a deputy for the department of the Seine. But when Napoleon III assumed power, Lamennais retired from politics. He died in 1854 without any formal reconciliation with the Church.

6. In a very general or broad sense of the term we can describe as traditionalists all those who saw the French revolution as a disastrous attack on the valuable political, social and religious traditions of their country and who advocated a return to these traditions. In the technical sense of the term however, the sense, that is to say, in which it is used in recounting the history of ideas in the decades following the revolution, traditionalism means the theory that certain basic beliefs, necessary for man's spiritual and cultural development and well-being, are not the result simply of human reasoning but have been derived from a primitive revelation by God and have been handed on from generation to generation through the medium of language. Obviously, traditionalism in the broad sense does not exclude traditionalism in the narrower sense. But it does not entail it. It hardly needs saying that a Frenchman could quite well support the restoration of the monarchy without the theory of a primitive revelation and without placing restrictions on the range of philosophical proof. Again, it was possible to adopt traditionalist theories in the technical sense and yet not to demand a restoration of the *ancien régime*. The two could go together; but they were not inseparable.

It may appear at first sight that traditionalism in the technical sense, with its attack on the philosophy of the Enlightenment, its insistence on divine revelation and its tendency to ultramontanism would be highly acceptable to ecclesiastical authority. But though ultramontanist tendencies were naturally pleasing to Rome, the traditionalist philosophy brought upon itself ecclesiastical censures. To attack this or that eighteenth-century philosophy on the ground that its premises were unwarranted or its arguments unsound was all very well. In fact it was a commendable activity. But to attack the thought of the Enlightenment on the ground that the human reason in unable to attain certain truth was quite another matter. If the existence of God could be known only on authority, how did one know that the authority was trustworthy? For the matter of that, how did the first man know that what he took to be revelation was revelation? And if the human reason was as powerless as the more extreme traditionalists made it out to be,[1] how could one show that the voice of Christ was the voice of God? It is understandable that ecclesiastical authority, while sympathizing with attacks on the Enlightenment and the revolution, was not enthusiastic about theories which left its claims without any rational support save questionable appeals to the consent of mankind.

To take one example. The second volume of Lamennais' *Essai sur l'indifférence* exercised a considerable influence on Augustin Bonnetty (1798–1879), founder of the *Annales de philosophie chrétienne*. In an article in this periodical Bonnetty wrote that people were beginning to understand that the whole of religion rested on tradition and not on reasoning. His general thesis was that revelation was the only source of religious truth, and he drew the conclusion that the scholasticism which prevailed in seminaries was an expression of a pagan rationalism which had corrupted Christian thought and had eventually born fruit in the destructive philosophy of the Enlightenment. In 1855 Bonnetty was required by the Congregation of the Index to subscribe to a number of theses, such as that the human reason can prove with certainty the existence of God, the spirituality of the soul and human freedom, that reasoning leads to faith, and that the method used by St. Thomas Aquinas, St. Bonaventure and the Scholastics does not lead to rationalism. A series of similar propositions had already been subscribed to in 1840 by Louis-Eugène–Marie Bautain (1796–1867).

It may very well occur to the reader that imposition by ecclesiastical authority of the thesis that the existence of God can be philosophically proved contributes little to showing how this is done. However it is clear that the Church came down on the side of what Bonnetty regarded as rationalism. And definitive pronouncements on this matter were made at the first Vatican Council in 1870, the Council which also marked the triumph of ultramontanism. As for the general idea that France could be regenerated only through a return to the monarchy in alliance with the Church, this idea was to find a fresh lease of life with the *Action française* movement, founded by Charles Maurras (1868–1952). But Maurras himself was, like some of his closer associates,

---

[1] Some traditionalists maintained that while reason divorced from tradition (in effect, revelation) could not prove God's existence, once man had the concept of God as handed on in society he could discern reasons for belief. But others seemed to imply that metaphysics should be rejected altogether.

an atheist,[1] not a believer such as de Maistre or de Bonald. And it is not altogether surprising if his cynical attempt to use Catholicism for political ends led eventually to a condemnation by Pope Pius XI. Incidentally, in his *Essai sur l'indifférence* Lamennais had included among 'systems of indifference' the view of religion as being simply a politically and socially useful instrument.

[1] Maurras, condemned to life imprisonment in 1945 for collaboration with the Vichy régime, was reconciled with the Church shortly before his death. But for most of his life he was an admitted atheist. As for his philosophy, this was not of course traditionalism in the technical sense.

CHAPTER II

THE IDEOLOGISTS AND MAINE DE BIRAN

The ideologists—Maine de Biran: life and writings—Philo-
sophical development—Psychology and knowledge—Levels of
human life.

1. As we have seen, the Traditionalists attacked the spirit and
thought of the Enlightenment, which they regarded as largely
responsible for the revolution. Those who welcomed the revolution
tended to take a similar view of the relation between eighteenth-
century thought and the revolution. To attribute the revolution
simply to the influence of *les philosophes* would be of course an
obvious exaggeration and too flattering a compliment to the
power of philosophy. Though however the philosophers of the
eighteenth century aimed not at violence, bloodshed and terror
but at the spread of knowledge and, through the diffusion of
knowledge, at social reform, they helped to prepare the way for
the overthrow of the *ancien régime*; and it hardly needs saying
that the influence of the Enlightenment was prolonged beyond the
revolution. Once conditions became sufficiently settled, the scientific work associated with a man such as d'Alembert (1717–83)[1]
began to develop and flourish. The demands of a Condorcet
(1743–94)[2] for an educational system based on a secular ethics
and free from theological presuppositions and ecclesiastical
influences were eventually fulfilled in the programme of public
education in France. And though Condorcet was himself to become
a victim of the revolution,[3] his vision of man's perfectibility and of
history as a process of intellectual and moral advance, together
with the interpretation of history expounded by Turgot (1727–81),[4]
prepared the way for the philosophy of Auguste Comte, which
will be considered in due course.

The immediate inheritors of the spirit of the Enlightenment,
and in particular of the influence of Condillac (1715–80)[5] were the
so-called ideologists (*les idéologues*). In 1801 Destutt de Tracy
(1754–1836) published the first volume of his *Elements of Ideology*

[1] On d'Alembert see Vol. VI of this *History*, pp. 43–7.
[2] See Vol. VI of this *History*, pp. 168–71.
[3] He committed suicide when under arrest.
[4] See Vol. VI of this *History*, pp. 56–8.   [5] See *ibid.*, pp. 28–35.

19

(*Éléments d'idéologie*); and it was from this work that the label
'ideologist' was taken. The members of the group included, besides
de Tracy, the Comte de Volney (1757–1820), and Cabanis (1757–
1808).[1] The group had two principal centres, the *École Normale*
and the *Institut National*, both of which were established in 1795.
It was not long however before the ideologists aroused the suspicions of Napoleon. Though for the most part they had been
favourable to his rise, they soon came to the conclusion that he
had failed to preserve and implement the ideals of the revolution.
In particular they resented and opposed his restoration of religion.
On his side the emperor came to attribute to what he regarded as
the 'obscure metaphysics' of the ideologists all the evils from which
France was suffering; and he held them responsible for a con-
spiracy against himself in 1812.

As used by Destutt de Tracy, the term 'ideology' should not be
understood in the sense in which we are accustomed to speak of
ideologies. It would be nearer the mark to think of the term as
meaning a study of the origin of ideas, of their expression in
language and of their combination in reasoning. In point of fact
however de Tracy was more concerned with the study of human
faculties and their operations. He regarded this as a basic study
contributing the foundation of such sciences as logic, ethics and
economics. We can say therefore that he was concerned with
developing a science of human nature.

Mention has been made of the influence of Condillac. It is
important however to understand that de Tracy rejected the
reductive analysis expounded by Condillac. We can recall that the
latter tried to show that all mental operations, such as judging
and willing, could be exhibited as what he called transformed
sensations. In other words, Condillac tried to improve on Locke
by reducing all mental operations in the long run to elementary
sensations and by arguing that the human faculties can be recon-
structed, as it were, from sensation alone. In de Tracy's view
however this was an artificial process of analysis and reconstruction, an ingenious account of how things might have been, without
any attention being paid to what we might describe as the
phenomenology of consciousness. In his view Condillac sometimes
confused what ought to be distinguished and at other times
separated what ought to be united. In any case de Tracy was
more concerned with discovering the basic human faculties as

----

[1] See *ibid.*, pp. 50–1.

revealed to immediate and concrete observation than with the genesis of ideas, with arguing that they were all derivable from sensations.

The basic faculties for de Tracy are feeling, remembering, judging and willing. The operation of judging can be seen as the foundation of both grammar (considered as the study of signs as used in discourse) and logic, which is concerned with the ways of attaining certainty in judgment.[1] Reflection on the effects of the will grounds ethics, considered mainly as the study of the origins of our desires and of their conformity or lack of it with our nature, and economics which is looked on as an enquiry into the consequences of our actions in regard to meeting our needs.

Passing over the details of ideology we can notice the following two points. First, when laying down the fundamental notions of ideology de Tracy turned from the reductive analysis of Condillac to immediate self-observation, from hypothetical reconstruction of man's psychical life out of its basis in elementary sensation to reflection on what we actually perceive to take place when we think and speak and act voluntarily. Secondly, de Tracy maintained that if Condillac's psychology, which laid all the emphasis on receptivity, was true, we could never know that there was an external world. We should be left with the insoluble problem of Hume. In point of fact the real ground of our knowledge of the external world is our activity, our motion, our voluntary action which meets with resistance.

If we bear these points in mind, it is easier to understand how de Tracy could exercise an influence on Maine de Biran, the forerunner of what is called the spiritualist movement in nineteenth-century French philosophy. The ideologists helped to turn his mind away from the empiricism of Locke and Condillac and stimulated him to set out on a path of his own.

It is worth noticing that Thomas Jefferson (1743–1826), who had a high opinion of the French ideologists, maintained a correspondence with Destutt de Tracy from 1806 until 1826. In 1811 Jefferson published a translation of de Tracy's commentary on Montesquieu's *De l'esprit des lois*. And he also published an edition of de Tracy's *Treatise on Political Economy* (1818).

2. François-Pierre Maine de Biran (1766–1824) was born at

---

[1] In logic de Tracy lays emphasis on the relation by which one idea contains another. He therefore plays down the role of logical rules and stresses the need for direct examination of the ideas which one employs to see whether in point of fact *a* contains or implies *b*.

Bergerac and educated at Périgueux. At the age of eighteen he went to Paris and enrolled in the royal guard. He was wounded in 1789, and not long after the dissolution of the guard in 1791 he retired to the castle of Grateloup near Bergerac and devoted his time to study and reflection. In 1795 he was appointed administrator of the department of the Dordogne, and in 1797 he was elected a member of the Council of Five Hundred. In 1810, under Napoleon, he was nominated a member of the *Corps législatif*, but at the close of 1813 he was associated with a group which publicly expressed opposition to the emperor. After the restoration of the monarchy he was re-elected a deputy for the department of the Dordogne. In 1816 he acted as a councillor of State, and he served on various committees.

In 1802 Maine de Biran published an essay, though without the author's name, on the *Influence of Habit on the Faculty of Thinking* (*Influence de l'habitude sur la faculté de penser*) which won for him a prize from the Institute of France. This essay was a revised version of one which he had submitted to the Institute in 1800 and which, while not winning the prize, had aroused the attention of the ideologists Destutt de Tracy and Cabanis. In 1805 he won another prize from the Institute for an essay on the analysis of thought (*Mémoire sur la décomposition de la pensée*) and was elected a member of the Institute. In 1812 he won a prize from the Academy of Copenhagen for an *Essay on the Relations of Physics and Morals in Man* (*Mémoire sur les rapports du physique et du moral de l'homme*). Neither of these essays was published by Maine de Biran himself; but in 1817 he published, again without giving his name, an *Examination of the Lectures on Philosophy of M. Laromiguière* (*Examen des leçons de philosophie de M. Laromiguière*). And in 1819 he wrote an article on Leibniz (*Exposition de la doctrine philosophique de Leibniz*) for the *Biographie universelle*.

It will be seen from what has been said above that Maine de Biran published very little himself, the essay of 1802, the *Examination* (both anonymously), and the article on Leibniz. In addition he published a number of papers, mainly on political topics. But he wrote copiously; and it appears that up to the end of his life he planned to produce one major work, a science of human nature or a philosophical anthropology, incorporating revised versions of early essays. This major work was never completed; but a good deal of the manuscript material[1] seems to represent various phases

---

[1] Some of the manuscript material was lost, but a great deal was preserved.

in the attempt to realize the project. For example, the *Essay on the Foundations of Psychology* (*Essai sur les fondements de la psychologie*), at which de Biran was working in the years 1811–12, represents one phase in the writing of the unfinished work.[1]

In 1841 Victor Cousin published an (incomplete) edition of Maine de Biran's writings in four volumes.[2] In 1859 E. Naville and M. Debrit brought out three volumes of the unpublished works (*Oeuvres inédites de Maine de Biran*). In 1920 P. Tisserand began publication of the *Works* in fourteen volumes (*Oeuvres de Maine de Biran accompagnées de notes et de d'appendices*). Tisserand actually published twelve volumes (1920–39). The last two volumes were brought out by Professor Henri Gouhier in 1949. Gouhier has also published an edition of Maine de Biran's journal in three volumes (*Journal intime*, 1954–7).

3. By temperament Maine de Biran was strongly inclined to introspection and self-communing. And in his youth, during the period of retirement at the castle of Grateloup, he was powerfully influenced by Rousseau, considered more as the author of the *Confessions*, the *Rêveries du promeneur solitaire* and the *Profession de foi du vicaire savoyard* than as the expounder of the social contract theory. 'Rousseau speaks to my heart, but sometimes his errors afflict me.'[3] For example, while Maine de Biran sympathized with Rousseau's idea of the inner sense or feeling as prompting belief in God and immortality, he rejcted decisively the modest natural theology proposed by the *vicaire savoyard*. As far as reasoning was concerned, agnosticism was the only proper attitude.[4]

Another point on which Maine de Biran finds fault with Rousseau is the latter's view of man as essentially good, good by nature. It does not follow that Maine de Biran looks on man as essentially bad or as having become prone to evil through a Fall. In his view man has a natural impulse to seek after happiness, and virtue is a condition of happiness. This by no means entails the conclusion however that man is naturally virtuous. He has the power to become either virtuous or vicious. And it is reason alone

---

[1] This *Essay*, as published by E. Naville, was a compilation made from several manuscripts.

[2] The fourth volume was a reprint of a volume which Cousin had already published in 1834.

[3] *Oeuvres*, I, p. 63. References to *Oeuvres* are to the Tisserand–Gouhier edition mentioned above.

[4] At this time Maine de Biran was also strongly anti-clerical, and he had no use for theologians' claims to possess knowledge of God and his will.

which can discover the nature of virtue and the principles of morals. In other words, the reason why Maine de Biran criticizes Rousseau's theory of man's natural goodness is that he looks on it as involving the doctrine of innate ideas. In point of fact 'all our ideas are acquisitions.'[1] There are no innate ideas of right and wrong, good and bad. Ethics can however be established by reason, by a process of reasoning or reflection, that is to say, based on observation or experience. This can be done without any dependence on religious belief.

Given his idea of reason, it was natural that when it was a question of developing a science of man Maine de Biran should turn to contemporary 'scientific' psychology, which professed to be based on the empirical facts. In addition to Locke, the natural writers to turn to were Condillac and Charles Bonnet (1720–93). But it required very little time for Maine de Biran to see the extreme artificiality of Condillac's reduction of men's psychical life to externally caused sensations and of his notion of reconstructing man's mental operations from this basis. For one thing, Condillac passed over the evident fact that externally caused sensation affects a subject endowed with appetite and instinct. In other words, Condillac was a theorist who constructed or invented a psychology according to a quasi-mathematical method and was quite prepared to ride roughshod over the evident fact that there is much in man which cannot be accounted for in terms of what comes from without.[2] As for Bonnet, de Biran at first thought highly of him; and a quotation from Bonnet was placed at the beginning of his essay on the *Influence of Habit*.[3] But, as in the case of Condillac, de Biran came to look on Bonnet as the constructor of a theory which was insufficiently based on empirical evidence. After all, Bonnet had never observed the movements of the brain and their connections with mental operations.

From Condillac and Bonnet, Maine de Biran turned to Cabanis and Destutt de Tracy. True, Cabanis was the author of some pretty crude materialist statements, such as his famous assertion that the brain secretes thought as the liver secretes bile. But he

---

[1] *Oeuvres*, I, p. 185.

[2] Condillac refused to admit any difference between philosophical and mathematical analysis.

[3] 'What are the movements of the soul except movements and repetitions of movements?' Bonnet emphasized the relation between mental operations and movements in the brain. But the quotation gives a very inadequate idea of Bonnet's anthropology. He believed, for instance, that the soul survives the death of the body.

saw that Condillac's picture of the statue gradually endowed with one sense-organ after another represented an extremely inadequate and one-sided theory of the genesis of man's mental life. For Cabanis the nervous system, interior or organic sensations, the inherited physiological constitution and other factors belonging to the 'statue' itself were of great importance. Cabanis was indeed a reductionist, in the sense that he tried to find physiological bases for all men's mental operations. But he studied carefully the available empirical data, and he tried to account for human activity, which could hardly be explained in terms of Condillac's statue model. As for de Tracy, Maine de Biran remarks in the introduction to his essay on the *Influence of Habit* that 'I distinguish all our impressions into *active* and *passive*',[1] and in a note he pays tribute to de Tracy for being the first writer to have seen clearly the importance of man's faculty of moving or 'motility' (*motilité*), as de Tracy called it. For example, de Tracy saw that the judgment about the real existence of a thing, or of our knowledge of external reality, could not be accounted for without experience of resistance, which itself presupposed 'motility'.

In fine, Maine de Biran reacted against the psychology of Condillac by insisting on human activity. 'It is *I* who move or who *will* to move, and it is also *I* who am moved. Here are the two terms of the relation which are required to ground the first simple judgment of personality *I am*.'[2] In a real sense Maine de Biran is re-echoing the conviction of Rousseau who in the first part of his *Discourse on the Origin of Inequality* asserted roundly that man differs from the animals by being a free agent. But among the physiological psychologists de Biran has found his stimulus in the writings of the ideologists. And it was natural that when he submitted the revised version of his first prize-winning essay, Cabanis and de Tracy, who were among the judges, should have given both it and him a warm welcome.

Though however the ideologists regarded Maine de Biran as one of themselves, he soon came to the conclusion that Destutt de Tracy had failed to exploit his own addition to the psychology of Condillac, namely the idea of the active power in man. He may at first have regarded himself as correcting the ideas of the ideologists where they tended to fall back into the Condillacian psychology, but he was gradually moving away from the reductionist

---

[1] *Oeuvres*, II, (1954), p. 20. The reference to de Tracy is on p. 22, note 1.
[2] *Ibid.*, p. 22.

tradition to which the ideologists really belonged, in spite of the improvements which they introduced. In his *Mémoire sur la décomposition de la pensée*, which won a prize in 1805, he is still writing as an ideologist; but he asks whether a distinction should not be made between objective and subjective ideology. An objective ideology would be based chiefly 'on the relations which link the sensitive being to external things, in regard to which it finds itself placed in a relation of essential dependence, both in regard to the affective impressions which it receives from them and in regard to the images which it *forms* of them.'[1] Subjective ideology, 'enclosing itself in the consciousness of the *thinking* subject, would endeavour to penetrate the intimate relations which it has with itself in the free exercise of its intellectual acts.'[2] De Biran does not deny the importance of physiological psychology. He has no intention of rejecting Cabanis and all his works. But he is convinced that something more is required, something which we can describe as the phenomenology of consciousness. The self experiences itself in its operations; and we can envisage a reflection in which knower and known are one.

This may sound as though Maine de Biran were engaged in reintroducing the metaphysical concept of the self as a substance, the thinking substance of Descartes. He insists however that he is doing nothing of the kind. Muscular effort, willed effort that is to say, is a primitive fact. And the real existence of the ego or I is to be found 'in the apperception of the effort of which it feels itself subject or cause'.[3] To be sure, we can hardly think or speak about the ego or self without distinguishing it from the willed effort or action as cause from effect. But we should not allow ourselves to be misled with the metaphysician into postulating a self as a *thing*, a soul which 'exists before acting and which can act without knowing its acts, without knowing itself'.[4] With willed effort apperception or consciousness arises in the human being, and with consciousness *personal* existence as distinct from the existence of a merely sensing being. 'The fact of a power of action and of *will*, proper to the thinking being, is certainly as evident to him as the very fact of his own existence; the one does not differ from the other.'[5] Again, 'here is the sensitive being without *I*; there begins an identical *personality*, and with it all the faculties of the intelligent and moral being.'[6] In other words, consciousness cannot be

[1] *Oeuvres*, III, 1, p. 41.   [2] *Ibid.*, pp. 40–1.   [3] *Ibid.*, p. 216.
[4] *Ibid.*, p. 127.   [5] *Ibid.*, p. 178.   [6] *Ibid.*

explained simply in terms of 'transformed sensations' as understood by Condillac. It must be related to willed effort, to human activity meeting with resistance. If it is asked why in this case personality is not intermittent, present only at the moment when we are engaged in willed effort, de Biran's reply is that it is a mistake to suppose that such efforts occur only occasionally or now and again. In some form or another it continues during waking existence and lies at the basis of perception and knowledge.

Perhaps we can say that through the process of reflection first on the psychology of Condillac and Bonnet, then on that of Cabanis and de Tracy, Maine de Biran arrives at a reassertion of Rousseau's statement that man differs from the animals by being a free agent. We must add however that the reflection on contemporary psychology is always carried out in the light of the facts, the phenomena, as de Biran sees them. In his view the ideologists have seen facts to which Condillac was blind, or at any rate the significance of which he did not understand properly. And he refers to Cabanis and de Tracy as agreeing that the ego or I resides exclusively in the will.[1] But it by no means follows that Maine de Biran feels himself at one with the ideologists. For while becoming reflectively aware of the distance which now separates him from Condillac, he has reluctantly arrived at the conclusion that de Tracy, so far from exploiting or developing his own insights, has been retreating backwards. Maine de Biran may look on himself as the heir of the ideologists. But his letters testify to his growing conviction that their paths are diverging.

4. The ideas which found expression in the *Essay on the Decomposition of Thought* were taken up again and reconsidered in the manuscript of the *Essay on the Foundations of Psychology* which Maine de Biran brought with him to Paris in 1812. In this essay metaphysics, in the sense in which it is acceptable to the author, is really the same as reflexive psychology. If we understand by metaphysics a study of things in themselves (of noumena, to use Kantian terminology), apart from their appearance in consciousness, it is excluded. This means that philosophy cannot provide knowledge of the soul as an 'absolute' substance, existing apart from consciousness. If however metaphysics is understood as the science of 'interior phenomena'[2] or as the science of the primitive data of the interior sense (*sens intime*), it is not only possible but also required. Metaphysics in this sense

---

[1] *Ibid.*, p. 180.   [2] *Oeuvres*, VIII, p. 270.

reveals the existence of the subject as the active ego or I in the relation of willed effort encountering resistance. Further, the subject perceives itself as one power or active force encountering a succession of resistances; and it perceives itself as self-identical inasmuch as it is one subject in relation to the same organism.

It may appear that Maine de Biran is in effect claiming that the ego intuitively perceives itself as a substance. His actual claim however is that the ego is aware of itself as cause. 'On the basis of the primitive fact of interior sense, one can assure oneself that every phenomenon relative to consciousness, every mode in which the I participates or unites itself in any manner, includes necessarily the idea of a *cause*. This cause is I if the mode is active and perceived as the actual result of a willed effort; It is *not-I* if it is a passive impression, felt as opposed to this effort or as independent of every exercise of the will.'[1] In other words, awareness of the ego or I as a causal agent is fundamental. The concept of the soul as an 'absolute' substance existing apart from self-consciousness is an abstraction. At the same time de Biran tries to include awareness of personal identity within the intuition of causal efficacy.

Part of the *Essay on the Foundations of Psychology* seems to have been ready for publication when Maine de Biran came to Paris in 1812. But conversation and correspondence with his friends such as Ampère,[2] Dégerando[3] and Royer-Collard,[4] convinced him that he ought to devote further attention to the development of his ideas. And the result was that he never completed and published the work.

If the existence of the ego or subject as active cause is given in intuition, it is natural to think of this cause as persisting, at any rate as a virtual cause, even when it is not actually conscious of its causal efficacy in willed effort. And in this case it is natural to think of it as a substance, provided at least that the concept of substance is interpreted in terms of active force or causality and not as the idea of an inert substratum. So it is not altogether surprising to find Maine de Biran writing to Dégerando that he 'believes' in the metaphenomenal subject or ego. 'If you ask me

---

[1] *Oeuvres*, IX, p. 335.
[2] André-Marie Ampère (1775–1836), physicist and mathematician, was the author of a *Mathematical Theory of Electromagnetic Phenomena, deduced solely from Experience* (1827) and of an *Essay on the Philosophy of the Sciences* (1834).
[3] Marie-Joseph Dégerando (1772–1842) was a member of the group of ideologists and author of a *Theory of Signs* (1800).
[4] Further reference to Pierre-Paul Royer-Collard, professor of the Sorbonne, will be made in the next chapter.

why and on what ground I *believe* it, I reply that I am made in this way, that it is impossible for me not to have this belief, and that it would be necessary to change my nature for me to cease to have it.'[1] In other words, we *perceive* or intuit the ego or I as an active cause or force in actual concrete relations, and we have a natural and irresistible tendency to *believe* in its metaphenomenal or noumenal existence as a permanent substantial force which exists apart from actual apperception. The phenomenal is the object of intuition, while the noumenal or 'absolute' is the object of belief. To put the matter in another way, the subject or I which reveals itself in willed effort is 'the phenomenal manner in which my soul manifests itself to the interior vision'.[2]

In the *Essay on the Foundations of Psychology* Maine de Biran conceived metaphysics as the science of principles, the principles being sought and found in the primitive facts or basic data of intuition. Now he is seeking principles outside the objects of intuition. For the ego or I of consciousness is regarded as the phenomenal manifestation of a noumenal and substantial soul, the 'absolute' which appears in the relation of consciousness as the active subject. The question arises therefore whether the existence of the noumenal self, which is the object of belief, not of knowledge, is inferred. In point of fact de Biran does sometimes speak of induction and also of deduction in this context. But what he seems to be claiming is that this belief is the result of a spontaneous movement of the mind rather than of a deliberately performed inferential operation. 'The spirit of man, which cannot know or conceive anything except under certain relations, always aspires to the absolute and the unconditional.'[3] This aspiration may appear to constitute a leap beyond the frontiers of knowledge into the sphere of the unknowable. But de Biran also asks himself whether 'from the fact that one cannot conceive an act or its phenomenal result without conceiving a being in itself by which the act is produced, it does not follow necessarily that the relation of causality comprises the notion of substance.'[4] In any case metaphysics seem to extend beyond a study of the primitive facts or data of intuition or the interior sense to include reflection on the metaphenomenal conditions of these facts.

In arriving at his new ideas Maine de Biran was stimulated not only by conversation and correspondence with his friends but also

[1] *Oeuvres*, X, p. 26.   [2] *Ibid.*, pp. 312–13.
[3] *Oeuvres*, X, p. 95, note 1.   [4] *Oeuvres*, XI, p. 272.

by reflection on eminent philosophers such as Descartes, Leibniz and Kant. As we have seen, his philosophizing was first situated for a time in the tradition of Francis Bacon, Locke, Condillac and Bonnet. And he had little use for the defenders of the theory of innate ideas or those who tried to prove the existence of meta-phenomenal realities. In the course of time however he came to believe that there was more in Descartes and Leibniz than he had imagined; and though he seems to have had no first-hand know-ledge of Kant's writings, he obtained some acquaintance of the German philosopher's thought from secondary sources, and he was clearly influenced by his reading.

In so far as the *Cogito, ergo sum* (I think, therefore I am) of Descartes could be taken as expressing not an inferential opera-tion but an intuitive apprehension of a primitive fact or datum of consciousness, Maine de Biran came to appreciate Descartes' insight. De Biran naturally preferred the formula *Volo, ergo sum* (I will, therefore I am), inasmuch as it was in the expression of willed effort encountering resistance that, in his opinion, the I of consciousness arose. But he certainly thought of the existence of the ego as given in its appearing to consciousness as a causal agent. The existence of the subject or ego which was given as a phenomenal reality was however precisely its existence 'for itself', as active subject, that is to say, within consciousness or apperception. Descartes' great mistake, in de Biran's opinion, was that he confused the phenomenal self with the noumenal or substantial self. For from the *Cogito, ergo sum* Descartes draws conclusions about the ego or I 'in itself', thus going beyond the sphere of objects of knowledge. Kant however avoids the confu-sion by his distinction between the I of apperception, the pheno-menal ego or the ego appearing to itself and existing 'for itself', and the noumenal, substantial principle. Not that Maine de Biran's position is precisely the same as that of Kant. For instance, whereas for Kant the free agent presupposed by moral choice in the light of the concept of obligation was the noumenal self, for Maine de Biran freedom is, to use Bergsonian language, an immediate datum of consciousness, and the phenomenal ego is the free causal agent. This does not alter the fact however that de Biran sees some affinity between his idea of the permanent soul as the object of belief rather than of knowledge and Kant's idea of the noumenal self. He states, for example, that 'the relative supposes something which pre-exists absolutely, but as this absolute ceases to be such and necessarily assumes the character of the relative directly we come to know it, a contradiction is implied in saying that we have any positive knowledge or idea of the *absolute*, although we cannot prevent ourselves from believing that it exists or admitting it as a primary datum inseparable from our mind, pre-existing before all *knowledge*.'[1] To say this is to come down on the side of Kant rather than on that of Descartes.

Maine de Biran is not however content with postulating an 'absolute' as existing independently of actual consciousness and claiming that nothing further can be said about it than that it is or that we believe that it is. After all, how can we assert the existence of something when we are unable to say *what* is supposed to exist? Here Leibniz comes to de Biran's aid. Provided that the concept of substance is rethought in terms of force, it becomes easier to claim that the substantial soul manifests itself within consciousness, namely as the active subject in the relation of consciousness, and that the concept required for thinking the soul, the concept of substance that is to say, is included in the explicitation of the inner experience of causal activity or efficacy. The area of 'metaphysics' is thus extended, and Maine de Biran can state that 'Kant is wrong in refusing to the understanding the power of conceiving anything beyond *sensible* objects, outside, that is to say, the qualities which constitute these sensible objects, and in asserting that things in themselves are unknowable by the understanding.'[2]

5. The idea of seeing in the phenomenal ego the self-manifestation of an 'absolute' or substantial soul may suggest the idea of seeing all phenomena as manifesting the Absolute or God as their ultimate ground or as the cause of their existence. Though however Maine de Biran did come to regard all phenomena as related to God, it seems unlikely that he would have arrived at this position, had it not been for his meditative and religiously oriented nature and for a felt need for God. To *argue*, in the manner of traditional metaphysics, from internal phenomena to the noumenal self and from external phenomena, or from all phenomena, to the Absolute or Unconditional was really foreign to his mind.[3] It was much

---

[1] *Oeuvres*, X, p. 124.   [2] *Oeuvres*, XI, p. 284.
[3] Maine de Biran did indeed say at an early date that he believed that the world was governed by a divine intelligence. But this was a matter of spontaneous conviction or of the interior sense (*sens intime*) rather than of any cosmological argument in the traditional style.

more a question of a broadening of de Biran's idea of man's inner life. Just as he came to see in the I (*moi*) of consciousness the substantial soul manifesting itself in a relation and thus to knowledge, so did he come to see in certain aspects of man's life a manifestation of the divine reality. As he grew older, Maine de Biran developed a deeply religious philosophy. But he remained a philosopher of man's inner life. And the change in his philosophical outlook expressed a change in his reflections on this life, not a sudden conversion to traditional metaphysics.

Reference has already been made to de Biran's insistence, while in retirement at Grateloup, that belief in God is not required to lead a moral life, but that man has it within his own power to live morally. An atheist can perfectly well recognise moral values and try to realize them through his actions. De Biran was influenced by Stoicism and admired the Stoic heroes, such as Marcus Aurelius; but he naturally brought his ethical ideas into connection with his psychology, so far as this was possible. The end or goal is happiness; and a condition of attaining it is that harmony and balance should be achieved in man's powers or faculties. This means in effect that the active thinking subject of consciousness should rule over or govern the appetites and impulses of the part of man's nature which is presupposed by the life of consciousness. In other words, reason should rule over the impulses of sense. To give content however to the ideas of virtue and vice we have to consider man in his social relations, man as acting on others and as being acted on by society. 'From the feeling of free and spontaneous action which, of itself, would not have any limits, there derive what we call *rights*. From the necessary social reaction which follows the individual's action and which does not exactly conform to it (seeing that men are not like material things which react without acting or originating action) and which often anticipate it, forcing the individual to coordinate his action with that of society, there arise duties. The feeling of obligation (duty) is the feeling of this social *coercion* from which every individual knows well that he cannot free himself.'[1]

Maine de Biran became however more and more conscious of the limitations of the human reason and will, when left to themselves. 'This Stoic morality, sublime as it is, is contrary to the nature of man inasmuch as it tends to bring under the dominion

---

[1] *Journal* (H. Gouhier), I, p. 87. The interpretation of the feeling of obligation in terms of social pressure reappears in Bergson's theory of the 'closed morality'.

of the will affections, feelings or causes of excitation which do not depend on it in any way, and inasmuch as it annihilates a part of man from which he cannot become detached. Reason alone is powerless to provide the will with the motives or principles of action. It is necessary that these principles should come from a higher source.'[1] To the two levels of human life which he has already distinguished, the life of man as animal, as a sensitive being, and the life of man precisely as man, the life, that is to say, of consciousness, of the thinking and free subject, Maine de Biran is thus led to add a third level or dimension, the life of the spirit, characterized by love communicated by the divine Spirit.[2]

The concept of the three levels of human life can be expressed in this way. It is possible for man to allow his personality and liberty to be submerged in abandonment 'to all the appetites, to all the impulses of the flesh'.[3] Man as man then becomes passive, yielding to his animal nature. It is possible for him to maintain, or at least try to maintain, the level on which 'he exercises all the faculties of his nature, where he develops his moral force, by fighting against the unruly appetites of his animal nature. . . .'[4] And it is possible for him to rise to the level of 'absorption in God',[5] the level at which God is for him all in all. 'The *I* (le *moi*) is between these two terms.'[6] That is to say, the level of personal and self-sufficient existence lies between the level of the passivity of self-abandonment to the impulse of sense and the level of the passivity involved in living in God and under his influence. The second level is however ordered to the third, the divinization of man.

If one considers first of all the psychology expounded in the *Essay on the Influence of Habit* and then the ideas presented in de Biran's *Journal* from 1815 onwards or in works such as *New Essays in Anthropology*, one is likely to receive the impression that a revolution has taken place in the author's outlook and that the ideologist, strongly influenced by the thought of the Enlightenment, has been transformed into a Platonist and religious mystic. To a certain extent the impression would be justified. A series of

---

[1] *Journal*, II, p. 67.
[2] The three levels are discussed in the *Journal* (in for example, the entries for December 1818, II, p. 188, and for October 1823, II, pp. 389 f., and in the *New Essays in Anthropology* (*Oeuvres*, XIV) where the third part is devoted to the life of the spirit.
[3] *Oeuvres*, XIV, p. 369.
[4] *Ibid.*, p. 370.
[5] *Ibid.*, p. 369.
[6] *Journal*, II, p. 188.

changes certainly occurred.[1] At the same time it is important to understand that when Maine de Biran conceived and developed the idea of the life of the spirit, he did not so much reject as add to his former psychological theories. For instance, he did not reject his theory of consciousness as relational, nor his view of the life of the free and active subject of consciousness as that which is peculiar to man and as the level on which personal existence arises. He came to believe that as there is a passivity which is presupposed by the life of consciousness, so is there a receptivity above the level of personal self-sufficient existence, a receptivity in relation to the divine influence which manifests itself, for example, both in mystical experience and in the attraction exercised by the great ideals of the good and the beautiful of which Plato speaks and which constitute ways in which the divine Absolute manifests itself.

To be sure, if we speak of an 'addition', we must recognize that the addition brings about a marked change in perspective. For the life of the autonomous subject, which for the eighteenth-century *philosophe* was the highest life for man, is now subordinated to the life of the spirit in which man is dependent on the divine action within him.[2] Obviously de Biran is quite aware of the change of perspective. Thus in a frequently quoted passage he remarks that he spent his youth in studying 'individual existence and the faculties of the *self* (*moi*) and the relations, grounded in pure *consciousness*, of this self to external or internal sensations, ideas and all that is *given* to the soul or to sensibility and received by the organs, the different senses etc.'[3] He then adds that he now accords 'the primacy of importance to man's relations with God and with the society of his fellows'.[4]

In the same entry in the *Journal* however Maine de Biran says that he still believes that a 'thorough knowledge of the relations between the *ego* (*moi*) or the soul of man with the entire human being (the concrete person) should precede in the order of *time* or of study all the theoretical or practical inquiries into the two first

---

[1] The changes are admirably presented in *Les conversions de Maine de Biran* (Paris, 1948) by Professor H. Gouhier, who is also at pains to illustrate the elements of continuity in de Biran's thought.

[2] Maine de Biran writes of the self's absorption in God, of the ego's self-consciousness being swallowed up in the awareness of God or of the divine influence. But he makes it clear that he is referring to a mystical absorption in a *psychological* sense, and that he is not asserting an ontological identification of the substantial soul with God.

[3] *Journal*, II, p. 376.   [4] *Ibid.*

relations.'[1] Further, 'it is experimental *psychology* or a science at first purely reflexive which should lead us in due order to determine our moral relations to the beings like ourselves and our religious relations to the infinite superior being, whence our soul issues and to which it tends to return through the exercise of the sublimest faculties of our nature.'[2] In other words, the psychological study of the self constitutes the basis for reflection in the ethical and religious spheres, and the method to be employed throughout is that of what de Biran calls 'experimental psychology', though 'reflexive psychology' would be preferable. Throughout phenomena of man's inner life constitute the point of departure. Referring to the life of the spirit, de Biran asserts that 'the third division, the most important of all, is that which philosophy has hitherto felt obliged to leave to the speculations of mysticism, although it can also be reduced to facts of observation, drawn, it is true, from a nature lifted above the senses but not one which is at all alien to the *spirit* which knows God and itself. This division will therefore comprise the facts or the modes and acts of this spiritual life. . . .'[3] We can say perhaps that under the label 'experimental psychology' de Biran includes a psychological approach to the phenomenal effects or influence of what theologians have called divine grace.

It has been claimed that de Biran turned from Stoicism to Platonism rather than to Christianity, and that though meditation on literature such as the *Imitation of Christ* and writings by Fénelon certainly brought him closer to Christianity, he was attracted by the idea of the Holy Spirit much more than by that of Christ as son of God in a unique sense. There seems to be a good deal of truth in this contention. However, de Biran's later writings express the conviction that the Christian religion 'alone reveals to man a third life, superior to that of the sensibility and to that of the reason or of the human will. No other system of philosophy has risen so high.'[4] In any case the onetime agnostic of Grateloup died as a Catholic, even if his religion had been a Platonizing Christianity.

Maine de Biran was not a systematic thinker in the sense of one who creates a developed philosophical system. But he exercised a very considerable seminal or stimulating influence in psychology and on the philosophical movement, passing through Ravaisson

---

[1] *Ibid.*, pp. 376–7. The two first relations are those to our fellows and to God.
[2] *Ibid.*, p. 377.   [3] *Oeuvres*, XIV, p. 223.   [4] *Ibid.*, p. 373.

and Fouillée and culminating in Bergson, which is known as the spiritualist movement or current of thought.[1] In the religious sphere the type of apologetics 'from within' which was represented, for example, by Ollé-Laprune and afterwards by Blondel owed something to de Biran. His influence however, being more by way of stimulus to personal reflection in this or that field (such as psychology of volition, phenomenology of consciousness, the concept of causality and religious experience) than by the creation of disciples, is so widely diffused and so mixed with other influences that specialist studies are required to disentangle it.

---

[1] Spiritualism in this sense has nothing to do with spiritualism in the ordinary English sense of the term.

CHAPTER III

ECLECTICISM

The label—Royer-Collard—Cousin—Jouffroy

1. MAINE de Biran derived stimulus from a variety of sources. He was well aware of the fact, and at one period at any rate he defended what he described as a policy of electicism. When however reference is made to the eclectics in French philosophy during the first half of the nineteenth century, it is primarily to Royer-Collard and Cousin, rather than to Maine de Biran. It is true that de Biran was a friend of Royer-Collard and that Cousin published an edition of his writings. It is also true that Royer-Collard and Cousin can be regarded as representatives of the spiritualist movement of which de Biran was the initiator in French philosophy after the revolution. But de Biran's influence was chiefly felt at a later date, in the fields of psychology and phenomenology, whereas Cousin developed an explicitly eclectic philosophy which constituted for a time a kind of official academic system and then suffered a demise. During his lifetime Cousin enjoyed an incomparably greater fame than de Biran had ever enjoyed; but his reputation had declined when de Biran's began to increase. And while Royer-Collard and Cousin are known specifically for their eclecticism, de Biran is known for his reflection on human consciousness.

To give a precise definition of eclecticism is not an easy task. The root-meaning is indeed clear enough. The term is derived from a Greek verb (*eklegein*) meaning to pick out or choose out; and, in general, the eclectic philosophers are those who select from different schools or systems the doctrines of which they approve and then combine them. The presupposition of this procedure is obviously that every philosophical system expresses or is likely to express some truth or truths or some aspect of reality or some perspective or way of looking at the world or human life which needs to be taken into account in any overall synthesis.[1] The

[1] Leibniz expressed this idea by suggesting that every system was right in what it asserted but wrong in what it denied. In other words, original philosophers have seen something which was there to be seen, but what each saw was not all that there was to be seen.

implications however of this presupposition may or may not be fully grasped. At one extreme there are the philosophers who are lacking in the power of original thought and who pursue a policy of syncretism, combining or juxtaposing logically compatible (one hopes) doctrines from various schools or traditions but without having any very clear idea of the criteria which are being employed and without creating an organic unity. Such philosophers can be described appropriately as eclectics. At the other extreme are those philosophers, such as Aristotle and Hegel, who see the historical development of philosophy as the process whereby the most adequate philosophy up to date, namely their own systems, comes into being, subsuming in itself the insights of past thinkers. To describe such philosophers as eclectics would be to misdescribe them. If a thinker derives stimulus from a variety of sources, this does not, by itself, make him an eclectic. Or, if it does, the meaning of the term becomes too extended to be of much use. It is probably best reserved for those philosophers who combine or juxtapose doctrines taken from various sources without creating an organic unity. For if a philosopher does create an organic unity, through the consistent overall use of basic principles or fundamental pervasive ideas, he has created a recognizable system which is more than a collection of juxtaposed doctrines.

Obviously, there can be borderline cases. For example, a man might select from various systems the elements which in his opinion possessed truth-value and think that he had welded them together into an organic unity, whereas his critics might be convinced that his claim was unjustified and that he was nothing but an eclectic. The critics would however be giving to the term 'eclecticism' the meaning which we have proposed above as the appropriate meaning. Cousin indeed proclaimed himself an eclectic and then tried to distinguish between eclecticism, as he understood it, and a mere juxtaposition of ideas taken from different systems. But even if he tried to create a unified system, his claims to have done so have met with persistent criticism.

It has often been said that French eclecticism represented or at any rate was closely connected with a political attitude. This statement is not simply the expression of a general tendency to interpret philosophical movements in terms of political categories. There is more to it than that. The leading eclectics were actively engaged in politics. And they believed in the desirability of a constitution which would combine in itself the valuable elements in monarchy, aristocracy and democracy. In other words, they supported constitutional monarchy. On the one hand they were opposed not only to any hankering after the return of absolute monarchy but also to the rule of Napoleon as emperor. On the other hand they were opposed to those who believed that the revolution had not gone far enough and needed to be renewed and extended. It has been said of them that they represented a spirit of bourgeois compromise. They themselves thought of their political theory as expressing a sane eclecticism, an ability to discern the valuable elements in conflicting systems and to combine them in a viable political and social structure.

We can find a similar attitude in the religious sphere. The eclectics were opponents of materialism and atheism and of the sensationalism of Condillac. At the same time, while believing in religious freedom and having no wish to see the Church subjected to persecution, they certainly did not admit the Church's claim to be the sole guardian of truth in the religious and moral spheres; nor had they any sympathy with the idea of an ecclesiastically inspired and controlled system of education. They aimed at promoting a philosophically-based religion, existing alongside official organized religion and working with it in important ways but not subject to ecclesiastical authority and destined perhaps to take the place of Catholicism as then known.

In fine, while Traditionalists such as de Maistre dreamed of a return to a strong monarchy and preached ultramontanism, and while the social theorists who will be mentioned later demanded the extension of the revolution,[1] the eclectics tried to steer a middle course between two extremes, claiming to effect a combination of the different valuable elements in conflicting positions. To what extent political attitudes influenced philosophical positions and to what extent philosophical ideas exercised an influence on political convictions is obviously open to discussion. It is not in any case a question which can be answered purely abstractly, without consideration of individual thinkers. What seems to be clear however is that what was described as eclecticism expressed an attitude which manifested itself outside the sphere of academic philosophy.

---

[1] The reference is not of course to an extension of the Terror. Rather was it a case of believing that while the revolution had destroyed the old régime it had failed to implement its ideals in a genuine social reform. For one thing, its progress had been hampered by the rise to power of Napoleon and the arrest of any movement towards socialism.

2. Paul Royer-Collard (1763–1845) was born at Sompuis in the department of the Marne. In 1792 he was a member of the Commune of Paris and in 1797 of the Council of the Five Hundred. Though his philosophical training was meagre, he became a professor of philosophy at the Sorbonne in 1811 and retained the post until 1814. He had no liking for Napoleon; but the emperor highly approved of the inaugural lecture in which Royer-Collard attacked Condillac. In Napoleon's eyes Royer-Collard's thought would be an instrument for discomfiting and routing the ideologists. After the emperor's final overthrow Royer-Collard became a deputy for the department of the Marne and a leading figure among the so-called *doctrinaires*, who believed that their political theories could be deduced from purely rational principles.

Apart from a lecture delivered to inaugurate his course on the history of philosophy, we possess only the fragments of Royer-Collard's philosophizing which were collected by Jouffroy. He is best known for his introduction into France of the philosophy of common sense of Thomas Reid.[1] In 1768 a French translation of Reid's *Inquiry* had been published at Amsterdam; but it received little attention. Royer-Collard introduced his hearers to the work and then went on to develop some ideas of his own, though the main object of his criticism was Condillac, whereas Reid had been concerned with attacking the scepticism of Hume.

Reid's reply to Hume was not very well thought out. But one of the distinctions which he made was between Locke's simple ideas and Hume's impressions on the one hand and perception on the other. For Reid the former were not the positive data on which knowledge is grounded, but rather postulates arrived at through an analysis of what actually is given in experience, namely perception. Perception always carries with it a judgment or natural belief, about, for example, the existence of the thing perceived. If we insist on starting with subjective impressions, we remain shut up in the sphere of subjectivism. Perception however comprises within itself a judgment about external reality. This judgment stands in need of no proof[2] and is natural to all mankind, thus belonging to the principles of 'common sense'.

[1] For Thomas Reid (1710–96) see Vol. 5 of this *History*, pp. 364–73.
[2] Besides tending to forget that Hume himself had insisted on the force of natural beliefs, Reid leaves his readers in some doubt about the precise logical status to be attributed to the judgment. He speaks of self-evidently true principles; but as the judgment that what we perceive really exists is said to be a contingent truth, it seems that its self-evidence can be interpreted in terms of a natural propensity to believe it.

Royer-Collard utilizes Reid's distinction in his attack on the sensationalism of Condillac. Descartes started the trouble by taking a self-enclosed ego as his point of departure and then trying to prove the real existence of physical objects and other persons. But Condillac completed the development of 'idealism' by reducing everything to fleeting sensations, which are of their nature subjective. On his premises he was unable to explain our ability to judge, an ability which shows clearly the activity of the mind. Judgment is involved in perception, inasmuch as the perceiver naturally judges both that there is a permanent and causally active self and that the object of externally directed perception really exists. By sensations Royer-Collard understands feelings of pleasure and pain. These are clearly subjective experiences. But perception gives us objects existing independently of sensation. The armchair sceptic may entertain doubts about the existence of a permanent self and of physical objects, reducing everything to sensation; but he, like everyone else, acts in accordance with the primitive and natural judgments that there is a causally active permanent self and that there are really existing physical objects. Such judgments belong to the sphere of common sense, and they constitute the basis for the further work of reason, which can develop inductive science and which can argue to the existence of God as ultimate cause. There is no need for any supernatural authority to reveal to man the basic principles of religion and morality. Common sense and reason are sufficient guides. In other words, rejection of the sensationalism of Condillac does not entail recours to Traditionalism or to an authoritarian Church. There is a middle way.

The thought of Royer-Collard has some interest as associating a middle way in philosophy with a middle way in politics. To judge however by the fragments of his philosophizing his theories stand in need of a clarification which they do not receive. For example, in his view the self and its causal activity are given immediately to consciousness or to internal perception. Thus in the phenomenon of deliberate attention I am immediately aware of myself as a causal agent. We might expect therefore that Royer-Collard would also claim that we enjoy intuitive knowledge of the existence of perceived objects and an immediate awareness of causal relations in the world. We are told however that each sensation is a 'natural sign'[1] which in some mysterious way

---

[1] *Les fragments philosophiques de Royer-Collard*, edited by A. Schimberg, p. 22 (Paris, 1913).

suggests not only the idea of an external existent but also the irresistible persuasion of its reality. Royer-Collard also implies that we are led irresistibly by an awareness of the self as a causal agent to find (non-voluntary) causal activity in the external world. As critics have pointed out, Hume explicitly admitted that we have a natural and, in practice, irresistible belief in the real existence of bodies independently of our impressions or perceptions. He could therefore quite well have said that this belief was a matter of common sense. But though Hume thought that the validity of the belief could not be proved, he at any rate inquired into its genesis, whereas Royer-Collard finds such inquiries uncongenial and leaves his hearers in some doubt about precisely what he is claiming. It is indeed clear that he rejects the reduction of the self and the external world to sensations and the attempt to reconstruct them on this basis. It is also clear that he lays emphasis on the idea of perception as distinct from sensation and as a means of overcoming subjectivism. But his treatment of the way in which perception establishes the existence of the external world is ambiguous. He seems to wish to find room for an inductive inference which leads to a conclusion which is certainly, and not simply probably true. But the point is not developed.

3. Victor Cousin (1792–1867) came of a family of poor artisans in Paris. It is related that in 1803, when playing in the gutter, he intervened to rescue a pupil of the Lycée Charlemagne from a gang of pursuing schoolmates, and that in gratitude the boy's mother undertook to provide for Cousin's education.[1] At the Lycée Charlemagne Cousin carried off the prizes, and on leaving the school he gained entry to the École Normale. As soon as he had finished his course of studies he was appointed assistant professor of Greek, being then twenty years old. In 1815 he lectured at the Sorbonne as a substitute for Royer-Collard on the Scottish philosophy of common sense. At the École Normale he had indeed attended lectures by Laromiguière[2] and Royer-Collard; but his knowledge of philosophy was at the time pretty limited. For the matter of that, so was Royer-Collard's.

Cousin then applied himself to learning something about Kant

[1] For such details see *Victor Cousin* (London, 1888) by Jules Simon, who had been a pupil of Cousin.
[2] Pierre Laromiguière (1756–1837) accepted the general method of Condillac, but he adopted a twofold point of departure by adding the motive power of attention to the receptivity of sensation. It has been already noted that Maine de Biran wrote on Laromiguière's *Lectures* (*Leçons*).

whose doctrine he soon mastered, in his own opinion at least if not in that of posterity. In 1817 he went to Germany to make the acquaintance of the post-Kantian philosophers. On this visit he met Hegel, while on a subsequent visit in 1818 he came to know Schelling and Jacobi. On a third visit to Germany in 1824 Cousin had an opportunity to widen his knowledge of German philosophy while in prison for six months, suspected by the Prussian police of being a conspirator.

In 1820 the École Normale was closed, and Cousin lost his chair. He then set about editing the works of Descartes and of Proclus and started translating Plato. In 1828 he was restored to his chair, and with the accession to the throne of Louis-Philippe his day had come at last. In 1830 he became a councillor of State, in 1832 a member of the Royal Council and director of the École Normale, in 1833 a peer of France and in 1840 minister of public instruction. In the years of his glory he was to all intents and purposes not only the official philosopher of France but also a philosophical dictator who described the French philosophers of philosophy as his 'regiment' and excluded from the teaching staff of the Sorbonne those of whom he disapproved, such as Comte and Renouvier. The revolution of 1848 however brought Cousin's philosophical dictatorship to an end, and he retired into private life. At the accession to power of Louis Napoleon he became a professor emeritus with a pension.

Cousin described the sensationalist theory of Condillac and his associates as 'sensualism'. Hence the title of his work *Sensualist Philosophy in the Eighteenth Century* (*Philosophie sensualiste au XVIIIe siècle*, 1819). Among other writings one can mention *Philosophical Fragments* (*Fragments philosophiques*, 1826). *On the True, Beautiful and the Good* (*Du vrai, du beau et du bien*, 1837), a *Course of the History of Modern Philosophy* (*Cours de l'histoire de la philosophie moderne*, 5 volumes, 1841) and *Studies on Pascal* (*Études sur Pascal*, 1842).

It was Cousin's conviction that the nineteenth century stood in need of eclecticism. It needed it in the political sphere, in the sense that monarchy, aristocracy and democracy should function as component elements in the constitution. In the philosophical sphere the time had arrived for a systematic policy of eclecticism, for a welding together of the valuable elements contained in different systems. Man himself is a composite being, and just as in man an harmonious integration of different powers and activities is a desirable goal, so in philosophy do we require an integration of different ideas, each of which is apt to be over-emphasized by one or other philosophical system.

According to Cousin, reflection on the history of philosophy reveals that there are four basic types of system, which are 'the fundamental elements of all philosophy'.[1] In the first place there is sensualism, the philosophy 'which relies exclusively on the senses'.[2] Then there is idealism, which finds reality in the realm of thought. Thirdly there is the philosophy of common sense. And in the fourth place there is mysticism, which turns its back on the senses and takes refuge in interiority. Each of these systems or types of system contains some truth, but no one of them contains the whole truth or is uniquely true. For example, the philosophy of sensation must obviously express some truth, as sensibility is a real aspect of man. It is not however the whole of man. In regard therefore to the basic kinds of system we have to be careful 'not to reject any one, and not to be the dupe of any of them'.[3] We have to combine the true elements. To do so is to practise eclecticism.

Eclecticism is presented by Cousin as the culmination of an historical process. 'The philosophy of a century arises from all the elements of which this century is composed.'[4] In other words, philosophy is the product of the complex factors which compose a civilization, even though, once arisen, it takes on a life of its own and can exercise an influence. At the close of the Middle Ages, according to Cousin, the new spirit which arose first took the form of an attack on the dominant medieval power, the Church, and so of a religious revolution. A political revolution came second. 'The English revolution is the great event of the end of the seventeenth century.'[5] Both revolutions expressed the spirit of freedom, which was then manifested in the science and philosophy of the eighteenth century. The spirit of freedom or liberty led indeed to the excesses of the French revolution; but subsequently it was given a balanced expression in a political system combining the elements of monarchy, aristocracy and democracy, in constitutional monarchy that is to say. It follows that the philosophy required by the nineteenth century is an eclecticism which combines independence of the Church with a rejection of materialism and atheism. In fine, an eclectic spiritualism is required which transcends the philosophy of sensation of the eighteenth century

---

[1] *Cours de philosophie. Histoire de la philosophie*, I, p. 141 (Brussels, 1840).
[2] *Ibid.*, p. 118.   [3] *Ibid.*, p. 141.   [4] *Ibid.*, p. 8.   [5] *Ibid.*, p. 11.

but does not fall back into subservience to ecclesiastical dogma and tutelage.

It would not be fair to Cousin to suggest that he is blind to the fact that this sort of interpretation of the history of development presupposes a philosophy, a definite stand in regard to criteria of truth and falsehood. He may speak on occasion as though he were an impartial observer, judging philosophy from outside; but he also admits explicitly that we cannot separate truth from error in philosophical systems without criteria which are the result of previous philosophical reflection, and that for this reason eclecticism 'assumes a system, starts from a system'.[1]

Cousin's rejection of the sensationalism of Condillac by no means entails a rejection of the method of observation and experiment in philosophy, nor indeed of starting with psychology. In his view Condillac's use of observation was deficient. As was seen by Laromiguière, observation gives us phenomena such as active attention which cannot be reduced to passively received impressions. And Maine de Biran threw light, by means of observation, on the active role of the self. If Condillac rightly asserted the existence and importance of human sensibility, de Biran rightly asserted the existence and importance of the human will, of voluntary activity. Observation however, Cousin insists, will take us further than this. For it reveals to us the faculty of reason, which is reducible neither to sensation nor to will and which sees the necessary truth of certain basic principles, such as the principle of causality, that are implicitly recognized by common sense. Psychology therefore reveals the presence of three faculties in man, namely sensibility, will and reason. And philosophical problems fall into three corresponding groups, concerned respectively with the beautiful, the good and the true.

To develop a philosophy of reality we have of course to go beyond the purely psychological sphere. It is the faculty of reason which enables us to do this. For with the aid of the principles of substance and causality it enables us to refer the interior phenomena of willed effort to the self or ego and passively received impressions to an external world or Nature. These two realities, the ego and the non-ego, limit one another, as Fichte held, and cannot constitute the ultimate reality. Both must be ascribed to the creative activity of God. It is thus reason which enables us to emerge from the subjective sphere and to develop an ontology in

[1] *Fragments philosophiques* (1838 edition), I, p. 41.

which the self and the not-self are seen as related to the causal activity of God.

The Traditionalists emphasized the impotence of the human reason in the metaphysical and religious spheres, when working independently of revelation. The Catholic Church eventually took a stand against this attitude; and it may thus appear that it should have been gratified by Cousin's metaphysics. But what Cousin was driving at was a middle way between Catholicism on the one hand and eighteenth-century atheism and agnosticism on the other. It is understandable therefore that his point of view was not altogether acceptable to those who believed that the bosom of the Church was the only viable and proper alternative to infidelity. Further, Cousin was accused of pantheism on the ground that he represented the world as a necessary actualization of the divine life. That is to say, he thought of God as necessarily manifesting himself in the physical world and in the sphere of finite selves. The world, in his opinion, was as necessary to God as God to the world; and he spoke of God as returning to himself in human consciousness.[1] Cousin denied that such ways of speaking entailed pantheism; but little weight was attached to his denial by critics who were convinced of the inherently irreligious tendencies of philosophy. To be sure, he advised philosophers to steer clear of talking about religion, by which he meant primarily Catholicism. But he certainly talked about God; and to his religious critics his way of speaking seemed to be at variance with what they believed to be true religion and to confirm their suspicions of philosophy.

As an exponent of a middle way, of a policy of compromise, Cousin was naturally faced with criticism from two sides. His metaphysics was acceptable neither to materialists and atheists nor to the Traditionalists. His political theories satisfied neither the republicans and the socialistically minded nor the authoritarian royalists. His more academic critics have objected that the transition which he makes from psychology to ontology is unjustified. In particular, Cousin gives no clear explanation how principles of universal and necessary validity, capable of grounding an ontology and a metaphysics, can be derived from inspection of the data of consciousness. He asserts that 'as is the method of a

[1] Cousin's ideas on this subject obviously show the influence of German metaphysical idealism. It was however his general habit to minimize foreign influence in his thought. He even went so far as to represent electicism as a specifically French contribution to philosophical thought.

philosopher, so will be his system', and that 'the adoption of a method decides the destiny of a philosophy'.[1] Those critics who find Cousin's eclecticism incoherent may be inclined to agree, adding that in his case a clearly defined method was conspicuous by its absence.

Though however Cousin's thought has been submitted to a good deal of patronizing or even contemptuous criticism, he made a considerable contribution to the development of academic philosophy in France, especially perhaps in the field of the history of philosophy. His view that there was truth in all systems naturally encouraged study of them; and he set an example by his historical writings. It is easy to write him off as a man who gave theoretical expression to the reign of Louis-Philippe. The fact remains that he left his mark on university philosophy in France.

4. Among the pupils of Cousin was Théodore Simon Jouffroy (1796–1842). He entered the École Normale in 1814 and after his studies became a lecturer there until his appointment in 1833 as professor of ancient philosophy at the Collège de France.[2] From 1833 he also served as a deputy in the Chamber. His writings include two sets of philosophical essays (*Mélanges philosophiques*, 1833, and *Nouveaux mélanges philosophiques*, 1842) and two courses, one on natural law (*Cours de droit naturel*, 2 volumes, 1834–42) and one on aesthetics (*Cours d'esthétique*, 1843). The second course, published posthumously, consists of notes of his lectures taken by a hearer.

In regard to philosophy, or at any rate to philosophical systems, Jouffroy shows a marked scepticism. In 1813 he realized that he had lost his Christian faith. That is to say, he found that the answers provided by Christian dogmas to problems about human life and destiny were no longer valid for him. In his view philosophy would or at least might one day take the place of Christian dogmas and solve the problems which could no longer be answered by the authoritative pronouncements of a religion claiming to embody divine revelation.[3] In this matter Jouffroy was more outspoken than Cousin who, whatever he may have thought, tended to emphasize the co-existence of philosophy and religion

---

[1] *Elements of Psychology*, translated by C. S. Henry, p. 28 (London, 1851).
[2] Previously to his nomination to this chair Jouffroy had lectured at the Sorbonne as well as at the École Normale.
[3] In 1825 Jouffroy published an article on the end of dogmas and their eventual replacement by philosophy.

rather than the replacement of the latter by the former.[1] Though however Jouffroy remained convinced that each individual had in fact a vocation, a task in life, he did not believe that anyone could know with certainty what his vocation was, nor that philosophy as it existed could provide definite answers to problems of this kind. In his opinion philosophical systems reflected the outlook, ideas, historical and social circumstances and needs of their times. Systems, in other words, express relative, not absolute truth. Like religion, they can have pragmatic value; but a final philosophical system is a remote ideal, not an actuality.

Jouffroy combined this partial scepticism in regard to philosophical systems with belief in principles of common sense which are prior to explicit philosophy and express the collective wisdom of the human race. Royer-Collard and Cousin aroused in him an interest in the Scottish philosophy of common sense, an interest which bore fruit in his translation into French of Dugald Stewart's[2] *Outlines of Moral Philosophy* and of Reid's works. Reflecting on the Scottish philosophy Jouffroy came to the conclusion that there are principles of common sense which possess a degree of truth and certainty which is not enjoyed by the philosophical theories of individuals.[3] To be sure, these theories cannot be simply the product of individuals, if philosophies express the spirit of their times. But the principles of common sense represent something more permanent, the collective wisdom of mankind or the human race, to which appeal can be made against the one-sidedness of a philosophical system. One philosopher, for example, may expound a materialist system, while another regards spirit as the sole reality. Common sense however recognizes the existence of both matter and spirit. Presumably therefore any adequate or universally true philosophy would be basically an explication of common sense, of the wisdom of mankind, rather than of the ideas, outlook, circumstances and needs of a particular society.

There are of course some pretty obvious objections to any sharp division between individual opinions and theories on the one hand

---

[1] As a kind of philosophical dictator, the official mouthpiece of philosophy in France, Cousin was anxious not to antagonize potentially hostile groups but to harmonize different points of view. As we have noted, his policy of compromise was not particularly successful. The point is however that his position encouraged adoption of a policy which a man such as Jouffroy, who did not share Cousin's ambitions, had much less interest in pursuing.

[2] For Dugald Stewart see Vol. 5 of this *History*, pp. 375–83.

[3] On this subject see Jouffroy's essay on philosophy and common sense in *Mélanges philosophiques*.

and the collective wisdom of mankind on the other. For example, common sense is said to express itself in self-evidently true propositions which lie at the basis of logics and ethics. But the truth of such principles is grasped by individual minds. And in his psychological reflections, where he treats of human faculties, their development and cooperation, Jouffroy certainly depicts reason as capable of apprehending truth. To a certain extent perhaps the tension between individualism and what we may perhaps, for want of a better word, call collectivism can be overcome by representing the fully developed human being as participating in the common mind or wisdom. But the tension in Jouffroy's thought remains. For instance, his view of common sense as expressing human solidarity might be expected, as historians have pointed out, to influence his political ideas in the direction of socialism, whereas in fact he spoke on occasion of society as a collection of individuals. Perhaps however Jouffroy would maintain that the integration of the common and the individual is an ideal towards which mankind moves. In the case of philosophy at any rate he believed that the divergence between one-sided systems and common sense would one day be overcome. And he seems also to have thought that nationalism was in process of giving way to internationalism as an expression of human fraternity.

We have seen that Cousin tried to base ontology on psychology. Jouffroy did not follow him here. He insisted that psychology should be kept free from metaphysics and studied with the same scientific detachment that we find in the physicist. At the same time he emphasized the distinction between psychology and physical science.[1] When the physicist observes a series or set of phenomena, he is not simultaneously presented with their cause or causes. Further inquiry is required. In inner observation or perception however the cause, namely the self, is a datum. This may sound like an excursion into metaphysics; but Jouffroy seems to be referring, in a manner reminiscent of Maine de Biran, to the ego which is aware of itself in consciousness or apperception rather than to a substantial soul.

In his lectures on natural law Jouffroy devoted his attention very largely to ethical themes. In a sense good and evil are relative. For every man has his own particular vocation in life, his life-task; and good actions are those which contribute to the

---

[1] See Jouffroy's essay on the legitimacy of the distinction between psychology and physiology in *Nouveaux mélanges philosophiques*.

fulfilment of this vocation, while evil actions are those which are incompatible with its fulfilment. We can say therefore that good and evil are relative to the individual's self-realization. But this is not all that can be said. Underlying all ethical codes and systems of law are the basic principles which belong to common sense. Further Jouffroy seems to regard all individual vocations as contributing to the development of a common moral order. And if a unified moral ideal cannot be fully realized in this life, it may perhaps be the case that it will be realized in another.

CHAPTER IV

SOCIAL PHILOSOPHY IN FRANCE

General remarks—The utopianism of Fourier—Saint-Simon and the development of society—Proudhon, anarchism and syndicalism—Marx on the French socialists.

1. THE Traditionalists, as we have seen, were concerned with what they regarded as the breakdown of social order exhibited in and consequent on the revolution, the revolution itself being attributed in large measure to the thought and influence of the eighteenth-century philosophers. To depict the Traditionalists as being reactionaries to such an extent as to envisage the restoration of the pre-revolutionary régime together with all the abuses which rendered change inevitable would be to do them an injustice. But they certainly believed that social reconstruction on a firm basis demanded a reassertion of traditional principles of religion and of monarchic government. In this sense they looked backwards, though a writer such as de Maistre was, as we have noted, a strong upholder of ultramontanism and no friend of the tradition of Gallicanism.

The ideologists, regarded by Napoleon as pestilential 'metaphysicians', were not much given to political pronouncements. But their methods had implications in the social field. For example, they insisted on careful analysis of empirical phenomena and on education through discussion. The emperor doubtless thought that the ideologists were concerned with trivialities and useless or unprofitable inquiries; but the fact of the matter is that they were opposed to the idea of moulding the youth to a pattern and to the educational system as envisaged by Napoleon, as well as to his restoration of the Catholic religion in France.

The eclectics favoured constitutional monarchy and a compromise policy, acceptable to the bourgeoisie. They were themselves active in political life; and they can be said to have represented a class which gained in status through the revolution and which did not desire further drastic experiments, whether imperialistic conquests or socialist programmes of change.

It is only to be expected however that there should have been other thinkers who were convinced that the revolution ought to be carried further, not indeed in the sense of a renewal of blood-shed but in the sense that the ideals of the revolution needed to be realized in a reformation of the structure of society. Liberty might have been achieved by the revolution; but the realization of equality and fraternity was by no means so conspicuous. These would-be social reformers who were convinced that the work of the revolution needed to be extended, were idealists,[1] and their positive proposals have often been described as utopian, especially by Marx and his followers. In some cases at any rate the description has an obvious foundation in fact. If the Traditionalists had their dreams, so had their opposite numbers. To admit this patent fact does not however entail the conclusion that Marxism is scientific as opposed to utopian socialism.[2] In any case a sharp distinction tends to conceal the fact that the ideas of the French social reformers in the first half of the nineteenth century con-tributed to the development of political theory on socialist lines.

2. It must be admitted that Karl Marx's view of François Marie Charles Fourier (1772–1837) as a well-meaning and myth-creating utopian socialist was not unjustified. For while Fourier certainly drew attention to a real problem, his solution contained elements which now and then bordered on the fantastic. His views were often eccentric; and some of his prophecies, as about the functions which animals might or would come to fulfil, amounted to highly imaginative science fiction. But he was a kindly man and was inspired by a genuine desire for the regenera-tion of society.

A native of Besançon, where he received his schooling from the Jesuits, Fourier was the son of a merchant and gained his liveli-hood in the world of trade. Apart from this occupation he devoted himself to the propagation of his views on human society. His writings include a *Theory of the Four Movements and of General Destinies* (*Théorie des quatres mouvements et des destinées générales*, 1808), a *Theory of Universal Unity* (*Théorie de l'unité universelle*, 1822) and a work entitled *The New Industrial and Social World*

---

[1] There is of course no reference to idealism in any technical philosophical sense.
[2] It is arguable at any rate that a more helpful distinction can be made between pragmatic socialism, which is of course inspired by at least implicit socio-ethical ideals but is comparatively free from ideological dogmatism, and doctrinaire socialism in which the interests of individuals and groups here and now may very well be sacrificed in the name of the society of the future, the advent of which is regarded either as the inevitable result of an historical process or as so over-whelmingly desirable that the measures supposed to be required for its attain-ment must take precedence over the correction of present abuses and evils.

(*Le nouveau monde industriel et sociétaire*, 1829). Except for his secondary schooling at Besançon he was a self-taught man who possessed plenty of intelligence, a lively imagination and a smattering of knowledge on a variety of topics.

Fourier was an uncompromising and outspoken critic of established society as he knew it. More accurately, he followed Rousseau in blaming civilization for the ills of mankind. Everywhere in civilized society, according to Fourier, we can see selfishness and self-interest masquerading as service to humanity. For example, doctors thrive on the spread of ailments among their fellow citizens, and the clergy desire the deaths of their wealthier parishioners in order to receive substantial fees for performing the funeral rites.[1] Moreover, civilized society is afflicted with hordes of parasites. Women and children, for instance, are domestic parasites, while soldiers and traders are social parasites. Obviously, not even Fourier's eccentricity goes so far as to suggest that women and children should be eliminated. What he means is that in civilized society women and children lead unproductive lives. In his opinion, women should be emancipated and free to take part in productive work, while children, he quaintly suggests, who love playing in the gutter, might well be employed in cleaning up the streets. As things are, only a comparatively small section of the population is engaged in productive work. Armies are engaged in destruction, not production; and in times of peace they are parasites on society. As for traders and merchants, 'commerce is the natural enemy of the producer.'[2] It by no means follows however that the producers are either happy or free from the prevailing selfishness. Their conditions of life are often deplorable, and 'each worker is at war with the mass and bears ill will towards it from personal interest'.[3] In fine, civilized society is infected thoughout with selfishness, discord and disharmony.

What is the origin of the evils of civilized society? According to Fourier it is the repression of the passions, for which civilization is

---

[1] Fourier evidently gives one-sided pictures or caricatures of the motives and outlooks of groups and classes. Caricature apart however, he is certainly quick to detect evidence of what he believes to be sham and humbug and to draw inferences from behaviour to motives of which the agents may not be consciously aware. In other words, his picture of society, though doubtless one-sided, exhibits some psychological insight. In the case of politicians, for example, claims to be concerned exclusively with the public welfare often arouse sceptical thoughts in minds which have never heard of Fourier.

[2] *Four Movements*, p. 332; *Universal Unity*, II, p. 217.

[3] *Four Movements*, p. 29.

responsible. The world was created by a good God who implanted in man certain passions which must therefore be good in themselves. Among the thirteen passions implanted by God Fourier includes, for example, the five senses, social passions such as love and family feeling, distributive passions such as that for variety (the 'butterfly' passion), and the crowning passion for harmony which unites or synthesizes the others.[1] Civilization has repressed these passions in such a way as to render harmony impossible. What is required therefore is a reorganization of society which will secure the release of the passions and, consequently, both the development of individuals and the attainment of concord or harmony between them.

The social organization to which Fourier pinned his hopes was what he called a 'phalanx', a group of men, women and children amounting in number to between one and a half and two thousand people.[2] The members of a phalanx would be persons of different temperaments, abilities and tastes. They would be grouped according to occupation or type of work; but no member would be given work for which he was unsuited or which he would find repugnant. If his tastes changed or he felt the need for other work, he could satisfy the 'butterfly' passion.[3] Thus each member of a phalanx would have full opportunity to develop his talents and passions to the full; and he would understand the significance of his particular work in the general scheme. There would be competition between sub-groups; but harmony would reign. Indeed, if only one phalanx was successfully established, the evident harmony, happiness and prosperity of its members would inevitably stimulate imitation. Relations between different phalanxes would be loose, though there would have to be provision for groups of workers to perform special temporary tasks in different phalanxes. There would not of course be any wars. Their place would be taken by gastronomic contests or competitions.[4]

Some of Fourier's ideas strike most readers as odd or bizarre. Thus he believed that human social regeneration would have remarkable effects not only in the animal kingdom but even among

---

[1] It is hardly necessary to say that by passion Fourier does not mean something excessive and disordered, as when we say of someone that he flew into a passion or that he was carried away by ungovernable passion.

[2] The ideal number, according to Fourier, would be 1620, as this would facilitate all combinations of the thirteen basic passions.

[3] The family would be retained in the phalanx. But release of the 'butterfly' passion would mean abolition of tabus in regard to conjugal fidelity.

[4] Fourier laid stress on 'gastrosophy'.

the heavenly bodies. But the oddity of some of his ideas does not alter the fact that he saw a real problem which is acute enough today, namely that of humanizing industrial society and labour and overcoming what is described as alienation. His solution obviously suffers from the defects of utopianism, such as the notion that there is only one ideal form of social organization. At the same time it had its points. To a certain extent it was a socialist solution; but Fourier did not envisage the abolition of private property, which he believed to be necessary for the development of the human personality. What he was suggesting was an experimental cooperative society with shareholders, the shares being allotted in stated proportion to labour, capital and talent, and the highest interest going to those who held the least stock.

Fourier himself never succeeded in realizing his project. But after his death a disciple called Godin founded a 'phalanstery' in France, while another disciple, Victor Considérant, experimented on Fourierist lines in Texas. Fourier's doctrines, trimmed of their more bizarre features, attracted a number of adherents both in France and America; but their effect was understandably limited and passing. He regarded himself as the Newton of social thought, the discoverer of the laws of social development and, in particular, of the transition from 'civilization' to the harmonious and perfect society which would realize the divine plan. His own estimate of himself has not been accepted. But while it is understandable that his ideas should be regarded as being to a large extent an historical curiosity, he was by no means devoid of perspicacity. Such problems as how to organize social and industrial structures in the service of man and how to harmonize individual and collective needs are obviously still with us.

3. A more influential precursor of socialism was Claude-Henri de Rouvroy, Comte de Saint-Simon (1760–1825). Scion of a noble though by no means wealthy family Saint-Simon received his education from private tutors, one of whom was the philosopher and scientist d'Alembert.[1] It was doubtless d'Alembert who stimulated in Saint-Simon's mind his faith in science as the source of enlightenment. At the age of seventeen Saint-Simon became an officer in the army and took part in the American war of independence. When the revolution broke out, he supported it up to a point, though his cooperation seems to have consisted mainly in buying confiscated property cheaply. In 1793 he was arrested,

---

[1] For d'Alembert see vol. 6 of this *History*, pp. 39–47.

under the name which he had adopted for his profitable enter-
prises, but was subsequently released. He was politically active
under the Directory but eventually gave himself entirely to the
development and publicization of his social ideas, at times in a
position of very considerable hardship.[1] In 1807–8 he published
his *Introduction to the Scientific Works of the Nineteenth Century*
(*Introduction aux travaux scientifiques de XIXe siècle*), and in 1813
his *Essay on the Science of Man* and *Work on Universal Gravitation*
(*Mémoire sur la science de l'homme* and *Travail sur la gravitation
universelle*). From 1814 until 1817 he worked in collaboration with
Augustin Thierry; and the work entitled *Reorganisation of
European Society* (*Réorganisation de la société européenne*, 1814)
appeared under both names. From 1818 Auguste Comte acted as
his secretary and collaborator until the two men quarrelled in
1824, the year before Saint-Simon's death. Comte owed a considerable debt to Saint-Simon and he could on occasion acknow-
ledge the fact; but, in general, he preferred not to.

Saint-Simon described the philosophy of the eighteenth
century as critical and revolutionary, whereas the philosophy of
the nineteenth century was destined to be inventive and organiza-
tional. 'The philosophers of the eighteenth century made an
Encyclopaedia to overthrow the theological and feudal system.
The philosophers of the nineteenth century should also make an
Encyclopaedia to bring into being the industrial and scientific
system.'[2] That is to say, the thinkers of the eighteenth century
subjected the old régime and the beliefs on which it rested to
destructive criticism. If, in Saint-Simon's opinion, the last kings of
France had had the good sense to ally themselves with the rising
industrial class instead of with the nobility, the transition to a
new system could have been affected peaceably. In point of fact
however the old régime was swept away in a violent revolution.
At the same time a political system cannot disappear entirely,
unless a new system, capable of taking its place, is waiting, so to
speak, in the wings. In the case of the French revolution the new
system, destined to take the place of the old, was not ready. It is
no matter for surprise therefore if after a time the monarchy was
restored. The nineteenth century however was destined to be a
period of new social construction and organization. And in the
fulfilment of this task the nineteenth-century thinkers had an

---

[1] In 1823 Saint-Simon attempted suicide.
[2] *Oeuvres complètes de Saint-Simon et Enfantin* (Paris, 1865–76), X, pp. 104–5.

important role to play, the thinkers, that is to say, who, like Saint-Simon himself, could point out the lines which the process of constructive organization should take.

Though however Saint-Simon emphasized the critical and destructive aspects of the philosophy of the eighteenth-century Enlightenment, there was another aspect of it which he regarded as providing the basis for later construction. This was its exaltation of the rational and scientific spirit. In Saint-Simon's opinion, it was science which had undermined the authority of the Church and the credibility of theological dogmas. At the same time it was the extension of the scientific approach from physics and astronomy to man himself which provided the basis for social reorganization. 'Knowledge of man is the one thing which can lead to the discovery of the ways of reconciling the interests of people.'[1] And knowledge of man can be attained only by treating man as a part of nature and by developing the idea, already prepared by certain writers of the Enlightenment and by Cabanis, of psychology as a department of physiology. Psychology however must also include study of the social organism. In other words, a new science is needed, described by Saint-Simon as social physiology.[2] Society and politics or, more generally, man in society can then be studied no less scientifically than the movements of the heavenly bodies. In fine, the application of Newtonian science to man himself, his psychology, his moral behaviour and his politics, is an indispensable basis for solving the social problems of Europe.

The sciences of astronomy, physics and chemistry have already been placed on a 'positive basis',[3] that is to say on observation and experiment.[4] The time has now come to place the science of man on a similar basis.[5] This will bring about the unification of the sciences and the realization of the ideal which inspired the *Encyclopaedia*. It is true that a completely unified and final scientific knowledge of the world remains an ideal towards which the human mind can approximate but which it cannot fully attain, inasmuch as advance in scientific knowledge is always possible.

---

[1] *Ibid.*, XI, p. 40.
[2] The term 'sociology' derives from Comte rather than from Saint-Simon.
[3] *Oeuvres*, XI, p. 17.
[4] Saint-Simon emphasizes the role of observation and experiment. Obviously, experimentation, in the sense in which we speak of experiments in chemistry, is hardly possible in astronomy. But the term can be understood in a wide sense. And nowadays the situation has altered from what it was in Saint-Simon's time.
[5] We are reminded of the famous passage in Hume's introduction to the *Treatise*, in which he envisages placing the science of man on a solid foundation of experience and observation.

At the same time Saint-Simon thinks in terms of the extension of the approach and method of classical physics, considered as definitive in its main lines, to the study of man. And he believes that this extension will complete the transition from the stage of human thought in which theology and metaphysics passed as knowledge to the stage of positive or scientific knowledge.

Some writers have seen a discrepancy between Saint-Simon's ideal of the unification of the sciences and his later insistence on the superior dignity of the science of man. It has been argued, that is to say, that the ideal in question implies that all sciences are on the same level, whereas to ascribe a higher dignity to the science of man is to assume that there is a qualitative difference between man and other beings and to fall back on the medieval notion that the dignity of a science depends on its subject-matter or 'formal object'.[1]

This may be the case. But it does not seem necessary to postulate any radical change in Saint-Simon's position. He does indeed come to hold that social physiology has a special subject-matter, namely the social organism, which is more than a collection of individuals. But he demands that society should be studied by means of the same sort of method which is employed in other sciences. And if he adds a value-judgment, this does not necessarily involve him in a radical shift of position, not at any rate if we interpret him as referring to the importance of the science of man rather than as implying that man is qualitatively different from other things to an extent which precludes scientific study of human society. This implication was obviously not intended.

Saint-Simon does not of course treat society in a purely abstract manner. Social and political institutions develop and change; and Saint-Simon assumes that there must be a law which governs such changes. To study human society scientifically involves therefore discovery of the law or laws of social evolution. If we take it that any such law can be discovered only inductively, by investigating and reflecting on the historical phenomena, it is obvious that a survey of the widest possible field is desirable. Or, if a preliminary statement of the law of social change is based on an inquiry into a limited field, inquiry into other fields is required in order to see whether the hypothesis is confirmed or falsified. Though however

---

[1] See, for example, what is said by E. Bréhier in the sixth volume of his *History of Philosophy* (*The Nineteenth Century: Period of Systems, 1800–1850*, translated by Wade Baskin, Chicago and London, 1968, p. 267).

Saint-Simon does make general remarks about historical stages in the process of social evolution, what really interests him is the transition from medieval to modern civilization, apart from what he has to say about the future.

In his general views of the transition from theological beliefs and metaphysical speculation to the era of positive or scientific knowledge, of the need for a science of human society, and of historical changes as law-governed, Saint-Simon obviously anticipates the positivism of Auguste Comte. The latter's disciples were inclined to belittle the former's influence; and some even tried to make out that it was Saint-Simon who was influenced by Comte rather than the other way round. But this contention cannot be defended successfully. To be sure, both men had their precursors in the eighteenth century, writers such as Turgot and Condorcet.[1] And during their period of collaboration Saint-Simon doubtless derived stimulus from Comte. The point is however that Saint-Simon arrived at his basic ideas well before the period of his association with Comte. And whatever some of his disciples may have said, Comte could bring himself on occasion, at any rate in correspondence, to recognize his debt to Saint-Simon. True, Comte worked out his ideas in his own way. But it is a question of deriving stimulus from Saint-Simon and being influenced by him in important respects rather than of slavish appropriation of ideas. In view of Comte's reputation as the founder of classical positivism it is as well to draw attention to the important role played by Saint-Simon.

In his account of social change Saint-Simon lays great emphasis on the basic importance of ideas. For example, the beliefs and ideas of the Middle Ages exercised a determining influence on the social and political institutions of the time,[2] while the development of the sciences and the transition to the stage of positive knowledge demands and leads to the creation of new social and political structures. In thus emphasizing the basic role played by ideas he is linked with Comte rather than with Marx. At the same time Saint-Simon also stresses the importance of man's economic life by what he has to say about the rise of the class of merchants and artisans. In his opinion the feudal society of the Middle Ages reached its culminating point in the eleventh century. After

---

[1] For Turgot and Condorcet, see Vol. 6 of this *History*, pp. 56–8 and pp. 168–71.
[2] Saint-Simon regards the medieval period as a necessary stage in historical development and has thus little sympathy with the eighteenth-century tendency to dismiss the Middle Ages as a period of darkness.

this time there emerged within it two factors which were the remote augurs of its dissolution. One was the introduction of scientific ideas from the Islamic world, while the other was the emergence of the communes, representing a class of producers in a sense in which the Church and the feudal nobility were not producers.[1] Within the medieval period itself neither factor became strong enough to constitute a real threat to existing authority. In the sixteenth century however the power of the Church was weakened by the challenge of the reformers; and it allied itself with, or subordinated itself to the monarchy instead of being, as in the Middle Ages, a rival to the temporal power. Scientific knowledge grew and threatened theological beliefs, eventually leading intellectuals at any rate to question all established authority and ideas. Further, as the French monarchs foolishly associated themselves with the nobility, once it had been reduced to a condition of submission, rather with the interests of the rising class of producers, violent revolution became in the end inevitable. The French revolution was simply the outcome of a process which had been going on 'for more than six centuries'.[2] It set the rising class free and rendered possible the transition to industrial society.

Saint-Simon looked on contemporary society as being in an intermediary phase, intermediate, that is to say, between the old régime and the establishment of a new society based on scientific knowledge and on industry. The conditions for a new society were already there. It would not matter if France were to lose the monarchy, the bishops and the landowners; but it would certainly matter if it lost the only really useful class, the producers or workmen. (The scientists must also be included of course as an indispensable element in society.) It by no means follows however that Saint-Simon demanded the development of social democracy or concerned himself with extension of the franchise to all citizens or with their participation in government. What he does look forward to is the rule of scientists and of captains of industry. In *L'Organisation* (1819) he envisaged three chambers of experts.

---

[1] It does not follow that Saint-Simon regarded the Church and the feudal nobility as parasites on medieval society. For him medieval society was 'organic', and he looked on the feudal nobility and the Church as performing useful functions within this society. He did not, for instance, regard religion simply as harmful superstition, but rather as an historical necessity, even though religious beliefs were destined to be supplanted by scientific knowledge.

[2] *Oeuvres*, V. p. 78.

The first, the chamber of invention, consisting of engineers and artists, would draw up plans or projects which would then be examined by the second chamber, consisting of mathematicians, physicists and physiologists.[1] The third chamber would be responsible for putting into execution projects proposed by the first chamber and examined and approved by the second. Saint-Simon called the third body the chamber of deputies. It would consist of elected representatives of agriculture and industry; but the electorate would consist only of producers.

There is no need to lay a great deal of emphasis on these proposals. In his work *On the Industrial System* (*Du système industriel*, 1821–22) Saint-Simon more or less contented himself with demanding that finances should be put into the hands of a chamber of industry and that the Institute of France should take over the role in education which had once been played by the Church. In any case, the concrete proposals express a number of general presuppositions. For example, it is presupposed that the scientists have become the intellectual élite and that they can be trusted to make and approve plans beneficial to society. Again, it is presupposed that in contemporary society the interests which bind men together and which call for common deliberation and action are no longer theological or military but economic. Government, when understood as coercive and as associated with military adventures is on its way to being transformed into a managerial administration concerned with promoting the real interests of society.

Industrial society, according to Saint-Simon, would be a peaceful society, at any rate when fully developed and given the appropriate form of government or administration. What he calls the industrial class includes not only captains of industry but also the workmen. And Saint-Simon assumes that their interests coincide or harmonize with one another. Further, the industrial class in, say, France has much more in common with the parallel class in England than it has with the French nobility. The rise of the industrial class therefore provides the basis for human solidarity and for overcoming national enmities. True, governments as they actually exist represent a prolongation of the old régime, a hangover, as one might express it, from an outmoded social structure. The transition however to a form of adminstration appropriate to the

---

[1] The term 'physiologist' must obviously be understood in Saint-Simon's sense as referring to specialists in the science of man. This second chamber would have also the function of controlling education.

new industrial society and devoted to its interests will justify confidence in international peace. This goal cannot be attained by alliance between or conferences between governments which do not properly represent the interests of the productive and naturally peaceful class. A fuller development of industrial society is first required.

Karl Marx showed considerable respect for Saint-Simon. But he obviously disagreed with the latter's assumption that the real or true interests of the captains of industry coincided with those of the workmen. From Marx's point of view Saint-Simon, while seeing the importance of man's economic life, had failed to understand the clash of interests between the bourgeoisie and the proletariat and the connection between bourgeois society and war. In brief, Saint-Simon was a utopian. We may indeed be inclined to think that in his own way Marx himself was a utopian, and that people living in glass houses would be well advised to refrain from throwing stones. But it can hardly be denied that Saint-Simon was over-optimistic in regard to the inherently peaceful nature of industrial society.

To do Saint-Simon justice however, he came to see that ignorance is not the only bar to progress, and that the spread of scientific knowledge and government by experts was not sufficient to secure realization of the ideal of human brotherhood, the ideal of *fraternité*. There was man's self-seeking and egoism to reckon with. And selfishness could not be overcome without an appropriate morality or ethics. In his *New Christianity* (*Nouveau Christianisme*, 1824) Saint-Simon found this morality in the Christian ethics of love. He was not recommending a return to the Christian system of dogmas which, in his view, had been superseded by positive scientific knowledge of the world. He was however convinced that the Christian ideal of fraternal love, which had been obscured by the Church's power-structure and by the policy of religious intolerance and persecution, possessed permanent value and relevance. The Catholic system was outmoded, while Lutheranism had emphasized an interiority divorced from political life. What was needed was the realization of the message of the Christian gospel in the social-political sphere.

As Saint-Simon's insistence on ethico-religious motivation was expressed in a work which appeared in the year preceding that of his death, it has sometimes been thought that it represented a radical change in his thought and pretty well a recantation of positivism. But this view is inaccurate. Saint-Simon does not appear to have ever been a complete positivist, if we understand the term as implying rejection of all belief in God. He seems to have believed in an impersonal immanent Deity, pantheistically conceived, and to have thought this belief quite compatible with his positivism. Further, he always regarded Christianity with respect. To be sure, he did not accept Christian dogmas. But he looked on the theological outlook of the Middle Ages not as deplorable superstition but as an historical necessity. And though the theological stage of thought had, in his opinion, been superseded by the scientific stage, he did not think of this transition as entailing abandonment of all Christian moral values. He did indeed become convinced that the new society needed a new religion, to overcome both individual and national egoism and to recreate in a new form the 'organic' society of the Middle Ages. But the new religion was for him the old religion, in regard, that is to say, to what he considered to be the essential and permanently valuable element in the old religion. We can say perhaps that Saint-Simon envisaged a 'secularized' Christianity. The 'new Christianity' was Christianity as relevant to the age of the industrial society and of positive science.

Saint-Simon was not a systematic thinker. He advanced numerous lines of thought but tended to leave them only partly developed and did not make any prolonged effort to combine them in a systematic manner. His ideas however aroused widespread interest; and after his death some of his disciples founded the journal *Le producteur* to propagate these ideas. In 1830 a newspaper entitled *Le globe* also became an organ of Saint-Simonianism. Saint-Amand Bazard (1791–1832), one of Saint-Simon's principal disciples, tried to present his master's doctrine in a systematic way, paying special attention to its religious aspects. His lectures on Saint-Simon attracted a good deal of attention. Shortly before his death however he quarrelled with the other founding father, Barthélemy Prosper Enfantin (1796–1864), who pretty well turned Saint-Simonianism into a religious sect, though not an austere one, as Enfantin advocated generous ideas in regard to love between men and women. Bazard had been much more of a logical thinker; Enfantin was both an impassioned publicist and inclined to take up one particular project or cause after another. In spite however of his activity the Saint-Simonian school started to decline after the split between himself and Bazard.

The influence of Saint-Simon was not confined to those who can be classified as disciples. Outside their ranks the two most important thinkers who derived stimulus from his thought were doubtless Auguste Comte and Karl Marx. Both Marx and Engels admired Saint-Simon. It is true that Marx criticized him, as we have already noted, for failing to understand the class antagonism between capitalists and workers and for concentrating, in Marx's opinion, on glorifying bourgeois society in comparison with feudalism. At the same time Marx thought that in *The New Christianity* Saint-Simon had spoken up for the emancipation of the proletariat. We know from Engels that Marx was generally accustomed to express his esteem for Saint-Simon, whereas he regarded Comte as a reactionary and a thinker of little value.

4. Fourier and Saint-Simon were at one with the Traditionalists in believing that after the overthrow of the old régime at the revolution a reorganization of society was required. Obviously the two groups had different ideas about the form which such reorganization should take. The Traditionalists looked back, in the sense that they insisted on the permanent validity and value of certain traditional beliefs and institutions, whereas Fourier and Saint-Simon looked forward to the creation of those new forms of social organization which they believed to be demanded by the march of history. Both groups however emphasized the need for social reorganization. It may appear therefore that Proudhon, as a professed anarchist, should be sharply differentiated from both Traditionalists and socialists, inasmuch as the term anarchy suggests an absence, or rather a rejection, of social organization. Though however Proudhon accepted the label 'anarchist' in 1840, he did not understand by anarchism a general social chaos, anarchy in the popular sense of the term, but rather the absence of centralized authoritarian government. What he desired was social organization without government. In Marxist terminology, he envisaged the withering away of the State. Up to a point therefore there was an affinity between Proudhon and Saint-Simon, inasmuch as the latter looked for the transformation of 'government' into 'administration'. At the same time Proudhon went further than Saint-Simon. For he hoped that the form of social organization which he considered desirable would render centralized administration unnecessary.

Pierre-Joseph Proudhon (1809–1865) was born at Besançon. After a short period of school education he became an apprentice in the local diocesan printing press[1] and later a partner in a firm of printers. Though however he had to leave school for work, he continued to educate himself, and in 1838 he obtained a scholarship which enabled him to go to Paris. In 1840 he published his essay *What is Property? (Qu'est-ce que la propriété?)*, in which he made his famous statement that property is theft. This was followed by two further essays on the subject (1841 and 1842), the second of which was regarded as inflammatory propaganda by the civil authorities.[2]

In 1843 Proudhon published a work *On the Creation of Order in Humanity (De la création de l'ordre dans l'humanité)*. In it he maintained that the human mind progresses through the two successive stages of religion and philosophy to the scientific stage. At this third stage it becomes possible for man to discover the serial laws operating in the world, both infra-human and human. The science which shows how man should apply his knowledge of these laws in society is called by Proudhon 'serial dialectic'. In maintaining that there are ascertainable laws governing social development Proudhon is obviously at one with Saint-Simon and, for the matter of that, with Montesquieu.[3]

For a time Proudhon worked at Lyons, with visits to Paris. At Lyons he consorted with socialists, while at Paris he made the acquaintance of Marx, Bakunin and Herzen. Introduced to the ideas of Hegel, he undertook to apply the Hegelian dialectic in the sphere of economics.[4] The result was his *System of Economic Contradictions or the Philosophy of Poverty (Système des contradictions économiques ou Philosophie de la misère,* 1846). The contradiction or antithesis between the system of equality-destroying property on the one hand and independence-destroying socialism (communism) on the other is resolved in 'mutualism' (or 'anarchy'), a society of producers united by means of free contracts. Marx, who had hailed Proudhon's first essay on poverty as representing 'scientific socialism',[5] hastened to attack this new work in his

---

[1] At this time Proudhon read widely in theology and learned Greek and Hebrew. Later he was to say that it is a duty of the thinking and free man to expel the idea of God from his mind.

[2] Proudhon's ideas were found difficult to follow, and he was acquitted.

[3] For Montesquieu see Vol. 6 of this *History*, pp. 9–15.

[4] Proudhon's knowledge of Hegel was never profound. And there is little point in discussing his degree of fidelity to Hegel's thought. Proudhon simply derived some stimulus from what he had read and from what he had been told by left-wing Hegelians.

[5] It is possible that Marx took over this phrase from Proudhon himself.

Poverty of Philosophy (*Misère de la philosophie*, 1847). The split between the two men is in no way surprising. For Proudhon was never a communist, and in Marx's eyes he expressed the interests of the *petite bourgeoisie*.

When the monarchy was overthrown in February of 1848 Proudhon gave only a very qualified support to the revolution.[1] However he showed activity in a variety of ways, by campaigning for the establishment of a People's Bank, by making popular speeches, and by founding an anarchist paper *The Representative of the People* (*Le représentant de peuple*). In June of 1848 he was elected to the National Assembly. But an attack in his paper on Louis Napoleon, then president, led to his being sentenced to imprisonment for three years.[2] In 1849 he wrote *Confessions of a Revolutionary* (*Les confessions d'un révolutionnaire*), and in 1851 he published his *General Idea of Revolution in the Nineteenth Century* (*Idée générale de la révolution au XIXe siècle*), in which he expounded his vision of the ideal free society.

At the end of 1851 Louis Napoleon made himself emperor; and when Proudhon was released from prison in 1852, he was subjected to police supervision. In 1853 he published his *Philosophy of Progress* (*Philosophie du progrès*) in which he denied the existence of any absolutes and of any permanence and asserted a theory of universal movement or change both in the universe at large and in particular spheres such as morals, politics and religion. When however he published *Justice in the Revolution and the Church* (*De la justice dans la révolution et dans l'église*, 1858), he got into trouble. This was not of course because Proudhon now rejected the idea of the resolution of thesis and antithesis in a synthesis and substituted an expression of belief in continuing antinomies which produce a dynamic, though unstable, equilibrium of forces or factors. He was charged with attacking religion, morality and the law. To escape further imprisonment he went to Belgium, remaining there even after he had been pardoned in 1860. While in Brussels he wrote several works, for example *War and Peace* (*La guerre et la paix*).

Returning to Paris in 1862, Proudhon published his work *On the Federal Principle* (*Du principe fédératif*, 1863) and wrote the *Theory of Property* (*Théorie de la propriété*), a revision of his

---

[1] Proudhon was no great believer in political revolutions. He wanted economic changes.

[2] The imprisonment was not particularly stringent. Proudhon was sometimes allowed out on parole. And he was able to write.

thoughts on this subject. This revision was published posthumously, as was also *On the Political Capacity of the Working Classes (De la capacité politique des classes ouvrières,* 1865).

Proudhon came of a family of peasant stock, and he remained always on the side of the small producer, whether peasant or artisan. When he said that property was theft,[1] he was not suggesting that a peasant who owned and worked a plot of land and lived by the fruit of his labours or that a man who lived by making and selling chairs and claimed ownership of the tools of his trade was a thief. By 'property' Proudhon really meant what he regarded as an abuse, what he called the right of escheat or *aubaine.* For example, the landowner who did not himself work the land but none the less took the profits derived from the labours of others was a thief. In Proudhon's language there could be a right of 'possession', of exclusive *use*; but there was no right of 'property' as this would mean a right to exploit other people. 'Possession' means a right to make use of an object, whether it be land or tools. As 'property' means the *misuse* of objects (as means to exploitation), there can be no right to it. It involves theft.

It is important to understand that when Proudhon denounced property, he was not simply denouncing exploitation by individual landowners and capitalists. He believed that for the maintenance of human independence and dignity peasants and artisans should 'possess' the land which they worked on or the tools which they used and that they should receive the fruit of their labours. And he was therefore opposed to any system of collective ownership which meant that the State would take the place of the nonproductive landowner or capitalist. When referring later to his rejection of property in the essay of 1840 he remarks that 'I rejected it for both the group and the individual, the nation and the citizen, and thus I am not advocating either communism or State ownership.'[2]

If we bear this point in mind, it becomes easier to understand how in his *System of Economic Contradictions* Proudhon could retain the idea of property as theft and at the same time offer a new definition of it as liberty. There is the constant possibility of abuse, of exploitation, which spells theft. At the same time property is a spontaneous creation of society and a bulwark against the ever-encroaching power of the State. Proudhon came to doubt whether his previous distinction between property and possession

---

[1] *What is Property?*, p. 131.   [2] *Theory of Property*, p. 16.

was as useful as he had once thought it. He came to the conclusion that 'property is the only power which can act as a counterweight to the State.'[1] It is understandable that Marx, who in his analysis of capitalism made use of Proudhon's idea of theft, later attacked the French writer as an upholder of the interests of the *petite bourgeoisie*. But though Proudhon may have changed his terminology, he had always been on the side of the small producer; and he was a consistent enemy of communist theories.

Revolution, the product of the conflict between opposed forces or factors, obviously has a negative side, in the sense that a revolution negates or destroys or overthrows something. This however is only one aspect of revolution. If revolution negates, it must also affirm. The French revolution asserted the ideals of liberty, fraternity and equality; but on the positive side it was incomplete, a partial failure. It produced a measure of political liberty and equality, but it failed to produce liberty and equality in the economic sphere. 'Society should afterwards have been organized in terms of labour and not in those of politics and war';[2] but this is not what happened. The task of the revolution, to establish 'an egalitarian industrial régime',[3] was not fulfilled. And Proudhon's social and economic theorizing is designed to contribute to this fulfilment. For Marx, needless to say, he is a utopian. And one can see why Marx says this. It is however relevant to notice that Proudhon does not believe in permanent solutions to social problems. Industrial democracy, as he puts it, must succeed industrial feudalism.[4] But no blueprint for the organization of society can be absolute and definitive truth. For oppositions of some sort are always latent in human society, and their emergence involves further change.

Property (or 'possession'), duly distributed, safeguards independence and equality. But human society obviously cannot exist without some form or forms of organization. Such organization may be imposed from above, by the authority of the State as represented by the government. But what Proudhon envisages is a transition from political to economic organization, when the economic organization or forms of association are not dictated from above but are produced by agreements or contracts freely made by producers. This is what he calls 'anarchy'. The centralized government State will, he hopes, wither away, its place

---

[1] *Ibid.*, p. 144.   [2] *General Idea of the Revolution*, p. 125.
[3] *Ibid.*   [4] *Manuel du spéculateur à la Bourse*, 1857, p. 499.

being taken by a social order arising out of associations freely entered into for economic reasons, such as the demands of production, the needs of consumption and the security of the producers. 'The notion of *anarchy* in politics is just as rational and positive as any other. It means that once industrial functions have taken over from political functions, then business transactions and exchange alone produce the social order.'[1] Writing towards the end of his life Proudhon remarks that he has always had 'a particular horror of regimentation'.[2] In his opinion, freedom can flourish only when associations and federations of associations are based on free contracts, contract being 'the dominant idea in politics'.[3] As he puts it, commutative justice or rule by contract must take the place of the old systems of distributive justice, associated with the rule of law and a centralized governmental régime.

In so far as Proudhon envisages the existence and self-maintenance of a coherent and stable industrial society in the form of a loosely knit system of producers' associations, with contracts instead of laws and industrial companies instead of armies, he can not unfairly be described as a Utopian. For he sees all citizens as cooperating harmoniously, inasmuch as private and collective interests will be identical, and as behaving in the manner which he considers rational. It must be remembered however that Proudhon's great slogan is progress, continual change. He does not claim that any form of social organization is free from all antimonies or tensions and can be considered as the final goal, one which will be fully attained and, when attained, will represent perfection. He is quite ready to admit that 'what we call anarchy and others fraternity'[4] is a more or less mythical symbol, a spur to stimulate men to realize the revolutionary ideal of fraternity which, in Proudhon's opinion, can be realized only through transformation of the intermediary régime consequent on the revolution into an industrial society of the kind which he envisages. He desires a more just society; but just as humanity itself changes and develops, so is the ideal of justice 'changing all the time'.[5] 'We cannot see beyond the antithesis which is suggested to us by the present.'[6] Proudhon's utopianism and his idea of laws of social change are balanced by a conviction that there are no

---

[1] *The Federal Principle*, p. 278.
[2] *Theory of Property*, p. 28.
[3] *The Federal Principle*, p. 315.
[4] *Correspondence*, IV, p. 157.
[5] *Justice*, I, p. 233.
[6] *Correspondence*, IV, p. 158.

absolutes and that we cannot make infallible judgments about the future.

Whatever we may think about the viability of the kind of industrial society envisaged by Proudhon, some of his ideas are clearly sensible enough. For example, his proposals about the education of workers, to overcome the sharp division between the literate and illiterate classes and to facilitate the profitable use of leisure, and about apprentices being taught a variety of skills in order to diminish the monotony of the slavish repetition of one particular task were not without point. Nor indeed were his ideas about a credit system and a People's Bank. As for influence, during his last years at Paris he had a considerable following among the workers; and in 1871 a large section of the Paris Commune consisted of Proudhonians. Subsequently Marxist communism came to the fore; but Proudhon's ideas, or some of them at any rate, continued to exercise an influence on the minds of a number of French socialists and syndicalists. Further, through Michael Bakunin (1814–1876) Proudhon can be said to have influenced the anarchist movement.

5. Obviously, if we were to take Proudhon's plans for a People's Bank and Fourier's proposals about the establishment of phalanxes by themselves, they would not justify our describing these two thinkers as philosophers. Both men however had general theories about history and historical progress, even if Proudhon's ideas were vaguer than Fourier's.[1] It may well be true that it is possible to consider Fourier's concrete proposals without reference to his theory of the stages through which mankind must pass. But the theory is there; and if we interpret the word 'philosophy' in a broad sense, Fourier can be said to have outlined a philosophical anthropology and a philosophy of history. As for Proudhon, his denial of any absolutes presumably counts as a philosophical theory. To be sure, both fall short of the standards of preciseness and close argument which philosophers might be expected to aim at. The point is however that to classify them simply as sociologists or as political scientists or as economists would be somewhat misleading. In other words, it does not seem altogether unreasonable to include mention of them in a history of philosophy,

---

[1] If we consider Proudhon's writings as a whole, it seems that he sometimes implies the inevitability of historical progress, while at other times he says pretty clearly that it is not inevitable. But it is arguable that it is a case not so much of inconsistency as of his changing his mind and of coming to emphasize man's freedom to solve his social problems when he understands them.

not at any rate if we are prepared to include political and social theory as part of philosophy.

It must be admitted however that Saint-Simon's theory of historical and social change is more impressive than Fourier's, not to speak of Proudhon's. Further, as writers on early French socialism have noted,[1] his view of the way in which society should be changed is connected with his conception of the law-governed movement of history. In other words, of the three writers Saint-Simon gives the most coherent and developed general view of the pattern of historical and social change. And we naturally think of him as a predecessor of Auguste Comte and Karl Marx.

Mention has been made more than once of the fact that Marx and Engels describe the early French socialists as utopians. The word 'utopian' naturally suggests the idea of an unrealistic or unpractical reformer, someone who proposes as a solution for man's social and political problems some ideal state of affairs which seems to us an impracticable and perhaps fantastic solution. In this sense the word may well apply to Fourier and Proudhon, but it might obviously be applied also to Marx himself, even if Marx was much less inclined than Fourier to provide any detailed account of the future utopia. Though however this sort of meaning may have been part of the meaning which Marx and Engels attached to the word, it was not the element on which they laid the most emphasis. When they described the French socialists as utopians, what they had primarily in mind was the French writers' failure to understand the nature of class-antagonism and the irreconcilable nature of class-interests. Though the early socialists certainly believed that the ideals which had found expression in the French revolution had only been partially and very imperfectly realized and that a further transformation of society was required, they tended to think that this transformation could be brought about in a peaceful manner, by men coming to understand the problems and needs of society and the appropriate way of solving the problems and meeting the needs. Marx and Engels however were convinced that the desired transformation of society could be achieved only by revolution, by, that is to say, a class-war in which the proletariat, led by the enlightened, would seize power. In their view it was simply an expression of 'utopianism' if anyone thought that the interests of the ruling class or classes and those of the exploited could be peacefully

[1] See, for example J. Plamenatz's *Man and Society*, Vol. 2, p. 42.

reconciled through a spread of knowledge or understanding. For the interest of the dominant class was precisely the preservation of the actual state of affairs, whereas it was in the interest of the exploited class that the actual state of affairs should be radically changed. To call for a transformation of society while failing to see that it could be achieved only through a proletarian revolution was unrealistic and utopian.

For the proletarian revolution envisaged by Marx and Engels to take place it was a pre-requisite that there should be men who understood the movement of history and who could turn the exploited class into a self-conscious united whole, a class not only 'in itself' but also 'for itself'. They thus had a considerable respect for Saint-Simon, not only because he conceived of history as law-governed (Fourier too had this concept) but also because in his case there was a much closer connection than in the case of Fourier between his theory of history and his idea of the desirable transformation of society. Moreover Saint-Simon, with his notion of social physiology, could be said to have expounded a 'materialist' interpretation of man. At the same time, if we bear in mind the role attributed by Saint-Simon to captains of industry in the transformation of society, it is clear that he too would be guilty of utopianism in the eyes of Marx and Engels. For though captains of industry might agree to changes within the existing social framework, it would not be in their interest to contribute to the radical transformation which was required.

In view of the great historical importance of Marxism it is natural enough to think of the early French socialists in terms of their relations to Marx and Engels. But though this approach is easily understandable, it is a rather one-sided approach if we insist on looking at them simply as predecessors of Marx. In any case they realized clearly enough that while the revolution had destroyed the old régime, it had failed to bring peace and harmony between individuals, groups and nations. So of course did the Traditionalists. But whereas the Traditionalists adopted a negative attitude towards the Enlightenment and the revolution, the socialists looked for a prolongation and more satisfactory application of the ideals which inspired these movements. Obviously, if we assume with Saint-Simon that the course of history is governed by laws, in a sense at any rate which makes historical progress inevitable and social changes predictable in principle, even if in fact only very wide or vague predictions are feasible, there arises the problem of harmonizing this view of history with the emphasis on the role of human initiative and action which we would expect to find in the writings of any social reformer. But this is a problem which arises in the case of Marx and Engels as well. If we consider simply the French socialists' ideas of desirable changes, it is clear that they disliked the idea of the centralized bureaucratic State. It is true that Saint-Simon saw the need for economic planning; but he envisaged the transformation of 'government' into managerial 'administration' and in this sense can be said to have anticipated the doctrine of the withering away of the State. As for Fourier and Proudhon, it is clear that they both mistrusted and disliked the increasing power of the State, the centralized political authority. In actual fact of course control by State bureaucracy has vastly increased in modern society. And it is ironic that it should be such a conspicuous feature of Soviet communism. In spite however of the rather fantastic ideas of Fourier and Proudhon, we can see in the French socialists a respect for the individual and a marked dislike of violence. Marx of course thought that they were over-optimistic in their conviction that radical changes could be brought about without revolutionary violence. But it is an optimism with which many people would sympathize, irrespective of the concrete proposals made by the French writers.

CHAPTER V

AUGUSTE COMTE

*Life and writings—The three stages in human development—
The classification and methodology of the sciences—Tasks of
the philosopher in the positive area—The science of man; social
statics and social dynamics—The Great Being and the religion
of humanity.*

1. THE impact of the development of natural science on philosophy was felt in the seventeenth century and became more
marked in the eighteenth. As we have seen, in the eighteenth
century the call was raised, as by Hume in England and by some
of the French philosophers, for an extension of the 'experimental'
method to the study of man, his conduct and his social life, while
in the last decades of the century Kant maintained that reflection
on the contrast between the solid and increasing knowledge
achieved in the scientific area on the one hand and the conflicting systems of metaphysics on the other led inevitably to a
radical questioning of the claim of traditional metaphysics to
provide anything which could properly be described as knowledge
of reality. It was of course possible for science to coexist with
theological beliefs and with metaphysical speculation, as it did in
the mind of Newton. But with the growth of a stronger sense of
historical development it was natural enough that the idea of
successive stages in human thought should be proposed, the idea,
that is to say, of a progressive development in which theological
beliefs and metaphysical speculation are succeeded by scientific
explanation and positive knowledge. This sort of idea had been
proposed by Turgot and Condorcet in the eighteenth century; and
in the last chapter attention was drawn to Saint-Simon's theory
of historical stages or epochs. It is however with the name of
Auguste Comte (1798–1857), the foremost exponent and representative of classical positivism[1] that the theory of the human
mind's development from a theological through a metaphysical
phase to that of positive scientific knowledge has become tradi-
tionally associated.

[1] 'Classical' in distinction from the neo-positivism or logical positivism of the
twentieth century.

74

Born at Montpellier, Comte was brought up as a Catholic and a royalist. At the age of fourteen however he declared that he was no longer a Catholic, and it seems that at the same age he became a republican. From 1814 until 1816 he was a pupil at the École Polytechnique, where he studied under the guidance of leading scientists. It was doubtless during this period that he formed the conviction that society should be organized by a scientific élite.

In 1816 Comte was expelled from the École Polytechnique which had been given a royalist reorientation. He remained in Paris however and continued his studies, which included the thought of the ideologists, such as Destutt de Tracy and Cabanis, and the writings both of political economists and of historians such as Hume and Condorcet. Then in the summer of 1817 he became secretary to Saint-Simon. The association between the two men lasted for seven years; and while the extent of Comte's debt to Saint-Simon is a matter of dispute, there can be no doubt of the important part played by their collaboration in the formation and development of Comte's thought. It is clear that Saint-Simon was the first to propose certain ideas which reappeared in Comte's philosophy. At the same time Comte developed these ideas in his own way. For example, while Saint-Simon tended to think in terms of one overall scientific method and of the application of this method in the development of a new science of man, Comte regarded each science as developing its own method in the historical process of its emergence and advance.[1] Both men however looked for a reorganization of society with the aid of a new science of human behaviour and of man's social relations.

An acrimonious quarrel, leading to the severance of relations, arose between the two men, when Comte came to the conclusion that he had good reasons for believing that Saint-Simon intended to publish a paper by Comte as the concluding part of a work of his own and without proper acknowledgement on the title-page. In 1826 Comte began lecturing on his positivist philosophy to a private audience. The course of lectures was however interrupted by a breakdown induced by overwork and by the strain consequent on an unfortunate marriage. Indeed, Comte made an unsuccessful attempt at suicide. In 1829 Comte was able to resume the course, and the lectures formed the basis of his *Course of Positive Philosophy* (*Cours de philosophie positive*, six volumes, 1830–42). The basis had already been provided by a *Plan of the Scientific*

---

[1] For the necessary qualifications to this statement see pp. 85–6.

Researches Necessary for Reorganizing Society,[1] which he wrote in 1822. The title of this sketch or outline of the positive philosophy gives clear expression to Comte's basic social concern.

In the *Discourse on the Positivist Outlook* (*Discours sur l'esprit positif*, 1844) and the *Discourse on Postitivism as a Whole* (*Discours sur l'ensemble du positivisme*, 1848) Comte's idea of the religion of humanity made its appearance. Some biographers see in this development the influence of Comte's religious upbringing, with the difference that Humanity is substituted for God as the object of devotion. Others however have seen it, perhaps rather fancifully, as an extension to the human race of the philosopher's attachment to Madame Clothilde de Vaux, whose husband had disappeared to avoid a prosecution for embezzlement and with whom Comte fell in love in 1844.[2]

Comte never occupied a university chair, and for some time he had to support himself by doing tutorial work for students of the École Polytechnique. In 1851–4 he published his four-volume *System of Positive Policy* (*Système de politique positive*) and in 1852 his *Positivist Catechism* (*Catéchisme positiviste*). In this period he was trying to bring together the scientific and religious aspects of his thought. In 1856 he produced the first volume of a *Synthesis or Universal System of Concepts Proper to the Normal State of Humanity* (*Synthèse subjective ou système universel des conceptions propres à l'état normal de l'humanité*). But this attempt at a synthesis of all the sciences in terms of their relations to normal human needs was brought to an end by Comte's death in 1867. He had been living mainly on funds provided by his own devoted followers.

2. In a preface to his *Course of Positive Philosophy* Comte remarks that the expression 'positive philosophy' is constantly used in his lectures 'in a rigorously invariable sense',[3] and that it is therefore superfluous to give a definition other than that contained in his uniform use of the term. He goes on however to explain that by 'philosophy' he understands what the ancients, and in particular Aristotle, understood by the word, namely 'the general system

---

[1] This *Plan des travaux scientifiques nécessaires pour réorganiser la société* is included in *Opuscules de philosophie sociale*, 1819–28, published in 1883.

[2] It is clear enough from what Comte himself says that his love for Madame de Vaux influenced his idea of the religion of humanity. But it does not necessarily follow that Humanity, as an object of devotion, is simply Madame de Vaux writ large. Though rejecting traditional theological beliefs, Comte admired the so-called Age of Faith, and he wished to give humanism a religious dimension.

[3] *Cours de philosophie positive* (second edition, Paris, 1864), I, p. 5. This edition will be referred to in footnotes as C.P.P.

of human concepts',[1] while by 'positive' he understands the idea
of theories as having for their aim 'the coordination of observed
facts'.[2] Comte's statement, however, if taken by itself, is somewhat misleading. For in his view it is the sciences which subsume
phenomena or observed facts under general laws which are
descriptive and not explanatory, while philosophy examines the
nature of scientific methods and effects a systematic synthesis of
the various particular sciences. But his statement can stand if we
take it as meaning that philosophy coordinates observed facts
indirectly, inasmuch as it aims at a general synthesis of the partial
coordinations achieved in the sciences.

Positive knowledge is restricted by Comte to knowledge of
observed facts or phenomena and to the coordinating and descriptive laws of phenomena. Use of the word 'phenomena' does indeed
express Comte's conviction that we know reality only as appearing
to us, but it should not be taken to imply that for him the human
mind knows only subjective impressions. On occasion he refers to
Hume with respect; but Humean scepticism is really foreign to
Comte's mind, except in regard to theological beliefs and to the
claims of metaphysics to provide us with knowledge of what
transcends the phenomenal level. He stands closer to his
eighteenth-century French predecessors than to Humean empiricism. That is to say, Comte insists that genuine philosophy
takes the form of a systematic extension of the use of what
d'Holbach described as 'good sense' or 'natural ideas'.[3] And for
him this means that only what can stand up to empirical testing
can count as knowledge. The formulation of general laws enables us
to predict, and so to test. That this is the way to attain real knowledge is for Comte a matter of common sense or 'popular good
sense'.[4] It is this good sense which dismisses 'absurd metaphysical
doubts'[5] about ,say, the existence of physical objects external to
the mind. Comte has little patience with speculations of this kind.
His 'positive philosophy' is not a sceptical philosophy in the sense
of suggesting that our knowledge is confined to sense-data.

The positive spirit or outlook presupposes of course the birth
and advance of the natural sciences and is the result of an historical development of the human mind. In Comte's view this
process depends on man's nature and is thus necessary. In its

[1] *Ibid.*,   [2] *Ibid.*,
[3] D'Holbach's work *Le bon sens, ou idées naturelles opposées aux idées sur-
naturelles* appeared in 1772 at Amsterdam.
[4] See Comte's *Discours sur l'esprit positif*, section 34.   [5] *Ibid.*, section 10.

historical development through the centuries the human mind passes through three main stages or phases, the theological, the metaphysical and the positive. These three stages in the intellectual development of mankind have their analogues however in the life of the individual man as he passes from infancy through adolescence to manhood. 'When contemplating his own history does not each of us recollect that he has been successively ... *theologian* in his infancy, *metaphysician* in his youth, and *physicist* in his maturity?'[1] Unless he dies prematurely, the individual normally passes from infancy to maturity by way of adolescence. And these three phases are reflected in the intellectual development of mankind as a whole. If the race continues to exist, the phases or stages of mental growth succeed one another in a certain pattern because man is what he is. In this sense it is necessary, hypothetically necessary, we might say.

It is indeed obvious enough that unless a person dies or unless some factor intervenes to prevent the natural course of development, the individual passes from infancy through adolescence to adulthood. But though Comte may have seen himself as a theologian in infancy and a metaphysician in adolescence, it is by no means everyone who would interpret his or her mental development in this way. Comte's theory of stages becomes much more plausible when applied to the general intellectual development of mankind. Indeed, it is clear that reflection on human history is the chief influence which leads Comte to formulate his theory,[2] even if he goes on to connect the stages with phases in the life of the individual and to see these phases writ large in history. In any case consideration of Comte's account of the three main stages in the history of mankind is a simple way of approaching his positivist philosophy.

The first stage, the theological, is understood by Comte as being that phase of man's mental development in which he seeks the ultimate causes of events and finds them in the wills of personal, superhuman beings or in the will of one such being. It is, in general, the age of the gods or of God. Subdivision is however required. In the infancy of the race man instinctively tried to explain phenomena, the real causes of which were unknown, by ascribing to objects passions and affects analogous to those of

---

[1] *CPP*, I, p. II.
[2] It is not intended to imply that the theory was brand new. Attention has already been drawn to Comte's predecessors.

human beings. In other words, man endowed physical objects with life, passions and will, in a vague manner. This animistic mentality represented what Comte describes as the stage of fetishism. In the course of time however the animating forces immanent in objects were projected externally in the form of the gods and goddesses of polytheism. Later on the deities of polytheistic religion were fused in the concept of the one God of monotheism. These three successive sub-stages of fetishism, polytheism and monotheism constitute together the theological stage.

The second general stage is described by Comte as the metaphysical stage. The description however is apt to give rise to misunderstanding. For what Comte has in mind is the transformation of personal deities or of God into metaphysical abstractions, not, for instance, the theistic metaphysics of medieval thinkers such as Aquinas or, later, of Bishop Berkeley. In the metaphysical stage, that is to say, instead of explaining phenomena in terms of the activity of a divine will the mind has recourse to such fictional ideas as ether, vital principles, and so on. The transition from the theological to the metaphysical stage takes place when the concept of a supernatural and personal Deity is succeeded by the concept of all-inclusive Nature and when explanations are sought in terms of abstract entities of one kind or another, such as force, attraction and repulsion.[1]

The third stage is the positive stage, namely that of the mature scientific outlook or mentality. Here there is no attempt to find ultimate explanatory causes or to discuss the 'real' but unobservable inner essence of things. The mind concerns itself with phenomena or observed facts, which it subsumes under general descriptive laws, such as the law of gravitation. These coordinating descriptive laws make prediction possible. Indeed, the mark of real positive knowledge is precisely the ability to predict and so, within limits, to control. Positive knowledge is real, certain and useful.

Though however Comte describes positive knowledge as certain, he also insists that it is in a sense relative. For we do not know the

[1] In his *De Motu* Berkeley attacked the idea that there are realities or entities corresponding to abstract terms such as 'attraction', 'force' or 'gravity'. The terms, Berkeley maintained, had their uses as 'mathematical hypotheses'; but it was a mistake to think that they stood for corresponding abstract entities. The view which Berkeley attacked is a good example of what Comte meant by metaphysics, when he spoke of the metaphysical stage in the development of human thought.

whole universe. We know it only as appearing to us. Positive knowledge is knowledge of our world, and the extent of our world, the world as appearing to us, is not something fixed and determined once and for all. Positive knowledge is also relative in the sense that the search for absolutes is abandoned. Even if there are ultimate causes, we cannot know them. What we know are phenomena. Hence the mind which appreciates the nature and function of positive knowledge will not waste time in profitless theological and metaphysical speculation.

The theory of the three stages as just summarized may seem to have little connection with a concern for the reorganization of society. In point of fact however each stage is associated by Comte with a distinct form of social organization. The theological stage is associated with belief in absolute authority and the divine right of kings and with a militaristic social order. That is to say, social order is maintained by the imposition of authority from above, and the warrior class is pre-eminent. In the metaphysical stage the former régime is subjected to radical criticism; belief in abstract rights and in popular sovereignty comes to the fore; and royal and priestly authority is replaced by the reign of law. Finally, the positive stage is associated with the development of industrial society. Man's economic life becomes the centre of attention; and there arises a scientific élite, whose vocation it is to organize and regulate industrial society in a rational manner. This type of society is regarded by Comte, as by some contemporaries, as naturally peaceful.[1] But for its proper development a new science is required, namely sociology. Natural science enables man to control, within limits, his physical environment. The science of man will enable him to organize a peaceful industrial society. The emergence of the positive spirit or mentality will thus be accompanied by a reorganization of society.

For Comte the ancient world and the Middle Ages represented the theological outlook or mentality, while the Enlightenment represented the metaphysical stage. In his own world he saw the beginning of the positive stage. Further, just as he regarded adolescence as a period of transition between childhood and maturity, so did he look on the metaphysical stage as a period of transition in which the beliefs and institutions of the theological stage were

---

[1] The idea that industrial society would be a peace-loving society was not confirmed to French socialists. In the second half of the nineteenth century Herbert Spencer defended the same point of view.

subjected to criticism and the way was being prepared for the development of the positive mentality.

If we confine ourselves to sweeping impressions, Comte's theory of the three stages can obviously appear plausible. That is to say, if we consider simply the dominant position of theology among the subjects studied in the Middle Ages, certain aspects of thought in the eighteenth-century Enlightenment and the subsequent development of a conviction that science is the only reliable way of increasing our knowledge of the world, it may seem perfectly reasonable to divide up European history into the theological, metaphysical and positive stages. When however we begin to look at European history in more detail, it at once becomes clear that if Comte's divisions are pressed in a rigid way, they cannot accommodate the facts. For instance, philosophy flourished in ancient Greece; and mathematics too underwent development. Again, natural science had made striking progress long before the end of what Comte describes as the metaphysical period.

It is hardly necessary to say that Comte is aware of such facts. And he does his best to accommodate them within his general scheme. For example, he recognizes that in the Middle Ages theology was accompanied by metaphysics, but he regards this metaphysics as tailored to the theological mentality and as really forming part of it. Again, Comte does not claim that science began only with the positive stage. He is perfectly well aware that mathematics was cultivated by the Greeks. But he maintains that in the development of science there was a progression from the most abstract science, mathematics, to the most concrete science, sociology, which is the peculiar contribution of the positive stage. As for physics, it certainly started to develop well before the positive stage; but at one time it expressed the metaphysical mentality by postulating abstract entities as explanatory causes. It is only with the beginning of the positive stage that the real nature of physical science and of its concepts and laws comes to be understood.

Comte is therefore quite prepared to recognize a measure of overlapping between the stages. 'Thus we shall have to regard, for example, the theological epoch as still existing to the extent in which moral and political ideas have retained an essentially theological character, despite the transition of other intellectual categories to the purely metaphysical stage, and even when the genuinely positive stage has already begun in regard to the simplest of such categories. Similarly, it will be necessary to prolong the metaphysical epoch, properly speaking, into the beginning of positivism. . . . By this manner of procedure, the essential aspect of each epoch will remain as pronounced as possible, while the spontaneous preparation of the following epoch is clearly brought out.'[1] In the case of a given individual, psychological features belonging to an earlier stage of growth may persist in the grown man and co-exist with features characteristic of maturity. Analogously, expressions of the mentality of a previous historical epoch may be discernible at a later stage. 'Even in our days what in reality, for a positive mind, is this cloudy pantheism in which so many profound metaphysicians, especially in Germany, take such pride but fetishism generalized and systematized?'[2]

Some of Comte's remarks, taken by themselves, are sensible enough. But the overall impression is that of a man intent on fitting facts into a general interpretative scheme, based on a certain initial vision of European history. Comte is of course perfectly entitled to approach European history with a general framework of interpretation and see how the facts fit it. But the more the adjustments which he has to make, so much the more fluid does the division into stages or epochs become. Further, if the succession of stages is understood as representing progress, in the intellectual and social spheres, a judgment of value or a set of value-judgments is clearly presupposed. In other words, Comte reads European history from the point of a view of a convinced positivist. This is not indeed a crime. But the result is not simply a neutral description, but rather a reconstruction from a certain point of view. In other words, the truth of positivism seems to be a presupposition of Comte's interpretation of history. He was not prepared to consider the possibility of a post-positivist stage of intellectual development. To be sure, Comte tried to support his theory of historical stages by a psychological account of the unfolding of man's mental life in the process of growth towards maturity. But it seems pretty clear that this account too presupposes the truth of positivism, in the sense that it is governed by the assumption that the mature mind and the scientific mentality as Comte understands it are one and the same thing.

Before we turn to Comte's classification of the sciences, we can

[1] *CPP*, V, p. 24.   [2] *Ibid.*, p. 33.

note two points. The first relates to religious belief. The natural way of understanding Comte is to interpret him as maintaining that just as man sheds belief in elves and fairies when he understands that there is no good reason for thinking that there are such beings, so does he progressively shed belief in a transcendent God, not because God's non-existence has been demonstrated, but because there is no positive reason for believing that there is a transcendent God. In other words, the spread of atheism is a feature of the mind's advance into maturity, not the result of a philosophical proof of God's non-existence. Though however this is a natural way of interpreting Comte's theory of the three stages, what he actually insists on as being progressively shed by the wayside is recourse to God as an hypothesis to explain phenomena. That is to say, the more man comes to look for scientific 'explanations' of events, the less does he seek a supernatural explanation. And when the mature mind is ignorant of the scientific explanation of an event, it expects one and looks for it, instead of having recourse to God to fill a gap. At the same time Comte does not assert atheism. In his opinion, theism and atheism are concerned with problems which cannot be solved. For no empirical test is possible. There may be an ultimate cause or ultimate causes. But whether this is the case or not, we do not and cannot know.

The second point relates to the way in which Comte correlates three main types of social organization with the three main stages of man's intellectual development. He is perfectly ready to admit that man's intellectual advance can outrun his social progress, and that the positivist spirit, for example, can make its appearance before the corresponding form of social organization has developed. Apart from any other consideration, Comte's insistence on the need for social planning by a scientific élite compels him to recognize the fact that mental advance can outrun social progress. At the same time he wishes to preserve the idea of the correlation of two aspects, cognitive and social, of one historical movement. He therefore insists that even when man's intellectual progress outruns his social progress, we can none the less discern the preparatory stages of the emergence of a new form of social organization. Further, once the transition to a properly organized industrial society has taken place, this will strengthen and consolidate the positivist outlook.

3. Progress in knowledge is for Comte progress in scientific knowledge. Science however takes the form of the particular

sciences. They are all concerned with the coordination of phenomena, but they treat either of different classes of phenomena or of
different aspects of things, having, as the Scholastics would say,
different 'formal objects'. Further, they have their 'characteristic
procedures'[1] or methods. There is thus a certain fragmentation of
science. And it is one of the philosopher's main tasks to achieve
a synthesis, not by obliterating differences by means of a
systematic classification.

If such a classification is to be made, the first requirement is to
ascertain the basic or fundamental sciences. To do so, we ought to
consider 'only scientific theories and in no way their application'[2].
That is to say, the use made of scientific theory in the field of
technology should be left out of account. Further, attention should
be paid to the more general or abstract sciences rather than to
those which really constitute branches or particular applications
of the former. For example, the general laws of physics belong to
abstract physics, whereas study of the earth in particular is a
concrete science and involves consideration of factors other than
the abstract laws of physics. Similarly, it pertains to abstract
science to formulate the general laws of life, whereas a science
such as botany is concerned with a particular kind or level of life.

In his *Course of Positive Philosophy* Comte discovers six basic
sciences, namely mathematics, astronomy, physics, chemistry,
physiology and biology, and social physics or sociology. It will be
noted that psychology does not appear in the list. The explanation is that on the one hand Comte rejects introspective psychology, while on the other he is writing before the period in which
empirical psychology underwent real development. Psychology
as he understands it is therefore divided between physiology and
sociology. In assigning to physiology, or biology, the study of man
as an individual Comte is walking in the footsteps of Condillac and
Cabanis. The study of human nature and behaviour as social
phenomena is assigned to social physiology, as Saint-Simon called
it, or sociology.

In later writings Comte found room for ethics as an additional
science. Ethics however meant for him not a normative science
concerned with determining values and moral rules but rather
social psychology, a study of man's overt social behaviour with a

---

[1] *CPP,* 1, p. 83. For example, chemistry lays stress on experiment, whereas
astronomy relies more on observation. It is not possible to remove a heavenly
body in order to discover the effect of this action.
[2] *Ibid.*, p. 56.

view to the formulation of laws enabling us to predict and to pursue social planning.

For the purpose of systematic classification, Comte insists, we should start with what is simplest and most general or abstract and proceed according to the logical order of dependence to the more complex and less general. Mathematics, for example, is more abstract than astronomy; and astronomy depends on mathematics in the sense that the former presupposes the latter. Similarly, physiology or biology, dealing with the general laws of life, is more abstract than sociology which treats specifically of man in society. If we proceed on these lines, we end with the hierarchy of basic sciences mentioned above, arranged in an order in which the mind starts with what is most abstract and most removed from specifically human phenomena, with mathematics that is to say, and ends with sociology, which is concerned with such phenomena to a greater degree than any of the other sciences.

Mention has already been made of the fact that whereas Saint-Simon tended to think in terms of one overall scientific method, Comte regarded each science as developing its own method. This statement however stands in need of qualification. If we have in mind Comte's use of the word 'method', he recognizes only one scientific method. 'For every *science* consists in the coordination of facts; if the different observations were entirely isolated, there would be no science.'[1] If therefore we mean by method the observation of facts or phenomena and their coordination through the formulation of laws, there is one method common to all the sciences. If however we have in mind what Comte calls 'procedures', it is true to say, in his view, that in the process of its development each science perfects its own procedure or technique, its own way of coping with the data. There are indeed procedures which are not restricted to any one particular science. The use of hypothesis, deduction and testing is a case in point. At the same time experiment plays a role in, say, chemistry which it cannot play in astronomy, while in sociology use has to be made of an historical approach.

A further qualification is required to the statement that Comte recognizes a plurality of methods. When classifying the basic sciences, Comte insists on a logical order being followed, each successive science in the hierarchy logically presupposing its predecessor. At the same time he is convinced that 'one does not

[1] *CPP*, I, p. 99.

know a science completely as long as one does not know its history'.[1] A science, that is to say, reveals its real nature in proportion as it is developed or perfected rather than in its origins[2]. For example, mathematics has as its original data phenomena considered under their quantitative aspects, and it sets out to determine the relations between given quantities. But in its development mathematics becomes progressively more abstract until it is 'completely independent of the nature of the objects examined and bears only on the numerical relations which they present'.[3] As it becomes 'purely logical, rational',[4] consisting of 'a more or less prolonged series of rational deductions',[5] it is transformed into what Comte describes as the science of the calculus. And in this form it constitutes 'the true rational basis of the entire system of our positive knowledge'.[6] In this purely abstract form mathematics enables us to coordinate phenomena in other sciences in a way which would not otherwise be possible. It is true of course that we cannot convert biology, for example, into pure mathematics. But biology becomes a real science in proportion as the relations between biological phenomena are mathematically determined.

Further, in its developed or perfected state mathematics is a purely deductive science and Comte regards it as the model of scientific method.[7] Physics, for instance, grows in perfection in proportion as the deductive method preponderates. If therefore we look at the sciences from this particular point of view, we might say that there is one model scientific method, exemplified at its purest in mathematics. Comte does not claim however that every basic science can be transformed into a purely deductive science. The further we move away from pure mathematics in the hierarchy of the sciences, the less possible does such a transformation become. For one thing, the phenomena become even more complex. In practice therefore each science, as it advances, develops its own 'procedure', though it makes use, when possible, of mathematics with a view to obtaining greater precision. Sociology cannot be simply converted into mathematics. Nor can it proceed purely deductively. But it will make use of mathematics when it can.

4. We have noted that for Comte one of the main functions of

[1] *Ibid.*, p. 65.   [2] This is evidently an Aristotelian point of view.
[3] *CPP*, I, p. 103. Comte tries to combine his view that all science is concerned with phenomena with a recognition of the abstract nature of mathematics.
[4] *Ibid.*, p. 104.   [5] *Ibid.*   [6] *Ibid.*, p. 109.   [7] *Ibid.*, p. 122.

philosophy is to achieve a unification or synthesis of the sciences. Part of this task is fulfilled in the systematic classification of the sciences treated of in the last section. But Comte also speaks of a doctrinal synthesis or of a unification of scientific knowledge. And the question arises, how is this doctrinal synthesis to be understood?

The aim of a science is to coordinate phenomena of a given type through the formulation of descriptive laws, such as the law of gravitation in Newtonian physics. At first sight therefore it may seem to follow that the aim of philosophy in the positive stage of its development must be to coordinate *all* phenomena in terms of one single law. That is to say, it may seem to follow that positive philosophy should aim at exhibiting the most general laws of the particular sciences as derivable from or as presupposing one all-embracing law. Comte however explicitly rejects this concept of the function of philosophy. 'According to my profound personal conviction I consider these attempts to achieve the universal explanation of all phenomena by one unique law as eminently chimerical, even when they are made by the most competent minds. I believe that the means at the disposal of the human mind are too feeble and the universe too complex for such a scientific perfection to be ever open to us. . . .'[1] We can unify the sciences in the sense that we can find a method which lies at the basis of their different procedures; but we cannot achieve a doctrinal unification in the sense just mentioned.

This means in effect that we cannot achieve a doctrinal synthesis by following an 'objective' method, by extending the process of coordinating phenomena, which is common to all the sciences, to the point of reducing all laws to one law. We can however achieve a doctrinal synthesis by means of a 'subjective' method, by viewing the sciences, that is to say, in their relations to humanity, to the needs of man as a social being. This means that the synthesizing principle must be looked for in sociology. Once the science of man has arisen, we can look back and see the development of science as a progress from consideration of non-human to consideration of human phenomena, as a movement from the external world to man himself. We can then unify the sciences from the point of view of the subject, when the subject is humanity in general rather than the individual subject of epistemology.

[1] *CPP*, I, p. 44.

Comte is not of course suggesting that sociology should or could absorb all the other sciences. He is suggesting that sociology, having as its subject-matter man in society, offers the organizing principle for the unification of scientific knowledge, namely the idea of humanity and its needs. From the historical point of view sociology was the last science to appear on the scene. Once however sociological theory has been freed from theological beliefs and ethical assumptions and has reached the positive stage of its development, we are entitled to invert, as it were, the historical order and give supremacy to the human or 'subjective' point of view. If objective scientific knowledge was to be attained, the subjective point of view had to be disregarded. But when the basic sciences, sociology included, have been firmly established as scientific disciplines, we can follow the policy of unifying them in terms of their several relations to human needs without impairing their scientific objectivity, whereas at an earlier stage this policy would have been detrimental to the advance of the sciences.

The positive philosophy however does not aim simply at effecting a theoretical unification of the sciences. It has also a practical aim. Comte refers to 'the immense social revolution in the midst of which we are living and to which the totality of preceding revolutions has really contributed only a necessary preliminary.'[1] A reorganization of society is called for. This task cannot however be performed without a knowledge of the laws of society as formulated in sociology. Without knowledge of the laws which coordinate the phenomena of Nature man cannot effectively control or mould his external natural environment. Similarly, without knowledge of the laws relating to man in society we cannot effectively promote and achieve social renovation and progress. It is this social reorganization which is the practical goal of the 'subjective' synthesis of the sciences, their unification in terms of their relations to humanity and its needs.

5. Sociology or social physics is regarded by Comte as presupposing the other basic sciences, as the culmination of the development of science and as the special contribution of the positive stage to man's intellectual advance. It is divided by him into social statics and social dynamics. Social statics studies the general laws of existence common to human societies, the essential conditions, that is to say, of social solidarity. Social dynamics studies the laws of the movement or development of societies, the laws of social

[1] *CPP*, IV, p. 37.

progress. In Comte's view social statics 'forms the direct link between the final science and the totality of the preliminary sciences, above all biology, from which it appears to be inseparable.'[1] It is itself presupposed by and looks forward to social dynamics, the laws of which are said to apply above all to politics, whereas those of social statics 'belong rather to morals'.[2] Sociology as a whole, comprising, that is to say, both social statics and social dynamics, conceives 'progress as the gradual development of order',[3] while it also 'represents order as manifested by progress'.[4]

Social statics finds the basis of society in man's nature as a social being and shows how in any society there must be both division of labour and coordination of human effort with a view to realizing a common purpose. It also exhibits the necessity and basic nature of government. Social statics is thus primarily concerned with the element of order which is essential to any society; and in this field Aristotle made a notable contribution to thought. Though however order is essential to any society, the result of canonizing a given form of social organization is petrifaction. It was the great fault of utopians such as Plato that they represented one possible form of social organization as the one ideal form of order. Indeed, even 'the most powerful mind of all antiquity, the great Aristotle, was so dominated by his century that he was unable even to conceive a society which was not necessarily founded on slavery. . . .'[5]

The idea of order is thus insufficient. The idea of progress is also required. And this is studied in social dynamics. Comte insists however on the intimate connection between social statics and social dynamics. Order without progress or development results in petrifaction or in decay; but change without order would spell anarchy. We have to see in progress the actualization of the inherent dynamic tendency of social order. 'Progress remains always the simple development of order';[6] and this means that social order assumes successively different forms. Progress is 'oscillatory',[7] in the sense that it covers cases of retardation or even of retrogression as moments in a general movement of advance.

---

[1] *Système de politique positive* (1825), II, p. 1. This work will be referred to in footnotes as *Pol.*
[2] *Ibid.*, p. 2.   [3] *Ibid.*, p. 2.   [4] *Ibid.*, p. 2.
[5] *CPP*, IV, p. 37.   [6] *Pol.*, III, p. 72.   [7] *Ibid.*

We have noted that Comte praises Aristotle's contribution to social statics. In the field of social dynamics he pays tribute to Montesquieu. 'It is to Montesquieu that we must attribute the first great direct effort to treat politics as a science of facts and not of dogmas.'[1] But just as Aristotle had his shortcomings, so had Montesquieu. The latter did not succeed in freeing his thought from metaphysics; he did not properly understand the necessary succession of different political organizations; and he ascribed an exaggerated importance to forms of government. To find a real advance we must turn to Condorcet who was the first to see clearly that 'civilization is subject to a progressive advance, the stages of which are rigorously linked to one another by natural laws which philosophical observation of the past can reveal. . . .'[2] Not even Condorcet however understood properly the natures of the successive stages or epochs. It was Comte himself who contributed this understanding[3].

According to Comte, 'the fundamental characteristic of the positive philosophy is to regard all phenomena as subject to invariable natural *laws*.'[4] The phrase 'all phenomena' includes of course human phenomena. Comte does not claim that the coordination of human phenomena by the formulation of laws has reached the same degree of development in sociology which it has reached in some other sciences. None the less he maintains that the philosopher should regard human phenomena as capable of being subsumed under laws. This means in effect that the successive forms of social-political organization must be correlated with the successive stages of man's intellectual development. As we have seen, Comte's view is that in the theological epoch society was necessarily a military society, organized for conquest, industry being simply such as was required for the maintenance of human life. In the metaphysical stage, which was a period of transition, society was also in a state of transition, 'no longer frankly military, and not yet frankly industrial.'[5] In the positive stage society is organized with a view to production, and it is by nature a peaceful society, aiming at the common good. In fine, the three successive modes of human activity, 'conquest, defence and labour',[6] 'correspond exactly with the three states of intelligence, fiction, abstraction and demonstration. From this basic correla-

---

[1] *Ibid.*, IV, p. 106 (of the General Appendix).   [2] *Ibid.*, p. 109.
[3] Obviously, Saint-Simon is not accorded due recognition.
[4] *CPP*, I, p. 16.   [5] *Pol.*, IV, p. 112 (of the General Appendix).
[6] *Ibid.*, III, p. 63.

tion there results at once the general explanation of the three
natural ages of humanity.'[1]

Man is not however simply an intellectual and active being. He
is also characterized by feeling. 'In every normal existence affec-
tion constantly dominates speculation and action, though their
intervention is indispensable for it to be able to undergo and
modify external impressions.'[2] Man has, for example, a social
instinct or sentiment. In antiquity it was directed to the city
(the *polis*), while in the Middle Ages it found expression in cor-
porations of various kinds. In the positive or industrial epoch the
social instinct tends, under the influence of the unifying factors of
science and industry, to take the form of love of humanity in
general. This idea provides Comte with a ground for claiming
that the third basic form of social organization is inherently
peaceful.

It is hardly necessary to say that just as Comte tries to reconcile his theory of the three stages of man's intellectual development with facts which seem to tell against the theory, so does he
attempt to reconcile with his account of the correlated forms of
social organization those historical facts which might be cited as
evidence against the truth of this account. For example, if evidence
is cited to show that even the more highly industrialized nations
can indulge in aggressive military action, Comte replies that the
process of industrialization begins and develops while ways of
thought and feeling characteristic of earlier epochs are still influential. He does not claim that no society in which industrialization is developing ever manifests an aggressive spirit or goes
to war. What he claims is that as industrial society grows to
maturity, the unification of mankind, promoted by common
scientific knowledge and by industrialization, will result, under
the guidance of a scientic élite, in a peaceful society in which
differences will be settled by rational discussion.

There is of course no reason why Comte should not try to accommodate facts within the framework of an hypothesis, provided
that he is ready to revise or even abandon the hypothesis if it
proves to be incompatible with the facts. But it is none too clear
why an increase in scientific knowledge must lead to the moral
improvement of mankind or why an industrial society must be
more peaceful than a non-industrialized society. After all, Comte
is not simply saying what, in his opinion, *ought* to happen, from

[1] *Ibid.*   [1] *Ibid.*, p. 67.

an ethical point of view. He is saying what *will* happen, in virtue of the law or laws governing man's development. And it is difficult to avoid the impression that the law of the three stages tends to become for Comte not so much a falsifiable hypothesis as the expression of a faith or of a teleological philosophy of history in the light of which the historical data have to be interpreted.

If the historical process is governed by law and the future is predictable, at any rate in principle, the question arises whether any room is left for social planning. What, for example, can a scientific élite do to influence society and the course of history? From one point of view perhaps there is no particular problem. As we have seen, Comte insists that while all science coordinates phenomena by subsuming them under laws, these laws are purely descriptive. If we found that man could produce effects in the physical world which were incompatible with hitherto accepted physical laws, we would obviously revise the laws in question. The laws, as descriptive generalizations, are revisible in principle. Similarly, as far as his professed theory of scientific laws is concerned, Comte could perfectly well maintain that the laws of sociology are subject to falsification and so revisible in principle. A law might be falsified by human action. When however it is a question of the law of the three stages, Comte tends to speak as though it were inviolable, and as though society will develop in the way indicated by this law whatever man may do. The question therefore inevitably arises whether it makes any sense to call for social planning by a scientific élite.

Comte is quite well aware of the need to answer this question. And he argues that there is no incompatibility between the idea of all phenomena being subject to laws and the idea of human planning and control. On the contrary, man's power to modify phenomena of any sort can be exercised only if there is 'a real knowledge of their respective natural laws'.[1] To take an example from the modern world, a knowledge of the relevant physical laws is an essential condition of successful space-exploration. Similarly, a knowledge of the laws of human behaviour is an essential condition of intelligent and effective social planning. According to Comte, social phenomena are more complex than physical phenomena; and this means that the laws formulated in sociology are less precise than physical laws, less amenable than

[1] *CPP*, IV, p. 220.

physical laws to mathematical formulation. None the less, the formulation of laws in sociology permits prediction. For social phenomena are 'as susceptible of prediction as all the other kinds of phenomena, within the limits of precision which are compatible with their greater complexity.'[1] And so far from being incompatible with social planning, this predictability is an essential condition of it.

This may seem sensible enough. But it does not quite answer the question, to what extent can human action affect the course of history? Comte replies by making a distinction. Man cannot change the order of the successive stages of historical development. But human action or inaction can accelerate or retard this development. The emergence of the positive stage of thought and of the correlated form of society is necessary, man being what he is. But the development of industrial society can be accelerated by intelligent planning. For social phenomena are 'by their nature at the same time the most modifiable of all and the ones which have the most need of being usefully modified according to the rational indications of science.'[2] This modifiability of social phenomena permits effective planning; but what can be actually achieved is limited by what is evidently taken to be the working out of an unalterable law. Social development is modifiable 'in its speed, within certain limits, by a number of physical and moral causes. . . . Political combinations belong to the number of these causes. This is the sole sense in which it is given to man to influence the march of his own civilization.'[3] Comte certainly wishes to allow room for human initiative and action. But the space allowed is limited by his interpretation of human history as governed by a law which man can no more alter than he can alter physical laws. And Comte is quite sure that he knows the law governing the development of human history.[4]

6. It was Comte's firm conviction that society should be organized by those who possessed real knowledge. On this matter he agreed with Plato. Comte had little use for democracy, if this is taken to imply that the will of the people, whatever it may happen to be, should prevail. He favoured paternalist government for the common good. Just as in the Middle Ages men were expected

[1] *Ibid.*, p. 226.   [2] *Ibid.*, p. 249.
[3] *Pol.*, IV, p. 93 (of the General Appendix).
[4] We find of course an analogous situation in Marxist philosophy. Room is left for revolutionary activity and social planning. But revolutionary activity can only accelerate the coming of what will come in any case.

to accept the teaching of the Church whether or not they understood the doctrines and the reasons for them, so would the citizens of the 'positive polity' be expected to accept the principles
laid down by the positivist élite, namely the scientists and positivist philosophers. In Comte's society of the future this élite
would control education and form public opinion. It would be in
fact the modern equivalent of the medieval spiritual power, while
the government, drawn from the managerial class, would be the
modern equivalent of the medieval temporal power. In the
exercise of its functions the government would (or rather 'will',
given the law of the three stages) consult the positivist élite, the
high priests of science. Though he thought of the medieval period
as succeeded by the metaphysical and then the positivist eras,
Comte was by no means a despiser of the Middle Ages. The
scientists and positivist philosophers would take the place of the
pope and bishops, while members of the managerial class would
exercise the functions of medieval monarchs and nobles.

Comte saw of course the French revolution as dissolving an
outdated régime which would have been quite unable to meet the
needs of the nascent society. But he had scant sympathy with
liberal insistence on the alleged natural rights of individuals. The
notion that individuals had natural rights independently of, and
even against society, was foreign to his mind. In his view this
notion was based on a failure to understand the fact that the basic
reality is humanity rather than the individual. Man as an individual is an abstraction. And the regeneration of society 'consists
above all in substituting duties for rights, in order better to
subordinate personality to sociability.'[1] 'The word *right* should be
as much erased from the true language of politics as the word
cause from the true language of philosophy. . . . In other words,
nobody possesses any other right than that of always doing his
duty. It is only in this way that politics can at last be subordinated to morals, in accordance with the admirable programme of
the Middle Ages.'[2] In the positive epoch society will indeed
guarantee certain 'rights' to the individual, as this is required for
the common good. But these rights do not exist independently
of society.

Comte is not of course suggesting that the positive society will
be characterized by governmental oppression of individuals.
His contention is that as the new society develops, the idea of

---

[1] *Pol.*, I, p. 361.   [2] *Ibid.*, p. 361.

performing one's duties to society and of serving the interests of humanity will prevail over the concept of society as existing to serve the interests of individuals. In other words, he is confident that the development of industrial society, when properly organized, will be accompanied by a moral regeneration involving the substitution of concern with the welfare of humanity for concern with the individual's private interests. We may well think that he is somewhat over-optimistic. But the trouble is not that he hopes for moral regeneration but rather his confidence that this regeneration will inevitably accompany the development of a society based on science and industry. It is difficult to see why this should be the case.

However this may be, the highest form of the moral life consists for Comte in the love and service of humanity. In the positive phase of thought humanity takes the place occupied by God in theological thought; and the object of positivist worship is the 'Great Being' (*le Grand Être*), Humanity with a capital letter. To be sure, humanity does not possess all the attributes once predicated of God. Whereas, for example, the world was conceived as God's creation and as dependent on him, humanity is 'always subject to the totality of the natural order, of which it constitutes only the noblest element'.[1] The Great Being's 'necessary dependence' does not however affect its relative superiority. And Comte works out a religious system based on the Catholicism in which he was brought up. Positivism will have its saints (the great benefactors of mankind), its temples, its statues, its commination of the principal enemies of mankind, its commemoration of the dead, its social sacraments, and so on.

John Stuart Mill, who sympathized with Comte's general positivist attitude, criticized sharply the way in which Comte aspired to subject people to the straitjacket of a dogmatic religion expounded by positivist philosophers.[2] Mill also maintained that Comte's positivist religion had no organic connection with his genuinely philosophical thought but was a superfluous, and indeed repugnant, addition. These two contentions are of course separable. That is to say, we can quite well regard as repugnant what T. H. Huxley described as Comte's Catholicism without Christianity without necessarily subscribing to Mill's view that it had no

[1] *Ibid.*, II, p. 65.
[2] For Mill's views on Auguste Comte see his *Auguste Comte and Positivism* (1865). His own concept of the religion of humanity can be found in *Three Essays on Religion* (1874). Mill's correspondence with Comte has been edited.

organic connection with positivism. And this view has in fact been challenged. In spite of what Mill's critics say, there is an important sense in which his contention seems to be fully justified. For the idea that theology and metaphysics have been succeeded by science, which alone gives us genuine and useful knowledge, does not entail the elevation of humanity into an object of religious worship, nor the establishment of an elaborate religious cult. Comte's positivist religion, which influenced a number of his disciples and led to the establishment of a positivist Church,[1] is not a logical consequence of a positivist theory of knowledge. At the same time it is certainly arguable that there is a psychological connection between Comte's positivist philosophy and his religion of humanity. It seems true to say that Comte was at one with the Traditionalists in believing that a moral and religious regeneration of society was required. Believing however that God was a fiction, he had to look elsewhere for an object of devotion. And thinking, as he did, that the basic social reality was humanity rather than separate individuals and that individuals could transcend egoism only by devoting themselves to the service of humanity, it is understandable that in his 'Great Being' he found a substitute for the focus of devotion and worship in the Middle Ages. An emphasis on the service of humanity does not indeed entail the establishment of a religious cult. But Comte evidently thought that in modern society the unifying and elevating function once performed by belief in God could be fulfilled only by a religious devotion to humanity. While therefore Mill is undoubtedly right in maintaining that a positivist theory of knowledge does not entail the religion of humanity, it is relevant to remember that Comte was concerned not only with a theory of knowledge but also with social regeneration, and that his positivist religion, bizarre though it may seem, was for him an integral part of this regeneration.

A pertinent question however is whether in his talk about the Great Being Comte does not relapse into the metaphysical stage of thought as he conceived it. To be sure, he is ready to admit that the Great Being acts only through individuals. But it seems clear that to be considered as a proper object of worship by individuals humanity has to be hypostatized, to be conceived as a totality

---

[1] Reference will be made in the next chapter to Comte's followers in France. For a brief mention of his disciples in England see Volume VIII of this *History*, pp. 113 f.

which is more than the succession of individual human beings. Indeed, Comte refers to 'one immense and eternal Being, Humanity'.[1] Perhaps such statements should not be taken too seriously. They might be understood as expressing a hope that humanity will not in fact be destroyed by the 'cosmological fatalities'[2] which might extinguish it. At the same time it is clear that humanity as an object of common worship becomes an hypostatized abstraction and thus an example of the metaphysical stage of thought as described by Comte. This aspect of the matter is illustrated by what Comte has to say about immortality. Sometimes he speaks of continued existence 'in the heart and mind of others'[3]; but when he speaks of our nature needing 'to be purified by death'[4] and of man becoming 'an organ of humanity'[5] in the second life, he seems to be regarding humanity as a persistent entity which is irreducible to the succession of human beings living in the world.

The matter can be put in this way. In the classical positivism of Comte, as distinct from the logical positivism of the twentieth century, the notion of meaninglessness does not function prominently. As we have seen, Comte was anxious to defend positivism against the charge of atheism. He did not assert dogmatically that there was no God. The thesis which he generally adopted was that the idea of God has become more and more of an unverified hypothesis, in proportion, that is to say, as man has substituted scientific for theological explanations of phenomena. At the same time it might be inferred from some of the things which he says that an unverifiable hypothesis would lack any clear meaning. And occasionally this view is explicitly stated. Comte asserts, for example, that 'any proposition which is not ultimately reducible to the simple enunciation of a fact, whether particular or general, would not present (*ne saurait offrir*) any real intelligible sense.'[6] If such utterances were pressed, it would seem difficult to maintain that the concept of the 'Great Being' (Humanity), considered as an object of worship and religious devotion, had any clearly intelligible meaning. For if the Great Being is reducible to phenomena and the relations between them, the religion of humanity becomes an extremely odd affair. Comte's

---

[1] *The Catechism of Positive Religion*, translated by R. Congreve (3rd edition, 1891), p. 45.
[2] *Ibid.*, p. 45.   [3] *Ibid.*, p. 55.   [4] *Pol.*, IV, p. 35.   [5] *Ibid.*, II, p. 60.
[6] *CPP*, VI, p. 600. Comte is here quoting himself from an earlier writing.

positivist religion requires that the Great Being should be regarded as a reality which is irreducible to a collection of individual men and women. Hence in proposing his religion he seems to slip back into the mentality of the metaphysical, if not the theological stage.[1]

[1] According to Comte, however, it is 'our metaphysicians' who reduce Humanity to individuals, considered in abstraction from the whole.

PART II

FROM AUGUSTE COMTE TO HENRI BERGSON

CHAPTER VI

POSITIVISM IN FRANCE

E. Littré and his criticism of Comte—C. Bernard and the experimental method—E. Renan; positivism and religion—H. Taine and the possibility of metaphysics—E. Durkheim and the development of sociology—L. Lévy-Bruhl and morals.

1. AUGUSTE Comte, the most famous French positivist of the nineteenth century, had his faithful disciples who accepted the master's thought as a whole, including his religion of humanity. Foremost among them was Pierre Lafitte (1825–1903) who became a professor of the Collège de France in 1892 and who was recognized as their leader by the London Positivist Committee which was founded in 1881 with J. H. Bridges (1832–1906) as its president.[1] There were however philosophers who accepted positivism as an epistemological theory but who had little use for it as a religious cult and who regarded Comte's political ideas and his teleological interpretation of human history as constituting a departure from the genuine spirit of positivism. An eminent representative of this line of thought was Émile Littré (1801–1881).

Littré studied medicine for a time[2]; but he is best known for his dictionary of the French language.[3] In 1863 his candidature for election to the French Academy was vehemently opposed by Bishop Dupanloup of Orléans, who was himself a member of the Academy; but in 1871 Littré was at last elected. In the same year he became a deputy, and in 1875 he was made a senator for life. It is with his philosophical thought that we are concerned here.

When Littré came to read Comte's *Course of Positive Philosophy* he had already shed theological beliefs and rejected metaphysics. The *Course* provided him with something positive and

---

[1] The London Committee broke away from the original group of English Comtists, led by Richard Congreve (1818–99). The two groups were later reunited.

[2] His *Dictionnaire de médecine* appeared in 1855.

[3] *Dictionnaire de la langue française* (4 volumes, 1863–72).

definite to hold on to. 'It was in 1840 that I came to know M. Comte. A common friend lent me his system of positive philosophy; M. Comte, on learning that I was reading the book, sent me a copy of it. . . . His book conquered me. . . . I became from then on a disciple of the positive philosophy, and such I have remained, without other changes than those imposed on me by the increasing effort to carry out, in the midst of other obligatory labours, the corrections and enlargements which it allows of.'[1] In 1845 Littré reprinted a number of articles as a book with the title *On the Positive Philosophy* (*De la philosophie positive*).

In 1852 Littré broke with Comte; but his disagreements with the high priest of positivism did not affect his adherence to the philosophical outlook expounded in the *Course*. And in 1863 he published *Auguste Comte and the Positive Philosophy* (*Auguste Comte et la philosophie positive*) in which he warmly defended what he regarded as the main and valuable ideas of Comte, while also expressing some criticism of points on which he disagreed. Further, in 1864 he wrote a preface[2] for the second edition of Comte's *Course*, while in 1866 he tried to defend Comte against J. S. Mill. In 1873 Littré published *Science from the Philosophical Point of View* (*La science au point de vue philosophique*), which included a number of articles which had appeared in the *Revue de philosophie positive*. In 1879 he brought out a second edition of his *Conservation, Revolution and Positivisme* (*Conservation, révolution et positivisme*) in which he revised some of the ideas expressed in the first edition of the work (1852).

In Littré's opinion, Comte filled a vacuum. On the one hand the mind seeks a general or overall view; and this was just what metaphysics provided. The trouble was however that the metaphysician developed his theories *a priori*, and that these theories lacked a solid empirical basis. On the other hand the particular sciences, while proposing empirically testable hypotheses, inevitably lacked the generality which was characteristic of metaphysics. In other words, the discrediting of metaphysics left a gap which could be filled only by the creation of a new philosophy. And it was Comte who met this need. 'M. Comte is the founder of the positive philosophy.'[3] Saint-Simon did not possess the necessary scientific knowledge. Further, by trying to reduce the

---

[1] *Auguste Comte et la philosophie positive*, p. 1 (preface). This work will be referred to in footnotes as *AC*.
[2] It bore the title *Préface d'un disciple*.   [3] *AC*, p. 38.

forces of nature to one ultimate force, namely gravitation, he relapsed into the metaphysical mentality.[1] Comte however 'has constructed what nobody before him had constructed, the philosophy of the six fundamental sciences'[2] and has exhibited the relations between them. 'By discussing the interconnection of the sciences and their hierarchic system (Comte) discovered at the same time the positive philosophy.'[3] Comte also showed how and why the sciences developed historically in a certain order from mathematics to sociology. Metaphysicians may reproach other philosophers with neglecting consideration of man, the subject of knowledge; but this reproach does not affect Comte, who established the science of man, namely sociology, on a sound basis. Moreover by excluding all 'absolute' questions[4] and by giving philosophy a firm scientific basis, Comte at last made philosophy capable of directing 'minds in research, men in their conduct and societies in their development'[5]. Theology and metaphysics tried to do this; but as they treated of questions which transcended human knowledge, they were necessarily ineffective.

The positive philosophy, Littré asserts, regards the world as consisting of matter and the forces immanent in matter. 'Beyond these two terms, matter and force, positive science knows nothing.'[6] We do not know either the origin of matter or its essence. The positive philosophy is not concerned with absolutes or with knowledge of things in themselves. It is concerned simply with reality as accessible to human knowledge. If therefore it is claimed that phenomena can be accounted for in terms of matter and its immanent forces, this is not equivalent to a dogmatic materialism, which professes, for example, to tell us what matter is in itself or to 'explain' the development of life or thought. The positive philosophy shows, for instance, how psychology presupposes biology, and biology other sciences; but it steers clear of questions about the ultimate cause of life or about what thought is in itself, apart from our scientific knowledge of it.

Though however Littré is keen on differentiating between positivism and materialism, it is not at all clear that he is successful in this attempt. As mentioned above, he maintains that the

---

[1] Littré minimized Saint-Simon's influence on Comte. And he denied that Comte was ever in a real sense Saint-Simon's disciple.
[2] *AC*, p. 105.   [3] *Ibid.*, p. 106.
[4] *AC*, p. 107. Littré is referring to such questions as those about the ultimate origin and end or purpose of things.
[5] *Ibid.*, p. 107.   [6] *CPP*, I, p. ix (Préface d'un disciple).

positive philosophy recognizes nothing beyond matter and the forces immanent in matter. It is true of course that this thesis is expressed in terms of an assertion about scientific knowledge, and not as an assertion about ultimate reality or about what is 'really real'. At the same time Littré finds fault with J. S. Mill for leaving the existence of a supernatural reality an open question; and he criticizes Herbert Spencer's attempt to reconcile science and religion by means of his doctrine of the Unknowable. Perhaps we can say that two lines of thought are discernible in Littré's mind. On the one hand there is the tendency to insist that the positive philosophy simply abstains from questions relating to realities the existence of which cannot be verified by sense-experience. In this case there is no reason why such questions should not be left open, even if they are considered unanswerable[1]. On the other hand there is a tendency to regard assertions about alleged realities which transcend the sphere of the scientifically verifiable as nonsensical. In this case of course it makes no sense to ask whether or not such realities exist. The questions cannot then be regarded as open questions, and Littré's criticism of Mill becomes understandable.

Though however Littré was and remained in substantial agreement with the ideas expressed by Comte in his *Course of Positive Philosophy*, he believed that in later writings Comte had pretty well betrayed the positivist outlook. For example, Littré had no use for the 'subjective method', in which human needs constitute the synthesizing principle,[2] as advocated by Comte in his *System of Positive Polity* and the one completed volume of the *Subjective Synthesis*. By the subjective method Littré understood a process of reasoning which set out from premises asserted *a priori* and arrived at conclusions which were warranted only by their formal logical connections with the premises. In his opinion, this was the method followed in metaphysics; and it had no place in positive philosophy. What Comte did was to introduce a confusion between the subjective method as followed by metaphysicians and the deductive method as developed in the scientific era. The deductive method in the second sense 'is subject to the twofold condition of having experimentally acquired points

---

[1] Bertrand Russell, we may note, maintained, on occasion at any rate, that it was one of the jobs of philosophy to keep alive an awareness of certain important problems which were yet, in his opinion, insoluble.

[2] The needs, that is to say, of social man or the human collectivity rather than of the individual as such.

of departure and experimentally verified conclusions'.[1] By reintroducing the subjective method, which deals with the logical connection between ideas or propositions without any real attention being paid to empirical verification, Comte 'let himself be conquered by the Middle Ages'.[2]

Among the particular points criticized by Littré are Comte's identification of mathematics with logic and his subordination of the mind to the heart or to the affective aspect of man. It is one thing to emphasize the cooperating role of feeling in human activity, and it is quite another thing to suggest, as Comte does, that the heart should dominate the intelligence or dictate to it. This suggestion, Littré insists, is quite incompatible with the positivist mentality. As for the religion of humanity, to a very limited extent Littré is prepared to agree with Comte on the need for religion, as distinct from theology. 'In my opinion, M. Comte followed a legitimate deduction by investing the positive philosophy of which he is the author with a role equivalent to that of religions.'[3] That is to say, if we mean by religion a general worldview, the positivist conception of the world can be described as a religion. Comte however goes very much further than this. For he postulates a collective being, humanity, and proposes it as an object of cult. Love of humanity is indeed a noble and admirable sentiment; but 'there is no justification for selecting for adoration either humanity or any other fraction of the whole or the great whole itself'.[4] What Comte does in effect is to relapse into the theological mentality. And 'for all this the subjective method is responsible'.[5]

As for ethics or morals, Littré blames Comte for having added morals to the list of sciences as a seventh member. This was a mistake; for 'morals does not at all belong, as do the six sciences, to the objective order'.[6] Rather oddly, Littré goes on to say, practically immediately, that there is need of a science of morals.[7] The apparent contradiction would indeed be eliminated if we were justified in interpreting Littré as finding fault with Comte for thinking that a normative ethics could be a science or have an integral place in positive philosophy and as himself maintaining that a purely descriptive study of ethical phenomena or of man's moral behaviour was needed. And he does indeed speak elsewhere

[1] *AC*, p. 536.   [2] *AC*, p. 562.   [3] *Ibid.*, p. 524.
[4] *Ibid.*, Littré had no use for pantheism.
[5] *AC*, p. 579.   [6] *Ibid.*, p. 677.   [7] *Ibid.*, p. 677.

about 'the observation of the phenomena of the moral order as revealed whether by psychology or by history and political economy',[1] as serving as a foundation for the scientific knowledge of human nature. But he also refers to human progress, conceived in positivist terms, as 'the source of profound convictions, obligatory for conscience'.[2]

We can reasonably conclude that Littré did not work out his ideas on ethics in a clear and consistent manner. It is however evident enough that his general quarrel with Comte's later writings is that they show serious departures from the positivist conviction that the only genuine knowledge of the world or of man is empirically verified knowledge. Or perhaps it might be better to say that in Littré's opinion Comte came to introduce into the positive philosophy ideas which had no legitimate place there and thus created a state of confusion. It was therefore necessary to return to the pure positivism of which Comte himself had been the great expounder.

3. The conviction that experimental science alone is the source of knowledge about the world was shared by the famous French physiologist, Claude Bernard (1813-78), professor of physiology at the Sorbonne and of medicine at the Collège de France. His best known work is his *Introduction to the Study of Experimental Medicine* (*Introduction à l'étude de la médecine expérimentale*), which he published in 1865. Three years later he was elected to the French Academy; and in 1869 he became a senator.

To include mention of Claude Bernard in a chapter devoted to positivism may seem to be quite inappropriate. For not only did he say that the best philosophical system is not to have one but he also explicitly condemned the positivist philosophy for being a system[3]. He wished to make medicine more scientific; and the better to promote this cause he undertook an investigation into the nature of scientific method. He was not concerned with creating a philosophical system, nor with defending an already existing one. At the same time Bernard insisted that the experimental method was the only one which could yield objective knowledge of reality. He did indeed speak of 'subjective truths' as absolute truths; but he was referring to mathematics, the truths of which are formal, independent, that is to say, of what is the case in the world.

---

[1] *CPP*, VI, '. xxxiv (Préface d'un disciple).
[2] *Ibid.*, p. xlviii.   [3] *Introduction*, p. 387.

By the experimental method Bernard meant the construction and empirical testing of verifiable hypotheses, an objective method which eliminated, as far as possible, the influence of subjective factors such as the desire that X rather than Y should be the case. Theologians and metaphysicians claimed that their unverified ideal constructions represented absolute or definitive truth. Unverifiable hypotheses however do not represent knowledge. Positive knowledge of the world, which is knowledge of the laws of phenomena, can be obtained only through the use of scientific method. And this yields results which are provisional, revisible in principle that is to say.

It is true that Bernard asserts that there is an 'absolute principle of science',[1] the principle of determinism, which states that a given set of conditions (together constituting a 'cause') infallibly produce a certain phenomenon or effect. Bernard's contention however is that this principle is 'absolute' simply in the sense that it is a necessary working assumption of science. The scientist necessarily assumes a regular causal order in the world. The principle is not 'absolute' in the sense of being an *a priori* metaphysical truth or a philosophical dogma. It is not equivalent, Bernard maintains, to fatalism. He does indeed sometimes write as though the principle of determinism were in fact an absolute truth which is known *a priori*. But though a measure of inconsistency may be discernible in his various utterances, his official position, so to speak, is that the determinism in question is methodological, involved, that is to say, in the scientific approach to the world, rather than a philosophical doctrine.

We have seen that Bernard refuses to recognize theology and metaphysics as sources of knowledge about reality. In this matter his attitude is clearly positivistic. At the same time he also refuses to rule out what are sometimes described as ultimate questions on the ground that they are meaningless or that they should not be asked. And though he was not himself a religious believer, he insisted on leaving a place for belief as well as knowledge. The two should not be confused; but belief of some sort is natural to man, and religious belief is quite compatible with scientific integrity, provided that it is recognized that articles of belief are not empirically verified hypotheses. Bernard is therefore critical of Comte's doctrine of the three stages. Theological beliefs and metaphysics cannot legitimately be regarded simply

[1] *Introduction*, p. 69.

as *past* stages of human thought. There are questions of importance to man which transcend the scope of science, and so the field in which knowledge is possible; but belief in certain answers is legitimate, provided that they are not proposed as assured truths about reality, and that there is no attempt to impose them on others.

If therefore the question is raised whether Bernard was or was not a positivist, we have to make a distinction. His idea of what constituted positive knowledge of reality was in line with the ideas of Comte. We can quite well speak of Bernard's positivist outlook. At the same time he rejected positivism as a dogmatic philosophical system, though he had no wish to substitute for it any other philosophical system. To be sure, anyone who writes, as Bernard did, on human knowledge, its scope and limits, is bound to make philosophical statements or statements which have philosophical implications. But Bernard tried to avoid the temptation to expound a philosophy in the name of science. Hence his insistence that his principle of determinism should not be regarded as a philosophical dogma. Again, while he was prepared to speak of the organism which functions in virtue of its physico-chemical elements, he also admitted that the physiologist must look on the living organism as an individual unity, the development of which is directed by a 'creative idea' or 'vital force'[1]. This may sound like a contradiction. But Bernard tried, whether successfully or not, to steer clear of any philosophical assertion either that there is or is not a vital principle in the organism. His point was that though physicists and chemists must describe the organism in physico-chemical terms, the physiologist cannot help recognising the fact that the organism functions as a living unity and not simply as a collection of distinct chemical elements. Bernard tried at any rate to distinguish between thinking of the organism in a certain way and making a metaphysical assertion about entelechies.

4. Joseph Ernest Renan (1823–92) is best known for his *Life of Jesus* (*La vie de Jésus*, 1863). In 1862 he was appointed professor of Hebrew at the Collège de France[2]; and his two main publications were his *History of the Origins of Christianity* (*Histoire des origines du christianisme*, 1863–83) and his *History of the People of*

[1] *Introduction*, p. 151.
[2] Renan's lecturing activity at the Collège de France was soon suspended, as a consequence of his clear denial of the divinity of Christ. But he resumed his teaching after 1870, and in 1878 he was elected to the French Academy.

Israel (*Histoire du peuple d'Israël*, 1887–93). He also wrote on the Semitic languages and published French versions, with critical introductions, of certain books of the Old Testament. It may seem therefore that he is a most unsuitable person for mention in a history of philosophy. Though however he was not a professional philosopher and was far from being a consistent thinker,[1] he published some philosophical writings, such as *The Future of Science* (*L'avenir de la science*, written in 1848–49, though not published until 1890), *Essays on Morals and Criticism* (*Essais de morale et de critique*, 1859), and *Philosophical Dialogues and Fragments* (*Dialogues et fragments philosophiques*, 1876). His philosophical thought was a curious amalgam of positivism and religiosity, ending in scepticism. It is with his relation to positivism that we are concerned here.

When Renan left the seminary of Saint-Sulpice in 1845, he became a friend of Marcelin Pierre Eugène Berthelot (1827–1907), who was to become professor of organic chemistry at the Collège de France and subsequently minister of education. Like Comte, Berthelot believed in the triumph of scientific knowledge over theology and metaphysics. And Renan, who had lost his faith in the supernatural (in, that is to say, the existence of a transcendent and personal God), shared this belief up to a point. In his *Memoirs of Childhood and Youth* he remarked that from the first months of 1846 'the clear scientific vision of a universe in which there is no perceptible action of a free will superior to that of man'[2] became for Berthelot and himself an immovable anchor. Similarly, in the preface to the thirteenth edition (1866) of the *Life of Jesus* Renan asserted that he had rejected the supernatural for the very same reason for which he rejected belief in centaurs, namely that they had never been seen. In other words, knowledge of reality is obtained through observation and the verification of empirical hypotheses. This was the view expressed in *The Future of Science*. The scientific view of the world did not indeed mean for Renan simply the natural scientist's view. He emphasized (naturally enough, given his own intellectual interests) the importance and role of history and philology. But positive knowledge of reality, he insisted, must have an experimental basis. This is

---

[1] Renan tended to take pride in this lack of consistency, on the ground that it was only by trying out different hypotheses that one could hope to see the truth once in one's life.

[2] *Souvenirs d'enfance et de jeunesse* (2nd edition, 1883) p. 337.

why the enlightened man cannot believe in God. 'A being who does not reveal himself by any act is for science a being which does not exist.'[1]

If this were all, we would know where we were. But it is far from being all that Renan has to say. He rejects the idea of a personal God who intervenes in history. The occurrence of divine interventions has never been proved. And events which seemed to past generations to be divine acts have been explained in other ways. But to reject the personal transcendent Deity is not to embrace atheism. From one point of view God is the developing totality of existence, the divine being which becomes, God *in fieri*. From another point of view God, considered as perfect and eternal, exists only in the ideal order, as the ideal end of the whole process of development. 'What reveals the true God, is the moral sentiment. If humanity were simply intelligent, it would be atheist; but the great races have found in themselves a divine instinct. 'Duty, devotion, sacrifice, all of them things of which history is full, are inexplicable without God.'[2] True, all statements about God are simply symbolic. But the divine none the less reveals itself to the moral consciousness. 'To love God, to know God, is to love what is beautiful and good, to know what is true.'[3]

To give a precise account of Renan's concept of God is probably something which exceeds human capacity. We can discern the general influence, to a certain extent, of German idealism. More basic however is Renan's own religiosity or religious feeling which expresses itself in a variety of ways, not always mutually consistent, and which makes him quite incapable of being a positivist in the style of Littré. Obviously, there is no reason why a positivist should not have moral ideals. And if he wishes to interpret religion as a matter of sentiment or of the heart[4] and religious belief as the expression of feeling, not of knowledge, he can combine religion with a positivist theory of knowledge. But if he introduces the idea of the Absolute, as Renan does in his letter to Berthelot of August 1863,[5] he clearly goes beyond the limits of what can reasonably be described as positivism without the term being deprived of definite meaning.

In view of what has been said above it is hardly surprising to

---

[1] *Dialogues* (1876), p. 246.   [2] *Ibid.*, pp. 321–22.   [3] *Ibid.*, p. 326.
[4] In a letter of August 1862, addressed to Adolphe Guéroult, Renan said that to believe in the living God he needs only 'to listen in silence to the imperative revelation of my heart' (*Dialogues*, p. 251), a statement reminiscent of Rousseau.
[5] This letter is included in *Dialogues*, pp. 153–91.

find that Renan's attitude to metaphysics is complex. In an essay on metaphysics and its future, which he wrote in reply to a work entitled *Metaphysics and Science* (*La métaphysique et la science*, 2 volumes, 1858) by Étienne Vacherot,[1] he insisted that man had both the power and the right 'to rise above facts'[2] and to pursue speculation about the universe. He also made it clear however that he regarded such speculation as akin to poetry or even to dreaming. What he denied was not the right to indulge in metaphysical speculation but the view of metaphysics as the first and fundamental science 'containing the principles of all the others, a science which can by itself alone, and by abstract reasonings, lead us to the truth about God, the world and man'.[3] For 'all that we know, we know by the study of nature or of history'.[4]

Provided that positivism is not understood as entailing the claim that all metaphysical questions are nonsensical or meaningless, this view of metaphysics is doubtless compatible with the positivist thesis that all knowledge of reality comes through the sciences. So perhaps is Renan's assertion that while he denies that metaphysics is a 'progressive' science, in the sense that it can increase our knowledge, he does not reject it if it is considered as a science 'of the eternal'.[5] For he is referring not to an eternal reality but rather to an analysis of concepts. In his view logic, pure mathematics and metaphysics do not tell us anything about reality (about what is the case) but analyse what one already knows. To be sure, an equation of metaphysics with conceptual analysis is not the same as an assimilation of it to poetry or dreams. For in the first case it can reasonably be described as scientific, while in the second it cannot be so described. But Renan might of course reply that the word 'metaphysics' can bear both senses, and that he rejects neither of them. In other words, metaphysics can be a science provided that it is regarded simply as conceptual analysis. But if it professes to treat of existing realities, such as God, which transcend the spheres of natural science and of history, it is not and cannot be a science. One is entitled to speculate, but such speculation no more increases our knowledge of reality than do poetry and dreaming.

Given these two views of metaphysics, it is rather disconcerting to find Renan saying that philosophy is 'the general result of all

---

[1] Vacherot (1809–97) maintained the view that metaphysics could be made into a science. Renan's reply is reprinted in *Dialogues*.
[2] *Dialogues*, p. 282.   [3] *Ibid.*, p. 283.   [4] *Ibid.*, p. 284.   [5] *Ibid.*, p. 175.

the sciences'.[1] Taken by itself, this statement might be understood in a Comtean sense. But Renan adds that 'to philosophize is
to know the Universe,'[2] and that 'the study of nature and of
humanity is then the whole of philosophy'.[3] It is true that he uses
the word 'philosophy', not the word 'metaphysics'. But philosophy considered as 'the science of the whole'[4] is, one would have
thought, one of the meanings not uncommonly ascribed to
'metaphysics'. In other words, philosophy as the general result of
all the sciences tends to mean metaphysics, though the precise
status attributed by Renan to philosophy in this sense is by no
means clear.

Renan was obviously a man who believed that positive knowledge about the world could be obtained only through the natural
sciences and through historical and philological inquiries. In other
words, science, in a broad sense of the word,[5] had taken the place
of theology and metaphysics as a science of information about
existing reality. In Renan's view, belief in the transcendent
personal God of Jewish and Christian faith had been deprived of
any rational ground by the development of science. That is to say,
such belief was incapable of being confirmed experimentally. As
for metaphysics, whether it was regarded as speculation about
problems which were scientifically unanswerable or as some form
of conceptual analysis, it could not increase man's knowledge of
what is the case in the world. In one aspect of his thought therefore Renan was clearly on the side of the positivists. At the same
time he was unable to rid himself of the conviction that through
his moral consciousness and his recognition of ideals man entered,
in some real sense, into a sphere transcending that of empirical
science. Nor could he rid himself of the conviction that there was
in fact a divine reality, even if all attempts at definite description
were symbolic and open to criticism.[6] It is evident that he wished
to combine a religious outlook with the positivist elements in
his thought. But he was not enough of a systematic thinker to
achieve a coherent and consistent synthesis. Further, it was
hardly possible in any case to harmonize all his various beliefs,
not at any rate in the forms in which he expressed them. How,

---

[1] *Ibid.*, p. 290.   [2] *Ibid.*, p. 292.   [3] *Ibid.*, p. 292.   [4] *Ibid.*, p. 304.
[5] Renan uses the word 'science' in several senses. Sometimes it just means
knowledge, while sometimes it means natural sciences and sometimes it includes
the historical sciences.
[6] For example, 'every phrase applied to an infinite object is a myth' (*Dialogues*,
p. 323).

for example, could one reconcile the view that experimental or empirical verification is required to justify the assertion that something exists with the following claim? 'Nature is only an appearance; man is only a phenomenon. There is the eternal ground (*fond*), there is the infinite substance, the absolute, the ideal ... there is ... *he who is*'.[1] Empirical verification, in any ordinary sense, of the existence of the Absolute seems to be excluded. It is therefore not altogether surprising if in the last years of his life Renan showed a marked tendency to scepticism in the religious sphere. We cannot *know* the infinite or even that there is an infinite, nor can we establish that there are absolute objective values. True, we can act as if there were objective values and as if there were a God. But such matters lie outside the range of any positive knowledge. To claim therefore that Renan abandoned positivism would be inaccurate, though it is evident that it did not satisfy him.

5. If Renan's thought contains different elements, so does that of Hippolyte-Adolphe Taine (1828–93). Neither of the two thinkers can be adequately described by labelling him as a positivist. But whereas with Renan the obvious feature of his thought as a whole is his attempt to revise religion in such a way that it can be combined with his positivist ideas, in the case of Taine the salient characteristic of his thought is his attempt to combine positivist convictions with a marked inclination to metaphysics, an inclination stimulated by study of Spinoza and Hegel. Further, while the interests of neither Renan nor Taine are confined to the area of philosophy, their main extra-philosophical activities are somewhat different. Renan, as we have noted, is well known for his works on the history of the people of Israel and on the origins of Christianity, whereas Taine is celebrated for his work in psychology. He also wrote on art, literary history and the development of modern French society. Both men however were influenced by the positivist outlook.

Taine was attracted to philosophy at an early age; but at the time when he was studying at the École Normale at Paris, philosophical studies were more or less dominated by the thought of Victor Cousin, with which Taine had little sympathy. For a time he turned to teaching in schools and to literature. In 1853 he published his *Essay on the Fables of La Fontaine* (*Essai sur les fables de La Fontaine*) and in 1856 an *Essay on Livy* (*Essai sur*

[1] *Dialogues*, p. 252.

Tite-Live). These writings were followed by *Essays in Criticism and History* (*Essais de critique et d'histoire*, 1858) and the four-volume *History of English Literature* (*Histoire de la littérature anglaise*).[1] In the philosophical field Taine published *The French Philosophers of the Nineteenth Century* (*Les philosophes français du dix-neuvième siècle*) in 1857. But philosophical ideas also found expression in the prefaces to Taine's other writings.

In 1864 Taine obtained a chair at the École des Beaux-Arts, and his *Philosophy of Art*[2] was the result of his lectures on aesthetics. In 1870 Taine published his *De l'intelligence* in two volumes.[3] He planned to write another work on the will; but he was too occupied with his five-volume work on *The Origins of Contemporary France* (*Les origines de la France contemporaine*, 1875–93), in which he treated of the old régime, the revolution and the later development of French society. Another volume of essays on criticism and history appeared in 1894. Taine also published some travel books.

Taine was brought up a Christian but lost his faith at the age of fifteen. Doubt and scepticism were not however to his taste. He looked for knowledge that was certain; and he hankered after comprehensive knowledge, knowledge of the totality. Science, developed through the empirical verification of hypotheses, seemed to be the only road to secure knowledge of the world. At the same time Taine believed that the continuation of a metaphysical world-view, a view of the totality as a necessary system, was not only a legitimate but also a necessary enterprise. And his persistent problem was that of combining his conviction that there was nothing in the world but events or phenomena and the relations between them with his conviction that a metaphysics was possible which would go beyond the results of the particular sciences and achieve a synthesis. From the chronological point of view the attraction which he felt for the philosophies of Spinoza and Hegel preceded the development of his positivist ideas. But it was not a case of positivism arriving on the scene and driving out metaphysics. Taine reasserted his belief in metaphysics and endeavoured to reconcile the two tendencies in his thought. Whether he was

---

[1] 1863–4. There is an English translation by H. van Laun (Edinburgh, 1873).
[2] *Philosophie de l'art* (1865) was published in New York in an English translation by J. Durand. An enlarged French edition appeared in 1880.
[3] In 1871 an English translation, *Intelligence*, by T. D. Hayes was published in London.

successful, and indeed whether he could have been successful,[1] is disputable. But there can be no doubt about what he was trying to do.

The general nature of this attempt is made clear by Taine himself in his work on the French philosophers of the nineteenth century,[2] in his study of John Stuart Mill (*Le positivisme anglais. Étude sur Stuart Mill*, 1864) and in his history of English literature. The English empiricists, in Taine's opinion, regard the world as a collection of facts. To be sure, they concern themselves with the relations between phenomena or facts; but these relations are for them purely contingent. For Mill, who represents the culmination of a line of thought starting with Francis Bacon, the causal relation is simply one of factually regular sequence. Indeed, 'the law which attributes a cause to every event has for him no other basis, no other value and no other bearing than an experience. ... It simply gathers together a sum of observations'.[3] By confining himself simply to experience and its immediate data Mill 'has described the English mind while believing that he was describing the human mind'.[4] The German metaphysical idealists however have had the vision of the totality. They have seen the universe as the expression of ultimate causes and laws, as a necessary system, not as a collection of facts or of phenomena which are related in a purely contingent manner. At the same time, in their enthusiasm for the vision of the totality they have neglected the limitations of the human mind and have tried to proceed in a purely *a priori* manner. They have tried to reconstruct the world of experience by pure thought.[5] In point of fact they have constructed imposing edifices which presently collapse in ruins. There is thus room for a middle way, a combination of what is true and valuable in both English empiricism and German metaphysics. The achievement of this synthesis is reserved for the French mind. 'If there is a place between the two nations, it is

---

[1] If we mean by positivism a philosophy which explicitly excludes metaphysics, it is evident that any attempt to combine positivism with metaphysics is excluded by definition, even if we think that positivism implies a metaphysics in the sense of a theory of being (say, *esse est percipi vel percipi posse*). But Taine himself did not of course look on the empiricist tendencies in his thought as excluding from the start the sort of metaphysics which he envisaged.

[2] This work was later entitled *The Classical Philosophers* (*Les philosophes classiques*).

[3] *Le positivisme anglais*, p. 102.   [4] *Ibid.*, p. 110.

[5] Taine apparently thinks of Hegel as trying to deduce even particulars, a task which the German philosopher in fact disclaimed, in spite of his remarks about the planets.

ours'.[1] It is the French mind which is called to correct the faults of both English positivism and German metaphysics, to synthesize the corrected outlooks, 'to express them in a style which everyone understands and thus to make of them the universal mind'.[2] The English excel in the discovery of facts, the Germans in the construction of theories. Fact and theory need to be brought together by the French, if possible by Taine.

One's mind may well boggle at the thought of combining English empiricism with German idealism, Mill with Hegel. But Taine is not concerned simply with stating an ideal which doubtless seems to many minds unrealizable and perhaps even silly. He indicates what he considers to be the ground on which a synthesis can be constructed, namely man's power of abstraction. Taine's use of the word 'abstraction' stands however in need of some explanation.

In the first place Taine does not mean to imply that we are entitled to assume that abstract terms refer to corresponding abstract entities. On the contrary, he attacks not only Cousin and the eclectics but also Spinoza and Hegel for making precisely this assumption. Words such as 'substance', 'force' and 'power' are convenient ways of grouping similar phenomena, but to think, for example, that the word 'force' signifies an abstract entity is to be misled by language. 'We believe that there are no substances, but only systems of facts. We regard the idea of substance as a psychological illusion. We consider substances, force and all the metaphysical beings of the moderns as a relic of Scholastic entities. We think that there is nothing in the world but facts and laws, that is to say events and their relations; and like you we recognize that all knowledge consists in the first instance in linking or in adding facts.'[3] In his work on intelligence Taine insists that there are no entities corresponding to words such as 'faculty', 'power', 'self'. Psychology is the study of facts; and in the self or ego we find no facts except 'the series of events',[4] which are all reducible to sensations. Even positivists have been guilty of the reification of abstract terms. A signal example of this is provided by Herbert Spencer's theory of the Unknowable, considered as absolute Force.[5]

In this line of thought, considered by itself, Taine goes as far as any empiricist could wish. 'We think that there are neither minds

[1] *Le positivisme anglais*, p. 147.   [2] *Ibid.*, p. 148.   [3] *Ibid.*, p. 114.
[4] *De l'intelligence*, I, p. 6.   [5] *Derniers essais de critique et d'histoire*, p. 199.

nor bodies, but simply groups of movements present or possible, and groups of thoughts present or possible'.[1] And it is interesting to observe Taine's insistence on the bewitching power of language, which induces philosophers to postulate unreal entities that 'vanish when one scrupulously examines the meaning of the words'.[2] His empiricism also shows itself in his rejection of the *a priori* method of Spinoza, a method which can do more than reveal ideal possibilities. Any knowledge of existing reality must be based on and result from experience.

By abstraction therefore Taine does not mean the formation of abstract terms or concepts which are then mistakenly thought to stand for abstract entities. But what does he mean by it? He describes it as 'the power of isolating the elements of facts and considering them separately'.[3] The assumption is that what is given in experience is complex and that it is analyzable into constituent elements which can be considered separately or in abstraction. The natural way of understanding this is in terms of reductive analysis as practised by Condillac in the eighteenth century or by Bertrand Russell in the twentieth. Analysis (*décomposition*) is said to give us the nature or essence of what is analyzed. But Taine takes it that among the constituent elements which form 'the interior of a being'[4] there can be found causes, forces and laws. 'They are not a new fact added to the first; they are a portion of it, an extract; they are contained in them, they are nothing else but the facts themselves.'[5] For example, proof of the statement that Tom is mortal does not consist in arguing from the premise that all men die (which, as Mill maintained, begs the question), nor in appealing to the fact that we do not know of any human being who has not eventually died, but rather by showing that 'mortality is joined to the quality of being a man',[6] inasmuch as the human body is an unstable chemical compound. To find out whether Tom will die or not, there is no need to multiply examples of men who have died. What is required is abstraction, which enables us to formulate a law. Every single example contains the cause of human mortality; but it has of course to be isolated by the mind, picked out or extracted from complex phenomena, and formulated in an abstract manner. To prove a fact, as Aristotle said, is to show its cause. This cause is comprised within the fact.

---

[1] *Le positivisme anglais*, p. 114. Taine agrees with Mill on the need for introducing the idea of possible sensations.
[2] *De l'intelligence*, I, p. 339.   [3] *Le positivisme anglais*, p. 115.
[4] *Ibid.*, p. 116.   [5] *Ibid.*, p. 116.   [1] *Ibid.*, p. 124.

And when we have abstracted it, we can argue 'from the abstract to the concrete, that is to say from cause to effect'.[1]

We can however go further than this. We can practise the operation of analysis on groups or sets of laws and, in principle at any rate, arrive at the most primitive and basic elements of the universe. There are 'simple elements from which derive the most general laws, and from these the particular laws, and from these laws the facts which we observe'.[2] If these simple or unanalyzable elements can be known, metaphysics is possible. For metaphysics is the search for first causes. And, according to Taine, the first causes are knowable, inasmuch as they are everywhere exemplified, in all facts. It is not as though we had to transcend the world in order to know its first cause or causes. They are everywhere present and operative; and all that the human mind has to do is to extract or abstract them.

Given his insistence that the ultimate causes of empirical facts are contained within the facts themselves and so within experience, Taine can think of himself as correcting and enlarging British empiricism, not as contradicting it flatly. As far as he is concerned, metaphysics is really continuous with science, though it has a higher degree of generality. It is however evident that he starts with the assumption that the universe is one rational or law-ordered system. The notion that laws are convenient or practically useful fictions of the mind is quite alien to his thought. He assumes that 'there is a reason for everything, that every fact has its law; that every composite is reducible to simple elements; that every product implies causes (*facteurs*); that every quality and every existence must be deducible from some superior and anterior term'.[3] Taine assumes too that cause and effect are really the same thing under two 'appearances'. These assumptions are obviously derived not from empiricism but from the influence on his mind of Spinoza and Hegel. When he envisages one ultimate cause, one 'eternal axiom' and 'creative formula',[4] he is clearly speaking under the influence of a metaphysical vision of the totality as a necessary system which exhibits in innumerable ways the creative activity of an ultimate (though purely immanent) cause.

As we have noted, Taine criticizes the German idealists for having tried to deduce *a priori* such 'particular cases' as the

[1] *Ibid.*, p. 125.   [2] *Le positivisme anglais*, p. 137.   [3] *Ibid.*, p. 138.
[4] *The French Philosophers of the Nineteenth Century*, p. 371.

planetary system and the laws of physics and chemistry. But he appears to be objecting not to the idea of deducibility as such, deducibility in principle that is to say, but rather to the assumption that the human mind is able to perform the deduction, even when it has ascertained the primitive laws or ultimate causes. Between, so to speak, the primitive laws and a particular exemplification in the world as given in experience, there is an infinite series, criscrossed, so to speak, by innumerable cooperating or counterbalancing causal influences. And the human mind is too limited to be able to take in the whole pattern of the universe. But if Taine admits, as he seems to do, deducibility in principle, this admission obviously expresses a general vision of the universe which he has derived not from empiricism but from Spinoza and Hegel. This vision includes in its scope not only the physical universe but also human history. In his view history cannot become a science in the proper sense until causes and laws have been 'abstracted' from the facts or historical data.[1]

Talk about a metaphysical 'vision' may seem to be simply a case of employing the philosophical jargon which was fashionable some years ago among those who rejected the claim of metaphysics to be able to increase our positive knowledge of reality but who were not prepared to write off metaphysical systems as sheer nonsense. The term 'vision' however has a special appositeness in Taine's case. For he never developed a metaphysical system. He is best known for his contribution to empirical psychology. In psychopathology he tried to show how the constituent elements of what is *prima facie* a simple state or phenomenon can be dissociated; and he also made use of neural physiology to exhibit the mechanism which underlies mental phenomena. In general, he gave a powerful impetus to that development of psychology in France which is associated with such names as Théodule Armand Ribot (1859–1916), Alfred Binet (1857–1911) and Pierre Janet (1859–1947). In the fields of literary, artistic and social-political history Taine is known for his hypothesis of the formative influence on human nature of the three factors of race, environment and time and for his insistence, when dealing with the origins of contemporary France, on the effects of excessive centralization as manifested in different ways in the old régime, in the republic and under the empire. Throughout his work however Taine had, as he

---

[1] See, for example, *Essais de critique et d'histoire*, p. xxiv.

put it, 'a certain idea of causes',[1] an idea which was not that of the empiricists. In his view the eclectic spiritualists, such as Cousin, located causes outside the effects, and the ultimate cause outside the world. But the positivists banished causality from science.[2] Taine's idea of causality was obviously inspired by a general view of the universe as a rational and deterministic system. This vision remained a vision, in the sense that while he looked on his idea of causality as demanding and making possible a metaphysics, he did not himself attempt to develop a metaphysical system which would exhibit the 'first causes' and their operation in the universe. What he insisted on was the possibility of and the need for such a system. And while he could and did speak in an empiricist way of the scientific method of 'abstraction, hypothesis, verification'[3] for the ascertaining of causes, it is pretty clear that he meant more by 'cause' than would be meant by the empiricist or positivist.

6. Auguste Comte gave a powerful impetus to the development of sociology, an impetus which bore fruit in the later decades of the nineteenth century. To say this is certainly not to claim that French sociologists such as Durkheim were devoted disciples of the high priest of positivism. But by insisting on the irreducibility of each of his basic sciences to the particular science or sciences which it presupposed in the hierarchy and by emphasizing the nature of sociology as the scientific study of social phenomena Comte put sociology on the map. To be sure, the beginnings of sociology can be traced back well beyond Comte to Montesquieu, for example, and to Condorcet, not to speak of Saint-Simon, Comte's immediate predecessor. But Comte's clear recognition of sociology as a particular science, with a character of its own, justified Durkheim in regarding him as the father or founder of this science,[4] in spite of the fact that Durkheim did not accept the law of the three stages and criticized Comte's approach to sociology.

Émile Durkheim (1858–1917) studied in Paris at the École

---

[1] *Les philosophes français du dix-neuvième siècle*, p. x.
[2] The positivists would claim of course that it was a question of interpreting the causal relation rather than of banishing causality from science. Taine's view of the matter was obviously the expression of a non-empiricist view of the causal relation.
[3] *Les philosophes français*, p. 363.
[4] Durkheim regarded sociology as having been developed mainly in France. He had a low opinion of J. S. Mill's originality in this field, but he valued the contribution of Herbert Spencer, though with certain reservations, as will be indicated in the text.

Normale Supérieure and then taught philosophy in various schools. In 1887 he started to lecture in the University of Bordeaux, where he was appointed to the chair of social science in 1896. Two years later he founded *L'année sociologique*, a periodical of which he became editor. In 1902 he moved to Paris, where he was appointed professor of education in 1906 and then, in 1913, of education and sociology. In 1893 he published *De la division du travail social*[1] and in 1895 *Les règles de la méthode sociologique*.[2] Further writings included *Le suicide*[3] and *Les formes élémentaires de la vie religieuse*,[4] which appeared respectively in 1897 and 1912. Posthumously published writings, representing ideas expressed in lecture-courses, include *Sociologie et philosophie*,[5] *L'éducation morale*[6] and *Leçons de sociologie: physique des moeurs et du droit*.[7] These works appeared respectively in 1924, 1925 and 1950.

Sociology was for Durkheim the empirically based study of what he described as social phenomena or social facts. A social fact meant for him a general feature of a given society at a given stage of its development, a feature or general way of acting which could be regarded as exercising a constraint on individuals.[8] A condition of the possibility of sociology as a science is that there should be in any given society 'phenomena which would not exist if this society did not exist and which are what they are only because this society is constituted in the way it is'.[9] And it is the business of the sociologist to study these social phenomena in the same objective manner in which the physical scientist studies physical phenomena. Generalization must result from a clear perception of social phenomena or facts and their interrelations. It should not precede

---

[1] Translated as *The Division of Labour in Society* by G. Simpson (Glencoe, Illinois, 1952).
[2] Translated as *The Rules of Sociological Method* by S. A. Solovay and J. H. Mueller (Glencoe, Illinois, 1950).
[3] Translated as *Suicide* by J. A. Spaulding and G. Simpson (Glencoe, Illinois, 1951).
[4] Translated as *The Elementary Forms of the Religious Life* by J. W. Swain (London, 1915).
[5] Translated as *Sociology and Philosophy* by D. F. Pocock (London and Glencoe, Illinois, 1953).
[6] Translated as *Moral Education* by H. Schnurer and E. K. Wilson (Glencoe, Illinois, 1961).
[7] Translated as *Professional Ethics and Civic Morals* by C. Brookfield (London, 1957).
[8] See, for example, the first chapter (*What is a Social Fact?*) of *The Rules of Sociological Method*.
[9] From *La Sociologia ed il suo dominio scientifico* (1900). Quoted from the English translation by K. H. Wolff in *Essays on Sociology and Philosophy*, edited by K. H. Wolff (New York, 1960), p. 363.

such perception or constitute an *a priori* framework of interpretation in such a way that the sociologist is studying not the social facts themselves but his ideas of them.

From a philosophical point of view it is difficult to make a clear distinction between a fact and one's idea of it. For one cannot study anything at all without conceiving it. But there is no great difficulty in understanding the sort of procedure to which Durkheim objects. For example, while he gives credit to Auguste Comte for seeing that social phenomena are objective realities which fall within the natural world and can be studied scientifically, he finds fault with Comte for approaching sociology with a preconceived philosophical theory of history as a continual process of the perfecting of human nature. In his sociology Comte finds what he wants to find, namely what will fit into his philosophical theory. It is thus not so much the facts as his idea of the facts which Comte studies. Similarly, Herbert Spencer was concerned not so much with studying social facts in and for themselves as with showing how they verify his general evolutionary hypothesis. In Durkheim's opinion, Spencer pursued sociology as a philosopher, to prove a theory, rather than by letting the social facts speak for themselves.

We have seen above that Durkheim relates a social fact to a given society. And he laid great emphasis on the plurality of human societies, each of which has to be studied first of all in itself. On this matter he saw a difference between Comte and Spencer. Comte assumed that there was one human society which developed through successive stages, each of which was correlated with and in a sense dependent on the corresponding stage of man's intellectual advance. His philosophy of history made him myopic in regard to the particular questions which arise out of the careful study of given different societies. Further, by incorporating sociology into a philosophical system Comte really ensured that his sociology would make no progress in the hands of his disciples. For development to be possible the law of the three stages had to be jettisoned.[1] In the case of Herbert Spencer however the situation is rather different. For he recognized the plurality of societies and tried to classify them according to their types. Further, he discerned the operation of obscure forces beneath the level of

---

[1] In an article published in 1915, in *La science française*, Durkheim refers to Comte's law of the three stages as possessing 'only an historical interest'. See *Essays on Sociology and Philosophy* (cf. note 83), p. 378.

thought and reason and avoided the exaggerated emphasis placed by Comte on man's scientific advance. At the same time in his *Principles of Sociology* Spencer started out with a definition of society which was an expression of his own *a priori* concept rather than the result of meticulous study of the relevant data or facts.[1]

These social facts are for Durkheim *sui generis*. It is the business of the sociologist to study these facts as he finds them and not to reduce them to some other kind of fact. When a new science is beginning to develop, one has to take models from already existing developed sciences. But a new science becomes a science only in so far as it attains independence. And this involves having its own subject-matter and its own set of concepts formed through reflection on this subject-matter. Durkheim is thus no reductionist. At the same time he believes that for sociology to make real progress it must, like previously developed sciences, emancipate itself from philosophy. This does not mean simply liberating itself from subordination to a philosophical system such as that of Comte. It also means that the sociologist should not allow himself to become entangled in philosophical disputes, such as the dispute between determinists and upholders of free will. All that sociology requires is that the principle of causality should be applied to social phenomena, and then only as an empirical postulate, not as a necessary *a priori* truth.[2] Whether it is in fact possible to avoid all philosophical presuppositions, as Durkheim supposes, is debatable. But he is not of course saying that philosophers should not discuss such topics as freedom of the will, if they wish to do so. He is saying that there is no need for the sociologist to do so, and that the development of sociology requires that he should in fact abstain from such discussion.

The subject-matter of sociology is provided by what Durkheim calls social phenomena or social facts. And reference has been made above to his idea of social facts as exercising constraint on the individual. Social facts in this sense include, for example, the morality and the religion of a given society. Use of the term 'constraint' need not therefore imply coercion in the sense of the use of force. In the process of upbringing a child is initiated into a set of valuations which come from the society to which he belongs rather than from himself; and his mind can be said to be

---

[1] In *The Rules of Sociological Method* (pp. 20 f.) Durkheim refers to Spencer's use of the idea of co-operation as a basis for classifying societies.

[2] See, for example, the conclusion to *The Rules of Sociological Method*.

'constrained' by his society's moral code. Even if he rebels against the code, it is there, so to speak, as that against which he rebels and so as governing his reaction. There is no great difficulty in understanding this sort of idea. But Durkheim speaks of social phenomena such as morality and religion as expressions of the social or collective consciousness or of the common spirit or mind. And something has to be said about this topic, as use of a term such as 'collective consciousness' can easily be misunderstood.

In his essay on 'Individual and Collective Representations' Durkheim blames individualistic sociology for trying to explain the whole by reducing it to its parts.[1] And elsewhere he says that 'It is the whole that, in a large measure, produces the part.'[2] If such passages were isolated and considered simply by themselves, it would be natural to conclude that according to Durkheim the collective consciousness was a kind of universal substance from which individualistic consciousnesses proceed in a manner analogous to that in which plurality was said to emanate from the Neoplatonist One. It would then be somewhat disconcerting to find Durkheim stating that the parts cannot be derived from the whole. 'For the whole is nothing without the parts which form it.'[3]

The term 'collective consciousness' is apt to mislead and is therefore unfortunate. What Durkheim is trying to say however is reasonably clear. When he speaks of a collective consciousness or of a common spirit or mind, he is not postulating a substance existing apart from individual minds. A society does not exist apart from the individuals which compose it; and the system of a society's beliefs and value-judgments is borne, as it were, by individual minds. But it is borne by them in so far as they have come to participate in something which is not confined to any given set of individuals but persists as a social reality. Individuals have their own sensory experiences, their own tastes, and so on. But when the individual learns to speak, he comes to participate, through language, in a whole system of categories, beliefs and value-judgments, in what Durkheim describes as a social consciousness. We can thus distinguish between individual and collective 'representations', between what is peculiar to an individual as such and what he owes to or derives from the society to which he belongs. In so far as these collective 'representations'

---

[1] This essay, which was first published in the *Revue de Métaphysique et de Morale* in 1898, is included in *Sociology and Philosophy*, pp. 1–34).
[2] *Essays on Sociology and Philosophy* (see note 83), p. 325.   [3] *Ibid.*, p. 29.

affect the individual consciousness, we can speak of the parts as derived from or explained by the whole. That is to say, it makes sense to speak of the social 'mind' as causally affecting the individual mind, as affecting it, as it were, from without. According to Durkheim, it is by participating in civilization, the totality of 'intellectual and moral goods'[1] that man becomes specifically human. In this sense the part depends on the whole. At the same time civilization could not exist without individual human beings. And in this sense the whole is nothing without the parts which constitute it. The social facts or phenomena, which for Durkheim constitute the data of the sociologist's reflection, are social institutions of one kind or another which are the products of man in society and which, when once constituted, causally affect the individual consciousness. For instance, the outlook of a Hindu is formed not only by his private sensory experience but also by the religion of his society and by the institutions connected with it. The religion however could not exist as a social reality without any Hindus.

The constraint exercised by 'collective representations' or by the collective consciousness can be seen clearly, according to Durkheim, in the field of morals. There are indeed moral facts, but they exist only in a social context. 'Let all social life disappear, and moral life will disappear with it. . . . Morality, in all its forms, is never met with except in society. It never varies except in relation to social conditions.'[2] Morality, in other words, does not originate in the individual considered precisely as such. It originates in society and is a social phenomenon; and it bears upon the individual. In the sense of obligation, for example, it is the voice of society which speaks. It is society which imposes obligatory rules of conduct, their obligatory character being marked by the attachment of sanctions to the infringement of such rules. For the individual as such the voice of society, speaking through the sense of obligation, comes, as it were, from without. And it is this relationship of externality (of the whole functioning as a social reality in regard to the part) which makes it possible to regard the voice of conscience as the voice of God. For Durkheim however religion is basically the expression of a 'collective ideal';[3] and God is an hypostatization of the collective consciousness. It is quite

---

[1] *Ibid.*, p. 325.
[2] *The Division of Labour in Society*, translated by G. Simpson, p. 399.
[3] *The Elementary Forms of the Religious Life*, translated by J. W. Swain, p. 423.

true that in relation to the individual consciousness moral precepts and the sense of obligation to obey them possess an *a priori* character, imposing themselves, as it were, from without. But the religiously minded person's voice of God speaking through conscience and Kant's Practical Reason are really simply the voice of society; and the sense of obligation is due to the participation of the individual in the collective consciousness. If we are thinking simply of the individual consciousness considered purely as such, society speaks from without. But it also speaks from within, inasmuch as the individual is a member of society and participates in the common consciousness or spirit.

It is obviously true that society is constantly exercising pressure on individuals in a variety of ways. But even if it is an incontestable rule of conduct, emanating from the social consciousness, that we should 'realize in ourselves the essential traits of the collective type',[1] many people are likely to think that there is a middle way between thoroughly anti-social behaviour and conformity to a common type, and that society is enriched by the development of the individual personality. Further, many people would be prepared to envisage cases in which the individual could justifiably protest against the voice of society in the name of a higher ideal. Indeed, how else can moral progress be realized?

While Durkheim insists that morality is a social phenomenon, he does not of course see this theory as entailing social conformism in a sense which would exclude the development of individual personality. His view is that with the development of civilization the collective type of ideal becomes more abstract and so admits of a much greater degree of variety within the framework of what is demanded by society. In a primitive society the essential traits of the collective type are defined in a very concrete manner. The man is expected to act according to a definite traditional pattern of behaviour; and so is the woman. In more advanced societies however the likenesses which are demanded between members of the society are less than in the more homogeneous primitive tribe or class. And if the collective type or ideal becomes that of humanity in general, it is so abstract and general that there is plenty of room for the development of the individual personality. The area of personal freedom thus tends to grow as society becomes more advanced. At the same time, if a modern industrial society does not impose all the obligations imposed by a primitive

---

[1] *The Division of Labour in Society*, p. 396.

tribe, this does not alter the fact that in every case it is society which imposes the obligation.

A point which needs to be mentioned is that 'society' for Durkheim does not necessarily mean simply the State or political society, at any rate not as a completely adequate source of an ethical code. For example, in modern society a large part of human life is passed in the industrial and commercial world where ethical rules are lacking. In economically advanced societies therefore, with their highly developed specialization or division of labour, there is need for what Durkheim calls occupational ethics. 'Functional diversity induces a moral diversity that nothing can prevent.'[1] In all cases however the individual as such is subject to social pressure to act or not to act in certain ways.

It is hardly necessary to say that Durkheim is trying to turn ethics into an empirical science, treating of social facts or phenomena of a particular kind. In his view both the utilitarians and the Kantians reconstruct morality as they think it ought to be or as they would wish it to be, instead of observing carefully what it is. According to Durkheim, if we look closely at the facts, we see that social pressure or constraint exercised by the collective consciousness in regard to the individual is the chief constituent of morality. Though however he insists that the approach of the utilitarians and the Kantians is wrong, the attempt, that is to say, to find a basic principle of morality and then to proceed deductively, he also makes an effort to show that his own ethical theory comprises in itself the elements of truth contained in the theories which he attacks. For example, morality does as a matter of fact serve useful purposes within the framework of society. And its utility can be examined and ascertained. At the same time the chief characteristic of the moral consciousness is the sense of obligation which is felt as a 'categorical imperative'. The rule, imposed by society, has to be obeyed simply because it is a rule.[2] We can thus find a place for Kant's idea of duty for duty's sake, though we can also find a place for the utilitarian's concept of usefulness to society. Morality exists because society needs it; but it takes the form of the voice of society demanding obedience because it is the voice of society.

One obvious comment is that whereas Kant's idea of the

---

[1] *Ibid.*, p. 361.
[2] See, for example, a review-article by Durkheim in *L'année sociologique* Vol. X (1905–6), in which he discusses works by Fouillée, Belot and Landry.

categorical imperative as issuing from the practical reason provides a basis for criticizing existing moral codes, Durkheim's
theory provides no such basis. If moral rules are relative to given
societies, expressing the collective consciousness of a particular
society, and if moral obligation means that the individual is
obliged to obey the voice of society, how can the individual ever
be justified in questioning the moral code or the value-judgments
of the society to which he belongs? Does it not follow that moral
reformers must be condemned as subversive elements? If this is
not the case, how can we reasonably equate morality with the
moral codes of particular societies? For the reformer appeals
against such a code to something which seems to him higher or
more universal.

Durkheim is not of course blind to this line of objection. He
sees that he can be accused of holding that the individual must
accept passively the dictates of society, whatever they may be,
without ever having the right to rebel.[1] And as he has no wish to
push the demand for social conformism to this point, he looks to
the idea of utility to provide him with a reply. 'No fact relating to
life—and this applies to moral facts—can endure if it is not of
some use, if it does not answer some need.'[2] A rule which once
fulfilled a useful social function may lose its usefulness as society
changes and develops. Individuals who are aware of this are justified in drawing general attention to the fact. Indeed, it may not be
simply a question of a particular rule of conduct. Social changes
may be taking place on such a scale that what amounts to a new
morality is demanded by these changes and begins to make its
appearance. If then society as a whole persists in clinging to the
traditional and outmoded order of morality, those who understand the process of development and its needs are justified in
challenging the old dictates of society. 'We are not therefore
obliged to bow to the force of moral opinion. In certain cases we
are justified even in rebelling against it. ... The best way of
doing so may appear to be to oppose these ideas not only theoretically but also in action.'[3]

This line of reply may be ingenious, but it is hardly adequate.
If it is society which imposes obligation, obedience to the actual
dictates of any given society is presumably obligatory. If however,
as Durkheim allows, there can be situations in which individuals

---

[1] See, for example *Sociology and Philosophy*, translated by D. F. Pocock, pp. 59f.
[2] *The Division of Labour*, p. 35.   [3] *Sociology and Philosophy*, p. 61.

are justified in questioning, or even in rebelling against, the dictates of society, some moral criterion other than the voice of society is required. The moral reformer, it may be said, appeals from the actual voice of society, as embodied in traditional formulas, to the 'real' voice of society. But what is the criterion for assessing the 'real' voice of society, what society ought to demand as distinct from what it does demand? If it is utility, a society's real interests, one should presumably adopt utilitarianism. One is then faced however with the task of supplying a criterion for assessing a society's real interests. Referring to the possibility that a modern society might lose sight of the rights of the individual, Durkheim suggests that the society could be reminded that the denial of rights to the individual would be to deny 'the most essential interests of society itself'.[1] He might claim that this refers simply to the interests of modern European society as it has in fact developed, and not, for instance, to a closely-knit primitive clan. But even in this case one would be appealing from the actual voice of society to what one believed ought to be its voice. And it is difficult to see how normative judgments of this kind can be included in a purely descriptive study of moral phenomena.

Like morality, religion is for Durkheim essentially a social phenomenon. In one place he asserts that 'a religion is a unified system of beliefs and practices relative to sacred things, that is to say, things set apart and forbidden—beliefs and practices which unite into one single moral community, called a Church, all those who adhere to them.'[2] When Durkheim insists that 'we do not find a single religion without a Church'[3] and that 'religion is inseparable from the idea of a Church',[4] he does not mean simply a Christian Church. He means a community of persons who represent the sacred and its relation to the profane in the same way, and who translate these beliefs and ideas into common practice. Obviously, there are different beliefs and different symbols in different religions. But 'one must know how to go underneath the symbol to the reality which it represents and which gives it its meaning'.[5] We then find that religion is 'the primary form of the *collective consciousness*'.[6] Indeed, 'I see in the divinity only society transfigured and symbolically expressed'.[7]

[1] *Ibid.*, p. 60.   [2] *The Elementary Forms of the Religious Life*, p. 47.
[3] *Ibid.*, p. 44.   [4] *Ibid.*, p. 45.   [5] *Ibid.*, p. 2.
[6] *The Division of Labour in Society*, p. 285.   [7] *Sociology and Philosophy*, p. 52.

In primitive or undeveloped societies, according to Durkheim, morality was essentially religious, in the sense that man's most important and numerous duties were those towards his gods.[1] In the course of time morality has become progressively separated from religious belief, partly through the influence of Christianity with its insistence on love between human beings. The area of the sacred has diminished, and the process of secularization has advanced. Religion 'tends to embrace a smaller and smaller sector of social life'.[2] At the same time there is a sense in which religion will always persist. For society always needs to represent to itself 'the collective sentiments and the collective ideas which make its unity and its personality'.[3] If however a new faith arises, we cannot foresee the symbols which will be used to express it.

It is of course in the light of his theory of the essential nature of religion that we have to understand Durkheim's assertion that 'in reality there are no religions which are false. All are true in their own fashion; all answer, though in different ways, to the given conditions of human existence'.[4] Obviously, Durkheim does not mean to imply that all religious beliefs, if considered as statements about reality, are equally true. He is thinking of different religions as all expressing, each in its own way, a social reality. One religion can be described as superior to another if, for example, it is 'richer in ideas and sentiments' and contains 'more concepts with fewer sensations and images'.[5] But no religion can properly be described as being simply false. For even the most barbarous rites and the most fantastic myths 'translate some human need, some aspect of life, either individual or social'.[6] This is not to say that a religion is true in so far as it proves useful. It is true in so far as it expresses or represents, in its own fashion, a social reality.

Durkheim obviously considers religion from a purely sociological and external point of view. Moreover, he assumes that if we wish to ascertain the essential features of religion, we have to examine primitive or elementary religion. And this assumption is open to criticism, quite apart from the fact that some of Durkheim's theories about the origins of religion are highly disputable. For unless we assume from the start that religion is essentially

[1] See L'éducation morale, p. 6.
[2] On the Division of Labour in Society, p. 143.
[3] The Elementary Forms of the Religious Life, p. 427.
[4] Ibid., p. 3.   [5] Ibid., p. 3.   [6] Ibid., p. 2.

a primitive phenomenon, why should not its nature be better manifested in the course of its development than in its origins? Durkheim could of course argue that in primitive society religion played a much greater part in social life than it does today, and that as it is a receding phenomenon, it is only reasonable to look for its essential features at a period when it was most notably a living force. But this line of argument, though reasonable up to a point, seems to presuppose a certain idea of religion, Durkheim's idea, which represents it as the expression of the collective consciousness. Further, just as in his treatment of morality Durkheim concentrates on what Bergson describes as 'closed' morality, so in his treatment of religion does he concentrate on what Bergson describes as 'static' religion. But this is a theme which is best left to the relevant chapter on the philosophy of Bergson.

7. Though Durkheim recognized successive distinguishable mentalities and outlooks, he did not make such a sharp dichotomy between the primitive and later mentalities as to exclude a theory of the development of the former into the latter. He saw the category of causality, for example, as being first developed and employed in an essentially religious context and outlook and then as being later detached from the framework. It was Lucien Lévy-Bruhl (1857–1939) who expounded the theory that the mentality of primitive peoples was pre-logical in character.[1] He maintained, for example, that the primitive mind did not recognize the principle of non-contradiction but operated according to an implicit idea of 'participation' which allowed a thing to be itself and at the same time something other than itself. 'Primitive mentality considers and at the same time feels all beings and objects to be homogeneous, that is, it regards them all as participating in the same essential nature, or in the same ensemble of qualities.'[2] Again, the primitive mind was indifferent to empirical verification. It credited things with qualities and powers when the presence in things of these qualities and powers was in no way verified by experience. In fine, Lévy-Bruhl found a sharp distinction between the primitive mentality, which for him was essentially

[1] This view was expressed in *Les fonctions fondamentales dans les sociétés inférieures* (1910). Other writings in the anthropological field were *La mentalité primitive* (1921) and *L'âme primitive* (1927). Though best known as an anthropologist, Lévy-Bruhl was in fact a professor of philosophy at the Sorbonne from 1899 until 1927.
[2] *The 'Soul' of the Primitive (L'âme primitive)*, translated by L. A. Clare (London, 1928), p. 19.

religious and even mystical, and the logical and scientific mentality. If considered in its pure state at any rate, in primitive man that is to say, and not as surviving in co-existence with a different emerging outlook, the former was different in kind from the latter.

Nowadays it would be generally agreed that Durkheim was justified in criticizing this dichotomy and Lévy-Bruhl's characterization of primitive mentality as 'pre-logical'. In many ways the world of primitive man was doubtless very different from ours, and he had many beliefs which we do not share. But it does not follow that his natural logic was entirely heterogeneous from ours, as Lévy-Bruhl at first asserted.

In 1903 Lévy-Bruhl published *La morale et la science des moeurs*.[1] Like Durkheim, he aimed at contributing to the development of a science of morals, something which had to be carefully distinguished from morals itself. Morality is a social fact and needs no philosopher to bring it into being. But the philosopher can examine this social fact. He then finds that it is a case of facts rather than of a fact. That is to say, in every society there is a set of moral rules, an ethical code, relative to that society. A theoretical and abstract system, elaborated by a philosopher, bears as little resemblance to the actual ethical phenomena as does an abstract philosophical religion to the historic religions of mankind. If a philosopher works out an abstract ethical system and describes it as 'natural ethics', the ethics of man as such, this is a misnomer. 'The idea of a "natural ethics", ought to give way to the idea that all existing ethics are natural.'[2] What we need to do first is to ascertain the historical data in the field of morals. It should then be possible, on the basis of positive knowledge so gained, to develop some guidelines for the future. But the result would be an empirically based art rather than an abstract or ideal system of ethics as conceived by some philosophers in the past.

The task of collecting historical data is hardly the business of the philosopher as such. And it is arguable that the task of seeing what practical use can be made of the knowledge obtained in this way can perfectly well be performed by the sociologist. It might therefore be suggested that if Lévy-Bruhl rejected, as he did, the idea of elaborating an abstract ethical system, he might have done well, if he wished to act as a philosopher, to concentrate on the

[1] Translated as *Ethics and Moral Science* by E. Lee (London, 1905).
[2] *Ethics and Moral Science*, p. 160.

analysis of ethical concepts and language. To a certain extent both he and Durkheim provided such analyses. But the analyses really consisted in giving a naturalistic interpretation of ethical terms. Lévy-Bruhl occupied a chair of philosophy; but he was primarily an anthropologist and a sociologist.

CHAPTER VII

NEO-CRITICISM AND IDEALISM

Cournot and inquiry into basic concepts—The neo-criticism and personalism of Renouvier—Hamelin and idealist metaphysics—Brunschvicg and the mind's reflection on its own activity.

1. It would be misleading to refer to thinkers such as Cournot and Renouvier as representing a neo-Kantian movement in nineteenth-century philosophical thought in France. For this way of speaking would imply a closer connection with and a greater dependence on the thought of Kant than was actually present. Renouvier, it is true, liked to regard himself as Kant's true successor and described his own thought as neo-criticism. But he attacked some of Kant's cherished theories; and though there were indeed features of his thought which justified its description as neo-criticism, there were other features which would make personalism a more appropriate label. As for Cournot, he did indeed conduct a critical inquiry into the role of reason and into certain basic concepts and has been described as a critical rationalist; but he rejected Kant's Copernican revolution and has therefore been sometimes described as a critical realist. To perpetrate a tautology, Cournot was Cournot. He was neither a Kantian nor a Comtean.

Antoine Augustin Cournot (1801–77) was a distinguished mathematician and economist who was also a philosopher. After preliminary studies, partly at a school in his native town of Gray near Dijon and partly alone, he entered the École Normale Supérieure at Paris with a view to continuing his studies in mathematics. In 1823 he became secretary to Marshal Saint-Cyr and tutor to the latter's son. After the Marshal's death Cournot held a post at Paris until he was appointed professor of analysis and mechanics at Lyon. Shortly afterwards however he was appointed head of the Academy at Grenoble, a post which he combined with that of inspector general of public education, until confirmation in this second post led to his taking up his abode in Paris in 1838. His published writings were in the fields of mathematics, mechanics, economics, education and philosophy. He contributed to the application of mathematics to economics. In the philosophical area he published in 1843 an *Exposition de la théorie des chances et des probabilités* (*Exposition of the Theory of Chance and of Probability*). This was followed in 1851 by his *Essai sur les fondements de nos connaissances et sur les caractères de la critique philosophique*.[1] In 1861 Cournot published a *Traité de l'enchaînement des idées fondamentales dans les sciences et dans l'histoire* (*Treatise on the Connection between the Fundamental Ideas of the Sciences and of History*). In 1872 there appeared his *Considérations sur la marche des idées et des événements dans les temps modernes* (*Reflections on the Movement of Ideas and Events in Modern Times*) and in 1875 *Matérialisme, vitalisme, rationalisme: Études sur l'emploi des données de la science en philosophie* (*Materialism, Vitalism, Rationalism: Studies on the Use of the Data of Science in Philosophy*).

Cournot was not at all the man to think that philosophy could profitably pursue an isolated path of its own, without reference to the development of the sciences. 'Philosophy without science soon loses sight of our real relations with the Universe.'[2] Philosophy needs to feed, so to speak, on science. At the same time Cournot resolutely refused to regard philosophy either as a particular science or as a synthesis of the sciences. In his view science and philosophy were interrelated in a variety of ways; they were none the less distinguishable. And because they were distinct lines of inquiry, there was no good reason for thinking that the progress of science entailed the gradual disappearance of philosophy.

While recognizing that 'innumerable meanings'[3] have been given to the term 'philosophy' in popular usage and by philosophers themselves, Cournot regards philosophy as having two essential functions, 'on the one hand the study and investigation of the reason of things and, on the other hand, the study of the forms of thought and of the general laws and processes of the human mind'.[4] By the reason of things Cournot means, in general, rational or intelligible interconnection; and he makes a distinction between reason and cause. Consider, for example, the Russian revolution. Obviously, a multitude of causal actions were involved. But to understand the Russian revolution we have to find an intelligible structure connecting all these causes and events. And if we decide that the reason for the revolution was the unyielding

---

[1] Translated by M. M. Moore as *An Essay on the Foundations of Our Knowledge* (New York, 1956). As the work is divided into consecutively numbered sections, references will be given as *Essai* followed by the number of the relevant section.
[2] *Essai*, section 323.   [3] *Ibid.*, section 325.   [4] *Ibid.*, section 325.

autocratic constitution or régime, we are not talking about an efficient cause in the sense in which, for instance, a certain action by one man is the efficient cause of injury to another. The reason explains the series of causes. It answers the question 'why did these events take place'? The reason of things is thus akin to Leibniz's sufficient reason, though Cournot, who greatly admired Leibniz, remarks that the word 'sufficient' is superfluous. An insufficient reason would not be the reason of things.

When Cournot says that 'the search for the explanation and the reason of things is what characterizes philosophical curiosity, no matter what the order of facts to which it is applied',[1] he is thinking of an objective reason, of something which is there to be discovered. But it is of course the human reason, subjective reason, which seeks to grasp the objective reason. And subjective reason can reflect on its own activity. It can be concerned with 'the evaluation of certain regulative and fundamental ideas or with criticism of their representative value'.[2] Critical inquiry of this sort is the second function of philosophy. But the two functions are closely interrelated. For example, the human reason, according to Cournot, is regulated by the idea of order, in the sense that order is what reason seeks to find and what it can recognize when found. In fact, reason is guided by the idea of the perfection of order, inasmuch as it compares possible arrangements of phenomena and prefers that which best satisfies its idea of what constitutes order. At the same time the mind does not simply impose order on phenomena: it discovers it. And it is in the light of such discovery that reason can evaluate its own regulative idea. Cournot likes to quote Bossuet to the effect that only reason can introduce order into things, and that order can be understood only by reason. When the two sides, the subjective and the objective, are in accord, there is knowledge.

Cournot is therefore not prepared to accept the theory that the mind simply imposes order on what is in itself without order or that it simply projects into things their 'reasons'.[3] There is a marked element of realism in his thought. He insists, for example, that whatever Kant may have said Newtonian physics 'implies the existence of time, space and geometrical relations outside the

---

[1] *Ibid.*, section 26.   [2] *Ibid.*, section 325.
[3] The ideas of order and of the reason of things are for Cournot closely related. Indeed, the two ideas are 'the same idea under two different aspects'. *Essai*, section 396.

mind'.[1] At the same time he maintains both that what we know are the relations between phenomena, and that our knowledge of these relations is never absolute but always revisible in principle. When the astronomer, for example, tries to determine the movements of the heavenly bodies, he is certainly concerned with objective knowledge; but the knowledge which he obtains is relative in several ways. For instance, the movements which he establishes are relative to a certain system; and he cannot determine absolute points of reference in space. The astronomer's knowledge is real and relative at the same time. It is subject to revision. Our hypotheses can possess varying degrees of probability; but they do not amount to absolute knowledge, even when they produce the subjective feeling of certainty.

The concept of probability is, like that of order, one of the basic ideas discussed by Cournot. He makes a distinction between mathematical probability and probability in a general sense or what he calls philosophical probability. The former is concerned with objective possibility and is described as 'the limit of *physical possibility*',[2] whereas in the case of the latter the grounds of our preference are not amenable to precise mathematical formulation. Suppose that we are confronted with three *prima facie* explanations of a phenomenon or set of phenomena. It may be that we can rule out one of them as mathematically impossible. In deciding however between the other two we introduce criteria which are not amenable to exact mathematical treatment. Moreover, even if we succeed in falsifying empirically one of the hypotheses and therefore feel subjectively certain about the truth of the other, it may be that further developments in scientific knowledge will demand revision. Apart from matters of purely logical or mathematical demonstration, we have to rely on 'variable, subjective probability'.[3] In formulating a law of phenomena, for example, reason refers to certain criteria, such as simplicity, and the mind may feel certain that it has found the law. But this feeling of certainty does not alter the fact that what we judge to be more probable depends on the limited extent of our present knowledge and thus on a variable factor.

According to Cournot therefore reason seeks and finds order in the world, even if its knowledge of the order or reason of things is not absolute. Cournot's world however also contains fortuitous events, the result of the operation of chance. And this idea needs

[1] *Ibid.*, section 142.   [2] *Ibid.*, section 35.   [3] *Ibid.*, section 51.

some explanation. By a chance event Cournot does not mean a rare or surprising event. It might of course be rare or surprising, but these characteristics are not included in the meaning of the term. Nor does Cournot mean a causeless event. 'Everything that we call an event must have a cause.'[1] A chance event is one which is brought about by the conjunction of other events which belong to independent series.[2] A simple example given by Cournot himself is that of a Parisian who takes a train to a destination in the country. There is a railway accident, and the Parisian is among the victims. The accident has of course its cause or causes; but the operation of these causes has nothing to do with the presence of the particular Parisian on the train. The accident would have occurred even if he had decided at the last moment to stay in the city instead of going to the country. In this sense his being killed or injured is a fortuitous event, resulting from the conjunction of two series of causes which were originally independent of each other.

Chance in this sense is for Cournot an objective or real feature of the world. That is to say, it is not something which is simply dependent on and relative to the limitations of our knowledge.[3] 'It is not accurate to say, as Hume does, that "chance is only our ignorance of real causes".'[4] In principle the mind, by using the calculus of probabilities, could foretell possible conjunctions of independent series of causes. And a superhuman intelligence could do so to a greater extent than we can. This does not show however that chance events are law-governed, or that it would be possible to foretell with certainty actual events due to the conjunction of independent series of causes. In other words, for Cournot, as for Boutroux after him, contingency is a metaphysical reality, in the sense that there is in the universe an irreducible element of indeterminacy. Not even in principle could estimation of the probability of possible events in the future be converted into complete objective certitude.

Though Cournot argues that there are certain basic concepts, such as order, which are common to the sciences, he also insists that actual examination of and reflection on the sciences shows us

---

[1] *Ibid.*, section 29.
[2] It is for Cournot a matter of common sense that there are independent or only externally related series of events. *Ibid.*, section 30.
[3] The idea of chance as an objective factor in the universe is found also in the philosophy of C. S. Peirce in America. See Vol. 8 of this *History*, pp. 323 f.
[4] *Essai*, section 36.

that different sciences have to introduce different basic concepts. It is therefore impossible to reduce all sciences to one science, such as physics. For example, it is the behaviour of the living organism which excludes the possibility of accounting for it simply in terms of the physico-chemical elements of the constituent parts or elements, and which forces us to introduce the idea of a vital energy or plastic force. This concept and its implications are not indeed altogether clear. We cannot suppose that life precedes organic structure and produces it. But neither can we suppose that organic-structure precedes life. We have to assume that 'in organic and living beings organic structure and life play simultaneously the roles of cause and effect through a reciprocity of relations',[1] which is *sui generis*. And though a term such as vital or plastic force 'does not give the mind an idea which can be clearly defined',[2] it expresses a recognition of the irreducibility of the living to the non-living.

This irreducibility implies of course that in the process of evolution there is emergence of what is new, of what cannot be described simply in terms of that out of which it emerges. It does not follow however that evolution is for Cournot a continuous process, in the sense that it takes the form of a linear series of ascending levels of perfection. In Cournot's view evolution takes the form of distinct creative impulses or movements, in accordance with a kind of rhythm of relative activity and rest; and in his *Traité* he anticipates Bergson's idea of divergent paths or directions of development. As however he is sharply opposed, like Bergson after him, to any purely mechanistic interpretation of evolution, he regards it as legitimate for the philosopher to think in terms of finality and of a creative divine intelligence. This does not mean that after asserting the reality of chance as a factor in the Universe Cournot then goes on to reject this idea and to represent the universe as rational through and through. We have seen that for him the concept of order which regulates the mind's inquiries is not simply a subjective form of thought which reason imposes on phenomena but also represents what the mind discovers. Both order and chance are real factors in the universe. And reason is justified in extending the concept of order into the sphere of 'trans-rationalism', provided that it is not used in such a way as to be incompatible with the idea of chance. In Cournot's view the reality of chance 'is not in conflict with the generally

---

[1] *Essai*, section 129.   [2] *Ibid.*, section 130.

accepted idea of a supreme and providential direction',[1] not at any rate if we avoid implying that all events are caused by God. Cournot's positive contribution to philosophical thought consists primarily in his critical inquiry into basic concepts, whether those which he regards as common to the sciences or those which particular sciences find it necessary to introduce if they are to develop and to handle their subject-matter satisfactorily. It is this aspect of his thought which justifies treatment of it under the general heading of critical philosophy or 'neo-criticism'. But though he approaches this theme through an inquiry into the sciences, we have seen that he insists on the distinction between science and philosophy. For one thing, 'the intuitions of the philosophers precede the organization of positive science.'[2] For another thing, the mind can let itself be guided by 'the presentiment of a perfection and harmony in the works of nature'[3] which is superior to anything discovered by the sciences. The mind can thus pass into the field of speculative philosophy, a field in which it crosses the boundaries of formal demonstration and of scientific testing and in which it has to rely on 'philosophical' probability which is not amenable to mathematical treatment. This field of transrationalism is not excluded by science; and though it goes beyond science, we have to remember that scientific hypotheses themselves cannot be more than probably true.

2. In comparison with his contribution in the field of economics Cournot's philosophical writing was at first largely neglected. He worked patiently at a number of problems, avoiding extreme positions and not allowing himself to be distracted by temporarily fashionable lines of thought. Moreover, though he rejected the positivist exclusion of metaphysics, he did not himself present any striking metaphysical vision of the universe. He hinted, it is true, at possible lines of thought; but it was left to other philosophers, such as Bergson, to develop them in a manner which aroused general interest. Nowadays Cournot is respected for his careful critical analysis; but it is easy to understand how Renouvier, who was influenced to a certain extent by Cournot, came to make a greater impression on his contemporaries.

Charles Bernard Renouvier (1815–1903) was born at Montpellier, the birthplace of Auguste Comte, and when he entered the École Polytechnique at Paris he found Comte there acting as instructor in mathematics. Renouvier never occupied an academic

---

[1] *Ibid.*, section 36.   [2] *Traité*, I, section 226.   [3] *Essai*, section 71.

position, but he was a prolific writer. He began by publishing several manuals, on modern and ancient philosophy in 1842 and 1844 respectively[1] and in 1848 a *Republican Handbook on Man and the Citizen*.[2] At this time Renouvier was strongly influenced by the ideas of Saint-Simon and other French socialists, and the last named work was intended for schoolteachers. His republican convictions suffered a severe blow when Napoleon III made himself emperor, and he gave himself to philosophical reflection and writing. In 1872 however Renouvier started a periodical entitled *Critique philosophique*, and in its first years it included a good many articles of a political nature, aimed at supporting the restored republic. Later this periodical became *L'année philosophique*, edited in collaboration with F. Pillon.

Renouvier's first major philosophical publication was his four-volume *Essais de critique générale* (1854–64). This work impressed William James, who remained an admirer of Renouvier and contributed a number of philosophical articles to his periodical. In 1869 Renouvier wrote a two-volume work on the science of morals, *La science de la morale*, and in 1876 a sketch of what might have been, but was not, the historical development of European civilization, to which he gave the title *Uchronie*.[3] In 1866 there appeared a two-volume *Esquisse d'une classification systématique des doctrines philosophiques* (*Outline of a Systematic Classification of Philosophical Doctrines*), and in 1901 two works on metaphysics, *Les dilemmes de la métaphysique pure* and *Histoire et solution des problèmes métaphysiques*.[4] Renouvier's book on personalism[5] was published in 1903, and his well known work on Kant, *Critique de la doctrine de Kant*, was brought out in 1906 by his friend Louis Prat.

In the preface to his *Essais de critique générale* Renouvier announced his acceptance of one basic principle of positivism, namely the restriction of knowledge to the laws of phenomena. Though however he was prepared to assert his agreement with Comte on this point, the philosophy which he developed was certainly not positivism. As has already been mentioned, Renouvier liked to describe it as 'neo-criticism'. But while he clearly

---

[1] *Manuel de philosophie moderne* and *Manuel de philosophie ancienne*.
[2] *Manuel républicain de l'homme et du citoyen*.
[3] The full title is *Uchronie, l'utopie dans l'histoire. Esquisse historique du développement de la civilisation européenne, tel qu'il n'a pas été, tel qu'il aurait pu être*.
[4] *The Dilemmas of Pure Metaphysics* and *History and Solution of Metaphysical Problems*.
[5] *Le personnalisme, suivi d'une étude sur la perception externe et sur la force*.

derived stimulus from Kant, in the introduction to his work on the German philosopher he roundly stated that he was concerned primarily not with exposition but with 'a critique of the Kantian *Critique*.'[1] The fact of the matter is that he used Kant's thought in developing his own personalist philosophy.

In Renouvier's eyes one of the most objectionable features of Kant's philosophy was the theory of the thing-in-itself. Kant assumed that the phenomenon was the appearance of something other than itself. But as this something other was on Kant's own view unknowable, it was simply a superfluous fiction, like Locke's substance.[2] It does not follow however that because phenomena are not appearances of unknowable things-in-themselves, they are for Renouvier simply subjective impressions. They are all that we can perceive and all about which we can make judgments. In other words, the phenomenal and the real are the same.[3]

Another feature of the Kantian philosophy attacked by Renouvier is the theory of antimonies.[4] Kant believed, for example, that it could be both proved and disproved that the world had a beginning in time and that space is limited or finite. Renouvier saw in this thesis a flagrant disregard of the principle of non-contradiction. This verdict rather misses the point. For Kant was not concerned with denying the principle of non-contradiction. He was concerned with arguing that if the human mind pursued the path of 'dogmatic' metaphysics and claimed to know the world as a whole, it became involved in antimonies which showed that the claim was bogus and that metaphysics of the traditional kind was a pseudo-science. Renouvier however was not prepared to accept Kant's dismissal of metaphysics. And in regard to the particular points at issue he maintained that it could be proved that an infinite series of phenomena was impossible, on the ground that it involved the contradictory idea of an infinite number,[5] that space must be limited or finite, and that the contrary theses could be

[1] *Doctrine de Kant*, p. 3.

[2] Renouvier collaborated with F. Pillon in translating Hume's *Treatise of Human Nature* into French; and he thought that Hume was right in eliminating the concept of substance as expounded by Locke.

[3] The word 'phenomenon' tends to suggest, as Renouvier admits, the idea of the appearance of a reality which does not itself appear. But for Renouvier the phenomenon is simply the thing as appearing or as capable of appearing.

[4] See Vol. VI of this *History*, pp. 286 f.

[5] If we like to look back to medieval philosophy ,we can say that Renouvier was at one with St. Bonaventure, who maintained that the impossibility of an infinite series could be demonstrated. See Vol. II of this *History*, pp. 262–5 and 366–7.

decisively disproved. In other words, no antimony arose, as only one of the opposed theses could be proved, not both as Kant thought.

Though however Renouvier criticizes Kant pretty sharply in regard to important features of the latter's philosophy, he associates his own doctrine of categories with Kant's, at any rate to the extent that he offers his own doctrine as an improvement on that of the German philosopher. For Renouvier the basic and most general or abstract of all categories is that of relation, inasmuch as nothing at all can be known except as related. Renouvier then proceeds to add the categories of number, position, succession, quality, becoming, causality, finality or purposiveness and personality, the movement being from the most abstract to the most concrete. It is evident that Renouvier's list of categories differs from Kant's. Further, no attempt is made to deduce the categories *a priori* by a transcendental method. As with Cournot, Renouvier's categories are based on or derived from experience. The connection with Kant is thus pretty loose. But this does not alter the fact that Renouvier derived some stimulus from Kant and liked to think of himself as Kant's true successor.

Similarly, we can see a connection between Kant's theory of faith as based on the practical reason or moral will and Renouvier's idea of the role played by the will in belief, an idea which appealed to William James. Here again however the connection is a loose one, being a matter of stimulus rather than of Renouvier actually adopting a Kantian doctrine. Kant made a sharp distinction between the sphere of theoretical knowledge and that of practical or moral faith; and this distinction presupposed that between the phenomenon and the noumenon. As Renouvier rejected this second distinction, it is not surprising that he refused to admit any sharp division between knowledge and belief. 'The Kantian separation between the speculative reason and the practical reason is an illusion.'[1] In the second *Essai* Renouvier insisted that certitude always involves an element of belief, and that belief involves the will to believe. This is applicable even to the *Cogito, ergo sum* of Descartes. For an act of the will is required to unite the I-subject and the me-object in the assertion of personal existence.

What Renouvier does is to extend the scope of Kant's account

---

[1] *Doctrine de Kant*, p. 164.

of practical faith beyond the sphere to which Kant confines it. The objection then arises that nothing much is being said. For example, suppose that I maintain that the will to believe enters even into science. And suppose that I then go on to explain that what I mean is that the scientist's activity rests on an act of choice, that he wills to embrace the hypothesis which seems to him most probable or most likely to prove fruitful in a scientific context, and that the actual decision to adopt an hypothesis which is in principle revisible involves an act of the will. The comment might be made that what I say is true, but that it has little to do with the will to believe in the sense in which this idea has given rise to objections. When however Renouvier rejects Kant's sharp division between the theoretical and practical uses of reason, he is claiming that in all knowledge there is a personal element, an intervention of the will. In other words, he is developing a theory of knowledge in the light of a personalist philosophy. We have seen that for him personality is the most concrete of the basic categories. And he insists that in the activity of the human person no absolute dichotomy between reason and will can legitimately be made, though in this or that sphere of activity there may be of course a predominance of reason or of will or of feeling. In the ethical field this personalist approach shows itself in Renouvier's disapproval of Kant's tendency to think that an action has moral worth in proportion as it is performed simply and solely out of a sense of obligation and without regard to inclination and feeling. As moral action is the expression of the whole person, duty and feeling, for Renouvier, should ideally accompany one another.

Sometimes Renouvier refers to phenomena in a quite general way, as when he maintains that phenomena and the relations between them constitute the objects of human knowledge. At the same time he insists that there are irreducible levels of reality, culminating in the level of personality. Man can of course try to interpret himself exclusively in terms of categories or concepts which are applicable at a non-human level. This attempt is possible because, while the mind cannot conceive any phenomenon except in terms of the basic category of relation, there is room for choice in the selection of more determinate categories. Though possible however, attempts at reductionism are bound to fail. For example, freedom is a datum of consciousness. While rejecting Kant's notion of man as noumenally free and phenomenally determined and insisting that man is free as a phenomenon,[1] Renouvier agrees with Kant in associating awareness of freedom with the moral consciousness. The possibilities of choice and action are of course limited in various ways. The moral agent, 'capable of contraries, does not cease from being circumscribed within a static or dynamic order of relations.'[2] But though the area of freedom should not be exaggerated, morality cannot be understood unless we conceive freedom as an attribute of the human person. Freedom is indeed a datum of the moral consciousness rather than something which can be demonstrated. For Renouvier however determinism cannot be held without the determinist involving himself in the absurdity of claiming that the man who asserts freedom is determined to assert that he sees himself to be free.

When Renouvier talks about the free moral agent, it is of course the individual person of whom he is speaking.[3] In the philosophical area he has no use for Spinozism or for theories of the Absolute as found in post-Kantian German idealism or, in general, for any philosophical theory which represents individuals as moments in the life of the One. His dislike for such theories extends to any form of positivism which represents history as a necessary process subject to a law or laws and, in the theological sphere, to beliefs which seem to him to make human beings puppets of a divine universal causality. In the political field Renouvier is vehemently opposed to any political theory which depicts the State as a subsistent entity over and above its members He is not indeed an anarchist. But the desirable society is for him one which is founded on respect for the individual person as a free moral agent. The State is not itself a person or a moral agent: it is a name for individuals organized in certain ways and acting collectively. In his work on the science of morals Renouvier lays emphasis on the fictional character of such concepts as 'the nation'[4] and he insists that if the State is regarded as a subsistent entity,

---

[1] In Renouvier's opinion this attempt to have things both ways is another example of Kant's neglect of the principle of non-contradiction. As for Renouvier's insistence that man is free as a phenomenon, it must be remembered that by this he means that man as we experience him is free. He is not of course thinking in terms of the Kantian distinction between phenomenon and thing-in-itself, which, as we have seen, he rejects.

[2] *Essais*, II, p. 466.

[3] Like Leibniz, Renouvier had an acute sense of differentiation. And in 1899 he published, in collaboration with L. Prat, a work entitled *The New Monadology* (*La nouvelle monadologie*).

[4] *La science de la morale*, II, chapter 96.

the conclusion will be drawn either that there is one morality for the State and another for the individual or that the State stands above the ethical sphere. The moral order can be built up only by persons acting together or in concert; but it is by individual persons that it is constructed and maintained, not by a fictional super-person.

As the title of his work *La science de la morale* clearly implies, Renouvier believes that there can be a science of ethics. For this to be possible there must of course be moral phenomena. And inasmuch as science is concerned with relations between phenomena, we might perhaps expect that he would confine the sphere of morality to relations between different persons. But this is not in fact the case. In Renouvier's opinion the concept of rights has meaning only within a social context. Rights as a moral phenomenon arise only in society. But though a man has rights only in relation to his fellows, and though in a social context rights and duties are correlative, the concept of duty is for Renouvier more fundamental than that of rights. It would be absurd to speak of an entirely isolated individual as possessing rights; but he would have moral duties. For in every individual there is a relation between what he is and his higher or ideal self, and he is under an obligation to realize this higher self in his character and conduct. Renouvier thus agrees with Kant that obligation is the basic moral phenomenon; but he distinguishes various aspects of obligation. There is obligation on the part of the will to be in conformity with the ideal (*devoir-être*); there is obligation on the part of persons to perform their duty (*devoir-faire*); and one can also say that certain things ought to be (*devoir-être*), through human agency that is to say.[1] In society the concept of justice arises and becomes effective; and justice demands respect for the value and rights of other persons who, as Kant maintained, should not be used simply as means to the attainment of one's own ends.

As Renouvier insisted on personality as the highest category and on the value of the human person, it is natural that he should be opposed not only to any exaltation of the State but also to dogmatism and authoritarianism in the religious sphere. He was a strong anti-clerical and a supporter of secular education;[2] and for a time he published an anti-Catholic supplement (*La critique*

---

[1] *La science de la morale,* I, p. 10.
[2] In 1879 Renouvier published a *Little Treatise on Morals for the Secular Schools* (*Petit traité de morale pour les écoles laïques*).

religieuse) to his philosophical periodical. Renouvier was not however an atheist. He regarded reflection on the moral consciousness as opening the way to and as rendering legitimate, thought not as logically entailing, belief in God. And he insisted that God must be conceived in terms of man's highest category, and so as personal. At the same time Renouvier's conviction that recognition of the existence of evil was incompatible with belief in an infinitely good, omnipotent and omniscient Deity led him to conceive of God as finite or limited. It was only this concept, he believed, which could allow for man's creative freedom and responsibility.

It has been said of Renouvier that he was the philosopher of radicalism and that he combined the outlook of the Enlightenment and the revolution's ideal of liberty with themes which reappeared in the spiritualist movement in French thought, while employing the Kantian philosophy to sever the link between these themes and traditional metaphysics. And there is doubtless truth in this view. It is significant however that the last work which he himself published was entitled *Personalism*. As has already been noted, Renouvier described his philosophy as neo-criticism. And in the posthumously published *Last Conversations* he is recorded as referring to a study of the categories as being the key to everything. But it is arguable that what most attracted Renouvier in Kant's thought were its personalist elements. And it was his own personalism which determined his attitude to German metaphysical idealism,[1] to Comte's idea of history as governed by a law, to determinism, to traditional theology, to the Catholic Church as he saw it, to deification of the State on the one hand and to communist ideas and projects on the other.

3. It is customary to describe Octave Hamelin (1856–1907) as a disciple of Renouvier. Indeed, this was the way in which he described himself. He dedicated his main work, an *Essay on the Principal Elements of Representation* (*Essai sur les éléments principaux de la représentation*, 1907) to Renouvier; and in his posthumously published book *The System of Renouvier*[2] he asserted that this system had been for him 'the object of long meditations'.[3] Though however Renouvier's neo-criticism certainly exercised a considerable influence on Hamelin, the latter,

---

[1] The reference is of course to doctrines of the Absolute.
[2] *Le système de Renouvier*, edited by P. Mouy (1927).
[3] *Le système de Renouvier*, p. 2.

who became a professor at the Sorbonne, used Renouvier's thought as a point of departure for his own thinking. He was not a disciple in the sense of someone who simply adopts, continues and defends the master's system. For the matter of that, Hamelin was influenced by other thinkers too, such as Jules Lachelier (1832–1918), whose philosophy will be considered in connection with the so-called spiritualist movement in French thought.

It would be untrue to say that in his theory of categories Renouvier simply juxtaposed a number of basic concepts without any serious attempt to exhibit their mutual relations. For he tried to show that the other categories, culminating in that of personality, were progressively more concrete specifications of the most abstract and universal category, namely relation. Further, he represented each category as a synthesis between a thesis and an antithesis. Number, for example, was said to be a synthesis of unity and plurality. In other words, Renouvier attempted a dialectical deduction of the categories. In Hamelin's opinion however Renouvier's procedure was insufficiently systematic. What was needed was to develop a systematic dialectical construction of the categories in such a way that they would together constitute a complete system. In this way 'M. Renouvier's table of categories would develop into a completely rational system'.[1] The more systematic thought becomes, the more complete it is.

Like Renouvier, Hamelin begins with the category of relation, which he tries to establish in this way. It is a primitive fact of thought that 'everything *posited* excludes an *opposited*, that every *thesis* leaves outside itself an *antithesis*, and that the two opposed factors have meaning only in so far as they are mutually exclusive.'[2] To this primitive fact however we must add another which completes it. As the opposed factors receive their meaning precisely through their mutual opposition, they form two parts of one whole. This synthesis is a relation. 'Thesis, antithesis and synthesis, here is the simplest law of things in its three phases. We shall call it by the single word *relation*.'[3]

Having established, to his satisfaction, the basic category of relation, Hamelin proceeds to deduce that of number. In what he describes as relation the two opposed factors, the thesis and antithesis, exist in mutual opposition. It can therefore be said that the one needs the other in order to exist. At the same time the inability of the one to exist without the other implies that in some way

---

[1] *Système de Renouvier*, p. 114.   [2] *Essai*, p. 1.   [3] *Ibid.*, p. 2.

(*en quelque façon*) the one must exist without the other, in the manner, that is to say, which is compatible with, or indeed necessitated by, their mutual opposition. And 'number is the relation in which one posits that the one is without the other'.[1] We cannot follow Hamelin through his whole deduction of the categories. Nor indeed would it be very profitable to do so. The list or table differs somewhat from Renouvier's. For example, the category of time is deduced before that of space. Both men however begin with relation and end with personality. According to Hamelin the category of personality is the synthesis of causality (efficient causality that is to say) and of finality, the synthesis taking the form of being existing for itself. To exist for oneself is to be conscious. 'The for-itself or consciousness: such is the synthesis to which we aspired.'[2] Inasmuch as all the other categories are progressively more concrete specifications of the most abstract category of relation, the final category must be itself a relation. Further, as final it must be a relation which does not give rise to or demand any further category. These conditions are fulfilled in consciousness, which is 'the synthesis of the ego and the non-ego, the reality outside which the one and the other possess existence only in an abstract sense'.[3]

Hamelin's approach to the deduction of the categories is, as he intended, much more *a priori* and rationalistic than Renouvier's. And the influence of German idealism is clear. Hamelin presents us with a series of categories which are supposed to constitute a complete and self-contained system in which, in a real sense, beginning and end coincide. 'The two extremes of the hierarchy are doubtless demonstrated the one by the other, but not in the same manner. The more simple derives from the more complex by a series of analyses: the more complex superimposes itself necessarily on the more simple by a series of syntheses.'[4] In other words, it is possible to start with self-consciousness or personality and proceed backwards, so to speak, by a process of analysis from the more complex and concrete to the more simple and abstract. And it is also possible to start with the most abstract and simple category and let the system develop itself towards the more complex and concrete through the dialectical process of thesis, antithesis and synthesis.

The question arises whether Hamelin regards himself as concerned simply with the deduction of human forms of representation,

[1] *Ibid.*, p. 31.　　[2] *Ibid.*, p. 266.　　[3] *Ibid.*, p. 267.　　[4] *Ibid.*, p. 15.

with human ways of conceiving things-in-themselves which are independent of consciousness. The answer is in the negative. 'The thing-in-itself can only be a fiction, because the idea of it is self-contradictory.'[1] The non-ego exists only in relation to the ego, for consciousness that is to say. If it seems to follow from this view that the world consists of relations, this does not deter Hamelin. 'The world is a hierarchy of relations. . . .'[2] it is constituted 'not of things but of relations'.[3] Representation is not a mirror. It 'does not reflect an object and a subject which would exist without it; it is object and subject, it is reality itself. Representation is being, and being is representation.'[4] In other words, mind or spirit is the Absolute. This last term would indeed be inappropriate, if it were understood as referring to an ultimate reality beyond all relations. 'But if by absolute one understands that which contains in itself all relations, we must say that Mind is the absolute.'[5]

Hamelin does not of course intend to assert that the whole world is the content of my consciousness, in the sense that it exists solely in relation to myself as this particular subject. Some might wish to argue that from a logical point of view idealism of this kind cannot avoid solipsism. For him the subject-object relation falls within the Absolute. What he is claiming is that reality is the dialectical unfolding of thought or consciousness through a hierarchy of grades. And his insistence that the dialectical advance from the more simple and abstract to the more complex and concrete is 'synthetic' rather than purely 'analytic' leaves room for a theory of creative emergent evolution, provided that the process is interpreted in an idealist sense, as the development of consciousness. Hamelin therefore denies that consciousness must always mean clear consciousness, 'that of which the psychologists ordinarily speak.'[6] We must allow for 'an indefinite extension of consciousness'.[7] As Leibniz maintained, every being perceives or mirrors the whole; 'and this sort of consciousness suffices.'[8] Reflective consciousness represents a level which is reached only through the progressive development of mind or spirit.[9]

This may sound as though Hamelin is simply claiming that we can look on reality as a unified process whereby potential con-

[1] *Système de Renouvier*, p. 50.   [2] *Essai, p.* 15.   [3] *Ibid.*, p. 272.
[4] *Ibid.*, p. 279.   [5] *Ibid.*, p. 363.   [6] *Ibid.*, p. 269.
[7] *Ibid.*, p. 269.   [8] *Ibid.*, p. 269.
[9] Like the German term *Geist*, the French term *esprit* is difficult to translate. Both 'mind' and 'spirit' have their drawbacks.

sciousness is progressively actualized. In point of fact however he tries to combine his idealism with theism. 'God, it goes without saying, is the spirit in which we have not hesitated to recognize the absolute.'[1] In other words, the Absolute is personal. In Leibnizian language, the existence of God, as absolute spirit, is a truth of reason; but the divine goodness, according to Hamelin, is a truth of fact. That is to say, 'it was not, it could not be necessary that the absolute spirit should become absolute goodness. . . . In the field of possibility there was offered to the spirit, besides absolute goodness, the vista (*perspective*) of some erroneous perversity such as that which pessimism torments itself by imagining.'[2] Like Schelling, Hamelin thinks of God as willing goodness freely, and of the divine freedom being reflected in man's capacity to choose good or evil.[3]

In some respects Hamelin's idealism has an obvious affinity with that of Hegel. But he does not seem to have made any prolonged study of Hegel's philosophy; and he appears to have regarded the Hegelian Absolute in much the same way as Hegel himself had regarded Schelling's theory of the Absolute in his so-called 'system of identity'. That is to say, Hamelin interpreted Hegel as maintaining that no positive terms could be predicated of the Absolute, with the result that, as far as our knowledge was concerned, the Absolute would be a void, the night in which all cows are black as Hegel sarcastically remarked with reference to Schelling's theory of the Absolute as the vanishing-point of all differences. Hamelin's interpretation of Hegel is clearly disputable. But it is understandable that Hamelin insists on the personal character of the Absolute. For he follows Renouvier in regarding personality as the highest category and as the developed form of the abstract category of relation. On Hamelin's premises, if the Absolute is the totality, the all-embracing relation, it must be personal. At any rate this description is entailed by his premises even if it is difficult to see what precisely is meant by it. For one thing, if we start with the human subject or ego as standing to the non-ego in a reciprocal relationship, it is none too easy to see how we can detach the world, considered as object for a subject, from the human subject and attach it to a divine subject. Indeed, it is difficult to see how solipsism can be successfully evaded, except

---

[1] *Essai*, p. 269.   [2] *Ibid.*, p. 370.
[3] Freedom is defined by Hamelin as 'the synthesis of necessity and contingency'; and a free action is said to be 'the same thing as a motivated action' *Ibid.*, p. 310.

by recourse to the demands of common sense. For another thing, while identification of God with reality as a whole has the advantage of making unnecessary any proof of God's existence, it is none too clear that this identification can be properly described as theism. In other words, Hamelin's idealist metaphysics seems to stand in need of a good deal of rethinking. But the philosopher was only fifty-one years old when he died in an attempt to save two persons from drowning. And it is obviously impossible to know what modifications, if any, he would have made in his system, had he lived longer.

4. To treat here of Léon Brunschvicg (1869–1944) is open to objection on the ground that reference should be made to him after discussion of Bergson and not before. But though the objection is doubtless valid on chronological grounds, it is convenient to include him in the chapter devoted to the critical philosophy in France. Brunschvicg was first and foremost a philosopher who reflected on the nature of mind or spirit as it reveals itself historically in its activity in various fields. And his reflections on mathematics and science have to be seen in this light.

Born at Paris, Brunschvicg studied first at the Lycée Condorcet and then at the École Normale where in 1891 he received the licentiate in both letters and science. In 1897 he published his doctoral thesis on *The Modality of Judgment*.[1] In 1909 he was appointed to a chair of philosophy at the Sorbonne. In 1940 he retired to the south of France. His publications included *Les étapes de la philosophie des mathématiques* (1912, *Stages in the Philosophy of Mathematics*), *L'expérience humaine et la causalité physique* (1922, *Human Experience and Physical Causality*), *Le progrès de la conscience dans la philosophie occidentale* (1927, *The Progress of Consciousness in Western Philosophy*) and *La philosophie de l'esprit* (1949, *The Philosophy of Mind*). Brunschvicg also wrote on Spinoza and Pascal, besides publishing a well known edition of the latter's *Pensées* in 1897.

In his work on the modality of judgment Brunschvicg asserts his idealist standpoint clearly enough. From the properly philosophical point of view 'knowledge is no longer an accident which is added from without to being, without altering it . . .; knowledge constitutes a world which is for us the world. Beyond it there is

---

[1] The second edition of *La modalité du jugement* appeared in 1934. The third edition, amplified by a French translation of the Latin thesis on the metaphysical force of the syllogism according to Aristotle, was published at Paris in 1964.

nothing. A thing which was beyond knowledge would be by definition inaccessible, non-determinable. That is to say, for us it would be equivalent to nothing.'[1] In philosophy the mind 'seeks to grasp itself in its movement, in its activity. ... Intellectual activity coming to consciousness of itself, this is the integral study of integral knowledge, this is philosophy.'[2] In other words, from the point of view of naïve common sense the object of knowledge is something external and fixed, something which, in itself, lies outside knowledge but which comes to be known. We make the transition to the philosophical point of view when we see that the distinction between subject and object arises within the sphere of reason, of the mind's activity. According to Brunschvicg therefore his own (or contemporary) idealism should not be confused with a subjective idealism which is opposed to a metaphysical realism. Critical or 'rational idealism'[3] does not entail a denial of any distinction between subject and object or between man and his environment. What it entails is the assertion that this distinction arises within consciousness, and that something beyond consciousness and knowledge would be for us nothing at all.

Brunschvicg's idea of philosophy as the mind's activity in coming to reflective consciousness of itself naturally recalls the transcendental philosophy of Kant. Though however Brunschvicg is perfectly well aware of Kant's influence on the development of idealism, he insists that the philosophy which he has in mind does not consist in an *a priori* deduction of supposedly unchangeable categories. He sees the mind as coming to know itself through reflection on its activity as manifested historically in, for example, the development of science. And through this reflection the mind sees that its categories change: it sees its own inventiveness and creativity and is open to new categories and ways of thought. The Kantian attitude leads to a sterile idealism. Genuine idealism is 'a doctrine of the living mind. ... All progress in the knowledge and determination of the mind is linked to the progress of science.'[4] It is not however simply a question of science. In the sphere of morals too genuine idealism remains open to a fresh understanding of moral principles in the light of social progress. As has been mentioned, Brunschvicg published a work on the progress of consciousness in western philosophy. The word *conscience* can mean conscience as well as consciousness. And just as Brunschvicg

[1] *La modalité du jugement* (1964 edition), p. 2.   [2] *Ibid.*, p. 4.
[3] *L'idéalisme contemporain* (1905), p. 5.   [4] *Ibid.*, p. 176.

rejects an *a priori* deduction of categories which would exclude any radical changes in scientific theory, so does he reject any *a priori* deduction of moral principles which would exclude advances in moral insight. The mind or spirit comes to know itself in its activity, but its activity has not ceased at any given point at which it reflects on itself. Science is capable of change and progress; so is society; and so is man's moral life. The mind may aspire to a comprehensive and final synthesis; but it cannot attain it. For the mind or spirit remains inventive and creative. It creates new forms and comes to know itself in and through its own creations.

Metaphysics, for Brunschvicg, is reducible to the theory of knowledge; the constitutive act of knowledge is the judgment; and judgment is characterized by the affirmation of being.[1] But what is affirmed or posited as being can be affirmed in two ways. In the first place it can be affirmed simply in the sphere of intelligibility, under the form of 'interiority'. That is to say, the being which is posited is constituted simply by an intelligible relation. An arithmetical judgment is of this type. The being of the copula is purely logical. In the second place the being affirmed can be that of existence, the judgment being the expression of the mind's recognition of a 'shock', of its being constrained or limited, as it were, by something external to itself and of its own activity in giving content to this experience of constraint.[2] We are not however faced with an irreducible dualism between purely formal judgments on the one hand and discrete judgments of perception on the other. For the mind or intellect seeks intelligibility, unity that is to say. The judgments which in the first instance belong to the purely intelligible sphere of interiority are applied, and the relations affirmed in the sphere of exteriority are subjected to the conditions or demands of intelligibility. In brief, the world of mathematical physics is constructed. This creation of the mind's activity cannot however be given the form of pure mathematics, an exclusively deductive form. There is a constant tension between 'interiority' and 'exteriority'. The scientist deduces; but he must also test empirically, having recourse to experience. In the area of pure mathematics necessity rules; in that of science probability holds sway. The world of science is the creation of the

[1] *La modalité du jugement*, p. 40.
[2] It is intelligence, according to Brunschvicg, which determines the object. That which is given in the 'shock' is completely undetermined. Any judgment of perception involves both interiority and exteriority.

human spirit;[1] but it is a creation which never reaches a final and absolutely irreformable state.

In his treatment of the moral sphere, that of the practical judgment, Brunschvicg again emphasizes the human spirit's movement towards unification. He sees human beings as moving towards assimilation through participation in the activity of consciousness as it creates values which transcend self-centredness. In the theoretical sphere reason creates a network of coherent relations, as it moves towards the ideal limit of an all-encompassing coherent system. In the sphere of the moral life too the human spirit moves towards the interrelations of justice and love. As for religion, there is no question with Brunschvicg of a personal God transcending the sphere of human consciousness. He uses the word 'God', it is true; but with him it signifies reason as transcending the individual as such, though immanent in him, and as moving towards unification. 'Man participates in the divinity inasmuch as he is *particeps rationis*.'[2] And human life has a religious dimension in so far as it overcomes the barriers between man and man.

Brunschvicg is better described as an idealist than as a philosopher of science. It would not however be fair to him, if one were to represent him simply as forcing science into an idealist framework of thought. He does indeed start with idealist presuppositions; and it is undeniable that they influence his interpretation of science. At the same time he insists that the nature of mind or spirit can be seen only by studying its activity. And though his idealism influences his interpretation of science, his reflection on science in its actual development influences his idealist philosophy. For example, he sees clearly enough that science militates against the idea that the process of arriving at knowledge can be represented as a purely deductive process. He also sees however that the scientist's inventiveness and creativity rules out pure empiricism. And it is perhaps worth noting that in Einstein's relativity theory he saw a confirmation of his view of science as revealing the mutual interdependence of reason and experience. He also saw in it of course a justification of his rejection of fixed categories and of space and time as realities which are antecedent to and independent of the activity of the mind. 'In all domains,

---

[1] So of course is the world of common sense or of the pre-scientific consciousness. Both are real.
[2] *Le progrès de la conscience*, p. 796. In 1939 Brunschvicg published *La raison et la religion (Reason and Religion)*.

from the analysis of Cauchy or of Georg Cantor to the physics of M. Planck or of M. Einstein the decisive discoveries have been made in the opposite direction to the schema which was predetermined by the doctrine of forms and categories. Instead of applying unchangeable principles to new matter, progress has consisted on the one hand in looking back to the classical principles in order to question their apodictic truth and on the other hand in bringing to birth novel and unforeseeable relations.'[1] Whatever we may think of the Fichtean elements in Brunschvicg's thought (his attempt, for example, to derive externality from the activity of reason), he certainly did not try to canonize certain scientific theories in the name of philosophy. For it was precisely changes in scientific theory which he saw as revealing the inventiveness and creativity of the mind, a creativity which he also saw in the ethical sphere.

[1] *Ibid.*, p. 705.

CHAPTER VIII

THE SPIRITUALIST MOVEMENT

*The term 'spiritualism'—The philosophy of Ravaisson—
J. Lachelier and the bases of induction—Boutroux and contingency—A. Fouillée on idées-forces—M. J. Guyau and the
philosophy of life.*

1. It hardly needs saying that when the term 'spiritualism' is
used as a philosophical label in the context of nineteenth-century
thought in France, it has nothing to do with the belief that the
living can communicate with departed spirits by means of practices which are thought appropriate for the purpose. To give to
the term a precise positive definition is however none too easy.
Victor Cousin used it to refer to his own eclecticism. And in his
Letter on Apologetics Maurice Blondel remarked that the label
should be relegated to the lumber-room, inasmuch as it shared the
discredit into which eclecticism had fallen.[1] In spite of Blondel
however Cousin's philosophy is still sometimes referred to as
'eclectic spiritualism' or 'spiritualist eclecticism'. And if by
'spiritualism' we mean a rejection of materialism and determinism
and an assertion of the ontological priority of spirit to matter, this
description of Cousin's philosophy is doubtless justified. But if the
term is understood in this wide sense, it covers all theistic philosophies and the various forms of absolute idealism, such as the
thought of Hamelin. It would then lack any specific reference to
modern French philosophy and could be used to describe the
philosophies of, say, Aquinas, Descartes, Berkeley, Schelling,
Hegel, Rosmini and Berdyaev.

Perhaps the best policy is to abandon any attempt to give a
precise abstract definition and to say simply that in the present
context the word 'spiritualism' is used to signify the current of
thought which recognizes Maine de Biran as a fountainhead and
which runs from Ravaisson through Lachelier, Fouillée and others
to Bergson. In other words, the term is used to signify a movement
in which Maine de Biran's insistence on the spontaneity of the
human will and his reflection on the human spirit's activity as a

---

[1] See the *Letter* as translated by A. Dru and I. Trethowan, p. 150 (London,
1964).

key to the nature of reality are seen as a counterblast to the materialism and determinism of some of the thinkers of the Enlightenment and as a return to what are regarded as the genuine traditions of French philosophy. Cousin's thought then qualifies for being described as spiritualist to the extent in which he derives stimulus from Maine de Biran or from ideas similar to those of de Biran. It must be added however that as the movement develops Maine de Biran's psychological approach and his emphasis on the spontaneity and freedom of the will come to take the form of a general philosophy of life. This is obvious enough in the case of Bergson. Indeed, though Bergson acknowledged an indebtedness to Maine de Biran and Ravaisson, it is arguable that in some respects Blondel stands closer than Bergson to de Biran, in spite of Blondel's recommendation that use of the term 'spiritualism' should be abandoned.

2. Jean Gaspard Félix Ravaisson-Mollien (1813–1900), commonly known simply as Ravaisson, was born at Namur and after studies at Paris attended Schelling's lectures at Munich. In 1835 he presented to the Academy of Moral and Political Sciences a prize essay on the metaphysics of Aristotle, which was published in a revised form in 1837 under the title *Essai sur la métaphysique d'Aristote*. A second volume was added in 1846. In 1838 Ravaisson presented two theses for the doctorate at Paris, a Latin thesis on Speusippus and a French thesis on habit, *De l'habitude*. He taught philosophy for a short while at Rennes; but differences with Victor Cousin, who was then pretty well dictator of philosophical studies in the universities, stood in the way of his pursuing an academic career at Paris. In 1840 he was appointed inspector general of libraries, and in 1859 he became inspector general of higher education. Ravaisson was interested not only in philosophy but also in art, especially painting, and in classical antiquities. He was elected to membership both of the Academy of Moral and Political Sciences and of the Academy of Inscriptions and Fine Arts. In 1870 he was appointed curator of classical antiquities at the Louvre.

In 1867 Ravaisson published, at the request of the government, a Report on *Philosophy in France in the Nineteenth Century* (*Rapport sur la philosophie en France au XIXe siècle*) in which he provided both a source of information about a large number of philosophers and a programmatic defence of the metaphysical tradition of spiritualist realism, which he saw as going back beyond the nineteenth century and as having been reasserted by Maine de Biran. Ravaisson took the opportunity of attacking not only positivism but also the eclecticism of Cousin, of which he took a dim view, regarding it as a pitiable mixture of the Scottish philosophy of common sense with some misunderstood ideas derived from Maine de Biran. In effect it was made pretty clear that de Biran's true successor was Ravaisson himself. His *Philosophical Testament and Fragments* was published posthumously in 1901 in the *Revue des deux mondes*.[1]

As the title indicates, Ravaisson's *De l'habitude* is devoted to a special topic; but his treatment of the theme exhibits a general philosophical outlook. Reflection on our habit-forming, according to the author, shows that in habit voluntary movement, which encounters resistance and is accompanied by the feeling of effort, is transformed into instinctive movement, the conscious tending to become unconscious. In habit the spontaneous activity of life submits, as it were, to its material conditions, to the sphere of mechanism, and in so doing provides a basis for the further activity of will, of the voluntary movement and effort of which, as Maine de Biran argued, we are conscious in ourselves. This can be seen in the formation of physical habits, which form the foundation and background of purposeful action. To take a simple example, if I decide to walk to a friend's house to visit him, the carrying out of my purpose presupposes the formation of physical habits such as those of walking. And we can see an analogous situation in the ethical sphere, where, according to Ravaisson, virtuous activity is at first achieved only by deliberate effort but can become habitual, thus forming a 'second nature' and providing a basis for the further pursuit of ideals.

More generally, Ravaisson sees in the world two basic factors, space as the condition of permanence or stability, time as the condition of change. To these two factors there correspond respectively matter and life. The former is the sphere of necessity and mechanism, the latter of the spontaneous activity which is manifested in living organisms and which in man rises to the level of 'freedom of the understanding'.[2] The point of intersection between the two spheres is habit, which combines in itself the mechanism of matter and the dynamic finality of life. If however habit

---

[1] There is a separate edition of the *Testament philosophique et fragments*, edited by C. Devivaise (Paris, 1932).

[2] *De l'habitude*, p. 28 (Revue de métaphysique et de morale, XII, 1894).

presupposes voluntary movement and effort[1] and is, so to speak, intelligence which has gone to sleep or has entered an infra-conscious state, and if it provides the basis for further activity by the will, this shows the priority, from the finalistic point of view, of the upward movement of life. Between the lowest limit of Nature and 'the highest point of reflective freedom there is an infinity of degrees which measure the development of one and the same power'.[2] Habit 'redescends' the line of descent and can be described as an intuition in which the real and the ideal are one.

In the emphasis which Ravaisson places on voluntary movement and effort and in his tendency to look within man for the key to the secret of the world we see of course the inspiration of Maine de Biran. In his theory of habit we can also see evidence of the influence of Schelling, for example in talk about the unity of the ideal and the real.[3] Looking forward, we can see a clear anticipation of Bergsonian themes. In the commemorative discourse which Bergson delivered on succeeding Ravaisson as a member of the Academy of Moral and Political Sciences he referred to *De l'habi-tude* and made the following comment. 'Thus habit gives us the living demonstration of this truth, that mechanism is not self-sufficient: it would be only, so to speak, the fossilized residue of a spiritual activity.'[4] In other words, Bergson sees in Ravais-son's thought an anticipation of his own theory of the *élan vital* and of Nature as obscured consciousness or dormant volition.

Ravaisson's theory of habit expresses his conviction that the lower has to be explained through reference to the higher. And this is indeed a basic element in his general philosophical outlook. Thus in his *Report* he finds fault with those philosophers who attempt to explain mental activity either in terms of physico-chemical processes or, as in phenomenalism, by reduction to impressions or in terms of abstract categories. The analytic intelligence or understanding tends by its very nature to explain phenomena by reduction to ultimate constituent elements. But though this procedure certainly has its legitimate role in natural science, Ravaisson insists that we cannot understand spiritual phenomena in this way. They have to be viewed in the light of

---

[1] In Ravaisson's view there can be no habits, properly speaking, in the inorganic sphere.

[2] *De l'habitude*, p. 34.

[3] On some points of course the influence of Aristotle can be discerned pretty clearly.

[4] *La pensée et le mouvant. Essais et conférences*, p. 296, (3rd edition, 1934).

their finality, of the goal-directed upward movement of life, both at the infra-conscious and conscious levels. This movement is grasped by a kind of intuition which apprehends it first of all in our inner experience of goal-directed effort. It is in inner experience that we can see the will as seeking the Good, which manifests itself in art as Beauty. The Good and Beauty, the ideal goals of the will, are God, or at any rate symbols of God. And in the light of this truth we can interpret the material world, considered as the sphere of necessity and mechanism, as the effect of the self-diffusion of the divine Good and as the setting for the upward movement of light.

It has been said of Ravaisson[1] that he combines the psychology of Maine de Biran with the metaphysics of Schelling, whereas in the discourse to which reference has been made above Bergson remarks that Schelling's influence on Ravaisson should not be exaggerated[2] and that the vision of the universe as the manifestation of an ultimate reality which gives of itself in liberality was to be found among the Greek philosophers.[3] Bergson prefers to emphasize the influence of the development of biological studies in nineteenth-century science.[4] Though however there is doubtless a good deal of truth in what Bergson says, the influence of Schelling cannot be discounted. Ravaisson's view of Nature clearly has some affinity with Schelling's picture of Nature as slumbering spirit, even if in his *Report* he refers more to contemporary psychological ideas and theories. Further, Ravaisson's tendency to regard creation as a kind of cosmic Fall and his emphasis on the idea of a return to God justifies reference to the influence of the German philosopher. In any case we can see in Ravaisson's distinction between the activity of the analytic intelligence on the one hand and, on the other, an intuitive grasp of the movement of life an anticipation of central themes in the philosophy of Bergson.

3. Though Ravaisson was never a professor at Paris, he none the less exercised a considerable influence. It was he who divined the philosophical capacity of Jules Lachelier (1832–1918), when the latter was a student of the École Normale, and who did his best to promote Lachelier's career. In his years as a professor at the École Normale (1864–1875) Lachelier was himself to have a powerful stimulative effect on the minds of students of philosophy. He was not however a prolific writer. In 1871 he published a work

[1] By R. Berthelot.
[2] *La pensée et le mouvant*, p. 291.
[3] *Ibid.*, p. 317.
[4] *Ibid.*, p. 303.

on induction, *Du fondement de l'induction*, which was his French thesis for the doctorate, the Latin thesis being on the syllogism.[1] He also published a number of essays, the best known of which deal with psychology and metaphysics (*Psychologie et métaphysique*, 1885) and with Pascal's wager (*Notes sur le pari de Pascal*, 1901). But his *Works*, which include inverventions during discussions at the French Society of Philosophy and annotations on draft entries for Lalande's *Vocabulaire*, form only two modest volumes.[2] When Lachelier retired from the École Normale in 1875, he was appointed inspector of the Academy of Paris; and in 1879 he became inspector general of public education. In 1896 he was elected a member of the Academy of Moral and Political Sciences.

There would be ample justification for considering the thought of Lachelier in the chapter on neo-criticism and idealism. For in his main work, that on induction, he approaches his theme in a Kantian manner, by inquiring into the necessary conditions of our experience of the world. And on this basis he outlines an idealist philosophy which makes him a predecessor of Hamelin. At the same time there are elements in his thought which exercised an influence on the spiritualist movement; and though Bergson was not actually a pupil of Lachelier, as a student he read the work on induction and regarded its author as his teacher. Further, Lachelier referred to his own thought as a form of spiritualism.

By induction Lachelier understands 'the operation by which we pass from the knowledge of facts to that of the laws which govern them'.[3] Nobody doubts that this process actually takes place in science. But it gives rise to a problem. On the one hand experience gives us only a certain number of observed cases of practical connections between phenomena; but it does not tell us that they must be always so connected. On the other hand in inductive reasoning we do not hesitate to draw a universal conclusion, applying to unobserved and future connections; and, according to Lachelier, this implies that we are confident of the reign of necessity in Nature. He does not intend to assert that induction is in practice always correct. 'In fact, induction is always subject to error.'[4] But the revisibility of scientific laws does not alter the fact that our attempts to formulate them rest on and express a confidence that there are necessary connections to be found. And

[1] *De natura syllogismi* (1871).   [2] *Oeuvres de Jules Lachelier* (Paris, 1933).
[3] *Oeuvres*, I, p. 21.   [4] *Ibid.*, p. 25.

the question arises, can this confidence be theoretically justified? Or, as Lachelier puts it, what is the principle in virtue of which we add to the data of experience the elements of universality and necessity?

In the first place induction implies that phenomena are organized in series of mechanically related members. To put the matter in another way, phenomena are intelligible only if they are subject to the law of efficient causality. But the principle of causality does not by itself provide a sufficient basis for induction. For inductive reasoning presupposes not only mechanically related series of phenomena but also complex and recurring groups of phenomena, functioning as wholes, each whole being of such a kind that it determines the existence of its parts. A whole of this kind is what we call a final cause. The concept of laws of nature, 'with the exception of a small number of elementary laws, seems therefore to be based on two distinct principles: the one in virtue of which phenomena form series in which the existence of the preceding (member) determines that of the following; the other in virtue of which these series form in their turn systems, in which the idea of the whole determines the existence of the parts.'[1] In a nutshell, 'the possibility of induction rests on the double principle of efficient causes and of final causes.'[2]

It is one thing however to claim that inductive reasoning rests on a certain principle (or, more accurately, on two principles), and it is another thing to validate or justify this principle. Lachelier is not prepared to follow the Scottish School and Royer-Collard in appealing to common sense. Nor does he wish to claim simply that the principle is a self-evident indemonstrable truth. But though he commends J. S. Mill for trying to justify induction, he does not believe that the attempt was, or indeed could be successful, given Mill's empiricist premises. Further, he sees that if a solution is offered simply in terms of the human mind's imposing its *a priori* categories or concepts, necessitated by its own nature or structure, on phenomena which are appearances of things-in-themselves, the question can be raised whether the result of this imposition can properly be described as knowledge. In other words, Lachelier wishes to show that the principles of efficient causality and of final causes are not *a priori* simply and solely in a subjective sense, but that they govern both thought and the object of thought. This involves showing not only that, in general,

[1] *Ibid.*, p. 27.   [2] *Ibid.*, p. 27.

'the conditions of the existence of phenomena are the very conditions of the possibility of thought.'[1] but also, in particular, that
the two principles on which induction rests are conditions of the
possibility of thought.

In regard to the first principle, that of efficient causality,
Lachelier tries to show that the serial linking of phenomena
through causal relations is necessarily involved by the unity of the
world, which is itself a condition of the possibility of thought.
His line of argument is somewhat difficult to follow; but it proceeds
on these lines. Thought would not be possible without the
existence of a subject which distinguishes itself from each sensation and which remains one despite the diversity of sensations,
simultaneous and successive. Here however there arises a problem.
On the one hand knowledge does not consist in the activity of a
subject shut up in itself and cut off from or external to its sensations. Lachelier tries to solve this problem by seeking the required
unity in relations between the sensations, the subject or self
being regarded not as something over and above and cut off
from its sensations but rather as the 'form' of diverse sensations.
But natural relations between our sensations cannot be different
from relations between the corresponding phenomena. 'The question of knowing how all our sensations are united in one single
thought is then precisely the same as that of knowing how all
phenomena compose one single universe.'[2] For Lachelier at any
rate a condition of phenomena constituting one world is that they
should be causally related. Mere succession would locate phenomena in space and time; but for a real link between phenomena
the causal relation is necessary. As therefore things exist for us
only in so far as they are objects of thought, the condition of
phenomena forming one world and the condition of the unity of
thought are one and the same, namely the principle of efficient
causality.

This point of view gives us only what Lachelier describes as 'a
sort of idealist materialism'.[3] The world which it presents is a
world in relation to thought, but it is a world of mechanical
causality, of the reign of necessity. To complete the picture we
have to consider the second principle of induction, namely final
causality. Induction, according to Lachelier, presupposes something more than mechanically related series of discrete phenomena.
It also presupposes complex and recurring groups of phenomena,

---

[1] *Ibid.*, p. 48.   [2] *Ibid.*, p. 51.   [3] *Ibid.*, p. 68.

functioning as wholes. And we cannot account for these wholes, existing at various levels, without introducing the regulative idea of immanent finality. The most obvious example of the sort of thing which Lachelier has in mind is obviously the living organism, in the case of which the 'reason' of the whole complex phenomenon is found in itself, in an immanent final cause which governs the behaviour of the parts. But it is not only of living organisms that Lachelier is thinking. He has in mind all complex groups of phenomena which function as unities. Indeed, he sees every phenomenon as the manifestation of a force which expresses a spontaneous tendency towards an end. Further, it is this idea of force which explains the varying intensity of our sensations and which lies at the basis of our conviction that the world is not reducible to our sensations considered as purely subjective. Final causality may be a regulative idea; but it is required for induction which presupposes an intelligible world, one that is penetrable by thought and so reveals in itself the functioning of unconscious thought as seen in the development of recurrent unities functioning as wholes. It is not a question of final causality simply replacing or annulling mechanical causality. The latter forms a basis for the former. But once we introduce the idea of final causality as penetrating the world of mechanical causality and subordinating the latter to itself, our concept of the world changes. Materialist idealism (or idealist materialism, as Lachelier also describes it) is transformed into 'a spiritualist realism, in the eyes of which every being is a force, and every force a thought which tends to a more and more complete consciousness of itself.'[1]

The concept of spiritualist realism is developed in the essay on psychology and metaphysics. Psychology is said to have as its demesne 'sensible consciousness' (*la conscience sensible*), whereas metaphysics is described as 'the science of thought in itself, of the light at its source'.[2] This statement may give the impression that for Lachelier metaphysics is really part of psychology. For how can we exclude from psychology the study of thought? Lachelier does not mean however that the psychologist's attention must be confined to the study of sensation and perception and feeling without any reference at all to thought or will.[3] What he insists on is that psychology is concerned with thought in so far as

---

[1] *Ibid.*, p. 92.   [2] *Ibid.*, p. 219.
[3] In the study of 'sensible consciousness' physiology has its own field, which, according to Lachelier, consists of the laws governing the succession of states.

thought becomes a datum of consciousness, an objectifiable factor in, for example, perception. Similarly, psychology is concerned with will in so far as it is manifested in man's perceptive and affective life. Philosophy or metaphysics is concerned with thought itself, pure thought, which is also pure liberty or freedom, the thought which works unconsciously in Nature, at successive levels, and which comes to think itself in and through man. Metaphysics is thus equivalent to what Lachelier elsewhere describes as the profounder spiritual realism. In the comments which he makes on the entry 'spiritualism' for Lalande's *Vocabulary* he remarks that every doctrine that recognizes the independence and primacy of spirit, in the sense of conscious thought, or that regards spirit as above Nature and irreducible to physical pressures can be described as spiritualist. He then goes on to claim that there is a profounder spiritualism which consists in seeking in spirit the explanation of Nature and in believing that the thought which operates unconsciously in Nature is the same as the thought which becomes conscious in man. 'It is this second spiritualism which was, as it seems to me, that of M. Ravaisson.'[1] Evidently, this 'second spiritualism' is metaphysics as Lachelier understands the term.

The thought which Lachelier has in mind is clearly absolute thought, the thought which 'posits *a priori* the conditions of all existence'.[2] And we might well feel inclined to comment that 'idealism' would be a more appropriate word than 'realism'. But by 'idealism' Lachelier tends to mean subjective idealism, in the sense of the theory that the world consists of *my* representations, actual and possible. A philosophy which recognizes a plurality of subjects and for which '*my* world' has become '*the* world' can be described as realism. At the same time Lachelier insists that in so far as different subjects attain universal truth this thought is to be considered as one, as the manifestation of the thought which operates unconsciously in Nature and consciously in man. And this point of view is generally described as objective idealism. Lachelier does indeed assert that the object of thought is other than thought itself, and that 'thought could not produce it (the object) out of itself'.[3] But he adds that this is because thought is not what it ought to be, namely intuitive in a sense which would make the object immanent to thought, so that the two would be

---

[1] *Ibid.*, II, p. 221. [2] *Ibid.*, I, p. 218. [3] *Ibid.*, II, p. 210.

one. He is presumably saying that human thinking cannot coincide entirely with absolute thought and so retains a realist outlook, even if it recognizes that the whole world is the self-manifestation of absolute thought or spirit.

Lachelier does indeed endorse Aristotle's definition of first philosophy or metaphysics as the science of being as being; but he interprets this in the sense of the science of thought in itself and in things. As this thought is the one ultimate reality or being, which, as we have seen, operates unconsciously in Nature and comes to self-awareness in and through man, Lachelier is quite prepared to admit that 'pure philosophy is essentially pantheistic'.[1] He goes on however to say that one can *believe* in a divine reality transcending the world. And at the close of his notes on Pascal's wager he remarks that 'the sublimest question of philosophy, but perhaps more religious than philosophical, is the transition from the formal absolute to the real and living absolute, from the idea of God to God.'[2] This transition is the transition from philosophy to religion. At the end of the essay on induction Lachelier asserts that spiritual realism, so far as he has presented it, is 'independent of all religion',[3] though the subordination of mechanism to finality prepares the way for an act of moral faith which transcends the limits of Nature and of thought. By 'thought' in this context he doubtless means philosophy. Religion goes beyond not only science but also philosophy. And though Brunschvicg tells us that Lachelier was a practising Catholic,[4] the latter's discussion with Durkheim makes it clear that for him religion has no intrinsic relation to a group but is 'an interior effort and consequently solitary'.[5] From the historical point of view Durkheim is justified in protesting against this rather narrow concept of religion. But Lachelier is evidently convinced that religion is essentially the individual's act of faith by which the abstract Absolute of philosophy becomes the living God.

4. Among Lachelier's pupils at the École Normale was Émile Boutroux (1845–1921). After finishing his studies at Paris Boutroux taught for a while in a lycée at Caen; but after he had received the doctorate he was given a University post, first at Montpellier, then at Nancy. From 1877 until 1886 he lectured at the École Normale at Paris, and from 1886 until 1902 he occupied a chair of philosophy at the Sorbonne. His best known work is his

---

[1] *Ibid.*, p. 201. [2] *Ibid.*, p. 56. [3] *Ibid.*, I, p. 92.
[4] *Ibid.*, I, p. xvi. [5] *Ibid.*, II, p. 171.

doctorate thesis *La contingence des lois de la nature*[1] which appeared in 1874, three years after the publication of Lachelier's work on induction. The ideas which Boutroux had expressed in his thesis were developed in a work which he published in 1895, *De l'idée de loi naturelle dans la science et la philosophie contemporaines.*[2] Other writings include *La science et la religion dans la philosophie contemporaine,*[3] which appeared in 1908, and, in the historical field, *Études d'histoire de la philosophie.*[4] The posthumously published collection of essays *La nature et l'esprit* (1926) includes the programme for Boutroux's Gifford Lectures on *Nature and Spirit* which were delivered at Glasgow in 1903–04 and 1904–05.

In his preface to the English translation of *De la contingence de lois de la nature* Boutroux remarks that philosophical systems seem to him to belong to three main types, 'the idealist, the materialist and the dualist or parallelist types.'[5] All three have a common feature, namely that they represent the laws of nature as necessary. In rationalist systems of philosophy the mind tries to reconstruct reality by means of a logical deduction of its structure from what it takes to be self-evidently true propositions. When the mind abandons this dream and turns to phenomena known through sense-perception in order to ascertain their laws, it imports the idea of logical necessity into that of natural law and depicts the world as 'an endless variety of facts, linked together by necessary and immutable bonds'.[6] The question arises however whether the concept of a necessary relation is actually exemplified in the relations between phenomena; and Boutroux proposes to argue that natural laws are contingent and that they are 'bases which enable us constantly to rise towards a higher life'.[7]

Boutroux starts, very properly, by inquiring what is meant in this context by a necessary relation. Absolute necessity, the necessity, that is to say, which eliminates all conditions and is reducible to the principle of identity ($A = A$), can be left out of account. For the laws of nature are not simply tautologies. What

---

[1] Translated by F. Rothwell as *The Contingency of the Laws of Nature* (London, 1916).
[2] Translated by F. Rothwell as *Natural Law in Science and Philosophy* (London, 1914).
[3] Translated by J. Nield as *Science and Religion in Contemporary Philosophy,* (London, 1909).
[4] Originally published in 1897, this work was translated by F. Rothwell as *Historical Studies in Philosophy* (London, 1912).
[5] *The Contingency of the Laws of Nature,* p. vi.
[6] *Ibid.,* p. 4.   [7] *Ibid.,* p. vii.

we are concerned with is not absolute but relative necessity, 'the existence of a necessary relation between two things.'[1] In other words, when we inquire into the alleged necessity of the laws of nature, we are looking not for purely analytic truth, but for necessarily true synthetic propositions. But here again we must make a distinction. If the laws of nature are necessarily true synthetic propositions, they cannot be *a posteriori* propositions. For while experience can reveal to us constant relations, it does not by itself reveal necessity. Nor can it do so. Hence the aim of our inquiry is to discover whether the laws of nature can properly be described as *a priori* synthetic propositions. If they can, then they must assert necessary causal relations.[2] The question therefore comes down to this. Are there *a priori* causal syntheses?

It will be noted that Boutroux's use of terminology is based on that of Kant. Moreover, he does not deny that the principle of causality can be stated in such a form that it is necessarily true. At the same time he maintains that this is not the sense in which the principle is actually used in the sciences. 'In reality, the word "cause", when used scientifically means "immediate condition".'[3] For scientific purposes it is quite sufficient, for the formulation of laws, that 'relatively invariable relations exist between the phenomena'.[4] The idea of necessity is not required. In other words, the principle of causality, as actually employed in science, is derived from experience, not imposed *a priori* by the mind. It is a very general and abstract expression of observed relations; and we do not observe necessity, though we can of course observe regular sequences. True, if we restrict our attention simply and solely to quantity, to the measurable aspects of phenomena, it may be in conformity with experience to assert an absolute equivalence between cause and effect. In point of fact however we find qualitative changes, a qualitative heterogeneity, which excludes the possibility of showing that the cause (immediate condition) must contain all that is required to produce the effect. And if the effect can be disproportionate to the cause from the qualitative point of view, it follows that 'nowhere in the real concrete world can the principle of causality be rigidly applied'.[5] To be sure, it can serve as a practical maxim for the scientist.

---

[1] *Ibid.*, p. 7.
[2] Boutroux rejects the idea that any end must necessarily be realized or that, given an end, the means are determined necessarily. He therefore restricts the field of inquiry to relations of efficient causality.
[3] *Ibid.*, p. 23.   [4] *Ibid.*, p. 24.   [5] *Ibid.*, p. 30.

But the development of the sciences themselves suggest that the laws of nature do not express objectively *necessary* relations and that they are not irreformable or unrevisible in principle. Our scientific laws enable us to deal successfully with a changing reality. It would be absurd to question their utility. But they are not definitive.

In his later work, *De l'idée de loi naturelle*, Boutroux carried the matter further. In pure mathematics there are of course necessary relations, depending on certain postulates. But pure mathematics is a formal science. It is obviously true that a natural science such as astronomy makes use of mathematics and could not have advanced without it. Indeed in certain sciences we can see clearly enough the attempt to fit Nature, as it were, to mathematics and to formulate the relations between phenomena in a mathematical manner. But there always remains a gap between Nature as it exists and mathematics; and this gap becomes more manifest as we shift our attention from the inorganic sphere to that of life. The scientist is justified in emphasizing the connection between biological and even mental phenomena on the one hand and physico-chemical processes on the other. But if we assume the reducibility of the laws governing biological evolution to the more general laws of physics and chemistry, it becomes impossible to explain the appearance of novelty. Despite their admitted utility, all natural laws are of the nature of compromises, approximations to an equation between reality and mathematics; and the more we proceed from the very general laws of physics to the spheres of biology, psychology and sociology, the clearer does this characteristic of approximation become. For we have to allow for creativeness and the emergence of novelty. For the matter of that, it is not certain that even on the purely physical level there is no variability, no breach in determinism.

Nowadays the idea that the structure of reality can be deduced *a priori* from basic propositions which are indemonstrable but self-evidently true can hardly be described as fashionable. And while we could not reasonably claim that there is universal agreement about the proper use of the term 'law of nature' or about the logical status of scientific laws, it is at any rate a common enough view that scientific laws are descriptive generalizations with predictive force and that they are synthetic propositions and therefore contingent. Further, we are all aware of the claim, based on Heisenberg's principle of uncertainty, that universal determinism has been disproved on the sub-atomic level. To be sure, it is not everyone who would admit that all propositions which are informative about reality are contingent.[1] Nor would everyone agree that universal determinism has in fact been disproved. The relevant point however is that a good deal of what Boutroux says about the contingency of the laws of nature represents lines of thought which are common enough today. For the matter of that, his anti-reductionism and his claim that there are qualitatively different kinds or levels of being do not appear startling. Obviously, talk about lower and higher levels of being is likely to elicit the comment that judgments of value are being made. But when Boutroux maintains that science takes the form of the sciences and that we cannot reduce all the other sciences to mathematical physics, most people would agree with him.

Boutroux is not however concerned simply with philosophy of science for its own sake. When, for example, he insists on the contingent character of the laws of nature and maintains that they cannot be reduced to and derived from an absolutely necessary truth, he is not simply pursuing an inquiry into the logical status of scientific laws. He is doing this of course; but he is also illustrating what for him are the limitations of science, with a view to arguing that there is room for a religious metaphysics which satisfies reason's demand for a unified and harmonious world-outlook. In the programme for the Gifford Lectures he remarks that 'in a general manner, science is a system of symbols with the task of providing us with a convenient and usable representation of realities which we cannot know directly. Now the existence and properties of these symbols can be explained only in terms of the original activity of the spirit.'[2] Similarly, in *Science and Religion* Boutroux asserts that science, so far from being something stamped by things on a passive intelligence, is 'an *ensemble* of symbols imagined by the mind in order to interpret things by means of pre-existent notions . . .'.[3] Science in its developed state does not presuppose a metaphysics;[4] but it does presuppose the creative activity of the mind or spirit or reason. The life of the spirit takes

---

[1] It would be claimed by some that there can be and are what, in Kantian terminology, would be classified as synthetic *a priori* propositions.
[2] *La nature et l'esprit*, p. 27. The words 'destiné à nous procurer' have been translated as 'having the task of providing us'.
[3] *Science and Religion in Contemporary Philosophy*, translated by J. Nield (London, 1909), p. 249.
[4] Cf. *La nature et l'esprit*, p. 15.

the form of scientific reason; but this is not the only form which it takes. The life of the spirit is something much wider, including morality, art and religion. The development therefore of the scientific use of reason, which 'seeks to systematize things from an impersonal standpoint',[1] does not exclude a 'subjective systematization',[2] based on the concept of the value of the person and on reflection on the life of the spirit in its various forms, a reflection which produces its own symbolic expression.

As Boutroux was a pupil of Lachelier, it is not surprising if we can see in his ideas about the limitations of science a certain measure of Kantian influence. His view of metaphysics however seems to have some affinity with that of Maine de Biran. For example, while allowing of course for psychology as a science, he suggests that 'it is impossible to find ·real frontiers between psychology and metaphysics'.[3] Similarly, 'metaphysics, to be legitimate and fruitful, must proceed not from outside to the inside, but from within outwards.'[4] He does not mean that metaphysics, 'an original activity of spirit,'[5] is science, whether psychology or otherwise, transformed into metaphysics. For a science which tries to convert itself into metaphysics is unfaithful to its own nature and aims. Boutroux means that metaphysics is spirit's reflection on its own life, which is considered in psychology from a scientific point of view but which overflows, as it were, the limits placed by this point of view.

In his general view of the universe Boutroux sees the world as a series of levels of being. A higher level is not deducible from a lower level: there is the emergence of novelty, of qualitative difference. At the same time heterogeneity and discontinuity are not the only features of the world. There is also continuity. For we can see a creative teleological process at work, a striving upwards towards an ideal. Thus Boutroux does not assert a rigid distinction between the inanimate and animate levels. There is spontaneity even at the level of so-called 'dead matter'. Moreover, in a manner reminiscent of Ravaisson, Boutroux suggests that 'animal instinct, life, physical and mechanical forces are, as it were, habits that have penetrated more and more deeply into the spontaneity of being. Hence these habits have become almost unconquerable. Seen from without, they appear as necessary laws.'[6]

[1] *Science and Religion*, p. 365.   [2] *Ibid.*, p. 365.
[3] *La nature et l'esprit*, p. 15.   [4] *Ibid.*, p. 37.   [5] *Ibid.*, p. 37.
[6] *The Contingency of the Laws of Nature*, p. 192.

At the human level we find conscious love and pursuit of the ideal, a love which is at the same time a drawing or attracting by the divine ideal which in this way manifests its existence. Religion, 'a synthesis—or, rather, a close and spiritual union—of instinct and intellect,'[1] offers man 'a richer and deeper life'[2] than the life of mere instinct or routine or imitation or the life of the abstract intellect. It is not so much a case of reconciling science and religion, considered as sets of theories or doctrines, as of reconciling the scientific and the religious spirits. For even if we can show that religious doctrines do not contradict scientific laws or hypotheses, this may leave unaffected the impression of an irreconcilable conflict between the scientific and religious spirits and attitudes. Reason however can strive to bring them together and to fashion, from their union, a being richer and more harmonious than either of them taken apart.[3] This union remains an ideal goal; but we can see that the religious life which, in its intense form, is always mysticism, has a positive value inasmuch as it lies 'at the heart of all the great religious, moral, political and social movements of humanity'.[4]

Bergson was a student for a while at the École Normale at Paris while Boutroux was teaching there. And the latter's *Contingency of the Laws of Nature* certainly exercised an influence on his mind, even if the degrèe of influence should not be exaggerated. In any case it is clear that Bergson carried on and developed some of Boutroux's ideas, though it does not necessarily follow of course that he actually derived them directly from this source.

5. Boutroux was clearly a resolute opponent not of course of science but of scientism and of positivist naturalism. When we turn to Alfred Fouillée (1838–1912), who lectured at the École Normale at Paris from 1872 to 1875,[5] we find him adopting a more eclectic attitude and envisaging a harmonization between the valuable and true ideas in the positivist and naturalist line of thought on the one hand and the idealist and spiritualist traditions on the other. The conclusions to which Fouillée came place him definitely within the spiritualist movement; but his intention was to effect a reconciliation between different currents of thought.

---

[1] *Science and Religion*, p. 378.   [2] *Ibid.*, p. 378.   [3] *Ibid.*, p. 400.
[4] *Ibid.*, p. 397. Boutroux is referring to active mysticism', not to what he describes as 'an abstract and barren form of mysticism' (*ibid.*).
[5] Before joining the staff of the École Normale Fouillée had been a professor in schools (*lycées*) at Douai and Montpellier and at the University of Bordeaux. He retired from the École Normale for reasons of health.

In spite of this ecumenical attitude, recalling Leibniz's notion that all systems were right in what they affirmed and wrong in what they denied, Fouillée was polemically inclined. In particular he attacked the philosophy of evolution as presented by Herbert Spencer and the epiphenomenalist theory of consciousness defended by T. H. Huxley.[1] Fouillée did not attack the idea of evolution as such. On the contrary, he accepted it. What he objected to was Spencer's attempt to account for the movement of evolution in purely mechanistic terms, which seemed to him a very limited and one-sided view of the matter. For the mechanistic conception of the world was, in Fouillée's opinion, a human construction; and the concept of force on which Spencer laid such emphasis was a projection of man's inner experience of effort and volitional activity. As for the epiphenomenalist theory of consciousness, this was irreconcilable with the active power of the mind and the evident fact of its ability to initiate movement and action. It was not necessary to follow the idealists in regarding thought as the one reality in order to see that in the process of evolution consciousness had to be taken into account as an effective contributing factor. It was *sui generis* and irreducible to physical processes.

In defence and explanation of his insistence on the effective causal activity of consciousness Fouillée proposed the theory which is especially associated with his name, namely the theory of what he called *idée-force* or thought-force. Every idea[2] is a tendency to action or the beginning of an action.[3] It tends to self-realization or self-actualization and is thus a cause. Even if it is itself caused, it is also a cause which can initiate movement and through physical action affect the external world. We are thus not faced with the problem of finding an additional link between the world of ideas and the world of physical objects. For an idea is itself a link, in the sense that it has the active tendency to self-realization. It is a mistake to regard ideas simply as representations or reflections of external things. They have a creative aspect. And as they are of course mental phenomena, to say that they exercise causal force is to say that the mind

[1] T. H. Huxley certainly proposed an epiphenomalist theory of consciousness. But he insisted that he had no intention of identifying mental activity with the physical processes on which it was dependent; and he rejected the label 'materialist'. Cf. Volume 8 of this *History*, pp. 104–7.

[2] For Fouillée an idea is a consciously conceived idea.

[3] We can compare this thesis with Josiah Royce's notion of the 'internal meaning' of an idea, described by him as 'the partial fulfilment of a purpose'. See Volume 8 of this *History*, pp. 270–3.

exercises causal activity. In this case it cannot be a mere epiphenomenon, passively dependent on physical organization and processes.

In his work on freedom and determinism (*La liberté et le déterminisme*, 1872) he uses the theory of *idées-forces* in an attempt to effect a reconciliation between the partisans of freedom and the determinists. At first he gives the impression of allying himself with the determinists, inasmuch as he subjects to criticism the views defended by such defenders of human liberty as Cournot, Renouvier and Lachelier. He rejects liberty of indifference as a misguided notion, refuses to associate freedom with the idea of chance, dismisses Renouvier's contention that determinism implies the human being's passivity, and expresses agreement with Taine's questioning of the theory that determinism deprives moral values of all significance. In Fouillée's opinion determinism does not necessarily imply that because something is all that it can be, it is 'thereby all that it should be'.[1]

Though however Fouillée is not prepared to make the sort of forthright attack on determinism which was characteristic of the spiritualist current of thought, he points out that even determinists have to find room for the idea of freedom. He then proceeds to argue that though a psychological explanation of the idea of freedom can be offered, this idea is an *idée-force* and thus tends to realize itself. The idea of freedom is certainly effective in life; and the stronger it becomes, the freer we are. In other words, even if the genesis of the *idée-force* can be explained on determinist lines, once it is formed it exercises a directive power or causal activity. It can obviously be objected that Fouillée reconciles determinism with libertarianism by the simple expedient of equating freedom with the idea or feeling of freedom. And he does indeed speak as though the two were the same. But he seems to mean that when we act in the consciousness of freedom, for example, in striving after the realization of moral ideals, our actions express our personalities as human beings, and that this is the real significance of freedom. With the idea of freedom we act in a specific way; and there can be no doubt that such action can be effective.

Fouillée developed his theory of *idées-forces* in works such as *The Evolution of Thought-Forces* (*L'évolutionisme des idées-forces*, 1890), *The Psychology of Thought-Forces* (*La psychologie des*

---

[1] *La liberté et le déterminisme* (4th edition), p. 51.

idées-forces, 2 volumes, 1893) and *The Ethics of Thought-Forces* (*La morale des idées-forces*, 1908). This last-named book elicited praise from Bergson, not least because in it Fouillée argued that consciousness of one's own existence is inseparable from consciousness of the existence of others, and that the attribution of value to oneself implies the attribution of value to other persons. Fouillée's ethical theory was characterized by a conviction in the attractive power of ideals, especially those of love and fraternity or brotherhood, and by belief in the growth of an inter-personal consciousness with common ideals as a principle of action.

It is interesting to note that Fouillée claimed to have anticipated Bergson (and Nietzsche) in holding that movement is real. In his opinion the associationist psychologists, for example, were deceived by the artifice of language and broke up movement into successive discrete states, which might be compared to instantaneous photographs of waves.[1] In Fouillée's terminology, they retained the terms but omitted the relations and so failed to grasp the current of life, of which we have the feeling in, say, the experiences of enjoyment, suffering and wishing. Though however Fouillée was prepared to speak of the grasping or consciousness of duration, he was not prepared to accept Bergson's theory of an intuition of pure duration. In a letter to Augustin Guyau he remarked that in his opinion pure duration was a limiting concept and not an object of intuition.

6. Augustin Guyau was the son of Fouillée's stepson, Marie Jean Guyau (1854–88), who was a professor at the Lycée Condorcet for a short while during the period when Bergson was a pupil at the school. As his dates show, M. J. Guyau's life was a short one; but he made his mark by a series of publications. His first two works were *La morale d'Épicure et ses rapports avec les doctrines contemporaines* (*The Ethics of Epicurus and Its Relations to Contemporary Doctrines*) and *La morale anglaise contemporaine* (*Contemporary English Ethics*), which appeared respectively in 1878 and 1879. He also wrote on aesthetics in *Problèmes de l'esthétique contemporaine* (1884, *Problems of Contemporary Aesthetics*) and in the posthumously published (1889) *L'art au point de vue sociologique* (*Art from the Sociological Point of View*). He is best known however for his *Esquisse d'une morale sans obligation ni sanction*[2] and

---

[1] *La psychologie des idées-forces*, II, p. 85.
[2] Translated by G. Kapteyn as *A Sketch of Morality Independent of Obligation or Sanction* (London, 1898).

L'irréligion de l'avenir.[1] Published respectively in 1885 and 1887 these books were known and esteemed by Nietzsche. *Education et hérédité*[2] was published posthumously in 1889, while *La genèse de l'idée de temps* (*The Origin of the Idea of Time*) appeared in 1890 and was reviewed by Bergson.[3]

To a certain extent M. J. Guyau agrees with his stepfather's theory of *idées-forces*. Thought is directed to action, and it is through action that 'those problems to which abstract thought gives rise'[4] are solved, in part even if not completely. But the relation of thought to action expresses something deeper and more universal, namely the creative movement of life. This idea should not indeed be understood in a theistic sense. The background of Guyau's philosophy was formed by the concept of an evolving universe, without any doctrine of a supernatural cause or creator of the universe. He looked on evolution however as the process by which life comes into being and in its creative activity brings forth successively higher forms. Consciousness is simply 'a luminous point in the great obscure sphere of life'.[5] It presupposes intuitive action, which expresses an infra-conscious will-to-live. If therefore we mean by 'ideas' ideas at the level of consciousness, their relation to action is the form taken at a particular level by the dynamism of life, its creative activity. 'Life is fecundity';[6] but it has no end save its own maintenance and intensification. The Bergsonian emphasis on becoming, life and the *élan vital* are already present in Guyau's thought, but without that belief in a creative God which was to become, eventually at any rate, a marked feature of Bergson's philosophy.

It is in terms of the concept of life that Guyau develops his ethical theory. In his opinion attempts to give morality a firm theoretical basis have been unsuccessful. We cannot find the required basis simply in the abstract concept of obligation. For this by itself provides us with little guidance. Further, people have felt under a moral obligation to pursue lines of conduct which we at any rate regard as immoral or as irrational. If however the Kantian type of morality will not do, neither will hedonism or utilitarianism. It is of course an empirical fact that human beings

[1] Translated as *The Non-Religion of the Future* (London, 1897) and reprinted at New York in 1962.
[2] Translated by W. J. Greenstreet as *Education and Heredity* (London, 1891).
[3] Guyau's essay on time first appeared in 1885 in the *Revue philosophique*. The posthumous republication (of an extended manuscript) by A. Fouillée was reviewed by Bergson in the *Revue philosophique* for 1891.
[4] *Esquisse*, p. 250.   [5] *Ibid.*, p. 10.   [6] *Ibid.*, p. 24.

tend to pursue what they have found to be pleasurable activities and to avoid what they have experienced as painful. But a much more fundamental tendency or urge is that of life to expand and intensify itself, a tendency which operates not only at the conscious but also at the infra-conscious and instinctive level. 'The end which in fact determines all conscious action is also the cause which produces all unconscious action; it is life itself. . . .'[1] Life, which by its nature strives to maintain, intensify and expand itself, is both the cause and the end of all action, whether instinctive or conscious. And ethics should be concerned with the means to the intensification and self-expansion of life.

The expansion of life is interpreted by Guyau largely in social terms. That is to say, the moral ideal is to be found in human cooperation, altruism, love and brotherhood, not in self-isolation and egoism. To be as social as one can is the authentic moral imperative. It is true that the idea of the intensification and expansion of life, when taken by itself, may appear to authorize, and indeed does authorize, actions which according to conventional moral standards are regarded as immoral. But for Guyau an important factor in human progress is the pursuit of truth and intellectual advance, and in his opinion intellectual development tends to inhibit purely instinctive and animal-like behaviour. The pursuit of truth however should go hand in hand with pursuit both of the good, especially in the form of human brotherhood, and of the beautiful. It can be added that the pleasures accompanying man's higher activities are precisely those which can most be shared in common. My enjoyment, for example, of a work of art does not deprive anyone else of a similar enjoyment.

Not only morality but also religion is interpreted by Guyau in terms of the concept of life. Religion as an historical phenomenon was largely social in character; and the idea of God was a projection of man's social consciousness and life. As man's moral consciousness developed, his concept of God changed too, from that of a capricious despot to that of a loving Father. But religion was throughout clearly linked with man's social life, expressing it and contributing to maintain it. Though however Guyau regards the idea of God as mythical, the title of his book *L'irréligion de l'avenir* is somewhat misleading. By 'religion' he means primarily acceptance of unverifiable dogmas imposed by religious organizations. A religion means for him an organized religious system.

[1] *Ibid.*, p. 87.

In his view religion in this sense is disappearing and ought to disappear, inasmuch as it inhibits the intensification and expansion of life, intellectual life for example. But he does not envisage the disappearance of religious feeling, nor of the ethical idealism which was a feature of the higher religions. For the matter of that, Guyau does not call for the rooting out of all religious beliefs in the ordinary sense. The attempt to destroy all religious belief is for him as misguided and fanatical as the attempt to impose such beliefs. Even if ethical idealism is in itself sufficient, there are likely to be in the future as in the past people with definite religious beliefs. If such beliefs are the spontaneous expression, as it were, of the personalities of those who accept them and are embraced as hypotheses which seem reasonable to the believer, well and good, provided that no attempt is made to impose such beliefs on others. In other words, the religion of the future will be a purely personal matter, something distinct from the transformation of 'religion' into freely embraced and commonly recognized ethical values.

Guyau has been compared with Nietzsche. He has also been described as a positivist. As for the first point, there is obviously some affinity between the two philosophers, inasmuch as each expounds a philosophy of the intensification of life and of ascending life. Equally obviously however, there are important differences. Guyau's insistence on human solidarity and brotherhood is markedly different from Nietzsche's insistence on rank and diversification. As for positivism, there are certainly positivist and naturalistic features in Guyau's thought. But his ethical idealism comes to occupy the centre of the stage. In any case, even if it may seem odd, from some points of view, to include Guyau among representatives of the 'spiritualist' movement, he has in common with them a firm belief in human liberty and in the emergence of what is new in the process of evolution; and his philosophy of life clearly has a place in the line of thought of which Bergson is the best known exponent.[1]

---

[1] The precise relationship between Guyau and Bergson is none too clear. For instance, though Guyau's treatment of time is psychological and less metaphysical than Bergson's, there are certain phrases which appear also in pretty well the same form in Bergson's writings. Bergson however maintained that when Fouillée prepared Guyau's work for posthumous publication, he introduced phrases taken from his own (Bergson's) *Time and Free Will*.

CHAPTER IX

HENRI BERGSON (1)

Life and works—Bergson's idea of philosophy—Time and freedom—Memory and perception: the relation between spirit and matter—Instinct, intelligence and intuition in the context of the theory of evolution.

1. HENRI Bergson (1859–1941) was born at Paris and studied at the Lycée Condorcet. He was attracted, as he himself relates, both to mathematics and to letters; and when he finally opted for the latter, his professor of mathematics visited his parents to expostulate. On leaving the lycée in 1878 Bergson became a student of the École Normale. During the period 1881–97 he taught successively in lycées at Angers, Clermont-Ferrand[1] and Paris. From 1897 until 1900 he was a professor at the École Normale, and from 1900 until 1924[2] at the Collège de France, where his lectures attracted hearers even from the non-academic and fashionable world of Paris.[3] Already a member of the Institute and of the Academy of Moral and Political Sciences, he was elected to the French Academy in 1914 and received the Nobel prize for literature in 1928.

After the first world war Bergson was active in the work of promoting international understanding, and for a time he was chairman of the committee for intellectual cooperation established by the League of Nations, until bad health forced him to retire. In the final year of his life Bergson came very close to the Catholic Church, and in his testament he said that he would have become a Catholic, had it not been for his desire not to separate himself from his fellow-Jews during their persecution by the Nazis.[4]

---

[1] At Clermont-Ferrand Bergson also lectured in the University.

[2] In 1921 reasons of health compelled Bergson to consign his lecturing work to Édouard Le Roy, who succeeded formally to Bergson's chair in 1924. In 1891 Bergson had married a cousin of Marcel Proust, Louise Neuberger.

[3] It is said that in order to attend Bergson's lectures hearers found themselves driven to sit through the preceding lecture.

[4] In point of fact Bergson's name appears to have been included in the list of eminent Frenchmen who were not to be molested on the German occupation of France.

Bergson's first well known work was his *Essai sur les données immédiates de la conscience*, which appeared in 1889. Its subject-matter is perhaps better indicated by the title given to the English translation, *Time and Free Will*.[1] This work was followed in 1896 by *Matière et mémoire*[2] which gave Bergson the occasion for a more general treatment of the relation between mind and body. In 1900 Bergson published *Le rire*,[3] and in 1903 his *Introduction à la métaphysique* appeared in the *Revue de la métaphysique et de morale*.[4] His most famous work *L'évolution créatrice*[5] appeared in 1907, and this was followed by *L'énergie spirituelle*[6] in 1910 and *Durée et simultanéité*.[7] In 1932 Bergson published his notable work on morals and religion, *Les deux sources de la morale et de la religion*.[8] A collection of essays entitled *La pensée et le mouvant*[9] followed in 1934. Three volumes of *Écrits et paroles* were edited by R. M. Mossé-Bastide and published at Paris in 1957–59, with a preface by Édouard Le Roy. The centenary edition of Bergson's works appeared in 1959.

2. Although Bergson once had a great name, his use of imagery and metaphor, his sometimes rather high-flown or rhapsodic style, and a certain lack of precision in his thought have contributed to his being depreciated as a philosopher by those who equate philosophy with logical or conceptual analysis and who attach great value to precision of thought and language. Obviously, this is true in the first place of countries in which the analytic movement has prevailed, and where the tendency has been to look on Bergson as more of a poet or even a mystic than as a serious philosopher. In some other countries, including his own, he has fallen into neglect for another reason, namely the eclipse of the philosophy of life by existentialism and phenomenology.

---

[1] Translated by F. L. Pogson (London and New York, 1910).

[2] Translated by N. M. Paul and W. S. Palmer as *Matter and Memory* (London and New York, 1911).

[3] Translated by G. C. Brereton and F. Rothwell as *Laughter, An Essay on the Meaning of the Comic* (New York, 1910).

[4] Translated by T. E. Hulme as *An Introduction to Metaphysics* (London and New York, 1912).

[5] Translated by A. Mitchell as *Creative Evolution* (London and New York, 1911).

[6] Translated by H. Wildon Carr as *Mind-Energy* (London and New York, 1910).

[7] Second edition, with three appendices, 1923.

[8] Translated by R. A. Audra and C. Brereton, with the assistance of W. Horsfall-Carter, as *The Two Sources of Morality and Religion* (London and New York, 1935).

[9] Translated by M. L. Andison as *The Creative Mind* (New York, 1946).

It may be true to say that in recent years the stir caused by the writings of Teilhard de Chardin has led to some revival of interest in Bergson, in view of the affinities between the two thinkers. But though the vogue enjoyed by Teilhard de Chardin and recognition of the relationship between him and his predecessor Bergson may have tended to make the latter's thought seem more actual and relevant, they do little to mitigate the force of objections brought by logical or conceptual analysts against Bergson's style of philosophizing. For similar objections can obviously be levelled against Teilhard de Chardin.

The accusations brought against Bergson's way of philosophizing are certainly not groundless. At the same time it is only fair to him to emphasize the fact that he was not trying to accomplish the sort of task to which logical analysts devote themselves, but failing signally to do so. He had his own idea of the nature and function of philosophy; and his way of philosophizing, and even his style, were connected with this idea. It is thus appropriate to begin by giving a brief explanation of his concept of philosophy.

In an essay which he wrote specially for the collection entitled *La pensée et le mouvant* Bergson began by asserting, perhaps somewhat surprisingly, that 'what has been most wanting in philosophy, is precision'.[1] What he had in mind were the shortcomings, as he saw them, of philosophical systems, which are 'not tailored to the reality in which we live'[2] but which are so abstract and vast as to try to comprise everything, the actual, the possible 'and even the impossible'[3]. It seemed to him at first that the philosophy of Herbert Spencer was an exception, inasmuch as, in spite of some vague generalities, it bore the imprint of the actual world and was modelled on the facts. At the same time Spencer had not delved deeply enough into the basic ideas of mechanics; and Bergson resolved to complete this work. In the course however of trying to do so he found himself brought to consider the subject of time. He was impelled to distinguish between the mathematical time of the scientist, in which time is broken up into moments and conceived in a spatial manner, and 'real' time, pure duration, continuity, which we can grasp in inner experience but can conceptualize only with difficulty.

Bergson therefore comes to conceive of philosophy or metaphysics as based on intuition, which he contrasts with analysis.

---

[1] *La pensée et le mouvant*, p. 7 (3rd edition, 1934).
[2] *Ibid.*, p. 7.   [3] *Ibid.*, p. 7.

By analysis he means the reduction of the complex to its simple constituents, as when a physical object is reduced to molecules, to atoms and finally to sub-atomic 'particles' or as when a new idea is explained in terms of a new arrangement of ideas which we already possess. By intuition he means the 'immediate consciousness'[1] or direct awareness of a reality. Bergson also contrasts the symbolization which is required by analytic thought with intuitive freedom from symbolization.[2] Even if however the intuitive perception of a reality may, in itself, be unexpressed in linguistic symbols, there can obviously be no philosophy without conceptualization and language. Bergson is of course well aware of this fact. An effort of reflection[3] is required to grasp the content of an intuition and to appreciate its significance and illuminative bearing. The idea which expresses an intuition seemes at first to be obscure rather than clear; and though appropriate terms, such as 'real duration', can be employed, the linguistic expression will not really be understood unless one participates in the intuition. The philosopher should indeed strive after clarity; but he cannot achieve this unless intuition and expression go, as it were, hand in hand or unless symbolization is checked by a return to intuitive awareness of what the philosopher is speaking about. Further, images may have a useful role to play by suggesting the content of an intuition and facilitating a participation in it[4].

It is all very well to say that philosophy is based on intuition. What is the object of such intuition? A general answer might be that it is movement, becoming, duration, that which can be known only through immediate or intuitive awareness, and not through a reductive analysis which distorts it or destroys its continuity. To say this is to say (within the framework of Bergson's thought) that the object of intuition is reality. For in the second of his Oxford Conferences he makes the often quoted statement that 'there are changes, but there are not, under the change, things

---

[1] *La pensée et le mouvant*, p. 35.   [2] Cf. *ibid.*, p. 206.

[2] When replying to critics who interpret intuition as consisting in hunches or feelings, Bergson says that 'our intuition is reflection' (*Ibid.*, p. 109). At first hearing at any rate this sounds like a contradiction in terms. But he may be thinking in part of the 'reflection' of Maine de Biran, the immediate awareness by the self of its inner life, reflexive psychology in other words. In any case, even if intuition itself is not reflection, Bergson certainly thinks of the philosopher's mind as appropriating the intuition, so to speak, through a process of reflection which tries to keep as close as possible to the intuition.

[4] In the case of exceptional intuitions, such as those enjoyed by the mystics, the use of imagery may be the most appropriate way of trying to convey some idea of the intuitions or experiences.

which change: change has no need of a support. There are movements, but there is no inert, invariable object which moves: movement does not imply a *mobile*.[1] In the first instance however the object of intuition is, as with Maine de Biran, the inner life of the self, of the spirit. Bergson remarks, for example, that existence is only given in experience. He then goes on to say that 'this experience will be called sight or contact, exterior perception in general, if it is a question of a material object: it will have the name "intuition" when it bears on the spirit'.[2] It is true that according to Bergson his first concern is with real duration. But he finds this in the life of the self, in 'the direct vision of the spirit by the spirit',[3] in the interior life.

Bergson can thus maintain that while positive science is concerned with the material world, metaphysics 'reserves for itself the spirit'.[4] This may seem to be patently untrue, given the existence of psychology. For Bergson however psychology as a science treats the spirit or mind as if it were material. That is to say, it analyses the life of the mind in such a way as to represent it on an analogy with spatial and material objects. The empirical psychologist does not necessarily assert that mental phenomena are material. But he extends reductive analysis from physical objects to the mind and considers it as something over against himself. The metaphysician however takes as his point of departure an intuitive or immediate awareness of the inner life of the spirit as it is lived; and he tries to prolong this intuition in his reflection.

Science and metaphysics therefore have different objects or subject-matters according to Bergson. He assigns 'matter to science and spirit to metaphysics'.[5] It is thus clear enough that he does not regard philosophy as a synthesis of the particular sciences. There is no question of claiming that philosophy can 'go beyond science in the generalization of the same facts'.[6] Philosophy 'is not a synthesis of the particular sciences'.[7] The objects of science and philosophy are different. So too are their methods.

---

[1] *La pensée et le mouvant*, p. 185. Bergson does not mean that there is no existing reality. His contention is that reality is a becoming, the past persisting in the present, and the present being carried into the future, the whole process being continuous throughout and divisible only through the artificial separation effected by the intelligence for its own purposes.
[2] *Ibid.*, p. 61.   [3] *Ibid.*, p. 35.
[4] *Ibid.*, p. 50. Bergson's use of the word 'metaphysics' in this context recalls to mind the use made of the term by Maine de Biran.
[5] *Ibid.*, p. 54.   [6] *Ibid.*, p. 155.   [7] *Ibid.*, p. 156.

For science is the work of the intelligence and works by analysis, whereas metaphysics is, or is based on and draws its life from, intuition.

To say however that science and metaphysics differ from one another in subject-matter and method is by no means the whole of the story. For in Bergson's view reality is change or becoming, real duration or the life of the spirit; and the material world of the physicist is regarded, by an extension of Ravaisson's theory of habit, as a kind of deposit made by the movement of life in its creative advance. If therefore we ask whether it is science or metaphysics which reveals reality to us, the answer must be that it is metaphysics. For it is only in intuition that the mind can have direct awareness of the actual movement of life.

Bergson endeavours to show that he is not concerned with depreciating science, nor with suggesting that the philosopher can profitably dismiss the findings of the scientist. He explains, for example, that when he insists on the difference between the positive sciences and philosophy he is concerned with the purification of science from 'scientism', from a metaphysics, that is to say, which masquerades as positive scientific knowledge, and with freeing philosophy from any misconception of itself as a super-science, capable of doing the scientist's work for him or of providing generalizations from the data of science which the scientist is unable to provide. Referring to accusations against him of being an opponent of science, Bergson remarks 'once again, we wanted a philosophy which would submit itself to the control of science and which could also contribute to its (science's) advance.'[1] The work of the intelligence is necessary for action; and science, the product of the intelligence, is required if man is to have conceptual and practical control of his environment. Moreover, science, Bergson suggests rather vaguely, can provide verification for metaphysics,[2] while metaphysics, as it is based on intuition of truth, can help science to correct its errors. While therefore they remain distinct, science and philosophy can cooperate; and neither of them should be depreciated. As they differ in subject-matter and method, disputes about relative dignity are otiose.

Obviously, Bergson is justified in emphasizing the need for the work of the intelligence, and so of science. To be sure, Bergson's ideas are by no means always clear and unambiguous. Sometimes, for example, he speaks as though the world of individual things,

---

[1] *Ibid.*, p. 82.   [2] *Ibid.*, p. 83.

of substances which change, is a fiction or fabrication of the intelligence. At other times he implies that in its individualizing activity the intelligence makes objectively grounded distinctions. His precise meaning is left obscure. At the same time it is obvious that we could not possibly live, in any recognizable sense of 'live', simply with the consciousness of a continuous flow of becoming. We could not live and act without a world of distinct things. And we could not understand and control this world without science. Hence Bergson is quite justified in claiming that he has no intention of attacking science as a superfluity. When all this is said however, it remains true that for him it is intuition, not intelligence, and metaphysics rather than science, which reveals to us the nature of reality, underlying the constructed, even if necessarily constructed, world of the scientist. And when Bergson speaks about metaphysics submitting itself to the control of science, he really means that in his view modern science is developing in such a way as to confirm rather than to falsify his philosophical theories. In other words, if we assume the truth of Bergson's position, it seems to follow that in important respects metaphysics must be superior to science, however much Bergson may have tried to disclaim such judgments of value.

Reference has already been made to Bergson's negative attitude to philosophical systems. It is hardly necessary to say that he has no liking for attempts to deduce the structure of reality *a priori* from allegedly self-evidently true propositions. A man who believes that 'philosophy has never frankly admitted this continuous creation of unforeseeable novelty'[1] is obviously not disposed to look with favour on any system of a Spinozistic type. Indeed, Bergson explicitly disclaims the intention of constructing any sort of comprehensive system. What he does is to consider distinct questions in succession, reflecting on the data in various areas.[2] Some of the questions which have seemed of great importance to metaphysical philosophers are dismissed by Bergson as pseudo-problems. 'Why is there something rather than nothing?' and 'Why is there order rather than disorder?' are given as examples of pseudo-problems or at any rate of badly formulated questions.[3] In view of his reputation for high-flown poetry or imaginative

---

[1] *Ibid.*, p. 132.
[2] In an interview (*Mercure de France*, 1914, p. 397) Bergson asserted that he did not know in advance to what conclusions his premises would lead.
[3] *La pensée et le mouvant*, pp. 121 f.

and imprecise language, it is only fair to Bergson to emphasize the fact that he intends to be as concrete and as faithful as possible to reality as experienced. It is true that a more or less unified world-outlook emerges from his successive writings. But this is due to a convergence of his various lines of thought rather than to any deliberate attempt to construct a comprehensive system. There are of course certain recurrent and pervasive key-ideas, such as intuition and duration; but they are not postulated in advance like the premises of a deductive system.

When Bergson is treating of the mental life, there is no great difficulty in understanding what he means by intuition, even if one does not care for the term. It is equivalent to the immediate consciousness of Maine de Biran. When however Bergson turns to a general theory of evolution, as in *L'évolution créatrice*, it is not so easy to see how this theory can be said to be based on intuition. Even if we are immediately aware of a vital impetus or *élan vital* in ourselves, a good deal of extrapolation is required in order to make this intuition the basis for a general view of evolution. The philosophy of *l'esprit* becomes very much wider in its scope than any kind of reflexive psychology. However there is not much point in trying to discuss such matters in advance of a treatment of Bergson's successive lines of inquiry.

3. In the preface to *Time and Free Will* Bergson announces his intention of trying to establish that 'every discussion between determinists and their opponents implies a previous confusion of duration with extension, of succession with simultaneity, of quality with quantity.'[1] Once this confusion has been cleared up, one may perhaps find that objections against freedom vanish, together with the definitions which have been given to it, and, 'in a certain sense, the very problem of free will'.[2] In this case Bergson has of course to explain the nature of the alleged confusion before going on to show how its dissipation affects determinism.

We conceive of physical objects, according to Bergson, as existing and occupying positions in 'an empty homogeneous medium',[3] namely space. And it is the concept of space which determines our ordinary idea of time, the concept of time as

---

[1] *Time and Free Will*, pp. xix–xx. References to this work are given to the English translation, for the convenience of the reader. But as I have myself translated from the French, there are slightly different wordings in places.
[2] *Ibid.*, p. xx.   [3] *Ibid.*, p. 95.

employed in the natural sciences and for purposes of practical life. That is to say, we conceive time according to the analogy of an unbounded line composed of units or moments which are external to one another. This idea gives rise to the sort of puzzles raised centuries ago by Zeno.[1] But it enables us to measure time and to fix the occurrence of events, as simultaneous or as successive, within the time-medium, which is itself empty and homogeneous, like space. This concept of time is in fact the spatialized or mathematicized idea of duration. Pure duration, of which we can become intuitively or immediately aware in consciousness of our own inner mental life, when, that is to say, we enter into it in depth, is a series of qualitative changes melting into and permeating one another, so that each 'element' represents the whole, like a musical phrase, and is an isolated unit not in reality but only through intellectual abstraction. Pure duration is a continuity of movement, with qualitative but not quantitative differentiations. It can thus be described as heterogeneous, not as homogeneous. Language however 'demands that we should establish between our ideas the same clear and precise distinctions, the same discontinuity, as between material objects'.[2] Discursive thought and language require that we should break up the uninterrupted flow of consciousness[3] into distinct and numerable states, succeeding one another in time, represented as a homogeneous medium. This concept of time however is 'only the ghost of space haunting the reflective consciousness',[4] whereas pure duration is 'the form taken by the succession of our states of consciousness when our ego lets itself live, when it abstains from making a separation between its present and preceding states'.[5] We can say in effect that the idea of pure duration expresses the nature of the life of the deeper self, while the concept of the self as a succession of states represents the superficial self, created by the spatializing intelligence. Pure duration is grasped in intuition, in which the self is coincident with its own life, whereas the self of analytic psychology is the result of our looking at ourselves as external spectators, as though we were looking at physical objects outside us.

Now suppose that we conceive the self as a succession of distinct

---

[1] As the individual units, which are conceived as constituting time in their succession, are 'virtual stoppages of time' (*La pensée et le mouvant*, p. 9).

[2] *Time and Free Will*, p. xix.

[3] To what extent Bergson was influenced by other writers, such as William James, is a matter of dispute.

[4] *Time and Freewill*, p. 99.   [5] *Ibid.*, p. 100.

states in spatialized time. It is then natural to think of a preceding state as causing the succeeding state. Further, feelings and motives will be regarded as distinct entities which cause or determine successive entities. This may sound far-fetched. But that this is not the case can be seen by reflecting on talk about motives determining choices. In such language motives are clearly hypostatized and given a substantial existence of their own. Bergson thus asserts a close link between determinism and the associationist psychology. And in his view no answer to determinism is possible, if the adequacy of this psychology is once assumed. For it makes little sense to picture one state of consciousness as oscillating between making two mutually exclusive choices and then opting for one choice when it might have opted for the other. If we once accept the associationist psychology as adequate, it is a waste of time to look for answers to determinism. We cannot refute the determinists on their own selected ground. What is needed is to challenge their whole concept of the self and its life. And, as Bergson sees things, this means setting the idea of pure duration against the spatialized or geometric concept of time. If time is assimilated to space and states of consciousness are conceived on an analogy with material objects, determinism is inevitable. If however the life of the self is seen in its continuity, its uninterrupted flow, it can also be seen that some acts spring from the totality, the whole personality; and these acts are free. 'We are free when our acts flow from our whole personality, when they express it, when they have with it that indefinable resemblance which one sometimes finds between the artist and his work.'[1]

Bergson thus carries on that insistence on human freedom which we find among his predecessors in the spiritualist movement. A good deal of what he has to say, especially by way of criticism or attack, is sensible enough. It is pretty clear, for example, that talk about a man's choices being determined by his motives is misleading, inasmuch as it suggests that a motive is a substantial entity which pushes a man, as though from without, into a certain course of action. Again, while character-determinism, as portrayed by writers such as J. S. Mill, can be made extremely plausible, talk about a man's actions being determined by his character implies that to the noun 'character' there corresponds a block-entity which exercises a one-way causal activity on the

---

[1] *Ibid.*, p. 172.

will. In general, Bergson's contention that the determinists, especially those who presuppose the associationist psychology, are held captive by a spatial picture is well argued.

It does not follow of course that Bergson is an upholder of 'liberty of indifference'. For as he conceives this theory, it involves the same sort of misleading picture which can be found with the determinists.[1] In Bergson's view 'any definition of freedom will ensure the victory of determinism'.[2] For a definition is the result of analysis, and analysis involves the transformation of a process into a thing and of duration into extension. Freedom is the indefinable 'relation of the concrete self to the act which it performs'.[3] It is something of which we are immediately aware, but it is not something which can be proved. For the attempt to prove it involves taking the very point of view which leads to determinism, the point of view from which time is identified with space or at any rate is interpreted in spatial terms.

Bergson does not of course maintain that all the actions performed by a human being are free actions. He distinguishes between 'two different selves, one of which is, as it were, the external projection of the other, its spatial and, so to speak, social representation'.[4] We are reminded here of Kant's distinction between the phenomenal and the noumenal self; but Kant is found fault with by Bergson for his account of time. For Bergson free acts are those which proceed from the self considered as pure duration. 'To act freely, is to regain possession of oneself, to get back into pure duration.'[5] But a great part of our lives is lived at the level of the superficial self, the level at which we are acted upon, by social pressure for instance, rather than act ourselves. And this is why we are rarely free.'[6] This theory may seem to enable Bergson to evade the awkward position of Kant, the notion, that is to say, that the same actions are determined from one point of view and free from another. Even for Bergson of course a free act, springing from the 'deeper' self or the whole personality, appears as determined if it is located, so to speak, in homogeneous and

---

[1] It implies, according to Bergson, the picture of the ego as traversing a number of distinct states and then as oscillating between two ready-made paths lying before it.
[2] *Time and Free Will*, p. 220.
[3] *Ibid.*, p. 219.
[4] *Ibid.*, p. 231.
[5] *Ibid.*, pp. 231-2.
[6] *Ibid.*, p. 231.

spatialized time. But he regards this point of view as erroneous, even if it is required for practical, social and scientific purposes. What Bergson has to say about the two levels of the self recalls to mind not only the Kantian philosophy but also the later existentialist distinction between authentic and inauthentic existence. There are of course considerable differences between the philosophy of Bergson and existentialism, as there are too between the various brands of existentialism. But it is not a question of representing existentialism as an historical development of the Bergsonian philosophy of life. Rather is it a matter of affinities. In the spiritualist movement and in existentialism too we can see an attack on 'scientism', showing itself in an insistence on human freedom and in an interpretation of freedom in terms of the idea of a deeper self of some kind. If we consider the philosophy of Karl Jaspers, we can see that his contention that if we adopt the position of external spectators, of the objectifying scientist, we cannot avoid an at any rate methodological determinism, whereas freedom is something of which the agent, as agent, is aware, is akin to the position of Bergson. The fact that the influences on Jaspers' thought were Kant, Kierkegaard and Nietzsche rather than Bergson does not alter the fact that there is some affinity between their lines of thought.

4. In *Matière et mémoire* Bergson tackles the problem of the relation between mind and body. In his introduction he says that the book asserts the reality of both spirit and matter, and that his position is thus frankly dualistic. It is true that he speaks of matter as an aggregate of images. But by using the word 'image' he does not mean to imply that a physical object exists only in the human mind. He means that an object is what we perceive it to be and not something entirely different. In the case of a red object, for instance, it is the object which is red. Redness is not something subjective. In fine, a physical object is 'an image, but an image which exists in itself'.[1] Among such physical objects there is one which I know not only by perception but also 'from within by affections. It is my body.'[2] What is the relation between my body and my mind? In particular, are mental processes identifiable with physical processes in the brain, so that talk about the former and talk about the latter are simply two languages or ways of

---

[1] *Matter and Memory*, p. viii. Page-references are given to the English translation, even when my own translation differs slightly.
[2] *Ibid.*, p. 1.

speaking which refer to the same thing? Or is the mind an epiphenomenon of the cerebral organism, so that it is completely and throughout dependent on the brain? To put the matter in another way, is the relation between mind and the brain of such a kind that anyone who had a complete knowledge of what was going on in the brain would thereby have a detailed knowledge of what was proceeding in consciousness?

Bergson remarks that 'the truth is that there would be one way, and one only, of refuting materialism, that of establishing that matter is absolutely what it appears to be.'[1] For if matter is nothing but what it appears to be, there is no reason for ascribing it to occult capacities such as thought. This is one reason why Bergson dwells at some length on the nature of matter. However, though what Bergson takes to be the position of common sense should suffice, philosophical reflection requires something more. And Bergson tackles his problem by means of a study of memory, on the ground that memory, as representing 'precisely the point of interaction between mind and matter',[2] seems to provide the strongest support for materialism and epiphenomenalism. A study of memory however involves also a study of perception, as perception is 'wholly impregnated with memory-images which complete it while interpreting it'.[3]

To cut a long story short, Bergson makes a distinction between two kinds of memory. In the first place there is the kind of memory which consists in motor-mechanisms which resemble or are habits. Thus one can learn by heart, as we say, a certain series of words, a lesson or a poem. And when the appropriate stimulus is provided, the mechanism starts to function. There is 'a closed system of automatic movements which succeed one another in the same order and occupy the same time'.[4] Memory in this sense of mechanical repetition is a bodily habit, like walking; considered precisely as such, it does not include mental representation of the past but is rather a bodily aptitude, an organic disposition to respond in a certain way to a certain stimulus. Memory in this sense is not confined to human beings. A parrot, for example, can be trained to respond to a stimulus by uttering certain words in succession. This kind of memory is different from what Bergson calls 'pure memory', which is representation and records 'all the events of our daily life',[5] neglecting no detail.

[1] *Ibid.*, p. 80.   [2] *Ibid.*, p. xii.   [3] *Ibid.*, p. 170.
[4] *Ibid.*, p. 90.   [5] *Ibid.*, p. 92.

Memory in this sense is spiritual, and to admit its existence is obviously to admit that part of the mind is infra-conscious. If the whole of my past is stored, as it were, in my mind in the form of memory-images, it is clear that only a few of these images are even recalled to consciousness at a given time. They must then be stored in the infra-conscious area of the mind. Indeed, if the whole of my past, including every detail, were present to my consciousness at once, action would become impossible. And here we have the key to the relation between the brain and pure memory. That is to say, the function of the brain, according to Bergson, is to inhibit the invasion of consciousness by the pure memory and to admit only those recollections which are related in some way to contemplated or required action. In itself pure memory is spiritual; but its contents are filtered, as it were, by the brain. Pure memory and memory as habit come together of course in practice, as in, for example, the intelligent repetition of something learned. But they should not be confused. For it is this confusion which leads support to materialism.

The concept of pure memory is linked by Bergson with that of pure duration. And he argues, with the help of a study of pathological phenomena such as aphasia, that there is no cogent evidence of memories being spatially located in the brain. In his view the brain is not a storehouse of memories but plays a role analogous to that of a telephone-exchange. If one could penetrate into the brain and see clearly all the processes taking place in it, all that one would find would probably be 'sketched-out or prepared movements'.[1] That is to say, the cerebral state represents only a small part of the mental state, namely 'that part which is capable of translating itself into movements of locomotion'.[2] In other words, Bergson tries to refute psycho-physical or psycho-neural parallelism by arguing that the state of the brain indicates that of the mind only in so far as the psychic life is turned towards action and is the remote beginning of or at least the preparation for action.

Perception, Bergson insists, is different in kind from recollection. In perception the perceived object is present as object of an intuition of the real, whereas in recollection an absent object is remembered. Though however perception is an intuition of the real, it is a mistake to suppose that perception as such is directed towards pure knowledge. On the contrary, it is 'entirely oriented

<hr />

[1] *Ibid.*, p. xiii.   [2] *Ibid.*, p. xiii.

towards action'.[1] That is to say, perception is basically selective with a view to possible action or reaction. It is utilitarian in character. At root, it concentrates on what can answer to a need or tendency. And we can assume that with animals perception is generally just this.[2] As we ascend the stages of the evolution of organic life, moving into the sphere of consciousness and freedom, the area of possible action and of the subjectivity of perception grows. But perception in itself, 'pure perception', is oriented to action. And it is not the same thing as memory. If our perceptions were all 'pure', simple intuitions of objects, the function of consciousness would be to unite them by means of memory. But this would not convert them into memories or acts of recollection.

In point of fact however pure perception is pretty well a limiting concept. 'Perception is never a simple contact of the mind with the present object. It is wholly impregnated with memory-images which complete it while interpreting it.'[3] Pure memory manifests itself in images; and these images enter into our perceptions. In theory we can distinguish between pure memory and pure perception. And for Bergson it is important that the distinction should be made. Otherwise, for instance, recollection will be interpreted as a weakened form of perception, when it is in fact different in kind and not simply in intensity. In practice however recollection and perception interpenetrate each other. In other words, perception in its concrete or actual form is a synthesis of pure memory and pure perception, and so 'of mind (*esprit*) and matter'.[4] In concrete perception the mind contributes memory-images which confer on the object of perception a completed and meaningful form. In Bergson's view this theory helps to overcome the opposition between idealism and realism and also throws light on the relation between mind or spirit and body. 'Mind (or spirit) borrows from matter the perceptions from which it draws its nourishment and restores them to matter in the form of movement on which it has stamped its own freedom.'[5] Pure perception

---

[1] *Ibid.*, p. 21.

[2] It may be objected that in the case of animals reference should be made to sensation rather than to perception. But Bergson is not prepared to regard sensation as more fundamental than perception. 'Our sensations are to our perceptions what the real action of our body is to its possible or virtual action' (*Ibid.*, p. 58). Virtual action precedes real action. A body's real action is manifested within itself in the form of affective sensations. A herbivorous animal, for instance, perceives grass. The nearer the grass is, the more does the virtual action prefigured in perception tend to become real action. Real action is of course accompanied by sensation.

[3] *Ibid.*, p. 170.   [4] *Ibid.*, p. 325.   [5] *Ibid.*, p. 332.

which, as a limiting concept, is the coincidence of subject and object, belongs to the side of matter. Pure memory, which exhibits real duration, belongs to the side of spirit. But memory, as a 'synthesis of the past and the present in view of the future',[1] brings together or unites the successive phases of matter to use them and to manifest itself by the actions which constitute the reason for the soul's union with the body. In Bergson's opinion spirit and matter, soul and body, are united for action; and this union is to be understood not in spatial terms[2] but in terms of duration.

As in the case of Bergson's other writings most readers of *Matière et mémoire* often find it difficult to make out his precise meaning. And they may well suspect that if they fail to find it, this is not their fault. However Bergson's general position can be summarized in this way. The body is 'an instrument of action, and of action only'.[3] Pure perception is virtual action, at any rate in the sense that it detaches from the field of objects the object which interests from the point of view of possible bodily action. 'The virtual action of things on our body and of our body on things is our perception itself.'[4] And the state of the brain corresponds exactly to the perception. Actual perception however is not 'pure perception' but is enriched and interpreted by memory which is in itself, as 'pure memory', 'something other than a function of the brain'.[5] Perception as we actually experience it therefore (impregnated, that is to say, with memory-images) is a point where spirit and matter, soul and body, intersect dynamically, in an orientation to action.[6] And while the 'pure perception' element corresponds exactly to the state of the brain or to processes in the brain, the 'pure memory' element does not. Spirit or mind is not in itself a function of the brain, nor an epiphenomenon; but as turned to action it depends on the body, the instrument of action, and virtual action, prefiguring or sketching out and preparing real action, is dependent on the brain. Damage to the brain may inhibit action; but it should not be thought of as destroying the mind or spirit in itself.[7]

---

[1] *Ibid.*, p. 294.
[2] This is said to be the mistake of 'ordinary dualism' (*ibid.*).
[3] *Ibid.*, p. 299.   [4] *Ibid.*, p. 309.   [5] *Ibid.*, p. 315.
[6] As mentioned above, memory is stated by Bergson to be the point of intersection. But we are speaking here of concrete and conscious perception, in which memory-images are always present, not of the limiting concept of pure perception.
[7] Bergson looks on this view not so much as a proof of immortality as removing a major obstacle to belief in it.

5. In *Time and Free Will* and *Matter and Memory* Bergson introduces his readers, in the contexts of particular problems, to his ideas of mathematical or spatialized time on the one hand and of pure duration on the other, of the analytical intelligence, dominated by the concept of space, on the one hand and of intuition on the other, of matter as the sphere of mechanism and of spirit as the sphere of creative freedom, of man as an agent rather than as a spectator and of the intelligence as serving the needs of action, even if man, through intuition, is capable of grasping the nature of becoming as manifested in his own inner life. In *Creative Evolution* he exhibits such ideas in a wider context.

The year of Bergson's birth, 1859, was the year in which *The Origin of Species* was published. Though however the theory of evolution in general permeated Bergson's thought, he found himself unable to accept any mechanistic interpretation of it, including Darwinism. The theory of 'natural selection', for example, in virtue of chance or random variations which adapt the organism for survival seemed to him quite inadequate. In the process of evolution we can see a development of complexity. But a higher degree of complexity involves a greater degree of risk. If survival-value were the only factor, one might expect evolution to stop with the simplest types of organism. As for chance or random variations, if these occurred in a part of a whole (such as the eye), the functioning of the whole might well be impeded. For the effective functioning of the whole there must be coordination or coadaptation; and to attribute this simply to 'chance' is to make too great a demand on credulity. At the same time an explanation of evolution in terms of finality seemed to Bergson unacceptable, if the idea of finality were taken to mean that the process of evolution was simply the working out or realization of a predetermined end. For this sort of theory eliminated all novelty and creativity and in some important respects resembled mechanism. It added of course the idea of a preconceived or predetermined end; but neither in the case of a mechanistic acconunt or in that of a teleological account[1] was any room left for the emergence of novelty.

In Bergson's view we are justified in looking to man's inner life

---

[1] The expression 'a teleological account' must be understood in the sense of an account of evolution which represents it as the progressive realization of a preconceived plan, the working out of a blueprint. Bergson is far from denying an immanent teleology in the organism. Nor does he exclude a general teleology which allows for the emergence of what is novel.

for the key to the evolution of life in general. In ourselves we are aware, or rather can be aware, of a vital impetus, an *élan vital*, manifested in the continuity of our own becoming or duration. As a speculative hypothesis at any rate we are justified in extrapolating this idea and postulating 'an *original impetus* of life, passing from one generation of germs to the following generation of germs by way of the developed organisms which form the uniting link between the generations of germs.'[1] This impetus is regarded by Bergson as the cause of variations, at any rate of those which are passed on, accumulate and produce new species.[2] Its mode of operation should not be regarded as analogous to that of the manufacturers who assemble ready-made parts to form a whole but rather as an organizing action[3] which proceeds from a centre outwards, effecting differentiation in the process. The *élan vital* encounters resistance from inert matter; and in its effort to overcome this resistance it tries fresh paths. In fact it is the meeting between the 'explosive' activity of the vital impetus and the resistance of matter which leads to the development of different lines and levels of evolution. In its creative energizing the vital impetus transcends the stage of organization which it has reached. Hence Bergson's comparison of the movement of evolution to the fragmentation of an exploding shell, provided that we imagine the fragments as being themselves shells which explode in turn.[4] When the vital impetus organizes matter successfully at a certain level, the impetus is continued at this level in the successions of individual members of the species in question. The creative energy of the *élan vital* is not however exhausted at a particular level but expresses itself anew.

The movement of evolution is seen by Bergson as following three main directions, that of plant life, that of instinctive life and that of intelligent or rational life. He does not mean to deny that the different forms of life had a common origin in more primitive and hardly differentiated organisms. Nor does he intend to imply that they have nothing in common. But they have not simply succeeded one another. Plant life, for example has not been

---

[1] *Creative Evolution*, p. 92. Page-references are to the English edition, though I have, once again, translated from the French.

[2] *Ibid.*, p. 92.

[3] Bergson admits that the term 'organization' suggests the assembling of parts to form a whole. But he insists that in philosophy the term must be given a sense other than that which it bears in the contest of manufacture and in a scientific context.

[4] Cf. *Creative Evolution*, p. 103.

superseded by animal life. Bergson thinks therefore that it is more reasonable to regard the three levels as fulfilling three divergent tendencies of an activity which has split up in the course of its development than as three successive degrees of one and the same tendency. The world of plants is marked by the predominance of the features of fixity or stability and of insensibility, whereas in the world of animals we find mobility and consciousness (in some degree) as predominating characteristics. Further, in the animal world we can distinguish between those species in which intuitive life has become the dominant characteristic, as in the case of insects such as bees and ants, and the vertebrate species in which intelligent life has emerged and developed.

Bergson is at pains to point out that his theory of the three divergent tendencies in evolution necessitates, for the purpose of discussion, the making of more clear-cut distinctions that can actually be found. 'There is scarcely any manifestation of life which does not contain in a rudimentary state, whether latent or virtual, the essential characteristics of the majority of other manifestations. The difference lies in the proportions.'[1] The group should thus be defined not by its simple possession of certain characteristics but rather by its tendency to accentuate them. For example, in actual fact intuitive life and intelligent life interpenetrate in varying degrees and proportions. But they are none the less different in kind, and it is important to consider them separately.

Both instinct and intelligence are defined by Bergson with reference to the making and using of instruments. Instinct is 'a faculty of using and constructing organized instruments',[2] instruments, that is to say, which are parts of the organism itself. Intelligence is 'the faculty of making and using unorganized instruments',[3] artificial instruments, that is to say, or tools. Psychical activity as such tends to act on the material world. And it can do so either directly or indirectly. If therefore we assume that a choice has to be made, we can say that 'instinct and intelligence represent two divergent solutions, equally elegant, of one and the same problem.'[4]

If therefore man is regarded historically, he should be described, according to Bergson, not as *homo sapiens* but as *homo faber*, man the worker, in terms of the construction of tools with a view to

---

[1] *Ibid.*, p. 112.   [3] *Ibid.*, p. 147.
[2] *Ibid.*, p. 147.   [4] *Ibid.*, p. 150.

acting on the material environment. For man is intelligent, and 'intelligence, considered in what appears to be its original application, is the faculty of fabricating artificial objects, in particular of tools to make tools, and of varying their manufacture indefinitely.'[1] Whatever intelligence may have become in the course of human history and of man's scientific advance, its essential feature is its practical orientation. It is, like instinct, at the service of life.

Inasmuch as the human intellect is primarily oriented to construction, to acting on man's material environment by means of the instruments which it creates, it is concerned first and foremost with inorganic solids, with physical objects external to and distinct from other physical objects, and, in such objects, with parts considered as such, clearly and distinctly. In other words, the human intellect has as its chief object what is discontinuous and stable or immobile; and it has the power of reducing an object to its constituent elements and of reassembling them. It can of course concern itself with organic living beings, but it tends to treat them in the same way as inorganic objects. The scientist, for example, will reduce the living thing to its physical and chemical components and try to reconstitute it theoretically from these elements. To put the matter negatively 'the intellect is characterized by a natural inability to comprehend life'.[2] It cannot grasp becoming, continuity and pure duration as such. It tries to force the continuous into its own moulds or categories, introducing sharp and clear-cut conceptual distinctions which are inadequate to the object. It is unable to think pure duration without transforming it into a spatialized, geometric concept of time. It takes, as it were, a series of static photographs of a continuous creative movement which eludes its grasp. In fine, the intellect, though admirably adapted for action and for making possible control of the environment (and of man himself, in so far as he can be turned into a scientific object), is not fitted for grasping the movement of evolution, of   life, 'the continuity of a change which is pure mobility'.[3] It breaks up the continuous becoming into a series of states, each of which is immobilized. Moreover, as the analytic understanding strives to reduce becoming to given elements and to reconstitute it from these elements, it cannot allow for the creation of what is novel and unforeseeable. The movement of evolution, the creative activity of the *élan vital*, is represented either as a mechanical process or as the progressive

[1] *Ibid.*, p. 146.   [2] *Ibid.*, p. 174.   [3] *Ibid.*, p. 171.

realization of a preconceived plan. In neither case is there room for creativity.

If we assume with Bergson that evolution is the creative activity of a vital impulse which uses and, so to speak, lights up matter in its onward continuous movement,[1] and if, as Bergson claims, the human intellect or intelligence is unable to grasp this movement as it really is, it follows that the intellect is unable to understand reality, or at any rate that it can apprehend it only by distorting it and producing a caricature. Bergson is thus far from holding that the primary function of the intellect is to know Reality with a capital letter and that its functions of scientific analysis and of technological invention are secondary or even low-grade employments. On the contrary, the intellect has developed primarily for action and for purposes of practical control of the environment, and its logical and scientific uses are natural to it, whereas it is unfitted by nature to grasp Reality. Man, as already remarked, is *homo faber* rather than *homo sapiens*, as far at any rate as his original nature is concerned.

In this case the question obviously arises whether we can know the nature of reality at all, as it is in itself that is to say. For what other means have we of knowing but the intellect? Instinct may be closer to life. It may be, as Bergson claims, a prolongation of life. But it is not reflective. To return to instinct would be to leave the sphere of what would ordinarily be called knowledge. If therefore conceptual thought is incapable of grasping the true nature of the real, of creative becoming, it seems to follow that we can never know it but that we are condemned to live simply with our own fictional representations of reality.

It should hardly be necessary to say that Bergson raises this sort of question himself, and that he attempts to answer it. His main line of thought can indeed be inferred from what has already been said. But in *L'évolution créatrice* it is set in the wide context of evolutionary theory and linked with the idea of divergent directions or tendencies in the process of evolution. Intelligence is concerned with matter, and 'by means of science, which is its work, will reveal to us more and more completely the secret of physical operations.'[2] It can however grasp life only by translating it in terms of inertia. Instinct is turned towards life, but it is without

---

[1] The vital impetus does not, for Bergson, actually create matter. It explodes creatively through matter and uses matter.

[2] *Creative Evolution*, p. 186.

reflective consciousness. If however instinct, which is a prolongation of life itself,[1] could extend its object and also reflect upon
itself, 'it would give us the key to vital operations'.[2] And this idea
is verified in intuition, which is 'instinct become disinterested,
conscious of itself, capable of reflecting on its object and of
enlarging it indefinitely'.[3] Intuition presupposes the development
of intelligence. Without this development instinct would have
remained riveted to objects of practical interest with a view to
physical movements. In other words, intuition presupposes the
emergence of reflective consciousness, which then splits up into
intelligence and intuition, corresponding respectively to matter
and life. 'This doubling of consciousness is thus related to the
twofold form of the real, and the theory of knowledge must be
dependent on metaphysics.'[4]

Let us assume with Bergson that intelligence is oriented to
matter, intuition to life. Let us also assume that developed intelligence creates the natural sciences. The obvious implication is
that philosophy, treating of life, is based on intuition. Indeed,
Bergson tells us that if intuition could be prolonged beyond a few
instants, philosophers would be in agreement.[5] The trouble is
however that intuition cannot be prolonged in such a way as to
make rival systems of philosophy immediately disappear. In
practice there has to be interchange between intuition and intelligence. Intelligence has to apply itself to the content of intuition;
and what intelligence makes of this content has to be checked and
corrected by reference to intuition. We have to make do, so to
speak, with the instruments at hand; and philosophy can hardly
attain the degree of purity which is attained by positive science
in proportion as it frees itself from metaphysical assumptions and
prejudices. Without intuition however philosophy is blind.

Bergson used the intuition of our own freedom, our own free
creative activity, as a key to the nature of the Universe. 'The
universe is not made, but is being made continually.'[6] More precisely, there is both making and unmaking. Bergson uses the
metaphor of a jet of steam issuing at high pressure from a vessel,
with drops condensing and falling back. 'So, from an immense
reservoir of life jets must be leaping out without ceasing, each of
which, falling back, is a world.'[7] Matter represents the falling

---

[1] Bergson describes instinct as 'sympathy' (cf. *ibid.*, 186).
[2] *Ibid.*, p. 186.   [3] *Ibid.*, p. 186.   [4] *Ibid.*, p. 188.
[5] *Ibid.*, p. 252.   [6] *Ibid.*, p. 255.   [7] *Ibid.*, p. 261.

back, the process of unmaking, while the movement of life in the world represents what remains of the direct upward movement in the inverted movement. The creation of living species is due to the creative activity of life; but from another point of view the self-perpetuating species represents a falling back. 'Matter or mind, reality has appeared to us as a perpetual becoming. It makes itself or it unmakes itself, but it is never something (simply) made.'[1]

What, we may ask, is Bergson's justification for this extrapolation of an experience of free creative activity in ourselves? Or does he claim that we can have an intuition of becoming in general, of the cosmic *élan vital*? In his *Introduction to Metaphysics* he asks the following question. 'If metaphysics should proceed by intuition, if intuition has for its object the mobility of duration, and if duration is psychological in essence, are we not going to shut up the philosopher in the exclusive contemplation of himself?'[2] Bergson replies that the coincidence, in intuition, with our own duration puts us in contact with a whole continuity of durations and so enables us to transcend ourselves. But it seems that this can be the case only if the experience of our own duration is an intuition of the creative activity of the cosmic vital impulse. And this is what Bergson appears to imply when he refers to a 'coincidence of the human consciousness with the living principle from which it emanates, a contact with the creative effort.'[3] Elsewhere he asserts that 'the matter and life which fill the world are also in us; the forces which work in all things, we feel them in ourselves; whatever the intimate essence of that which is and of that which makes itself may be, we participate in it.'[4] So presumably it is our participation in the *élan vital* or its operation in us which enables Bergson to base a general philosophical theory on an intuition which, in the first instance, is of duration in man himself.

The concept of the *élan vital* bears some resemblance at any rate to that of the soul of the world as found in ancient philosophy and in some modern philosophers such as Schelling. Bergson also speaks of the vital impulse as 'supra-consciousness'[5] and likens it to a rocket, the extinguished fragments of which fall back as

---

[1] *Ibid.*, p. 287.   [2] *La pensée et le mouvant*, p. 233.
[3] *Creative Evolution*, p. 391. Bergson is speaking of the intuition which, he claims, is the basis of philosophy and enables the philosopher to treat of becoming in general.
[4] *La pensée et le mouvant*, p. 157.   [5] *Creative Evolution*, p. 275.

matter. In addition he uses the word 'God', God being described as 'a continuity of leaping out'[1] or, more conventionally, as 'unceasing life, action, freedom'.[2] In *Creative Evolution* therefore the concept of God is introduced simply in the context of evolutionary theory, as signifying an immanent cosmic vital impulse which is not creator in the Judaeo-Christian traditional sense but uses matter as the instrument of the creation of fresh forms of life. However Bergson's ideas of God and religion are much better left to the next chapter, where his work on the subject will be considered.

Reference has already been made to Bergson's lack of linguistic precision. But if conceptual thought cannot grasp reality as it is in itself, we can hardly expect a high degree of precision. 'Comparisons and metaphors will suggest here what one does not succeed in expressing. ... As soon as we begin to treat of the spiritual world, the image, even if it aims only at suggesting, can give us the direct vision, while the abstract term, which is of spatial origin and which claims to express, leaves us on most occasions with metaphor.'[3] As there does not seem much that can usefully be said on this matter, in view, that is to say, of Bergson's premises, we can go on to remark that in this chapter we have made no attempt to assess the influences on Bergson's thought. There can be little doubt, for example, that he was influenced by Ravaisson's idea of the inverse movement of matter and of mechanism as a kind of relapse of freedom into habit. But though Bergson refers to some eminent philosophers of the past, such as Plato, Aristotle, Spinoza, Leibniz and Kant, and, among the moderns, to Herbert Spencer and to a number of scientists and psychologists, he makes very little reference to his immediate predecessors. He acknowledged some debt to Plotinus, to Maine de Biran and to Ravaisson; but even if it can be shown, despite his disclaimers, that he had probably read some essay or book by an immediate predecessor or a contemporary,[4] it does not necessarily follow that he simply borrowed the idea in question. Disputes about his originality or lack of it are apt to be inconclusive. Nor is the matter of any great importance. Wherever they may have originated, the ideas appropriated by Bergson are part of his philosophy.

---

[1] *Ibid.*, p. 262.　　[2] *Ibid.*, p. 262.　　[3] *La pensée et le mouvant*, p. 52.
[4] Though Bergson was not actually a pupil of Lachelier, he read the latter's book on induction while he was a student, and he liked to regard Lachelier as one of his teachers.

CHAPTER X

HENRI BERGSON (2)

Introductory remarks—Closed morality—Open morality: the interpretation of the two types—Static religion as a defence against the dissolvent power of intelligence—Dynamic religion and mysticism—Comments.

1. BERGSON's general procedure or way of going about things has been illustrated in the last chapter by reference to *Time and Free Will*, *Matter and Memory* and *Creative Evolution*. He selects certain sets of empirical data which interest him and arrest his attention and tries to interpret them in terms of some coordinating hypothesis or basic concept. For example, if the immediate data of consciousness suggest the mind's transcendence of matter while scientific research seems to point in the direction of epiphenomenalism, the question of the relation between mind and body (or between soul and body) presents itself once more and calls for the development of a theory which will accommodate both sets of data. While however Bergson is often certain that a given theory is inadequate or erroneous, he is not given to the dogmatic proclamation of his own theories as the definitive and finally proved truth. He shows us a picture which in his opinion is a better portrayal of the landscape than other pictures and provides persuasive arguments to show that this is the case; but he often shows himself conscious of the tentative and speculative character of his explanatory hypotheses.

In his last main work *The Two Sources of Morality and Religion* Bergson follows his customary procedure by taking as his point of departure sets of empirical data relevant to man's moral and religious life. In the field of morals, for example, he sees that there are facts exhibiting connections between codes of conduct and particular societies. At the same time he sees the part played in the development of ethical ideas and convictions by individuals who have risen above the standards of their societies. Similarly, in the area of religion Bergson sees the sociological aspects of religion and its social functions in history, while he is also aware of the personal and deeper levels of the religious consciousness. True, for information about the empirical data he relies to a considerable extent on the writings of the sociologists such as Durkheim and Lévy-Bruhl and, in regard to the mystical aspects of religion, on writers such as Henri Delacroix and Evelyn Underhill. The point is however that his theory of *two* sources of morality and religion is based on his conviction that there are distinguishable sets of empirical data which cannot be accounted for without a complex theory or explanation of this kind.

Bergson does not begin his treatment of morals by formulating explicitly certain problems or questions. But the nature of his questions emerges more or less clearly from his reflection on the data. One way of formulating his question would be to ask, what is the part played by reason in morality? He has of course to assign some role to reason; but it is not that of being a source. In his view there are two sources of morality, one infra-rational, the other supra-rational. Given his treatment of instinct, intelligence and intuition in *Creative Evolution*, this position is what might have been expected. In other words, the convictions which Bergson has already formed certainly (and naturally) influence his reflections on the data relevant to man's moral and religious life. At the same time his religious ideas are developed in the *Two Sources* well beyond anything that was said in *Creative Evolution*. In fine, the Bergsonian general world-outlook, as has already been stated, emerges from or is built up by a series of particular inquiries or lines of thought which are linked together through the pervasive presence of certain key-concepts, such as duration, becoming, creativity and intuition.

2. Bergson begins his treatment of morals with reflection on man's sense of obligation. He is far from agreeing with Kant's derivation of morality from the practical reason. Nor is he prepared to give to the concept of obligation the pre-eminent position which it occupies in Kantian ethics. At the same time Bergson recognizes of course that the sense of obligation is a prominent feature of the moral consciousness. Further, he agrees with Kant that obligation presupposes freedom. 'A being does not feel itself obliged unless it is free, and every obligation, taken separately, implies freedom.'[1] It is not possible to disobey laws of nature. For they are statements of the way in which things actually behave; and if we find that some things act in a manner contrary to an alleged law we reformulate the law in such a way as to cover the

---

[1] *The Two Sources*, p. 19. Page-references are to the English translation, though the wording of my translation from the French sometimes differs slightly.

exceptions. But it is quite possible to disobey a moral law or rule. It is thus a case not of necessity but of obligation. Talk about obeying the laws of nature should not be taken literally. For such laws are not prescriptive but descriptive.[1] Obedience and disobedience to moral prescriptions however are familiar phenomena.

The question which Bergson raises concerns the cause or source of obligation. And the answer which he gives is that society is the source. That is to say, the sense of obligation is a sense of social pressure. The voice of duty is not something mysterious, coming from another world; it is the voice of society. The social imperative bears on the individual as such. This is why he feels obliged. But the individual human being is also a member of society. Hence for a great part of the time we observe social rules without reflection and without experiencing any resistance in ourselves. It is only when we do experience such resistance that we are actually aware of a sense of obligation. And as such cases are infrequent in comparison with the number of times in which we obey pretty well automatically, it is a mistake to interpret the moral life in terms of doing violence to oneself, of overcoming inclination, and so on. As man has his 'social self', his social aspect, he is generally inclined to conform to social pressure. 'Each of us belongs to society as much as to himself.'[2] The further we delve into the personality, the more incommensurable it becomes. But the plain fact of the matter is that on the surface of life, where we mainly dwell, there is a social solidarity which inclines us to conform to social pressure without resistance.

Bergson is at pains to argue that this sort of view does not imply that an individual living alone would be aware of no duties, no sense of obligation. For wherever he goes, even to a desert island, he carries with him his 'social ego'. He is still joined in spirit to society which continues to speak to him in his thinking and language, which have been formed by society. 'Generally, the verdict of conscience is that which would be given by the social self.'[3]

We can now ask two questions. First, what does Bergson mean by 'society'? Secondly, what does he mean by 'obligation'? The first question is answered fairly easily. By society Bergson means in the context any 'closed society', as he expresses it. This may be

---

[1] Bergson did not think of the laws of nature as necessary in the absolute sense. But the scientist would not speak of a law of nature unless he conceived it as exemplified in every member of a class of phenomena.
[2] *The Two Sources*, p. 6.   [3] *Ibid.*, p. 8.

a primitive tribe or a modern State. Provided that it is a particular society which is conscious of itself as *this* society, distinct from other social groups, it is, in Bergson's language, a closed society. It is from society in this sense that obligation emanates; and the function of the social pressure which gives rise to the sense of obligation in individual members of the society is to maintain the society's cohesion and life.

The second question is more difficult to answer. Sometimes he seems to mean by obligation the feeling or sense of obligation. We can then say that, for him, an empirical fact, namely social pressure, is the cause of a specifically ethical feeling. Sometimes however Bergson speaks as though the awareness of obligation were the awareness of social pressure as such. In this case obligation seems to be identified with a non-moral empirical fact. To complicate matters, Bergson introduces the idea of the essence of social pressure, which he also describes as the totality of obligation and defines as the 'concentrated extract, the quintessence of the thousand special habits which we have contracted of obeying the thousand particular demands of social life.'[1] It is perhaps natural to understand this as referring to a generalization from particular obligations, so that 'the totality of obligation' would be logically posterior to particular obligations. But this interpretation can hardly be accepted. For the totality of obligation is also described as 'the habit of contracting habits';[2] and though this is said to be the aggregate of habits, it is also the necessity or need for contracting habits and a necessary condition for the existence of societies. In this case it is presumably logically prior to social rules.

Though however Bergson uses the word 'obligation' in a lamentably loose manner, in several senses that is to say, it is at any rate clear that for him the efficient cause of obligation is the pressure exercised on its members by a closed society, and that its final cause is the maintenance of the society's cohesion and life. Obligation is thus relative to the closed society and has a social function. Further, its origin is infra-intellectual. In a society such as those of bees and ants instinct takes care of social cohesion and service of the community. If however we imagine a bee or an ant becoming self-conscious and capable of intellectual reflection, we can picture it asking why it should continue to act as it has been hitherto acting by instinct. At this point we can see social

[1] *Ibid.*, p. 13.   [2] *Ibid.*, p. 17.

pressure making itself felt through the insect's social self, the awareness of this pressure being a sense of obligation. If therefore we personify Nature, as Bergson is inclined to do, we can say that social pressure and obligation are the means used by Nature to secure society's cohesion and preservation when man emerges in the process of creative evolution. The morality of obligation is thus of infra-intellectual origin in the sense that it is the form taken in human society by the instinctive activity of members of infra-human societies.

Preservation of a society's cohesion is obviously not secured simply by pressure to observe rules which would be classified as moral rules by members of an advanced society, accustomed to differentiate between social conventions and ethical norms. A primitive society, when looked at from one point of view, extends the coverage of moral obligation to rules of conduct which we would be unlikely to classify as moral norms. As experience widens and civilization progresses, the human reason starts to discriminate between rules of conduct which are still necessary or genuinely useful to society and those which are no longer necessary or useful. It also begins to discriminate between rules which are seen to be required for the cohesion and maintenance of any tolerable society and conventions which differ from society to society. Further, when a traditional code of conduct has once been subjected to radical questioning by human intelligence, the mind will look for reasons to support the code. There is thus plenty of scope for reason in the ethical field. But this does not alter the fact that the ethics of obligation as such as of infra-intellectual origin. Reason does not originate it. It gets to work on what is already there, clarifying, discriminating, tidying up and defending.

3. The morality of obligation, relative to the closed society, is not regarded by Bergson as coterminous with the whole field of morality. He is well aware that the moral idealism of those individuals who have embodied in their own lives values and standards higher and more universal in their effect than the current ethical codes of the societies to which they belonged cannot be easily explained in terms of the social pressure of a closed group. He therefore asserts the existence of a second type of morality which is different in kind from the morality of obligation, which is characterized by appeal and aspiration, and which relates to man as man or to the ideal society of all human beings rather than to the closed group in any of its forms. Consider, for example, an

historical figure who not only proclaims the ideal of universal love but also embodies it in his own personality and life. The ideal, so embodied, acts by way of attraction and appeal rather than by way of social pressure; and those who respond to the ideal are drawn by example rather than impelled by the sense of obligation which expresses the pressure of a closed group.

This open and dynamic morality[1] is, for Bergson, of suprarational origin. The morality of obligation is, as we have seen, of infra-intellectual origin, being the analogue at the human level of the constant and never failing pressure of instinct in infra-human societies. The open morality however originates in a contact between the great moral idealists and prophets and the creative source of life itself. It is, in effect, the result of a mystical union with God, which expresses itself in universal love. 'It is the mystical souls which have drawn and continue to draw civilized societies in their wake.'[2]

There is a natural inclination to think that it is all a question of degree, and that love of the tribe can become love of the nation and love of the nation love of all men. Bergson however rejects this view. The closed and open moralities are for him different in kind and not simply in degree. Though the open morality does in fact involve the ideal of universal love, it is essentially characterised not so much by its content (which, taken in itself, could logically be an extension of the content of closed morality) as by a vital impetus in the will which is quite different from social pressure or obligation. This vital impetus, also described by Bergson as 'emotion', is of supra-rational origin. In terms of the theory of evolution it expresses the creative movement of ascending life, whereas the closed morality represents rather a certain fixed deposit of this movement.

As Bergson insists on the difference between the two types of morality, he naturally treats them successively. Though however he thinks of primitive human society as dominated by the closed mentality, he recognizes of course that in society as we know it the two types not only coexist but interpenetrate. In a Christian nation, for example, we can find both types showing themselves. Just as we can consider pure memory and pure perception separately though

---

[1] 'Open' in the sense that it is essentially universal, aspiring to union between all human beings; 'dynamic' in the sense that it strives to change society, not simply to preserve it as it is.
[2] *The Two Sources*, p. 68.

they interpenetrate in concrete perception, so we can and ought to distinguish and consider separately the closed and open moralities, though in our actual world they coexist and mingle.

An important factor in the bringing together of the two types of morality is the human reason or intelligence. Both the infra-intellectual drive of social pressure and the supra-intellectual appeal are projected, as it were, onto the plane of reason in the form of representations or ideas. Reason, acting as an inter-mediary, tends to introduce universality into the closed morality and obligation into the open morality. The ideals presented by the open morality become effective in society only in so far as they are interpreted by the reason and harmonized with the morality of obligation, while the closed morality receives an influx of life from the open morality. In its actual concrete form therefore morality includes both 'a system of *orders* dictated by *impersonal* social demands and a group of *appeals* made to the conscience of each one of us by *persons* who represent the best that there is in humanity.'[1]

Though the closed and open moralities intermingle with one another, there remains a tension between them. The open morality tries to infuse fresh life and new vistas into the closed morality, but the latter tends to bring down, as it were, the latter by turning what is essentially appeal and aspiration into a fixed code and by minimizing or whittling away ideals. We can however envisage the possibility of man's moral advance. In the final chapter of *The Two Sources* Bergson remarks that modern technology has made pos-sible the unification of man in one society. This might of course be brought about by the triumph of an imperialism which would simply represent the closed mentality writ large. But we can also imagine a truly human society in which man's free response to the highest ideals would be the uniting factor rather than the tyran-nical force and power of a world-imperialism. In such a society obligation would not disappear, but it would be transformed by man's response to ideals which are ultimately the expression of an influx of divine life as mediated to society by persons who have opened themselves to the divine life.

4. We have already had occasion to refer to a religious theme, mysticism, in connection with open morality. Bergson however distinguishes, as one might expect, between two types of religion,

---

[1] *Ibid.*, p. 68.

described respectively as static and dynamic. They correspond of course to the two types of morality, static religion being infra-intellectual in origin and dynamic supra-intellectual.

Let us once more imagine a bee or an ant suddenly endowed with intelligence and self-consciousness. The insect will naturally tend to pursue its private interests instead of serving the community. In other words, intelligence, when it emerges in the course of evolution, is a potentially dissolving power in regard to the maintenance of social cohesion. Reason is critical and questioning; it enables man to use his initiative and so endangers social unity and discipline.[1] Nature however is not at a loss what to do. What Bergson calls the myth-making faculty gets to work; and the protective deity of the tribe or the city appears 'to forbid, threaten, punish'.[2] In primitive society morality and custom are the same; and the sphere of religion is coterminous with that of social custom. The god protects the structure of custom by ordering the observance of the customs and punishing disobedience, even if the infringement is not known by a man's fellows.

Again, though the vital impulse turns animals away from the image of death and though there is no reason for supposing that any animal can argue to the inevitability of its own death, man is certainly able to conceive the fact that he will inevitably die. What does Nature do? 'To the idea that death is inevitable she opposes the image of continuation of life after death; this image, thrown by her into the field of intelligence, puts things in order again.'[3] Nature thus attains two ends. She protects the individual against the depressing thought of the inevitability of death; and she protects society. For a primitive society requires the presence and continuing authority of the ancestors.

Once more, as primitive man is extremely limited in his power to influence and control his environment, and as he is being constantly confronted with and reminded of the gap between the actions which he takes and the results for which he hopes, Nature or the vital impulse conjures up in him the image of and belief in

---

[1] Bergson remarks that though reason can convince a person that by promoting the happiness of others he promotes his own, it took centuries of culture to produce J. S. Mill, and he 'has not convinced all philosophers, let alone the mass of mankind' (*ibid.*, p. 101).

[2] *Ibid.*, p. 101. Bergson also discusses tabu and magic; but we cannot follow him into this discussion. We confine our remarks to polytheism.

[3] *Ibid.*, p. 109. Bergson explains that he is not denying immortality as such but maintaining that primitive man's image of life after death is 'hallucinatory'.

friendly powers interested in his success, to whom he can pray and who will help him.[1]

In general therefore static religion can be defined as 'a defensive reaction of nature against what could be depressing for the individual and dissolvent for society in the exercise of intelligence'.[2] It attaches man to life and the individual to society by means of myths. In the first instance it is found with primitive man, in some form or other; but it does not follow of course that it ceased with primitive man. On the contrary, it continued to flourish. But to say this is to say that the primitive mentality survived in civilization. Indeed it still survives, though the development of natural science has of course contributed powerfully to discrediting the religious myths. In Bergson's view, if in a modern war both parties express confidence that God is on their side, the mentality of static religion is showing itself. For though both sides may profess to be invoking the same God, the God of all mankind, each tends to treat him in practice as a national deity. Again, religious persecution was an expression of the primitive mentality and of static religion. For universal belief by a society was a criterion of its truth. Hence unbelief could not be regarded with equanimity. Common belief was considered a necessary ingredient of social solidarity or cohesion.

5. As for dynamic religion, its essence is mysticism, the ultimate end of which is 'a contact, and consequently a partial coincidence, with the creative effort of which life is the manifestation. The effort is of God, if it is not God himself. The great mystic is an individual who transcends the limits assigned to the species by its material nature and who thus continues and prolongs the divine action. Such is our definition.'[3] For Bergson therefore complete mysticism means not only a movement upwards and inwards which culminates in a contact with the divine life but also a complementary movement downwards or outwards by which a fresh impulse from the divine life is communicated through the mystic to mankind. In other words, Bergson thinks of what he describes as complete mysticism as issuing in activity in the world. He therefore regards a mysticism which concentrates simply on turning away from this world to the divine centre or which results in an intellectual grasp of the unity of all things, coloured by

---

[1] Bergson adds that a logical consequence of belief in friendly powers is a belief in unfriendly or antagonistic powers. But this second belief is, he maintains, derivative and even degenerate, as the vital impulse is optimistic (*ibid.*, p. 117).
[2] *Ibid.*, p. 175.   [3] *Ibid.*, p. 188.

sympathy or compassion but not by dynamic activity, as incomplete. And he finds a mysticism of this sort represented especially, though not exclusively, in the East, whereas 'complete mysticism is in effect that of the great Christian mystics'.[1] We cannot undertake to discuss here Bergson's views on oriental and western mysticism. But there are one or two points worth noticing. In the first place Bergson raises the question whether mysticism provides us with an experimental approach to problems about the existence and nature of God. 'Generally speaking, we judge that an existing object is one which is perceived or which could be perceived. It is therefore given in a real or possible experience.'[2] Bergson is aware of the difficulties, or at any rate some of them, involved in proving that a given experience is an experience of *God*. But he suggests that reflection on mysticism can serve as confirmation of a position already reached. If, that is to say, the truth of creative evolution has been established, and if we can envisage the possibility of an intuitive experience of the principle of all life, reflection on the data of mysticism can add probability to the thesis that there is a transcendent creative activity. In any case mysticism, according to Bergson, can throw light on the divine nature. 'God is love, and he is object of love: this is the whole contribution of mysticism.'[3] Bergson writes, as usual, in an impressionistic manner; and he is far from tackling the logical difficulties in a professional way. His general position however is clearly that while reflection on evolution can bring us to the conviction that there is an immanent creative energy operative in the world, reflection on 'dynamic religion' or mysticism sheds further light on the nature of this principle of life, revealing it as love.[4]

In the second place, if 'the creative energy must be defined as love',[5] we are entitled to conclude that creation is the process whereby God brings into being 'creators, in order to have, beside himself, beings worthy of his love.'[6] In other words, creation appears as having an end or goal, the coming into being of man and his transformation through love. In the final chapter of *The Two Sources* Bergson sees the advance of technology as the progressive construction of what one might describe as one body (the

[1] *Ibid.*, p. 194.   [2] *Ibid.*, p. 206.   [3] *Ibid.*, p. 216.
[4] Needless to say, it was largely Bergson's reflections on mysticism which brought him to the point of contemplating formal adherence to Catholicism.
[5] *The Two Sources*, p. 220.   [6] *Ibid.*, p. 218.

unification of mankind on the levels of material civilization and of science), and the function of mystical religion as that of infusing a soul into this body. The universe thus appears as 'a machine for the making of gods',[1] a deified humanity, as transformed through an influx of divine love. Objections based on man's physical insignificance are rejected. The existence of man presupposes conditions, and these conditions other conditions. The world is the condition for man's existence. This teleological conception of creation may seem to contradict Bergson's previous attack on any interpretation of evolution in finalistic terms. But he was then thinking of course of the sort of finalistic scheme which would entail determinism.

In the third place Bergson sees mysticism as shedding light on the problem of survival. For in mystical experience we can see a participation in a life which is capable of indefinite progress. If it has already been established that the life of the mind cannot in any case be properly described in purely epiphenomenalistic terms, the occurrence of mysticism, which 'is presumably a participation in the divine essence',[2] adds probability to belief in the soul's survival after bodily death.

Just as Bergson sees the closed and open types of morality interpenetrating one another in man's moral life as it actually exists, so does he see actual religion as a mingling of various degrees of static and dynamic religions. For example, in historical Christianity we can see the impulse of dynamic religion recurrently manifesting itself; but we can also discern plenty of evidence of the mentality characteristic of static religion. The ideal is that static religion should be transformed by dynamic religion; but, apart from limiting cases, the two intermingle in practice.

6. If anyone asks what Bergson means by closed and open morality, static and dynamic reality, there is no great difficulty in mentioning examples of the sets of phenomena to which these terms refer. It does not necessarily follow that Bergson's interpretation of the historical or empirical data has to be accepted. It is clear that he interprets the data within the framework of the conclusions to which he has already come about evolution in general and about the roles of instinct, intelligence and intuition in particular. The picture which he already has in his mind predisposes him to split up morality and religion into distinct types, different in kind. Obviously, his reflections on ethical and religious

[1] *Ibid.*, p. 275.   [2] *Ibid.*, p. 227.

data seem to him to confirm his previously embraced conclusions; and the picture which he forms of man's moral and religious life reacts on the concept of the world which he already has in his mind. At the same time it is possible to admit the facts which Bergson mentions (facts, for example, about the relation between different codes of conduct and different societies) but to accommodate them in a different interpretative scheme or overall picture. It is not of course a question of blaming Bergson for painting an overall picture. It is simply a question of pointing out that other pictures are possible, which do not involve the Bergsonian dualism.

How far are however we to press this theme of dualism? That Bergson asserts a psychological dualism of soul and body is clear enough. It is also clear that in his theory of morals and religion there is a dualism of origin. That is to say, closed morality and static religion are said to be of infra-intellectual origin, while open morality and dynamic religion are said to be of supra-intellectual origin.[1] But Bergson attempts to bring together soul and body by means of the concept of human action. And in his theory of morals and religion the different types of morality and religion are all ultimately explained in terms of the divine creative activity and purpose. In spite therefore of the dualistic features of his philosophy Bergson provides the material for a line of thought, such as that of Teilhard de Chardin, which is more 'monistic' in character.

In any case it is really the overall picture, the painting as a whole, which counts. It is possible of course to take particular points for consideration, such as Bergson's account of moral obligation. And then it is easy to criticize his sometimes inconsistent and often imprecise use of language and his failure to carry through a sustained and careful analysis. It is also possible to dwell on the influence exerted by particular views, such as the vital or biological primary function of intelligence. But it is probably true to say that Bergson's widest influence was exercised by his general picture,[2] which offered an alternative to mechanistic and positivist pictures.

---

[1] In theological terms one might perhaps say that they are, for Bergson, of natural and supernatural origin respectively.

[2] By the general picture, that is to say, conveyed by his writings up to and including *Creative Evolution*. Between 1907, when this work was published, and 1932, when *The Two Sources* appeared, there was a considerable gap. The climate of thought had changed a good deal in the meantime. Further, *The Two Sources* showed how Bergson's mind had been moving closer to Christianity than anyone might have expected from *Creative Evolution*.

In other words, this picture exercised a liberating influence on many minds. For it offered a positive and to many people appealing interpretation of the world, an interpretation which was neither confined to criticism of and attack on other views nor a return to past ways of thought. It did not seem to be a philosophy thought out by someone fighting a rearguard action but rather the expression of an outlook for the future. It was capable of arousing excitement and enthusiasm, as something new and inspiring,[1] and as putting the theory of evolution in a fresh light.

Bergson had some disciples, such as Édouard Le Roy (1870–1954), who succeeded him in his chair at the Collège de France.[2] But there was no Bergsonian school in any strict sense. Rather was it a question of a diffused influence, which it is often difficult to pin down. For example, William James hailed the appearance of *Creative Evolution* as marking a new era in thought; and he was doubtless influenced to some extent by Bergson. At the same time Bergson has been accused of basing his idea of real duration on James's theory of the stream of consciousness. (Bergson denied this, while paying tribute to James and recognizing similarities in thought.) Again, there are ideas, such as the originally biological or practical function of intelligence, which were certainly features of Bergson's philosophy but which could also have been derived from German philosophy, the writings of Schopenhauer for example.[3] If we pass over learned research into the particular ways in which Bergson influenced or may have influenced other philosophers in France and in other countries, it is sufficient to say that in his heyday Bergson appeared as the spearhead of the vitalist current of thought or philosophy of life and that, as such, he exercised a wide but not easily definable influence. It is worth adding however that this influence was felt outside the ranks of professional philosophers, as by the well known French writer Charles Pierre Péguy (1873–1914) and the revolutionary social

---

[1] One can of course find anticipations of a large number of Bergson's ideas in previous French philosophers. And some writers have challenged Bergson's originality. But this is really a matter for historians. As far as the general public are concerned, Bergson's thought was novel.

[2] Le Roy interpreted scientific theories and laws as useful fictions, making possible effective action to meet human needs. In *Dogma and Criticism* (*Dogme et critique*, 1906) he gave a pragmatist interpretation of religious dogmas, interpreting them as directives for moral action.

[3] How far Bergson himself was influenced by nineteenth-century German philosophers, such as Schopenhauer and Eduard von Hartmann, has been matter for dispute. It seems probable however that any influence was indirect, by way of French thought, rather than direct.

and political theorist Georges Sorel (1847–1922). Before he became a Thomist, Jacques Maritain was a disciple of Bergson; and though he criticized the Bergsonian philosophy, he retained a profound respect for his onetime master. Finally, as has already been mentioned, Pierre Teilhard de Chardin (1881–1955) had obvious affinities with Bergson and can be regarded as having continued his way of thinking into the contemporary world, provided at any rate that one does not give the erroneous impression that Teilhard simply borrowed his ideas from Bergson or Le Roy.

PART III
FROM BERGSON TO SARTRE

CHAPTER XI

PHILOSOPHY AND CHRISTIAN APOLOGETICS

Ollé-Laprune on moral certitude—Blondel and the way of immanence—Laberthonnière and Christian philosophy—Some remarks on modernism.

1. During the eighteenth-century Enlightenment Christian apologetics tended to follow a rationalistic pattern. The arguments of atheists were countered by philosophical proofs of the existence of God as cause of the world and as responsible for order in the universe, while the deists' attacks on revealed religion were met by arguments to prove the trustworthiness of the New Testament accounts of the life of Christ, including the accounts of miracles, and the fact of revelation. In the Age of Reason, that is to say, the arguments of rationalists, whether atheists or deists, had as their counterpart a kind of Christian rationalism.

After the revolution apologetics in France underwent a change. The general influence of the romantic movement showed itself in a turning away from rationalistic philosophy of the Cartesian type and in an emphasis on the way in which the Christian religion fulfilled the needs of man and society. As we have seen, Chateaubriand explicitly stated the need for a new type of apologetics and appealed to the beauty or aesthetic qualities of Christianity, maintaining that it is the intrinsic excellence of Christianity which shows that it comes from God rather than that it must be judged excellent because it has been proved to have come from God. The Traditionalists, such as de Maistre and de Bonald, appealed to the transmission of a primitive divine revelation rather than to metaphysical arguments for the existence of God. Lamennais, while making some use of traditional apologetics, insisted that religious faith requires a free consent of the will and is far from being simply an intellectual assent to the conclusion of a deductive inference. He also laid emphasis on the benefits conferred by religion on individuals and societies as evidence for its truth. The Dominican preacher Henri-Dominique Lacordaire (1802–61), who was for a time associated with Lamennais, tried to show the truth of Christianity by exhibiting the content and implications of the Christian faith itself and showing how it fulfils man's needs and the legitimate demands of human society.

It was obviously a strong point in the new line of apologetics in France in the first half of the nineteenth century that it tried to show the relevance of Christian faith by relating it to man's needs and aspirations both as an individual and as a member of society, rather than by proceeding simply on the plane of abstract metaphysical proofs and historical arguments. At the same time appeals to aesthetic considerations, as with Chateaubriand, or to the actual or possible beneficial social effects of Christianity could easily give the impression of attempts to stimulate the will to believe. That is to say, in so far as persuasive arguments were substituted for the traditional proofs, the substitution might be seen as expressing a tacit admission that religious faith rested on the will rather than on the reason.

Unless however Christian faith was to be regarded as being of the same nature as intellectual assent to the conclusion of a mathematical demonstration, some role had to be attributed to the will. After all, even those who were convinced of the demonstrative character of traditional metaphysical and apologetic arguments could hardly maintain that the unbeliever's withholding of his assent was always and exclusively due to his failure to understand them. It was natural therefore that the role of the will in religious belief should be explored, and that an attempt should be made to combine recognition of this role with avoidance of a purely pragmatic or voluntarist interpretation of Christian faith. Thus the question was raised, can there be a legitimate certitude, legitimate from the rational point of view, in which the will plays an effective role?

The name which first comes to mind in connection with this question is that of Léon Ollé-Laprune (1839–98). After completing his studies at the École Normale at Paris, Ollé-Laprune taught philosophy in lycées until he was given a post at the École Normale in 1875. In 1870 he published a work on Malebranche, *La Philosophie de Malebranche*, and in 1880 a book on moral certitude, *De la certitude morale*. An essay on the ethics of Aristotle, *Essai sur la morale d'Aristote*, appeared in 1881,[1] while *La philosophie*

---

[1] A Latin version had already been presented as one of the dissertations for the doctorate.

et le temps présent and a work on the value of life, *Le prix de la vie*, were published respectively in 1890 and 1894. Among other writings are two posthumously published works, *La raison et le rationalisme* (1906) and *Croyance religieuse et croyance intellectuelle* (1908, *Religious Belief and Intellectual Belief*).

It was a firm conviction of Ollé-Laprune that the will had a role to play in all intellectual activity. And there is of course a sense in which this is obviously true. Even in mathematical reasoning attention is required; and intention implies a decision to attend. It is also clear that there are areas of inquiry where there is room for the influence of prejudice of one sort or another and where the effort to be open-minded is required. Though however Ollé-Laprune liked to lay emphasis, in a general way, on thinking as a form of life, of action, he was particularly concerned with the search for truth in the religious and moral spheres. Here above all there was need for thinking 'with the whole soul, with the whole of oneself'.[1] In arriving at this conviction Ollé-Laprune was influenced by the thought of Pascal[2] and by Newman's *Grammar of Assent*,[3] as well as by Ravaisson and by Alphonse Gratry (1805–72). Gratry was a priest who maintained in his writings that though Christian faith could not be attained simply by human effort, it none the less satisfied man's deepest aspirations and that the way to it could be prepared if a man sought truth with his whole being and if he tried to live in accordance with moral ideals.

In his work on moral certitude Ollé-Laprune begins by examining the nature of assent and of certitude in general. As one would expect in the case of a French philosopher, there are frequent references to Descartes. A prominent feature however of Ollé-Laprune's reflections is the stimulus derived from Newman's *Grammar of Assent*. For example, he agrees with Newman that assent itself is always unconditional;[4] and he also accepts Newman's distinction between real and notional assent, though he expresses it as a distinction between two types of certitude. 'There is then a certitude which one can call *real* and another which one can call *abstract*. The latter is related to *notions*, the former to *things*.'[5] Ollé-Laprune also distinguishes between implicit certitude, preceding reflection, and actual or explicit certitude, which arises as a result of a reflective appropriation of

---

[1] *La philosophie et le temps présent*, p. 264.
[2] See Volume 4 of this *History*, pp. 153–173.
[3] For Newman see Appendix A to Volume 8 of this *History*.
[4] *De la certitude morale* (3rd edition, 1898), p. 22. [5] *Ibid.*, p. 23.

implicit knowledge. As for the role played by the will, no truth can be perceived without attention; and attention is a voluntary act. Further, when it is not a question of assent to self-evidently true 'first principles' but a matter of reasoning, of the discursive activity of the mind, an effort of the will is obviously required to sustain this activity. But Ollé-Laprune is not prepared to accept the view of Descartes that judgment, in the form of affirmation or of denial, is in itself an act of the will. In the case of legitimate certitude it is the light of the evidence which determines assent, not an arbitrary choice by the will between affirmation and denial. At the same time truth may, for example, be displeasing, as when I hear a critical statement about myself, the truth of which I do not want to accept. An act of the will is then required to 'consent' to what I really perceive to be the truth. Consent (*consentement*) must however be distinguished from assent (*assentiment*), even if the two are often intermingled. '*Assent* is involuntary, but the *consent* which is added to it, or rather which is present as by way of implication, is voluntary.'[1] It is true that the intervention of the will may be required to overcome hesitation in giving assent; but this intervention is legitimate only when the hesitation is judged to be unreasonable. In other words, Ollé-Laprune wishes to avoid any implication that truth and falsity depend on the will and at the same time to attribute to the will an effective role in man's intellectual life.

This general treatment of assent and certitude constitutes a basis for reflection on man's assent to moral truths. A moral truth in the strict sense is an ethical truth. But Ollé-Laprune extends the range of meaning of the term to include metaphysical truths which, in his view, are closely connected with ethical truth. The moral life is defined as any exercise of human activity which implies the idea of obligation; and a truth of the moral order is 'any truth which appears as a *law* or a *condition* of the moral life'.[2] Thus 'all together, moral truths in the proper sense and metaphysical truths, form what one may call the order of moral things (*choses*), the moral order. One can also say that it is the religious order, if we abstract from positive religion.'[3] Moral truths can be summed up under four main headings: the moral law, liberty, the existence of God, and the future life.[4]

[1] *Ibid.*, p. 65.   [2] *Ibid.*, p. 4.
[3] *Ibid.*, p. 3. Ollé-Laprune means that he is abstracting from revelation.
[4] *Ibid.*, p. 98.

The influence of Kant can be seen not only in the close connection which Ollé-Laprune makes between man's moral life and his religious belief, but also in particular lines of thought. For example, Ollé-Laprune agrees with Kant that moral obligation implies freedom; and he approaches belief in the future life by arguing that recognition of the moral law and of a moral order warrants conviction that this order will triumph, and that its triumph demands human immortality. Though however Ollé-Laprune often refers appreciatively to Kant, he has no intention of accepting that Kantian position that religious beliefs are objects not of theoretical knowledge but solely of practical faith. And he criticizes at length the views of philosophers, such as Kant, Pascal, Maine de Biran, Cournot, Hamilton, Mansel and Spencer, who either deny or severely restrict the mind's power to prove moral truths. To put the matter in another way, the title of the work, *On Moral Certitude*, can be misleading. The word 'moral' refers to the moral dispositions which, according to Ollé-Laprune, are required for the full recognition of truths in the moral order. But it is not intended to indicate that in the case of moral truths a firm assent is given to a more or less probable hypothesis, still less that it is given simply because one wants the relevant propositions to be true. Ollé-Laprune can therefore claim of his book that it establishes, as against the fideists, that truth is 'independent of our will and of our thought, and that we have to recognize it, not create it.'[1]

The fact of the matter is that Ollé-Laprune was a devout Catholic whose sense of orthodoxy prevented any substitution of the will to believe for the perception of adequate rational grounds for assent. When therefore he undertakes to show, as against the *'dry rationalists* who admit only a kind of logical mechanism',[2] that in regard to the recognition of moral truths the will has a particular role to play, he has to stop short of any view which would entail the conclusion that these truths cannot be known to be true. At one end, so to speak, he can maintain that effective recognition of such truths requires personal dispositions of a moral nature which are not required for recognition of the truth of, say, mathematical propositions. For example, a man may refuse to recognize a moral obligation which entails consequences that, for lack of the requisite dispositions, he is reluctant or unwilling

---

[1] *Ibid.*, p. vii.   [2] *Ibid.*, p. vii.

to accept. And an effort of will is required to overcome this aversion to the truth. At the other end Ollé-Laprune can maintain that a purely intellectual assent to the conclusion of a proof of God's existence cannot become 'consent' and be transformed into a living faith without a personal commitment of the whole man, including the will. 'Complete certitude is *personal*: it is the total act of the soul itself embracing by a free choice, no less than by a firm judgment, the truth which is present to it. . . .'[1] Ollé-Laprune can also admit that in the case of moral truths an effort of the will may be required to overcome the hesitation occasioned by 'obscurities' which are not present in the case of purely formal truths, such as mathematical propositions. If, for instance, a man contemplates only 'the ordinary course of nature',[2] appearances seem to tell against immortality; and the man may therefore hesitate to assent to any argument in favour of human survival. Ollé-Laprune insists however that though an intervention of the will is required to overcome such hesitation, this intervention derives its justification not simply from the desire to believe but rather from recognition of the fact that hesitation to give assent is unreasonable and therefore ought to be overcome.

It is understandable that to some minds Ollé-Laprune should have appeared as a pragmatist or as a pioneer of modernism, in spite of his efforts to safeguard the objective truth of religious beliefs. But even the most orthodox theologian could hardly object to the claim that it is not simply by a process of reasoning that philosophy passes into religion, and that for a living faith what Ollé-Laprune describes as *consentement* is required. Moreover, from the theological point of view it is considerably easier to see how room is left for the activity of divine grace in Ollé-Laprune's account of religious belief than it is in the case of the purely rationalist apologetics which he criticizes. To be sure, Ollé-Laprune writes from the standpoint of a convinced believer; and what appear to some people as adequate grounds for not believing are presented by him as occasions for doubts and hesitations which the genuine seeker after truth can see that he is morally obliged to overcome. But though the arguments which he presents to establish the truth of the beliefs which he judges of importance for human life may appear unconvincing to many minds, he himself regards them as possessing a force which, for the man of good will, should outweigh the force of contrary

[1] *Ibid.*, p. 79.　　　[2] *Ibid.*, p. 107.

appearances. In other words, he has no intention of expounding a pragmatist theory of truth.

2. Mention has been made of the fact that Ollé-Laprune regarded thought as a form of action. But this theme is best considered in connection with his pupil Maurice Blondel (1861–1949), author of *L'action*.

Blondel was born at Dijon; and after studying at the local lycée he entered the École Normale at Paris, where he had Ollé-Laprune and Boutroux as his teachers and Victor Delbos as his fellow-student.[1] Blondel experienced considerable difficulty in getting action accepted as the subject for a thesis, though he eventually succeeded.[2] After two failures he obtained the *agrégation* in 1886 and was appointed to teach philosophy in the lycée at Montauban. In the same year he was transferred to Aix-en-Provence. In 1893 his thesis, *L'Action*, was submitted to the Sorbonne. His application for a university post was at first refused, on the ground that his thought was not properly philosophical. He was then offered a chair of history. But in 1894 the then minister of education, Raymond Poincaré, appointed him professor of philosophy in the University of Aix-en-Provence. Blondel held this post until 1927, when he retired because of failing eyesight.

The original edition of *L'Action* appeared in 1893.[3] This was also the date of Blondel's Latin thesis on Leibniz.[4] What is generally known as Blondel's *Trilogy* appeared in 1934–7. It consisted of *Thought* (*La Pensée*, 2 vols., 1934), *Being and Beings* (*L'être et les êtres*, 1935) and *Action* (2 vols., 1936–7). This last-mentioned work should not be confused with the original *L'Action*, which was reprinted in 1950 as the first volume of Blondel's *Premiers écrits* (*First Writings*). *La philosophie et l'esprit chrétien* (*Philosophy and the Christian Spirit*) was published in two volumes in 1944–6, and *Exigences philosophiques du christianisme* (*Philosophical Requirements of Christianity*) appeared posthumously in 1950.

---

[1] Victor Delbos (1862–1916) became a professor of the Sorbonne and published studies on Spinoza, Kant and German idealism. He was a friend and correspondent of Blondel.

[2] Blondel's preliminary reflections can be found in *Carnets intimes*.

[3] *L'Action. Essai d'une critique de la vie et d'une science de la pratique*. There were three versions, the thesis itself, a printed version and a version revised and added to by Blondel.

[4] *De vinculo substantiali et de substantia composita apud Leibnitium*. A French version, *Une énigme historique: le 'Vinculum substantiale' d'après Leibniz*, appeared in 1930.

In addition Blondel published a considerable number of essays, such as his Letter on the *Requirements of Contemporary Thought in the Matter of Apologetics* and *History and Dogma*.[1] The correspondence between Blondel and the Jesuit philosopher Auguste Valensin (1879–1953) was published in three volumes at Paris in 1957–65, while Blondel's *Philosophical Correspondence* with Laberthonnière, edited by C. Tresmontant, appeared in 1962. There is also a collection of philosophical letters written by Blondel to Boutroux, Delbos, Brunschvicg and others (Paris, 1961).

Blondel has often been described as a Catholic apologist. So indeed he was, and so he saw himself. In the project for his thesis *L'Action*, he referred to the work as philosophical apologetics. In a letter to Delbos he stated that for him philosophy and apologetics were basically one.[2] From the start he was convinced of the need for a Christian philosophy. But in his opinion 'there has never yet been, strictly speaking, any Christian philosophy.'[3] Blondel aspired to meet this need, or at any rate to point out the way to do so. Further, he spoke of trying to do 'for the Catholic form of thought what Germany has long since done, and continues to do for the Protestant form'.[4] But there is no need to multiply references to justify the description of Blondel as·a Catholic apologist.

Though however the description is justifiable, it can be extremely misleading. For it suggests the idea of a heteronomous philosophy, a philosophy, that is to say, which is used to support certain theological positions or to prove certain preconceived conclusions which are considered to be both philosophically demonstrable and an essential propaedeutic to or theoretical basis for Christian belief. In other words, the description of a philosophy as Christian apologetics suggests the idea of philosophy as a handmaid or servant of theology. And in so far as the business of Christian philosophy is conceived to be that of proving certain theses dictated by theology or by ecclesiastical authority, the

---

[1] These two long essays, published respectively in 1896 and 1904, have appeared in English translation, with an introduction, by Alexander Dru and Illtyd Trethowan (London, 1964).

[2] *Lettres philosophiques*, p. 71.

[3] *Lettre sur les exigences* (1956), p. 54. (*Letter on Apologetics*, English translation, p. 171).

[4] *Lettres philosophiques*, p. 34. Blondel's interest in German thought was stimulated by the lectures of Boutroux and by the studies of his friend Delbos, as well as by his own reading.

conclusion is likely to be drawn that Christian philosophy is not philosophy at all but theology in disguise.

Blondel recognized of course that philosophical concepts could be used in the explicitation of the content of Christian faith. But he insisted, rightly, that this process was internal to theology.[1] Philosophy itself, he was convinced, should be autonomous, in fact and not simply in theory. Christian philosophy too should therefore be autonomous. But an autonomous Christian philosophy did not, in his opinion, exist. It was something to be created. It would be Christian in the sense that it would exhibit man's lack of self-sufficiency and his opening to the Transcendent. In the process it would exhibit its own limitations as human thought and its lack of omnicompetence. Blondel was convinced that autonomous philosophical reflection, consistently and rigorously pursued, would in fact reveal in man an exigency for the supernatural, for that which is inaccessible to human effort alone. It would open the horizon of the human spirit to the free self-communication of the divine, which answers indeed to a profound need in man but which cannot be given through philosophy.[2] In brief, Blondel envisaged a philosophy which would be autonomous in its reflection but, through this reflection, self-limiting, in the sense that it pointed to what lay beyond itself. He was considerably influenced by Pascal, but he had a greater confidence in systematic philosophy. Perhaps we can say that Blondel aimed at creating the philosophy which was demanded by the thought of Pascal. But it must be philosophy. Thus in one place Blondel asserts that 'apologetical philosophy ought not to become a philosophical apologetics'.[3] That is to say, philosophy ought to be a process of autonomous rational reflection, not simply a means to an extra-philosophical end.

Blondel therefore wished to create something new or at any rate to make a substantial contribution to its creation. But he was not of course thinking of creation out of nothing, of bringing into existence, that is to say, a novelty without relation to past

[1] Mathematics, for example, is an autonomous discipline. But mathematical concepts might be used by a theologian. And if he uses such concepts, this does not convert theology into mathematics.

[2] Blondel was of course concerned, as was Augustine, with man in the concrete, who, from the point of view of Christian faith, is called to a supernatural end. For Blondel man as he is exhibits the need for the supernatural, for what transcends his own powers but towards which he reaches out.

[3] From the letter to Charles Denis, editor of *Annales de philosophie chrétienne* (*Lettre sur les exigences*, p. 3).

thought. We cannot enter here into any detailed discussion of the influence exercised upon his mind by particular movements and individual thinkers.[1] But a general, even if very sketchy account of the sort of way in which he interpreted the development of western philosophy seems to be required for the elucidation of his aims.

In Aristotelianism Blondel saw a remarkable expression of rationalism, of the tendency of reason, that is to say, to assert its omnicompetence and to absorb religion into itself. With Aristotle thought was divinized, and theoretical speculation was represented as man's highest activity and end. In the Middle Ages Aristotelianism was of course harmonized with Christian theology in a way which limited the scope of philosophy. But the harmonization was a conjunction of two factors, one of which, left to itself, would aspire to absorb the other; and the limitation of philosophy was imposed from outside. Philosophy may have been autonomous in theory; but in practice it was heteronomous. When the external control weakened or was lifted, rationalistic philosophy once more asserted its omnicompetence.[2] At the same time new lines of thought came into being. For example, whereas medieval realism had concentrated on objects of knowledge, Spinoza, though one of the great rationalists, started with the active subject and the problems of human existence and man's destiny. To this extent he pursued the way of 'immanence'; but he also understood that man can find his true fulfilment only in the Absolute which transcends himself.[3]

A step forward was made by Kant, with whom we see philosophy becoming self-critical and self-limiting. It is not, as in the Middle Ages, a question of limitations imposed from outside. The limitations are self-imposed as the result of self-criticism. The act of limiting is therefore compatible with the autonomous character of philosophy. At the same time Kant drove a wedge

---

[1] There are several books on aspects of this subject. For example, *The Blondelian Synthesis* by J. J. McNeil (Leiden, 1966) deals with Blondel's relation to Spinoza, Kant and the great German idealists, while *Hegel and Blondel* by P. Henrici (Munich, 1958) deals with his relation to Hegel in particular. For remarks by Blondel himself see *L'itinéraire philosophique de Maurice Blondel*, edited by F. Lefèvre (Paris, 1928).

[2] Blondel saw Luther's hostility to rationalism and his separation between philosophy and theology as having the practical effect of encouraging philosophy to assert its independence and to invade the sphere of theology.

[3] Blondel was fully conscious of course of Spinoza's pantheism and of his intellectualist interpretation of love and union with God. But when referring to past philosophers Blondel is more concerned with their significance for him than with exegesis.

between thought and being and between theory and practice or action, whereas Spinoza had aimed at overcoming the gulf between thought and being. Syntheses were attempted by the great German idealists, from whom the philosopher has much to learn.[1] But with Hegel especially we see a tendency to divinize reason, to identify human and absolute thought, and to absorb religion into philosophy. As a counterweight we can turn to the tradition from Pascal through Maine de Biran up to Ollé-Laprune and others which starts with the concrete active subject and reflects on the exigencies of its activity. What is wanting in this tradition however is a method which will make possible the construction of a philosophy of immanence which at the same time leads or points to transcendence.

From what has been said it should be clear that Blondel was no supporter of the 'Back to Aquinas' movement.[2] In his opinion the Christian thinker, concerned with the development of philosophy of religion, should not attempt to go back but rather to enter into the development of modern philosophy and to go beyond it from within. One great contribution of modern thought, he was convinced, was the concept of autonomous but self-limiting philosophy. This rendered possible for the first time a philosophy which would both point to the Transcendent and refrain, through its own critical self-limitation, from trying to capture the Transcendent in a rationalistic network. It would thus leave room for the divine self-revelation. Another contribution of modern philosophy (though foreshadowed in earlier thought) was the approach to being by way of the active subject's reflection on its own dynamism of thought and will, the method of immanence in other words. In Blondel's opinion it was only by means of this approach that a philosophy of religion could be developed which would mean

---

[1] For example, Blondel had considerable sympathy with Schelling's later philosophy of religion, though he regarded the division between negative and positive philosophy (or between philosophy of essence and philosophy of existence) as something which needed to be overcome.

[2] In earlier writings, such as the *Letter on Apologetics*, Blondel made some pretty sharp comments about Thomists and Scholasticism. As several writers have pointed out, what he had in mind was a form of Thomism which held aloof from modern thought or mentioned it only to criticize it, often caricaturing it in the process, and which suspected heresy in any Catholic philosopher who did not follow the party-line. Blondel's remarks about pseudo-philosophizing would not apply, for example, to Maréchal who tried to do one of the very things which Blondel thought necessary, to develop a Kantian line of thought beyond the position reached by Kant himself. Later Blondel devoted some more study to Aquinas himself and became more sympathetic. The Thomists whom Blondel castigated obviously paid little attention to the *spirit* of Aquinas.

something to modern man. For God to become a reality for him and not simply an object of thought or of speculation, man must rediscover God from within, not indeed as an object which can be found by introspection but by coming to see that the Transcendent is the goal of his thought and will.

If however Blondel was convinced that Catholic philosophers should throw themselves into the stream of modern thought, he did not mean to imply that modern philosophers had solved all the major problems which they raised. For example, whereas Aristotle in the ancient world had exalted thought to the detriment of practice or action, Kant in the modern world had emphasized the moral will at the expense of the theoretical reason, doing away with reason, as he put it, to make way for faith. The problem remained of uniting thought and will, thought and action or practice. Again, the *method* of immanence, the approach to being through critical reflection on the subject, could easily be converted and had in fact been converted, into a *doctrine* of immanence, asserting that nothing exists outside human consciousness or that the statement that anything so exists is devoid of meaning. There remained therefore the problem of pursuing the method of immanence while avoiding the doctrine or principle of immanence.

To be sure, some of Blondel's critics accused him of immanentism, in the sense that they attributed to him the principle or doctrine of immanence and concluded that on his premises man could never emerge from the prison-house of subjective impressions and ideas and assert the existence of any reality except as a content of human consciousness. Though however they were able to select certain passages in support of this interpretation, it is evident that he had no intention of proposing any doctrine which would entail subjective idealism. It is indeed true that he derived stimulus from a number of philosophers who enclosed all reality within the realm of thought.[1] But one of his aims was to close the gap between thought and being (considered as object of thought) without reducing being to thought. And though he was obviously

---

[1] In the case of a philosopher such as Hegel it was not of course a question of enclosing all reality within the realm of human thought as such. Hegel was not a subjective idealist. Reality was for him the self-expression of absolute thought, in which the human mind participates, at any rate at certain levels. In Blondel's opinion however Hegelianism was in fact an apotheosis of the human reason. And Blondel wished to open man's mind to the Transcendent, not to divinize the human reason.

aware of the fact that God cannot be conceived except through consciousness, he had no intention of suggesting that God is identifiable with man's idea of him. He wished to pursue a method of immanence which would lead to an affirmation of the Transcendent as an objective reality, in the sense of a reality which was not dependent on human consciousness.

For the solution of his problems Blondel looked to a philosophy of action. The term 'action' naturally suggests the idea of something which may be preceded by thought or accompanied by it but is not itself thought. But as Blondel uses the term, thought itself is a form of action. There are of course thoughts, ideas and representations which we tend to conceive as contents of consciousness and possible objects of thought. More fundamental however is the act of thinking which produces and sustains thought. And thought as activity or action is itself the expression of the movement of life, the dynamism of the subject or of the whole person. 'There is nothing in the properly subjective life which is not act. That which is properly subjective is not only what is conscious and known from within . . .; it is what causes the fact of consciousness to be.'[1] Action might perhaps be described as the dynamism of the subject, the aspiration and movement of the person seeking self-fulfilment. It is the life of the subject considered as integrating or synthesizing pre-conscious potentialities and tendencies, as expressing itself in thought and knowledge, and as reaching out towards further goals.

Blondel makes a distinction between what he calls 'the will-willing' (*la volonté voulante*) and 'the will-willed' (*la volonté voulue*). The latter consists of distinct acts of volition. One wills first this, then that. The former, the will-willing, is 'the movement which is common to every will'.[2] Blondel does not of course mean to imply that there are in man two wills. His contention is that there is in man a basic aspiration or movement (*la volonté voulante*) which expresses itself in willing distinct finite objects or ends but which can never be satisfied with any of them but reaches out beyond them. It is not itself the object of psychological introspection but rather the condition of all volitions or acts of will and at the same time that which lives and expresses itself in them and passes beyond them, as they are inadequate to it. Moreover, it is the operation of the basic will which leads to thought and knowledge. 'Knowledge is nothing more than the middle term, the fruit of

[1] *L'Action*, p. 99.   [2] *Ibid.*, p. xxi.

action and the seed of action.'[1] Thus even mathematics can be seen as 'a form of the development of the will'.[2] It does not follow that truth is simply what we decide that it is to be. What Blondel means is that man's life of thought and knowledge, whether in the sciences or in philosophy, is rooted in man's basic activity and must be seen in relation to it. In his view the genesis and the meaning or end of science and philosophy can be properly understood only in terms of the subject's fundamental and dynamic orientation.

It hardly needs saying that in his insistence on the basically dynamic character of the subject or ego Blondel stands within the general current of thought to which Maine de Biran gave such a powerful stimulus. But he also derived inspiration from his reflection on the thought of the German philosophers, as he understood it. Though, for example, he wished to overcome the Kantian dichotomies between theoretical and practical reason, the noumenal and phenomenal selves, and the spheres of freedom and necessity, he was certainly influenced by Kant's emphasis on the primacy of the practical reason or moral will. Again, we can find links between Blondel's concept of *la volonté voulante*, Fichte's idea of the pure ego as activity and Schelling's theory of a basic act of will or primitive choice which expresses itself in particular choices. But it is a question not of Blondel's taking or borrowing this idea from one philosopher and that idea from another philosopher but rather of his developing his own ideas in dialogue with the ideas of other thinkers either as expressed directly in their writings or as conveyed to him through the works of his friend Delbos. And we cannot discuss this process of dialogue here.

The philosophy of action can be described as a systematic inquiry into the conditions and dialectic of the dynamism of the subject, or as critical reflection on the *a priori* structure of the will-willing, seen as determining or expressing itself in man's thought and action, or perhaps as critical reflection on the basic orientation of the active subject as manifested in the genesis of morality, science and philosophy. The word 'subject' should not be understood in the narrow sense of the Cartesian ego or of the transcendental ego of German idealism. For action is the life of the 'human composite, the synthesis "of body and soul".'[3] But it is the basic orientation of the person as aiming at a goal with which Blondel

[1] *Lettres philosophiques*, p. 84.   [2] *L'Action*, p. 55, *n*. 1.
[3] *Lettres philosophiques*, p. 82.

is concerned. In other words, he is using the method of immanence to solve what he sees as the problem of human destiny.

To take an example, Blondel tries to show that the idea of liberty or freedom arises on the basis of the determinism of nature. The will is subject to desires and tendencies, but in its potential infinity it transcends the factual order and reaches out towards ideal ends. On the basis of a determinism of nature the subject becomes aware of its freedom. But at the same time it substitutes for the determinism of nature that of reason and obligation. Obligation is 'a necessary postulate of the will'[1] and a synthesis of the ideal and the real. Morality or the moral order does not represent therefore an imposition from without: it arises in the dialectical self-unfolding of the dynamism of the subject. But the feeling of obligation, the awareness of a moral imperative, can arise only through the subject transcending the factual, in the sense that it learns to find the motive of its behaviour in the ideal. In other words, the moral consciousness involves an implicit metaphysics, an implicit recognition of the natural or factual order as related to a metaphysical or ideal sphere of reality.

As one might expect, Blondel proceeds to argue that the total activity of the human subject cannot be understood except in terms of an orientation to a transcendent Absolute, to the infinite as final end of the will. This does not mean of course that the Transcendent can be discovered as an object, whether internal or external. Rather is it a question of the subject becoming aware of its dynamic orientation to the Transcendent and of being faced with an option, the choice between asserting and denying the reality of God. Philosophical reflection, that is to say, gives rise to the idea of God; but precisely because God is transcendent, man can either affirm or deny the reality of God. Blondel sees man as beset by what an existentialist might call 'anxiety', as seeking an adequation between the will-willed and the will-willing. In his view the adequation cannot be attained except through God. But the method of immanence can lead only to the necessity of an option. As Sartre was to say after him, Blondel tells us that 'man aspires to be God'.[2] This means however that he is faced with the choice between substituting his own will for the divine will, thus choosing against God with the idea of God,[3] and becoming God (united with God) only through God. Ultimately, what a man

---

[1] *L'Action*, p. 302.   [2] *L'Action*, p. 356.
[3] As Nietzsche may be said to have done.

becomes depends on his will. Is his will to live sufficient, to speak paradoxically, to die 'by consenting to be supplanted by God',[1] his will being united with the divine will? Or will he seek to be self-sufficient and autonomous without God? The choice is man's. At a point in the dialectic of man's basic movement or aspiration the idea of God as a reality necessarily arises. But it still remains open to man to affirm or to deny God as a reality.

Blondel's theory of the option was understood by some critics as implying that in his view the existence of God was incapable of proof, and that assertion of it was simply the result of an act of the will, of the will to believe that is to say. In point of fact however Blondel did not reject all proofs of God's existence. He regarded the philosophy of action as itself constituting a proof, inasmuch as the way of immanence showed the necessity of the idea of God. It was not a question of rejecting, for example, the argument from contingency as worthless but rather of interiorizing it and trying to show how the idea of the necessary being arises through the subject's reflection on its own orientation or movement and aspiration. As for the option, Blondel regards this as necessary if God is to be a reality 'for us'.[2] Speculative knowledge may precede the option; but without the option, without the subject's free self-relating to God, there can be no *effective* knowledge. 'The living thought which we have of him (God) is and remains living only if it turns towards practice, if one lives by it and if one's action is nourished by it.'[3] This however demands a voluntary act of self-relating not to the idea of God but to God as being.

Catholic critics also understood Blondel as claiming that supernatural revelation and life were not gratuitous but necessary, fulfilling, that is to say, a demand in the nature of man, a demand which man's creator had to satisfy. Though however Blondel's statements sometimes provided ground for this interpretation, it is clear that 'the supernatural' which is demanded by the method of immanence is simply the 'undetermined supernatural', in the sense that the philosophy of action shows, for Blondel, that man should accept and surrender himself to the Transcendent. Christian revelation is the positively determined form of the supernatural; and man should accept it, if it is true. But the method of immanence cannot prove that it is true. At the same time nobody could accept the positively determined supernatural, unless there were something in him to which it answered and responded.

[1] *L'Action*, p. 354.   [2] *L'Action*, p. 426.   [3] *Ibid.*, p. 354.

Otherwise it would be irrelevant. And the method of immanence shows that this something, a dynamic orientation to the Transcendent, is really there.[1]

Of course, if we say, as we have said above, that the philosophy of action reveals the necessity of the idea of 'God', the impression can easily be given that Blondel regards the method of immanence as leading to the specifically Christian belief in God. Looking back however on modern philosophy Blondel sees some systems as resolutely trying to exclude the Transcendent and others as trying to take the Transcendent by storm, as it were, and producing only an idol or caricature. In his view the method of immanence, as pursued in the philosophy of action, opens man's mind and will to the Transcendent, while leaving room for God's self-revelation. In this sense a truly critical philosophy is a Christian philosophy and a Christian apologetics, not in the sense that it tries to prove the truth of Christian doctrines but rather in the sense that it leads man to the point at which he is open to God's self-revelation and to the divine action. 'Philosophy cannot directly demonstrate or procure (for us) the supernatural'.[2] But it can proceed indirectly by eliminating incomplete solutions to the problem of human destiny and showing us 'what we inevitably have and what is necessarily lacking to us.'[3] Philosophy can show the insufficiency of the natural order for providing the goal of the dynamic orientation of the human spirit. At the same time philosophy's self-criticism reveals its own incompetence to provide man with the beatitude to which he aspires. It thus points beyond itself.

Though Blondel made it clear enough that he had no intention of identifying God with the immanent idea of God, and though he was opposed to the historicism of the modernists, to anyone who is aware of the situation in the Catholic Church during the modernist crisis it is not surprising that Blondel came under suspicion and was thought by some to have been involved in the condemnation of 'religious immanentism' in the encyclical *Pascendi* which Pope Pius X issued in 1907. Matters were not improved by Blondel's opposition to the *Action Française* movement, which he regarded as an unholy alliance between positivist sociology and a reactionary Catholicism. For though Charles

---

[1] For a discussion of Blondel's position in regard to the supernatural see *Blondel et le christianisme* by Henri Bouillard (Paris, 1961).
[2] *Lettre sur les exigences*, p. 85 (*Letter on Apologetics*, p. 198).   [3] *Ibid.*, p. 85.

Maurras was an atheist who endeavoured to make use of the
Church for his own ends, the movement was supported by a
number of distinguished but very traditional theologians and
Thomists who disliked Blondel's originality and independence,
considered him corrupted by German thought, and did not
hesitate to accuse him of modernism. In point of fact Blondel's
ideas were never condemned by Rome, in spite of efforts in this
direction. But it is probably fortunate for him that he had not
become a priest, as he had once thought of doing. It must be
added however that he did not indulge in the kind of ardent
polemics carried on by his friend Laberthonnière. And the obscurity of his style or, if preferred, the fact that he was a highly
professional philosopher and not a popularizer may well have
contributed some protection.

In any case Blondel weathered the years of controversy and
criticism and, as has already been mentioned, he at length
produced his trilogy (*La Pensée*, *L'Être et les êtres* and the second
L'Action), followed by *Philosophy and The Christian Spirit*. Some
writers on Blondel have pretty well neglected the later works,
perhaps regarding them as an expression of second thoughts
under the pressure of criticism and as being tamer and more
traditional than the original *L'Action*. Other writers have insisted
that the trilogy represents the philosopher's mature thought,
sometimes adding that the emphasis placed in it on ontological
and metaphysical themes shows that it is a mistake to describe
him as an apologist on the basis of the first *L'Action* and the *Letter on
Apologetics*. In some instances they have been glad of the opportunity to assimilate his thought to the metaphysical tradition
passing through St. Thomas Aquinas.[1] Though however the
trilogy obviously does represent Blondel's mature thought and
though he did indeed come to have a greater respect for Aquinas,
Blondel continued to be concerned with developing an autonomous philosophy which would be at the same time open to
Christianity. In this sense he remained an apologist, even if in his
later writings he emphasized the ontological implications and
presuppositions of his thought as previously presented.

In *La Pensée* Blondel inquires into the antecedent conditions
of human thought and defends the theory of 'cosmic thought'
(*la pensée cosmique*). In his view we cannot justifiably make a sharp

[1] See, for example, *Introduction à la métaphysique de Maurice Blondel* by
Claude Tresmontant (Paris, 1963).

dichotomy between human beings as thinking subjects on the one
hand and Nature as mindless matter on the other. On the contrary, Leibniz was right in maintaining that the material always
has its psychical aspect. Indeed, the intelligible organic universe
can be described as 'a subsistent thought',[1] not of course conscious
thought but thought 'in search of itself'.[2] In the process of the
world's development conscious thought arises on the basis of a
hierarchy of levels, each successive level prerequiring the antecedent levels, introducing something new and creating problems, as
it were, the solution of which demands a higher level. In man the
spontaneous, concrete thought present in Nature persists; but
there also arises abstract analytic thought which deals with
symbols.[3] The tension between them had been noted by some
previous philosophers. The Scholastics spoke of 'reason' (*ratio*) and
'intellect' (*intellectus*), Spinoza of degrees of knowledge, Newman
of notional and real assent. Together with advertence to the
distinction between different types of thought there has gone the
vision of a synthesis at a higher level, as with the Scholastics and
Spinoza in their several ways. The condition of any such synthesis,
of the self-perfecting of thought, is participation in the life of
absolute thought, in a union with God in which vision and love are
one. But the attainment of this goal of the dialectic of thought lies
beyond the competence of philosophy and of human effort in
general.

In *L'Être et les êtres* Blondel turns from thought to being and
interrogates, as it were, different kinds of things to discover
whether they merit being described as beings. Matter fails to pass
the test. It is not a being. It is 'less a thing than the common
condition of the resistances, which all things oppose to us and
which we oppose to ourselves.'[4] It is indeed, to use the language of
Aristotelianism, the principle of individuation and multiplicity,
and it thus provides a good ground for the rejection of monism,
but it is not itself substantial being. The living organism, with its
specific unity, its spontaneity and relative autonomy, presents a
better claim; but though it transmits an *élan vital*, its activity is
counterbalanced by passivity, and it lacks both real autonomy
and immortality. As for human persons, they present a still better
claim. At the same time their lack of self-sufficiency can be shown

---

[1] *La Pensée*, I, p. 4.   [2] *Ibid.*, p. 6.
[3] Blondel adds to his distinction between will-willing and will-willed a distinction between *cogitatio ut natura* (*La Pensée*, I, p. 495) and thought-thought.
[4] *L'Être*, p. 80.

in many ways. It may seem therefore that it is the universe in its totality which alone merits the name of being. But the universe is becoming rather than being. It participates in being; but it is not being itself.

In these reflections Blondel obviously takes it that there is in man an implicit and real idea of 'Being in itself',[1] which is found not to be fully instantiated in matter, organisms, persons or even in the universe considered as a developing totality. But he does not claim that this implicit idea is able to provide a basis for the ontological argument of St. Anselm. Hence he is bound to ask whether there is justification for asserting that the idea refers to a reality. While not rejecting arguments of a traditional nature from the world to God, Blondel maintains that 'our idea of God has its source, not in a light which belongs to us, but in the illuminating action of God in us.'[2] 'The fundamental and congenital aptitude of the spirit for knowing and desiring God is the initial and supreme cause of the whole movement of nature and thought, so that our certainty of being is thus grounded on Being itself.'[3]

In the second *Action* Blondel says that in the original work of this name he had deliberately left on one side 'the redoubtable metaphysical difficulties of the problem of secondary causes'[4] and had considered action only in man and with a view to a study of human destiny. In the second *Action* however he widens his horizon to include action in general, and he includes themes which had been passed over in the first version. He argues, for example, that the pure and complete concept of action is verified only in God, who is absolute activity (*l'Agir absolu*) and who is the productive course of all finite things. At the same time there are graded approximations, so to speak, to the absolute divine activity; and the question arises, how is it possible for God to create finite beings as free and responsible moral agents? Blondel tries to combine recognition of man's creative activity and moral responsibility with the belief in divine creation and with his theory of the basic orientation of the human spirit to the Transcendent and of the perfecting of human nature through the union of the human will with the divine.

This broadening of horizons to cover wide-ranging ontological and metaphysical themes undoubtedly gives to the trilogy a different flavour, as it were, from that of the original *L'Action* and

---

[1] *Ibid.*, p. 156.   [2] *Ibid.*, p. 163.   [3] *Ibid.*, p. 167.
[4] *L'Action* (trilogy), I, p. 298.

the *Letter on Apologetics*. But though the trilogy widens the scope of reflection, it does not constitute a repudation of the first *L'Action*. Blondel remains profoundly convinced of the basic dynamic orientation of the human spirit to God; and the widening of horizons can be seen as a covering of problems implicit in his original line of thought. The change in Blondel's ways of expressing his thought and the respectful attitude which he often shows to Aquinas can be misleading. For instance, though in *La Pensée* Blondel is careful to allow for the role of traditional-type proofs of God's existence, he makes it clear that if they are taken in isolation and as exercises in theoretical metaphysics, they lead to an *idea* of God, and that for God to be a living reality for man, the God of the religious consciousness, something more is required. He may avoid use of the word 'option'; but the fundamental idea remains. Blondel will not allow that there is a final and unbridgeable dichotomy between 'the God of the philosophers' and 'the God of religion'. The difference arises because there are different types of thought in man; but the ideal is an integration of conflicting tendencies within man. And this ideal was obviously present in the original *L'Action*.

It is difficult to see how Blondel can ever be a popular writer. He writes for philosophers rather than for the general public. Moreover, a good many readers, even if they are philosophers, are probably often left wondering precisely what he means. But he is notable as a Catholic thinker who developed his ideas in dialogue with modern philosophy in its spiritualist, idealist and positivist movements. He did not call simply for a return to the medieval past, when brought into line with modern science. Nor did he adopt an attitude of discipleship in regard to any given thinker. We can of course discern lines of thought which link him with Augustine and Bonaventure, just as we can see affinities with Leibniz, Kant, Maine de Biran and others. But he was throughout an original thinker. And the general idea of a philosophy which should be intrinsically autonomous but at the same time self-critical and self-limiting and open to Christian revelation is presumably acceptable in principle to all Catholic thinkers who have any use for metaphysical philosophy.[1] Some may of course believe that the approach to metaphysics 'from within', by way of reflection on the active subject, which was characteristic of

[1] How far Blondel's philosophy really is 'autonomous' is of course open to discussion.

Maine de Biran and which is especially noticeable in the first *Action*, smacks of subjectivism. In this case they will welcome the widening of horizons in the trilogy as equivalent to an acknowledgement of the inadequacy of the way of immanence. But Blondel's approach does at any rate have the merit of trying to exhibit the relevance of religion. And he recognized the fact, also seen by the so-called transcendental Thomists, that the traditional proofs of God's existence, based on the external world, rest on presuppositions which can be justified only by systematic reflection on the activity of the subject in thought and volition.

3. Among Blondel's correspondents was Lucien Laberthonnière (1860–1932).[1] After studying in a seminary at Bourges Laberthonnière became an Oratorian in 1886 and taught philosophy in the Oratorian school at Juilly and then at a school in Paris. In 1900 he returned to Juilly as rector of the College; but when the Combes government had passed its legislation against religious orders and congregations in 1902, he went to live in Paris. In 1903 he published *Essays in Religious Philosophy* (*Essais de philosophie religieuse*) and in 1904 *Christian Realism and Greek Idealism* (*Le réalisme chrétien et l'idéalisme grec*). In 1905 Blondel made him editor of the *Annales de philosophie chrétienne*. In the following year however two of his writings were placed on the Index. In 1911 he published *Positivism and Catholicism* (*Positivisme et catholicisme*); but in 1913 he was prohibited by the ecclesiastical authorities from further publication. In this period of enforced silence one or two writings of Laberthonnière were published under the name of friends.[2] But the bulk had to await posthumous publication. In 1935 Louis Canet started to publish these works at Paris under the general title *Oeuvres de Laberthonnière*.

In spite of the treatment which he received Laberthonnière never broke with the Church. Still less did he abandon his deep Christian faith. It is indeed both probable and natural that the placing of two of his books on the Index and the later veto on further publication increased his hostility not only to authoritarianism but also to Aristotelianism and Thomism.[3] But this hostility certainly did not originate in reaction to the measures taken by ecclesiastical authority. It was a reasoned attitude,

---

[1] This correspondence has been edited by C. Tresmontant, *Correspondance philosophique, Maurice Blondel–Lucien Laberthonnière* (Paris, 1961).

[2] For example, P. Sanson's *L'inquiétude humaine* was really written by Laberthonnière.

[3] Laberthonnière was much more polemically inclined than Blondel.

based on his view of human life, of the nature of philosophy and of the Christian religion. If it had not been for his reduction to silence, his ideas might have made a much greater impression. As it was, other philosophers were coming to the fore by the time when his works were at length published. One must add however that whereas Blondel concentrated on expounding his own thought, Laberthonnière tended to work out and exhibit his ideas while discussing those of other thinkers, sometimes in a markedly polemical manner. Thus the first volumes of the *Works* as published by Louis Canet contain Laberthonnière's *Studies on Descartes* (*Études sur Descartes*, 1935) and his *Studies in Cartesian Philosophy* (*Études de philosophie cartésienne*, 1938) while the *Outline of a Personalist Philosophy* (*Esquisse d'une philosophie personnaliste*, 1942) presents a philosophical outlook which is developed, in large measure, by way of critical discussion of the ideas of other philosophers, such as Renouvier, Bergson and Brunschvicg. One part, for example, is entitled 'the pseudo-personalism of Charles Renouvier'. It does not follow of course that Laberthonnière's ideas are not of value. Moreover, Blondel too developed his thought through a process of dialogue with other philosophers. At the same time in the original *L'Action* and in the trilogy the reader is much less distracted from the author's own line of thought by polemical and historical excursions than in the case of Laberthonnière's main works.

In the notes which form the preface to his *Studies on Descartes* Laberthonnière asserts that 'every philosophical doctrine has as ts end to give a meaning to life, to human existence'.[1] Every philosophy has a moral motivation, even if the philosopher gives to his thought a quasi-mathematical form. This can be seen even in the case of Spinoza, in whose thought the geometrical structure is really subordinate to the underlying aim and motivation. Further, the test of a philosophy's truth is its viability, its capacity for being lived. Laberthonnière is actually referring to the need for detecting the animating principle, the underlying and pervasive moral motivation, in any philosophy studied. But what he has to say expresses of course his own idea of what philosophy should be. 'There is only one problem, the problem of ourselves, from which all the others derive.'[2] What are we? And what ought we to be?

[1] *Études sur Descartes*, I, p. 1.
[2] *Études de philosophie cartésienne* (1938), p. 1.

The animal, Laberthonnière asserts, is certainly not a machine; but it does not enjoy the self-consciousness which is required for raising problems in regard to the world and itself. For the matter of that, the human will-to-live is in origin akin to that of the animal. That is to say, the human will-to-live is oriented first of all to 'the things of time and space'.[1] The living organism, impelled by the will-to-live, learns empirically to seek for some things as satisfying desires and needs and to shun other things as causing suffering or menacing its existence. With the awakening of self-consciousness however the situation changes. Man becomes conscious of himself not as something already made and complete but rather as something which is to be and ought to be. In fact, according to Laberthonnière we are carried, as it were out of or beyond ourselves by the aspiration to possess the plenitude of being. Here however several paths lie open to man.

In the first place man finds himself in a world of things, which self-consciousness sets over against him. On the one hand he can make of this world of things a spectacle, an object of theoretical or aesthetic contemplation, possessing things, so to speak, without being possessed by them. This is the attitude exemplified in Aristotle's idea of contemplation. On the other hand man can strive to discover the properties of things and the laws governing the succession of phenomena in order to obtain mastery over things, to use them and to produce or destroy phenomena as he wills. Both attitudes can be described as pertaining to physics. But in the first case we have a physics of contemplation, while in the second case we have a physics of exploitation, such as has been practised from the time of Descartes onwards.

In the second place however man does not find himself simply in a world of things. He is not simply an isolated individual face to face with a material and non-self-conscious environment. He finds himself also in a world of persons who, like him, can say 'I' or 'I am'. This world of persons forms already a certain unity. We live and feel and thnk and will in a social world. Within however this material unity human beings can obviously experience hostility to one another. Beyond the basic natural unity there is a moral unity which is something to be achieved rather than something given. In this field the aspiration to possess the plenitude of being takes the form of the sense of obligation to become one with others, to achieve a moral unity of persons. Laberthonnière

[1] *Ibid.*, p. 2.

distinguishes between 'things' and 'beings', reserving the word 'being' for the self-conscious subject, who is characterized by an interiority which the 'thing' does not possess. This self-conscious subject aspires to possess the plenitude of being through union with other subjects.

How is this unity to be achieved? It is of course possible to attempt to achieve it by means of an authority, of whatever kind, which dictates what men should think and say and do, treating human beings as animals which have to be trained. But this procedure can produce no more than an external unity which, according to Laberthonnière, simply transfers conflict from the external to the internal spheres. The only efficacious way of achieving unity between beings which exist in and for themselves is by each person overcoming his egoism and giving himself by setting himself at the service of others, so that the unification is the fruit of an expansion from within, so to speak, and not imposed from without. There is of course a place for authority, but for an authority which maintains a common ideal and tries to help persons to develop themselves as persons rather than to mould them by coercion or to reduce them to the level of sheep.

What Laberthonnière has to say on this matter obviously has its implications both in the political and in the ecclesiastical sphere. For example, when referring in one place to what he regards as the wrong use of authority, he mentions 'Caesarist or Fascist'[1] domination. It does not follow however that emphasis on Fascist totalitarianism is accompanied by a blindness to the possible shortcomings of democracy. For instance, in a note he speaks of democracy which 'instead of being a dynamic movement (*élan*) towards the ideal through the spiritualization of human life has become a stampede towards the goods of the earth through a systematic materialization of life'.[2] In other words, modern western democracy, though animated originally by an impulse directed to ideal goals, has become materialistic and cannot therefore simply be contrasted with political authoritarianism as the good is contrasted with the bad. As for the ecclesiastical sphere, it is obvious that Laberthonnière was opposed to the policy of trying to impose uniformity from above and to the sort of methods from which he personally was to suffer. He had, as it were, a post-Vatican II mentality long before the second Vatican Council. The same kind of ideas about the development of persons as

---

[1] *Ibid.*, p. 5.   [2] *Ibid.*, p. 5*n*.

persons and of their union through personally willed acceptance of common ideals came out in his theory of education.

According to Laberthonnière therefore there is a natural unity. 'All men constitute one humanity by nature.'[1] There is also a unity which remains to be achieved, as a willed ideal. This shows that we have a common origin and a common goal. Beings (self-conscious subjects, that is to say) proceed from God and can attain their end only through union with the divine will. God is not so much a problem as 'the solution of the problem which we are for ourselves'.[2] Without reference to God we cannot answer such questions as 'what are we?' and 'what ought we to be?'. Or, rather, in attempting to answer these questions we are inevitably led into the sphere of religious belief.

Laberthonnière was influenced by Maine de Biran and Boutroux, and also by Blondel. Philosophy was for him the science of life, human life; and its point of departure was '*ourselves* as interior and spiritual realities having consciousness of ourselves'.[3] The word 'science' however must not be misunderstood. Science in the ordinary sense is a science of things, a physics of some kind, even if it takes human beings in their phenomenal reality into consideration. But metaphysics, to have a meaning for us, must illuminate the problems of life; and it must be livable. Biology deals with life and psychology with mind; and they have of course their value. But metaphysics is concerned with the self-conscious active subject as oriented to an ideal and a goal; and it is a science of life in the sense that it illuminates the nature and goal of the life of this subject (or of the person) considered as such.

There is no great difficulty in understanding Laberthonnière's hostility to Aristotelianism and traditional Thomism, an hostility which led him to take a dim view of what he regarded as the weak concessions made by Blondel to Aquinas and the Thomists. In Laberthonnière's opinion Aristotelianism was a physics rather than a metaphysics, even if part of it was labelled 'metaphysics'. And the God of Aristotle, wrapped up in himself, bore little resemblance to the living and active God of religion. As for Spinoza and other monists, they denied to all intents and purposes the irreducible distinctness of persons, while the positivists cut off the goal of unity-in-distinction from its ultimate transcendent and at the same time immanent foundation.

---

[1] *Ibid.*, p. 11.   [2] *Ibid.*, p. 11.
[3] *Esquisse d'une philosophie personnaliste* (1942), p. 7.

The reader is likely to conclude that Laberthonnière's idea of philosophy and his critical discussions of other philosophers, such as Aristotle, Descartes, Spinoza and Bergson, were influenced by his Christian belief. This conclusion would be obviously correct. But in the case of Laberthonnière all was out in the open; there was no attempt at concealment. In his view it was wrong to suppose that Christianity could be superimposed on a philosophy which had already been constructed or which was developed independently of Christian faith. For Christianity is 'itself *the* philosophy in the etymological sense of the word, that is to say wisdom, the science of life which explains what we are and, on the basis of what we are, what we ought to be.'[1] The question whether or not there can be a Christian philosophy rests on a false assumption if one is thinking of a philosophy worked out independently of Christian belief and which would serve as a 'natural' basis on which Christianity could be superimposed as a 'supernatural' superstructure. This is the sort of idea which followed in the wake of the invasion of Aristotelianism in the Middle Ages. Christianity is itself the true philosophy. And by the very fact that it is the true philosophy it excludes every other system. For 'every philosophy which deserves this name . . . presents itself, if not as exhaustive, at least as exclusive of what is not itself.'[2]

Laberthonnière obviously does not mean to imply that a man who is not a Christian is unable to raise and reflect on metaphysical problems. For it is clear that human life or existence can give rise to problems in anyone's mind, whether he is a Christian or not. Laberthonnière's thesis is rather that it is Christianity which provides the most adequate solution available to man. Or, better, Christianity is for him the saving wisdom, the true 'science of life', by which man can live. As he explicitly recognizes, Laberthonnière thus returns to the point of view of St. Augustine and other early Christian writers who looked on Christianity as being itself the true and genuine philosophy which fulfilled and supplanted the philosophies of the ancient world. The separation and subsequent conflict between philosophy and theology was a disaster. St. Thomas Aquinas did not baptize Aristotle; he aristotelianized Christianity, introducing into it 'the pagan conception of the world and of life'.[3] To be sure, if we once make a sharp separation between philosophy and theology, it appears inappropriate to describe Christianity as a philosophy,

[1] *Ibid.*, p. 13.   [2] *Ibid.*, p. 13.   [3] *Ibid.*, p. 643.

even as the true philosophy. But there is no compelling reason to make the separation. It may seem that philosophy is the work of 'pure reason' and belongs to the natural level, whereas theology is the fruit of revelation proceeding from the supernatural sphere. But according to Laberthonnière it is a mistake to look on the natural and the supernatural as two worlds, of which the latter is superimposed on the former. The terms 'natural' and 'supernatural' should be understood not in terms of a metaphysical dualism but as referring to 'two opposed manners of being and acting, of which one corresponds to what we are, to what we think and to what we do in virtue of our innate egocentricism, while the other corresponds to what we have the obligation of being, of thinking and of doing through willed generosity.'[1] If therefore metaphysical philosophy is regarded as dealing with the problems of what we are and what we ought to be, it is in no way derogatory to Christianity to describe it as the true philosophy. For it is precisely on these problems that it throws light, with a view to enabling man to become what he ought to be.

Given this point of view, it is natural enough that Laberthonnière should emphasize the close connection between truth and life. 'One does not demonstrate that God exists, no more than one demonstrates any existence. One finds him in seeking him. But one seeks only because one has already found him, only because he is present and active in the consciousness which we have of ourselves.'[2] In regard to Christian dogmas too Laberthonnière thoroughly dislikes the idea of them as pieces of information, so to speak, which come from a supernatural world and which we simply have to accept on authority. He certainly rejects a purely relativistic view of Christian dogmas, but he looks on them from the point of view of their capacity to illuminate human problems and to be guides for life. Without relevance for human life they would have no real meaning for us. It is not, Laberthonnière insists, a case of making man the measure of all truth, including revealed truth. For by considering truth in relation to ourselves and our lives we thereby measure ourselves by the truth rather than the other way round. If we understand the term 'pragmatism' as covering the view that truth in the religious sphere becomes '*our* truth' when we see its relevance to our lives, we can of course

---

[1] *Ibid.*, p. 15. The distinction, Laberthonnière remarks, is really the same as that between St. Paul's carnal and spiritual man.
[2] *Ibid.*, p. 19. This is basically Augustinian doctrine.

describe Laberthonnière as a pragmatist. But if we understand pragmatism as implying, for example, that the assertion of God's existence is true only in the sense that it is useful for man to make this assertion, he was certainly not a pragmatist. For he believed that we cannot know ourselves properly without recognizing the *reality* of God.

From one point of view Laberthonnière's view of the nature of philosophy and metaphysics is a matter of terminology. That is to say, if we decide to mean by 'metaphysics' the saving wisdom, it is clear that for the Christian Christianity itself must be '*the* metaphysics'.[1] And if Laberthonnière were accused of reducing the Christian religion to the level of a philosophy, he could reply that the accusation rested on a misunderstanding of his use of the word 'philosophy'. At the same time, when he says that metaphysics, identified with Christian doctrine as 'the science of our life',[2] has *ourselves* as its point of departure, one can understand theologians suspecting him of pure immanentism, especially if they take such propositions out of the context in which he is distinguishing between what he means by metaphysics and what Aristotle meant.

It may seem that Laberthonnière has really no place in a history of philosophy. But this judgment obviously presupposes a concept of philosophy which he rejects. In any case his thought is of some interest. It continues the approach to metaphysics from within which was characteristic of Maine de Biran, but in its concept of the relation between metaphysics and Christianity it goes back to St. Augustine. By his attitude to Aquinas's attempt to incorporate Aristotelianism into a comprehensive theological-philosophical world-vision Laberthonnière recalls to our minds the reaction which produced and followed on the condemnations of 1277. But his hostility to Aristotle and Aquinas is motivated not so much by veneration for the *sancti* and for tradition as such as by his own personalist and, to a certain extent, existentialist approach. For instance, his attack on the Aristotelian theory of matter as the principle of individuation is made in the name of a spiritualist personalism. He is in a real sense a modern Augustinian who develops his thought through dialogue with other philosophers such as Descartes, Bergson and Brunschvicg. His insistence on Christian doctrines becoming truths for us, *our* truths, in proportion as we discern and appropriate their relevance to human life

---

[1] *Ibid.*, p. 7.   [2] *Ibid.*, p. 7.

may assimilate him to the modernists. But he combines this insistence with a genuine attempt to avoid a relativism which would exclude the claim that there are objective and abiding Christian truths.

4. The term 'modernism' was first used in the early years of the twentieth century and seems to have been coined by opponents of the movement, though it was also used by writers such as Buonaiuti, who published *The Programme of the Modernists* (*Il programma dei modernisti*) in 1907. It is easy enough to mention names of persons who are universally classified as modernists. In France there is Alfred Loisy (1857–1940), in Italy Ernesto Buonaiuti (1881–1946) and in Great Britain George Tyrrell (1861–1909). But it is a great deal more difficult to give a clear account of the content of modernism, and still more difficult to define it. Perhaps the easiest way of coping with the matter is to give an historical account, as proper attention can then be paid to differences in interests and lines of thought.[1] One can of course attempt to delineate modernism as a system, in an abstract manner; but one then exposes oneself to the pertinent objection that modernism as a clearly defined system was created not by the modernists themselves but by the ecclesiastical documents condemning them, such as the decree *Lamentabili* and, much more, the encyclical *Pascendi*, both of which appeared in 1907.[2] It would however be quite out of place to attempt to give a history of the modernist movement in this chapter. And the primary purpose of the following remarks is to show why thinkers such as Blondel and Laberthonnière were suspected of modernism, and how the thought of Blondel at any rate differed from modernism in the sense in which modernism was condemned by Rome.

The term 'modernism', taken by itself, might be understood in terms of modernization, in the sense of an attempt to bring Roman Catholic thought into line with contemporary scholarship and intellectual developments. In view of his positive attitude towards the greatly increased knowledge of Aristotelianism which

---

[1] Among general works on the subject mention can be made of *Le modernisme dans l'église* by J. Rivière (Paris, 1929), *The Modernist Movement in the Roman Church* by A. R. Vidler (London, 1934) and *Histoire, dogme et critique dans la crise moderniste* by E. Poulat (Paris, 1962).

[2] In the papal encyclical *Pascendi* it is explicitly stated that the document gathers together views which are expressed separately in the writings of the modernists and arranges them in a systematic manner, so that their presuppositions and implications can be clearly seen. In other words, the document undertakes to make explicit what is regarded as an implicit system.

was creating a stir in the thirteenth century, St. Thomas Aquinas has been spoken of as a modernist.[1] Again, Catholic scholars such as Louis Duchesne (1843–1922), who were concerned with applying to the origins of Christianity the methods of historical criticism which had developed in liberal Protestantism, especially in Germany, can be described as modernist in this general sense of the term. So of course can writers such as Blondel who insisted on the need for a more positive appreciation of modern philosophy.

As used however with reference to a current of thought in the Catholic Church at the end of the nineteenth century and in the first decade of the present century, the term 'modernism' is obviously more specific than modernization or *aggiornamento* in a general sense. In the case of Loisy, for example, it refers to his conclusions about what was required or implied by the updating of historical and biblical studies. For instance, Loisy believed that Jesus as the Son of God was the creation of Christian faith reflecting on and transforming the man Jesus of Nazareth. This transformation involved also a deformation inasmuch as, for example, it involved attributing to the man Jesus miraculous actions the acceptance of which as historical events was ruled out by modern thought and knowledge. The task of historical criticism was to rediscover the historical figure hidden beneath the veils which faith had woven about it. In brief, Loisy maintained in effect that the historian of Christianity must approach his subject as he would approach any other historical theme, and that this approach demanded a purely naturalistic account of Christ himself and of the origins and rise of the Christian Church. We may of course wish to distinguish between historical inquiry in itself and 'higher criticism' as it developed in liberal Protestantism and then influenced some Catholic thinkers, but it is understandable that Loisy's ideas did not commend themselves to the authorities of the Church. For these ideas pretty well undermined the Church's claims.

Loisy was not a professional philosopher and was quite prepared to admit that philosophy was not his speciality.[2] At the same time

---

[1] Étienne Gilson suggested that St. Thomas's 'modernism' was the only one which had proved successful. Laberthonnière retorted, 'successful in what?'. In Laberthonnière's view the success consisted in Aristotelian Thomism eventually receiving an official blessing from ecclesiastical authority, a result which was a matter for regret rather than for rejoicing.

[2] Loisy makes this admission in his *Simple Reflections* on *Lamentabili* and *Pascendi* (*Simples réflexions sur le décret du Saint-Office 'Lamentabili sane exitu' et sur l'encyclique 'Pascendi dominici gregis'*, Paris, 1908, p. 198). Buonaiuti was more given to philosophy than was Loisy.

in his remarks about belief in God he can be said to assume that the human mind cannot attain knowledge of the Transcendent. God is really the Unknowable of Spencer, that which transcends the reach of what Kant described as theoretical knowledge. We think of God in terms of symbols, and from a practical point of view we are warranted in acting as though there were a personal divine will having a claim on the human will. But in the moral and religious sphere we cannot prove the absolute truth of any belief. In this sphere truth, as related to man's good, is as subject to change as man himself. There are no absolutely true and immutable revealed truths. What is called revelation is man's interpretation of his experience; and both experience and interpretation are subject to change.

Later on Loisy approached the position of Auguste Comte. That is to say, he saw in the history of religion an expression of the experience not of the individual but of the community. Christianity had promoted the ideal of a united humanity and was passing into the religion of humanity. Finally, Loisy seems to have returned to the idea of a transcendent God, not however to any belief in revelation or in the Church as custodian of revelation. For present purposes however we can emphasize simply his relativistic and pragmatist view of truth in the ethico-religious sphere.

In general, the modernists tended to assume that modern philosophy had shown that the human mind cannot transcend the sphere of consciousness. In one sense of course this is a truism, in so far, that is to say, as it means that we cannot be conscious of anything without being conscious of it or think of anything without thinking of it. But immanentism was understood as excluding any proof of God's existence by, for example, a causal argument. What is given in man is a need for the divine which, rising into consciousness, takes the form of a religious feeling or sense which is equivalent to faith. Revelation is man's interpretation of his religious experience. This interpretation is expressed of course in conceptual or intellectual forms. But these can become antiquated and stifling, so that new forms of expression have to be sought. Revelation in a general sense can be considered as the work of God, even if from another point of view it is man's work. But the idea of God revealing absolute truths from outside, as it were, truths which are promulgated by the Church in the form of unchangeable statements of unchanging truths is incompatible with the concept of evolution, when applied to man's cultural and religious life, and with the accompanying relativistic view of religious truth.

The foregoing remarks are of course a partial summary of views expressed in writings by different authors.[1] But they may suffice to show how Catholic philosophers such as Blondel and Édouard Le Roy could be accused of modernism or of modernist leanings. For Blondel, as we have seen, pursued what he called the method of immanence and approached God in terms of the human spirit's basic orientation as manifested in its activity, while Le Roy, through his acceptance and application of the Bergsonian views of intelligence and intuition, appeared to attribute to religious dogmas a purely pragmatic value. Blondel however never accepted immanentism as a doctrine. Nor could he, as he tried, by means of the method of immanence, to open the mind to the transcendent divine reality and lead it to the stage at which there was a point of insertion, so to speak, for God's self-revelation. As for Le Roy, he certainly expounded a pragmatic interpretation of scientific truth and applied it also to religious dogmas. But he defended his position and was never separated from the Church, either by his own action or by that of ecclesiastical authority. According to Laberthonnière, who was given to such remarks, what Le Roy did was to reduce not Christianity to Bergsonism but Bergsonism to Christianity.

The main theme of this chapter has been philosophy as apologetics. The new approach in apologetics was represented by Ollé-Laprune, Blondel and Laberthonnière. Their thought had indeed some points in common with views expressed by the modernists. But they were primarily concerned with philosophical approaches to Christianity, whereas the modernists were primarily concerned with reconciling Catholic faith and beliefs with freedom in historical, biblical and scientific research. While therefore Blondel, as a professional philosopher, was careful not only to stop short of pronouncements about revelation but also to justify this stopping short in terms of his own concept of the nature and

---

[1] Tyrrell spoke of revelation as being man's statements about his spiritual experiences rather than God's statements to man. But he did not deny that in and through these experiences man encounters God. According to Tyrrell God is known only in and through his effects. These effects are divine impulses in man, which man interprets in his own categories and language. And the test of the interpretations is their spiritual fruitfulness. Tyrrell certainly felt at times a strong inclination or temptation to agnosticism. But he tried to hold on to belief in God as a reality.

scope of philosophy, the modernists were naturally compelled to reconsider the nature of revelation and of Catholic dogma. In other words, they occupied themselves with theological topics in a way in which Blondel did not. And as their idea of what was demanded by modern historical and biblical research was a radical one, they naturally fell foul of ecclesiastical authorities who were convinced that the modernists were undermining the Christian faith. Looking back, we may think that the authorities were so much concerned with the conclusions at which the modernists arrived that they failed to consider whether or not the modernistic movement expressed recognition of genuine problems. But we have to see things in their historical perspective. Given the actual situation, including the attitude of the authorities on the one hand and the concept of 'modern' scholarship and knowledge on the other hand, one could hardly expect events to be other than what they were. Moreover, from the philosophical point of view the thought of Blondel is of considerably more value than the ideas of the modernists.

CHAPTER XII

THOMISM IN FRANCE

Introductory remarks; D. J. Mercier — Garrigou-Lagrange and Sertillanges — J. Maritain — E. Gilson — P. Rousselot and A. Forest—J. Maréchal.

1. IT would be incorrect to say that the Thomist revival in the nineteenth century originated with the publication in 1879 of Pope Leo XIII's encyclical letter *Aeterni Patris*. But papal assertion of the permanent value of Thomism and the encyclical's exhortation to Catholic philosophers to draw their inspiration from Aquinas while developing his thought to meet modern intellectual needs certainly gave a powerful impetus to an already existing movement. Papal endorsement of Thomism had of course several effects. On the one hand it encouraged the formation, especially in clerical circles and in ecclesiastical seminaries and academic institutions, of what one might describe as a party-line, a kind of philosophical orthodoxy. In other words, it could be used in support of the subordination of philosophy to theological interests and of the activities of the rigid and narrow-minded Thomists who were suspicious of and hostile to the more original and independent-minded Catholic thinkers, such as Maurice Blondel. On the other hand the call to look back to the thought of an outstanding thinker of the Middle Ages and to apply the principles of his thought to problems arising in the modern cultural situation undoubtedly helped to promote a great deal of serious philosophical reflection. Whatever one may think about the perennial value of Aquinas's thought, there was a lot to be said in favour of approaching philosophy by way of the system of an outstanding thinker and of thinking on systematic lines, in terms, that is to say, of certain basic philosophical principles and of their application instead of following the rather wishy-washy eclecticism which had tended to prevail in ecclesiastical academic institutions.

Exaggeration should be avoided. Official approval of a certain line of thought could and did produce a party-spirit which was narrow and polemical. At no time indeed was Thomism as such imposed on Catholic philosophers in a way which would imply that it was part of the Catholic faith. In theory the autonomy of philosophy was upheld. It is however undeniable that in some circles there was a marked tendency to depict Thomism as the only line of philosophical thought which really fitted in with Catholic theology. The theory was of course that it fitted in because it was true rather than it must be thought of as true because it fitted in. But one can hardly shut one's eyes to the fact that in many ecclesiastical institutions Thomism, or what was considered such, came to be taught in a dogmatic manner analogous to that in which Marxism-Leninism is taught in Communist-dominated education. At the same time the 'back to Aquinas' movement could obviously stimulate more able minds to endeavour to recapture the spirit of Aquinas and to create a synthesis in the light of the contemporary cultural situation. And there certainly have been Thomist philosophers who have embraced Thomist principles not because they were taught to do so but because they came to believe in their validity, and who have tried to apply these principles in a constructive way to modern problems. To this positive development of Thomist thought France has made a signal contribution; and it is with this contribution that we are concerned here.

In its earlier days the Thomist revival owed a great deal to Désiré Joseph Mercier (1851–1926) and to his collaborators at Louvain. After having taught philosophy in the seminary at Malines Mercier was appointed professor of Thomist philosophy in the University of Louvain in 1882. In 1888 he founded the Philosophical Society of Louvain, and in 1889 he became the first president of the newly established Institute of Philosophy of the University. The *Revue néo-scolastique* (now the *Revue philosophique de Louvain*) was started by the Philosophical Society under Mercier's editorship. In his years as a professor Mercier laboured strenuously to develop Thomism in the light of modern problems and of modern philosophy. Among his writings are two volumes on psychology (1892), a work on logic (1894), a book on general metaphysics or ontology (1894) and a work on the theory of knowledge, *Critériologie générale* (1899). In general, Mercier concerned himself with developing a realist metaphysics in critical dialogue with empiricism, positivism and the philosophy of Kant. But he was also particularly insistent on the need for a first-hand knowledge of science and for a positive relation between philosophy and the sciences. He himself wrote on experimental psychology, and through the Institute of Philosophy he encouraged the formation of a band not only of philosophers but also of scientists, such as the experimental psychologist Albert-Édouard Michotte (1881–1965) who had studied in Germany with Wundt and Külpe. Nowadays Mercier's philosophical writings may seem rather old-fashioned; but there can be no doubt of his real contribution to bringing Thomism into closer touch with contemporary philosophical and scientific thought and with making it intellectually respectable. In 1906 he was appointed archbishop of Malines, and in the following year he was made a Cardinal.

Though Mercier admired Kant in some respects, he criticized at length what seemed to him to be Kant's subjectivism and his restriction of the scope of metaphysics. For a considerable time Kant was one of the principal bogeymen of the Scholastics. At a later date however another Belgian, Joseph Maréchal, of whom more will be said later, adopted a much more positive approach, trying to appropriate Kant, as it were, and then to go beyond him. Some people doubt whether the so-called transcendental Thomism which stems from Maréchal can properly be described as Thomism. But at any rate its development is one expression of the marked change in the attitude of Thomists to other currents of thought in modern philosophy. Nowadays the orthodox Thomist of the type of Jacques Maritain has become comparatively rare.

The relaxing of polemical attitudes on the part of Thomist philosophers through a genuine effort to enter into, understand and evaluate other currents of thought has been accompanied in recent years by a notable diminution in the Church's attempt to encourage and promote a philosophical party-line. For example, the second Vatican Council was careful not to make pronouncements in the philosophical area. Besides, a number of Catholic theologians are understandably anxious to emphasize the independence of faith from any philosophical system, including Thomism, while others prefer to look for a philosophical basis in, say, the anthropology of Martin Heidegger. Again, certain developments in theological thought have tended to weaken the idea that Christian beliefs need to be expressed in categories borrowed from a particular philosophical tradition. It is indeed questionable whether theologians can get along without philosophy quite as easily as some of them seem to assume. The point is however that the 'handmaid of theology' situation, to which reference was made above, has greatly changed.

Given the changed situation, it is arguable that the impetus of the Thomist revival is spent. With diminished official backing and with the development of tendencies in theology which are hostile to the use of metaphysics for apologetic purposes, if not to metaphysics as such, it is natural that there should be a marked reaction against Thomism. There may of course be a renewal of interest in the spirit and ways of thought of Aquinas. The present writer is however happily not called upon to indulge in hazardous prophecies. His task is to make some remarks about Thomism in France.

2. France has made a signal contribution to the development of Thomism in the modern world. Among the pioneers Réginald Garrigou-Lagrange (1877–1964), a well known Dominican philosopher and theologian, has indeed appeared to a good many people as a rather narrow representative of neo-Thomism, intent on maintaining and promoting an orthodox party line. But despite his rather limited outlook[1] he contributed by his writings to raising the standard of thought in Thomist circles. An opponent of modernism, in 1909 he published *Le sens commun, la philosophie de l'être et les formules dogmatiques (Common Sense, the Philosophy of Being and Dogmatic Formulas)*. His well known book on natural theology, *Dieu, son existence et sa nature*, appeared in 1915.[2] In 1932 he published *Le réalisme du principe de finalité (The Realism of the Principle of Finality)*, and in 1946 *La synthèse thomiste*.[3] He also published theological works and books on Christian spirituality and mysticism, a number of which have been translated into English.

Another name which should be mentioned is that of Antonin-Dalmace Sertillanges (1863–1948), also a Dominican. Sertillanges was a prolific writer, who tried to exhibit the applicability and fruitfulness of Thomist principles in a variety of spheres and who devoted special attention to the relation between philosophy and Christianity. His best known work is probably his two-volume study of St. Thomas, *S. Thomas d'Aquin*, the first edition of which appeared in 1910.[4] Other publications on Aquinas include a study of his ethics, *La philosophie morale de S. Thomas*

---

[1] Garrigou-Lagrange would claim of course that if his outlook was limited, it was limited by a perception of the truth of perennial philosophical principles on the one hand and by divine revelation on the other.

[2] An English translation by B. Rose appeared in two volumes in 1934, *God, His Existence and His Nature*.

[3] There is an English translation by P. Cummings, *Reality. A Synthesis of Thomist Thought* (London, 1950).

[4] It was later entitled *La philosophie de S. Thomas d'Aquin*.

d'Aquin (1914, later edition 1942) and *Les grandes thèses de la philosophie thomiste*[1] which appeared in 1928. A two-volume work on the relation between philosophy and Christianity, *Le christianisme et les philosophies* appeared in 1939–41, and another two-volume work on the problem of evil, *Le problème du mal*, in 1949–51. Among other writings we can mention a book on socialism and Christianity, *Socialisme et christianisme* (1905), and one on the thought of Claude Bernard, *La philosophie de Claude Bernard* (1944).

3. The two names however which are most associated with putting Thomism on the map, with, that is to say, bringing it out of a rather narrow and predominantly ecclesiastical circle and making it respectable in the eyes of the academic world, are Jacques Maritain and Étienne Gilson. Professor Gilson of course is widely known for his historical studies which have won him respect even among those who are not particularly sympathetic to Thomism. Maritain is first and foremost a theoretical philosopher. Gilson, as befits an historian, has concerned himself with exhibiting the thought of Aquinas in its historical setting and therefore in its theological context. Maritain has been more concerned with exhibiting Thomism as an autonomous philosophy which can enter into dialogue with other philosophies without appealing to revelation and the principles of which are relevant to the solution of modern problems. Given the suspicion of metaphysics which is not infrequently encountered among theologians, including Catholic theologians, and given the natural reaction in Catholic colleges and seminaries to past indoctrination in what amounted to a Thomist party line, it is understandable if Maritain in particular is commonly regarded as old-fashioned and if his writings no longer have the vogue which they once enjoyed.[2] But this does not alter the fact that his was probably the greatest single contribution to the Thomist revival to which impetus was given by the encyclical letter *Aeterni Patris* in 1879.

Jacques Maritain was born at Paris in 1882. When he went to the Sorbonne as a student, he looked to science to solve all problems; but he was liberated from scientism by the influence of the lectures of Henri Bergson. In 1904 Maritain married Raissa

---

[1] There is an English translation by G. Anstruther under the title *The Foundations of Thomistic Philosophy* (London, 1931).

[2] This is applicable more to Maritain than to Gilson, as the value of Gilson's historical studies does not depend on one's attitude to Thomism as a philosophy for today.

Oumansoff, a fellow student, and in 1906 they were converted to Catholicism under the influence of Léon Bloy (1846–1917), the famous French Catholic writer and vigorous opponent of bourgeois society and religion. In 1907–08 Maritain studied biology at Heidelberg with Hans Driesch, the neovitalist.[1] He then devoted himself to studying the works of Aquinas and became an ardent disciple. In 1913 he delivered a series of conferences on the philosophy of Bergson;[2] and in 1914 he was appointed to lecture on modern philosophy at the Institut Catholique at Paris. He has also taught at the Pontifical Institute of Medieval Studies at Toronto, at Columbia University and at Notre Dame, where a centre was set up in 1958 to encourage studies on the lines of his thought. After the second world war Maritain was French ambassador to the Holy See from 1945 until 1948 and then taught at Princeton University. Later he lived in retirement in France. He died in 1973.

It has sometimes been said that whereas Gilson rules out the so-called critical problem as a pseudo-problem, Maritain admits it. This statement is however misleading, if taken by itself, for it suggests that Maritain starts his philosophizing either with trying to prove, abstractly, that we can have knowledge or with following Descartes in taking self-consciousness as undeniable and then attempting to justify our natural belief that we have knowledge of objects external to the self or that there are things corresponding to our ideas of them. If the critical problem is understood in this sort of way, Maritain excludes it just as much as Gilson does. He does not try to prove *a priori* that knowledge is possible. And he sees clearly that if we once shut ourselves up in the circle of our ideas, there we remain. He is a realist, and he has always insisted that when I know Tom, it is Tom that I know, not my idea of Tom.[3] At the same time Maritain certainly admits the critical problem, if by this is meant reflection by the mind on its pre-reflexive knowledge with a view to answering the question, what is knowledge? To ask in an abstract manner whether there can be knowledge and to attempt to answer this question in a

---

[1] See Vol. 6 of this *History*, pp. 383–4.
[2] Published as *La philosophie bergsonienne* (1914). English translation, *Bergsonian Philosophy and Thomism*, by M. L. Andison and J. G. Andison (N.Y., 1955).
[3] Obviously, objections can be raised. But Maritain has clung tenaciously to the view that though from a psychological point of view ideas are mental modifications, the intentional object, considered precisely as such, is not different from the object referred to. In scholastic language, he has always refused to transform the *medium quo* into a *medium quod*.

purely *a priori* manner is to enter a blind alley. The only way out is the way we came in. But there can perfectly well be an inquiry leading to knowledge of knowledge, the result of the mind's reflecting on its own activity in knowing something. The question, 'what is knowledge'? suggests however that there is only one kind of knowledge, whereas Maritain's concern has been with inquiring into distinguishable ways of knowing reality. He has written a good deal in the field of theory of knowledge; but his best known work on the topic is probably *Distinguer pour unir, ou Les degrés du savoir*, the first edition of which appeared in 1932.[1] One of his preoccupations, here and elsewhere, is to interpret knowledge in such a way that it does count as knowledge of the world but yet not only leaves room for but also demands philosophy of Nature in particular and metaphysics in general. In *The Degrees of Knowledge* Maritain expresses his agreement with Meyerson that a concern with ontology, with causal explanation that is to say, is not foreign to science as it actually exists (as distinct from what may be said about it); but he argues that the mathematical nature of modern physics has resulted in the continuation of a world which is so remote from the world of ordinary experience as to be practically unimaginable. He is not of course objecting to the mathematicization of physics. 'To be experimental (in its matter) and deductive (in its form, but above all in regard to the laws of the variations of the quantities involved), such is the ideal proper to modern science.'[2] But in Maritain's view 'the encounter of the law of causality, which is immanent in our reason, and of the mathematical conception of Nature has as a result the construction in theoretical physics of more and more geometrized universes in which fictional causal entities with a basis in reality (*entia rationis cum fundamento in re*), the function of which is to serve as support for mathematical deduction, come to include a very detailed account of empirically determined real causes or conditions.'[3] Theoretical physics certainly provides scientific knowledge, in the sense that it enables us to predict and to master Nature. But the functions of its hypotheses are pragmatic. They do not provide certain knowledge of the *being* of things, their ontological structure. And in *The Range of Reason* Maritain commends the views on science advanced by the Vienna Circle. As one would expect, he rejects the thesis that 'whatever

[1] English translation, *The Degrees of Knowledge*, by G. B. Phelan (N.Y., 1959).
[2] *Les degrés du savoir* (1932 edition), p. 90.   [3] *Ibid.*, p. 87.

has no meaning *for the scientist* has no meaning *at all'*.[1] But in
regard to the logical structure of science itself and in regard to
what has meaning for the scientist as such, 'the analysis of the
School of Vienna is, I believe, generally accurate and well-
founded'.[2] Maritain is still convinced however that though science
constructs *entia rationis* possessing pragmatic value, it is inspired
by a desire for a knowledge of reality, and that science itself gives
rise to 'problems which go beyond the mathematical analysis of
sensory phenomena'.[3]

Theoretical physics for Maritain is therefore a cross, as it were,
between purely observational or empirical science on the one hand
and pure mathematics on the other. It is 'a mathematicization of
the sensible'.[4] Philosophy of Nature however is concerned with the
essence of 'mobile being as such and the ontological principles
which account for its mutability'.[5] It deals with the nature of the
continuum, of quantity, of space, motion, time, corporal substance, vegetative and sensitive life, and so on. Metaphysics is
concerned not with mobile being as such but simply with being as
being. It therefore has a wider range and, according to Maritain,
goes deeper. All this is set in the framework of a theory of degrees
of abstraction based on Aristotle and Aquinas. The philosophy of
Nature, just like science, abstracts from matter as the individuat-
ing principle (that is to say, it is not concerned with particular
things as such); but it is still concerned with the material thing as
that which can neither exist without matter nor be conceived
without it. Mathematics is largely concerned with quantity and
quantitative relations *conceived* in abstraction from matter, though
quantity cannot *exist* without matter. Finally, metaphysics
includes knowledge of that which not only can be conceived
without matter but can also exist without it. It is 'at the purest
degree of abstraction because it is furthest removed from the
senses: it opens up on the immaterial, on a world of realities
which exist or can exist in separation from matter.'[6]

It is hardly necessary to say that Maritain is reasserting the
concept of the hierarchy of the sciences derived from Aristotle and
Aquinas. He has of course to fit modern science into this scheme;

---

[1] *The Range of Reason*, p. 6.   [2] *Ibid.*, p. 6.   [3] *Ibid.*, p. 4.
[4] *Les degrés du savoir*, pp. 269–70.   [5] *Ibid.*, p. 346.
[6] *Ibid.*, pp. 11–12. Maritain does not mean to imply that metaphysics (the
'first philosophy' of Aristotle) treats solely of what transcends sensible reality.
Its subject-matter is being as being. But as it abstracts from materiality, it can
proceed to the sphere of spiritual reality.

for physical science as it has developed since the Renaissance is not the same as what Aristotle called 'physics'.[1] Basically however the scheme is the same, though, like Aquinas, Maritain leaves room at the apex of the sciences for Christian theology, based on revealed premises. Theology apart, metaphysics is the highest of the sciences, science being conceived in Aristotelian fashion as knowledge of things through their causes. Nobody could accuse Maritain of lacking the courage to express his convictions. He admits of course that metaphysics is 'useless', in the sense that it is contemplative, not experimental, and that from the point of view of one who wishes to make empirical discoveries or to increase our mastery of Nature metaphysics cuts a very poor figure in comparison with the particular sciences. But he insists that metaphysics is an end, not a means, that it reveals to man 'authentic values and their hierarchy',[2] that it provides a centre for ethics, and that it introduces us to the eternal and absolute.

Maritain insists that if he adopts the principles of Aristotle and Aquinas, this is because the principles are true, not because they come from these venerable figures. As however his metaphysics is substantially that of Aquinas, at any rate when separated from Christian theology, it would be inappropriate to outline the content here.[3] It is sufficient to say that Aquinas, with his emphasis on *esse* (being in the sense of existence) is represented as the genuine 'existentialist', though Maritain is not the man to despise 'essences', which he thinks of as grasped within the existent, though the mind considers them in abstraction. Rather than attempting to recapitulate Thomist metaphysics it is preferable to draw attention to the two following points.

In the first place, though Maritain is the last man to despise the activity of the discursive reason and though he criticizes what he regards as Bergson's exaggerated depreciation of the intelligence and of the cognitive value of concepts, he has always been ready to recognize other ways of knowing than those exemplified in the 'sciences'. For example, he claims that there can be a non-

---

[1] What Aristotle called physics corresponds more with Maritain's philosophy of Nature.

[2] *Les degrés du savoir*, p. 10.

[3] See, for example, *Sept leçons sur l'être* (1934) (translated as *A Preface to Metaphysics: Seven Lectures on Being*, London and N.Y., 1939) and *Court Traité de l'existence et de l'existent*, (1947) (translated as *Existence and the Existent* by L. Galantière and G. B. Phelan, N.Y., 1948). But Maritain's books on knowledge, such as *The Degrees of Knowledge*, also treat of metaphysics. For knowledge and metaphysics are for him closely related.

conceptual, pre-reflective knowledge. Thus there can be an implicit knowledge of God which is not recognized by the person who has it as knowledge of God. In virtue of the internal dynamism of the will choice of the good, as against evil, involves an implicit affirmation of God, the Good itself, as the ultimate goal of human existence. This is 'a purely practical, non-conceptual and non-conscious knowledge of God which can co-exist with a theoretical ignorance of God.'[1] Again, Maritain has written about what he calls 'knowledge by connaturality'. This is found, for example, in religious mysticism. But it also plays a part in our knowledge of persons. And another form of it, distinct from mysticism, is 'poetic knowledge', arising 'through the instrumentality of emotion, which, received in the preconscious life of the intellect, becomes intentional and intuitive',[2] and tends by its nature to expression and creation. Knowledge by connaturality is also prominent in moral experience. For though moral philosophy[3] belongs to the conceptual, discursive, rational use of reason, it by no means follows that a man actually arrives at his moral convictions in this way. On the contrary, moral philosophy presupposes moral judgments which express a knowledge by connaturality, a conformity between the practical reason and the essential inclinations of human nature.

In the second place Maritain has tried to develop Thomist social and political philosophy, applying its principles to modern problems. If Aquinas had lived in the time of Galileo and Descartes, he would, according to Maritain, have freed Christian philosophy from the mechanics and astronomy of Aristotle, while remaining faithful to the principles of Aristotelian metaphysics. If he were living in the modern world, he would free Christian thought from 'the images and fantasies of the *sacrum imperium*'[4]

---

[1] *The Range of Reason*, p. 70. Obviously, this view is relevant to Maritain's assessment of atheism. In addition to 'practical atheists' (who believe that they believe in God but deny him by their conduct) and 'absolute atheists' he admits a class of 'pseudo-atheists' (who believe that they do *not* believe in God but who in fact believe in him unconsciously). Cf. *Ibid.*, pp. 103 ff.

[2] See also *Art et scolastique*, first published in 1920. *Art and Scholasticism and The Frontiers of Poetry*, translated by J. W. Evans (N.Y., 1962) contains also an English version of *Frontières de la poésie* (1935). See also *Creative Intuition in Art and Poetry* (N.Y., 1953).

[3] Maritain's writings on this subject include *Neuf leçons sur les notions premières de la philosophie morale* (*Nine lectures on the First Notions of Moral Philosophy*) published in 1951, and *La philosophie morale*, vol. 1, which appeared in 1960 (English translation, *Moral Philosophy*, by M. Suther and others, 1964).

[4] *Humanisme intégral* (1936), p. 224. There is an English translation, *True Humanism*, by M. R. Adamson (London, 1938).

and from worn-out temporal systems. In outlining a philosophical basis for the fulfilment of such a task Maritain has recourse to the distinction, also encountered in the personalism of Mounier, between 'individual' and 'person'. Accepting the Aristotelian-Thomist theory of matter as the principle of individuation, he describes individuality as 'that which excludes from oneself all other men' and as 'the narrowness of the ego, foreover threatened and forever eager to grasp for itself'.[1] Personality is the subsistence of the spiritual soul as communicated to the composite human being and as characterized by self-giving in freedom and love. In the concrete human being individuality and personality are of course combined, as man is a unity. But there can be societies which disregard man as a person and consider him simply as an individual. They emphasize individuals precisely as distinct particulars, neglecting the universal, as in bourgeois individualism, which corresponds, philosophically, to nominalism. Or they may emphasize the universal to such an extent that the particulars are completely subordinated to it. This happens in totalitarian societies of various kinds, which correspond, philosophically, to ultra-realism, for which the universal is a subsistent reality. The 'moderate realism' of St. Thomas would be expressed, in the social-political sphere, in a society of persons, which would indeed satisfy the needs of human beings as biological individuals but would at the same time be grounded on respect for the human person as transcending the biological level and, indeed, any temporal society. 'Man is by no means for the State. The State is for man.'[2] It may be added that during the Spanish Civil War Maritain supported the Republic and thus incurred a good deal of opprobrium in certain circles. Politically speaking, he has been on the left rather than on the right.

4. Étienne Henri Gilson was born at Paris in 1884 and did his university studies at the Sorbonne. After the first world war, in which he served as an officer, he was appointed professor of philosophy at Strasbourg. In 1921 however he accepted the chair of history of medieval philosophy at the Sorbonne, a post which he held until he was appointed to a similar chair at the Collège de France in 1932. He founded and directed the *Archives d'histoire doctrinale et littéraire du moyen âge* and also the series *Études de*

---

[1] *The Person and the Common Good*, p. 27 (English translation, 1947, of *La Personne et le bien commun*).
[2] *Man and the State* (Chicago, 1951), p. 13.

philosophie médiévale. In 1929 he cooperated in founding the Institute of Medieval Studies at Toronto, and after the second world war he acted as its director. In 1947 he was elected a member of the French Academy. On the advice of Lévy-Bruhl Gilson studied the relations between Descartes and Scholasticism. His main doctorate thesis was on freedom in Descartes (*La liberté chez Descartes et la théologie*, 1913) while the minor thesis was entitled *Index scolastico-cartesien* (1913). But the main fruit of the research suggested by Lévy-Bruhl was Gilson's *Études sur le rôle de la pensée médiévale dans la formation du système cartésien* (*Studies on the Role of Medieval Thought in the Formation of the Cartesian System*), which appeared in 1930. Meanwhile Gilson had studied Aquinas, and in 1919 he published the first edition of *Le thomisme. Introduction à l'étude de S. Thomas d'Aquin*.[1] The first edition of *La philosophie au moyen âge* was published in 1922.[2] Works followed on St. Bonaventure,[3] St. Augustine,[4] St. Bernard,[5] Dante[6] and Duns Scotus.[7] Gilson has also collaborated in the production of volumes on modern philosophy.

Despite his astonishing productivity in the historical field, which is not confined to the writings mentioned above, Gilson has also published works in which he presents personal philosophical positions, even if his views are often developed in an historical setting or context.[8] One of the features of his philosophical outlook is his rejection of the primacy of the so-called critical problem. If we cancel out, as it were, all our actual knowledge and then try to decide *a priori* whether knowledge is possible, we create for

---

[1] There have been a number of editions. There is a version in English, *The Christian Philosophy of St. Thomas Aquinas* (N.Y., 1951).
[2] The 1944 edition was practically a new work. And the English *History of Christian Philosophy in the Middle Ages* (London, 1955) is also a work on its own.
[3] *La philosophie de S. Bonaventure* (1924). The English translation, *The Philosophy of St. Bonaventure*, appeared in 1938. There was a second French edition in 1943.
[4] *Introduction à l'étude de S. Augustin* (1929 and subsequent editions). There is an English translation, *The Christian Philosophy of St. Augustine*, by L. E. M. Lynch (London, 1961).
[5] *La Théologie mystique de S. Bernard* (1934, 2nd edition 1947).
[6] *Dante et la philosophie* (1939; 2nd edition 1953).
[7] *Jean Duns Scotus. Introduction à ses positions fondamentales* (1952).
[8] We can mention, for example, *The Unity of Philosophical Experience* (N.Y., 1937; London, 1938), *Being and Some Philosophers* (Toronto 1949, an English version of *L'être et l'essence*, 1948 and 1962), *Painting and Reality* (N.Y., 1958), *Elements of Christian Philosophy* (N.Y., 1960), *Le philosophe et la théologie* (Paris, 1960; English version, *The Philosopher and Theology*, N.Y., 1962), and *Introduction aux arts du beau* (Paris, 1963).

ourselves a pseudo-problem. For we could not even raise the question unless we knew what knowledge is. And we know this through actually knowing something. In other words, it is in and through the act of knowing something that the mind becomes aware of its capacity to know. In Gilson's opinion Aquinas's attitude on this matter was far superior to that of those modern philosophers who have believed that the proper way of starting philosophy was to wrestle with the question whether we can know anything at all outside the subjective contents of our own minds.

Gilson's realism is also evident in his criticism of what he describes as 'essentialist' philosophy. If we try to reduce reality to clear and distinct concepts, universal by their nature, we omit the act of existence which is an act of singular or individual things. According to Gilson, this act is not conceptualizable, as existence is not an essence but the act by which an essence exists. It can be grasped only in and through essence, as its act, and it is affirmed in the existential judgment, which must be distinguished from the descriptive judgment. Thomism, as concerned with existing reality, is the authentic 'existentialism'. It does not, like the philosophies which are nowadays described as existentialist, interpret 'existence' narrowly, in the sense of something peculiar to man. Nor does it exclude essence. But it is primarily concerned with reality as existing and with the relation between received or participated existence and the infinite act in which essence and existence are indentical. One of the chief representatives of essentialist philosophy, in Gilson's eyes, was Christian Wolff; but he traces the origin of this line of thought back into the Middle Ages, where Aquinas is for him the chief exponent of existential philosophy.

Another feature of Gilson's thought is his refusal to extract a purely self-contained Thomist philosophy from the total thought of Aquinas. He does not indeed deny that the distinction made by St. Thomas between philosophy and theology is a valid distinction. But he insists on the artificiality of tearing from its theological setting a philosophy in which the selection and ordering of themes is determined by theological ends or by their theological context. Further, it seems clear to Gilson that theological beliefs, in free divine creation for example, have had a great influence on philosophical speculation, and that whatever some Thomists may say, they do in fact philosophize in the light of their Christian beliefs, though it by no means follows that their philosophical reasoning must be invalid or that they have to appeal to theological premises. In other words, Gilson has maintained that there can be a Christian philosophy which is genuinely philosophical. Its Christian character would not indeed be ascertainable simply by inspecting its logical arguments. For if this were the case, it would be theology rather than philosophy. But comparison between philosophies shows that there can be a philosophy which, while remaining genuinely philosophical, does not deprive itself of the light afforded by revelation. This point of view has given rise to a good deal of discussion and controversy. Some writers have maintained that to speak of a Christian philosophy is as inappropriate as to speak of a Christian mathematics. But Gilson has persisted in maintaining his thesis. In so far as this is the historical judgment of a scholar who sees clearly the influence exercised on philosophy by Christian belief, especially in the patristic and medieval periods, there is no difficulty in accepting it. For it can hardly be denied that under the influence of Christian belief concepts derived from Greek thought were often given a new stamp or character, fresh themes were suggested, and philosophy, pursued for the most part by theologians, was used to extend a general Christian world-vision. Whereas however many people would claim that philosophy became adult only through separation from Christian theology and the attainment of complete autonomy, Gilson insists that there is still room for genuine philosophy pursued not simply by Christians but by philosophers *as Christians*. He is doubtless justified in rejecting the claim that Christians who develop natural theology, for example, are in no way influenced by their antecedent beliefs. But some would conclude that it is then a case of apologetics, not of authentic philosophy. The retort might be made that the complete autonomy of philosophy is a myth, and that if it is not the handmaid of theology, it is the handmaid of something else, being always 'parasitic'. However, the question whether philosophizing pursued in the interests of the development of a comprehensive Christian world-view is genuine philosophizing or not, is probably best answered by inspecting examples.

From the titles of books mentioned above it will be seen that Gilson, like Maritain, has written on aesthetics. In a general sense his point of view is Thomist. Art is regarded as a making or production of beautiful objects which cause contemplative enjoyment or pleasure. Gilson however derives from this view of art as creative the conclusion that it is a great mistake to think that imitation belongs to its essence or nature. Abstract art as such needs no special justification. Whether a given picture, for example, is or is not a genuine work of art is clearly not a question which can be settled by philosophical reasoning. But if art is creative, there can be no good reason for regarding non-representational works as deficient, still less as disqualified from counting as works of art.

5. Mention has been made of Garrigou-Lagrange, Sertillanges, Maritain and Gilson. It is neither possible nor desirable to list all French Thomists here. In view of his influence however mention should be made of Pierre Rousselot (1878–1915), a Jesuit theologian and philosopher who was killed on service in the first world war. In theological circles he is known for his views on the analysis of faith; but his main publication is *L'intellectualisme de S. Thomas d'Aquin*[1] in which he argues that the movement of the intellect to Being is the expression of a dynamism of the will, of love that is to say, which can find its goal only in God. In other words, he tries to dispose of the view that Aquinas was an arid intellectualist by revealing the dynamic orientation of the human spirit which underlies and gives rise to the movement of the mind in philosophical reflection.

Sime similar ideas can be found in the writings of Aimé Forest (b. 1898), who was appointed professor of philosophy at Montpellier in 1943. Author of works on Aquinas,[2] he is best known for his development of the idea of 'consent' to being,[3] in which he shows the influence of modern French philosophers. In the first place consent to being means consent to a movement of the human spirit whereby it does not stop short at empirical reality but transcends it towards the ultimate ground of all finite being. As the mind can stop short, or attempt to stop short, at the empirically given, consent or option is required to recognize the realm of values and to pass beyond to God, who alone makes empirical reality intelligible. In the second place consent to being involves regarding finite existence as a gift, arousing a response in the human spirit. In other words, with Forest the metaphysics of being assumes a religious and also ethical character.

---

[1] This work, published in 1908, was translated into English by F. James as *The Intellectualism of St. Thomas* (London, 1935).
[2] *S. Thomas d'Aquin* (1933) and *La structure métaphysique du concret selon S. Thomas d'Aquin* (1931, 2nd edition, 1956).
[3] *Du consentement à l'être* (1936, *On Consent to Being*) and *Consentement et création* (1943, *Consent and Creation*).

6. Garrigou-Lagrange obviously looked on most modern philosophers as 'adversaries', as defending positions which were to a greater or lesser degree opposed to the truth as represented by St. Thomas Aquinas. With Maritain and Gilson we find indeed intelligent discussions of the development and currents of modern philosophical thought; but their realism was such that they could not but regard the procedures of, say, Descartes and Kant as aberrations. It by no means follows, for example, that Gilson is unable to appreciate the achievement of Kant, given the latter's premises. But it is clear that for Gilson the premises should be avoided in the first place. An outstanding thinker doubtless shows his talent in the way in which he develops the implications of his premises and steers clear of any patchwork eclecticism which tries to combine elements which do not really fit together. But constructive talent of this kind does not entail the validity of the premises.

A much more positive attitude to modern philosophy, especially in regard to Kant, was shown by Joseph Maréchal (1878–1944), a Belgian Jesuit who was a professor of philosophy in the Jesuit house of studies at Louvain from 1919 until 1935. A doctor of science of the University of Louvain, he had also studied experimental psychology and psychotherapy in Germany; and his interest in the psychology of religion found expression in the two volumes of his *Études sur la psychologie des mystiques*[1] which appeared respectively in 1924 and 1937. He is best known however for his *Point de départ de la métaphysique*,[2] particularly for the fifth Cahier or volume on Thomism in confrontation with the critical philosophy of Kant (*Le Thomisme devant la philosophie critique*). Maréchal is not of course so foolish as to claim that St. Thomas Aquinas in the thirteenth century provided in advance all the solutions to problems raised centuries later by Immanuel Kant in a different historical context. He does however claim that the Kantian antimony between understanding and pure reason, with its implications for metaphysics, can be overcome by developing a synthesis in terms of an idea of intellectual dynamism which is virtually present, in his opinion, in the thought of St. Thomas

[1] There is a partial translation, *Studies in the Psychology of the Mystics*, by A. Thorold (London, 1927).
[2] The first, second, third and fifth Cahiers were published in 1922–6. The fourth Cahier, on idealism in Kant and the post-Kantians, was published posthumously (from notes) in 1947. There was to have been a sixth Cahier which, Maréchal remarked, would have clarified his personal position.

and to which Kant, given his view of the mind's activity, should have devoted greater attention. In other words, Maréchal does not simply confront the Kantian philosophy as it stands with traditional Thomism and then argue that the latter is superior. He uses an idea which he believes to be basic in the thought of St. Thomas to develop the critical philosophy in such a way that the antimony between understanding and pure reason is overcome and the Kantian agnosticism is transcended.

The fifth Cahier contains two complementary parts. Both have as their point of departure the immanent object, immanent, that is to say, in consciousness. The first part is devoted to what Maréchal describes as a metaphysical critique of the object, and the second to a transcendental critique. In the first critique the object is regarded as strictly intentional and so as having ontological reference, while in the second the object is taken as a phenomenon. But we cannot enter into details. To cut a long story short, Maréchal enters by Kant's door and inquires into the *a priori* conditions of knowledge or of the possibility of objectification. It his view the most important *a priori* condition, overlooked by Kant, is the intellectual dynamism of the subject as oriented to absolute Being. No more than Kant does Maréchal postulate an intellectual intuition of the Absolute or of God in himself. But he sees the act of judgment, which sets the subject over against the object, as a partial realization of the intellect's dynamic orientation and as pointing beyond itself. In other words, every judgment implicitly affirms the Absolute, which reveals itself not as the direct object of an intellectual intuition but as the *a priori* condition of all objectification and the ultimate goal of the movement of the intellect. Affirmation of the existence of God is thus a speculative necessity, and not simply a practical postulate.

It has been objected against Maréchal that he assumes illegitimately that the Kantian method of transcendental reflection is 'neutral', in the sense that it can be used to enable us to reach conclusions which go beyond anything contemplated by Kant, in particular to establish the existence of God. If, it is contended, we once adopt the Kantian point of departure and method, we shall try in vain to overcome the Kantian agnosticism. It has also been objected that Maréchal confuses the intellect with a natural appetite or pre-reflexive volitional tendency. Maréchal's thesis however is that we cannot justifiably make a dichotomy between the formally cognitive function of the intellect and its dynamic tendency. The former has to be interpreted in the light of the latter. Further, the fact that Kant recognized the activity of the mind shows that he ought to have reflected on the intellect's dynamism as an *a priori* condition of knowledge. For Maréchal at any rate his development of Kant does not contradict the exigencies of the critical approach.

We are entitled to regard Maréchal as initiating the movement of thought which is customarily described as transcendental Thomism. To say this is not to deny that there were other antecedent influences, the thought of Blondel for example. But Maréchal regarded Blondel as inclining too much to voluntarism; and he himself emphasized an intellectual dynamism which he believed to be implicit in the philosophy of Aquinas and which, if developed, would enable Thomism to satisfy the demand of modern philosophy, as represented by Kant and Fichte, for the 'transcendental turn', as it is sometimes described, and at the same time to overcome the agnosticism which had made Kant the bogeyman of the neo-Scholastics. For, as we have seen, he was convinced that use of the method whereby thought reflects on its own object-oriented activity would show that absolute Being is an *a priori* condition of the possibility of this activity. Instead of rejecting the critical philosophy as a pernicious influence, he thought that it was necessary to adopt the transcendental method and at the same time to bring to light a condition of the possibility of the mind's intentional acts to which Kant himself had failed to do justice. As however Maréchal believed that use of the transcendental method was a justifiable development of what was virtually present in the thought of Aquinas and that it could show the legitimacy of a metaphysics which Kant rejected, he regarded himself as a Thomist. He thus prepared the way for the development of transcendental Thomism.[1] But it would be misleading to describe the transcendental Thomists as Maréchal's 'disciples'. In the case of writers in German, such as J. B. Lotz and

---

[1] The objection has been raised that transcendental Thomism is Thomist only in the sense that a method derived from Kant and German idealism, supported in some cases by strong doses of phenomenology and of Heidegger's existentialist philosophy, is used to reach Thomist conclusions or at any rate conclusions which are in agreement with Thomism. (See, for example, the second Appendix to Leslie Dewart's *The Foundations of Belief*, London 1969). The retort can be made however that whatever traditional Thomists may say, the philosophy of Aquinas makes presuppositions which the transcendental Thomists try to make explicit and to justify in a systematic manner.

E. Coreth (an Austrian), the contributory influence of other factors, notably the thought of Martin Heidegger,[1] is clear enough. And in France the influence of other French philosophers, such as Blondel, has to be taken into account. Still, Maréchal is the patron saint, so to speak, of the movement.

Maréchal, as we have seen, was concerned in a special way with Kant. That is to say, it was the critical philosophy of Kant, at any rate when regarded in the light of subsequent idealist developments, which provided the setting or context for Maréchal's approach to transcendental philosophy. And in his fifth Cahier Maréchal was particularly concerned with the problem set by Kant's antimony between the understanding and pure reason and his rejection of traditional metaphysics. Some of the transcendental Thomists however have used the transcendental method to outline at any rate a general system of thought without noticeable emphasis on or preoccupation with Immanuel Kant. It would be inappropriate here to speak of non-French representatives of the movement. But a very brief mention can be made of André Marc (1892–1961), a French Jesuit who was a professor of philosophy first at Jesuit houses of study and then at the Institut Catholique at Paris. In his *Psychologie réflexive*[2] he used the method whereby thought takes itself in act as object of reflection to start with language as revelatory of the nature of man and then to develop a philosophical anthropology. In doing so he also deduced 'from our act of knowledge and its structure, as well as from the structure of its object, the diversification of the sciences, at any rate in outline.'[3] In a subsequent volume, *Dialectique de l'affirmation*, which has as its subtitle *Essai de métaphysique réflexive*, Marc developed a metaphysics, employing the 'reflexive method', thought's reflections on its own acts, to study 'the laws of being as such'.[4] In another volume, *Dialectique de l'agir* (Paris-Lyon, 1954) Marc devoted his attention to the development of an ethics, defining the moral destiny or vocation of man in the light of his theories of man's metaphysical nature and of the structure

---

[1] The writings of B. Lonergan, the Canadian Thomist, seem to be free of Heideggerian influence. As for Coreth, the influence of Heidegger is clear enough. But so is that of Fichte, by whom Maréchal himself was influenced.

[2] Two volumes, Paris, 1948–9.

[3] *Dialectique de l'affirmation* (Paris, 1952), p. 17.

[4] *Ibid.*, p. 43. The method involves reductive analysis, to get back to the proper point of departure, followed by a deductive and dialectical process of reflection.

of being. Other writings dealt with the possibility and conditions of an acceptance of Christian revelation.[1]

There are of course other French thinkers who have been influenced to some extent by Maréchal, such as Jacques Édouard Joseph de Finance (b. 1904), a professor of philosophy at the Gregorian University in Rome, who has given special attention to freedom and man's moral vision and action. But instead of making further brief and inadequate remarks about individuals we can conclude this section by suggesting one or two general features of transcendental Thomism. In the first place the transcendental Thomists seem intent on developing a presuppositionless philosophy or at any rate going back to an unquestionable point of departure. This can be seen in the first moment or phase of the transcendental method, the reductive or analytic phase. In the second place they seem intent on developing metaphysics as a deductive science, systematically deduced, that is to say, from the point of departure.[2] And in the third place they try to develop philosophy as the conscious subject's reflection on its own activity. It can hardly be claimed that this procedure is in accordance with the traditional presentation of Thomism. This does not of course show that the procedure is misguided. But it provides some ground for the critics' claim that 'Thomism' as a misnomer, and for the suggestion that harmony between the results or conclusions of transcendental Thomism and traditional Thomism is due as much to common religious beliefs and preoccupations as to any factor intrinsic to purely philosophical argumentation. This is not however a question which can be settled by dogmatic *a priori* pronouncements on either side. Instead we can remark that several philosophers have tried to make philosophy properly scientific by taking as a point of departure an unquestionable datum or proposition. Descartes was one of them, Husserl another. And the transcendental Thomists join the company. Even if however it is allowed that the attempt to develop a presuppositionless philosophy is legitimate, the question arises whether idealism does not result if the subject is taken as the basis of all philosophical reflection. Needless to say, the transcendental Thomists

---

[1] For example, *L'être et l'esprit* (Paris-Louvain, 1958) and *Raison et conversion chrétienne* (Paris, 1961).

[2] The transcendental Thomists are not all in agreement about the proper point of departure. For example, whereas Lotz starts with analysis of the judgment as an act of absolute affirmation, Coreth thinks that the philosopher must go further back, to what he calls the question.

do not believe that this is the case. Indeed, they would claim to have demonstrated that it is not the case. The more old-fashioned Thomists however remain unconvinced. What Aquinas himself would have said about the matter, whether he would have approved of Maritain or preferred Maréchal, we obviously cannot know.

CHAPTER XIII

PHILOSOPHY OF SCIENCE

H. Poincaré — P. Duhem — G. Milhaud — E. Meyerson —
A. Lalande — G. Bachelard.

1. Mention has already been made of a number of philosophers who concerned themselves with reflection on the natural sciences. Reference has been made for example, to Comte and to writers belonging more or less to the positivist line of thought, such as Bernard and Taine, to the neo-critical philosophers Cournot and Renouvier, and to thinkers such as Ravaisson, Lachelier and Boutroux, who belong to the spiritualist movement. We can now take a brief glance at the ideas of a few writers who can more easily be described as philosophers of science.

A well known name in this group is that of Jules Henri Poincaré (1854–1912)[1]. Born at Nancy, he studied mining engineering; but from an early age he was interested in mathematics, and in 1879 he started to teach mathematical analysis at Caen. In 1881 he went to the University of Paris where he lectured on mathematics, physics and astronomy. In 1887 he was elected a member of the Académie des Sciences and in 1908 of the Académie Française. In 1902 he published *La science et l'hypothèse*,[2] in 1905 *La valeur de la science*[3] and in 1908 *Science et méthode*.[4] His *Dernières Pensées* appeared in 1912.[5]

The best known feature of Poincaré's philosophy of mathematics and science is probably the element of conventionalism which it contains. When referring, for example, to geometry, he remarks that geometrical axioms are neither synthetic *a priori* intuitions nor experimental facts. 'They are conventions.'[6] And this means that they are definitions in disguise'.[7] It does not follow, Poincaré insists, that the axioms are decided purely arbitrarily. For though our choice is free and limited only by the need to

---

[1] Raymond Poincaré, who became President of the Republic, was a cousin.
[2] Translated by W. J. Greenstreet as *Science and Hypothesis* (London, 1905; New York, Dover Publications, 1952).
[3] Translated by G. B. Halsted as *The Value of Science* (London, 1907).
[4] Translated by F. Maitland as *Science and Method* (London, 1914).
[5] Translated by J. W. Bolduc as *Mathematics and Science: Last Essays* (New York, 1963).
[6] *Science and Hypothesis*, p. 50.   [7] *Ibid.*, p. 50.

avoid any contradiction, by the demands of logical consistency that is to say, it is also guided by the experimental facts. One system of geometry is not in itself truer than any other system. But it can be more convenient than another system or more suitable for a specific purpose. We cannot justifiably claim that Euclidean geometry is truer than the non-Euclidean geometries. We might just as well claim that a decimal coinage is truer than a non-decimal coinage. But a decimal coinage may be the more convenient. And for most purposes, though not for all, Euclidean geometry is the most convenient system.

Such conventions or disguised definitions play a role in physical science too. A proposition can start as an empirical generalization or hypothesis and end as a convention, inasmuch as this is what the physicist makes it to be. For example, 'it is *by definition* that force is equal to the product of the mass and the acceleration; this is a principle which is henceforth beyond the reach of any future experiment. Thus it is by definition that action and reaction are equal and opposite.'[1] Science begins with observation and experiment; but with the development of mathematical physics the role played by conventions grows too.

It would however be a great mistake to think that according to Poincaré science consists entirely of conventions in the sense of disguised definitions. This is a view which he describes as nominalism, attributes to Édouard Le Roy and attacks. For Le Roy 'science consists only of conventions and it is solely to this circumstance that it owes its apparent certainty. . . . Science cannot teach us the truth, it can serve us only as a rule for action.'[2] To this theory Poincaré objects that scientific laws are not simply like the rules of a game which can be altered by common agreement in such a way that the new rules serve as well as the old ones. One might of course construct a set of rules which would not serve their purpose because they were mutually incompatible. But, this point apart, we cannot properly speak of the rules of a game as being verified or falsified, whereas the empirical laws of science are rules of action in so far as they predict, and the predictions are open to falsification. In other words, empirical hypotheses are not simply conventions or disguised definitions: they have a cognitive value. And even though absolute certainty is not attainable, inasmuch as an empirical generalization is always revisable in principle, in some cases at any rate science attains a high degree

[1] *Ibid.*, p. 104.   [2] *La valeur de la science*, p. 214.

of probability. In mathematical physics conventions have a part to play; and, as we have seen, what was originally an empirical generalization may be so interpreted that it is transformed into a disguised definition which is not open to falsification, as it is not allowed, so to speak, to be falsifiable. But this does not alter the fact that science aims at knowledge of the relations between things, that it predicts, and that some predictions are verified, even if not conclusively, while others are falsified. It cannot therefore be legitimately claimed that science consists entirely of conventions, and that, given internal consistency, any scientific system would serve as well as any other.

Poincaré's use of language is sometimes open to question. For example, when distinguishing between different kinds of hypotheses he includes the disguised definitions which, he tells us, are to be found especially in mathematics and mathematical physics.[1] And it is obviously arguable that he ought to reserve the name 'hypotheses' for empirical hypotheses which are open to falsification. However this may be, it is perfectly clear that for Poincaré the natural sciences can increase our knowledge, and that this increase is attained by testing empirical generalizations which permit prediction. It is true that he regards some empirical statements of natural science as resoluble into a principle or convention and a provisional law, an empirical hypothesis, that is to say, which is revisible in principle. But the mere fact that he makes this distinction shows that he does not regard science as consisting simply of principles in the sense of conventions or disguised definitions. Conventionalism therefore is only one element in his philosophy of science.

Science, for Poincaré, aims at attaining truth about the world. It rests indeed on presuppositions or assumptions, the basic ones being the unity and the simplicity of Nature. That is to say, it is presupposed that the parts of the Universe are interrelated in a manner analogous to that in which the organs of the living body are interrelated. And the simplicity of Nature is presupposed in the sense at any rate that if two or more generalizations are possible, so that we have to choose between them, 'the choice can only be guided by considerations of simplicity.'[2] Though however science rests on presuppositions, it none the less aims at truth.

---

[1] *Science and Hypothesis*, pp. xxii–xxiii.
[2] *Ibid.*, p. 146. Poincaré also talks about 'simple facts'. Cf. *Science et méthode*, pp. 10 f.

'In my eyes it is knowledge which is the end, and action which is the means.'[1]

What however is it that science enables us to know? It is certainly not the essences of things. 'When a scientific theory claims to tell us what heat is, or what electricity is, or what life is, it is condemned in advance: all that it can give us is a rough image.'[2] The knowledge which we obtain through science is knowledge of the relations between things. Poincaré sometimes uses a sensationalist language and maintains that what we can know are the relations between sensations.[3] But he does not wish to assert that there is nothing of which our sensations are the reflection. And it is simpler to say that for him science tells us the relations between things rather than the inner natures of things. For example, a theory of light tells us the relations between the sensible phenomena of light rather than what light is in itself. Indeed, Poincaré is prepared to claim that 'the only objective reality is the relations between things, from which the universal harmony derives. Without doubt these relations, this harmony, could not be conceived apart from a mind which conceives or perceives them. But they are none the less objective inasmuch as they are, will be or will remain common to all thinking beings.'[4]

The impression may perhaps have been given that while Poincaré certainly did not regard all scientific laws as conventional, he looked on pure mathematics as dependent entirely on conventions. This is not however the case. For while he was quite ready to see certain axioms as disguised definitions, he believed that mathematics also comprised certain synthetic *a priori* propositions, the truth of which was discerned intuitively. He was thus not prepared to accept the view that Kant's view of mathematics had been simply exploded. Nor was Poincaré favourably disposed to the thesis, as maintained, for example, by Bertrand Russell, that mathematics is reducible to formal logic. On the contrary, he criticized the 'new logics', 'of which the most interesting is that of M. Russell.'[5]

In his sensationalism Poincaré was influenced by the thought of Ernst Mach,[6] while his view of mechanics seems to have been influenced by Heinrich Rudolf Hertz (1857–94).

---

[1] *La valeur de la science*, p. 220.   [2] *Ibid.*, p. 267.
[3] Sensations, Poincaré says, are non-transmissible. 'But it is not the same with relations between sensations'. *Ibid.*, p. 263.
[4] *Ibid.*, p. 271.   [5] *Science et méthode*, p. 172. See also *Dernières pensées*.
[6] For some brief remarks on Mach see Volume VII of this *History*, p. 359.

2. We have seen that according to Poincaré science is concerned not with the nature of things in themselves but with the relations between things as appearing to us or between sensations. The same sort of view was advanced by Pierre Maurice Marie Duhem (1861–1916), who was both a theoretical physicist and a philosopher and distinguished historian of science. In 1886 Duhem published at Paris a work on thermodynamics,[1] and in the following year he began to lecture in the Faculty of Science at Lille. In 1893 he went to Rennes, and in 1895 he was appointed to a chair in the University of Bordeaux. His most important theoretical publication was *La Théorie physique, son objet et sa structure*, the first edition of which appeared at Paris in 1906.[2] Duhem also published several works on the history of science,[3] the best known being *Le système du monde. Histoire des doctrines cosmologiques de Platon à Copernic (The System of the World. A History of Cosmological Doctrines from Plato to Copernicus)*, consisting of eight volumes (Paris, 1913–1958). In Duhem's opinion study of the history of science was not simply a learned luxury, so to speak, which could be neglected without any detriment to one's study of actual scientific problems. As he saw the matter, one could not fully understand a scientific theory or concept without knowledge of its origins and development and of the problems which it was designed to solve.

One of Duhem's principal aims is to make a clear theoretical separation between physics and metaphysics. The metaphysician, in Duhem's view, is concerned with explanation, to explain being, 'to strip reality of the appearances covering it like a veil, in order to see the bare reality itself.'[4] But it is only metaphysics which raises the question whether there is a reality underlying or distinct from sensible appearances. As far as physics is concerned, phenomena or sensible appearances are all that there is. Hence it cannot aim at explanation in the sense mentioned. 'A physical theory is not an explanation. It is a system of mathematical propositions, deduced from a small number of principles, which aim at

---

[1] *Le potentiel thermodynamique et ses applications à la mécanique chimique et à la théorie des phénomènes électriques.*

[2] The second edition has been translated by P. P. Wiener as *The Aim and Structure of Physical Theory* (Princeton, 1954). This work will be referred to as *Physical Theory*.

[3] These include *L'évolution de la mécanique* (Paris, 1903), *Les origines de la statique* (Paris, 1905–6) and studies on Leonardo da Vinci (*Études sur Léonard da Vinci*, Paris, 1906–13).

[4] *Physical Theory*, p. 7.

representing as simply, as completely and as exactly as possible a set of experimental laws.'[1] A theory however is not exclusively a representation of experimental laws: it is also a classification of them. That is to say, by deductive reasoning it exhibits these laws as consequences of certain basic hypotheses or 'principles'. And the test of a theory, a theory of light for example, is its agreement or disagreement with the experimental laws which themselves represent relations between phenomena or sensible appearances. 'Agreement with experiment is the sole criterion of truth for a physical theory.'[2] A physical theory does not explain the laws, though it coordinates them systematically. Nor do the laws explain reality. Duhem is at one with Poincaré in insisting that what we know are the relations between sensible phenomena. He adds indeed that we cannot avoid the feeling or conviction that observed relations correspond to something in things apart from their sensible appearances to us. But he insists that this is a matter of natural faith or belief and not something which can be proved in physics.

Duhem is aware of course that scientific theories permit prediction. We can 'draw some consequences which do not correspond to any of the experimental laws previously known and which simply represent possible experimental laws'.[3] Some of these consequences are empirically testable. And if they are verified, the value of the theory is increased. If however a prediction which represents a legitimate conclusion from a theory is falsified, this shows that the theory must be modified, if not abandoned altogether. In other words, if we assume the truth of a given hypothesis and then deduce that on this assumption a certain event should occur in certain circumstances, the actual occurrence of the event in these circumstances does not prove the truth of the hypothesis. For the same conclusion, namely that in certain circumstances a certain event should occur, might also be deducible from a different hypothesis. If however the event which ought to occur does not occur, this shows that the hypothesis is false or that it stands in need of revision. If therefore we leave out of account other reasons for changing or modifying theories, such as considerations of greater simplicity or economy, we can say that science advances through the elimination of hypotheses rather than through verification in a strong sense. A scientific hypothesis can be conclusively falsified and so eliminated, but

---

[1] *Ibid.*, p. 19.   [2] *Ibid.*, p. 21.   [3] *Ibid.*, p. 28.

it cannot be conclusively proved. There is not and cannot be a 'crucial experiment' in Francis Bacon's sense of the phrase. For the physicist can never be sure that there is not another conceivable hypothesis which would cover the phenomena in question.[1] 'The truth of a physical theory is not decided by heads or tails.'[2]

Though Duhem agrees with Poincaré on a number of issues, he refuses to admit that there are scientific hypotheses which are beyond the reach of experimental refutation and must be regarded as definitions which remain unaffected by empirical testing. There are indeed hypotheses which, if taken in isolation, have no 'experimental meaning'[3] and which cannot therefore be directly confirmed or falsified by experiment. But these hypotheses do not in fact exist in isolation. They constitute foundations of wide-ranging theories or physical systems; and it always remains possible that the consequences of the system taken as a whole will be subjected to experimental refutation on such a scale that the whole system will crumble, together with those basic hypotheses which, if considered in isolation, cannot be directly refuted.

According to Duhem his interpretation of physics is 'positivist in its conclusions as well as in its origins'.[4] Physical theories, as he sees them, have nothing to do with metaphysical doctrines or with religious dogmas; and it is a mistake to attempt to use them for apologetic purposes. For example, the attempt to prove the creation of the world from thermodynamics (the law of entropy) is misguided. But it by no means follows that Duhem is a positivist in the sense that he rejects metaphysics. He is concerned with making a sharp distinction between physics and metaphysics, not with condemning the latter. Whether we can in fact make such a rigid distinction as Duhem has in mind is doubtless open to dispute. But it is obviously true that science has progressively developed its autonomy; and it is also arguable that those writers who have tried to base metaphysical or religious doctrines on revisible physical theories have been misguided. In any case Duhem is not an anti-metaphysician. As for religion, 'I believe

[1] Duhem makes his point clear by considering two different hypotheses. But he insists that what a physicist actually subjects to experimental testing is a group of hypotheses, not an isolated one. (We have seen that for him a physical theory combines and coordinates a set of hypotheses.) Falsification of a prediction therefore indicates that some member of the group must be modified or changed. But if the prediction is the result of a deduction based on the set or group, its non-fulfilment does not by itself indicate which member of the group should be revised.
[2] *Physical Theory*, p. 190.   [3] *Ibid.*, p. 215.   [4] *Ibid.*, p. 275.

with all my soul in the truths which God has revealed to us and which he has taught us through his Church.'[1]

3. A certain measure of affinity with the ideas of Poincaré and Duhem is evident in the philosophy of science of Gaston Milhaud (1858–1918), who after having been professor of philosophy at Montpellier[2] went to Paris in 1909 to occupy a newly created chair in the history of philosophy in its relationship to the sciences.[3] For example, in his *Essay on the Conditions and Limits of Logical Certitude* (*Essai sur les conditions et les limites de la certitude logique*, 1894, second edition 1897), Milhaud asserts that what we know of things are the sensations which they arouse in us.[4] At the same time he is at one with Poincaré and Duhem in emphasizing the mind's activity in reflection on experience and in the development of scientific hypotheses. Milhaud is less inclined to talk about 'conventions'; but he insists, as in his work *The Rational* (*Le rationnel*, 1898) on the spontaneity of the human reason.

While however Duhem was anxious to claim that his idea of science was positivistic, with the aim of making a sharp distinction between natural science and metaphysics, Milhaud draws attention to the shortcomings of positivism, by which he meant the ideas of Auguste Comte in particular. For example, in the introduction to his work on *The Geometer-Philosophers of Greece* (*Les philosophes géomètres de la Grèce*, 1900) he alludes to the naïvely confident way in which Comte undertook to assign the precise limits at which knowledge could arrive and in which he rejected in advance any attempt to effect a radical change in accepted scientific theories. Comte wanted 'to attribute to the system of already acquired scientific knowledge the power of immediately organizing society on unshakable foundations, or, once society was organized, to prescribe the submission of all to him or to those who would have in their hands the rational direction of mankind.'[5] The dogmatism of Comte was thus in opposition not simply to scepticism but even 'to the spirit of free inquiry'.[6] It is true that Comte believed in progress; but he thought of progress as an advance towards a determinate goal or limit, the point at which science could constitute the basis for the sort

---

[1] *Ibid.*, p. 273.
[2] Before becoming a professor in the University of Montpellier, Milhaud taught mathematics at a school in the same town.
[3] Milhaud published several works on the history of Greek and modern science in its relationship to philosophy.
[4] *Essai*, p. 2.   [5] *Les philosophes géomètres*, p. 4 (second edition, 1934).
[6] *Ibid.*, p. 4.

of society which he considered desirable. Comte therefore had no use for the dreams of never-ending progress indulged in by eighteenth-century thinkers. In his view science had already arrived 'if not at the final term of its advance, at any rate at the state of consolidation in which no further radical transformations were to be foreseen, in which the fundamental concepts were definitely fixed, and in which new concepts could not differ much from the old ones.'[1] We cannot however set bounds in this way to the creativity of the human mind.

At first Milhaud made a sharp distinction between pure mathematics, which rests on the principle of non-contradiction, and empirical science. But he soon came to emphasize the element of rational decision which is present in all branches of science. He had indeed no intention of suggesting that scientific hypotheses are purely arbitrary constructions. He saw them as based on or suggested by experience and as constructed in such a way as to satisfy logical demands of consistency and also practical and aesthetic requirements. But he refused to admit that scientific theories were necessitated either by logic or by experience. They express the creativity of the human mind, though this creative activity is guided in science by rational decision and not by caprice. Further, we can never say that scientific knowledge has attained its final form. We cannot exclude radical transformations in advance. There is indeed an ideal goal, but it is an ever-receding goal, even though progress is real. If we think of Comtean positivism are representing the third stage of human thought, we must add that this stage has to be transcended, as it constitutes an obstacle to the mind's creative activity.[2]

4. We have seen that Duhem made a sharp distinction between science on the one hand and metaphysics or ontology on the other. A rather different view of the nature of science was taken by Émile Meyerson (1859–1933). Born at Lublin of Jewish parentage, he studied classics and then chemistry in Germany.[3] In 1882 he took up his abode at Paris, and later, after the 1914–18 war, he became a naturalized French citizen. He never occupied any official academic post, but he was an influential thinker. In 1908 he published at Paris his well known book *Identité et réalité*[4] and in

---

[1] *Études sur la pensée scientifiques chez les grecs et chez les modernes* (1906), p. 230.
[2] See *Le positivisme et le progrès de l'esprit* (1902).
[3] Meyerson's chemical studies were pursued under R. W. Bunsen.
[4] Translated by K. Loewenberg as *Identity and Reality* (London and New York, 1930).

1921 a two-volume work on explanation in the sciences (*De l'explication dans les sciences*). These publications were followed by a book on relativity theory (*La déduction relativiste*, 1925), a three-volume work on the ways of thought (*Du cheminement de la pensée*, 1931) and a small book on quantum theory (*Réel et déterminisme dans la physique quantique*, 1933). A collection of essays (*Essais*) appeared posthumously in 1936.

In the first place Meyerson is strongly opposed to a positivist view of science as concerned simply with prediction and control or action. According to the positivist science formulates laws which represent the relations between phenomena or sensible appearances, laws which enable us to predict and so serve action and our control of phenomena. Though however Meyerson has no wish to deny that science does in fact enable us to predict and extend the area of control, he refuses to admit that this is the primary goal or operative ideal of science. 'It is not accurate to say that science has action as its sole end, nor that it is governed solely by the desire of economy in this action. Science seeks also to make us *understand* Nature. It tends in fact, as M. Le Roy expresses it, to the 'progressive rationalization of the real'.[1] Science rests on the presupposition that reality is intelligible; and it hopes that this intelligibility will become ever more manifest. The mind's drive towards understanding lies at the basis of all scientific inquiry and research. It is therefore a mistake to follow Francis Bacon, Hobbes and Comte in defining the goal of science simply in terms of prediction with a view to action. 'The positivist theory rests at bottom on a palpable error in psychology.'[2]

If science rests on the presupposition that Nature is intelligible and seeks to discover its intelligible character, we cannot legitimately maintain that scientific hypotheses and theories are simply intellectual constructions which are devoid of ontological import. 'Ontology is joined to science itself and cannot be separated from it.'[3] It is all very well to claim that science should be stripped of all ontology and metaphysics. The fact of the matter is that this very claim involves a metaphysics or theory about being. In particular, science cannot get away from the concept of things or substances. A positivist may claim that science is concerned simply with formulating laws and that the concept of things or substances

[1] *Identité et realité*, p. 438 (my translation); English version, p. 384.
[2] *De l'explication dans les sciences* (1927), p. 45. This work will be referred to as *Explication*.
[3] *Identité et realité*, p. 439; English version, p. 384.

which are independent of the mind can be thrown overboard; but the idea of law as expressing relations presupposes the idea of related things. If it is objected that the concept of things, existing independently of consciousness, belongs to the sphere of naïve common sense and must be abandoned at the level of science, the reply can be made that 'the hypothetical beings of science are really more *things* than the things of common sense'.[1] That is to say, atoms or electrons, for example, are not direct objects of sense or sense-data; and they thus exemplify the concept of a thing (as existing independently of sensation) more clearly than the sensible objects of the level of common sense. Science has its point of departure in the world of common sense; and when it transforms or abandons common sense concepts, 'what it adopts is as ontological as what it abandons.'[2] According to Meyerson, those who think otherwise fail to grasp the nature of science at work, in its actual reality; and they themselves produce theories about science which have ontological implications of which they seem to be blissfully unaware. The positivist idea of separating science from all ontology 'corresponds neither with science today nor with that which humanity has known in any epoch of its development'.[3]

Reference has been made to common sense. One of Meyerson's strongest convictions is that science is 'only a prolongation of common sense'.[4] We ordinarily assume that our perception of objects is something simple and primitive. If we analyze perception, we arrive in the long run at states of consciousness or sensations. To build up perception out of primitive subjective data, we have to introduce memory. Otherwise we could not account for our belief in permanent possibilities of sensation. But in the construction of the world of common sense we go further than this. We use, though not of course explicitly or with conscious reflection, the principle of causality to construct the concept of permanent physical objects. Common sense is thus shot through with ontology or metaphysics. We explain our sensations in terms of physical objects as causes of our sensations. On the level of common sense we hypostatize our sensations as far as we can, attributing, for example, colour and other qualities to objects, whereas science transforms the objects. But science has its point of

---

[1] *Explication*, pp. 39–40.   [2] *Ibid.*, p. 39.
[3] *Identité et realité*, p. 439; English version, p. 384.
[4] *Ibid.*, p. 402; English version, p. 354.

departure in common sense, and it prolongs our use of the causal principle. The entities postulated by the scientist may differ from those of common sense; but physics can no more get along without the concept of things or substances or without causal explanation than common sense can. The concept of law, establishing relations between phenomena, is not enough by itself.

Given this point of view, it is understandable that Meyerson insists that science is explanatory and not simply descriptive. Comte and others may have tried to expel explanation and explanatory theories from science; but 'the existence of explanatory science is a *fact*',[1] a fact which cannot be got over by ingenious accounts of what the scientist is about. A phenomenon is explained in so far as it is deduced from antecedents which can be described as the cause of the phenomenon or, to use Leibnizian terminology, as its sufficient reason, sufficient, that is to say, to produce the phenomenon in question. 'The cause can be defined as the point of departure of a deduction of which the phenomenon is the point of arrival.'[2] It is true, according to Meyerson, that in science we do not actually find deductions corresponding fully with an abstract concept of what deductive explanation should be. But though this shows that in science, as elsewhere, man pursues a goal which transcends his grasp, it does not show that the pursuit does not exist. The drive to explain phenomena involves the presupposition that reality is intelligible or rational. The attempt to understand reality meets with resistance, in the form of the irrational, of that which cannot be rendered fully intelligible. But this does not affect the fact that science aims at explanation.

It is clear that Meyerson assimilates the causal relation to that of logical implication. Indeed, he regards causal explanation as a process of identification. In so far as a phenomenon is explained by deducing it from its antecedents, it is identified with these antecedents. 'The principle of causality is simply the principle of identity applied to the existence of objects in time.'[3] That the mind seeks persistence through motion and time can be seen, for example, in its formulation of principles such as those of inertia, of conservation of matter and conservation of energy. When pushed however to the limit the demand for causal explanation is a demand for an identification of cause and effect such that the two would coincide, time would be eliminated and nothing would

[1] *Explication*, p. 57.   [2] *Ibid.*, p. 66.
[3] *Identité et realité*, p. 38; English version, p. 43.

happen. In other words, the reason aspires after an Eleatic world, 'a universe eternally immutable,'[1] a universe in which, paradoxically, there is no causality and nothing ever happens. As a limiting concept, the world which would fully satisfy the will to identification would be one in which distinct bodies had been eliminated by their reduction to space, and so to nonentity. For that which does not act and is not the cause of anything is as if it were not.

Meyerson has not of course taken complete leave of his senses. He does not in fact believe that science will ever arrive at acosmism as a final conclusion. He is known indeed as a philosopher of science; but in the first instance he is an epistemologist, in the sense that he is interested in developing a critique of reason. He wishes, that is to say, to discover the principles governing human thought.[2] To achieve this task he turns neither to introspection nor to *a priori* reflection but to an '*a posteriori* analysis of expressed thought'.[3] In other words, he examines the products of thought. And his attention is focussed for the most part, though not exclusively, on physical science. In this area he finds that the mind aims at understanding phenomena through causal explanation, that the principle of causality, in its pure form so to speak, is the principle of identity applied to objects in time, and that the *a priori* drive of the reason is thus to identification. The mind in its activity is governed by the principle of identity. He proceeds to show what sort of universe, in his opinion, would satisfy this will to identification, if it were able to proceed unchecked and without encountering any resistance. In point of fact however it does not proceed unchecked; and it does encounter resistance. We cannot get over the irreversibility of time and the reality of becoming or change. 'Identity is the eternal framework of our mind';[4] but science has come to be increasingly dominated by empirical elements which militate against the will to identification. The universe as presented to us by science is thus not a Parmenidean universe. This remains a limiting concept, a projected goal of the mind's inborn or *a priori* drive to identification, if we suppose that it encounters no resistance.

Perhaps the matter can be expressed in this way. Whatever the positivists may have asserted, science is explanatory. It

---

[1] *Ibid.*, p. 256; English version, p. 230.
[2] As Meyerson puts it, using a Leibnizian term, he seeks to know the nature of 'the intellect itself' (*intellectus ipse*). Needless to say, he is aware of the affinity between his inquiry and Kant's; but his approach and method are different.
[3] *Essais*, p. 107.   [4] *Identité et realité*, p. 322; English version, p. 284.

exemplifies a drive to understanding by means of causal explanation, a drive which belongs to the human mind as such and is already present and operative on the level of common sense. This approach presupposes that reality is intelligible or rational. And as, according to Meyerson, the search for causal explanation is governed by the principle of identity, reality, if completely rational, would be one self-identical being, the cause of itself, or *causa sui*. But the completely self-identical being would be equivalent to not-being. Science cannot arrive at a *causa sui*. Further, reality is in any case not fully rational in the sense mentioned. In modern science we have become more and more aware of the irreversibility of time and of the emergence of novelty. Reality, as constructed by science, will not fit into the schema of rationalism. It does not follow from this that science is not explanatory. That is to say, it always embodies the drive to understanding by means of causal explanation. But science can never find a final resting-place. The 'irrational', in the sense of what is unforseen and unforeseeable, breaks in, as in quantum physics. The behaviour of living things cannot be simply deduced from what we know of the behaviour of inorganic bodies. And even if some apparently irrational phenomena come to be explained, there is no guarantee whatever that the scientist will not be faced with new ones, or that new theories will not supplant or profoundly modify their predecessors. We have had an Einstein. There may be others. 'We shall never be able really to *deduce* Nature, . . . We shall always have need of new experiences and these will always give rise to new problems, will cause new contradictions to break out (*éclater*), according to Duhem's term, between our theories and our observations.'[1] The drive or impulse of reason remains the same. 'Everyone, always and in every circumstance, has reasoned and reasons still in an essentially invariable way.'[2] But reason cannot attain its ideal goal. It has to adapt itself to empirical reality. And science as it exists exemplifies the dialectic between the drive of reason, which postulates the completely rational character of reality, and the obstacles which it constantly encounters.

Meyerson was interested in philosophical systems and applied his ideas to, for example, Hegel's philosophy of Nature. Hegel tried to subject what he regarded as the irrational to the dominion of reason. And we cannot legitimately object to the attempt to understand and explain. For 'reason must tend to subject to

---

[1] *Explication*, p. 230.   [2] *Ibid.*, p. 703.

itself all that does not come from it; it is its proper function, for it is this which we call *reasoning*. We have seen moreover, in our previous book, that explanatory science is nothing but an operation pursued entirely according to this pattern.'[1] But the fact of the matter is that reality cannot be taken by storm in the manner envisaged by those who construct comprehensive deductive systems. They are sure to meet with a check. And this check constitutes precisely a demonstration of the fact that the 'irrational' cannot be totally mastered by the deductive reason.

Evidently, in a certain sense Meyerson sympathizes fully with the mathematical deductive ideal of knowledge. This is what, in his view, reason strives after and will always strive after. But Nature exists independently of us, even though it becomes known only through our sensations, through the sensible appearances of things. We cannot simply reconstruct Nature deductively. We have to have recourse to experience. The ways of Nature can be different from those of pure reason. And this fact sets limits to our power of conceptual mastery. The philosopher who produces a comprehensive deductive system tries to subject Nature completely to the demands of reason. But Nature is refractory; it takes its revenge. Hence science as it exists must be both deductive and empirical. It advances in the process of understanding; but it must always be ready for shocks and for the revision of its theories. Reason seeks an ideal goal, which is set by the essence or nature of reason; but the attainment of the goal is an ever-receding limit of aspiration. In one sense reason suffers frustration. But in another sense it does not. For if the goal were completely attained, there would be no science.

5. According to Meyerson, as we have just seen, reason, governed in its operation by the principle of identity, seeks a Parmenidean One, a *causa sui* in which diversity is overcome and complete self-identity is realized. To be sure, this limiting goal can never be attained. For novelty and the unforeseeable break in and prevent reason coming to any final rest. But the ideal limit remains, that of a complete explanation of all events or phenomena through identification with their ultimate cause. In Kantian language this ideal limit is a regulative idea of the reason.

We can perhaps see some affinity at any rate between Meyerson's idea of reason and that of André Lalande (1867–1964), the editor of the well known *Vocabulaire technique et critique de la*

---

[1] *Explication*, p. 402.

philosophie.[1] With Lalande the Eleatic overtones are missing, but he lays emphasis on a movement towards homogeneity and unification and of the role played by reason in this movement as found in human life. In 1899 he published a thesis in which he opposed Herbert Spencer's contention that the movement in evolution is one of differentiation, a movement from homogeneity to heterogeneity.[2] Lalande did not of course deny that there is a process of differentiation; but in his view the movement of what he called 'dissolution' or 'involution'[3] was of wider significance. In Nature this movement can be seen in entropy, in the increasing unavailability of thermal energy and the tendency towards an equilibrium which would result in a kind of thermal death.[4] In the organic sphere we do indeed find a process of differentiation, a movement from the homogeneous to the heterogeneous; but the movement of life can be likened to that of an object thrown into the air. The vital energy or impetus is finally spent, and living things relapse in the end into inanimate matter. In the long run it is homogeneity which prevails over heterogeneity, assimilation over differentiation.

In point of fact Herbert Spencer, in his general theory of èvolution, allowed for an alternation of differentiation and dissolution or, as Lalande would say, involution.[5] But as a resolute champion of individual liberty and a strong opponent of the organic theory of the State,[6] Spencer clearly regarded increasing differentiation, increasing heterogeneity, as the desirable goal in the development of human society and as the mark of progress. Here Lalande parts company with him. He does not regard processes in Nature as proper objects of moral judgments. But in the sphere of human life he looks on the movement towards homogeneity as desirable and as constituting progress. In other words, Lalande sees man's biological nature and tendencies as impelling him to self-centredness and egoism, as separating human beings. The desirable

---

[1] Lalande began publishing his *Technical and Critical Vocabulary of Philosophy* in 1902. In 1904 he was appointed to a philosophical chair at Paris.

[2] *L'idée directrice de la dissolution opposée à celle de l'évolution.* A revised edition appeared in 1930 with the title *Les illusions évolutionistes* (*Evolutionist Illusions*).

[3] The word 'involution' was substituted for 'dissolution' in the revised version of the thesis.

[4] Extension of the second law of thermodynamics from a closed thermal system to the universe is now commonly regarded as illegitimate.

[5] For Herbert Spencer see Vol. 8 of this *History*, chapter V.

[6] By the organic theory of the State I mean the theory of the State as an organism which is more than the sum of its members.

movement is the one which tends to make men not more unlike
but more like one another, not indeed through an imposed uniformity or one which would eliminate our human freedom, but
rather through a common participation in the realm of reason,
morality and art. The movement of biological life is differentiating,
divisive. Reason tends to unify and to assimilate.

In science the unifying function of reason is obvious. Particulars
are grouped under universals, in classes that is to say; and the
tendency is towards the coordination of phenomena under ever
fewer and more general laws. In the spheres of logical thought
and of scientific inquiry reason assimilates in the sense that it
tends to make people think alike, even if they feel differently.
Obviously, feeling can influence thought; but the point is that in so
far as reason triumphs, it unites men rather than divides them.
It may seem that the more science is given a technological application, the more individuals are identified with their functions,
becoming simply members of a social organism. But according to
Lalande the growth of technology serves to liberate the individual. It is true that in modern society men and women tend to
become more alike, and that a certain uniformity is produced;
but in this very process they are liberated from ancient tyrannies,
such as that of the patriarchal family, and increasing specialization sets people free to enjoy common cultural values, such as
aesthetic values. The assimilating tendency of modern society,
with the breakdown of old hierarchies, is at the same time a process of liberation for the individual. Man becomes free to enter
more fully into his common cultural heritage.

As we are all aware, some writers have seen in the development
of modern society a process of levelling-out which tends to produce
a uniform mediocrity prejudicial to the individual personality,
while others have emphasized the identification, as they interpret
it, of the individual with his social function. The growth of
homogeneity can be interpreted as equivalent to the growth of
what Nietzsche described as the 'Cold Monster' or as leading in the
direction of a totalitarian society. Lalande proposes a different
point of view, seeing modern society as potentially liberating the
individual for his self-enrichment by entering into the common
cultural world of reason and art. Biological urges are divisive;
reason and morals and aesthetics are unifying factors. It is therefore not surprising that in a work on *Reason and Norms* (*La
raison et les normes*), which appeared in 1948, he criticized

phenomenologists and existentialists. For example, while phenomenologists emphasized the origins of the concepts of space and
time in the experience of the individual as a being in the world,
Lalande emphasized the common space and time of mathematicians and physicists, in which he saw the unifying work of reason.

Lalande did indeed write specifically about the philosophy of
science. Thus in 1893 he published the first of the numerous
editions of *Lectures sur la philosophie des sciences* (*Readings in the
Philosophy of the Sciences*) and in 1929 *Les théories de l'induction
et de l'expérimentation* (*Theories of Induction and Experimentation*).
But his thought was much wider than what could usefully be
described as philosophy of science. For his concern was with
emphasizing the movement of 'involution' and the role played in it
by what he called 'constituting reason'. Science is one field in which
reason unifies. But morals is another, where reason is capable of
promoting agreement and producing a lay or secular ethics. In
general, reason fosters mutual understanding and cooperation
between human beings. The effort devoted by Lalande to editing
and re-editing his *Vocabulary* was based on this assumption.

6. Meyerson and Brunschvicg both emphasized the impulse to
unification which is manifested in science. This was natural
enough, not only because this emphasis fitted into or was demanded
by their general philosophies but also because unification of
phenomena clearly constitutes a real aspect of science. It is not
necessary to talk about identification or to follow Meyerson in
introducing Parmenidean themes in order to see that when the
mind is faced with a plurality of phenomena conceptual unification forms a real aspect of understanding. Conceptual mastery
cannot be obtained without unification. Or, rather, it is a process
of unification. At the same time it is possible to emphasize the
pluralism in science, the elements of discontinuity and the plurality of theories. Brunschvicg, as we have seen, allowed for this
aspect. But there is a difference between finding room for the facts
within the framework of an idealist philosophy which emphasizes
the nature of mind or spirit as a unity and singling out and laying
emphasis on aspects of the history of science which it is not so easy
to harmonize with the general idea of reason as progressively
imposing its own unity and homogeneity on phenomena.

Emphasis on plurality and discontinuity was characteristic of
the philosophy of science of Gaston Bachelard (1884–1962). After
having been employed in the postal service he obtained a degree

in mathematics and science and then taught physics and chemistry in his home town, Bar-sur-Aube. In 1930 he was appointed professor of philosophy in the university of Dijon,[1] and after ten years he went to Paris as professor of the history and philosophy of science. He published a considerable number of works, in 1928 an *Essai sur la connaissance approchée* (*Essay on Approximative Knowledge*), in 1932 *Le pluralisme cohérent de la chimie moderne* (*The Coherent Pluralism of Modern Chemistry*), in 1933 *Les intuitions atomistiques* (*Atomistic Intuitions*), in 1937 *La continuité et la multiplicité temporelles* (*Temporal Continuity and Multiplicity*) and *L'expérience de l'espace dans la physique contemporaine* (*The Experience of Space in Contemporary Physics*), in 1938 *La formation de l'esprit scientifique* (*The Formation of the Scientific Mind*), in 1940 *La philosophie du non* (*The Philosophy of No*), in 1949 *La rationalisme appliqué* (*Applied Rationalism*), in 1951 *L'activité rationaliste de la physique contemporaine* (*The Rationalist Activity of Contemporary Physics*), and in 1953 *Le matérialisme rationnel* (*Rational Materialism*). Bachelard was also interested in the relation between the activity of the mind in science and its activity in poetic imagination. In this field he published a number of works, such as *La psychoanalyse du feu* (1938, *The Psychoanalysis of Fire*), *L'eau et les rêves* (1942, *Water and Dreams*), *L'air et les songes* (1943, *Air and Dreams*), *La terre et les rêveries de la volonté* (1948, *Earth and the Reveries of the Will*), *La poétique de l'espace* (1957, *The Poetics of Space*) and *La flamme d'une chandelle* (1961, *The Flame of a Candle*).

In Bachelard's view existentialist talk about the absurdity or meaninglessness of the world is an illegitimate exaggeration. It is indeed true that scientific hypotheses and theories are the creation of mind; but experiment or empirical testing is necessary to science, and the interplay of reason and experience in the development of scientific knowledge does not support the view that the world is completely unintelligible in itself and that intelligibility is nothing but a mental imposition. When however we consider the nature and course of this interplay of reason and experience, we find that scientific progress cannot properly be regarded as a continuous advance in which reason simply adds to the coherent system of knowledge already attained. It is all very well for some philosophers to lay down first principles and then to interpret reality as exemplifying them and as filling in the preconceived

---

[1] Bachelard received the doctorate in 1927.

outline of a picture. They can always regard refractory material as of little significance or as illustrating the contingent or even irrational nature of the given. Their philosophy remains 'a philosopher's philosophy'[1] and has little to do with science. In the growth of scientific knowledge discontinuity is an essential feature. That is to say, new experiences force us to say 'no' to old theories; and for an old model of interpretation we may have to substitute a new one. Indeed, we may have to change concepts or principles which have seemed basic. The genuinely scientific mind is open. It will not do, for example, to reject quantum mechanics, with its recognition of a measure of indeterminism, simply because it will not fit into a sacrosanct framework. Conceptual frameworks may have to be negated in favour of new ones, though these too of course are themselves open to negation in the future. The philosophy of science must itself be pluralistic, open to a variety of perspectives. The old rationalistic deductive ideal of Descartes and others is untenable and discredited. Reason has to follow science. That is to say, it must learn the various forms of reasoning from seeing them at work in the sciences.[2] 'The traditional doctrine of an absolute and changeless reason is only a philosophy. It is a philosophy which has perished.'[3]

In his *Philosophie du non* Bachelard does not of course understand by 'no' a mere negation. The new physics, for example, does not simply deny or cancel out the classical physics. Classical concepts are given fresh meanings in a new framework. The negation is dialectical rather than pure rejection. At the same time the emphasis is laid by Bachelard on discontinuity, on rupture in thought and on 'transcendence' of previous levels. For instance, the world as represented in science transcends the pre-scientific world. There is a rupture between the naïve consciousness and the scientific consciousness. But within science itself there are ruptures. Science, for example, was once a kind of organized common sense, treating either of concrete objects or of objects which sufficiently resembled the concrete things of common sense for them to be imaginable. With the advent however of non-Euclidean geometries, of theories of the world which can be expressed only mathematically and of concepts of 'objects' which are not imaginable things like those of common sense, science has become

---

[1] *La philosophie du non*, p. 8 (5th edition, 1970).
[2] Here Bachelard says much the same as Brunschvicg.
[3] *La philosophie du non*, p. 145.

concerned, according to Bachelard, with relationships rather than with things. It looks beyond things and immediate objects to mathematically formulable relationships. And there has thus taken place a 'dematerialization of materialism'.[1] Thought tends to become fossilized in a realistic outlook; but the crisis of discovery forces it forward into the process of abstraction which is made possible by mathematics. There arises therefore a scientific world which is not communicable to the non-scientific mind and which is far removed not only from the world of naïve consciousness but also from that of the imaginable world of earlier science.

The creative activity of the mind is exemplified, Bachelard insists, both in the work of scientific reason and in the poetic imagination, their roots being, in his view, discoverable by psychoanalysis. Though however both science and poetry (or art in general) manifest the creative activity of the mind, they take different directions. In art man projects his dream, the product of the imagination, on things, while in modern science the mind transcends both subject and object towards mathematically formulable relationships. In regard to this sphere of the scientific reason Bachelard obviously agrees with Brunschvicg both in the rejection of fixed categories and models and in the view that reason comes to know its nature through reflection on its actual work, on its historical development. For Bachelard the nature of reason is thus revealed as pluriform and as plastic or changing. But if we ask why reason in its creative activity constructs the world of science, the answer, even if it is not clearly given by Bachelard, must presumably be similar to that given by Brunschvicg, namely that the mind pursues unification. Emphasis on discontinuity, on revisibility and on the non-final character of scientific concepts, models and theories does not really affect the issue. For Brunschvicg himself did not envisage a complete and final unification or assimilation as actually attainable. To be sure, the obviously idealist presuppositions and ideas of Brunschvicg are absent from Bachelard's thought. But the latter's view of modern man as projecting or creating an extremely abstract world of relationships, in which materialism is left behind or at any rate transformed, might perhaps be given an idealist setting, if one wished to do so.

We have noted the lively interest shown by recent French philosophers of science in epistemological themes. In this field the

---

[1] *Le nouvel esprit scientifique*, p. 67.

philosophers mentioned above manifested a strong reaction to positivism on the one hand and to the Cartesian ideal of knowledge on the other. They emphasized the inventiveness and creativity of the mind and the approximating and revisible character of its interpretation of reality. Duhem was something of an exception. For though he agreed, in large measure, with the conventionalism of Poincaré, he was concerned with separating science from ontology and metaphysics. Generally speaking however the sciences were looked on as embodying the mind's urge to understand the world through the unification of phenomena. And the ideas of the inventiveness and creativity of the mind and of the essentially revisible character of scientific hypotheses and theories were obviously grounded in reflection on the history of science. In other words, it was science in its actuality which prompted the conclusion that both the purely rationalistic and deductive picture of the mind's operation and Comte's rather naïve conception of positive knowledge were alike discredited. Again, philosophers such as Brunschvicg and Bachelard saw clearly that neither pure rationalism nor pure empiricism could provide a satisfactory account of science as it existed. We may of course be inclined to think that the French philosophers of science were too 'philosophical'. But at any rate they tried to make their philosophical positions clear and explicit, even if their success was not always conspicuous.

CHAPTER XIV

PHILOSOPHY OF VALUES, METAPHYSICS, PERSONALISM

General remarks — R. Polin — Metaphysics of values: R. Le Senne and the philosophy of spirit — R. Ruyer and J. Pucelle — L. Lavelle and the philosophy of act — The personalism of E. Mounier.

1. It hardly needs saying that moral philosophy in one form or another has been a prominent feature of French thought from the time of the Renaissance. Even Descartes, whose name is primarily associated with methodology, metaphysics and the view of the world as a machine, emphasized the practical value of philosophy and envisaged a science of ethics as its crown. The philosophers of the eighteenth-century Enlightenment were concerned with setting ethics on its own feet, separating it, that is to say, from theology and metaphysics. In the nineteenth century ethical themes were prominent in the writings of positivists such as Durkheim, of spiritualists such as Guyau and Bergson[1] and of thinkers such as Renouvier who belonged to the neo-critical movement. In spite however of this tradition of ethical thought the philosophy of values was a comparative latecomer on the French scene, in comparison with Germany that is to say; and it met at first with some suspicion and resistance. Obviously the concept of the good and of desirable ends had been familiar enough, and philosophers had discussed moral ideals as well as truth and beauty. In a sense ethical discussion had always included discussion of values. At the same time the French moral philosophers had tended to focus their attention on ethical phenomena as an empirical or given point of departure for reflection; and there was some doubt about the utility of the abstract analysis of values, especially as this sort of language suggested the idea of subsistent essences 'out there'. Besides, the explicit philosophy of values as practised by Max Scheler and Nicolai Hartmann was connected with phenomenology, which developed in Germany and

---

[1] Bergson's ethical writing belongs of course to the twentieth century. But his philosophy was the culmination of a movement which began and developed in the nineteenth century.

at first had little impact in France.[1] There was of course Nietzsche's discussion of values. But for a considerable time Nietzsche was regarded in France more as a poet than a philosopher.

From a phenomenological point of view it can reasonably be argued that values are recognized or discovered. Consider, for example, the case of someone who judges that love is a value, something to be valued, whereas hatred is not. It is clearly arguable that his attitude is one of recognizing or seeing love as a value and hatred as a disvalue. Whatever his theory of values may be, it can be argued that as far as his immediate consciousness is concerned, love imposes itself on his mind as a value. Similarly, from the phenomenological point of view it is reasonable to use the language of recognition or discovery in regard to truth and beauty considered as values. In other words, our experience of values provides a ground or basis for the idea of values as objective and as transcendent, in the sense that they do not depend simply on one's own choice of them. To be sure, one has to find room for different and even incompatible value-judgments. But we can always refer, as some phenomenologists have done, to the possibility of a blindness to values and of varying degrees of insight into the field of values. And these ideas can be applied both to societies and to individuals.

From an ontological or metaphysical point of view however it seems absurd, to most people at any rate, to conceive values as existing in some ethereal world of their own. We can of course substitute the word 'subsist' for the word 'exist'; but it is doubtful if this verbal change really improves the situation. If therefore we wish to assert the objectivity of values, and if at the same time we wish to avoid committing ourselves to the view that universals such as love or truth or beauty can exist or 'subsist' in a Platonic world of their own, we can either regard values as objective qualities of things and actions in addition to other qualities, or we can try to work out some general metaphysics which will permit us to talk about the objectivity of values without committing ourselves to the concept of a realm of subsistent universal essences.

If may of course seem very much simpler to deny the objectivity of values, if this is taken to imply that values have an ontological status of their own, whether as ethereal substances or as objective qualities of things, persons and actions. That is to say, it may seem

[1] In Germany there was also of course the Neo-Kantian School of Baden. See Vol. 7 of this *History*, pp. 364–6.

much simpler, and also more sensible, to throw all the weight on the value-judgment or on the act of valuation and to maintain, for example, that to assert that beauty is a value is to express the act of attributing value to beautiful things or persons. We can maintain, in other words, that it is through the act of attributing value that human beings create values. Values depend on and are relative to the human will and choice.

If we adopt this line of thought, we have of course to account in some way for the feeling of recognizing or discovering values. For this seems to be a datum of consciousness. We can try to explain this feeling by referring it to the bearing of the collective consciousness, as conceived by Durkheim, on the individual consciousness. Or, if we wish to speak only in terms of individuals, we might adopt a line of thought represented by Sartre and see the individuals' particular value-judgments as determined by an original *projet* or a basic operative ideal.

Leaving aside for the moment not only the existentialism of Sartre, which will be discussed later, but also those who have tried to give a metaphysical foundation to values, we can turn first to a philosopher, Raymond Polin, who has discussed a variety of axiological theories and attitudes and who himself comes down on the anti-objectivist side.

2. Raymond Polin was born in 1910. After studying at the École Normale and obtaining the doctorate in letters, he taught philosophy first in several lycées, such as the Lycée Condorcet at Paris, and then as professor of ethics in the university of Lille. In 1961 he became a professor at the Sorbonne. His publications include *La création des valeurs* (1944, *The Creation of Values*), *La compréhension des valeurs* (1945, *The Understanding of Values*), *Du laid, du mal, du faux* (1948, *On the Ugly, the Evil and the False*) and *Éthique et politique* (1968, *Ethics and Politics*). Polin has also published works on Hobbes and Locke.[1]

Phenomenology, Polin asserts, seems to offer 'the most adequate method for the study of values',[2] inasmuch as for the consciousness which thinks or conceives them values coincide with their meaning (*signification*). He envisages two steps, first a phenomenological reduction giving access to the pure axiological consciousness (the consciousness of value) with a view to defining the

---

[1] *Philosophie et politique chez Thomas Hobbes* (1953) and *La politique morale de John Locke* (1960).
[2] *La création des valeurs*, p. 1.

essence of values, and secondly a movement of liberation, freeing the mind, that is to say, both from the pressure exercised by received values and from the influence of all existing theories of value. In other words, he wishes to take a fresh and unprejudiced view of the matter. The mind should place itself in a position of neutrality in regard to any determinate hierarchy of values and in regard to all existing theories. It should prescind from all authority, including that of society.

As Polin refers frequently to 'values', using the noun that is to say, one may be tempted to conclude that for him there is a realm of essences which have some sort of existence of their own or which have to be given an ontological or metaphysical foundation. Indeed, the subtitle of his work on the creation of values is *Recherches sur le fondement de l'objectivité axiologique* (*Inquiries into the Foundation of Axiological Objectivity*). We have already noted however that for him a value coincides with its meaning for the consciousness which thinks it. It thus has intentional objectivity, in the sense that the act of thinking or conceiving a value-meaning is a reality. But a value does not exist as an object 'out there', independently of the subject which thinks it. As for finding a foundation for values, other than the act of evaluating, this would have to be different from the values themselves (if it were to serve as a foundation) and at the same time to stand in an intelligible and necessary relation to the values which it founded. But how can there be a necessary relation between what is not a value and a value? Or to express the matter in a different and more familiar way, how can a factual statement entail a value-judgment?

In point of fact Polin's talk about values is somewhat misleading. He is really concerned with the act of evaluation, by which values are constituted. In his view evaluation cannot be understood apart from the concept of human action. 'Phenomenological inquiry into the essence of values is vain and futile unless it constitutes the introduction to a philosophy of action.'[1] Human action presupposes and expresses evaluation, which is an act of the free subject. The free subject outruns or transcends the empirically given, creating its own values with a view to action. The values created have of course a certain exteriority, in the sense that they are the objects of an intentional and teleological consciousness. But it is a mistake to think that there is an axiological reality or

---

[1] *Ibid.*, p. 3.

realm of values apart from the consciousness which creates them. The only given reality is empirical reality; but this is evaluated in relation to action. Values are grounded in the self-transcending creative subject. And this is the only foundation which they have or require.

According to Polin therefore values are not real objects 'out there' waiting to be known. On the contrary, there is an irreducible distinction between knowledge of things, in which the 'noetic' consciousness is absorbed in the object, and the axiological consciousness which transcends what is given and creates the 'unreal'. In other words, we must not confuse truth and value. 'Truth is not a value,'[1] and we ought not to speak of the truth of values. But there is a truth of action. That is to say, while theoretical truth is attained through the conformity of thought with reality, truth in action is attained through the conformity produced in the reality (work) created by action 'with the axiological project and intention'.[2] We know a fact when our thought is conformed to an objective state of affairs. In the sphere of action however truth consists in the conformity between what we achieve or bring about and our value-laden intention. But this is not all there is to be said. For through his action a man creates not simply his work but also himself. 'This is why the truth of action embraces the totality of the work and its creator. It is at the same time the work and the man who accomplishes the work.'[3]

In his insistence that it is man who feely creates values Polin stands in the Nietzschean line of thought. And in this and some other respects, such as his view that through the process of evaluation and action man creates himself, he obviously stands close to Sartre. But what, we may ask, does Polin make of the social aspect of morality? In his view, 'action is social by its essence, by its object, by its conditions; it is inconceivable without the presence of the other.'[4] This means that vlaues, as the expression of a creative will, tend to become norms; and norms, as universalizable, are essentially social. Moreover, whereas values (valuations) are personal and cannot be imposed, norms can be imposed by others. A society or group, for example, can accept certain norms and try to enforce or impose acceptance on its individual members or on another group. Norms then become values rendered static; and they can be accepted servilely or because people are looking for a secure foothold or a refuge from personal decision which is always

[1] *Ibid.*, p. 296.   [2] *Ibid.*, p. 296.   [3] *Ibid.*, p. 297.   [4] *Ibid.*, p. 259.

a venture, as it means going beyond or transcending the given. At the same time values can also present themselves not as constraining norms or rules or commandments but as attracting or exercising an appeal. To their creator values can appear as attracting ideals and ends; and they can appear in the same way to others. 'The commandment is replaced by an appeal.'[1] The creator then 'owes his domination over others simply to the influence of the values which he creates'.[2] In this line of thought we can see perhaps a resumption of Bergson's theme of the closed and open moralities.

In his analysis of 'axiological attitudes' Polin begins by examining what he describes as the contemplative attitude. Here the subject conceives transcendence not in the form of creative human action but in that of 'a static and given being: the transcendent'.[3] Values are conceived not as 'unreal' entities which are realized only through human action but as realities existing independently of man. Polin admits that values, as so conceived, can provide a 'model of a perfect human activity';[4] but, as objects of contemplation, they do not, in his view, 'give rise to any efficacious *action*'.[5] A value is not, as it were, a moment in the total process or cycle of human action, but rather a detached object of contemplation which exists, or if preferred, subsists, independently of human consciousness.

Polin does not of course share this axiological attitude. And most of us would probably find it difficult to accept a theory which postulated a world of subsistent value-essences, which would really be subsistent universals, in addition to particular individual things. At the same time it is arguable, as has already been noted, that from the phenomenological point of view there is such an experience as recognizing or discovering values. That is to say, there is an experience which seems to demand the use of such terms. And even if one is determined to avoid the literal implication of a term such as 'discovery', namely the implication that there is a pre-existing reality waiting to be discovered, any adequate theory of values must at any rate allow for the type of experience which prompts the use of terms which are potentially misleading. Hence it is perfectly understandable that some philosophers are not content with any theory which interprets values simply as free creations of the individual subject. And even if

---

[1] *La compréhension des valeurs*, p. 134.   [2] *Ibid.*, p. 134.
[3] *Ibid.*, p. 58.   [4] *Ibid.*, p. 58.   [5] *Ibid.*, p. 58.

in some cases it involves retracing our steps from the chronological point of view we can consider briefly two or three French philosophers who have tried to link up a theory of values with a general metaphysics.

3. A name which comes at once to mind in this connection is that of René Le Senne (1882–1954). A pupil of Hamelin at the École Normale, Le Senne taught in lycées at Chambéry, Marseilles and then Paris, becoming a professor of moral philosophy at the Sorbonne in 1942. Together with his friend Louis Lavelle he founded and edited the series entitled *Philosophie de l'esprit* (*Philosophy of Spirit*), published by Aubier at Paris. Among his works we can mention his *Introduction to Philosophy* (*Introduction à la philosophie*, 1925, revised and enlarged edition 1939), his doctorate thesis entitled *Duty* (*Le Devoir*, 1930, second edition 1950), *Obstacle and Value* (*Obstacle et valeur*, 1934), a general treatise on ethics (*Traité de morale générale*, 1942), a work on characterology (*Traité de caractérologie*, 1945), *Personal Destiny* (*La destinée personnelle*, 1951), and the posthumously published work *The Discovery of God* (*La découverte de Dieu*, 1955).

In an essay entitled *La philosophie de l'esprit*[1] Le Senne remarks that to follow the development of French philosophy from Descartes to Hamelin, or even to Bergson, is to understand the fecundity of Cartesianism.[2] From one point of view this may seem to be an odd assertion. Is there not, we may ask, a very great difference between the rationalism of Descartes, with his mathematical model of reasoning, and his appeal to clear and distinct concepts, and Bergson's appeal to intuition and his philosophy of duration and of the movement of life? It hardly needs saying however that Le Senne is perfectly well aware of the differences. When he refers to the continuity between the thought of Descartes on the one hand and the spiritualist and idealist movements in nineteenth-century French philosophy on the other, he is thinking not of Descartes' mathematical model nor of his view of the material world as a machine but of the emphasis placed by Descartes on the thinking and active self or ego and of the relation which is asserted between the self and God. Le Senne is thinking,

---

[1] *Philosophic Thought in France and the United States*, edited by Marvin Farber (Buffalo, N.Y., 1950), pp. 103–20. The fact that in the American version of the work the title of Le Senne's essay is given in French is perhaps significant. The word *esprit* can indeed be translated as 'mind'. But though mind is included in its range of meaning, *esprit* has, in the context, metaphysical and religious connotations which favour use of the word 'spirit'.

[2] *Ibid.*, p. 103.

in other words, of elements in Cartesianism which were preserved and developed in the movement of thought from Maine de Biran onwards, but which were menaced by positivism in its various forms and by certain aspects of technological civilization. Obviously, Le Senne makes a judgment of value about what constitutes authentic philosophy. And one characteristic of authentic philosophy, in his view, is that it transcends the initial empiricist attitude of common sense, which 'leads to *realism* and even to *materialism*',[1] and discovers the self as that which thinks the objective world and is conscious of itself. In this movement of thought however there is a dialectic or dialogue between intellectualism or idealist rationalism on the one hand and, on the other, opposition to the reduction of existence to thought. 'As against Descartes, Pascal, Malebranche combines in his philosophy the demands of Cartesianism with the Augustinian inspiration. From Condillac comes Biran, but the latter reacts against the former. At the beginning of this century the dialogue is continued between Hamelin and Bergson.'[2] These two philosophers 'have maintained with the same fidelity the ideal of a knowledge which seeks the reason or the one and indivisible source of all that is and is thought'.[3] As for French existentialism, Le Senne sees, as one would expect, a great difference between the religiously oriented and 'optimistic' philosophy of thinkers such as Marcel and the 'negative' and 'pessimistic' existentialism of Sartre.[4]

As one would expect of a philosopher influenced by Hamelin, there are evident idealist elements in Le Senne's thought. He asserts, for example, that 'the celebrated formula of Berkeley *Esse est percipi vel percipere* (to be is to be perceived or to perceive) is false only inasmuch as it is too narrow. To perceive, to think abstractly, to feel, to will, to love, to have a presentiment of, to regret, and so on indefinitely, so that no experience of the spirit is omitted, this is reality and the whole of reality.'[5] Le Senne adds however a note to explain that while he denies that matter is a thing in itself, in the sense that it exists independently of any spirit, he does not intend to imply that matter has no reality at all. It exists only in relation to spirit, but in this relation it is real and functions 'sometimes as obstacle, sometimes as a support, in

---

[1] *Introduction à la philosophie* (2nd edition, 1947), p. 7.
[2] *Ibid.*, p. 134.   [3] *Ibid.*, p. 135.
[4] We cannot discuss here the use of the words 'existentialism' and 'existentialist'. This must be left until we come to treat explicitly of Marcel and Sartre.
[5] *Introduction à la philosophie*, p. 250.

regard both to action and to contemplation.'[1] In other words, matter exists only in relation to spirit; and in regard to the human spirit it can function either as an obstacle or a help in spirit's fufillment of its vocation.

The question arises of course, what does Le Senne mean by spirit? Let us begin with the human spirit. 'When I affirm that I am a spirit, I mean that I distinguish myself from things by the consciousness which I have correlatively of them and of myself, that the multiplicity of determinations and qualities with which I furnish space and time are accessible to me only by reason of an envelopment of which I am the centre.'[2] This enveloping is however an active synthesis. 'I will say therefore of spirit, as I grasp it in myself, that it is a dynamic unity of linking together (*liaison*), in the widest sense of the last term, according to which to distinguish and to exclude is still to link together.'[3] But what I grasp in myself, according to Le Senne, is simply a finite reflection of spirit in itself, which can be defined as 'the operative unity of an active relation (*une relation en exercice*), interior to itself, between itself as infinite Spirit and the multitude of finite spirits.'[4] In other words, absolute Spirit is one and many. One can conceive it as 'the relation between itself as one and therefore as unlimited and itself as many, in short as the union of God . . . and of finite consciousnesses.'[5] By distinguishing itself from the non-self and from other selves the finite spirit experiences limits and obstacles. It cannot achieve an all-embracing synthesis. This is realized only in and through infinite Spirit, which is at the same time other than and immanent in and inseparable from the finite spirit. Spirit in the most general sense is the relation between the two terms, God and the finite self.

In Le Senne's philosophy of spirit there seems to be a certain tension between absolute idealism and the theism which he certainly accepts. However this may be, his spiritualist metaphysics forms the setting for his theory of values. He sees the human spirit as oriented to value. '*That which is worthy of being sought after* is what everyone calls value.'[6] The statement that value is that which *is* worthy of being sought after indicates that for Le Senne value is not simply the creation of the human will. At the same time a value which was not a value for anyone would not be a value. '*If it does not exist through the subject, it is for the*

[1] *Ibid.*, p. 252.   [2] *Ibid.*, p. 254.   [3] *Ibid.*, p. 254.   [4] *Ibid.*, p. 257.
[5] *Ibid.*, p. 258.   [6] *Traité de morale générale* (3rd edition, 1949), p. 693.

subject.[1] Recognition of value unites persons, and value 'can have meaning only for them'.[2] It does not follow of course that everyone makes the same value-judgments, nor that all human beings give precedence to the same value or values. One man may regard the aesthetic value of beauty as taking precedence, when another man gives the precedence to truth or to moral value. But the search for value plays a central role in the constitution of personality; and human beings are united by a common recognition of values. This is obvious, for example, in regard to both truth and love. Such recognition implies the transcendence of values, in the sense that they do not depend simply on man's arbitrary decree; but they are for man, in the sense that they are not values unless they can be appropriated, so to speak, in experience and realized in life.

Le Senne admits therefore that there is a plurality of values. Moral value, which he links with the idea of acting in accordance with duty or moral obligation, is not the only value. Truth, beauty and love are also values. Consider, for example, a mother who performed those actions in regard to her child which love would prompt but who did so simply and solely out of a sense of moral obligation. She 'would be a moral mother; but it would be false to say that she loved her child.'[3] For love involves the heart. No value can be identified with a particular thing. The aesthetic value of beauty, for example, cannot be identified with this or that empirical reality of which we say that it is beautiful. But this does not alter the fact that there are distinct values, irreducible to one another or to one particular 'cardinal' value, such as moral value or truth or beauty.

Though positive, values have also a negative aspect. A particular value exists only in opposition to a correlative non-value. Thus love is opposed to hatred; courage has meaning only in opposition to cowardice; truth is correlative to falsity; and so on. Further, one particular value can exclude another, so that precedence has to be given to one or the other. Le Senne does not however try to unify values in terms of a systematically graded hierarchy of particular values.[4] He seeks the principle of unity in

---

[1] *Introduction à la philosophie*, p. 365. The original text is *si elle n'est pas par lui, elle est pour lui. Lui* refers to *le sujet.*
[2] *Obstacle et valeur*, p. 192.
[3] *Introduction à la philosophie*, p. 381.
[4] For some summary lines of objection to this procedure see *Traité de moral générale*, p. 698.

absolute value, 'one and infinite'.[1] All particular values are for him relative and phenomenal. They are the ways in which pure or absolute value appears to the human consciousness or mediates itself to us. Absolute value is not the highest member of a hierarchy. It transcends and at the same time grounds all particular values. These constitute for us the phenomena or appearances of the Absolute, which is their source and is yet immanent in them.[2] Man's destiny or vocation is 'an exploration oriented to value, which is identical with the absolute'.[3] He experiences value 'in a given historical situation';[4] but he can transcend the determinate situation and conceive the value abstractly. He can also transcend particular values towards absolute value; but he discovers it only in and through its appearances, so that value is essentially 'a relational unification between its source, which is independent of the self, and the self.'[5] By realizing particular values, such as truth or love, in his life man attains authentic personality and participates in absolute value, inasmuch as the latter is at the heart of every relative value.

In one place Le Senne asserts that 'value is the knowledge of the Absolute'.[6] Elsewhere he speaks of the Absolute as being itself pure and infinite value. And as infinite value must comprise, in an eminent way, the value of personality, the Absolute 'must be called God'.[7] Hence Le Senne can give to the eighth chapter of his *Introduction to Philosophy* the heading 'Value or God', which implies that the two terms are synonymous. Whether these various ways of speaking can be harmonized is open to discussion. We have indeed noted Le Senne's statement that a value which was completely self-enclosed and incapable of being a value *for* anyone would not be a value. So it is understandable if he speaks of value, even of absolute value, in terms of a relation. But this way of speaking seems to fit in better with the view of the Absolute itself as relational, as comprising the two related terms of infinite spirit and finite spirit, than with the theory of the divine transcendence which is also defended by Le Senne.

Le Senne's theory of value calls Platonism to mind, at any rate if we are prepared to identify the absolute Good of the *Republic* with the Beauty in itself of the *Symposium* and the *One* of the

---

[1] *Obstacle et valeur*, p. 180.
[2] Le Senne refers to Bradley's theory of the Absolute.
[3] *Introduction à la philosophie*, p. 265.   [4] *Traité de moral générale*, p. 694.
[5] *La destinée personelle*, p. 210.   [6] *Obstacle et valeur*, p. 181.
[7] *Traité de morale générale*, p. 693.

Parmenides, the difference being that Le Senne's absolute value is identified with the personal God of the Christian religion. And unless we are inclined to write off all metaphysics as so much nonsense, we can presumably form some idea of what he means. For example, he claims that there is a transcendent divine reality which reveals itself not simply in the physical world as experienced by man but also in the axiological world or world of values, which constitutes a constituent element in experience. Though however Le Senne's theory of values is doubtless religiously edifying, and though we can have a general impression of its meaning, there are a good many questions to which no very clear answers are provided. For example, how would Le Senne analyze the value-judgment? It is indeed clear that he would not accept an analysis which interpreted it simply as expressing man's feelings or emotive attitudes or desires. For in his view value is neither simply psychological nor simply metaphysical but psycho-metaphysical.[1] Perhaps he would claim, for instance, that to say of something that it is beautiful is to say that it participates in beauty and, by implication, that it reflects the Absolute in a limited and finite way. But the metaphysics of participation itself gives rise to questions, as Plato was well aware.

4. There are of course other attempts in recent French philosophy to integrate a theory of values into a general world-view. We can just mention, for instance, Raymond Ruyer,[2] whose work *La conscience et le corps* (1937, *Consciousness and Body*) expressed an abandonment of his former mechanistic outlook and the development of a theory according to which every being manifests a teleological activity. That is to say, subjectivity or consciousness is present in all beings, though it is only at a certain level that the distinction between subject and object emerges. In the case of every being therefore its activity in the spatio-temporal sphere[3] is directed to an end, though it is only at the level of man that there is actual awareness of values belonging to an axiological realm which transcends space and time. The meaning of the activity of any being cannot be understood without reference to the realm of

---

[1] *Ibid.*, p. 697.

[2] Born in 1902, Ruyer was appointed a professor of the university of Nancy in 1945. In 1946 he published *Éléments de psycho-biologie* (*Elements of Psychobiology*), in 1952 *Néo-finalisme* (*Neo-finalism*) and in 1958 *La genèse de formes vivantes* (*The Genesis of Living Forms*).

[3] Objectivity, the spatio-temporal sphere, is conceived by Ruyer as phenomenal. All genuine activity is rooted in and proceeds from subjectivity.

values; but it is only at the level of man that such reflective understanding arises.

Ruyer has devoted special studies to the theory of values, *Le monde des valeurs* (1948, *The World of Values*) and *Philosophie de la valeur* (1952, *Philosophy of Value*). The unification of the phenomenal world of space and time and the world of subjectivity and of values is sought in the idea of God, conceived both as the ultimate source of all activity in the world and as the perfect qualitative unity of all values, their point of convergence.

The philosophy of Ruyer is to some extent a revival of lines of thought expounded by Leibniz. When we turn to Jean Pucelle, who is a professor in the University of Poitiers,[1] we find an approach to the subject of values which seems to represent both a reaction to the existentialist theory of values as the creation of the individual[2] and a desire to avoid any objectivist theory which postulates values as entities existing out there, independently of consciousness. Further, Pucelle is concerned with integrating the concepts of value and norm, instead of separating them sharply in the manner of those who tend to regard norms as static hindrances to liberty. It is true that norms belong to the juridical sphere, and that if human behaviour were dictated simply by norms and rules, it would degenerate into legalism. At the same time norms arise out of the recognition of values and serve as a condition or matrix for the exercise of creative liberty.

Pucelle allows that we can distinguish between the judgment of fact and the judgment of value. But he insists that 'it is only by abstraction that one distinguishes them'.[3] In his view, that is to say, no concrete factual judgment is entirely free of valuational elements. He traces back the value-judgment to the subject-object relation, in the sense that it presupposes both desire of an object and a distantiation (*détachement*) of the self from the object, whereby one transforms the actually desired into the desirable. At the same time the transition from felt desire to the value-judgment, by detaching, as it were, the self from the object, opens up the field of evaluation. And ideal values arise on the plane of intersubjectivity. Recognition of the value of love, for example, presupposes actual love between persons. The ideal value is

[1] Pucelle's publications include *La source des valeurs* (1957, *The Source of Values*) and *Le règne des fins* (1959, *The Kingdom of Ends*).
[2] The reference is of course to the Sartrian type of existentialism.
[3] *La source des valeurs*, p. 34.

clearly not a thing out there; but it is objectified for consciousness in the value-judgment. We have to avoid the extremes of pure subjectivism on the one hand and a reifying objectivism on the other and recognize that values are relational. 'Truth is a privileged relation *between* terms *for* at least one mind,'[1] though we can go on to argue that truth has meaning only in the context of intersubjectivity.

In Pucelle's opinion 'intersubjective relations are the source of all values'.[2] He extends this idea to cover 'the appeal of God and man's response'[3] in the Judaeo-Christian ethical tradition. He also insists that axiology has to be set within an ontology and introduces the idea of the presence of Being and of man's consent to Being. Here he seems to come close to Le Senne by seeing the ultimate foundation of values in a 'theandric' relation. For example, it is because value is a relation between Being and beings that every existence has value. And it is because the presence of Being can be sought or unknown or ignored by man that the field of one's valuational vision can be very restricted.

When the word 'Being' with a capital letter is introduced and there is talk of the presence of Being and of consent to Being, some philosophers are inclined to give up.[4] This point apart however, it might perhaps be asked whether, given Pucelle's initial interpretation of the value-judgment, it is really necessary to look for a metaphysical foundation of values. Or is it a case not so much of being compelled to look for a foundation outside the world of human persons in their relationship to one another and their environment as of fitting the recognition of values into a pre-existing religious world-outlook? One might perhaps reply that reflection on an experience of values naturally suggests a religiously metaphysical complement or framework, unless one rejects such a framework on other grounds. But we cannot prolong discussion of such issues.

The work by Pucelle from which we have quoted above is

[1] *Ibid.*, p. 155.
[2] *Ibid.*, p. 164. Though Pucelle begins by considering the subject-object relation in the individual, he does not intend to imply that we can make a complete distinction between private and inter-subjective consciousness.
[3] *Ibid.*, p. 165.
[4] It might be simpler to use the word 'God', if this is what is meant. Being of course sounds more metaphysical or ontological; but a religious person at any rate can more easily find meaning in talk about the presence of God and response to God than about the presence of and consent to Being. The reply might be made however that the concept of God (as personal) is a determination of the concept of Being.

dedicated to the memory of Louis Lavelle and René Le Senne, the co-founders and editors of the series *The Philosophy of Spirit*. Something has already been said about Le Senne as a philosopher of values. We can now turn briefly to a consideration of the metaphysics of Lavelle.

5. Louis Lavelle (1883–1951) was a pupil at Lyons of Arthur Hannequin (1856–1905), author of a well known thesis on the atomic hypothesis[1] in which he maintained that science knows only what it creates and in which he looked to metaphysics to overcome the agnosticism implied by this Kantian-inspired view and to reveal the nature of reality. Later Lavelle came under the influence of Hamelin's writings. Indeed, he combined in his own thought a considerable variety of influences. That of the French spiritualist tradition was prominent; but Lavelle was also open to the problems raised by existentialists, though he tried to solve them in a different manner from philosophers such as Sartre. In 1932 Lavelle was appointed to a chair of philosophy at the Sorbonne. From 1941 he was a professor at the Collège de France. He was a prolific writer.[2]

In a sense Lavelle goes back to Descartes and builds his metaphysics on the foundation of the *Cogito, ergo sum*, on consciousness of the self. Consciousness is an act, and by this act I give myself being. That is to say, the act of consciousness is the genesis of the self. It is not a question of my coming through consciousness to contemplate a self which is already there. Rather is it a question of bringing the I to birth in and through consciousness, by opposing it to the non-self. In other words, the ego grasps itself as activity, an activity which first creates itself. This may seem to be absurd. How, we may ask, can the ego bring itself into being? Lavelle however insists that we cannot distinguish between an ego which confers consciousness and an ego on whom consciousness is conferred. Being and act are identical. This identity, revealing the nature of being, is thus discovered in self-consciousness. And it follows that the proper approach to metaphysics is through subjectivity, through, that is to say, reflection on the self as activity rather than through reflection on the multiplicity of phenomena which the ego opposes to itself under the form of externality. We have to retreat inwards, so to speak, rather than outwards, when 'outwards' refers to the external world. 'Metaphysics rests on

---

[1] *Essai Critique sur l'hypothèse des atomes dans la science contemporaine* (1895).
[2] For Lavelle's works see the Bibliography.

a privileged experience which is that of the act which makes me be.'[1]

It is in the act of consciousness that I become aware of being. But I am certainly not the plenitude of being. 'Being overflows the self and at the same time sustains it.'[2] There is not and cannot be anything outside Being, whether selves or external objects. Being is the whole in which I participate. The word Being with a capital letter, taken by itself, suggests the idea of a Parmenidean One; and Lavelle's insistence in *De l'être* on the universal and univocal character of Being tends to support this idea. But we have seen that in *De l'acte* he argues that in self-consciousness I grasp being as act, which is the 'interiority' of being. Being with a capital letter therefore, the Whole from which I derive my existence and in which I participate, must be pure and infinite Act. 'Being does not exist in front of me as a motionless object which I seek to attain. It is in me by the operation which makes me give being to myself.'[3] Being is infinite Act, infinite Spirit; but it is at the same time the *immanent* cause of all finite selves, giving them the act by which they constitute themselves. As for the non-self, external reality or the world, this must ultimately be correlative to pure Act as the infinite self. But the world comes to be for me, my world arises, only in correlation with myself as active subject. To be sure, I find myself in a world, which is for me something given. Indeed, it is the condition of there being a plurality of selves. The self comes into being only in correlation with a world, to which it gives meaning in terms of its ideas, its evaluations, its activity. But to say this is to say that in giving me the act by which I came to be a self pure Act also gives me the world as a datum. In other words, the world, for Lavelle, must be correlative to an active self. There is no world which is independent of all consciousness whatsoever. It does not follow however that the world is a mere phantom. It is at the same time the condition for the plurality of finite selves, the field of their activity, and the instrument of mediation between consciousnesses, and thus the basis of human society. It is also the 'interval' between pure Act and participated act. It is by transcending the limits and obstacles posited by the world that the human person fulfils its destiny or vocation and tends to realize on the level of consciousness its oneness with infinite Act.

---

[1] *De l'acte* (*On Act*), p. 11. This work is the second volume of Lavelle's *La dialectique de l'éternel présent*, the first being *De l'être* (*On Being*).
[2] *Ibid.*, p. 59.   [3] *Ibid.*, p. 72.

Any reader who is well acquainted with German idealism is likely to be struck by the resemblances between much of what Lavelle has to say and the philosophy of Fichte. For example, Fichte's theories of the pure or absolute ego as activity, of the positing of the limited ego and non-ego, of the world as the field for and instrument of man's moral vocation and of the world as the appearance to us of absolute Being, are all present in some form in Lavelle's thought. It does not follow however that Lavelle borrowed his ideas from German idealism. It is a question of noting certain similarities rather than of asserting direct influence.

Mention has already been made of Lavelle's insistence in *De l'être* on the universal and univocal character of Being. This view is repeated in *De l'acte*. 'To say that Being is universal and univocal is to say that we all form part of the same Whole and that it is the same Whole which gives us the same being which belongs to it and outside which there is nothing.'[1] This combination of the theory of Being as univocal, whether considered in itself or in its creations, with the whole-and-part language obviously suggests a monistic pantheism. But Lavelle uses the doctrine of the univocal character of the concept of Being to support the conclusion that the Absolute is not only the source of personal existence but also itself personal, indeed a person 'which must be distinguished from all other persons'.[2] In other words, he has no intention of simply throwing theism overboard. He wishes to maintain that God, considered in himself, is not in any way diminished through creation of finite selves and the world. and he has recourse to a theory of participation. 'Participation obliges me therefore to admit that there are at the same time homogeneity and heterogeneity not only between the participant and the participated, but also between the participated and the participable.'[3] And this theory of participation is regarded as implying a distinction between Act and Being, between, that is to say, the divine Act and the totality of Being. 'The totality is the very unity of Act considered as being the unique and indivisible source of all the particular modes, which seem to be always contained eminently, and, so to speak, by way of excess, in the very impulse (*élan*) which produces them and in which all beings participate according to their power.'[4] The totality of Being, in other words, is not something achieved, accomplished, static. There is a creative process of totalization, which is the expression

---

[1] *Ibid.*, p. 78.   [2] *Ibid.*, p. 140.   [3] *Ibid.*, p. 72.   [4] *Ibid.*, p. 80.

of pure Act, the source and immanent cause of all finite beings but at the same time distinguishable from them.

Lavelle's philosophy is of course an example of the tendency in religiously oriented metaphysics to get away from pictorial or imaginative theism, with its concept of a God 'out there' or 'up there', without however relapsing into Spinozism or into a monism which would exclude the concept of a personal God. This tendency to a panentheism designed to avoid two extremes is perfectly understandable. But it is very difficult to state this sort of theory in any satisfactorily consistent and coherent manner. Ferdinand Alquié,[1] a redoubtable opponent of monism in all its forms and of the objectivation of Being, may be unfair in interpreting Lavelle in a monistic sense. But the latter certainly speaks of Being as the totality, even if the whole is conceived in an Hegelian rather than in a Parmenidean way. And though Lavelle tries to save the situation, from a theistic point of view, by making a distinction between pure Act and the totality of Being, regarding the former as the creative inwardness or interiority of the latter, it is obviously open to dispute whether his various assertions are in fact compatible. It can be claimed of course that language is bound to reveal its inadequacy when we try to talk about the Absolute and the relation of particulars to the Absolute. But the retort might be made that in this case silence would be the best policy. Indeed, according to Alquié Being as such remains inaccessible to us. For though it grounds all that is given in experience, it cannot itself be a datum.

6. Although in the philosophy of spirit as represented by Le Senne and Lavelle there is a strong dose of metaphysics, there is also a prominent emphasis on the idea of the destiny or vocation of the human person. Indeed Le Senne published a book with the title *La destinée personelle* and Lavelle one entitled *Le moi et son destin*. Further, Lavelle, as we have seen, starts with the act which in his view brings the human person into being. Again, it is clear that those philosophers who have been generally labelled existentialists have also been concerned with the person. Marcel, for example, talks a great deal about personal relationships, while Sartre has laid emphasis on man's creative freedom. Thomists

---

[1] Ferdinand Alquié, born in 1906, was a professor in the university of Montpellier from 1947 until 1952 and was appointed to a chair in the Sorbonne. Among his works are *La nostalgie de l'être* (1950, *The Nostalgia of Being*), *Philosophie du surréalisme* (1955, *Philosophy of Surrealism*), *Descartes, l'homme et l'oeuvre* (1956, *Descartes, the Man and his Work*) and *L'expérience* (1957, *Experience*).

too, such as Jacques Maritain, have stressed the personalist elements in their own thought. To go further back in time, Renouvier, who influenced William James, entitled his last work *Le personnalisme*. In other words, emphasis on the nature and value of the human person and on the idea of the human person as relevant to our general interpretation of reality has not been confined to any one School or group in recent French philosophy. One can find the roots of personalism in the spiritualist tradition in French philosophy; and one can connect the fairly widespread emphasis on the person in recent French thought with a shared reaction to both intellectual and social-political tendencies which appear to treat man simply as an object of scientific study or to reduce him to his function in the economic sphere or in the social-political totality. In some cases of course, as with Le Senne and Lavelle as also with such different thinkers as Marcel and Maritain, there is also a strong religious motivation. The human person is seen as oriented by nature to a super-empirical end or goal.

When however reference is made to personalism in recent French philosophy, it may be primarily to the thought of Emmanuel Mounier (1905–50), editor of *Esprit*, and of certain other writers such as Denis de Rougemont, a Swiss Protestant, and Maurice Nédoncelle, a French priest. It is in this restricted use of the term that personalism will be understood in this section. And it is therefore important to emphasize the fact that the restriction should not be interpreted as implying that the writers mentioned here are the only French philosophers who have expressed characteristically personalist ideas. The point is rather that Mounier conducted a specific campaign in support of personalism as such, whereas with other thinkers personalist ideas have often formed part, even if an important part, of a philosophy to which another label has been attached, such as philosophy of spirit or existentialism or Thomism.

Emmanuel Mounier was born at Grenoble and studied philosophy first in his home town and then at Paris. He was influenced by the writings of Charles Péguy (1873–1914), and in 1931 he published, in collaboration, a book on Péguy's thought.[1] He was also influenced by the famous Russian philosopher, Nikolai Berdyaev (1874–1948), who had settled in Paris in 1924. Mounier taught philosophy in schools for some years; and in 1932 he

[1] *La pensée de Charles Péguy* (*The Thought of Charles Péguy*).

undertook the editorship of the newly founded periodical *Esprit*, which continued publication until 1941 when it was banned by the Vichy government.[1] After the war he revived *Esprit* as an organ of personalism.

In 1935 Mounier published *Révolution personnaliste et communautaire* (*Personalist and Communal Revolution*), in 1936 a work entitled *De la propriété capitaliste à la propriété humaine* (*From Capitalist Property to Human Property*) and a personalist manifesto, *Manifesto au service du personnalisme*. In some Catholic circles his writings won him the reputation of being pretty well a Marxist. In 1946 he published an introduction to the existentialist philosophies, *Introduction aux existentialismes*,[2] and a work on character, *Traité du caractère*. Among other post-war publications we can mention *Qu'est-ce que le personalisme?* (1947, *What is Personalism?*) and *Le personnalisme* (1950, Personalism).

At the beginning of his work on the existentialist philosophies Mounier remarks that in very general terms the existentialist movement might be described as 'a reaction of the philosophy of man against the excesses of the philosophy of ideas and the philosophy of things'.[2] By the philosophy of ideas in this context he means the type of philosophizing which concentrates on abstract universal concepts and devotes itself to classification in terms of ever more comprehensive categories to such an extent that particulars are given a subordinate place and are regarded as objects of philosophical reflection only in so far as they can be subsumed under universal ideas and deprived of their singularity and, in the case of man, of freedom. This line of thought, starting in ancient Greece, is looked on as reaching its culmination in the absolute idealism of Hegel, at any rate as interpreted by Kierkegaard. The philosophy of things means the kind of philosophical thought which assimilates itself to natural science and regards man purely 'objectively', as an object among other objects in the physical universe. Mounier recognizes that rationalism on the one hand and positivism on the other have involved 'excesses'. But in his opinion the existentialist reaction, especially in its atheistic form, has also been guilty of exaggeration. In a general way personalism is for him akin to existentialism, as expressing a reaction against systems such as those of Spinoza and Hegel on

---

[1] Mounier himself was arrested in 1942 and spent some months in prison before being released. He was an active member of the Resistance.

[2] *Existentialist Philosophies*, translated by E. Blow (London, 1948), p. 2.

the one hand and positivism, materialism and beheaviourism on the other. But he also sees in existentialism 'a dual tendency to solipsism and pessimism, which separates it radically from personalism as we understand it'.[1]

Personalism, Mounier insists, is 'not a system'.[2] For its central assertion is the existence of free and creative persons, and it thus introduces 'a principle of unpredictability'[3] which resists definitive systematization. By a 'system' Mounier evidently understands a philosophy which tries to understand all events, including human actions, as necessary implications of certain first principles or as necessary effects of ultimate causes. A 'system' excludes all creative freedom in human persons. To say however that personalism is not a system is not the same thing as saying that it is not a philosophy and cannot be expressed in terms of ideas, or that it is simply an attitude of mind. There is such a thing as a personalist universe, seen from the perspective of man as a free and creative person; and there is such a thing as a personalist philosophy. More accurately, there can be different personalist philosophies. For there can be an agnostic personalism, whereas Mounier's personalism is religious and Christian. But they could not be appropriately described as personalist philosophies, unless they had some basic idea in common. This idea however is also a call to action. And Mounier himself was always a campaigner, a fighter. In the foreword to his *Traité de caractère* he states explicitly that his science is 'a fighting science'.[4] In being a campaigner Mounier resembles Bertrand Russell. But while Russell made a sharp distinction between his activity as a campaigner and his role as a professional philosopher, Mounier regarded his philosophical convictions as expressing themselves by their very nature in the sphere of action.

In its view of man the personalism of Mounier is of course opposed to materialism and the reduction of the human being simply to a complicated material object. But it is also opposed both to any form of idealism which reduces matter, including the human body, to a mere reflection of spirit or to appearance and to psycho-physical parallelism. Man is not simply a material object; but it does not follow either that he is pure spirit or that he can

---

[1] *Be Not Afraid*, translated by C. Rowland (London, 1951), p. 184. This volume contains two of Mounier's publications; and the quotation comes from the second part, which is a translation of *Qu'est-ce que le personalisme?*
[2] *Personalism*, translated by P. Mairet (London, 1952), p. vii.
[3] *Ibid.*, p. viii.   [4] *Une science combattante; Traité de caractère*, p. 7.

be neatly divided into two substances or two sets of experiences. Man is 'wholly body and wholly spirit',[1] and subjective existence and bodily existence belong to the same experience. Man's existence is embodied existence; he belongs to Nature. But he can also transcend Nature in the sense that he can progressively master it or subdue it. This mastery of Nature can of course be understood simply in terms of exploitation. But for the personalist Nature presents man with the opportunity of fulfilling his own moral and spiritual vocation and of humanizing or personalizing the world. 'The relation of the person to Nature is not purely exterior but a dialectic of exchange and of ascension.'[2]

Personalism can thus be seen as man's reassertion of himself against the tyranny of Nature, represented on the intellectual plane by materialism. And it can also be seen as a reassertion by the person of his own creative freedom against any totalitarianism which would reduce the human being to a mere cell in the social organism or would identify him with his economic function. But it by no means follows that personalism and individualism are the same thing. The individual, in the pejorative sense in which personalists are inclined to use the term, is the egocentric man, the atomistic individual in abstraction from society. The term also signifies man as devoid of a sense of moral vocation. Thus Denis de Rougemont describes the individual as 'a man without destiny, a man without vocation or reason for existing, a man from whom the world demands nothing.'[3] The individual is man centralized in himself. For Mounier this egocentricism represents a degeneration of or a falling away from the idea of the person. 'The first condition of personalism is his (man's) decentralization,'[4] that he may give himself to others and be available for them in communication or communion. The person exists only in a social relationship, as a member of the 'we'. It is only as a member of a community of persons that man has a moral vocation. De Rougemont interprets the idea of vocation in a frankly Christian manner. Person and vocation are possible 'only in their unique act of obedience to the order of God which is called the love of the neighbour . . . Act, presence and commitment, these three words define the person, but also what Jesus Christ commands us to be: the neighbour.'[5] Mounier is no less Christian in his outlook.[6] But

---

[1] *Personalism*, p. 3.   [2] *Ibid.*, p. 13.   [3] *Politique de la personne*, p. 56.
[4] *Personalism*, p. 19.   [5] *Politique de la personne*, pp. 52-3.
[6] See, for example, *Personnalisme et Christianisme* (*Personalism and Christianity*), reprinted in *Liberté sans conditions* (1946).

he gives a more general and 'sufficient' statement of the personalist point of view, 'that the significance of every person is such that he is irreplaceable in the position which he occupies in the world of persons'.[1] In other words, every human being has his or her vocation in life, in response to recognized values; but this vocation presupposes the world of persons and of interpersonal relations. If we prescind from the religious aspect of vocation (the response to the divine appeal), man's vocation, the exercise of his creative freedom in the realization of values, is his unique contribution, as it were, to the building-up of the world of persons and the humanization or personalization of the world.

In his personalist *Manifesto*, which appeared in *Esprit* in October 1936, Mounier, while maintaining that no strict definition of the concept of person could be given, offered the following definition or description as passing muster. 'A person is a spiritual being constituted as such by a manner of subsistence and of independence in being; it maintains this subsistence by its adhesion to a hierarchy of values, freely adopted, assimilated and lived, by a responsible self-commitment and by a constant conversion; it thus unifies all its activity in liberty and develops, moreover, by means of creative acts, its own unique vocation.' The concept of constant conversion is presumably more or less equivalent to Kierkegaard's idea of repetition and Marcel's idea of fidelity or faithfulness. As for self-commitment, Mounier regarded personalism as having implications in the social and political spheres; and it has already been noted that he looked on it not simply as an exercise in theoretical understanding but also as a call to action.

We have remarked above that personalism can be regarded as a reaction against collectivism or totalitarianism. This description is however one-sided and inadequate, as Mounier himself is not slow to point out. To be sure, personalism is opposed to the reduction of the human person to a mere cell in the social organism and to the complete subordination of man to the State. 'The State is meant for man, not man for the State.'[2] In totalitarianism the value of the person is overlooked. Indeed, the 'person' is reduced to the 'individual', even if the individual is regarded on an analogy with the cell in an organic whole. But it by no means follows that Mounier is prepared to defend bourgeois capitalist democracy. It is not simply a question of flagrant abuses which can be and to a certain extent have been overcome within the

[1] *Personalism*, p. 41.   [2] *Personalism*, p. 112.

capitalist system. Mounier sees the developing capitalist system as containing within itself factors which point to and demand the transition to socialism. It is all very well to propose idealistic schemes according to which political authority and all constraint would be suppressed in favour of personal relations. Anarchism may be idealistic, but it is also unrealistic. It does not understand that the links which bind together persons as persons must find expression in political structures and authority. Personalism aims at a social reorganization which will meet the requirements of economic life as it has developed but which will at the same time be grounded on recognition of the nature and rights of the human person. In important respects capitalism is inhuman. But so is totalitarianism. And anarchism is no solution. In brief, personalism demands the rethinking of our social and political structures with a view to the development of a personalized socialism.

Mounier does not of course confine himself simply to generalities. But we cannot discuss his more concrete suggestions here. It must suffice to point out that he is well aware of attempts to exploit personalism (the defence of the person) in the interests of 'the narrowest form of social conservation'[1] or in the service of bourgeois democracy. He emphasizes the inadequacy of simply using words such as 'person' and 'community'. To preserve the revolutionary edge of personalism we must also say, 'the end of western bourgeois society, the introduction of socialist structures, the proletarian role of initiative.'[2] At the same time Mounier is very conscious of the tendency of all societies, political or religious, to become closed societies or groups and so to stand in the way of advance towards the unification of mankind which is demanded by the nature which, despite Sartre, human beings have in common. Moreover, although in his analysis of capitalism Mounier tends to think in a manner similar to that of Marx, he does not of course regard man's vocation or destiny as realizable simply in a terrestrial society, even an ideal one. His Christian faith is always there. But he refuses to use it as an excuse for passivity or for neglect of tasks in the social-political sphere. And if he had lived longer, he would most probably have sympathized with attempts to develop dialogue between Christians and Marxists on the themes of man and humanism.

With Maurice Nédoncelle we find a much more contemplative

[1] *Personalism*, p. 187.   [2] *Ibid.*, p. 186.

attitude. Personalism takes the form of a phenomenology and metaphysics of the person, special attention being paid to the basic structure of human consciousness as expressed in the I–thou relationship (consciousness of the I or self is inseparable from consciousness of the other) and in its religious bearing and significance.[1] Though however Nédoncelle's view of man is in basic agreement with that of Mounier, he has expressed his hesitation in speaking of the political and social implications of personalism. He admits that in a general sense personalism has social implications. For example, any form of social organization which denies the rights of the person as person or devalues the person is to this extent incompatible with the personalist outlook. But he will not allow that personalism can legitimately be used in support of 'any party';[2] and he shows a measure of pessimism, doubtless often justified, in regard to hopes of solving social and political problems by revolution or by the hasty realization of some ideal scheme. It is wise 'not to expect too much from collective life'.[3] In Nédoncelle's view 'it is perhaps in *religious philosophy* that the repercussions of personalism are the most considerable'.[4] Obviously, his attitude differs somewhat from that of Mounier.[5]

---

[1] See especially *La réciprocité des consciences. Essai sur la nature de la personne. (The Reciprocity of Consciousness. An Essay on the Nature of the Person)*, 1942.
[2] *Vers une philosophie de l'amour et de la personne (Towards a Philosophy of Love and of the Person)*, 1957, p. 267.
[3] *Ibid.*, p. 266.   [4] *Ibid.*, p. 259.
[5] I do not mean to imply that Mounier was a blind optimist. He was not. But he was definitely committed in the social–political field.

CHAPTER XV

TWO RELIGIOUS THINKERS

Teilhard de Chardin — G. Marcel — Differences in outlook.

1. ONE of the more surprising phenomena of recent years has been the very widespread interest in the thought of a Jesuit priest, Pierre Teilhard de Chardin (1881–1955). The interest is surprising in the sense that though there have been distinguished Jesuit astronomers and scholars, one does not normally expect from this source a world-view of a sufficiently original and striking nature as to win attention not only from readers belonging to different Christian traditions but also from people who profess no religious beliefs in the ordinary sense of the term. It is true that Teilhard de Chardin was unable to obtain permission from his ecclesiastical superiors to publish the writings with which his name is chiefly associated. But it would be absurd to attribute his fame to the difficulties which he experienced in the matter of publication. The interest taken in the writings which have appeared after his death has been due to the content of his world-vision. This assumes an evolutionary view of the world and of man, not grudgingly or apologetically but enthusiastically, and extends this view in the form of a world-vision which is not only metaphysical but also Christological. This mingling of scientific theory with philosophical speculation and Christian themes is understandably uncongenial, if for different reasons, to a number of scientists, philosophers and theologians, especially perhaps as the whole is presented as a persuasive world-vision rather than in the form of conclusions to closely reasoned arguments. But a world-vision of this kind, which synthesizes in itself science, a metaphysics of the universe and Christian belief and is at the same time markedly optimistic, is just the sort of thing which many people have looked and hoped for and have not found elsewhere. And it has been able to appeal even to some, such as Sir Julian Huxley, who feel themselves unable to go all the way with Teilhard de Chardin. Teilhard's new-style apologetics may not fare as well when the prolonged attention of the coldly analytic reason is directed to it; but there can be no doubt of its meeting a felt need.

Teilhard de Chardin was born in the Auvergne, not far from

Clermont-Ferrand. Educated at a Jesuit school, he entered the Society of Jesus as a novice in 1898. Ordained priest in 1911, he served in the first world war in the medical corps of the French army. Interested in geology from an early age, he had developed an enthusiasm for palaeontology during a period when he was teaching in a Jesuit school in Cairo before beginning his theological studies at Ore Place near Hastings;[1] and in 1908 he published an article on the eocene strata of the region of Minieh (*L'éocène des environs de Minieh*). After the war Teilhard studied natural science at the Sorbonne, and in 1922 he successfully defended his doctorate thesis on the mammals of the Lower Eocene period in France and their strata. In 1923–4 Teilhard was a member of a palaeontological team in China. By this time he had already formed his idea of cosmogenesis, his view, that is to say of the world as a dynamic evolutionary movement in which any dualism between matter and spirit is dissolved.[2] Matter is not simply the opposite of spirit; but spirit emerges from matter, and the movement of the world is towards the further development of spirit.[3] For Teilhard man naturally came to occupy a central place in the evolutionary movement; and the profound Christian faith which he possessed from youth led him to the notion of the cosmic Christ, evolution being placed in a Christocentric setting.

In 1920 Teilhard started teaching in the Institut Catholique at Paris, and he returned there after his first visit to China. But as a result of excursions outside the field of science, such as attempts to harmonize the doctrine of original sin with his evolutionary outlook, he was asked by his religious superiors to leave Paris and to confine his writing to scientific topics. From 1926 until 1927 he was in China, and then, after a brief interlude in France, he went to Ethiopia and thence back again to China, where he continued geological and palaeontological research. Apart from visits to France, America, England, India and some other eastern countries, he remained in China until 1946. In 1926 he wrote *Le milieu divin*,[4] a religious meditation in which the Christocentric character

---

[1] In 1902 the French Jesuits left France for English territory, as the result of the laws passed under the anticlerical government of Combes; and Teilhard did his earlier studies as a Jesuit on the island of Jersey.

[2] Teilhard read and was influenced by Bergson. But he did not accept Bergson's idea of divergent paths of evolution. He opted for the idea of convergence.

[3] It seems that it was in about 1925 that Teilhard conveived the idea of the 'noosphere', a term which was adopted by his friend Édouard Le Roy, then a professor at the Collège de France.

[4] An English translation by Bernard Wall appeared in 1957 with the title *Le Milieu Divin. An Essay on the Interior Life.*

of his world-vision comes out clearly, while *Le phénomène humain*[1] was begun in 1938 and completed in 1940; but he was not permitted to publish his major works in the non-scientific field. Indeed, in 1947 he was told to keep off philosophy.

From 1946 until 1951 Teilhard was in Paris. In 1948 he was offered a chair at the Collège de France, as successor to the Abbé Breuil; but he was directed by his religious superiors to decline the offer. However, in 1947 he had been elected a member of the Académie des Sciences, and in 1950 he was elected a member of the Institut de France. In 1951 Teilhard left France for a visit to South Africa, after which he went to New York where he remained until his death, apart from a second visit to Africa, under the auspices of the Wenner Gren Foundation, various trips in the United States and a visit to France in 1954. He died of a heart attack on Easter Sunday, 1955. He had taken the advice of a French Jesuit friend to leave the manuscripts of his unpublished works in safe hands, and publication began in the year of his death.

The statement that Teilhard de Chardin starts with the world as represented in scientific theory and that he extends what he considers to be the scientific view of the world into the spheres of metaphysical speculation and religious belief is doubtless true; but it is a partial truth and can be misleading. For from the beginning the world presents itself to him as the totality of which we are members and as having value. We can of course ask precisely what is meant by claiming that the world has value; and it is difficult to find an answer which would satisfy an analytic philosopher. But there is no doubt that for Teilhard the world is not simply a complex system of interrelated phenomena, a system which just happens to be there, but rather the totality which has value and significance. In the first instance the world presents itself in experience as a complex of phenomena of varied types. From one point of view science breaks up the things of experience into smaller centres of energy, as in the atomic theory; but at the same time it exhibits their interrelations and shows them as unified through the transformation of energy and as constituting one complex network or system. The world thus forms not simply a collection but a totality, one whole. Further, this totality is not static but developing. For Teilhard evolution is not simply a

---

[1] This work has been published in an English translation by Bernard Wall, with an introduction by Sir Julian Huxley, under the title *The Phenomenon of Man* (London, 1959).

theory about the origin of living species, a biological theory; it is a concept which applies to the world or universe as a whole. Natural science obviously presupposes consciousness. For without consciousness there could be no science. But science has tended to discount consciousness as much as possible and to concentrate on the quantitative and measurable, so that the sphere of mind, consciousness, spirit, appears as something over against the material world or as an epiphenomenon. For Teilhard life and consciousness are potentially there, in matter, from the beginning. As Leibniz saw, there is nothing which does not possess a psychic aspect, an inner force, so to speak. The world thus appears as a totality, a whole, which is developing towards an end, an increasing actualization of spirit. Human beings are members of an evolving organic whole, the universe, which possesses spiritual value and appears as a manifestation of the divine. According to Teilhard, humanity has been spontaneously converted 'to a kind of religion of the world'.[1] And he can say that he believes in matter or that he believes in the world, when belief obviously means much more than belief in the existence of matter or of the world.

Teilhard does not of course present us simply with this very general sketchy vision of the world. He distinguishes, for example, two components in energy, tangential energy, linking one element or particle with others of the same degree of complexity in the universe, and radial energy, drawing the element or particle towards increasing complexity and 'continuity' or consciousness.' Again, he argues that if we resolve what he describes as 'the stuff of the universe' into a dust of particles, in this 'pre-vital' stage the 'within' of things corresponded point by point with their 'without', with their external aspect or force, so that a mechanistic science of matter is not excluded by the view that all elements of the universe have their internal or vital aspect. From the outside point of view it is only with the emergence of the cell that the biosphere or sphere of life begins. And Teilhard opts for the hypothesis that the genesis of life on earth was a unique and, once it had happened, unrepeatable event. In other words, it is a

---

[1] *Science et Christ*, p. 151. The quotation comes originally from a paper published in 1933.
[2] See *The Phenomenon of Man* (English translation), pp. 63–6, where Teilhard offers a line of solution in regard to the problem of reconciling his view of increasing energy (especially 'radial' energy) in the universe with the laws of thermodynamics.

moment in a process of evolution which is moving towards a goal. Teilhard is of course perfectly well aware that many or most scientists would deny, or would see no reason for asserting, that the process of evolution in general, or of life in particular, is directed to any goal. But he is convinced that he can trace within the natural history of living things a movement towards the emergence of consciousness and thought. With the appearance of consciousness and thought there is born the noosphere, in embryo indeed but moving through personalization towards a hyper-personal focus of union which Teilhard calls 'Omega Point', the union of the personal and the collective on the planes of thought and love. Indications of this convergence towards Omega Point are to be seen, for example, in the increasing intellectual unification of mankind, as in science, and in the pressures which make for social unification.

A good many writers have noted the affinity between the thought of Teilhard de Chardin and the philosophy of Hegel. When Teilhard says, for example, that man is evolution becoming conscious of itself[1] and proposes the concept of the noosphere, the sphere of universal thought and knowledge which exists not as a separate entity but in and through individual consciousnesses, unifying them and forming a one-in-many, we are reminded of Hegel's doctrine of the self-development of Spirit. To be sure, Hegel himself lived before Darwin and did not regard the evolutionary hypothesis, with its idea of temporal succession, as relevant to the logical dialectic of his philosophy of Nature. As far as biological evolution is concerned, Teilhard obviously stands much closer to Bergson than to Hegel. Moreover, Teilhard thought of Hegel as expounding an *a priori* logical dialectic which was very different from his own scientifically-based concept of evolution. But this does not alter the fact that Teilhard's general idea of the developing world or universe as coming to self-consciousness in and through the human mind, of the noosphere as presupposing the biosphere and the biosphere as presupposing a stage which makes mechanistic physics a possibility bears a striking resemblance to Hegel's vision of self-actualizing Spirit. The historical contexts of the two philosophers are of course different. Hegelianism has to be seen in the context of the development of post-Kantian German idealism, a context which is evidently not that of the thought of Teilhard de Chardin. But the degree of

[1] *The Phenomenon of Man*, p. 221.

difference which we find between the two lines of thought depends to a certain extent on our interpretation of Hegel. If we interpret Hegel as postulating the pre-existence, so to speak, of a logical Idea which actualizes itself with dialectical necessity in cosmic and human history, we are likely to emphasize the difference between Hegel's approach and that of Teilhard, with his point of departure in empirical science. If however we believe that Hegel has been unjustly represented as a despiser of empirical science, and if we bear in mind the fact that for both men the process of 'cosmogenesis' is a teleological or goal-directed process, we are likely to emphasize the resemblances between them. For if Teilhard seriously thinks of evolution as directed towards a goal, Omega Point, the process must presumably be in some sense the working-out of an Idea. There is no question of course of claiming that Teilhard borrowed the framework of his thought from Hegel. He seems to have known little of Hegel and, in regard to what little he did know, to have emphasized differences rather than resemblances. But similarity can exist between the general lines of thought of two thinkers without any borrowing having taken place. One can perfectly well deny that X borrowed from Y and at the same time assert the existence of similarities between their lines of thought.

Even if however there are some similarities between the thought of Teilhard de Chardin and the philosophy of Hegel, it is essential to add that Teilhard is not really concerned with developing a metaphysical system.[1] As a Christian believer he is anxious to show that Christianity has not become too small and too dated to be able to meet the needs of modern man's world-consciousness. He wishes to integrate his interpretation of cosmic evolution with his Christian beliefs or, better, to show how Christian belief is able to subsume in itself and enrich a view of the world attained by what he describes as 'phenomenology', a reflective interpretation of the significance of man as appearing to himself in his experience and science.[2] To some admirers of Teilhard the specifically Christian themes in his thought naturally tend to appear as an extra, the expression of a personal faith which they feel themselves

---

[1] Referring to Plato, Spinoza and Hegel, Teilhard says that while they developed views which compete in breadth with the perspectives opened up by belief in the incarnation, 'none of these metaphysical systems advanced beyond the limits of an ideology' (*The Phenomenon of Man*, p. 295).

[2] Obviously, Teilhard uses the term 'phenomenology' in a different sense from that in which it was used by Husserl.

unable to share. Though however Teilhard is aware that in introducing belief in the incarnation and in the cosmic role of Christ he is going 'beyond the plane of phenomenology',[1] his Christocentricism is for him an integral feature of his total world-vision, the vision which he tries to communicate in his writings taken as a whole.

Teilhard's way of thinking was of course opposed not only to any sharp dualism between matter and mind or spirit but also to any bifurcation of reality into natural and supernatural spheres cut off from one another or so related that the supernatural is simply superimposed on the natural. And his mind was so filled with the idea of the organic unity of the developing universe, of its convergence on man and of human consciousness and knowledge of the world as the world's self-reflection in and through man as part of the totality that some of the lyrical passages in which he praised or exalted the universe gave to some readers the impression that for him the universe was itself divine and that he denied the divine transcendence. In spite however of his reverential feeling for the material world as pregnant with spirit and as evolving creatively towards a goal he insisted that the source of the whole process and the centre of unification 'must be conceived as pre-existing and transcendent'.[2] Further, as a Christian he believed that God had become incarnate in Christ, and he thought of the risen Christ as the centre and consummation of the movement towards Omega Point. He saw Christ as progressively uniting all men in love, and in the light of his Christian belief he interpreted Omega Point as the point at which, in St. Paul's words, God becomes 'all in all'.[3] For Teilhard, 'evolution has come to infuse new blood, so to speak, into the perspectives and aspirations of Christianity. In return, is not the Christian faith predestined, is it not preparing, to save and even to take the place of evolution?'[4] Evolution in the widest sense of the term becomes a process not simply of 'hominization' but also of divinization in and through the risen Christ.

This optimistic vision of the cosmic process constitutes a form of apologetics, not indeed in the old sense of apologetic arguments designed to serve as external buttresses or supports to an act of faith in revealed truths but rather in the sense that Teilhard hopes to make people *see* what he sees, the relevance of

---

[1] *The Phenomenon of Man*, p. 308, n 2.   [2] *Ibid.*, p. 309.
[3] I *Corinthians*, xv, 28.   [4] *The Phenomenon of Man*, p. 297.

Christianity to an evolutionary view of the world and the significance conferred on the process of evolution when the process is
conceived in the context of Christian belief. In a sense Teilhard's
world-vision renews the ancient idea of the 'emanation' from God
and the return to God. But with him the return does not take the
form of the individual turning his back on an alien world and
seeking an ecstatic union with the One, Plotinus's 'flight of the
alone to the Alone'. The evolutionary process is itself the process of
return, and individuals are envisaged as becoming a one-in-many
in and through Christ. Nietzsche refused to admit that man as he
existed was the peak-point of evolution and proclaimed the idea of
Superman, a higher form of man.[1] Teilhard sees man as attaining
a higher form of existence through following the lines of evolution
converging to the point at which the person, while remaining a
person, is united with all other persons in a whole which is greater
than himself. And this point turns out to be what we might
perhaps describe as the 'Christosphere'. From one point of view
the universe is seen as interiorizing itself, as taking more and more
the form of self-reflection (through man) in the noosphere. From
the point of view of Christian faith this process of cosmogenesis is
seen as a process of Christogenesis, the total Christ that is to say,
Christ in his mystical body.

It is of course easy enough to find objections against Teilhard's
world-vision. It can be objected, for example, that though the
theory of evolution is accepted by practically all scientists, it
remains an hypothesis, and that in any case the scientific hypothesis is insufficient to bear the weight of the edifice which Teilhard builds on it. Again, it can be objected that a distinction must
be made between the scientific hypothesis of evolution and the
optimistic idea of progress for which Teilhard opts and which is
clearly connected with his religious beliefs. Further, the objection
can be made that in outlining his optimistic world-vision Teilhard
devotes too little attention to the negative side, to the facts of
evil and suffering and to the possibility of shipwreck and failure.
Some have complained that Teilhard mixes up science, metaphysics and Christian faith, and that he sometimes presents
as conclusions of a scientist ideas which are due rather to free

---

[1] By saying this I do not intend to imply that Nietzsche believed that Superman would necessarily emerge as a product of inevitable evolution. He does indeed
talk about evolution; but it seems evident to me that the concept of Superman is
intended much more as a spur and goal to the human will than as a prediction of
something which will come to pass through an inevitable process of evolution.

metaphysical speculation or to personal religious convictions. In general it can be, and often has been objected that he presents us with vague impressions and concepts which are not clearly defined. The whole thing, it may be said, is a mixture of science, poetry and religious faith, which impresses only those who are unable or unwilling to respect ideals of preciseness of thought and clarity of language. The Teilhardian world-vision may thus appear as at best elevating and hope-inspiring poetry and at worst as a large-scale confidence-trick which tries to put across under the guise of science a world-view which has really little to do with science.

It would take an ardent disciple to claim that such objections are completely groundless. But as the expression of the outlook of a man who was both a scientist and a convinced Christian and who tried not simply to reconcile but rather to integrate what he regarded as a scientific world-view with a Christocentric faith, Teilhard's vision of reality has an indubitable sweep and grandeur which tend to make the objections appear as pedantic or irrelevant. It may be said that he was a visionary or seer who presented in broad and sometimes vague and ambiguous outlines a prophetic programme, so to speak, which others are called upon to investigate in detail, to clarify, render more precise and justify with sustained argument. There is indeed the possibility that an original world-vision will be drained of its life and power when it is submitted to this sort of treatment.[1] Hegel towers above Hegelians, Nietzsche above Nietzscheans. But Teilhard's bold extension of the concept of evolution into a profoundly religious world-view, not by way of mere additions or superimpositions but rather through a process of broadening out so as to include distinguishable dimensions in an integrated and comprehensive vision, can of course provide an inspiring programme for further reflection. Some have thought the scientific hypothesis of evolution irreconcilable with Christian orthodoxy. Others have found it reconcilable but with certain reservations. Teilhard is not really bothered with 'reconciling', except when criticism by others drives him to it. The concept of evolution is taken as the perspective

---

[1] I am not referring of course to Teilhardian scholarship. Like Aristotelian or Kantian scholarship, this can command respect, even when it is not particularly exciting. I am referring to devoted disciples who are concerned with propagating the master's views but who lack his power of vision and who 'scholastize' his theories. What they say may of course be reasonable enough; but it is apt to be much more pedestrian than the original, at any rate if the disciples are not really caught in the grip of the problems which stimulated the master's intellectual activity.

from which modern man must see the world, if he is to see it rightly. And Teilhard tries to show how this way of seeing the world broadens out, or can broaden out, to take the form of a Christocentric vision of the world and of human existence. In so doing he gives hostages to fortune, in the sense that the scientific theories on which he bases his world-vision are, from the logical point of view, revisable in principle. But it would be a mistake to think of him as claiming that religious faith is logically dependent on the truth of certain scientific hypotheses. He is concerned with showing that a marriage, so to speak, between the evolutionary view of man and Christian belief bears fruit in a general world-vision in which Christianity is seen neither as something parochial and outdated nor as despising this world and concentrating on another but as a world-affirming faith and as the religion for present and future man. It is sometimes said that the idea that science and religion are incompatible is dead. For with some exceptions Christians do not now interpret Biblical texts in a manner which produces a clash with science. But even if there is no logical incompatibility between religion and science, there can obviously be divergent mentalities or outlooks. For example, belief in God can appear not as logically incompatible with science but as superfluous and irrelevant. Teilhard, with his firm belief in the value of scientific knowledge and theory and his deep religious faith, tries to display their interrelations in one unified outlook.

2. When we turn to Gabriel Marcel, we are turning to a very different kind of thinker. Teilhard de Chardin did indeed lay great emphasis on man; but he did so in the context of the general process of cosmogenesis. His eyes were fixed on the universe, the world. Gabriel Marcel explores a different kind of world. To say that he is concerned with an inner world would be misleading. For it suggests the notion of self-concentration or introspection, whereas interpersonal relationships constitute a central datum for Marcel's reflection. Science hardly figures in his thought. Whereas Teilhard asserts enthusiastically his belief in science,[1] Marcel is much more likely to assert his belief in the value and significance of personal relationships. A comparison between Teilhard and thinkers such as Hegel, Bergson and Whitehead makes sense at any rate. But in

---

[1] It might of course be questioned whether to say 'I believe in science' is a sensible way of speaking. But Teilhard obviously means in particular that he believes firmly in the truth and the wider significance of the theory of evolution, and, in general, that he accepts the scientific view of the world as a point of departure.

the case of Marcel it would be a matter of pointing out radical differences rather than of drawing attention to similarities.[1] Further, even if Teilhard is often vague and impressionistic in his utterances, it is possible to say, in outline, 'what he holds', whereas Marcel's thought is so elusive that to ask what his 'doctrines' are would be pretty well tantamount to inviting either silence or the reply that the question should not be put, as it rests on a false assumption.

Gabriel Marcel has often been classified (by Sartre among many others) as a Catholic existentialist. But as he himself has repudiated the label, it is best abandoned.[2] It is doubtless natural enough to look for a label of some sort, but there is no general label which really fits. Marcel has sometimes been described as an empiricist. But though he certainly bases his reflections on experience and does not try to deduce a system of ideas *a priori*, the word 'empiricism' is too much associated with the reductive analysis of Hume and others for it to be anything but thoroughly misleading if applied to the thought of Marcel. Again, though Marcel certainly develops what can be described as phenomenological analyses, he is no disciple of Husserl, or indeed of anyone else. He has gone his own way and cannot be treated as a member of any definite school. He tells us however that a pupil once suggested that his philosophy was a kind of neo-Socratism. And on reflection Marcel concluded that the term might be the least inexact which could be applied, provided that his questioning or interrogating attitude was not understood as implying scepticism.[3]

Marcel was born at Paris in 1889. His father, a Catholic turned agnostic, was for a time French minister to Sweden and later director of the Bibliothèque Nationale and of the Musées Nationaux. His mother, who came of a Jewish family, died while

[1] One might perhaps compare some of Marcel's reflections with parts of Hegel's *Phenomenology of Spirit*. But Marcel's philosophy in general bears little resemblance to absolute idealism.

[2] There was a time when Marcel at any rate tolerated the label 'existentialist', even if he did not care for the addition of 'Christian', on the ground that people who did not regard themselves as Christians could adhere to existentialism as he understood it. Indeed, in an autobiographical essay he referred to 'my first existentialist statements' (*The Philosophy of Existence*, translated by Manya Harari, London, 1948, p. 89). However, Marcel has indeed definitely repudiated the label 'existentialist', probably largely to avoid confusion with the philosophy of Sartre. And in this case it is better not to use it.

[3] See Marcel's preface to the English translation of his *Metaphysical Journal* (translated by B. Wall, London, 1952).

he was a small child; and he was brought up by his aunt, a convert to Protestantism[1] and a woman of strong ethical convictions. When he was eight, Marcel spent a year with his father at Stockholm; and not long after his return to Paris he was sent to the Lycée Carnot. He was a brilliant pupil, but he loathed the educational system to which he was subjected and took refuge in the world of music and of the imagination. Thus he started writing plays at an early age. After his studies at the lycée he went to the Sorbonne, and in 1910 he obtained the Agrégation in philosophy. Attracted for a time by idealism, especially by the thought of Schelling, he soon turned against it. Fichte irritated him, and he mistrusted Hegel, while admiring him. For F. H. Bradley he had a profound regard; and much later he was to publish a book on Josiah Royce. But idealism did not seem to him to come to terms with concrete existence; and the first part of his *Metaphysical Journal* expresses his criticism of idealist ways of thought from a point of view which was still influenced by idealism. His experience with the French Red Cross in the first world war[2] confirmed him in his conviction of the remoteness of abstract philosophy from concrete human existence. For a few years Marcel taught philosophy in various lycées; but for most of his life he was a freelance writer, publishing philosophical works and plays and acting as a literary, dramatic and musical critic. In 1948 he received the Grand Prix de Littérature of the French Academy, in 1956 the Goethe Prize and in 1958 the Grand Prix National des Lettres. In 1949–50 Marcel gave the Gifford lectures at Aberdeen. He was elected a member of the Institut de France. He died in 1973.

If we understand by a philosophical system a philosophy which is developed by a process of deduction from a point of departure which is taken as certain, there is no such thing as Gabriel Marcel's system. He has no use for systems in this sense. What he does is to develop a series of 'concrete approaches'. These approaches are of course convergent, in the sense that they are not incompatible and that they can be regarded as contributing towards a general interpretation of human experience. But it would be a great mistake to think that Marcel regards these 'concrete approaches' as providing a series of results or conclusions or solutions to

---

[1] Marcel's aunt does not appear to have had much more belief in Protestant doctrines than his father had in Catholic ones.

[2] Marcel's state of health disqualified him from serving as a soldier. He was employed in obtaining news for families of wounded soldiers and in trying to locate the missing.

problems, which can be put together to constitute a set of proved theses. To use one of his analogies,[1] if a chemist invents a certain product, it can then, let us suppose, be bought by anyone in a shop. Once made, the product can be sold and bought without reference to the means by which it was first discovered. In this sense the result is separable from the means whereby the result was obtained. But for Marcel this is certainly not the case in philosophy. The result, if one may use the word, is inseparable from the process of research or inquiry leading to it. Inquiry must of course start somewhere, with some dis-ease or exigence or situation which gives rise to the inquiry. But a philosophical exploration is for Marcel something intensely personal; and we cannot simply separate the result from the exploration and pass it on as an impersonal truth. Communication is possible. But this is really a matter of participation in the actual process of philo-sophizing. And if it is objected that in this case philosophy in-volves a repeated starting again and that there can be no set of proved or verified results which can serve as a foundation for further reflection, Marcel's reply is 'this perpetual beginning again . . . is an inevitable part of all genuinely philosophical work'.[2]

There are of course pervasive themes in Marcel's philosophizing. And we can try to indicate one or two of them. If however it is the actual process of reflection which counts, rather than results or conclusions, any attempt at summarizing Marcel's thought in a brief review of it is bound to be inadequate and unsatisfactory. When referring to someone who asked him to express the essence of his philosophy in a couple of sentences, Marcel remarked that the question was silly and could really only be answered by a shrug of the shoulders.[3] If however an historian is writing about recent French philosophy, he can hardly omit the thought of one of the best known thinkers. So he just has to reconcile himself to his remarks being inadequate.

There is however one point which should be clarified in advance. Reference has already been made to the description of Marcel as a 'Christian existentialist'. And he is well known as a devout Catholic. The conclusion may therefore be drawn that his philo-sophy is dependent on his Catholic faith. But it would be mistaken.

---

[1] The Mystery of Being. I, Reflection and Mystery, translated by G. S. Fraser, London, 1950, pp. 4 f.
[2] The Philosophy of Existence, p. 93.   [3] Reflection and Mystery, p. 2.

Marcel's *Journal Métaphysique* was published in 1927, and its entries date from the beginning of 1914 until the spring of 1923. He became a Catholic in 1929; and it is much truer to say that his conversion was part of the general development of his thought than that his philosophy was the result of his conversion. Indeed the second statement is patently false. His adherence to Catholicism has doubtless confirmed his conviction that the philosopher should pay attention to certain themes, but reflection on religious faith is a prominent feature of the first part of his *Journal*.

In 1933 Marcel published a play with the title *The Broken World* (*Le Monde cassé*). As a philosophical postscript he wrote an essay on 'the ontological mystery'[1], in which the broken world is described as the functionalized world. 'The individual tends to appear both to himself and to others as an agglomeration of functions.'[2] There are the vital functions, and there are the social functions, such as those of the consumer, the producer, the citizen, the ticket-collector, the commuter, the retired civil servant, and so on. Man is, as it were, fragmented, now a churchgoer, now a clerk, now a family man. The individual is medically overhauled from time to time, as though he were a machine; and death is written off as a total loss. This world of functionalization is, for Marcel, an empty or devitalized world; and in it 'the two processes of atomization and collectivization, far from excluding each other as a superficial logic might be led to suppose, go hand in hand and are two essentially inseparable aspects of the same process of devitalization.'[3] In such a world there is of course room for problems, technological problems for example. But there is a blindness to what Marcel describes as 'mysteries'. For they are correlative to the person; and in a broken world the person becomes the fragmented individual.

This brings us to Marcel's distinction, which he regards as very important, between problem and mystery. He admits that no clear line of demarcation can be drawn, as reflection on a mystery and the attempt to state it inevitably tend to transform it into a problem. But it would obviously be futile to use the two terms unless it were possible to give some indication of the difference in meaning. And we must try to give such an indication. Happily, Marcel supplies some examples.

---

[1] *Positions et approches concrètes du mystère ontologique,* an English translation is included in *Philosophy and Existence.*
[2] *Philosophy and Existence,* p. 1.　　　　[3] *Reflection and Mystery,* p. 27.

A problem, in Marcel's use of the term, is a question which can be answered purely objectively, without the questioner himself being involved. Consider a problem in mathematics. I may of course be interested in the problem, perhaps intensely so. Solving it may be for me a matter of importance, as it would be, for instance, if I were tackling an examination and success was essential to my career. But in my attempt to solve the problem I hold it over against me, as it were, considering it purely objectively and leaving myself out of the picture. I am the subject, the problem the object. And I do not enter into the object. It is true of course that the solving is done by me. But it could be done in principle not only by anyone else but also by a machine. And the solution, once attained, can be handed on. The problem moves, so to speak, purely on the plane of objectivity. If it is a question of solving problems relevant to putting a man into space and bringing him back again safely, it is clear that the more the people concerned tackle the problems purely objectively and leave themselves outside, so much the better will it be for everybody.

The term 'mystery' can be misleading. It does not refer to mysteries in the sense in which theologians have used the word, namely truths revealed by God which cannot be proved by reason alone and which transcend the comprehension of the human mind. Nor does the term mean the unknowable. In the essay referred to above Marcel describes a mystery as 'a problem which encroaches upon its own data, invading them, as it were, and thereby transcending itself as a simple problem.'[1] Elsewhere, in *Être et avoir*, he gives the same description and adds that 'a mystery is something in which I am myself involved, and which is therefore thinkable only as a sphere where the distinction between what is in me and what is before me loses its significance and its initial validity.'[2] Suppose, for example, that I ask 'what am I?' and that I answer that I am a soul or a mind which has a body. To answer in this way is to objectify my body as something over against me, something which I can have or possess, as I might have an umbrella. It is then quite impossible to reconstitute the unity of the human person. I *am* **my** body. But I am obviously not identifiable with the body in the sense which the term 'body' bears when it has been distinguished from 'soul' and objectified as a

---

[1] *Philosophy of Existence*, p. 8.
[2] *Être et avoir*, p. 169 (*Being and Having*, translated by K. Farrer, London, 1949, p. 117).

thing which I can consider, as it were, from outside. To grasp the unity of the human person I have to return to the lived experience of unity which precedes the mental separation into two data or factors. If, in other words, I separate myself into soul and body, objectify them as data for the solution of a problem and try to link them together, I shall never be able to do so. I can grasp the unity of myself only from within. One has to try to explore on the level of second reflection 'that massive, indistinct sense of one's total existence'[1] which is presupposed by the dualism produced by primary reflection.

We have just alluded to primary and secondary reflection. The distinction can perhaps be elucidated in this way. John and Mary love one another. They think of one another, but they do not, let us suppose, think of love in an abstract way and raise problems about it. There is simply the concrete unity or communion of mutual loving in which both John and Mary are involved. Let us then suppose that John stands back, as it were, from the actual experience or activity of loving, objectifies it as an object or phenomenon before him and asks, 'what is love?'. Perhaps he tries to analyse love into constituent elements; or he interprets it as something else, in terms, for instance, of the will to power. This analytic process is an example of first reflection, and love is considered as setting a problem to be solved, the problem of the nature of love, which is solved by means of reductive analysis of some kind. Let us further suppose that John comes to see the remoteness of this analysis from the actual experience of loving or from love as a lived communion between persons. He returns to the actual togetherness of love, the communion or unity which was presupposed by primary reflection, and he tries to grasp it in reflection but as from within, as a lived personal relationship. This is an example of second reflection.

Bradley, it may be remembered, postulated an original experience of the unity of reality, of the One, on the level of feeling or immediacy, a unity which analytic reflection breaks up or fragments but which metaphysics tries to restore, to recapture on the level of thought. Marcel is not of course an absolute idealist; but the project of grasping in reflection what is first present in feeling, on the level of immediacy, and is then distorted or broken up by analytic thought is a basic feature of his philosophy as it is of Bradley's. For example, my relation to my body, a relation

[1] *Reflection and Mystery*, p. 93.

which is *sui generis* and irreducible, is experienced on the level of
'feeling'. On the level of first reflection the unity of this feeling-
experience is broken up by analytic thought. That which is in
itself irreducible is subjected to reductive analysis and thus
distorted. It by no means follows that first reflection is devoid of
value. It can serve practical ends.[1] But in order to grasp the
sui generis relation between myself and my body it is necessary
to return to the original feeling-experience at the level of second
reflection.

The general idea of recuperating a lost unity at a higher
level is understandable. It is rather like the idea of recovering a
primitive innocence at a higher level which presupposes its loss
and recovery.[2] Implementation of the project however presents
some difficulty. For it may well appear that reflection or mediation
cannot be combined with immediacy, but that the latter is necessarily
transformed by the former. In other words, is not second reflection a dream? John, it may be said, is either involved in the
immediacy of loving or committed to playing the part of a spectator and objectifying love as an object of reflection. He cannot
combine the two at a higher level, however much he may dream
of doing so.

Marcel is aware of the difficulty. He admits that second reflection can easily degenerate into first reflection. At the same time
he envisages second reflection as an exploration of the metaphysical significance of experience. For example, he sees love as an
act of transcendence on the part of the human person and as a
participation in Being. And he asks, what does this experience
reveal to me of myself as a human person and of Being? Marcel's
use of the term 'Being' is somewhat perplexing. He insists that
Being is not and cannot be made into an object, a direct object of
intuition for instance. It can only be alluded to indirectly. However, it is clear that he sees in personal relationships such as love
and in experiences such as hope keys to the nature of reality
which are not available on the level of objectifying scientific
thought. John loves Mary, but Mary has died, and science offers
no assurance of her continued existence or of her reunion with

---

[1] Bradley recognized of course that science was not possible without analytic
thought, though he regarded science as manifesting a drive towards unification
which could not fully attain its goal on the level of science.

[2] We can note that at the end of *Être et avoir* Marcel includes an essay on
Peter Wust (1884–1940), the German philosopher who wrote about the second
'naïvety' or piety which is a recuperation of the first religious faith subsequent
to the work of the critical intelligence.

John.[1] For love and hope in union however there remains a communion, a 'we', which enables John to transcend the level of empirical evidence and to be confident in Mary's continued existence and of their future reunion. From the point of view of common sense this act of transcendence is simply an instance of wishful thinking. For Marcel it is grounded in a mysterious presence which is a participation in Being. On the level of first reflection an object cannot be described as present to me, unless it is locatable, according to specifiable criteria, in space and time. On the level of intersubjectivity and personal communion another person can be present to me, even after his or her bodily death, as a 'thou'. The bond is broken on the physical plane. But on the metaphysical plane it persists for 'creative fidelity', which is 'the active perpetuation of presence'.[2]

It hardly needs saying that Marcel is not prepared to regard God as an object, the existence of which is asserted as a conclusion that solves a problem. Faith is a matter not of believing *that* but of believing *in*; and God is for Marcel, as for Kierkegaard,[3] the absolute thou.[4] He is thus encountered rather than proved. The human being, according to Marcel, has an exigence of Being, which in religious language is an orientation to the absolute Thou. But there are various ways in which the orientation to God can be appropriated. That is to say, there are various concrete approaches to God. God is 'absolute presence', and he can be approached through the intersubjective relationships, such as love and creative fidelity, which are sustained by and point to him. Or a man can encounter God in worship and prayer, in invocation and response. The various ways are not of course mutually exclusive. They are ways of coming to experience the divine presence. But man can shut his eyes to this presence. In discussing personal relationships Marcel makes much of the concept of availability (*disponibilité*). If I am available to another, I thereby transcend my egoism; and

[1] It should be added perhaps that Marcel has had a continuing interest in meta-psychical experiences; but his metaphysic of hope does not rest on parapsychology. For a definition of hope see the end of Marcel's essay on a metaphysic of hope, which is included in *Homo Viator* (translated by E. Craufurd, London, 1951).

[2] *The Philosophy of Existence*, p. 22.

[3] Marcel's ideas on this subject were formed before he read Kierkegaard. On reading him he recognized of course certain points of similarity. We can also draw attention to the affinity between Marcel and Martin Buber, in regard to the I–Thou relationship.

[4] In his *Metaphysical Journal* (p. 281) Marcel raises the question, how is it possible to conceive a *thou* which is not also a *he* (in the sense of an object)?

the other is present to me on the plane of intersubjectivity. If I am not available for or open to a person, I shut the person out, so to speak, and he or she is not present to me except perhaps in a purely physical sense. It is also possible for me to shut out God and deny him, refusing invocation. This is, for Marcel, an option, an act of the will.

For some readers Marcel is undoubtedly a disconcerting writer. When looked at under certain aspects his thought gives the impression of being thoroughly realistic and down to earth. For example, with him there is no question of starting with a self-enclosed ego and then trying to prove the existence of an external world and of other people. Man is essentially 'incarnate', embodied, in the world. He finds himself in a situation, in the world; and his self-consciousness grows correlatively to his awareness of others. But for many readers Marcel becomes progressively elusive. We find him taking familiar terms, such as 'have', 'presence', 'love', 'hope', 'testimony', and proceeding to inquire into their meaning. And we are prepared, if not for exercises in linguistic analysis, at any rate for phenomenological analyses. The analyses however open up into what seems to be a peculiarly elusive form of metaphysics, in regard to which we may be left wondering not only whether we have really grasped what has been said but also whether in fact anything intelligible has been said. And it is understandable if some readers are tempted to regard Marcel's philosophizing as a kind of poetry or as highly personal meditations, rather than as public-property philosophy.

That Marcel's thought is elusive and also highly personal can hardly be denied. His own value-judgments reveal themselves clearly enough. It is important however to realize that he is not trying to explore what transcends all human experience. He is concerned throughout with human experience. What he tries to do is to reveal or to draw attention to the metaphysical significance hidden in the familiar, to the pointers to eternity which are present, as he sees it, in the personal relationships to which he attaches great positive value and to an all-pervading and unifying presence. His philosophy centres round personal relationships and the relationship to God. This doubtless tells us a good deal about Marcel. But if his philosophizing has no further significance for us than an indication of what he himself most values in life, he might comment that our outlook has obviously been so conditioned by this 'broken world' that we are unable, or at least find it extremely difficult, to discern the metaphysical dimensions of experience. Heidegger has written about Hölderlin. Marcel has written about Rilke as a witness to the spiritual.[1] He is aware of course of Rilke's increasing opposition to Christianity and refers to it. But he sees the poet as open to and perceptive of dimensions of our being and world which are hidden from many eyes. And we can look on Marcel's essays in 'second reflection' as attempts to facilitate our perception of these dimensions.

3. Teilhard de Chardin and Gabriel Marcel are both Christian thinkers. But there are obvious differences between them. Teilhard's attention is focussed on the evolving universe. Nothing is for him completely lifeless. Matter is pregnant with life and with spirit, the spirit which comes to birth in man and which develops towards a hyper-personal consciousness. The whole process is teleological, oriented to Omega Point when the world reaches its fulfilment in the union of all men in the cosmic Christ. Modern science and our modern technological civilization are preparing the way for a higher consciousness in which man as we know him will be surpassed. In brief, Teilhard's world-vision is thoroughly optimistic. With Gabriel Marcel however we hear little about the universe in Teilhard's sense of the word. To be sure, Marcel insists, like Teilhard, on man's situation as a being in the world. But it is not the material changing world on which he focusses his intention. When speaking of man as a traveller, he remarks that anything connected with evolution must be eliminated from the discussion.[2] Evolution, that is to say, is quite irrelevant to his 'second reflection', and to his exploration of 'mysteries'. The act of transcendence is for him an entering into communion with other people and with God, not the movement from the biosphere to the noosphere and so to Omega Point. Attention is directed, to speak paradoxically, to the beyond within, to the revelatory significance and metaphysical dimensions of the relationships which are possible for actual persons at any time. Marcel shows a great sensitivity to uniting relations between human beings; but we can hardly imagine him hymning the world or the universe in the way that Teilhard did. And while some readers of Teilhard have found difficulty in distinguishing between the world and God, such an impression would scarcely be possible in the case of Marcel, for whom God is the absolute Thou. Moreover, though it

[1] The two lectures on Rilke are included in *Homo Viator*.
[2] *Homo Viator*, p. 7.

would be wrong to describe Marcel as a pessimist, he is very conscious of the precariousness of what he values and of the ease with which depersonalization can take place. To regard the other person as an object and to treat him as such is common enough both in private relationships and in wider social contexts. For Marcel our world is '*essentially* broken';[1] and he seems to see in our modern civilization an increasing depersonalization. In any case the idea that the world is inevitably proceeding from good to better is certainly not his. In 1947 he discussed with Teilhard the question, to what degree does the material organization of humanity lead man to spiritual maturity? While Teilhard of course maintained an optimistic view, Marcel was sceptical. He saw in collectivization and in our technological society a Promethean spirit expressing itself in a refusal of God. Marcel believes indeed in the eschatological triumph of goodness; and he admits that an optimistic view can be maintained on religious grounds, in the light of faith, that is to say. But for him invocation and refusal have always been two possibilities for men and always will be. And the dogma of progress is 'a completely arbitrary postulate'.[2] In other words, while Teilhard can reasonably be regarded as trying to capture the Hegelian and Marxist views of history for Christianity (or to interpret Christianity in such a way as to assimilate and transcend them), Marcel will have nothing to do with a point of view which, in his opinion, obscures human freedom, is oblivious, in theological language, of the effects of the Fall, and fails to take real account of evil and suffering.

The differences in outlook between the two men should not of course be exaggerated. For example, Marcel's position does not entail rejection of the scientific hypothesis of evolution, an hypothesis which stands or falls according to the strength or weakness of the empirical evidence. He regards the scientific theory as irrelevant to philosophy as he conceives it; and what he objects to is the inflation of a scientific hypothesis into a metaphysical world-view which incorporates a doctrine of progress which he regards as unwarranted. Again, there is no question of suggesting that Teilhard attached no value to those personal relationships in which Marcel sees the expression of genuine human personality. In his private life he set great store by such relationships; and in a real sense the movement of cosmogenesis was for him a movement from exteriority to interiority, to the full actualization of spirit.

---

[1] *Reflection and Mystery*, p. 34.   [2] *Faith and Reality*, p. 183.

At the same time the perspectives of the two men are clearly different, despite their common religious allegiance. And they appeal to different types of mind. One can see this in their respective attitudes to notable thinkers such as Marx and Bergson. Neither Teilhard nor Marcel is a Marxist; but their respective evaluations of Marxism are understandably different. As for Bergson, it is natural to think of Teilhard as continuing his general line of thought. Though however Marcel pays tribute to Bergson's distinction between the 'closed' and the 'open', he then gives to the idea of 'openness' an application which fits in with his own perspective and interests. If we mentally associate Teilhard with Bergson, we associate Marcel with thinkers such as Kierkegaard and Jaspers, though Marcel did not derive his ideas from the former and though he had considerable reservations in regard to the latter's philosophy. What unites Teilhard and Marcel is their Christian faith and their regard for man. But whereas Teilhard takes an optimistic view of man's future,[1] seeing it in the light of his philosophy of evolution, Marcel is much more conscious, as Pascal was, of ambiguity, fragility and precariousness.

---

[1] Teilhard was prepared to say that he had no intention of stating dogmatically that the future *must* be rosy. At the same time he obviously came down decisively on the side of optimism.

CHAPTER XVI

THE EXISTENTIALISM OF SARTRE (1)

Life and writings — Pre-reflexive and reflexive consciousness: the imagining and the emotive consciousness — Phenomenal being and being in itself — Being for itself — The freedom of being for itself — Awareness of others — Atheism and values.

1. IN his popular lecture *Existentialism and Humanism* Sartre informs his audience that there are two kinds of existentialists, Christian and atheist. As representatives of Christian existentialism he mentions 'Jaspers and Gabriel Marcel, of the Catholic confession',[1] while as representatives of atheist existentialism he mentions Heidegger and himself. In point of fact Karl Jaspers was not a Catholic and, moreover, came to prefer a descriptive label for his philosophy other than 'philosophy of existence' (*Existenzphilosophie*). Gabriel Marcel is indeed a Catholic; but, as we have noted, he eventually repudiated the label 'existentialist'. As for Heidegger, he has explicitly dissociated himself from Sartre; and, though he is certainly not a Christian, he does not like being described as an atheist. Though therefore books on existentialism generally include treatments of all the philosophers named by Sartre, and often of others as well, as far as definite acceptance of the label 'existentialist' is concerned we seem to be left with Sartre, who has described himself in this way and has expounded what he considers to be the essential tenet of existentialism.

It may thus appear somewhat disconcerting when we find Sartre telling us in recent years that Marxism is the one living philosophy of our time. It does not follow however that Sartre has definitely turned his back on existentialism and adopted Marxism instead. As will be explained in the next chapter, he looks for a fusion of the two, a rejuvenation of ossified Marxism through an injection of existentialism. The present chapter will be devoted to an exposition of Sartrian existentialism as such, as developed in *Being and Nothingness* and other writings before he turned his hand to the task of a systematic fusion of existentialism and Marxism.

---

[1] *L'existentialisme est un humanisme*, p. 17 (Paris, 1946). English translation by P. Mairet, *Existentialism and Humanism*, p. 26 (London, 1948).

There are fashions in the world of philosophy as elsewhere; and the vogue of existentialism has declined. Further, as Sartre has published a considerable number of novels and plays which have made his name well known by many people who would be disinclined to tackle his philosophical works, there is a not unnatural tendency to regard him as a literary figure rather than as a serious philosopher. Indeed, it has sometimes been said, though unfairly, that he derives all his philosophical ideas from other thinkers, especially German ones. And his long-standing flirtation with Marxism, culminating in his attempt to combine it with existentialism, has perhaps encouraged this impression. But while Sartre as a philosopher may have been overvalued by his fervent admirers in the past, he can also be undervalued. The fact that he is a novelist, a dramatist and a campaigner for social and political causes does not entail the conclusion that he is not an able and serious thinker. He may have written in Parisian cafés; but he is an extremely intelligent man, and his philosophy is certainly not without significance, even if it is no longer as fashionable in France as it once was. We are concerned here with Sartre as a philosopher, not as a dramatist or novelist.

Jean-Paul Sartre was born at Paris in 1905.[1] His higher studies were done at the École Normale from 1924 until 1928. After obtaining the *agrégation* in philosophy he taught philosophy at lycées in Le Havre, Laon and then Paris. From 1933 until 1935 he was a research student first at Berlin and then at the University of Freiburg, after which he taught in the Lycée Condorcet at Paris. In 1939 he joined the French army and was captured in 1940. Released in 1941, he returned to teaching philosophy and was also an active participant in the Resistance movement. Sartre has never occupied a University chair.

Sartre started writing before the war. In 1936 he published an essay on the ego or self[2] and a work on the imagination, *L'imagination. Étude critique*,[3] while in 1938 he published his famous novel *La nausée*.[4] In 1939 there appeared a work on the emotions,

---

[1] Sartre's reminiscences of his childhood, *Les mots*, appeared in 1964. There is an English translation, *Words*, by I. Clephane (London, 1965). Simone de Beauvoir's memoirs contain other biographical material.

[2] *La transcendance de l'égo: esquisse d'une description phénoménologique*, translated into English by F. Williams and R. Kirkpatrick as *The Transcendence of the Ego* (New York, 1957).

[3] There is an English translation by F. Williams, *Imagination: A Psychological Critique* (Ann Arbor, Michigan, 1962).

[4] Translated by Robert Baldick as *Nausea* (Harmondsworth, 1965).

Esquisse d'une théorie des émotions[1] and several stories under the title *Le Mur*.[2] During the war, in 1940, Sartre published a second book on the imagination, *L'imaginaire: psychologie phénoménologique de l'imagination*,[3] and his main philosophical tome, *L'être et le néant: essai d'une ontologie phénoménologique* appeared in 1943.[4] His play *Les mouches*[5] was performed in the same year. The first two volumes of the novel *Les chemins de la liberté* appeared in 1945,[6] and also the well known play *Huis clos*.[7] Two other plays appeared in 1946, the year of publication of the lecture to which reference has been made above[8] and also of *Réflexions sur la question juive*.[9]

In subsequent years Sartre has published a considerable number of plays, while collections of essays under the title *Situations* have appeared in 1947, 1948, 1949 and 1964.[10] Sartre was one of the founders in 1945 of the review *Les temps modernes*, and some of his writings have appeared in it, such as the 1952 articles on Communism. His attempt to combine existentialism and Marxism has led to the production in 1960 of the first volume of the *Critique de la raison dialectique*.[11] Sartre has also published an introduction to the works of Jean Genet, *Saint Genet: comédien et martyr*.[12]

2. In one of his essays Sartre remarks that for three centuries Frenchmen have been living by 'Cartesian freedom', with, that is to say, a Cartesian intellectualist idea of the nature of freedom.[13]

---

[1] There are two English translations, one by P. Mairet under the title *Sketch for a Theory of Emotions* (London, 1962).

[2] An English translation by Lloyd Alexander, *Intimacy*, is available in paperback in Panther Books. It appeared originally at London in 1949.

[3] *The Psychology of the Imagination*, translated by B. Frechtman (London, 1949).

[4] *Being and Nothingness*, translated by H. Barnes (New York, 1956; London, 1957).

[5] *The Flies*, translated by S. Gilbert, is contained in *Two Plays* (London, 1946).

[6] The first two volumes, *L'âge de la raison* and *Le sursis*, have been translated by E. Sutton as *The Age of Reason* and *The Reprieve* (London, 1947). The third volume, *La mort dans l'âme* (1949) has been translated by G. Hopkins as *Iron in the Soul* (London, 1950).

[7] Translated by S. Gilbert as *In Camera* and included in *Two Plays* (London, 1946).

[8] See note 1.

[9] There are two translations, one by E. de Mauny, *Portrait of an Anti-Semite* (London, 1948).

[10] Some of these essays have been translated by A. Michelson as *Literary and Philosophical Essays* (London, 1955).

[11] The first section of this volume has been translated by H. Barnes as *Search for a Method* (New York, 1963; London, 1964).

[12] Translated by B. Frechtman as *Saint Genet* (New York, 1963).

[13] *Literary and Philosophical Essays*, p. 169.

However this may be, it is hardly an exaggeration to say that the shadow of Descartes lies across French philosophy, not of course in the sense that all French philosophers are Cartesians but in the sense that in many cases personal philosophizing begins through a process of reflection in which positions are adopted for or against the ideas of the foremost French philosopher. We can see this sort of influence at work in the case of Sartre. But he has also been strongly influenced by Hegel, Husserl and Heidegger. Here again he is no more a disciple of any German philosopher than he is of Descartes or his successors. The influence of Heidegger, for example, is shown clearly enough in *Being and Nothingness*, even if the German philosopher is often criticized by Sartre and has himself repudiated association with Sartrian existentialism. From an academic point of view[1] Sartre's thought has developed partly though reflection on the methods and ideas of Descartes, Hegel, Husserl and Heidegger, whereas British empiricism hardly enters his field of vision,[2] and materialism, in its non-Marxist forms at any rate, is not a philosophy for which he seems to have much use.

The influence of the background formed by Cartesianism and phenomenology shows itself not only in Sartre's essay of 1936 on the ego but also in his works on imagination and emotion and in the attention given to consciousness in the introduction to *Being and Nothingness*. At the same time Sartre makes clear the differences between his position and those of Descartes and Husserl. For Sartre the basic datum is what he calls the pre-reflexive consciousness, awareness, for example, of this table, this book or that tree. What Descartes starts with however in his *Cogito, ergo sum* is not the pre-reflexive but the reflexive consciousness, which expresses an act whereby the self is constituted as object. He thus involves himself in the problem of passing from the self-enclosed ego, as object of consciousness, to a warranted assertion of the existence of external objects and of other persons. This problem does not arise if we go behind the reflexive consciousness to the pre-reflexive consciousness, which is 'transcendent', in the sense that it posits its object as transcending itself, as that

---

[1] As distinct, that is to say, from his own experience of and reflections on life and the world.

[2] In *Being and Nothingness* there is some discussion of Berkeley's *esse est percipi*, and Hume is mentioned twice. The philosophers whose names appear most frequently are Descartes, Hegel, Heidegger, Husserl, Kant and Spinoza. In *L'imaginaire* Sartre does however quote from Hume on ideas as images, but only to dismiss his theory as illusion. See *L'imaginaire*, p. 17 (English translation, pp. 12–13).

towards which it reaches.[1] 'All consciousness, as Husserl has shown, is consciousness *of* something. This means that there is no consciousness which is not the *positing* of a transcendent object, or, if one prefers, that consciousness has no "content".'[2] Suppose, for example, that I am aware of this table. The table is not *in* my consciousness as a content. It is in space, near a window or near the door or wherever it may be. And when I 'intend' it, I posit it as transcending, and not as immanent in consciousness. In this case of course Husserl's policy of bracketing existence, of treating all the objects of consciousness as purely immanent and suspending judgment, as a matter of principle, about their objective reference, is misguided. As far as perception is concerned, the object of consciousness is posited as transcendent and as existent. When I perceive this table, the table itself, and not a mental representation of it, is the object of the intentional act; and it is posited as existing. Sartre therefore follows Heidegger in rejecting Husserl's claim that the bracketing of existence is essential to phenomenology.[3]

Sartre is not of course claiming that we never make mistakes about the nature of the object. Suppose, for example, that in the twilight I think that I see a man in the wood, and that it turns out to be the stump of a tree. I have obviously made a mistake. But the mistake does not consist in my having confused a real thing, namely the stump of a tree, with a mental content, the representation of a man, which was the object of consciousness. I perceived an object, positing it as transcendent; but I misread or misinterpreted its nature. That is to say, I made an erroneous judgment about a real object.

What then of images and imagination? Imagination, as a form of consciousness, is intentional. It has its own characteristics. 'Every consciousness posits its object, but each does so in its own way.[4] Perception posits its object as existent; but the imagining consciousness, which manifests the mind's freedom, can do so in several ways. For example, it can posit its object as non-existent.

---

[1] In this context words such as 'transcendence' and 'transcend' should obviously not be understood as referring to what transcends the world or the limits of human experience. To say that consciousness is transcendent is to say that it is not confined to purely immanent objects, subjective ideas or images or copies of external things.

[2] *L'être et le néant*, p. 17 (English translation, p. 11).

[3] Husserl's approach led him eventually into the development of an idealist philosophy.

[4] *L'imaginaire*, p. 24 (English translation, p. 20).

Sartre is more concerned however with arguing that just as perception intends an object posited as transcendent and not a
mental content which stands in place of the extramental object, so
does the imagining consciousness intend an object other than the
image as image. One can of course reflect on the first-order
imagining consciousness and say, whether felicitously or not, 'I
have an image'. But in the first-order imagining consciousness
itself the image is not the intended object but a relation between
consciousness and its object. What Sartre means is seen most
easily in a case such as my imagining Peter as present, when
Peter is a real but absent friend. The object of consciousness is
Peter himself, the real Peter; but I imagine him as present, the
image or picture being simply a way in which I relate myself to
Peter or make him present to me. Reflection of course can distinguish between image and reality; but the actual first-order imagining consciousness intends or has as its object Peter himself. It is
'the imaginative consciousness of Peter.'[1] It may be objected
that though this line of interpretation holds good in cases such as
the one just mentioned, it is hardly applicable to cases in which
the imagining consciousness freely creates an unreal anti-world,
as Sartre puts it, of phantom objects, which represents an escape
from the real world, a negation of it.[2] In such cases does not
consciousness intend the image or images? For Sartre at any rate
it is the reflexive consciousness which, through reflection, constitutes the image as such. For the actual imagining consciousness
the image is the way in which consciousness posits an unreal
object as non-existing. It does not posit the image as an image
(this is what reflection does); it posits unreal objects. Sartre is
prepared to say that this unreal 'world' exists 'as unreal, as
inactive';[3] but that which is posited as non-existent obviously
'exists' only as posited. If we consider a work of fiction, we can
see that its unreal world 'exists' only through and in the act of
positing; but in first-order consciousness attention is directed to this
world, to the saying and doings of imagined persons, not to images
as images, as, that is to say, psychical entities in the mind.[4]

[1] *Ibid.*, p. 17 (English, p. 14).
[2] For Sartre negation is involved in imagination. When, for instance, I imagine the
absent Peter as present, I do not deny that he is absent (for I posit him as real but
absent); but I try to overcome or negate the absence by imagining him as present.
[3] *L'imaginaire*, p. 180 (English, p. 157). Elsewhere (p. 17, *n* 1; English, p. 15,
n 1), Sartre remarks that the chimera exists neither as an image nor otherwise.
[4] In *L'imaginaire* Sartre writes at some length about the pathology of the
imagination and about dreams. But we cannot pursue these themes here.

In his book on the emotions Sartre insists on the intentionality of the emotive or emotional consciousness. 'Emotional consciousness is at first consciousness *of* the world.'[1] Like the imagining consciousness, it has its own characteristics. For example, the emotive way of apprehending the world is 'a transformation of the world',[2] the substitution, though not of course an effective substitution, of a magical world for the world of deterministic causality. But it is always intentional. A man who is afraid is afraid *of* something or someone. Other people may think that there is no real objective ground for his fear. And the man himself may say in subsequent reflection, 'there was nothing to be afraid of after all.' But if he genuinely felt fear, his first-order emotive or affective consciousness certainly intended something or someone, even if vaguely conceived. 'Emotion is a certain way of apprehending the world';[3] and the fact that one may clothe objects or persons with qualities which they do not possess or read a malign significance into a person's expression or words or actions does not alter this fact. The projection of emotive significance on a thing or person clearly involves intending the thing or person as object of consciousness. In *L'imaginaire* Sartre repeats the same basic point. To feel hate towards Paul is 'the consciousness *of* Paul as hateful';[4] it is not consciousness of hatred, which pertains to the reflexive consciousness. The theme of emotion is also pursued in several sections of *Being and Nothingness*.

We have seen that Sartre insists on the distinction between the pre-reflexive and the reflexive consciousness. To love Peter, for example, is not the same act as to think of myself as loving Peter. In the first case Peter himself is the intentional object, whereas in the second case myself-loving-Peter is the intentional object. The question arises therefore whether or not Sartre confines self-consciousness to the level of reflection, so that first-order or pre-reflexive consciousness is regarded as unaccompanied by self-consciousness. To answer this question we can turn to the 1936 essay on the transcendence of the ego.

In this essay Sartre asserts that 'the mode of existence of consciousness is to be conscious of itself'.[5] And if we take this statement by itself, it may seem to follow that self-consciousness

[1] *Esquisse d'une théorie des emotions*, p. 29 (Frechtman's translation, p. 51).
[2] *Ibid.*, p. 33 (English, p. 58).   [3] *Ibid.*, p. 30 (English, p. 52).
[4] *L'imaginaire*, p. 93 (English, p. 82).
[5] *The Transcendence of the Ego*, p. 40.

belongs to the pre-reflexive consciousness. But Sartre adds immediately that consciousness is consciousness of itself insofar as it is consciousness of a transcendent object. In the case of pre-reflexive consciousness this means that consciousness of, say, a table is indeed inseparably accompanied by consciousness of itself (it is and must be, so to speak, conscious consciousness); but the 'self-consciousness' which is an essential feature of pre-reflexive consciousness is, in Sartre's jargon, non-positional or non-thetic in regard to the ego. An example may clarify the matter. Let us suppose that I am absorbed in contemplating a particularly splendid sunset. Consciousness is directed wholly to the intentional object; there is no place in this consciousness for the ego. In the ordinary sense of the term therefore there is no self-consciousness, inasmuch as the ego is not posited as an object. Only the sunset is posited as an object. The positing of the ego arises on the level of reflection. When I turn consciousness of the sunset into an intentional object, the ego is posited. That is to say, the 'me' arises as an object for (reflexive) consciousness.

For phenomenology therefore the basic datum for Sartre is the pre-reflexive consciousness, in which the ego of reflexive consciousness does not appear. But we cannot of course think or talk about pre-reflexive consciousness without objectifying it, turning it into an intentional obect. And in this reflexive consciousness the ego and the world are posited as correlative to one another. The ego is the 'me', posited as the unity to which all my states of consciousness, experience and actions are ascribed, and posited also as the subject of consciousness, as in 'myself imagining Peter' or 'myself loving Mary'. The world is posited as the ideal unity of all objects of consciousness. Husserl's transcendental ego is excluded or suppressed; and Sartre thinks that in this way he can avoid following Husserl into idealism.[1] His line of thought also enables him to avoid Descartes's problem of proving the existence of the external world. For reflexive consciousness the ego and the world arise in correlation, as the subject in relation to its transcendent object. To isolate the subject and treat it as though it were a datum given in isolation is a mistake. We have

---

[1] Sartre distinguishes between the 'I' and the 'me' as two aspects or functions of the ego. But in *The Transcendence of the Ego* he represents the ego and the world as objects of 'absolute consciousness' which, according to him, is impersonal and without a subject. It is rather as though one adopted Fichte's theory of the constitution of the limited or finite subject and its object while omitting the transcendental ego.

not got to infer the world from the self, nor the self from the world: they arise together in correlation.

All this may seem very remote from anything that we ordinarily associate with existentialism. But it provides Sartre with a realist basis, the self in relation to its transcendent object. Further, though the self is not created by its object, any more than the object is created by the self (for they are posited together in correlation), the self is derivative, appearing only for reflexive consciousness, for consciousness, that is to say, which reflects on pre-reflexive consciousness. The self emerges or is made to appear from the background of first-order consciousness, as one pole of consciousness. The way thus lies open for Sartre's analysis of the self as derivative and fugitive. Further, as the ego is posited as the point of unity and the source of all one's experiences, states and actions, it is possible for man to try to conceal from himself the boundless freedom or spontaneity of consciousness and to take refuge in the idea of a stable self which ensures regular patterns of conduct. Afraid of boundless freedom, man can attempt to avoid his responsibility by attributing his actions to the determining causality of the past as precipitated, so to speak, in the self or ego. He is then in 'bad faith', a theme on which Sartre likes to dwell.

These ideas however are best considered in the context of Sartre's analysis of the self-conscious subject and of Being in *Being and Nothingness*. The analysis is indeed involved. But given the fact that Sartre is well known as a dramatist and novelist, it is desirable to make it clear that he is a serious and systematic philosopher and not simply a dilettante. He is not of course the creator of a system such as that of Spinoza, a system formed on a mathematical model. At the same time his existentialist philosophy can be seen as the systematic development of certain basic ideas. It is certainly not a mere juxtaposition of impressionistic views.

3. Consciousness, as we have seen, is for Sartre consciousness *of* something, something other than itself and in this sense transcendent. The transcendent object appears to or for consciousness, and it can thus be described as a phenomenon. It would however be a mistake to interpret this description as meaning that the phenomenal object is the appearance of an underlying reality or essence which does not appear. The table of which I am now aware as I sit before it is not the appearance of a hidden noumenon or of a

reality distinct from itself. 'The phenomenal being manifests itself, it manifests its essence as well as its existence.'[1] At the same time the table is obviously more than what appears to me here and now in a given act of awareness or consciousness. If there is no hidden and non-appearing reality of which the phenomenal table is the appearance, and if at the same time the table cannot be simply equated with one individual appearance or manifestation, it must be identified with the series of its manifestations. But we can assign no finite number to the series of possible appearances. In other words, even if we reject the dualism between appearance and reality and identify a thing with the totality of its appearances, we cannot simply say with Berkeley that to be is to be perceived. 'The being of that which *appears* does not exist *only* in so far as it appears.'[2] It surpasses the knowledge which we have of it and is thus transphenomenal. And according to Sartre the way thus lies open for inquiry into the transphenomenal being of the phenomenon.

If we ask what being in itself is, as revealing itself to consciousness, Sartre's answer recalls to our minds the philosophy of Parmenides: 'Being is. Being is in itself. Being is what it is.'[3] Being is opaque, massive: it simply is. As the foundation of the existent, it cannot be denied. Such remarks, taken by themselves, are perhaps somewhat baffling. Consider however a table. It stands out from other things as being a table and not something else, as being suitable for this purpose and not for that, and so on. But it appears for consciousness as a table precisely because human beings give it a certain meaning. That is to say, consciousness makes it appear as a table. If I wish to spread out my books and papers on it or to set a meal, it obviously appears primarily as a table, an instrument for the fulfilment of certain purposes. In other circumstances it might appear for consciousness (be made by consciousness to appear) as primarily firewood or a battering-ram or a solid object to hide under or an obstacle in my flight from an attacker or as a beautiful or an ugly object. It has a certain meaning or significance in its relation to consciousness. It does not follow however that consciousness creates the object. It indubitably is or exists. And it is what it is. But it acquires an instrumentalist meaning, standing out from its background as this sort of thing and not another, only in relation to consciousness.

---

[1] *L'être et le néant*, p. 12 (English, p. xlvi).
[2] *Ibid.*, p. 29 (English, p. lxii).   [3] *Ibid.*, p. 34 (English, p. lxvi).

In general, the world considered as a system of interrelated things with instrumental significance is made to appear for consciousness. In his theory of the conferring of meaning on things in terms of perspectives and purposes Sartre derives stimulus from Martin Heidegger. And in developing his theory of the way in which this is done he discusses Hegel's dialectic of being and not-being. For Sartre being in itself is logically prior to not-being and cannot be identified with it; but the table, for example, is constituted as a table through a negation. It is a table and not something else. All differentiation within being is due to consciousness, which makes something to appear by differentiating it from its background and in this sense negating the background. The same sort of thing can be said about spatial and temporal relations. A thing appears as 'near' or as 'far away' in relation to a consciousness which compares and relates. Similarly, it is for consciousness that this event appears as happening 'after' that event. Again, the Aristotelian distinction between potency and act arises only through and for consciousness. It is in relation to consciousness, for example, that the table is potentially firewood. Apart from consciousness, it simply is what it is.

In fine, it is for consciousness that the world appears as an intelligible system of distinct and interrelated things. If we think away all that is due to the activity of consciousness in making the world appear, we are left with being in itself (*l'en-soi*, the in-itself), opaque, massive, undifferentiated, the nebulous background, as it were, out of which the world is made to appear. This being in itself, Sartre tells us, is ultimate, simply there. It is 'without reason, without cause and without necessity'.[1] It does not follow that being is its own cause (*causa sui*). For this is a meaningless notion. Being simply is. In this sense being is gratuitous or *de trop*, as Sartre puts it in his novel *Nausea*.[2] In this work Roquentin, sitting in the municipal garden at Bounville, has an impression of the gratuitous or superfluous character of the being of the things about him and of himself. That is to say, there is no reason for their being. 'To exist is simply *to be there*.'[3] Being in itself is contingent, and this contingency is not an 'outward show', in the sense that it can be overcome by explaining it with

[1] *Ibid.*, p. 713 (English, p. 619).

[2] *Being and Nothingness* presents in systematic form the point of view expressed in *Nausea*.

[3] *La nausée*, p. 171 (English, Penguin edition, p. 188).

reference to a necessary being. Being is not derivable or reducible. It simply is. Contingency is 'the absolute itself and consequently perfectly gratuitous'.[1] 'Uncreated, without reason for being, without any relation to another being, being-in-itself is gratuitous for all eternity.'[2]

It is clear enough that there are different perspectives and that things can appear differently to different people. And we can make sense of the statement that it is consciousness which makes things to appear in certain ways or under certain aspects. To the climber or would-be climber a mountain appears as possessing certain characteristics, while to someone else who has no intention of trying to climb it but who is contemplating it aesthetically from a distance other characteristics stand out. And if one wishes to speak of each consciousness as making the object appear in a certain way or under certain aspects by negating other aspects or relegating them to a foggy background, this way of speaking is understandable, even if it is somewhat pretentious. Again, in so far as human beings have common interests and purposes, things appear to them in similar ways. It is not unreasonable to speak of human beings as conferring meanings on things, especially when it is a case of instrumental meaning. But Sartre carries this line of thought beyond the limit to which many people would be prepared to accompany him. For example, we have noted that in his view distinctions between things are due to consciousness, inasmuch as they are due to the act of distinguishing (of negation, in Sartrian terminology, or of denying that this is that). This is obviously true in a sense. Without consciousness there can be no distinguishing. At the same time most people would probably wish to claim that the mind is not confined to designating distinctions in what is in itself without distinction, but that it can recognize objective distinctions. And if Sartre disagrees, it is difficult to avoid the impression that he is carrying his line of thought as far as he can, without falling into what he would recognize as idealism, in order to be able to present being in itself in the way that he does. To be sure, there is no need to deny that the sort of impression or experience which Roquentin is represented as having in the gardens of Bouville can occur. But it by no means follows that Sartre is justified in drawing from this sort of impression the ontological conclusions which he in fact draws. He does indeed argue in *Being and Nothingness* that to

---

[1] *Ibid.*, p. 171.   [2] *L'être et le néant*, p. 34 (English, p. lxvi).

ask why there is being is to ask a question devoid of meaning, as it presupposes being.[1] But when making this statement he obviously cannot be referring to beings. For he has already said that it is consciousness which makes beings appear as such, as distinct that is to say. He is presumably arguing that it is meaningless to ask why there is being, inasmuch as being is what he has declared it to be, *de trop*, 'just there'. He might of course have raised difficulties in regard to the presuppositions involved in the use of the word 'why'. But what he actually does is to disallow the question 'why is there being'? on the ground that it presupposes being. And it is difficult to see how the question can be excluded on this ground, unless the being referred to is understood in the sense of trans-phenomenal and ultimate being, the Absolute. Sartre does indeed argue against other views. Something will be said later about his criticism of theism. But his own view seems to be the result of thinking away or abstracting from all in the object that he considers to be due to consciousness and then declaring the residue to be the Absolute, *l'en-soi* opaque and, in itself, unintelligible.

4. The concept of 'the in-itself' (*l'en-soi*) is one of the two key concepts of *Being and Nothingness*. The other key concept is that of consciousness, 'the for-itself' (*le pour-soi*). And it is hardly surprising if most of the work is devoted to this second theme. For if being in itself is opaque, massive, self-identical, there is obviously little that can be said about it. Besides, as an existentialist Sartre is primarily interested in man or, as he likes to put it, the human reality. He insists on human freedom, which is essential to his philosophy; and his theory of freedom is based on his analysis of 'the for-itself'.

Once more, all consciousness is consciousness *of* something. Of what? Of being as it appears. In this case it seems to follow that consciousness must be other than being, not-being that is to say, and that it must arise through a negation or nihilation of being in itself. Sartre is explicit about this. Being in itself is dense, massive, full. The in-itself harbours no nothingness. Consciousness is that whereby negation or nihilation is introduced. By its very nature consciousness involves or is distantiation or separation from being, though if it is asked what separates it from being, the answer can only be 'nothing'. For there is no intervening or separating entity. Consciousness is itself not-being, and its activity, according to Sartre, is a process of nihilation. When I am

[1] *Ibid.*, p. 713 (English, p. 619).

aware of this piece of paper, I distantiate myself from it, deny that I am the paper; and I make the paper appear, stand out from its background, by denying that it is anything else, by nihilating other phenomena. 'The being by which nothingness comes into the world is a being in which, in its own being, there is question of the nothingness of its being: *the being by which nothingness comes into the world must be its own nothingness.*'[1] 'Man is the being through whom nothingness comes into the world.'[2]

The language employed by Sartre is clearly objectionable. Consciousness is said to be its own nothingness; but it is also referred to as a being, as indeed it must be if it is to be described as exercising the activity attributed to it. Of course, one can see easily enough what Sartre means by ascribing to consciousness a process of nihilation. If I fix my attention on a particular picture in a gallery, I relegate the others to an indeterminate background. But one might emphasize equally well, or perhaps better, the positive activity involved in the intentional act.[3] Still, if we assume that being in itself is what Sartre says that it is, and if being is made to appear as the object of consciousness, consciousness of being must presumably involve the distantiation or separation of which he speaks, and in this sense not-being. If we object to the language, as well we may, we had better examine the premises which lead to its employment.

How does consciousness arise? It is difficult to see how being in itself, if it is as Sartre describes it, could give rise to anything at all, even to its own negation. It is equally difficult, if not more so, to see how consciousness could originate itself, as *causa sui*. As for the ego-subject, this arises, as we have seen, not on the level of pre-reflexive consciousness but on that of reflexive consciousness. It comes into being through the reflection of consciousness on itself; and it is thus made to appear as object. In this case there is no transcendental ego which could originate consciousness. However, that consciousness has arisen is an indubitable fact. And Sarte depicts it as rising through the occurrence of a fissure or rupture in being, resulting in the distantiation which is essential to consciousness.

It does not seem to the present writer that Sartre offers any really clear account of the origin of consciousness. However, as it

---

[1] *Ibid.*, p. 59 (English, p. 23).   [2] *Ibid.*, p. 60 (English, p. 24).
[3] So-called nihilation is itself a positive activity of course. But I am referring to the actual focussing of attention.

arises through the occurrence of a fissure or gap in being in itself, it must presumably come in some way or other out of being, even if by a process of negation, and so be derivative. As we have seen, Sartre excludes the question 'why is there being'? But he allows the question 'why is there consciousness'? True, he relegates explanatory hypotheses to the sphere of 'metaphysics' and says that phenomenological 'ontology' cannot answer the question. But he ventures the suggestion that *'everything takes place as if the in-itself, in a project to ground itself, gave itself the modification of the for-itself'*.[1] How the in-itself could have such a project is none too clear. But the picture is that of the Absolute, being in itself, undergoing a process or performing an act of self-diremption whereby consciousness arises. It is as though being in itself tries to take the form of consciousness while remaining being. But this goal cannot be achieved. For consciousness exists only through a continuous separation or distantiation from being, a continuous secretion of the nothing which separates it from its object. Being in itself and consciousness cannot be united in one. They can be united only by the for-itself relapsing into the in-itself and ceasing to be for-itself. Consciousness exists only through a process of negation or nihilation. It is a relation to being, but it is other than being. Arising out of being in itself through a process of self-diremption in being it makes beings (a world) to appear.

5. Being in itself, massive, opaque and without consciousness, is obviously not free. The for-itself however, as separated from being (even if by nothing), cannot be determined by being. It escapes the determination of being in itself and is essentially free. Freedom, according to Sartre, is not a property of human nature or essence. It belongs to the structure of the conscious being. 'What we call freedom is thus impossible to distinguish from the *being* of the 'human reality.'[2] Indeed, in contrast with other things man first exists and then makes his essence. 'Human freedom precedes the essence of man and makes it possible.'[3] Here we have the belief which, Sartre tells us, is common to all existentialists, namely that 'existence precedes essence'.[4] Man is the not-already-made. He makes himself. His course is not predetermined: he does not proceed, as it were, along a pair of rails from which he cannot diverge. He makes himself, not of course in the

---

[1] *L'être et le néant*, p. 715 (English, p. 621).
[2] *Ibid.*, p. 61 (English, p. 25).   [3] *Ibid.*, p. 61 (English, p. 25).
[4] *L'existentialisme est un humanisme*, p. 17 (English, Mairet, p. 26).

sense that he creates himself out of nothing but in the sense that what he becomes depends on himself, on his own choice.

It is not necessary to hold a theory of occult essences, hidden away inside things, in order to find difficulty in the notion of man's existence preceding his essence. In his lecture on existentialism and humanism Sartre explains that in his view there is no God who creates man according to some idea of human nature, so that each human being exemplifies human essence. Well and good, all atheists would obviously agree. But we are concerned here with man himself, not with the question whether or not he was created by God. Quite irrespective of man's relation to God, Sartre maintains that in man existence precedes essence. What then exists in the first instance? The answer is presumably a reality capable of making itself, of defining its own essence. But has this reality no characteristics other than freedom? Whether there is a human nature or essence which is fixed, immutable, static, non-plastic, is another question. The point is that it is very difficult to suppose that there is no human nature in any sense, distinguishable from the natures of lions or roses. Indeed, even if we take literally what Sartre says, it is clear that human beings have a certain common essence or nature, namely that they are the beings which make themselves to be what they become. After all, Sartre can talk about the 'human reality' or about human beings with the conviction that people will recognize what he is talking about. However, we need not really worry very much about Sartre's pronouncements taken in a literal sense. His main contention is clearly that man is wholly free, that whatever he does is the result of free choice, and that what he becomes depends entirely on himself.

At first sight this appears highly implausible. Sartre is not of course talking about reflex acts, which cannot be counted as human actions in the proper sense. But even if we confine our attention to acts which can be ascribed to the for-itself, to consciousness, the contention that we are totally or absolutely free may seem to be quite incompatible with facts. Quite apart from determinist theory, it may be said, our freedom is surely limited by all sorts of internal and external factors. What about the limiting, if not determining influence of physiological and psychological factors, of environment, upbringing, education, of a social pressure which is exercised continuously and generally without our being reflectively aware of it? Again, even if we reject determinism and admit freedom, must we not recognize the fact that people tend to act in accordance with their characters, and that we often believe that we can predict how they will act or react in a given set of circumstances? True, people sometimes act in unexpected ways. But do we not then tend to conclude that we did not know them as well as we thought, and that if we had known them better, we would have made more accurate predictions? The thesis that the human being is totally or absolutely free is surely at variance with the empirical facts and with our ordinary ways of thinking and speaking.

It is hardly necessary to say that Sartre is well aware of such lines of objection and has his answer ready. He sees the for-itself as projecting its own ideal goal and striving to attain it. In the light of this project certain things appear as obstacles. But it depends entirely on my choice whether they appear as obstacles to be overcome, as stepping-stones, so to speak, on the path of my exercise of freedom or whether they appear as insurmountable obstacles in the way. To take a simple example of a kind used by Sartre himself. I desire to take a holiday in Japan. But I lack the money to do so, and consequently cannot go. My lack of money appears to me an insurmountable obstacle only because I have freely formed the project of taking my holiday in Japan. If I freely choose to go to Brighton instead, for which I have the money, my financial situation no longer appears as an obstacle at all, let alone an insurmountable one. Or suppose that I have strong inclinations to act in ways which are incompatible with the ideal which I have projected for myself and my conduct. It is I myself who make these inclinations appear in this or that way. In themselves they constitute a kind of in-itself, a datum, the meaning or bearing of which is constituted by myself. If I give way to them completely, this is because I have chosen to regard them as insurmountable obstacles. And this choice shows in turn that my real project, my actually operative ideal, is not what I told myself that it was, deceiving myself. A man's actually operative ideal is revealed in his actions. It is all very well for Garcin in the play *Huis Clos* (*In Camera*) to claim that he was not actually a coward. As Inez says, it is what one does that reveals what one is, what one has chosen to be. In Sartre's opinion, to be 'overcome' by a passion or emotion, such as fear, is simply a way of choosing, though it is obviously a comparatively unreflective way of reacting to a given situation. Similar remarks can be made about, say, the influence of environment. It is consciousness itself which gives meaning to the environment. To one man it appears as an opportunity, to another as something which, as it were, sucks him down and absorbs him. In both cases it is the man himself who makes his environment appear in a certain way.

Sartre is not of course blind to the fact that we are often unable to alter external factors, in the sense of physically removing them or of removing oneself from them. Practically speaking, I may not be able to alter my place and environmental situation. And even though I can do so in theory and perhaps also in practice, I must be in some place and in some environmental situation. Sartre's contention is that the meaning which such factors have for me is chosen by myself, even if I fail or decline to recognize the fact. Similarly, I cannot alter the past in the sense of bringing it about that what I have done should not have been done. If I betrayed my country, this fact has become frozen, as it were, unalterable. It belongs to myself as *facticité*, as something already made. But, as we have seen, being in itself is not, for Sartre, temporal. It makes no sense to speak of being in itself as comprising succession. Temporality is *'the mode of being* peculiar to being-for-itself'.[1] That is to say, the for-itself is a perpetual flight from what it was towards what it will be, from itself as something made towards itself as something to be made. In reflection this flight grounds the concepts of past, present (as present to being) and future. In other words, the self is beyond its past, what it has made of itself, surpassing it. If it is asked what separates the self in its flight from itself as already made, as its past, the answer is 'nothing'. To say this however is to say that the self negates itself as made and so surpasses it and is beyond it. The self as already made relapses into the condition of the in-itself. And one day, at death, the for-itself becomes wholly something already made and can be regarded purely objectively, as by the psychologist or the historian. But as long as it is the for-itself, it is ahead of itself as past and so cannot be determined by itself as past, as essence.[2] As has been noted, the self cannot alter its past, in the sense of bringing it about that what happened did not happen or that actions

---

[1] *L'être et le néant*, p. 188 (English, p. 142). Temporality is discussed at length in chapter two of the second part of the work. See also the following chapter, on transcendence. Sartre is strongly influenced by Heidegger; but he dismisses and criticizes the views of some other philosophers too.

[2] Sartre makes play with Hegel's saying *Wesen ist, was gewesen ist* (Essence is what has been).

performed were not performed; but it depends on its own choice what meaning the self gives to its past. And it follows that any influence exercised by the past is exercised because one chooses that it should. One cannot be determined by one's past, by oneself as already made.

According to Sartre therefore freedom belongs to the very structure of the for-itself. In this sense one is 'condemned' to be free. We cannot choose to be free or not: we simply are free by the fact that we are consciousnesses. We can however choose to try to deceive ourselves. Man is totally free; he cannot but choose and commit himself in some way; and in whatever way he commits himself, he ideally commits everyone else.[1] The responsibility is entirely his. Awareness of this total freedom and responsibility is accompanied by 'anguish' (*angoisse*), akin to the state of mind experienced by a man standing on a precipice who feels both attracted and repelled by the abyss. Man may therefore try to deceive himself by embracing some form of determinism, by throwing the responsibility on to something apart from his own choice, God or heredity or his upbringing and environment or what not. If however he does so, he is in bad faith. That is to say, the structure of the for-itself is such that a man can be, as it were, in a state of knowing and not-knowing at the same time. Radically, he is aware of his freedom; but he can see himself, for example, as being what he is not (his past), and he then draws a veil over, or masks for himself, the total freedom which gives rise to *angoisse* as a kind of vertigo.[2]

This may sound as though for Sartre all human actions are absolutely unpredictable, as though no intelligible pattern can be found in a man's life. That this is not at all what he means can be seen by recalling what he says in his lecture on existentialism and humanism about the young man who during the second world war asked for advice whether he should remain in France to look after his mother, who was estranged from his collaborating father and whose other son had been killed in 1940, or whether he should attempt to get to England in order to join the Free French forces. Sartre refused to give an answer. And when, in the discussion after

---

[1] If I commit myself to Communism, for example, I choose ideally for others too.
[2] Bad faith is not, for Sartre, the same thing as lying. One can lie to other people, telling them what one knows perfectly well to be untrue. In bad faith or self-deception there is a mixture of knowing and not-knowing, the possibility of which is based on the fact that the for-itself is not what it is (its past) and is what it is not (its possibilities or future).

the lecture, M. Naville said that advice should have been given, Sartre replied not only that the decision was up to the young man and could not be made for him but also that 'I knew moreover what he was going to do, and that is what he did'.[1] In Sartre's opinion the for-itself makes an original or primitive choice, projecting its ideal self, a projection implying a set of values; and particular choices are informed, as it were, by this basic free projection. A man's operative ideal way of course may be different from his professed ideal, from what he says is his ideal. But it is revealed in his actions. The original project *can* be changed, though this demands a radical conversion or change. Apart however from this radical change a man's particular actions implement and reveal his original choice or *projet*. A man's actions are thus free, inasmuch as they are contained in his original free choice; but the more clearly the external observer sees a man's basic *projet* revealed in his actions, so much the more can the observer predict how the man will act in a given situation. Besides, if someone asks advice from a particular man, whose ideas and attitudes are known to him, he has in effect already decided. For he has chosen to hear what he wants to hear.

What we have said about the possibility of conversion obviously implies that different people can have different projects, which reveal themselves in their actions. Underlying all such projects however, there is, according to Sartre, a basic project which belongs to the very structure of *le pour-soi*. The for-itself is, as we have seen, a flight from the past into the future, from itself as something already made towards its possibilities, towards the being which it will be. It is thus a flight from being to being. But the being which it seeks and strives after is not simply *l'en-soi*, devoid of consciousness. For it seeks to preserve itself, the for-itself that is to say. In fine, man reaches out to the ideal project of becoming the in-itself-for-itself, being and consciousness in one. This ideal however corresponds with the concept of God, self-grounded conscious being. We can say therefore that 'to be man is to strive towards being God; or, if one prefers, man is fundamentally the desire to be God.'[2] 'Thus my freedom is the choice of being God, and all my acts, all my projects, translate this choice and reflect it in a thousand and one ways, for there is an infinity of ways of being and of having.'[3] Unfortunately, the idea of God is

---

[1] *L'existentialisme est un humanisme*, p. 141 (English, Mairet, p. 70).
[2] *L'être et le néant*, pp. 653–4 (English, p. 566).   [3] *Ibid.*, p. 689 (English, p. 599).

contradictory. For consciousness is precisely the negation of being. Sartre therefore draws the somewhat pessimistic conclusion that 'man is a useless striving'.[1] The for-itself aspires after Deity; but it inevitably relapses into the opacity of *l'en-soi*. Its flight is terminated not in realization of its basic project but in death.

6. So far we have paid little attention to the plurality of consciousnesses. We cannot follow Sartre into his discussion of the theories of other philosophers, such as Hegel, Husserl and Heidegger,[2] about our knowledge of the existence of other persons. But something at any rate should be said about his own line of thought. And we can draw attention at once to his rejection of the idea that the existence of other minds or consciousnesses is simply inferred from observation of bodies and their movements. If I see a body walking in the street and infer that there is in it a consciousness similar to my own, this is simply conjecture on my part.[3] If the other self lies right outside my experience, I can never prove that what I take to be a human being is not in fact a robot. At best I might claim that whereas my own existence is certain (*Cogito, ergo sum*), the existence of the Other is probable. And this is not a position which Sartre considers tenable. He wishes to show that there is a real sense in which the *Cogito* reveals to me 'the concrete and indubitable presence of this or that concrete Other'.[4] He is not looking for reasons for believing that there are other selves but for the revelation of the Other as a subject. He wishes to show that I encounter the Other directly as a subject which is not myself. And this involves exhibiting a relation between my consciousness and that of the Other, a relation in which the Other is given to me not as an object but as a subject.

It is therefore not a question of deducing the existence of other selves in an *a priori* manner, but of giving a phenomenological analysis of the sort of experience in which the Other is revealed to me as subject. And Sartre's line of thought is perhaps best illustrated by summarizing one of the examples which he actually gives. Complaints are sometimes made that Sartre does not offer proofs of what he asserts. Even if however such complaints are sometimes justified, it should be remembered that in a context

---

[1] *Une passion inutile. Ibid.*, p. 708 (English, p. 615).
[2] In Sartre's opinion Husserl cannot escape solipsism, and Hegel's theory, though chronologically prior, is much superior. Heidegger made further progress.
[3] There is indeed the possibility of embracing behaviourism. But this is not a solution to whch Sartre is prepared to give favourable consideration.
[4] *L'être et le néant*, p. 308 (English, p. 251).

such as the present one it is in his view sufficient 'proof' if attention is drawn to situations in which the Other is clearly revealed
as a subject to one's consciousness, within one's experience. If it is
said that other people are always objects for oneself and never
subjects, Sartre tries to refute the statement by giving examples
of situations in which it is falsified. Whether he is successful or not,
there does not seem to be anything disreputable in this procedure,
except perhaps in the eyes of those who think that philosophers
should assert only what they have deduced *a priori* from some
unquestionable point of departure.

Let us imagine that I am squatting down in the corridor of a
hotel looking through a keyhole. I am not thinking of myself at
all; my attention is absorbed in what is going on inside a room.
I am in a state of pre-reflexive consciousness. Suddenly I become
aware that an employee or a fellow guest of the hotel is standing
and watching me. I am at once ashamed. The *cogito* arises, in the
sense that I become reflexively aware of myself as object, as
object, that is to say, of another consciousness as subject. The
other's field of consciousness, so to speak, invades mine, reducing
me to an object. I experience the Other as a free conscious subject
through his look (*regard*), whereby he makes me an object for
another. The reason why common sense opposes an unshakable
resistance to solipsism is that the Other is given to me as an evident
presence which I cannot derive from myself and which cannot
seriously be doubted. The consciousness of the Other is not of
course given to me in the sense that it is mine; but the fact of the
Other is given in an incontestable manner in the reduction of
myself to an object for a transcendence which is not mine.

In view of the way in which Sartre tackles the subject of one's
encounter with the Other it is not surprising to find him saying
that 'conflict is the original meaning of being-for-others'.[1] If the
Other's look reduces me to an object, I can try either to absorb
the Other's freedom while leaving it intact or to reduce the Other
to an object. The first project can be seen in love, which expresses
a desire 'to possess a freedom as freedom',[2] whereas the second can
be seen in, for example, indifference, sexual desire and, in an
extreme form, sadism. Both projects are however doomed to
failure. I cannot absorb another person's freedom while leaving
it intact; he or she always eludes me, as the other self necessarily
transcends myself, and the look which reduces me to objectivity

---

[1] *Ibid.*, p. 431 (English, p. 364).   [2] *Ibid.*, p. 434 (English, p. 367).

is always reborn.[1] As for the reduction of the Other to an object,
this can be completely achieved through destruction, killing; but
this is a frustration of the project of reducing a subject as such to
the condition of an object. As long as there is another for-itself, the
reduction cannot be carried through; and if it is carried through,
there is no longer a for-itself.

Sartre's preoccupation with the existential analysis of phenomena such as masochism and sadism naturally gives the impression that he regards love as doomed to frustration and that he is
not prepared to recognize genuine community, the we-consciousness. He does not however intend to deny that there is such a
thing as an experience of 'we'. For example, during a theatrical
performance or a football match there is or can be what Sartre
describes as a non-thetic we-consciousness. That is to say, though
each consciousness is absorbed in the object (the spectacle), the
spectators at a cup final, for instance, are certainly co-spectators,
even though they are not reflecting on the we-subject. The non-
thetic we-consciousness shows itself clearly enough in a spontaneous outburst of applause.

On the level of the reflexive consciousness however the emphasis
is laid by Sartre on the we-subject as arising in confrontation with
Others. Consider, for example, the situation of an oppressed class.
It experiences itself or can come to experience itself as an Us-
object for the oppressors, as an object of the look of a They. If
subsequently the oppressed class becomes a self conscious revolutionary class, the We-subject arises, which turns the tables on the
oppressors by transforming them into an object. There can therefore perfectly well be a we-consciousness in which one group
confronts another.

What however about humanity as a whole? According to
Sartre, as one would indeed expect, the human race as a whole
cannot become conscious of itself as an Us-object without postulating the existence of a being which is the subject of a look comprising all members of the race. Humanity can become an Us-
object only in the posited presence of the being who looks at but
can never be looked at. 'Thus the limiting concept of humanity
(as the totality of the Us-object) and the limiting concept of God
imply one another and are correlative.'[2] As for the experience of a

---

[1] In connection with this project Sartre examines devious ways, such as
masochism, of wooing, as it were, another's freedom.
[2] *L'être et le néant*, p. 495 (English, p. 423).

universal We-subject, Sartre insists that this is a purely psycho-logical or subjective event in a single consciousness. One can indeed conceive the ideal of a We-subject representing all humanity; but this ideal is conceived by a single consciousness or by a plurality of consciousnesses which remain separate. The actual constitution of a self-conscious intersubjective totality remains a dream. Sartre can therefore conclude that 'The essence of the relations between consciousnesses is not the *Mitsein*; it is con-flict.'[1] The for-itself cannot do away with the basic dilemma. It must attempt to turn the Other into an object or allow itself to be objectified by the Other. As neither of these projects can be really successful, it can hardly be claimed that *Being and Nothingness* provides a promising basis for any such concept as Teilhard de Chardin's theory of a hyper-personal consciousness.

7. We have noted that according to Sartre humanity as a whole can become for itself an Us-object only if the existence of an omnipotent and all-seeing God is posited. And if there were a God, humanity could become a we-subject, in striving, for instance, to master the world in defiance of God. But Sartre does not believe that there is a God. In fact he is convinced that there cannot be a God, if by 'God' we mean an infinite self-conscious Being.[2] He does indeed represent belief in God as the result of an hypostatizing of 'the look' (*le regard*), a point of view which finds expression in *Les mots*[3] and in the account in *The Reprieve* of Daniel's conversion, as well as in *Being and Nothingness*, where Sartre refers to Kafka's *The Trial* and remarks that 'God is here only the concept of the Other pushed to the limit'.[4] This account of the origin of man's idea of God, if taken simply by itself, would leave open the possibility of there being a God. For all we know, there might be an all-embracing 'look'. But Sartre also argues, as we have already noted, that the concept of God is self-contra-dictory, inasmuch as it tries to unite two mutually exclusive concepts, that of being in itself (*l'en-soi*) and that of the for-itself

---

[1] *Ibid.*, p. 502 (English, p. 429). *Mitsein*, to be with or being with. Sartre's contention is that Heidegger's *Mitsein* is a psychological experience which does not reveal a basic ontological relation between consciousnesses.

[2] It is sometimes said that Sartre denies the existence of God only as conceived by theists. But such remarks are not so important as the people who make them seem to think that they are. If, for example, we care to call *l'en-soi* God, then of course Sartre does not deny the existence of God. But given the ordinary use of terms in the West, it would be extremely misleading or confusing to say that Sartre believes in God because he postulates the existence of *l'en-soi*.

[3] *Words* (Penguin edition), p. 65.

[4] *L'être et le néant*, p. 324 (English, p. 266). Cf. *ibid.*, p. 341 (p. 281).

(*le pour-soi*). It is indeed pretty obvious that if consciousness is the negation of being in itself, there cannot be a self-grounded and non-derived consciousness, and that the concept *l'en-soi-pour-soi* is self-contradictory.

It is hardly necessary to say that the validity of this logical demonstration of atheism depends on the validity of Sartre's analysis of his two basic concepts. And here there is a formidable difficulty. For the more he assigns to consciousness the active role of conferring meanings on things and constituting an intelligible world, so much the less plausible does it become to represent consciousness as a negation of being. It is true of course that being in itself is depicted as self-identical in a sense which excludes consciousness, so that the rise of consciousness can be represented as a negation of being. But the contention that being as so depicted is the Absolute, in so far as there is an Absolute, depends for its validity on the further contention that *le pour-soi* not only involves a negation or 'nihilation' of being as depicted by Sartre but is also in itself a negation, not-being. And it is very difficult to see how this position can be maintained, if consciousness is as active as Sartre says that it is. In other words, the force of his demonstration of the self-contradictory nature of theism seems to depend on the assumption that being in itself must be without consciousness, an assumption which requires, if it is to be justified, a proof that consciousness is not-being. And this cannot be proved in terms of the assumption which it is used to justify. In the long run Sartre appears simply to assume or to assert that infra-conscious being, when stripped of all the intelligibility conferred on it by consciousness, is absolute being.

However this may be, what role does atheism play in the philosophy of Sartre? Sometimes he says that it does not make any difference whether God exists or not. But what he seems to mean by this is that in either case man is free, inasmuch as he *is* his freedom. For freedom belongs to the very structure of the for-itself. In *The Flies* (*Les mouches*) therefore, when Zeus says that he created Orestes free in order that he might serve him (Zeus), Orestes replies that once he had been created free, he ceased to belong to Zeus and becme independent, able to defy the god if he so wished. In this sense it makes no difference, according to Sartre, whether God does or does not exist. But it by no means follows that atheism plays no important role in Sartrian existentialism. Indeed, Sartre himself has explicitly stated that it does.

In his lecture on existentialism and humanism he asserts that 'existentialism is nothing else but an attempt to draw all the conclusions from a coherent atheist position'.[1] A conclusion which he mentions is that if God does not exist, values depend entirely on man and are his creation. 'Dostoievsky wrote, "if God did not exist, everything would be permitted". This is the point of departure of existentialism.'[2] Sartre could of course refer also to Nietzsche, who had no use for the idea that one could reject belief in God and still maintain belief in absolute values or in a universally obligatory moral law.

Sartre's position can be expressed in this way. Man is free; and this means that it depends on man what he makes of himself. He cannot however avoid making something of himself.[3] And what he makes of himself implies an operative ideal, a basic project, which he has freely chosen or projected for himself. It is not therefore a question of man being under an *a priori* moral obligation to choose his values. For he does so in any case. Even if he endorses, so to speak, a set of values or of ethical norms which he receives from society, this endorsement is an act of choice. The values become *his* values only through his own act. This would apply to acceptance of commands and prohibitions which the religious believer conceived as emanating from God. God could indeed punish a man for disobedience; but if man is free, it depends on him whether or not he accepts the divine commands as his ethical norms. From this point of view therefore we can say that it makes no difference whether there is a God or not. Even if God existed, man would still have to pursue goals which he had chosen. At the same time, if there is no God, there can obviously be no fore-ordained divine plan. There can be no one common ideal of human nature which man has been created to realize through his actions. He is thrown back entirely on himself, and he cannot justify his choice of an ideal by appealing to a divine plan for the human race. In this sense the existence or non-existence of God does make a difference. It is true that if a man accepts the ethical norms which he believes to have been promulgated by God, this implies that he has freely projected his ideal as that of a God-fearing man. The point is however that if in fact there is no God who has created man for a purpose, to attain a determinate end or

---

[1] *L'existentialisme est un humanisme*, p. 94 (English, Mairet, p. 56).
[2] *Ibid.*, p. 36 (English, p. 33).
[3] Even if a man commits suicide, he has made something of himself.

goal, there is no given moral order to which man can appeal to justify his choice. The notion that there are absolute values subsisting in some celestial realm of their own, apart from a divine mind, is quite unacceptable to Sartre. It may indeed be the case that he could have approached the matter in a simpler way by interpreting 'values' simply in terms of the act of evaluation. But he would still insist of course that if there is no God, there is no possibility of justifying man's act of evaluation, say as 'rational', by appealing to a divinely determined ideal of human nature which is the measure of self-fulfilment or self-realization. To be sure, Sartre himself sees man as striving after the realization of a basic project, that of becoming *l'en-soi-pour-soi* or God. But he adds that the project is doomed to frustration, inasmuch as the concept of the unity of being in itself and consciousness is a self-contradictory concept. And in this sense the (necessary) non-existence of God makes a difference.

Sartre is anxious to dissipate the impression that he is concerned with promoting moral anarchy or encouraging a purely capricious choice of values and ethical norms. He argues therefore that to choose between *x* and *y* is to assert the value of what we choose (that *x*, for example, is better than *y*), and that 'nothing can be good for us without being good for all'.[1] That is to say, in choosing a value one chooses ideally for all. If I project a certain image of myself as I choose to be, I am projecting an ideal image of man as such. If I will my own freedom, I must will the freedom of all other men. In other words, the judgment of value is intrinsically universal, not of course in the sense that other people necessarily accept my judgment but in the sense that to assert a value is to assert it ideally as a value for everyone. Sartre can therefore claim that he is not encouraging irresponsible choice. For in choosing values and deciding on ethical norms 'I am responsible for myself and for all'.[2]

The validity of the contention that in choosing a value one chooses ideally for all men is perhaps not so clear as Sartre seems to think that it is. Is it logically inadmissible for me to commit myself to a course of action without claiming that anyone else in the same situation ought to commit himself in the same way? It may be so; but further discussion would be appropriate. Indeed, a philosophical ethics would have to consist, on Sartre's premises,

---

[1] *L'existentialisme est un humanisme*, pp. 25–6 (English, p. 29).
[2] *Ibid.*, p. 27 (English, p. 30).

in an analysis of the judgment of value and of the moral judgment as such. It is true of course that within the frame of reference of his personally chosen values Sartre could develop a moral philosophy with concrete content. And within this frame of reference he can pass judgment on other people's attitudes and actions. But his personally chosen system of ethics could not legitimately be presented as entailed by existentialism, not, that is to say, if existentialism illuminates possibilities of choice while leaving the actual choice entirely to the individual. It has indeed appeared to some readers that Sartre really regards freedom as an absolute value, and that the outline of an ethical system could be deduced from existentialist premises. In this case however existentialism would stand in need of some revision. The idea of there being a common human nature would reappear.[1] And it is perhaps not surprising that Sartre denies that he looks on freedom as an absolute value. Freedom makes possible the creation or choice of values; but it is not itself a value. It can hardly be claimed however that Sartre successfully avoids making statements which imply that recognition by the for-itself of its total freedom and realization of this freedom in action are intrinsically valuable.

[1] It appears in any case of course, given Sartre's analysis of the common basic structure of the for-itself. His attempt to admit a universality of condition (such as being-in-the-world) while denying a universal human nature is not conspicuously successful.

CHAPTER XVII

THE EXISTENTIALISM OF SARTRE (2)

Sartre and Marxism — The aims of the Critique *— Individual praxis — The anti-dialectic and the domination of the practico-inert — The group and its fate — Critical comments.*

1. SARTRIAN existentialism as outlined in the last chapter by no means excludes personal self-commitment in a given historical situation. Provided therefore that Sartre did not claim that the values which he was defending were absolute in a metaphysical sense, there was no incompatibility between his existentialist philosophy and his support of the Resistance in the second world war. In regard however to his support of Marxism the situation is more complex. If it were simply a question of collaborating with a political Party with a view to realizing certain social ends which were considered desirable, such collaboration would hardly be incompatible with existentialism from a logical point of view, even if we felt inclined to question the wisdom of a champion of human freedom making common cause with a Party whose dictatorial ways are notorious. Marxism however is a philosophy with doctrines, not to say dogmas, which cannot be reconciled with Sartrian existentialism. For example, whereas Sartre represents the for-itself as the source of all meaning, Marxism depicts history as being in itself an intelligible process, a process which can be discerned by the human mind and which, when stated in the form of dialectical materialism, represents scientific knowledge rather than metaphysical speculation. The question arises therefore to what extent Sartre has come to accept Marxism as a philosophy, and, if he accepts it, whether he has abandoned existentialism or tries to combine it with Marxism.

In 1946 Sartre published in *Les temps modernes* a long article on materialism and revolution.[1] In it he accepts Marx's view of man as self-alienated and of the need for revolution if this alienation is to be overcome. He objects however to Marxist materialism. He is indeed prepared to admit that, historically speaking, materialism

---

[1] Reprinted in *Situations III* (1949). An English translation is included in *Literary and Philosophical Essays.*

has been 'bound up with the revolutionary attitude',[1] and that from the short-term view of the politician or the political activist it is 'the *only myth* which suits revolutionary requirements'.[2] At the same time Sartre insists that this is precisely what materialism is, namely a myth and not the expression of scientific knowledge or of absolute truth. Further, dogmatic materialism makes it impossible to understand man as the free self-transcending subject. To be sure, the Marxists protest that their materialism is dialectical and different from old-fashioned materialism. And in practice they obviously call for and rely on man's free activity. This simply shows however that even if materialism has a temporary pragmatic value, a genuine philosophy of revolution must discard this myth. For such a philosophy must be able to accommodate and explain the movement of transcendence, in the sense of the human subject transcending the present social order towards a society which does not yet exist, which is therefore not clearly perceived, and which man seeks to create but which will not come about automatically or inevitably. This possibility of transcending a given situation and grasping it in a perspective which unites understanding and action 'is precisely what we call freedom'.[3] And it is this which materialism is incapable of explaining.

The article to which we have been referring certainly reads like a sustained attack on Marxism and, by implication at any rate, as a defence of existentialism. Sartre asserts however that 'the Communist Party is the only revolutionary party',[4] and in a subsequently added note he explains that his criticism was directed not so much against Marx himself as against 'the Marxist scholasticism of 1949'.[5] In other words, Sartre looks on the Communist Party as the spearhead of social revolution and as the organ of man's transcendence in a given situation. And in his articles on the Communists and peace in *Les temps modernes* (1952 f.) he defends the Party and exhorts workers to join it. He has not himself joined it however, and he has continued to believe that Marxism has become a dogmatism which stands in need of rejuvenation through a rediscovery of man as the free active subject. As long as dialectical materialism retains its present form, existentialism must continue to exist as a distinct line of thought. If however

---

[1] *Literary and Philosophical Essays*, p. 207. The implication is that theism, for example, is linked with a conservative outlook.
[2] *Ibid.*, p. 208.   [3] *Ibid.*, p. 220.   [4] *Ibid.*, p. 238.   [5] *Ibid.*, p. 185, *n* 1.

Marxism were rejuvenated by basing itself on man rather than on Nature, existentialism would cease to exist as a distinct philosophy. This point of view finds expression in Sartre's *Question de méthode*,[1] which is prefaced to the first volume of his *Critique de la raison dialectique*.[2] In no age, according to Sartre, is there more than one living philosophy, a living philosophy being the means by which the ascending class comes to consciousness of itself in an historical situation, whether clearly or obscurely, directly or indirectly.[3] Between the seventeenth and twentieth centuries Sartre finds only three epochs of real philosophical creation. 'There is the "moment" of Descartes and of Locke, that of Kant and of Hegel, finally that of Marx.'[4] The philosophy of Marx is thus the living philosophy of our time; and it cannot be surpassed as long as the situation out of which it arose remains unsurpassed.[5] Unfortunately, the philosophy of Marx has ceased to grow and is affected with sclerosis. 'The open concepts of Marxism have become closed; they are no more *keys*, interpretative schemata; they are asserted in themselves, as already achieved knowledge.'[6] In Kantian terminology, regulative ideas have been transformed into constitutive ideas; and heuristic schemes have become dogmas imposed by authority. This has meant that the Marxists have misrepresented historical events, such as the Hungarian revolution of 1956, by forcing them into a rigid theoretical framework,[7] while the heuristic principle of seeking the universal in its particulars has been converted into the terrorist principle 'liquidate particularity',[8] a liquidation which under Stalin at any rate assumed an obviously physical form.

A living philosophy is for Sartre a process of 'totalization'. That is to say, it is not a totality or finished whole, like a fully constructed machine, but rather a unifying or synthesizing process,

---

[1] Translated by H. Barnes as *Search for a Method* (New York, 1963).
[2] Paris, 1960. This work will be referred to in footnotes as *C.R.D.*
[3] For example, the consciousness of the bourgeoisie is said to have been expressed obscurely 'in the image of universal man proposed by Kantianism' (*C.R.D.*, p. 15).
[4] *C.R.D.*, p. 17.
[5] According to Sartre, any attempt to go beyond Marxism is in effect a return to a pre-Marxist position.
[6] *C.R.D.*, p. 28.
[7] It is of course true that events such as the Hungarian revolution and the liberalization of the régime in Czechoslovakia under Dubcek were misrepresented by theoreticians and publicists of the Soviet Union. But it is also pretty obvious that the actions of the Soviet authorities were influenced by other factors besides ideological blinkers.
[8] *C.R.D.*, p. 28.

bringing together past and present and oriented to a future
which is not determined in advance. The philosopher is within an
ongoing process, and he cannot take the place of God and see all
history as a totality. This is however precisely what the Marxists
try to do when they speak of the future as assured and of the
inevitable march of history towards a certain goal. Moreover, they
thus make nonsense of human freedom and creativity, even though
their political activism demands and presupposes human freedom.

A natural conclusion to draw from Sartre's criticism is that
Marxism is certainly not the living philosophy of our time, even
if it is the official ideology of a powerful social-political movement.
Sartre however will not allow that the sclerosis of Marxism is the
result of senility. 'Marxism is still young, almost in infancy; it has
hardly begun to develop. It remains therefore the philosophy of
our time.'[1] The original inspiration of Marxism has indeed been
forgotten by theoreticians of the Communist Party. And if the
Marxist follows Engels in finding the dialectic at work in Nature
itself, quite independently of man, and regards human history as
the prolongation of natural processes which develop inevitably,
man is reduced to the condition of a passive instrument of an
hypostatized dialectic. Though however Marxism has been
distorted, it is capable of rediscovering its original inspiration and
its basic humanism. Sartre quotes the well known statement by
Engels in a letter to Marx that it is human beings themselves who
make their history, though they do so in a situation which conditions their activity.[2] He uses texts of this kind to support his contention that Marxism can rediscover within itself the idea of man
as defined by his project, by his movement of transcendence
towards his possibilities, towards a future which, though conditioned by the present, can be realized only through man's free
action.

If Marxism returns to its original inspiration and rediscovers the
human dimension within itself, 'existentialism will no longer
have any reason to exist.'[3] That is to say, it will cease to be a
distinct line of thought and will be absorbed, preserved and
surpassed in 'the totalizing movement of philosophy',[4] in the one
living and developing philosophy of our time. Marxism is the only
philosophy which really expresses the consciousness of man living
in a world of 'scarcity' (rareté), in a world in which there is an
unequal distribution of material goods and which is therefore

[1] Ibid., p. 29.   [2] Ibid., p. 60.   [3] Ibid., p. 111.   [4] Ibid., p. 111.

characterized by conflict and class antagonism. And a humanized Marxism (an existentialized Marxism, one might say) would be the only genuine philosophy of revolution. If however the social revolution were to be realized and a society were to come into being from which scarcity and class antagonism were absent, Marxism would have fulfilled its destiny and would be succeeded by another 'totalizing' philosophy, a philosophy of freedom.[1] In other words, to say that Marxism is the one living philosophy of our time is not to say that it is the final philosophy for all future time.

2. We have been referring to the essay on method (*Question de méthode*), which was originally entitled *Existentialism and Marxism*. Sartre tells us[2] that though this essay was written before the *Critique of Dialectical Reason* and has been used as an introduction to it, the *Critique* is prior from the logical point of view, inasmuch as it provides the critical foundations of the essay on method. This does not alter the fact that the essay is considerably easier to read than the *Critique* itself, which is long, rambling and turgid.

In the *Critique* Sartre is concerned with dialectical thinking as the only way of understanding history. He makes a distinction between analytical and dialectical rationalism. The analytical reason, represented by eighteenth-century rationalism and by positivism, adopts the position of a spectator, of an external judge. Further, it tries to explain new facts by reducing them to old facts; and it is thus incapable of understanding the emergence of novelty. The dialectical reason however, which moves through thesis, antithesis or negation, and the negation of the negation, does not reduce the new to the old; nor does it attempt to explain the whole by reducing it to its constituent parts. It expresses an irreversible movement, oriented to the emergence of novelty. It can be described, Sartre tells us, as 'the absolute intelligibility of an irreducible novelty *in so far* as it is an irreducible novelty'.[3] It understands the 'parts', such as particular historical situations and social groups, not in the light of a totality, in the sense of a finished or complete whole, but in terms of an ongoing process of totalization, oriented to the new.

Sartre agrees therefore with the Marxists that the movement of

---

[1] Sartre is referring of course to freedom from the slavery of material production as hitherto experienced, not to freedom as the structure of *le pour-soi*. For the latter is an ever-present reality.

[2] *C.R.D.*, p. 9.   [3] *Ibid.*, p. 147.

history can be understood only by dialectical thinking. He finds fault with them however for not grounding the dialectical method in an *a priori* manner. He himself proposes to establish *a priori* 'the heuristic value of the dialectical method, when it is applied to the sciences of man, and the necessity, whatever may be the fact envisaged, provided that it is *human*, of setting it in the ongoing totalization (*dans la totalisation en cours*) and of understanding it in this context.'[1] For example, Sartre wishes to grasp, in and through the real alienations of concrete history, alienation as an '*a priori* possibility of human *praxis*'.[2] In the first volume of the *Critique* he is not concerned with adding to our knowledge of historical facts, nor with playing the part of a sociologist by studying the development of particular societies or groups. Rather is he concerned with asking 'on what conditions is the knowledge of *a history* possible? Within what limits can the connections which are brought to light be *necessary*? What is dialectical rationality, what are its limits and its foundations'?[3] Sartre therefore entitles his work a *Critique* of the dialectical reason, the term being obviously suggested by Kant's use of the term *Kritik*. Indeed, in one place Sartre remarks that, to 'parody' Kant, his aim might be described as that of laying the foundations of a 'Prolegomena for every future anthropology'.[4]

Mention of Kant can however be misleading. For though Sartre is concerned with the conditions of possibility for history being an intelligible but not determined process, he does not regard his inquiry as purely formal, as a reflection by the mind on a pattern of thought which it imposes on a process which is not itself dialectical in structure. The word 'dialectic', he remarks, can be used in two ways, as meaning either a method, a movement of thought, or a movement in the object of thought. He claims however that the two meanings are simply two aspects of one process. The dialectical reason has indeed to reflect on itself. For it 'can be criticized, in the sense in which Kant understood the term',[5] only by itself. But to grasp the basic structures of dialectical thought is also to grasp the basic structures of the movement of history. The dialectical reason's reflection on itself can thus be seen as history becoming conscious of itself.

What Sartre tries to do in the first volume of the *Critique* is to

---

[1] *Ibid.*, p. 153.
[2] *Ibid.*, p. 154. By *praxis* Sartre means human action. Philosophy as oriented to the future, is itself a form of action and can thus be subsumed under *praxis*.
[3] *Ibid.*, p. 135.   [4] *Ibid.*, p. 153.   [5] *Ibid.*, p. 120.

reconcile the thesis that it is man who makes history, and so the dialectic, with recognition of the fact that human activity is subject to and limited by antecedent conditions to such an extent that he can appear to be 'undergoing' the dialectic rather than making it. To put the matter in another way, Sartre is determined to preserve his existentialist view of man as a free agent, defined by his project, while he is also determined to adopt and justify the Marxist interpretation of history as a dialectical process. His determination to make human freedom the basic factor in history means that he cannot accept any mechanistic interpretation of history which would imply that human beings are simply puppets or instruments of a dialectical law which operates in Nature apart from man and continues to govern human history. In the *Critique* he does not seem prepared to state roundly that talk about a dialectical process in Nature in itself, apart from man, is nonsensical. But he makes it clear that the claim that there is such a process is for him no more than an unverified hypothesis which should be disregarded. And he confines his attention to human history, insisting that it is made by man, whereas Nature 'in itself' is obviously not man's creation. At the same time Sartre's determination to do justice to the contention of Marx and Engels that human activity is subject to antecedent conditions means that he has to place a greater emphasis than in *Being and Nothingness* on the influence of man's situation. Man exists, for example, in a material environment; and though he works on the environment, the environment (or Nature not 'in itself' but in relation to man) acts on him and conditions his activity. Within limits man can change his environment; but then the changed environment constitutes a new objectivity, a new set of antecedent conditions which influence and limit human activity. In other words, the relationship between man and Nature is a changing dialectical relationship. And analogous remarks can be made about the relationship between man and his social environment. Societies and groups are created by man; but every human being is born into a social environment, and the fact of social pressure is undeniable, even though man is capable of transcending a given social situation in view of a projected goal which, if realized, constitutes a new objectivity or set of antecedent conditions.

The reconciliation of the two theses, that man makes history and that his activity is subject to and limited by antecedent conditions, can be found, according to Sartre, only by discovering the roots of the whole dialectical process of history in human *praxis* or action. Sartre tells us that in the first volume of the *Critique* he looks 'exclusively for the intelligible foundations of a structural anthropology, in so far, it is understood, as these synthetic structures constitute the very condition of an ongoing totalization which is perpetually oriented.'[1] He treats first of what he calls the constituting dialectic. This is grasped in and through reflection on the individual's *praxis*, on his productive work; and it is in fact the dialectic of the worker, considered as an individual. Sartre then tries to show how the constituting dialectic gives rise to its negation, the anti-dialectic, in which man becomes a prisoner of his own product, of the 'practico-inert'. This is of course the sphere of alienation, the sphere in which human beings are united in 'collections', like the individuals who are brought together by being concerned with the maintenance and running of a certain machine. Thirdly, the transition from the negation to the negation of the negation is effected by the constitution of the 'group', in which human beings are united by sharing a common end or project and transcend their given situation towards possibilities to be realized through concerted free action. The third phase therefore, described as the constituted dialectic, is in effect the dialectic of the group. The whole process, in all its phases, is rooted in human *praxis*, in man's productive action. And if we can say that in the dialectical reason's self-reflection history becomes conscious of itself, this means that human *praxis* becomes conscious of itself and of its dialectical developments as free activity which presupposes antecedent conditions.

In the first volume of the *Critique* therefore Sartre pursues what he describes as a regressive method, working back to the underlying dialectical structure of the relations between man and Nature and between human beings. He inquires into the fundamental structures which make it possible to claim with truth that it is men who make history but that they do so as the basis of antecedent conditions. It is clear however that human action can have results which are different from those envisaged by the agents. A group may carry out concerted action which appears as successful to the members of the group, though the long-term result, the 'diachronic' effect as Sartre puts it, may be different from what the group intended or extended. To take a simple example, 'the victory of 1918 creates in the common field of

[1] *Ibid.*, p. 156.

Europe the possibility of the defeat of 1940.'[1] It may thus appear that in the long run it is not so much a question of men freely making history as of their suffering or undergoing a necessity which is beyond their control. There is need therefore for use of the method of 'synthetic progression' to unify the multiplicity of human actions or, rather, to show how they ceaselessly 'totalize' themselves in an intelligible but open-ended historical process. And Sartre informs us that in the promised second volume of the *Critique* he 'will try to establish that there is *one* human history, with *one* truth and *one* intelligibility'.[2]

The development of an overall philosophy of history is not quite what one would expect from the author of *Being and Nothingness*. But critical comment is best left until we have outlined, in an inevitably brief and sketchy manner, some of the lines of thought contained in the one published volume of the *Critique*. For the moment it is sufficient to note that Sartre is determined to prove a thesis, to justify the view that Marxism is the one living philosophy of our time, even if it needs rejuvenation through an injection of existentialism.

3. As we have already indicated, Sartre begins by considering the action or *praxis* of the individual. For if it is men who make history, and if history is a dialectical totalization of the actions of individuals, it is essential to show that human action possesses an inherently dialectical structure. '*The whole of the historical dialectic rests on individual praxis which is already dialectical*, that is to say in the measure in which action is in itself a negating transcendence of a contradiction, a determination of a present totalization in the name of a future totality, a real and efficacious working of matter.'[3]

This tiresome jargon is used to refer to quite ordinary situations. Sartre assumes the existence of man as a living organism. That is to say, the organic negates the inorganic. Man however experiences need (*besoin*). He needs food, for example. And this need is said to be a negation of the negation, in the sense that the organism transcends itself towards its material environment. By doing so it totalizes its environment as the field of possibilities, as the field, that is to say, in which it seeks to find satisfaction of its needs and so to conserve itself as an organic totality in the future. The action proceeding from the need is a working of matter.

By totalizing his environment in this way man constitutes it as

[1] *Ibid.*, p. 635.   [2] *Ibid.*, p. 635.   [3] *Ibid.*, pp. 165–6.

a passive totality. 'Matter revealed as a passive totality by an organic being which endeavours to find therein its being, here is Nature in its first form.'[1] Nature however, as so constituted, reacts on man by revealing itself as a menace to the life of the human organism, as an obstacle and threat of possible death. In this sense Nature negates man. Sartre preserves the point of view maintained in *Being and Nothingness* that it is consciousness which confers meaning on being-in-itself. For it is the organism's transcending towards its natural environment which reveals this environment as threatening or menacing. Nature's negating of man is thus due to man himself. This does not however alter the fact that Nature does appear as a menace or a threat of destruction. And to protect himself man has, according to Sartre, to make himself 'inert matter'. That is to say he has to act on matter by means of a tool, whether it is a tool in the ordinary sense or his own body treated as a tool. This action however is inspired by a *projet* and thus has a mediating function between present and future, in the sense that man's acting on his material environment is directed to his own conservation, as a present totality, in the future. 'Praxis is at first nothing else but the relation of the organism as an exterior future to the present organism as a threatened totality.'[2] It is therefore through his productive labour, and so through the mediation of Nature, that man totalizes himself, linking himself as a present totality to himself as a future possibility, as the goal of his movement of transcendence. According to Sartre the relations between man and his material environment thus take the form of 'dialectical circularity',[3] man being 'mediated' by things to the extent in which things are 'mediated' by man.

Even on the level of individual praxis however there are obviously relations between individuals, though the genuine group does not belong to this phase of the dialectic. Consider, for example, two workers who agree on an exchange of products. Each voluntarily becomes a means for the other, in and through his product. And we can say that each recognizes the other's *praxis* and project. But unity does not go further than this. In a world of scarcity of course one man represents a menace or threat to the other. But this situation leads to conflict rather than to genuine unity, even if one man succeeds in compelling another to serve as an instrument for the attainment of his own end. In Sartre's view

[1] *Ibid.*, p. 167.   [2] *Ibid.*, p. 168.   [3] *Ibid.*, p. 165.

'unity comes from outside',[1] a theme already familiar from *Being and Nothingness*. In some cases unification is affected simply in the consciousness of the third party. One of the examples given by Sartre is that of a bourgeois on holiday, who watches from a window two workers, one working on a road, the other in a garden. The watcher negates them by differentiating himself, as a bourgeois on holiday, from the two workers, but by doing so he unites them in terms of their praxis. This unification has of course a foundation in fact, inasmuch as the two men are actually workers; but the unification takes place in the mind of the watcher, not in the minds of the labourers who are *ex hypothesi* unaware of one another. In other cases however the unification (or totalization) is effected in a plurality of consciousnesses through the mediation of a third party. For example, in the presence of the exploiting boss a we-consciousness, that of the exploited, can arise in the minds of the workmen.

As has been noted, explicit treatment of such themes as exploitation does not really belong to consideration of the first phase of the dialectic. For individual praxis as such does not involve either exploitation or the formation of a group. At the same time the possibility of such developments is prefigured in individual praxis. And this is the point which Sartre wishes to make. He is arguing that the conditions of possibility of the dialectic of history, interpreted of course on Marxian lines, are present from the start in individual praxis, so that human action is the foundation of the whole dialectic. To put the matter in another way, he wishes to maintain the position of *le pour-soi* in *Being and Nothingness* as the giver of meaning. For example, Sartre argues that in Nature in itself there is no scarcity. Scarcity is present in Nature only through the mediation of man, in relation, that is to say, to human needs. Once present in the material environment, making Nature appear as a threat to man's life, scarcity then rebounds, so to speak, onto man himself, making his fellow men appear to the individual as a threat. This situation in turn makes possible not only conflict, violence[2] and exploitation but also the forming of genuine groups. Thus while he finds room for Marx's concept of man as standing in a dialectical relationship to his environment before the development of conflict and class antagonism, at any rate in a logical sense of 'before', Sartre can also assert that the conditions of possibility of the whole dialectic of history are

[1] *Ibid.*, p. 197.   [2] For Sartre violence is interiorized scarcity.

precontained in man's free action, and that history is thus made by man.

4. When speaking of scarcity Sartre refers to scarcity of products, scarcity of tools, scarcity of workers, scarcity of consumers. The basic reference however is to shortage of the goods required for the maintenance of human life. Scarcity in this sense grounds the possibility of social division into haves and have-nots or at any rate into consumers and sub-consumers, and so of class division. Such division can of course take place as the result of war, when one population is compelled to work for another. But what is inevitable is that in a world of scarcity there should be class divisions of some kind. As for determinate social relations and structures, Sartre accepts the Marxian doctrine that they depend on the mode of production. 'The essential discovery of Marxism is that work as an historical reality and as the utilization of determinate tools in an already determinate social and material milieu is the real basis of the organization of social relations. This discovery *can no more* be questioned. . . . In the milieu of scarcity all the structures of a determinate society rests on its mode of production.'[1] At the same time Sartre tries to go back behind social division and struggle, the negation of man by man, 'the negation of man by matter considered as the organization of his being outside himself in Nature.'[2]

The point of view which finds expression in this typical specimen of Sartrian jargon can be illustrated in the following way. To overcome scarcity man acts on his material environment and invents tools to do so. But then matter worked on by man (*matière œuvrée*) turns against man, becoming 'counter-man'. Thus the Chinese peasants won arable soil 'against Nature'[3] by pursuing a policy of deforestation. The result of this was a series of inundations against which there was no protection. Nature exhibited a 'contra-finality' and affected human praxis and social relations. Again, the invention of machines and the development of industrialization was intended to overcome scarcity but in fact produced a further negation of man by making human beings the slaves of machines. Man thus falls under the domination of the 'practico-inert' which he himself has created. Man makes the machine; but the machine then reacts on man, reducing him to the level of the practico-inert, to what can be manipulated. To be sure, man remains the *for-itself*, and so free. At the same time hs becomes subject to the

[1] *Ibid.*, pp. 224–5, notes.   [2] *Ibid.*, p. 223.   [3] *Ibid.*, p. 232.

domination of the worked matter (*matière œuvrée*) which he himself has made and which represents man as outside himself, as
objectified in matter. Man is thus alienated or estranged from
himself.

Sartre lays great emphasis on the power of worked matter to
affect social relations. 'It is the object and the object alone which
combines human efforts in its inhuman unity.'[1] For example, it is
the demands of the machine which differentiate workers into
skilled and unskilled. It is also the practico-inert which determines
the stratification of classes, a class being for Sartre a collective
or collection. In the collection human beings are united by something outside themselves in the way that a number of people
waiting for an already crowded bus are united. They constitute a
'series', not in the sense that they are all standing in a line but in
the sense that each member is a unit, interested in his getting a
place in the bus, a unit for which other members of the series are
potential rivals or enemies. Similarly, each worker in a factory is
intent on gaining his livelihood; and what brings the workers
together in this particular collection is the machine or set of
machines. Again, it is worked matter or the practico-inert which
lies at the basis of class-division. To use an Hegelian term, Sartre
is speaking of the class 'in itself', not of the class 'for itself'. And
he accepts the Marxist view that the mode of production determines the nature of class division.

This domination of man by matter represents the sphere of what
Sartre describes as the anti-dialectic.[2] And he lays such emphasis
on it that some writers have seen in his attitude an almost
Manichaean view of matter as evil or at any rate as the source of
evil. However this may be, it should be remembered that worked
matter is for Sartre man exteriorized and that man's subjection to
the practico-inert is in a sense subjection to himself, though in a
form which involves self-estrangement or self-alienation. Though
enslaved to his creation, man remains free. And just as the
constituting dialectic contains within itself the possibility of an
anti-dialectic, so does the anti-dialectic contain within itself the
possibility of the constituted dialectic. Thus the class in itself can

---

[1] *Ibid.*, p. 350.
[2] The sphere or phase of the anti-dialectic is associated by Sartre with the
analytical reason, the mode of thought characteristic of the bourgeoisie. This is
one reason why Sartre describes the bourgeois intellectuals who discovered the
dialectical reason as 'traitors' to their class. Obviously, the word 'traitor' is used
descriptively, and not in a condemnatory sense.

become the class for itself, and the series can be transformed into the group.

5. This transition is not for Sartre inevitable or automatic but depends on human freedom, on individuals negating the domination of the practico-inert and transcending the social situation created by this domination towards a new social form, with a view to constituting or making it 'on the basis of the anti-dialectic'.[1] The unification of the workers as a genuine group, taking concerted action in view of a common end, must come from within. The transformation of the series into a group or of the class in itself into the class in and for itself comes about through a synthesis, a marriage as it were, of the original freedom which expresses itself in individual praxis, in the constituting dialectic, with the externally produced totalization in a series which pertains to the phase of the anti-dialectic.

The original constitution of the group expresses an upsurge of freedom. But Sartre is under no illusion about the group's stability. Once its immediate aim is attained, the storming of the Bastille for example, it tends to fragment or fall apart. The threat of atomization is met, if it is met, by 'the oath' (*le serment*), a term which should be understood not in the sense of a formal oath or of a social contract but rather in that of the will to preserve the group. This will however is inevitably accompanied by the exercise of constraint on members of the group whose actions tend to disintegrate it. In other words, the preservation of a group is accompanied by the development of authority and institutionalism. There then arises the temptation on the part of the leader or leaders of the group to represent his or their will as the 'real' will of all, considered as constituting an organic totality. But Sartre refuses to admit that the group is or can be an organic entity over and above its interrelated members. It is true that the leader may succeed not only in imposing his will but also in getting it accepted by the other members as their will. But the individual member is then reduced to the status of a quasi-inorganic entity, while 'the group is the machine which the sovereign makes to function *perinde ac cadaver*'.[2] The group can thus come to resemble an inorganic entity, a machine; but when constraint is removed, its members tend to break apart, thus manifesting the fact that while they are individual organic entities, the group is not.

[1] *C.R.D.*, p. 376.
[2] *Ibid.*, p. 601. *Perinde ac cadaver*, like a corpse.

The State is for Sartre the group of organizers and administrators to which the other groups composing a given society have conceded authority, probably more out of impotence than because they positively willed to do so. It is true that the organized State is required for the protection of groups; but it is not an organic entity with some sacred status. And its legitimacy consists in its ability to combine and manipulate other collections and groups. 'The idea of a diffused popular sovereignty which embodies itself in the sovereign is a mystification. There is no diffused sovereignty. The legitimacy of the sovereign is simply one of empirical fact, the ability to govern. 'I obey because I *cannot* do otherwise.'[2]

Sartre rejects therefore any deification of the State. And, as one would expect, he accepts the Marxist view that in the class struggle the State acts as 'the organ of the exploiting class (or classes)'.[3] At the same time he recognizes that even if the State acts as the organ of a dominant class, it none the less claims to represent the national interest and that it may conceive a 'totalizing' view of the common good and impose its mediating policy even on the dominant class. To say this however is to say that the group which constitutes the State tries to maintain itself as the accepted legitimate sovereign 'by serving the interests of the class from which it proceeds, and, *if needed, against its interests.*'[4] In plain English, a government composed of people from a particular class may take a wider view than that which would be suggested by the *prima facie* interests or advantage of the class in question. If so, this is to be interpreted in Marxist terms as a subtle way of preserving the position of the dominant class, which might otherwise be threatened.

To do him justice, Sartre is quite prepared to extend his rather cynical view of the State to the Communist State. In his opinion it is in the interest of the dominant group in the State to reduce other groups to collections or series and at the same time to condition the members of these series in such a way that they have the illusion of belonging to a genuine totality. This was what the Nazi government tried to do. And it can also be seen in the case of the so-called dictatorship of the proletariat. Talk about the proletariat exercising a dictatorship is for Sartre 'mystification'. The plain fact is that the dominant group takes good care to see that no other genuine groups arise and combines coercion with

---

[1] *Ibid.*, p. 609.   [2] *Ibid.*, p. 609.   [3] *Ibid.*, p. 610.   [4] *Ibid.*, p. 612.

conditioning to preserve the illusion that its own interest is that of the totality.

6. There is an obvious difference in atmosphere between *Being and Nothingness* on the one hand and the *Critique of Dialectical Reason* on the other. In the earlier work it is the totally free individual who stands in the centre of the picture, the individual who chooses his own values and is constantly transcending himself towards his future possibilities in the light of his freely chosen basic operative ideal, until at death he relapses into the facticity of *l'en-soi*, the in-itself. In spite of topical examples, the work can be looked on as an abstract analysis of the two fundamental concepts of the for-itself and the in-itself and as applying to man at all times. In the later work, the *Critique*, the general movement of history comes to the fore, and a much greater emphasis is laid on the group and concerted action by a group as it transcends a given social situation towards the realization of a new society. Again, though in the earlier work Sartre certainly recognizes the fact that every human being exists and acts in a given historical situation, and the fact that the exercise of human freedom is influenced by a variety of factors, environmental, physiological, and psychological, he is chiefly intent on arguing that limitations on human freedom are limitations only because the individual confers on them this significance. In the *Critique* this point of view does indeed reappear; but there is clearly a much greater emphasis on the constraining pressure of antecedent conditions on human activity. 'Above all, let no one proceed to interpret us as saying that man is free in all situations, as the Stoics claimed. We want to say exactly the contrary, namely that all men are slaves in so far as their experience of life develops in the field of the practico-inert and in the precise measure in which this field is originally conditioned by scarcity.'[1]

To draw attention to differences between *Being and Nothingness* and the *Critique of the Dialectical Reason* is not however to deny that there is any discernible continuity. In the earlier work, we can say, there is a dialectical relationship between the for-itself and the in-itself, between consciousness and being. The former arises through a negation of the latter; and it thus presupposes and depends on being in itself. At the same time being in itself requires consciousness in order to possess meaning and to be revealed as a world. In the *Critique* this dialectical relationship

[1] *Ibid.*, p. 369.

takes the form of that between man and his material environment. Man presupposes a material environment and acts on it; but the environment is revealed as Nature only through the mediation of man. Again, in *Being and Nothingness* there is a dialectical relationship between distinct consciousnesses, inasmuch as the for-itself is said to negate and yet to require the Other. The Other's 'look' both threatens the self and reveals it to itself. In the *Critique* the threat represented by the Other is described in terms of the concept of scarcity rather than in that of the look; but the basic dialectical relationship remains. Moreover, in spite of the prominence which Sartre gives to the idea of the group, his account of the genesis, nature and disintegration of the group shows clearly enough that for him the individual free agent is still the basic factor. And even though in the *Critique* a much greater emphasis is placed on the constraining influence of antecedent conditions, the domination of man by matter is represented as man's subjection to himself as exteriorized, as a self-estrangement which can be freely transcended.

As Sartre has not simply abandoned existentialism for Marxism but has tried to combine the two by re-interpreting Marxism in the light of an existentialist anthropology, it is only to be expected that we should find in his thought elements both of continuity and of discontinuity. It does not necessarily follow however that his existentialized Marxism is free of all ambiguity. As we have seen, he tries to combine two positions. On the one hand there is the thesis that it is man himself who makes history, and that he does so in a sense which excludes the claim that a certain social situation in the future is assured, as, that is to say, the inevitable result of the working out of a dialectical law which governs the historical process. On the other hand there is the thesis that the dialectical pattern is not simply imposed on history by the human mind but that history possesses a dialectical structure of such a kind that it makes sense to speak of man undergoing or suffering the dialectic. Sartre wishes to retain the concept of man as the free agent and at the same time to make room for the idea of man as the slave of the practico-inert. He wishes to say on the one hand that it is man who freely makes the dialectical movement of history, while on the other hand he proposes the view that history is one intelligible open-ended process. If by claiming that history is intelligible Sartre meant simply that historians can write intelligible accounts of historical events and movements, there would be no difficulty, other than the puzzles which the philosopher can propose about the relation between, for instance, an historian's reconstruction in the present and a past which no longer exists. But when Sartre claims that history is intelligible, he obviously does not mean simply that historiography is possible. He is claiming that history as a whole, though an unfinished whole, a process of 'totalization', embodies one intelligible movement. And the more this claim is pressed, the closer does Sartre come to a teleological view of history which implies the very conclusion which he wishes to avoid, namely that history is governed by a dialectical law of which man is the instrument.

Sartre can reply, for example, that the statement that it is man who makes history and thus its dialectical pattern is not incompatible with the statement that man does not simply impose the pattern but finds or recognizes it. For man finds what he has made. If he finds in history his own self-alienation and his enslavement to the practico-inert, he is recognizing in reflection what he himself has brought about. It does not follow that man deliberately caused his enslavement. The fact of the matter is that man's activity is conditioned from the start by an antecedent or given situation. He acts freely, but not in a vacuum. His action has results which constitute antecedent conditions for the actions of others. And so on. Given man's basic situation, the course of his history is what one might expect. But it is none the less the story of the activity of free agents. History should not be represented as an entity over and above human action and as determining it. It is human action, as subject to the constraining pressure of antecedent conditions. And this pressure can amount to enslavement, though it does not destroy man's basic freedom and his ability to transcend his enslavement.

Though however Sartre can make a good job of reconciling positions which may appear at first sight to be incompatible, it is difficult to feel satisfied. As we have noted, Sartre looks in man himself for the conditions of possibility of the dialectic of history. This enables him to claim that it is man himself who makes history and its dialectical pattern and that there is no impersonal dialectical law working independently and using man as an instrument. As however man acts in a situation, we may well be inclined to draw the conclusion that the movement of history is simply the unfolding or development of the original or basic dialectical relationship between man and his environment. In other words,

Sartre's grounding of the dialectic in man himself is not free from ambiguity. It might imply that man happens to have chosen to act in a certain way, when he could have acted in another way. Or it might imply that the dialectical movement of history is the development of a basic situation, a development which is predictable in principle. In this second case it would seem reasonable to speak of the operation of a law, even if the law were a law of man's nature as existing in a certain environment. As the second volume of the *Critique* has not yet appeared, it is obviously difficult to know how precisely Sartre proposes to develop his view of human history as possessing '*one* truth and *one* intelligibility'[1] without implying that the historical process is necessary. It would not be surprising however if he found the task rather difficult and was driven to talk about the analytical reason's inability to grasp the movement of dialectical thought.

The foregoing remarks relate of course simply to certain difficulties which arise if a philosopher tries to fuse Sartrian existentialism with Marxism. But we can very well go on to ask why Sartre or anyone else should make this attempt. It is not sufficient to answer that Marxism has become fossilized and that it needs an injection of humanism. This may very well be the case. But why choose Marxism in particular for rejuvenation? As we have seen, Sartre's reply is that Marxism is the one living philosophy of our time. Why however does he think this? He assumes of course that history can be divided up into epochs, and that in each epoch there is only one living philosophy. And even if we are prepared to grant the first assumption or at any rate to pass over it in silence, the second assumption is clearly questionable. There are other philosophies besides Marxism which are alive today. What makes Marxism more living than the others? It can hardly be because Marxism has practical implications, whereas so-called linguistic analysis, for example, is not practically oriented. For Sartre tells us that 'every philosophy is practical, even that which appears at first to be the most contemplative'.[2]

The answer is of course simple enough. Sartre assumes that in every epoch there is one ascending class. And the living philosophy of an epoch is for him the philosophy which brings to explicit expression the needs, interests, aspirations and goal of this class. It need not be thought out by members of the class in question. Marx and Engels were members of the bourgeoisie. But they

---

[1] *Ibid.*, p. 635.   [2] *Ibid.*, p. 16.

developed the philosophy which turned the proletariat from a class in itself into a class in and for itself and transformed it, or part of it, from a series of collections into a group. Marxism brings to explicit expression the consciousness of the ascending class and enables it to transcend the existing social situation towards a future to be realized by concerted revolutionary action. It is the one genuine revolutionary philosophy of our time, and it is there-fore the one living philosophy of our time.

It is true that Sartre sometimes speaks of philosophy in what appears at first sight to be a different way. For example, he tells his readers that philosophy 'must present itself as the totalization of contemporary knowledge. The philosopher achieves the unifi-cation of all branches of knowledge.'[1] Taken by itself, this state-ment of the function of philosophy sounds like a reintroduction of the concept of a synthesis of the sciences as found in classical positivism. Sartre goes on however to say that the philosopher unifies contemporary knowledge by means of directive schemata which express 'the attitudes and the techniques of the ascending class in relation to its epoch and to the world'.[2] So the living philosophy is still the philosophy of the ascending class, in spite of talk about unification of the sciences.

It may well be true to say that every statement of the nature of philosophy expresses a philosophical stance, unless perhaps it is a case of a statement simply about linguistic usage. However this may be, it seems pretty clear that Sartre's concept of living philo-sophy expresses a previous acceptance of Marxism. For the matter of that, it is a previous acceptance of a Marxist point of view which governs his selection of historical examples and even his definition or description of man as 'a practical organism living with a multi-plicity of organisms in a field of scarcity'.[3] Man is doubtless what Sartre says that he is, even if this is not all that he is. But the selection of certain aspects of man and his situation for particular emphasis is clearly governed by a previous conviction that Marxism is the one living philosophy of our time. In the long run we can hardly avoid the conclusion that it is Sartre's personal social and political commitment which is basically responsible for his choice of Marxism as the philosophy which he proposes to rejuvenate.

If the living philosophy of an epoch represents the self-con-sciousness and aspirations of the ascending class, the natural conclusion to draw is that it is true only in a relative sense. For

[1] *Ibid.*, p. 15.   [2] *Ibid.*, p. 15.   [3] *Ibid.*, p. 688.

there have been other epochs, with other ascending classes and other living philosophies. Sartre however does not wish to tie Marxism in an exclusive manner to the rising class. In the *Critique* he insists that Marxism is the philosophy of alienated man, not simply of the alienated worker. And, as we have seen, he tries to give Marxism a foundation in an anthropology or doctrine of man which exhibits the possibility of man's enslavement but is none the less logically prior to the emergence of the class struggle, inasmuch as it goes back to the basic situation of man as such. When looked at under this aspect, Marxism seems to be presented not simply as the philosophy of a particular class but rather as the true philosophy of man and of his history. To a certain extent a harmonization of the two points of view is perhaps possible. For it may be claimed, as the Marxist would doubtless claim, that the triumph of the proletariat will bring with it, sooner or later, the liberation of man in general. The salvation of man will be achieved through the proletarian revolution. But in this case Marxism would seem to be not simply the living philosophy of our time, in the sense mentioned above, but the one true philosophy, which would have been true at any time. Perhaps in the second volume of the *Critique* Sartre will devote some careful reflection to the question of precisely what truth-claims he wishes to make on behalf of his rejuvenated Marxism. As things stand, he does not seem to have made the matter very clear.

To many people however criticism of this kind has little value. Those who can swallow the contention that Marxism is the living philosophy of our time will regard such criticism as just the sort of tiresome exhibition which one might expect from an obscurantist bourgeois philosopher. Those however who believe that Marxism has life and power only because it has become the official ideology of a powerful, self-perpetuating and authoritarian Party and that, left to itself, it would go the way of other notable systems, may be impatient for another reason. They may think that Sartre has devoted his very considerable talents to pouring new wine into old skins, and that there are more valuable occupations than pointing out inconsistencies or ambiguities in his attempt to rejuvenate a philosophy which belongs to the nineteenth century rather than to the second half of the twentieth century. Perhaps so. But Marxism still has a powerful appeal. It possesses an obvious importance, even today. This however is compatible with its being a powerful myth, powerful, that is to say, when it is believed. It is arguable that Sartre has become fascinated by this myth because he sees in it the expression and instrument of a cause to which he has committed himself. At the same time it is a myth which can be misused and turned into the instrument of an oppressive group intent on the preservation of its power. Hence the attempt to rejuvenate the myth and to give it fresh life as a revolutionary call to the creation of a new society.

CHAPTER XVIiI

THE PHENOMENOLOGY OF MERLEAU-PONTY

A. Camus; the absurd and the philosophy of revolt — Merleau-Ponty; the body-subject and its world — Merleau-Ponty and Marxism — Lévi-Strauss and man.

1. IF a philosopher wishes to discuss such themes as human freedom, authenticity, self-commitment and personal relationships, his treatment is inevitably abstract and expressed in terms of general or universal concepts. Karl Jaspers, for instance, made a sharp distinction between the scientific objectification of man and the philosopher's endeavour to illuminate man's inner awareness of his freedom with a view to clarifying for man his basic possibilities of self-transcendence.[1] But even Jaspers had to write *about* man, employing universal concepts, even if he insisted on the need for special categories for this purpose. It is therefore understandable if in addition to their more professional philosophical writings certain thinkers, such as Sartre and Marcel, have published plays and, in Sartre's case, novels too, in which they have been able to exhibit 'problems of life' in terms of the actions, predicaments, options and relationships of individuals. Such works may give concrete and dramatic expression to themes which have already been treated in a more abstract way, or, as in Marcel's case, they may precede the more abstract and philosophical expression. In both cases however the two kinds of works have a recognizable relationship to one another which is lacking in cases in which a writer sets his philosophy aside and produces popular detective stories to augment his income.

If however the thought of Sartre is discussed in accounts of French philosophy, it is because of the writings which profess to be and are philosophical works, not on account of plays such as *The Flies* or *In Camera*, even if the latter stand in a recognizable relationship to the former. And the question arises whether one is

---

[1] Jaspers' point of view might be expressed in this manner. Considered as an object of scientific study, man is something already made, and individuals are classifiable in various ways by physiologists, psychologists and so on. For the philosophers of 'existence' (*Existenz*) man is the free agent who makes himself: he is always 'possible existence'. And each individual is unique, a unique possibility of self-transcendence.

justified in including mention of literary figures who are commonly thought of as having philosophical significance but who not only did not publish philosophical works in the academic sense but also refrained from making any claim to be philosophers. It is difficult to determine rules to which no exception can reasonably be taken. If we think of philosophy as a science which is concerned with proving that certain propositions are true, we shall be unlikely, for example, to include a treatment of Dostoievsky in a history of Russian philosophy. And though mention of his name occurs fairly frequently in, for instance, the work by N. O. Lossky,[1] he is mentioned incidentally and not listed among Russian philosophers. At the same time it is possible to take a wider view of philosophically significant writing; and no great surprise would have been caused if aspects of Dostoievsky's thought had been considered. In fact, the *Encyclopedia of Philosophy* edited by Paul Edwards contains an article devoted to the great Russian novelist.

In regard to recent French thought similar questions can be raised in regard to A. Camus.[2] He was not indeed a professional philosopher, nor did he ever claim to be. But in view of the themes of which he wrote he has been commonly mentioned in accounts of existentialism in France, even though he denied that he was an existentialist. And the insertion of some remarks about him seems defensible, though not obligatory.

Albert Camus (1913–60) was born and educated in Algeria. In 1940 he went to Paris, where he participated actively in the Resistance. In 1942 he published his novel *L'étranger*[3] and a well known essay entitled *Le mythe de Sisyphe*.[4] After the war he continued to be involved in political activity, and a number of his political essays, which originally appeared in the newspaper *Combat* and elsewhere, have been reprinted in the three volumes of *Actuelles*.[5] Camus' famous novel *La Peste* appeared in 1947,[6]

[1] *History of Russian Philosophy* (New York, 1951).
[2] There are of course a good many French literary figures whose writings possess philosophical significance but who cannot be all discussed in a history of philosophy. Georges Bataille, author of *L'expérience intérieure* (1943), *Sur Nietzsche* (1945) and other works is a case in point.
[3] Translated by S. Gilbert as *The Outsider* (London, 1946) and *The Stranger* (New York, 1946).
[4] Translated as *The Myth of Sisyphus and Other Essays* by J. O'Brien (New York and London, 1955).
[5] Paris, 1950–8. A selection of these articles have been published in an English translation by J. O'Brien entitled *Resistance, Rebellion and Death* (New York and London, 1961).
[6] Translated as *The Plague*, by S. Gilbert (London and New York, 1948).

and in 1951 he published *L'homme revolté*,[1] an essay which led to a breach in relations between himself and Sartre. The novel entitled *La chute*[2] appeared in 1956. In the following year Camus received the Nobel prize for literature. But in 1960 he was killed in a motor accident. His *Notebooks (Carnets)* have been translated into English[3] and also some of his plays.[4]

Camus is well known for his statement that 'there is only one really serious philosophical problem, that of suicide. To judge that life is or is not worth the trouble of being lived, this is to reply to the fundamental question of philosophy.'[5] On the face of it this may seem a very eccentric view of philosophy. The presupposition however is that man seeks a meaning in the world and in human life and history which would ground and support his ideals and values. Man wants to be assured that reality is an intelligible teleological process, comprising an objective moral order. To put the matter in another way, man desires metaphysical assurance that his life is part of an intelligible process directed to an ideal goal, and that in striving after his personal ideals he has the backing and support, so to speak, of the universe or of reality as a whole. The great religious leaders and creators of metaphysical systems and world-views have tried to supply this need. But their interpretations of the world cannot stand up to criticism. In the end the world is revealed, to the clear-sighted man, as without any determinate purpose or meaning. The world is not rational. Hence arises the feeling of the absurd (*le sentiment de l'absurde*). Strictly speaking, the world is not absurd in itself: it simply is. 'The absurd arises from this confrontation between man's appeal and the irrational silence of the world. . . . The irrational, human nostalgia and the absurd which arises from their confrontation, those are the three personages of the drama . . .'[6] The feeling of the absurd can arise in a variety of ways, through, for example, the perception of Nature's indifference to man's values and ideals, through recognition of the finality of death, or through the shock caused by the

---

[1] Translated as *The Rebel* by A. Bower (London, 1953; revised version, New York, 1956).
[2] Translated as *The Fall* by J. O'Brien (London and New York, 1957).
[3] *Notebooks 1935-42*, translated by P. Thody (New York and London, 1963). *Notebooks 1942-51*, translated by J. O'Brien (New York, 1965).
[4] *Caligula and Three Other Plays*, translated by S. Gilbert (London and New York, 1958).
[5] *Le mythe de Sisyphe* (new French edition, Paris, 1942), p. 15.
[6] *Ibid.*, p. 45. Camus distinguishes between the feeling of the absurd and the idea or conviction (the clear consciousness) of the absurd.

sudden perception of the pointlessness of life's routine. Some thinkers understand the absurd but then pursue a policy of escapism. Thus Karl Jaspers leaps from the 'shipwreck' of human longings to the Transcendent, while Leo Chestov makes a similar leap to a God who is beyond reason. But the man who, like Nietzsche, is able to look the absurdity of human existence in the face sees the meaning of the world disappear. Hence the problem of suicide. For 'to see the meaning of this life dissipated, to see our reason for existing disappear, that is what is unbearable. One cannot live without meaning.'[1]

Suicide is not however the action recommended by Camus. In his opinion suicide means surrender to the absurd, capitulation. Human pride and greatness are shown neither in surrender nor in the sort of escapism indulged in by the existential philosophers (*les philosophes existentiels*, such as Jaspers) but in living in the consciousness of the absurd and yet revolting against it by man's committing himself and living in the fullest manner possible. There are indeed no absolute standards which permit us to dictate to a man how he should live. As Ivan Karamazov says, all is permitted. But it does not follow that the absurd 'recommends crime. This would be puerile. . . . If all experiences are indifferent, that of duty is as legitimate as any other. One can be virtuous by caprice.'[2] The man of the absurd (*l'homme absurde*) can take various forms. The Don Juan who enjoys to the full, as long as he is able, experiences of a certain type, while conscious that none of them possesses any ultimate significance, is one form. So is the man who recognizes the meaninglessness of history and the ultimate futility of human action but who none the less commits himself to a social or political cause in his historical situation. So is the creative artist who sees clearly enough that both he and his works are doomed to extinction but who none the less devotes his life to artistic production. And in *La peste* Camus raises the question whether there can be an atheist saint. The man of the absurd lives without God. But it by no means follows that he cannot devote himself in a self-sacrificing manner to the welfare of his fellow men. Indeed, if he does so without hope of reward and conscious that in the long run it makes no difference how he acts, he exhibits the greatness of man precisely by this combination of recognition of ultimate futility with a life of self-sacrificing love. It is possible to be a saint without illusion.

---

[1] From the play *Caligula*.   [2] *Le mythe de Sisyphe*, p. 94.

In maintaining the meaninglessness of the world and of human history (in the sense that they have no goal or purpose which is given independently of man) Camus is substantially at one with Sartre, though the latter does not dwell so much as the former on the theme of 'the absurd'. Sartre is not however the source of Camus' assumption. We should not of course speak as though an original writer such as Camus simply borrowed his ideas from a predecessor. But it is clear that it was Nietzsche who provided a stimulating influence. Camus believed that Nietzsche had rightly seen the advent and rise of nihilism; and, like the German philosopher, he looked to man as the only being capable of overcoming nihilism. At the same time it does not follow that Camus can be properly described as a Nietzschean. For one thing, Camus came to be more and more concerned with injustice and oppression in human society in a manner in which Nietzsche was not. Camus did not indeed renounce his belief 'that this world has no ultimate meaning';[1] but he came to lay more and more stress on revolt against injustice, oppression and cruelty rather than on revolt against the human condition as such. Indeed, he became convinced that the feeling of the absurd, taken by itself, can be used to justify anything, murder included. 'If one believes in nothing, if nothing makes sense, if we can assert no value whatsoever, everything is permissible and nothing is important. . . . One is free to stoke the crematory fires or to give one's life to the care of lepers.'[2] In point of fact revolt presupposes the assertion of values. True, they are man's creation. But this does not alter the fact that if I revolt against oppression or injustice, I assert the values of freedom and justice. With Camus, in other words, cosmic absurdity, so to speak, tends to retreat into the background; and a moral idealism comes to the fore, a moral idealism which did not call for the production of an élite, an aristocracy of higher men, at the expense of the herd, but which insisted on freedom and justice for all, real freedom and justice moreover, not oppression or enslavement masquerading under these honoured names.

Camus was no admirer of bourgeois society. But he became acutely aware of the way in which revolt against the existing order can end with the imposition of slavery. 'The great event of the twentieth century was the forsaking of the values of freedom by the revolutionary movement, the progressive retreat of socialism based on freedom before the attacks of a Caesarian and military

---

[1] *Resistance, Rebellion and Death*, p. 21.　　　[2] *The Rebel*, p. 13.

socialism.'[1] Man cannot play the part of a spectator of history as a whole; and no historical enterprise can be more than a risk or adventure for which some degree of rational justification can be offered. It follows that no historical enterprise can rightly be used to justify 'any excess or any ruthless and absolutist position'.[2] For example, killing and oppression in the name of the movement of history or of a terrestrial paradise to be attained at some indefinite future date are unjustified. If absolute nihilism can be used to justify anything, so can absolute rationalism, in which God is replaced by history. In regard to their consequences, 'there is no difference between the two attitudes. From the moment that they are accepted, the earth becomes a desert.'[3] We have to get away from absolutes and turn to moderation and limitation. 'Absolute freedom is the right of the strongest to dominate'[4] and thus prolongs injustice. 'Absolute justice is achieved by the suppression of all contradiction: therefore it destroys freedom.'[5] It is on behalf of living human beings not on behalf of history or of man in some future age that we are called upon to rebel against existing injustice and oppression, wherever it may be found. 'Real generosity towards the future lies in giving all to the present.'[6]

As has already been noted, the publication of *The Rebel* (*L'homme revolté*) led to a breach of relations between Camus and Sartre.[7] The latter had been coming closer to Communism, though without joining the Party, and he was already engaged in the project of combining existentialism and Marxism. Camus, while disclaiming the label 'existentialist', was convinced that the two were incompatible, and that Marxism, with its secularization of Christianity and substitution of the movement of history for God, led straight to the death of freedom and the horrors of Stalinism. As for bourgeois democracy, which replaced eternal divine truths by abstract principles of reason, the trouble has been, according to Camus, that the principles have not been applied. In the name of freedom bourgeois society has condoned exploitation and social injustice; and it has sanctioned violence. What then does Camus wish to put in the place of Communism, Fascism, Nazism and bourgeois democracy? Apart from some

---

[1] *Resistance, Rebellion and Death*, p. 67.   [2] *The Rebel*, p. 253.
[3] *Ibid.*, p. 253.   [4] *Ibid.*, p. 251.   [5] *Ibid.*, p. 252.   [6] *Ibid.*, p. 268.
[7] A critical review of the work was published by Francis Jeanson. Camus replied in the form of a letter addressed to the editor, Sartre himself. And this elicited a combative counterblast from Sartre.

remarks about the benefits to man which have been obtained
through trade unionism, he gives no clear picture. And Sartre of
course sees him as criticizing various movements but offering only
vague and abstract ideas. Camus however has no intention of
offering a blueprint. His philosophy of revolt is mainly concerned
with moral values and the development of moral responsibility;
and he insists that though the rebel must act because he believes
that it is right to do so, he must also act with the recognition that
he might be wrong. The Communist will not entertain the idea that
he might be wrong. Hence his ruthlessness. The only hope for the
future is an open society, in which the passion of revolt and the
spirit of moderation are in constant tension.[1]

It does not follow however that Camus is an optimist with
unbounded faith in man, provided that unjust institutions can
be overthrown. In *The Fall* he makes his central character,
Clamence, refer to 'the basic duplicity of the human being',[2]
as though he located the root of evil in man himself. This is not
indeed incompatible with what he has to say about social institutions. For they are made by man. At the same time there seems to
be a shift of emphasis in his thought from the absurdity which
arises in the confrontation between man and the world to social
evils, and from social evils to the evil in the heart of man. How his
thought would have developed if it had not been for his untimely
death, it is obviously impossible to say.

Camus was a man who found himself unable to accept Christian
belief but who not only had high moral ideals but was also pas-
sionately concerned with human freedom, social justice, peace
and the elimination of violence. He was not anti-Christian in the
sense in which this term would be ordinarily understood. What he
objected to was not so much Christianity as such (he had Christian
friends whom he admired) but the compromise and ambiguous
attitude in regard to social and political evils which he regarded
as a betrayal of the original Christian inspiration. 'When man
submits God to moral judgment, he kills him in his own heart.'[3]
The question then arises, what is the basis of morality? If we deny
God in the name of justice, 'can the idea of justice be understood
without the idea of God?'[4] Camus was not sufficiently interested

---

[1] Camus laid great emphasis on the reduction of violence. This included for
him the elimination of capital punishment. See his 'Reflections on the Guillotine'
in *Resistance, Rebellion and Death*.
[2] *The Collected Fiction of Albert Camus* (London, 1960), p. 282.
[3] *The Rebel*, p. 57.   [4] *Ibid.*, p. 57.

in professional philosophy to devote time and energy to prolonged reflection on such problems. He was convinced however that man cannot live without values. If he chooses to live, by that very fact he asserts a value, that life is good or worth living or should be made worth living. Man as man can revolt against exploitation, oppression, injustice and violence, and by the very fact that he revolts he asserts the values in the name of which he revolts. A philosophy of revolt has therefore a moral basis; and if this basis is denied, whether explicitly or in the name of some abstraction such as the movement of history or through a policy of expediency, what began with revolt, with the expression of freedom, turns into tyranny and the suppression of freedom. Camus tended to leave his assertions without any developed theoretical support; but he undoubtedly threw light, as the citation asserted when he was awarded the Nobel Prize, on the problems of human conscience in our times. He was genuinely and deeply concerned with these problems, and in treating of them he displayed, as writers on him have noticed, a combination of commitment and detachment. He was certainly committed; but at the same time he preserved the measure of detachment which enabled him to avoid the lamentable but not uncommon tendency to fulminate against the evils of one political system while excusing similar or even worse evils in another system or country. In other words, Camus' commitment was basically moral rather than political in character.

2. In turning from Albert Camus to Maurice Merleau-Ponty (1908–61) we turn from a socially and politically committed essayist, novelist and dramatist to a professional philosopher. Not that Merleau-Ponty can be described as uncommitted. For he believed that ethics cannot be divorced from political action; and up to a point he supported the Marxists, even if he had little use for Marxist dogmatism. Whereas however we cannot consider Camus' thought apart from his social and political commitment, there are large areas of Merleau-Ponty's philosophy which can be treated on a purely theoretical level.

After studying at the École Normale in Paris and taking his agrégation in philosophy, Merleau-Ponty taught in a lycée and then at the École Normale. After the war, during which he served as an officer, he became a professor first at the University of Lyon and then at the Sorbonne. In 1952 he was appointed to the chair of philosophy at the Collège de France. Merleau-Ponty was one of the founders of *Les temps modernes* and a co-editor, along with

Sartre. He has sometimes been described as an existentialist;[1] but though there is indeed ground for associating him with atheist existentialism, he is better described as a phenomenologist. This label helps at any rate to differentiate him from Sartre. It is true of course that Sartre has developed phenomenological analyses. The point is however that the label 'existentialist', together with the fact that Merleau-Ponty was for a time associated with Sartre, tends to give the impression that the former was a junior partner or even disciple of the latter, whereas he was really an independent and original thinker.

Merleau-Ponty's first main publication was *La structure du comportement*,[2] which appeared at Paris in 1942. This was followed in 1945 by *Phénoménologie de la perception*.[3] In 1947 Merleau-Ponty published *Humanisme et terreur, essai sur le problème communiste*, in which he examined the problem of the use of terror by the Communists. A collection of essays, entitled *Sens et non-sens*, appeared in 1948.[4] The inaugural lecture given by Merleau-Ponty at the Collège de France was published in 1953 under the title *L'éloge de la philosophie*.[5] In 1955 he published *Les aventures de la dialectique*, which includes a criticism of Sartre, and this was followed in 1960 by *Signes*.[6] Before his death Merleau-Ponty had started on a new work, *Le visible et l'invisible*, intended as a fresh statement of his philosophy. The part of the work which he had written was published in 1964, together with notes for the projected parts.

In a lecture which he gave at Geneva in 1951 Merleau-Ponty asserts that the twentieth century has erased the dividing line between body and mind and 'sees human life as through and through mental and corporeal, always based upon the body and always (even in its most carnal modes) interested in relationships between persons'.[1] This statement refers of course to the overcoming of dualism on the one hand and of a reductive materialism on the other. And the reader may wonder whether it is not perhaps

---

[1] For example, there is one excellent work on his thought by A. de Waehlens entitled *Une philosophie de l'ambiguité: l'existentialisme de Maurice Merleau-Ponty* (Louvain, 1951).
[2] Translated by A. L. Fisher as *The Structure of Behaviour* (Boston, 1963).
[3] Translated by C. Smith as *Phenomenology of Perception* (London and New York, 1962).
[4] Translated by H. L. and P. A. Dreyfus as *Sense and Nonsense* (Evanston, Ill., 1964).
[5] Translated by J. Wild and J. M. Edie as *In Praise of Philosophy* (Evanston, Ill., 1963).
[6] Translated by R. C. McCleary as *Signs* (Evanston, Ill., 1964).

too sweeping. Sartre, for example, is certainly a twentieth-century writer; but as far as his analysis of the concepts of 'the in-itself' and 'the for-itself' is concerned, the distinction between the two seems to be sharpened into an antithesis, a pretty obvious dualism. Merleau-Ponty is however quite well aware of this fact. When he refers to twentieth-century thought, he is clearly referring to what he considers its most significant and valid trend, a more adequate self-awareness by man, an awareness which is expressed in, though not confined to, Merleau-Ponty's own philosophy. He sees the line of thought which he sums up in his concept of the 'body-subject' as triumphing over dualism on the one hand and materialism and behaviourism on the other and, to put the matter in another way, as going beyond the antithesis between idealism and materialism. In existentialism man is indeed conceived as essentially a being in the world, dialectically related to it in the sense that man cannot be understood apart from the world, apart from his situation, while what we call 'the world' cannot be understood apart from the meanings conferred on it by man. This sort of idea is of course present in Sartre and expresses the trend of thought to which Merleau-Ponty refers. But Sartre also presses the distinction between consciousness and its object in such a way as to give new life to a version of the Cartesian dualism against which Merleau-Ponty vigorously reacts.

By dualism Merleau-Ponty understands the view of man as a composite of body and spirit or mind, the former being considered as a thing among things, subject to the same causal relations which are found between other material objects, while the latter is looked on as the source of all knowledge, freedom and openness to others or, to use Merleau-Ponty's term, as 'existence'. Obviously, Merleau-Ponty does not deny that the body can be treated as an object and considered as such in scientific inquiry and research. But in his view this possibility presupposes the human body as being itself a subject, in dialogue with the world and with other persons. It is not a question of maintaining that there is in the body a distinct soul or spirit, in virtue of which the composite being can be described as a subject. It is the body which is subject. This view obviously entails understanding body in a sense rather different from that in which it would be understood within a dualistic framework of thought, namely as opposed to mind or spirit. It is precisely this opposition which Merleau-Ponty wishes

¹ *Signs*, pp. 226–7.

to overcome and thinks that he has overcome through his concept of body-subject. If we start with dualism and then try to overcome it by making the one or other factor primary, we either reduce mind to body or identify the real man with an incorporeal soul or spirit. Merleau-Ponty however rejects such reductionism and insists that the human body is one reality which is at the same time material and spiritual. He is of course aware that there are factors in the situation which provide an at any rate *prima facie* ground for dualism; and he is aware of the very great difficulty which we encounter if we try to avoid language which implies dualism. In other words, he admits that the concept of the body-subject is difficult to express, and that one has to look for a new language to express it. He is convinced however that this is precisely what philosophers ought to try to do, and that they should not tamely let themselves remain imprisoned in old linguistic and conceptual fetters.

It may seem that Merleau-Ponty's project bears a marked similarity to that of Gilbert Ryle in his work *The Concept of Mind.* So it does in some respects. Both philosophers are opponents of dualism, but neither wishes to reduce man to a machine. For each of them the human being is one single 'incarnate' reality which lives, desires, thinks, acts, and so on. At the same time there is also a clear dissimilarity. One of Ryle's contentions is that all mental operations should be understood in terms of public or witnessable activities.[1] It is natural therefore that he should devote his attention to the mental phenomena of which we are easily aware; and as a counterblast to dualism he constantly cites examples of what we are accustomed to say in ordinary language, to expressions which militate against the idea of purely private and occult mental activities, and so against the notion of 'the ghost in the machine'. Merleau-Ponty however is intent on showing that mental activities, in the sense of activities at the level of more or less clear consciousness, do not constitute a mental life which accrues to a body that is itself without subjectivity, but that they presuppose the body-subject. He is not trying to reduce psychical to physical processes. He argues that already at a preconscious level the body is subject. In other words, he wishes to explore a territory which underlies and is presupposed by the various activities that give rise to the dualistic expressions of

---

[1] It is this aspect of his thought which has given rise to the accusation of behaviourism, the validity of which Ryle rejects.

ordinary language. It is understandable therefore that he insists on the need for fresh concepts and modes of expression.

The field specially chosen for investigation by Merleau-Ponty is perception. In a paper which he wrote in connection with his candidacy for a chair at the Collège de France he says that his 'first two works sought to restore the world of perception'.[1] If we simply state however that Merleau-Ponty develops a phenomenology of perception, the statement is apt to mislead. For the word 'perception' may suggest the activity of describing the essential structure of this conscious activity when it has been turned into an object of reflection. Merleau-Ponty however is concerned with perception as the mode of existence of the body-subject at a pre-conscious level, with, that is to say, the dialogue between the body, as subject, and its world at a level which is presupposed by consciousness. In this case of course the phenomenological method, as employed by him in this context, cannot take the form of a faithful description of an immediate datum of reflective awareness or consciousness. It is a case of delving into the region of obscurity; and Merleau-Ponty admits that any complete illumination of this obscure field is unattainable. One can only feel one's way, grope, and try to let in as much light as one can. He believes however that it is important to make the effort. For 'the perceived world is the always presupposed foundation of all rationality, all value and all existence'.[2] It is not a case of maintaining that thought, for example, consists of transformed sensations. It is a case of trying to penetrate to the presupposed foundation of thought and of all conscious activity and trying to elucidate its structure. The philosopher, as Merleau-Ponty conceives him, is very much an explorer.

In his first main work, *La structure du comportement* (*The Structure of Behaviour*) Merleau-Ponty approaches the theme of the relations between man and his environment through an examination of certain modern physiological and psychological theories, such as behaviourism and the *Gestalt* psychology. In other words, he places himself on the level of scientific theories and confronts these theories with what he believes to be the facts of man's perceptual behaviour. He argues, for example, that we cannot account for the facts by interpreting the relation between

[1] *The Primacy of Perception and Other Essays*, edited by J. M. Edie (Northwestern University Press, 1964), p. 3.
[2] *Ibid.*, p. 13.

the human body and its environment in terms which imply that the body is a machine with pre-established mechanisms which are set in motion simply by reaction to external stimuluses. 'The true stimulus is not the one defined by physics and chemistry; the reaction is not this or that particular series of movements; and the connection between the two is not the simple coincidence of two successive events'.[1] Science, for its own purposes, can legitimately consider the body as a thing among things; but the scientific point of view is formed through a process of abstraction from a level of real behaviour at which the organism exhibits a kind of prospective activity, behaving as though it were oriented towards certain meanings or goals. The organism's capacity for meaningful response can be exercised of course only within limits and in dependence on conditions in its environment. It is not however a question simply of a 'blind' response. The organism exhibits 'subjectivity', though at a pre-conscious level.

Merleau-Ponty's line of thought can be expressed in this way. The relation between the human organism and its environment cannot be expressed simply in terms of mechanistic reciprocal causality. That is to say, we cannot reduce the reciprocal action between the terms of the relation 'to a series of uni-directional determinations'.[2] There is indeed causal interaction. For example, food acts on the organism, and the organism acts on the food by assimilating it. But the food is *food* only in virtue of the structure, needs and activity of the organism. The effect produced by x cannot be understood simply in terms of x. There is a complex dialectical relationship. And subjectivity is present when for one of the factors in the relationship all other factors constitute a world. Merleau-Ponty does not mean to imply that the perceived world (at the level of experience under consideration) is consciously perceived by the body-subject as a world. But he insists that on the level of perceptual behaviour there is already a global environment or milieu as a term in a dialectical relationship, correlative to the aptitudes (the 'can' or ability) of the subject. As we ascend the levels of experience and consciousness, the environment takes on new forms or shapes, in correlation with the meaning-conferring activity of the subject. But these presuppose a pre-conscious level on which the human organism unconsciously confers meaning and constitutes a milieu or environment. It does not of course confer meaning on nothing; nor does it create the things about it.

---

[1] *The Structure of Behaviour*, p. 99.   [2] *Ibid.*, p. 161.

But if we can talk about the ego and its world at the level of consciousness, we can also talk about the body-subject and its world or milieu at the pre-conscious level. The epistemological distinction between subject and object is not yet there. But there is none the less a *lived* dialectical relationship, which forms the constantly presupposed basis for higher levels of experience, though a higher level differs qualitatively from a lower level.

To assert that there is a dialectical relationship between man and his environment is to assert that man is from the beginning a being in the world, and that both terms of the relationship are real. In this sense Merleau-Ponty is a realist. At the level of reflective consciousness it becomes possible for philosophers to advance theories which subordinate the object to the subject, idealist theories that is to say; but this sort of theory distorts the original and basic relationship between man and his environment which is presupposed by every level of behaviour and experience. At the same time to say that this relationship is dialectical or that it is a continual dialogue between man and his environment is to say, among other things, that the meanings of things are determined not only by the object but also by the subject. To take a simple example, if that tree appears as far away, it is for me, in relation to myself, that it appears as far off. I am the centre in relation to which one tree appears as near, another as far. On the scientific level of course one can freely adopt the frame of reference which suits one's purpose; but on the level of perceptual behaviour spatial relations 'appear' within the dialogue between the human organism and its environment. Similarly, colours are neither purely objective nor purely subjective; they appear in the lived dialogue between the body-subject and the world. Obviously, the environment or situation changes. So does the subject, not simply as an effect of external stimuli but also through its own active responses which contribute to determining the meanings of the stimuli. The dialectical relationship is not static; the active dialogue is perpetual, as long as the subject exists. But it is within the dialogue between the body-subject and its environment that 'the world' comes to appear, though its appearances change.

In *La structure du comportement* Merleau-Ponty considers, as we have already mentioned, certain modern psychological theories. He tries to show that the facts discovered by these psychologists are at variance with and do not fit their presuppositions and implied ontological perspectives. On the contrary, the facts demand neither the reduction of the subject to a thing or object nor an idealist theory of a consciousness which creates the object but rather a recognition of the basic situation of an 'incarnate' subject involved in the world and in constant dialogue with it. In other words, Merleau-Ponty takes certain theories and tries to delve into the obscure region which is presupposed by all thought and knowledge. In his subsequent work *Phénoménologie de la perception* (*Phenomenology of Perception*) he instals himself from the first in perceptual behaviour 'in order to pursue the analysis of this exceptional relation between the subject and its body and its world'.[1] We cannot however reproduce the contents of this remarkable work. It must suffice to draw attention to a few points.

It may well have occurred to the reader that inasmuch as the passage just quoted makes a distinction between subject and body, it is hardly compatible with what we have been saying about Merleau-Ponty's concept of the body-subject as one single reality. But it is necessary to make some distinctions. We can of course consider the body purely objectively, and then we naturally distinguish between the body as object and the subject. However, 'the objective body is not the truth of the phenomenal body, the truth, that is to say, of the body as we live it. It is only an impoverished image thereof, and the problem of the relations between soul and body do not concern the objective body, which has only a conceptual existence, but the phenomenal body.'[2] The body considered as a purely physical object distinct from the subject is an abstraction, legitimate enough for a variety of purposes but not an expression of the body as lived or experienced. The latter is the body-subject. At the same time the body-subject is temporal: it transcends itself, and there are distinguishable levels. For example, the body considered as a group of habits can be considered as 'my body' by the subject or 'I' as it transcends the already given. 'We do not say that . . . the subject *thinks itself* as inseparable from the idea of the body.'[3] Indeed, Merleau-Ponty sometimes speaks of 'the soul', as a higher level of the subject's self-organization. But he insists that such distinctions refer to distinguishable aspects of one reality, and that they should not be understood in a dualistic sense. All such distinctions are made within a unity, the body-subject.

Merleau-Ponty's rejection of any dualistic interpretation of the

[1] *The Primacy of Perception*, pp. 4–5.
[2] *Phénoménologie de la perception*, p. 493.   [3] *Ibid.*, p. 467.

human being is naturally accompanied, or followed, by a rejection of any real distinction between language and thought. It is true of course that when linguistic expressions have once been created and have become the common possession of a given society, with meanings determined by convention, they can be repeated and handed on from generation to generation. The 'spoken word',[1] language as already constituted, thus forms a datum which human beings appropriate in the course of education. And as, given this datum, it is possible for writers to invent new expressions to express new concepts, thus adding 'the speaking word'[2] to the 'spoken word', there is a natural inclination to regard thought as an inner activity which is distinct from language. One thinks and then gives verbal expression to the thought. Merleau-Ponty however regards this as a mistaken interpretation of the situation. In the case of the 'speaking word' the meaning is indeed in a state of coming to be; but it by no means follows that it comes to be *before* its symbolic or linguistic expression. We may talk, for example, of the poet seeking words to express his thoughts but the thought takes shape in and through its expression. He does not first have his poem 'in his mind' in an unexpressed state and then express it. For if he has it in his mind, he has already expressed it. Whether he has written it down or spoken it aloud is irrelevant. If the poem can be said to be present in his mind, it is present as expressed. It is precisely in the case of the 'speaking word' that the relation between thought and language becomes most clearly apparent. They are two aspects of one reality. If we separate them, words become mere physical occurrences, *flatus vocis*, to use a medieval term.

The general view maintained by Merleau-Ponty of the relation between thought and language is of course in harmony with that of the so-called 'linguistic analysts', who are opposed to the idea of a separation or real distinction between an occult activity, thought, on the one hand and the public phenomenon of language on the other. Like Gilbert Ryle, Merleau-Ponty recognizes the absurdity of complaining that we have only the words of a philosopher of the past, such as Plato or Hegel, and do not enjoy access to his thoughts or to his mind. For the philosopher's thoughts are expressed in his writings; and access to his words is access to his mind. The philosophers of ordinary language however are principally concerned with what Merleau-Ponty calls

---

[1] *Ibid.*, p. 229, *La parole parlée.*   [2] *Ibid.*, *La parole parlante.*

'the spoken word'. Inasmuch as they do not exclude in principle either the revision of ordinary language or the invention of fresh terms, they leave room for the 'speaking word'. At the same time the emphasis is laid on the 'spoken word', whereas Merleau-Ponty lays emphasis rather on 'the speaking word'. For he is intent on exhibiting the connections between his theory of language and his theory of the body-subject. He recognizes a kind of pre-linguistic understanding by the body of its world, a 'practognosis' as he calls it,[1] which is not distinct from the bodily behaviour in question. But thought in any proper sense of the word comes to exist in and through linguistic expression. The social aspects of the subject are of course manifested in the 'spoken word'. The human subject however is capable of transcending the already given or acquired; and this aspect is exhibited in the 'speaking word', in the creativity of scientists, poets and philosophers. But even with them thought and expression go together; and this shows that thought is anchored, so to speak, in the body-subject. There are successive levels of subjectivity; but the subject is always the 'incarnate' subject which, as it develops its poten-tialities, gives new meanings to the world. Thought represents one aspect of the body-subject, its subjectivity, while language represents another aspect, its corporeality. But just as the body-subject is one single reality, even if there are distinguishable aspects, so are thought and language one reality.

We have spoken of man's dialogue with his environment. This environment is not however simply the physical world of things or objects. Man is born into an historical and cultural situation. 'I do not have only a physical world, I do not live only in the milieu of the earth, air and water, I have around me roads, plantations, villages, streets, churches, utensils, a bell, a spoon, a pipe. Each of these objects bears stamped on it the mark of the human action for which it serves.'[2] Though however the human being is born into a world of cultural objects, it is obviously not a question of inferring the existence of other persons from such objects. This would give us at best an anonymous One. 'In the cultural object I experience the near presence of the Other under a veil of anonymity.'[3] Must we then say that we infer the existence of other persons from their overt behaviour, from their bodily movements? It is difficult to see what else one could say, if the

---

[1] *Ibid.*, p. 164. *Praktognosie* is the word coined by Merleau-Ponty.
[2] *Ibid.*, p. 399.   [3] *Ibid.*, p. 400.

body were understood in the sense required by dualism. But if the subject is not something hidden away in a body but the body itself, the body-subject, we can see that the existence of other subjects is experienced in man's pre-reflective dialogue with the world. The small child does not *infer* the existence of its mother from the smile which it sees on her face or from the movements of her hands. It has a pre-reflective perception of its mother in the dialogue of their behaviours. We have indeed to admit that a conflict can arise between different subjects, and that one subject can try to reduce another to the level of an object. But such conflicts obviously presuppose awareness of the existence of other persons. It may be objected that it is only as appearing for me or to me that other persons come to exist in my world. But it does not follow that they do not appear for me as other subjects. Certainly, I cannot *be* the other subject. Communication cannot be total and complete: the self is always involved in a certain solitude. But the solitude of real life is not that of solipsism. 'Solitude and communication ought not to be regarded as the two terms of an alternative, but as two moments of a single phenomenon, since, in fact, other people exist for me.'[1] To exist is to exist in a world which includes a social dimension; and the theoretical puzzles which can be raised on the level of reflection in regard to our knowledge of others presuppose an experienced or lived dialogue with other subjects.

In the *Phenomenology of Perception* Merleau-Ponty has some sensible remarks to make on the subject of freedom. He begins by recapitulating briefly the theory of Sartre in *Being and Nothingness*. For Sartre freedom is absolute. Our decisions are not determined by motives. For 'the alleged motive does not exercise weight on my decision; on the contrary, it is my decision which gives the motive its force.'[2] Again, it depends on me whether I see human being as things or as human beings, as objects or as free subjects; and it depends on my will to climb it that a rock appears to me as unclimbable or as a difficult obstacle. Merleau-Ponty objects that if freedom is said to be absolute and without limits, the word 'freedom' is deprived of all definite meaning. 'If, in effect, freedom is equal in all our actions and even in our passions . . . one cannot say that there is any *free action*. . . . It (freedom) is everywhere, if you like, but it is also nowhere.'[3] It is obviously true that it is I who give to

[1] *Ibid.*, p. 412.   [2] *Phénoménologie de la perception*, p. 497.
[3] *Ibid.*, p. 499.

this precipice the meaning of being an 'obstacle' to the ascent of the mountain which I envisage; but my dialogue with the world, in which this meaning arises, *is* a dialogue, not a monologue. The relation between the precipice and my body does not depend simply on me. When I give the precipice the significance of being an obstacle, I am already in a situation. Similarly, my past behaviour and the habits which I have formed constitute a situation. It does not follow that my present choice is determined. What follows is that freedom is never absolute but always 'situated'. This does not mean that a free action is divisible, as it were, into a part which is free and a part which is determined. It means that man is not a pure consciousness, but that the level of consciousness and freedom is conditioned by a pre-conscious level. To take an example given by Merleau-Ponty,[1] the bourgeois intellectual who breaks with his class and identifies himself with the proletarian revolutionary movement does so freely; but he reaches his decision not as a pure consciousness, existing apart from all social classes, but as one who is already situated by birth and upbringing. His decision, though free, is the decision of a bourgeois intellectual; he chooses precisely as such, and though in the end he may succeed in closing the gap between bourgeois intellectual and member of the proletarian class, he cannot do so through one initial decision to break with his own class and espouse the cause of another. His exercise of freedom is conditioned by a pre-existing situation.

Merleau-Ponty did not claim to have provided definitive solutions of the problems which he considered. His thought was exploratory; and he regarded himself as making a contribution which opened the way to further reflection. In general, he was faced with the problem of harmonizing belief that man, the existing subject, confers meanings on his world with the evident fact that, as conscious beings, we find ourselves in a world already clothed with meaning. His treatment of perception and perceptual behaviour at a pre-conscious level was a contribution to the solution of this problem. But Merleau-Ponty never intended to imply that all levels of experience could be reduced to pre-conscious experience, or that the structures characteristic of higher levels could be described or analyzed simply in terms of the structures characteristic of the level of perception. The realm of perception, the 'life-world', constituted for him the basis of other

[1] *Ibid.*, pp. 509–10.

levels. We all continue to live in the realm of perception. At the same time the higher levels require individual treatment; and Merleau-Ponty planned to follow up *The Structure of Behaviour* and the *Phenomenology of Perception* with works on such subjects as the origin of truth and the sociological significance of prose literature. In point of fact the planned volumes were not written; but he developed ideas on a number of subjects in important essays. An example is his paper on the phenomenology of language (1951) in which he maintains that 'when I speak or understand, I experience that presence of others in myself or of myself in others which is the stumbling-block of the theory of intersubjectivity.'[1] Another example is the notable essay *L'oeil et l'esprit* (*Eye and Mind*), which appeared in 1961.[2] This was the last piece of writing which Merleau-Ponty himself published. In it he expressed his view of operational science as having lost touch with the 'real world' and of art as drawing on the fabric of meaning which modern science 'would prefer to ignore'.[3] Reflection on art is used to support the basic idea of the body-subject as a perceiving and perceptible reality, the reality in the world through which Being becomes partially visible or is revealed. The author refers to music as representing 'certain outlines of Being—its ebb and flow, its growth, its upheavals, its turbulence';[4] but he concentrates his attention on painting as giving direct expression to concrete realities. Merleau-Ponty is not of course suggesting that science is useless or that it should be done away with. He is suggesting that it cuts itself off from the real world to which the artist has direct access.

What does Merleau-Ponty mean by Being? In his last writings, particularly in the part of *The Visible and the Invisible* which he was able to finish before his death, his phenomenology takes a more metaphysical turn, and the theme of an ultimate or basic reality comes to the fore. Man is a perceptible reality, and as such he belongs to Nature or the world. He is also a perceiving reality, in dialogue with the world. But it does not follow that as subject man is a consciousness apart from or outside the world. What follows is that in his act of vision the world becomes visible to itself, in and through man. To put the matter in another way, man's awareness of Nature is Nature's awareness of itself,

---

[1] *Signs*, p. 97.
[2] An English translation is included in *The Primacy of Perception*.
[3] *The Primacy of Perception*, p. 161.
[4] *Ibid.*, p. 161.

inasmuch as man belongs to Nature and is rooted in it. This is the metaphysical significance, so to speak, of the statement that man is both a perceiving and a perceptible reality. Though however man as perceiving constitutes his world (not in the sense that he creates it but in the sense that he makes structures appear), reality is more than becomes visible or perceptible. And that which becomes visible and which underlies the distinction between subject and object is Being. Being in itself is invisible. To speak paradoxically, it manifests itself as the non-appearing foundation of that which appears in the dialogue between the body-subject and its environment. It is not itself a perceptible structure but the field of all structures. Being becomes visible to itself in and through man, but only in the form of perceptible structures. What Merleau-Ponty calls 'the flesh of the world' grounds both subject and object and thus logically precedes them. It manifests itself both in perceptible structures and to thought (in the sense that man can become intellectually aware of its reality); but, considered in itself, it remains hidden.

It is perfectly reasonable to see in this theory of Being a significant development in Merleau-Ponty's thought. And it is understandable if some of those who admire him as a philosopher but who are distressed by his earlier exclusion of such concepts as the Absolute and God like to dwell on a metaphysical development which recalls Schelling's idea of Nature coming to know itself in and through man and of Being as hidden in itself but as grounding both subject and object. At the same time we should not read too much into Merleau-Ponty's concept of Being. Being is for him the invisible dimension of the visible. It is indeed the ultimate reality, in the sense that it becomes visible in the structures of the world; but it is not the God of theism. And even if this metaphysical turn in his thought would make it easier for him to find an opening to religious belief, there is no real justification for trying to annex Merleau-Ponty for Christianity.

3. What we have said hitherto may have given the impression that Merleau-Ponty stood aloof from social and political issues and confined himself to abstract philosophy. In point of fact he was strongly attracted by Marxism. One reason for this was obviously the emphasis laid by Marx on the basic situation of man as a being in the world and on man's dialogue with his environment. Merleau-Ponty may have tended to interpret Marx in terms of his own philosophy; but he was genuinely impressed by the

close connection made by Marxism between ideals and social realities and between ethics and politics. He was never the man to accept an ideology on authority or to submit his mind to the requirements of a Party line, and he had little use for a deterministic view of history. But in *Humanisme et terreur* he asserted that Marxism was 'the simple statement of those conditions without which there would be neither any humanism ... nor any rationality in history',[1] and that as a criticism of existing society and of other humanist theories it could not be surpassed. Though however in this work Merleau-Ponty did his best to understand sympathetically the use of terror in the Soviet Union and the purges instituted by Stalin, he later became not only highly critical of Soviet policy and of Communist orthodoxy but also prepared to admit that Communist practice was the logical consequence of Marx's adoption of a theory of history which enabled the Communist leaders to lay claim to scientific knowledge of the movement and demands of history and to justify their actions and dictatorial and repressive behaviour in a manner analogous to that in which the Inquisitors would have justified their actions in the name of their knowledge of divine truth and of the divine will.[2] Merleau-Ponty never lost his admiration for Marx as a thinker; but he had little use for the idea of a philosophy which had become science and could be used to justify dictatorship. He was certainly not an upholder of capitalism. But neither was he a Communist. And it seems reasonable to claim that at no time was he really a Marxist. What attracted him to the thought of Marx were the elements which fitted in with his own philosophy. And whereas he at first tried to dissociate Marx himself from the developments in Communism which he disliked, he later came to think that the origins of these developments could be found in Marx's later ideas.

In an essay Merleau-Ponty remarks that ever since Nietzsche the humblest student would flatly reject a philosophy which did not teach him to live fully.[3] The context of the remark is provided by the statement that we do not accuse painters of escapism, whereas philosophers are liable to be reproached in this way. Context apart however, would Merleau-Ponty's philosophy serve as a guide to life? It is difficult to say, when it remained incomplete. As it stands, it can be seen as demanding reciprocal

---

[1] *Humanisme et terreur*, p. 165.   [2] See *Les aventures de la dialectique.*
[3] *The Primacy of Perception*, p. 161 (in the essay, *The Eye and the Mind*).

recognition among human beings, a respect for human freedom and a self-commitment to the cause of social liberation without the claim to absolute knowledge and to the right to coerce human beings in the name of this alleged knowledge. In other words, Merleau-Ponty's philosophy can be regarded as a form of humanism. But if he is remembered, it will presumably be for his phenomenological inquiries. And these, we may suppose, will be considered not as definitive treatments (which Merleau-Ponty never claimed that they were) but as stimulating explorations, as points of departure.

4. One of Merleau-Ponty's essays is entitled *From Mauss to Claude Lévi-Strauss*,[1] and Lévi-Strauss dedicated his work *La pensée sauvage*[2] to the memory of Maurice Merleau-Ponty, his colleague at the Collège de France. Lévi-Strauss was born in the same year (1908) as Merleau-Ponty, and after his studies he taught philosophy for a time in secondary schools (*lycées*). But in 1935 he accepted the chair of sociology at the University of Sao Paulo in Brazil, where he remained until 1939. After the war he acted as cultural attaché to the French ambassador in Washington; but in 1947 he returned to France, He became Director of Studies at the École des Hautes Études at Paris, and in 1959 he was appointed to the chair of social anthropology at the Collège de France. He is first and foremost an anthropologist;[3] but his ideas have, or have been given, philosophical implications. Structuralism has been presented as embodying or implying a view of man rather different from the existentialist view. Indeed, it has been represented by Michel Foucault[4] as completing Nietzsche's 'death of God' by the 'death of man'. Though therefore the present writer would not be competent to discuss anthropological themes, even if considerations of space permitted such discussion, we can hardly leave French philosophy without some remarks, however inadequate, about the structuralist movement in recent French thought.

In the first and last chapters of his *Structural Anthropology* Lévi-Strauss discusses the use of such terms as ethnography,

---

[1] *Signs*, pp. 114–125.

[2] Translated as *The Savage Mind* (London, 1962).

[3] Lévi-Strauss discusses the use of terms such as ethnology, social and cultural anthropology, and sociology in chapter XVII of his *Anthropologie structurale* (1958; English translation by C. Jacobson and B. G. Schoerf, *Structural Anthropology*, New York and London, 1963).

[4] Author of *Les mots et les choses* (Paris, 1966).

ethnology, physical anthropology, social anthropology and cultural anthropology. In his view ethnography, ethnology and anthropology do not constitute three different disciplines but rather 'three stages, or three moments of time, in the same line of investigation'.[1] Ethnography, for example, 'aims at recording as accurately as possible the respective modes of life of various groups';[2] it is concerned with observation and description. The movement of the mind is then one of synthesis, in which ethnology forms a stage. Synthesis however is concerned primarily with the relations between social phenomena; and anthropology aims at establishing basic structural relations underlying man's whole social life and organization. The sociologist, as Lévi-Strauss sees him, is concerned with the observer's own society or with societies of the same type, whereas the anthropologist seeks to formulate theories which are applicable 'not only to his own fellow countrymen and contemporaries, but to the most distant native population'.[3] Further, the anthropologist, while not of course neglecting man's conscious processes, should include also his unconscious processes, with a view to bringing to formulation the basic structures of which all social and cultural institutions are projections or manifestations. In other words, anthropology is concerned with what Marcel Mauss described as the total social phenomenon. While however it is not indifferent to highly developed societies which express man's conscious endeavour or to the historical processes which led to their development, its aim is to go behind the sphere of conscious ideas and purposes and that of historical processes to 'the complete range of unconscious possibilities'.[4] These possibilities, according to Lévi-Strauss, are limited in number. If therefore the anthropologist can determine the relations of compatibility and incompatibility between these different possibilities or potentials, he can formulate a logical framework for all historical-social developments. Lévi-Strauss quotes the statement of Marx that while men make their own history, they do not know that they are making it; and he comments that while the first part of the statement justifies history, the second part justifies anthropology.

In coming to his idea of structural analysis in anthropology Lévi-Strauss was influenced by linguistics which, in his view, was the social science which had made the most notable progress.

---

[1] *Structural Anthropology*, p. 356.   [2] *Ibid.*, p. 2.
[3] *Ibid.*, p. 363.   [4] *Ibid.*, p. 23.

This progress was achieved through the development of structural linguistics by N. Troubetzkoy and others. In his *Psychologie du langage*[1] Troubetzkoy assigned four basic operations to structural linguistics: the study of the unconscious infrastructure of linguistic phenomena, concentration on the relations between terms, exhibition of the structures of phonemic systems (systems of vocal sounds), and the discovery of general laws which would formulate basic necessary relationships. Lévi-Strauss does not claim that the method of structural linguistics can be simply abstracted and then applied literally in anthropology. For the anthropologist concerns himself with human behaviour and attitudes which cannot be reduced to systems of terminology or shown to be nothing but expressions of language. While he interprets society in terms of a theory of communication, Lévi-Strauss does not restrict communication to language. Nor does he regard all other forms of communication as derivatives of language. At the same time he insists on collaboration between linguistics and anthropology and on their mutual relations, and the method of structural linguistics has served him as a model in formulating a method of anthropology. He looks on the relations between social phenomena as providing the material for the construction of abstract models[2] which should make the observed facts intelligible. The anthropologist will endeavour to go behind (or beneath) conscious models to unconscious models and, by studying the relations between types of models, to bring to light the necessary relationships which govern man's mental, affective, artistic and social life. Further, while not claiming that all social phenomena must be susceptible of numerical measurement, Lévi-Strauss envisages the possibility of the use of mathematics as a tool in anthropological analysis.

The matter can be clarified somewhat in this way. In *La pensée sauvage* Lévi-Strauss rejects the distinction, made, for example, by Lévy-Bruhl, between the logical mentality of civilized man and the prelogical mentality of primitive man. 'The savage mind is logical in the same sense and the same fashion as ours, though as ours is only when it is applied to knowledge of a universe

---

[1] Paris, 1933.
[2] A structural model, we are told, must have the characteristics of a system, in the sense that none of its elements should be able to undergo a change without changes being effected in other elements. Further, it should be possible, in the case of any given model, to state a series of transformations which result in a group of models of the same type.

in which it recognizes physical and semantic properties simultaneously.'[1] In this case of course there must be a logic in myths. And when writing about mythology in *Le cru et le cuit* (1964) Lévi-Strauss argues that there is no arbitrary disorder or mere fantasy in the choice of images or in the ways in which they are associated, opposed or limited. The reason is that the myths express unconscious mental structures which are the same for all. These structures however are purely formal in character. That is to say, they do not provide content, like the archetypes of Jung, but rather the formal structures or patterns which condition all forms of mental life. In spite of the obvious differences between myths and science, the same formal structures are expressed in both. In a sense the basic structures correspond to the *a priori* categories of Kant. But they are not referred to any transcendental subject or ego. They belong to the sphere of the unconscious, and Lévi-Strauss evidently thinks of them as having their origin behind man, not in a metaphysical but in a naturalistic sense.

Lévi-Strauss has written on a number of particular themes, such as kinship structures (*Les structures élémentaires de la parenté*, 1949), totemism (*Le totémisme aujourd'hui*, 1962, and *La pensée sauvage*, 1962) and, as we have seen, on mythology. He has utilized both the relevant anthropological literature and his own field work; and he naturally, and rightly, regards himself as an anthropologist, not as a philosopher. Moreover, philosophies seem to be for him phenomena which, like myths, provide material for the anthropologist's inquiry and research, inasmuch as they embody the formal structures which express themselves in the whole of human life and culture. At the same time the scope of anthropology, as dealing with the total social phenomenon and as concerned with discovering the formal bases of man's mental life, becomes so wide that it is difficult to draw any clear line of demarcation between anthropology as a social science[2] and philosophical anthropology. Further, the fact that Lévi-Strauss does not claim to be a philosopher does not necessarily prove that he has no personal philosophical point of view which is implied by and sometimes finds more or less explicit expression in his anthropological writings.

[1] *The Savage Mind*, p. 268.
[2] Lévi-Strauss allows that anthropology can be described as a social science. But he rejects any tendency to consider it as an isolated discipline. Through physical anthropology it is linked with the natural sciences, and it is also linked to humanistic studies through, for example, linguistics and archaeology.

A philosophy of man is clearly implied by some remarks made by Lévi-Strauss in the ninth chapter of *La pensée sauvage*. When discussing Sartre's concept of the dialectical reason, he admits that in Sartre's terminology he can be described as 'a transcendental materialist and aesthete'.[1] He is a 'transcendental materialist' inasmuch as he regards dialectical reason not as something other than analytical reason but as something additional within analytical reason. 'Sartre calls analytical reason reason in repose; I call the same reason dialectical when it is raised to action, tensed by its efforts to transcend itself.'[2] Reason's effort to transcend itself is not however an effort to grasp the Transcendent but the effort to find the ultimate bases of language, society and thought or, to express the matter more provocatively, 'to undertake the resolution of the human into the non-human'.[3] As for the term 'aesthete', Lévi-Strauss says that it applies to himself inasmuch as Sartre uses it to describe anyone who studies men as if they were ants. Indeed, the ultimate goal of the human sciences is 'not to constitute, but to dissolve man'.[4]

It is hardly necessary to say that Lévi-Strauss has no intention of denying that there are human beings. Man is the subject of his study. The word 'dissolve' is to be understood in terms of reduction. But Lévi-Strauss insists that he does not mean by this the reduction of a 'higher' to a 'lower' level. The level which is to be reduced must be conceived in all its distinctive characteristics and qualities; and if it is reduced to another level, some of its richness will be communicated retroactively to this other level. For example, if we were to succeed in understanding life as a function of inert matter, we would find that 'the latter has properties very different from those previously attributed to it'.[5] It is not a question of reducing the complex to the simple, but of replacing a less intelligible complexity by one which is more intelligible. Thus to reduce man's mental, social and affective life to unconscious formal structures or patterns is not to deny that the former is what it is: it is to make the complexity of the forms of social and cultural phenomena intelligible in the light of a complex structure which is expressed in and unifies the phenomena but from which the phenomena cannot simply be deduced *a priori*. For we have also to take into account the dialectic between man and his environment and between man and man.

---

[1] *The Savage Mind*, p. 246.   [2] *Ibid*., p. 246.
[3] *Ibid*., p. 246.   [4] *Ibid*., p. 247.   [5] *Ibid*., p. 248.

Lévi-Strauss doubtless believes that these ideas fall within the scope of anthropology, and that it is a mistake to represent them as philosophical theories. While however he does not develop them as a philosophy, it seems clear enough that they imply a naturalism which is different from the crude reductionism of some eighteenth-century *philosophes*. If Lévi-Strauss is prepared to accept the Sartrian label 'transcendental materialist', his materialism is of the somewhat ambiguous type represented by dialectical materialism, which has indeed exercised a certain influence on his thought. In any case he opposes a view which reintegrates man into Nature to the Sartrian dichotomy between the for-itself and the in-itself, and a conditioning of man's thought and activity by formal structures which underlie consciousness to the absolute freedom proclaimed by the author of *Being and Nothingness*.

Structuralism has its antecedents in, for example, structural psychology and, more recently, structural linguistics, as well of course as in the theories of Durkheim and Mauss. Its principal field of application is the human sciences, where it concentrates on the relations and supposedly invariant laws of combination between the relevant phenomena. It does not neglect historical development, the 'diachronic' element; but it concentrates on the 'synchronic' element, the basic formal structures which are believed to be independent of historical change. This approach has been applied in a variety of fields, such as literary criticism, art, psychology and the interpretation of Marxism; and in so far as it is a question of a heuristic method, there can obviously be no cogent objection to experimenting with it and evaluating the results. The method however is connected with hypotheses which can reasonably be seen as implying a naturalistic philosophy which differs from both existentialism and Marxism, even if elements from both sources are incorporated. Given the emphasis on heuristic method, it is doubtless an exaggeration to speak of a system of structuralist philosophy. Equally, given the wide area of application of the method in the human sciences, one can justifiably speak of a current of thought which differs from both existentialism and Marxism and which can perhaps be described as a new naturalism, based on reflection in the field of social and cultural anthropology.

A SHORT BIBLIOGRAPHY

In the bibliography at the end of Volume VII of this work a number of general histories of philosophy were mentioned, the titles of which have not been repeated here. Encyclopaedias have not been listed, except for the two mentioned under General Works below. Nor have bibliographies been provided for all the philosophers whose names appear in the text of this volume.

General Works

Balodi, N. *Les constantes de la pensée française*. Paris, 1948.

Benrubi, J. *Contemporary Thought of France*. London, 1926. *Les sources et les courants de la philosophie contemporaine en France*. 2 vols. Paris, 1933.

Boas, G. *French Philosophies of the Romantic Period*. New York, 1925, reissued 1964. *Dominant Themes of Modern Philosophy*. New York, 1957.

Bréhier, E. *Histoire de la philosophie. La philosophie moderne. Tome 2; deuxième partie, XIXe et XXe siècles*. Paris, 1944. *The History of Philosophy. Vol. VI, The Nineteenth Century, Period of Systems, 1800–1850*, translated by W. Baskin. Chicago, 1968.

Charlton, D. G. *Positivist Thought in France during the Second Empire, 1852–1870*. Oxford, 1959.

Collins, J. *A History of Modern European Philosophy*. Milwaukee, 1954. (includes chapters, with bibliographies, on Comte and Bergson).

Cruickshank, J. (editor). *The Novelist as Philosopher. Studies in French Fiction, 1935–60*. London 1962.

Edwards, P. (editor). *The Encyclopedia of Philosophy*. 8 vols. New York and London, 1967. (Besides a general article on French philosophy there are articles on distinct movements and on a considerable number of individual philosophers.)

Enciclopedia Filosofica. Second edition, 6 vols. Florence, 1967.

Farber, M. (editor). *Philosophic Thought in France and the United States. Essays representing Major Trends in Contemporary French and American Philosophy*. Buffalo, N.Y., 1950.

Gouhier, H. *Les grandes avenues de la pensée philosophique en France depuis Descartes*. Paris, 1966.

Gunn, J. Alexander. *Modern French Philosophy. A study of the Development since Comte*. London 1922.

Lavelle, L. *La philosophie française entre les deux guerres*. Paris, 1942.

Lévy-Bruhl, L. *A History of Modern Philosophy in France*. Translated by G. Coblence. London and Chicago, 1899.

Mandelbaum, M. *History, Man and Reason. A Study in Nineteenth-Century Thought*. Baltimore and London, 1971. (A general study, but includes a treatment of several French philosophers.)

Parodi, D. *La philosophie contemporaine en France*. Paris, 1919.

Pierce, R. *Contemporary French Political Thought*. London, 1966.

Plamenatz, J. *Man and Society. A Critical Examination of Some Important Social and Political Theories from Machiavelli to Marx*. Vol. 2, London, 1963. (This volume is devoted mainly to Hegel and Marx, but it includes a treatment of the early French socialists.)

Randall, J. H., Jr. *The Career of Philosophy: Vol. 2, From the German Enlightenment to the Age of Darwin*. New York and London, 1965. (Includes a brief treatment of French philosophy from the Revolution up to Comte.)

Ravaisson, F. *La Philosophie en France au XIXᵉ siècle*. Paris 1868.

Simpson, W. J. S. *Religious Thought in France in the Nineteenth Century*. London, 1935.

Smith, C. *Contemporary French Philosophy. A Study in Norms and Values*. London, 1964.

Soltan, R. *French Political Thought in the Nineteenth Century*. New Haven, 1931.

Trotignon, P. *Les philosophes français d'aujourd'hui*. Paris, 1967.

Wahl, J. *Tableaux de la philosophie française*. Paris, 1946.

Chapter I

1. General Works relating to Traditionalism

Boas, G. *French Philosophies of the Romantic Period*. New York, 1925, reissued 1964.

Ferraz, M. *Histoire de la philosophie en France au XIXᵉ siècle: Traditionalisme et ultramontanisme*. Paris, 1880.

Foucher, L. *La philosophie catholique en France au XIXᵉ siècle*. Paris, 1955. (First four chapters.)

Hocedez, E. *Histoire de la théologie au XIXᵉ siècle*, I–II. Brussels and Paris, 1948–52.

Hötzel, N. *Die Uroffenbarung im französischen Traditionalismus*. Munich, 1962.

Lacroix, J. *Vocation personnelle et tradition nationale*. Paris, 1942.

Laski, N. *Authority in the Modern State*. New Haven, 1919.

Roche, A. V. *Les idées traditionalistes en France*. Urbana, 1937.

Menzer, B. (editor). *Catholic Political Thought (1789–1848)*. Westminster, Maryland, 1952.

2. De Maistre

Texts

Oeuvres complètes. 14 vols. 1884–7.

The Works of Joseph de Maistre (Selections), translated by J. Lively. New York, 1965.

Considérations sur la France. Neuchâtel, 1796.

Essai sur le principe générateur des constitutions politiques. Paris, 1814 (and Lyons, 1929).

Du Pape. 2 vols. Lyons, 1819.

Soirées de Saint-Pétersbourg. 2 vols. Paris, 1821.

Examen de la philosophie de Bacon. Paris, 1836.

Studies

Bayle, F. *Les idées politiques de Joseph de Maistre.* Paris, 1945.

Brunello, B. *Joseph de Maistre, politico e filosofo.* Bologna, 1967.

Gianturco, E. *Joseph de Maistre and Giambattista Vico.* Washington, DC, 1937.

Goyau, G. *La pensée religieuse de Joseph de Maistre.* Paris, 1921.

Huber, M. *Die Staatsphilosophie von Joseph de Maistre im Lichte des Thomismus.* Basel and Stuttgart, 1958.

Lecigne, C. *Joseph de Maistre.* Paris, 1914.

Rhoden, P. R. *Joseph de Maistre als politischer Theoretiker.* Munich, 1929.

2. *De Bonald*

Texts

Oeuvres complètes. 7 vols. Paris, 1857–75 (3rd edition).

Oeuvres, edited by J. P. Migne. 3 vols. Paris, 1859.

Théorie du pouvoir politique et religieux dans la société civile. 3 vols. Constance, 1796. There is an edition by C. Capitan, Paris, 1965.

Essai analytique sur les lois naturelles de l'ordre social. Paris, 1800.

La législation primitive. 3 vols. Paris, 1802.

Recherches philosophiques sur les premiers objets des connaissances morales. 2 vols. Paris, 1818.

Démonstration philosophique du principe constitutif de la société. Paris, 1827.

Studies

Adams, A. *Die Philosophie de Bonalds.* Münster, 1923.

Faguet, E. *Politiques et moralistes du XIXe siècle.* Series 1, Paris, 1891.

Moulinié, H. *De Bonald.* Paris, 1915.

Quinlan, M. H. *The Historical Thought of the Vicomte de Bonald.* Washington, DC, 1953.

Reinerz, H. W. *Bonald als Politiker, Philosoph und Mensch.* Leipzig, 1940.

Soreil, A. *Le Vicomte de Bonald.* Brussels, 1942.

3. *Chateaubriand*

Texts

Oeuvres complètes. 20 vols. Paris, 1858–61.
Essai historique, politique et moral sur les révolutions. London, 1797.
Génie du christianisme. 5 vols. Paris, 1802.

Studies

Bertrin, G. *La sincérité religieuse de Chateaubriand.* Paris, 1899.
Döhner, K. *Zeit und Ewigkeit bei Chateaubriand.* Ghent, 1931.
Giraud, V. *Le christianisme de Chateaubriand.* 2 vols. Paris, 1925–8.
Lemaître, J. *Chateaubriand.* Paris, 1912.
Maurois, A. *Chateaubriand.* Paris, 1938.
Sainte-Beuve, C. A. *Chateaubriand et son groupe littéraire sous l'Empire.* Paris, 1869.

4. *Lamennais*

Texts

Oeuvres complètes. 12 vols. Paris, 1836–7.
Oeuvres choisies et philosophiques. 10 vols. Paris, 1837–41.
Oeuvres posthumes, edited by E. D. Forgues. 6 vols. Paris, 1855–9.
Oeuvres inédites, edited by A. Blaize. 2 vols. Paris, 1866.
Essai sur l'indifférence en matière de religion. 4 vols. Paris, 1817–1824.
Défense de l'Essai sur l'indifférence. Paris, 1821.
Paroles d'un croyant. Paris, 1834.
Esquisse d'une philosophie. 4 vols. Paris, 1841–6.

Studies

Boutard, C. *Lamennais, sa vie et ses doctrines.* 3 vols. 1905–13.
Derré, J. R. *La Mennais, ses amis et le mouvement des idées à l'époque romantique (1824–34).* Paris, 1962.
Duine, M. *La Mennais, sa vie, ses idées, ses ouvrages.* Evreux, 1922.
Gibson, W. *The Abbé de Lamennais and the Liberal Catholic Movement in France.* London and New York, 1896.
Janet, P. *La philosophie de Lamennais.* Paris, 1890.
Le Guillon, L. *L'évolution de la pensée religieuse de Félicité Lamennais.* Paris, 1966.
Mourre, M. *Lamennais, ou l'hérésie des temps modernes.* Paris, 1955.
Roe, W. G. *Lamennais and England. The Reception of Lamennais' Religious Ideas in England in the Nineteenth Century.* Oxford, 1966.
Verucci, G. F. *Lamennais. Dal cattolicesimo autoritario al radicalismo democratico.* Naples, 1963.

Chapter II

1. *The Ideologists*

Texts

Destutt de Tracy. *Éléments d'idéologie.* 4 vols. Paris, 1801–15. *Traité de la volonté et de ses effets.* Paris 1805. *Commentaire sur l'esprit des lois de Montesquieu.* Liège, 1817. Translated by Thomas Jefferson as *A Commentary and Review of Montesquieu's Spirit of Laws.* Philadelphia, 1811.

Studies

Cailliet, E. *La tradition littéraire des idéologues.* Philadelphia, 1943.
Chinard, J. *Jefferson et les idéologues.* Baltimore, 1925.
Picavet, F. *Les idéologues.* Paris, 1891. (The standard work).
Riverso, E. *I problemi della conoscenza et del metodo nel sensismo degli ideologi.* Naples, 1962.
Van Duzen, C. *The Contributions of the Idéologues to French Revolutionary Thought.* Baltimore, 1935.

2. *Maine de Biran*

Texts

Oeuvres de Maine de Biran, edited by P. Tisserand and H. Gouhier. 14 vols. Paris, 1920–9. (This edition entirely supersedes Victor Cousin's four-volume edition of de Biran's *Oeuvres Philosophiques.* Paris, 1841.)
Journal intime, edited by H. Gouhier. Paris, 1954–7.
The *Mémoire sur l'habitude* (1802) has been translated by M. Boehm as *The Influence of Habit on the Faculty of Thinking.* Baltimore, 1929.
De l'apperception immédiate. Mémoire de Berlin 1807, edited by J. Echeverría, Paris, 1963.

Studies

Ambrosetti, G. *La filosofia sociale di Maine de Biran.* Verona, 1953.
Antonelli, M. T. *Maine de Biran.* Brescia, 1947.
Buol, J. *Die Anthropologie Maine de Birans.* Winterthur, 1961.
Cresson, A. *Maine de Biran.* Paris, 1950.
De la Valette Monbrun, A. *Maine de Biran. Essai de biographie historique et psychologique.* Paris, 1914.
Delbos, V. *Maine de Biran et son œuvre philosophique.* Paris, 1931.
Drevet, A. *Maine de Biran.* Paris, 1968.
Ghio, M. *Maine de Biran e la tradizione biraniana in Francia.* Turin, 1962.
Fessard, P. *La méthode de réflexion chez Maine de Biran.* Paris, 1938.

Funke, H. *Maine de Biran. Philosophisches und politisches Denken zwischen Ancien Régime und Bürgerkönigtum in Frankreich.* Bonn, 1947.

Gouhier, H. *Les conversions de Maine de Biran.* Paris, 1947. (Highly recommended.)

Hallie, P. P. *Maine de Biran, Reformer of Empiricism.* Cambridge (Mass.), 1959.

Henry, M. *Philosophie et phénoménologie du corps. Essai sur l'ontologie biranienne.* Paris, 1965.

Lacroze, R. *Maine de Biran.* Paris, 1970.

Lassaigne, J. *Maine de Biran, homme politique.* Paris, 1958.

Lemay, P. *Maine de Biran.* Paris, 1946.

Le Roy, G. *L'expérience de l'effort et de la grâce chez Maine de Biran.* Paris, 1937.

Madinier, G. *Conscience et mouvement.* Paris, 1939.

Monette, A. *La théorie des premiers principes selon Maine de Biran.* Montreal and Paris, 1945.

Moore, F. C. T. *The Psychology of Maine de Biran.* Oxford, 1970.

Paliard, J. *La raisonnement selon Maine de Biran.* Paris, 1925.

Robef, I. *Leibniz et Maine de Biran.* Paris, 1927.

Thibaud, M. *L'effort chez Maine de Biran et Bergson.* Grenoble, 1939.

Tisserand, P. *L'anthropologie de Maine de Biran, ou la science de l'homme intérieur.* Paris, 1909.

Voutsinas, D. *La psychologie de Maine de Biran.* Paris, 1964.

There are some collections of articles, such as those in the number of the *Revue internationale de Philosophie* dedicated to Maine de Biran on the occasion of the second centenary of his birth (Brussels, 1966).

Chapter III

1. *Royer-Collard*

Texts

Les fragments philosophiques de Royer-Collard, edited by A Schimberg. Paris, 1913.

Studies

De Barante, A. *La vie politique de M. Royer-Collard, ses discours et ses écrits.* 2 vols. Paris, 1878 (3rd edition).

Nesmesdesmarets, R. *Les doctrines politiques de Royer-Collard.* Montpellier, 1908.

Spuller, E. *Royer-Collard.* Paris, 1895.

2. *Cousin*

Texts

Philosophie sensualiste au XVIIIe siècle. Paris, 1819.
Fragments philosophiques. Paris, 1826.

Cours de l'histoire de la philosophie. 3 vols. Paris, 1829.
De la métaphysique d'Aristote. Paris, 1835.
Du vrai, du beau et du bien. Paris, 1837.
Cours de l'histoire de la Philosophie moderne. 5 vols. Paris, 1841.
Études sur Pascal. Paris, 1842.
Justice et charité. Paris, 1848.

Studies

Cornelius, A. *Die Geschichtslehre Victor Cousins.* Geneva, 1958.
Dubois, P. F. *Cousin, Jouffroy, Damiron, souvenirs publiés avec une introduction par Adolphe Lair.* Paris, 1902.
Janet, P. *Victor Cousin et son œuvre.* Paris, 1885.
Mastellone, S. *Victor Cousin e il risorgimento italiano.* Florence, 1955.
Saint-Hilaire, J. B. *Victor Cousin, sa vie, sa correspondance.* 3 vols. Paris, 1895.
Simon, J. *Victor Cousin.* Paris, 1887. There is an English translation by M. B. and E. P. Anderson, Chicago, 1888.

3. *Jouffroy*
Texts

Mélanges philosophiques. Paris, 1833.
Nouveaux mélanges philosophiques, edited by F. Damiron. Paris, 1842.
Cours de droit naturel. 2 vols. Paris, 1834–42.
Cours d'esthétique. Paris, 1843.

Studies

Lambert, L. *Der Begriff des Schönen in der Ästhetik Jouffroys.* Giessen, 1909.
Ollé-Laprune, L. *Théodore Jouffroy.* Paris, 1899.

Chapter IV

1. *Fourier*
Texts

Oeuvres complètes. 6 vols. Paris, 1841–5.
Théorie des quatre mouvements et des destinées générales. 2 vols. Lyons, 1808.
Théorie de l'unité universelle. 2 vols. Paris, 1822.
Le nouveau monde industriel et sociétaire. Besançon, 1829.
La fausse industrie morcelée, répugnante, mensongère, et l'antidote: l'industrie naturelle, combinée, attrayante, véridique, donnant quadruple produit. 2 vols. Paris, 1835–6.
(For manuscript work see *Les cahiers manuscrits de Fourier* by E. Poulat, Paris, 1957.)

Studies

Bourgin, H. Fourier, *Contribution à l'étude du socialisme français.* Paris, 1905.

Lehouck, E. *Fourier aujourd'hui.* Paris, 1966.

Manuel, F. E. *The Prophets of Paris.* Cambridge (Mass.), 1962.

Tosi, V. *Fourier e il suo falansterio.* Savona, 1921.

Vergez, A. *Fourier.* Paris, 1969.

2. Saint-Simon

Texts

Oeuvres complètes de Saint-Simon et Enfantin. 47 vols. Paris, 1865–76.

Oeuvres. 6 vols. Paris, 1966.

Textes choisis, edited by J. Dautry. Paris, 1951.

Selected Writings, translated with an introduction by F. M. H. Markham. Oxford, 1942.

Lettres d'un habitant de Genève à ses contemporains. Geneva, 1802–03. Edited by A. Pereire, Paris, 1925.

Introduction aux travaux scientifiques du XIXe siècle. 2 vols. Paris, 1807–08.

Esquisse d'une nouvelle Encyclopédie. Paris, 1810.

Mémoire sur la science de l'homme. Paris, 1813.

Travail sur la gravitation universelle. Paris, 1813.

De la réorganisation de la société européenne. Paris, 1814. (In collaboration with A. Thierry.)

L'industrie. Paris, 1818.

La politique. Paris, 1819.

L'organisation. Paris, 1819–20.

Catéchisme des industriels. Paris, 1824.

Studies

Charléty, S. *Essai sur l'histoire du saint-simonisme.* Paris, 1896.

Dondo, M. M. *The French Faust, Henri de Saint-Simon.* New York, 1955.

Durkheim, E. *Le socialisme, sa définition, ses débuts. La doctrine saint-simonienne.* Edited by M. Mauss. Paris, 1928. Translated into English by C. Sattler as *Socialism and Saint-Simon*, Yellow Springs (Ohio), 1958.

Fazio, M. F. *Linea di sviluppo del pensiero di Saint-Simon.* Palermo, 1942.

Gurvitch, G. *Les fondateurs français de la scociologie contemporaine: Saint-Simon et P.-J. Proudhon.* Paris, 1955.

Leroy, M. *La vie véritable du comte de Saint-Simon.* Paris, 1925.

Manuel, F. E. *The New World of Henri de Saint-Simon.* Cambridge (Mass.), 1956.

Muckle, F. *Henri de Saint-Simon, Persönlichkeit und Werk*. Jena, 1908.
Vidal, E. *Saint-Simon e la scienza politica*. Milan, 1959.

3. Proudhon

Texts

Oeuvres complètes. 26 vols. Paris, 1867–71.
Correspondance. 14 vols. Paris, 1875.
Oeuvres complètes, edited by C. Bouglé and H. Moysset. 11 vols. Paris, 1920–39 (incomplete).
Selected Writings of Pierre-Joseph Proudhon, edited with an introduction by S. Edwards and translated by E. Fraser. London, 1970.
Qu'est-ce que la propriété? Paris, 1840. Translated by B. Tucker as *What is Property?* Princeton, 1876.
De la création de l'ordre dans l'humanité. Paris, 1843.
Système des contradictions économiques ou Philosophie de la misère. Paris, 1846. Translated by B. Tucker as *System of Economic Contradictions*. Boston, 1888.
Idée générale de la révolution du XIXe siècle. Paris, 1851. Translated by J. B. Robinson as *General Idea of the Revolution in the Nineteenth Century*, London, 1923.
La justice dans la révolution et dans l'église. Paris, 1858.
La guerre et la paix. Paris, 1861.
Du principe féderatif et de la nécessité de reconstituer le parti de la révolution. Paris, 1863.
De la capacité des classes ouvrières. Paris, 1865.

Studies

Ansart, P. *Sociologie de Proudhon*. Paris, 1967.
Brogan, C. *Proudhon*. London, 1936.
De Lubac, H. *Proudhon et le christianisme*. Paris, 1945. Translated by R. E. Scantlebury as *The Un-Marxian Socialist: A Study of Proudhon*. 2 vols. Paris, 1896.
Diehl, C. *P.-J. Proudhon, seine Lehre und sein Leben*. 3 vols. Jena, 1888–96.
Dolléans, E. *Proudhon*. Paris, 1948 (4th edition).
Gröndahl, B. *P.-J. Proudhon*. Stockholm, 1959.
Heintz, P. *Die Autoritätsproblematik bei Proudhon. Versuch einer immanenten Kritik*. Cologne, 1957.
Jackson, J. H. *Marx, Proudhon and European Socialism*. New York, 1962.
Lu, S. V. *The Political Theories of P.-J. Proudhon*. New York, 1922.
Prion, G. *Proudhon et syndicalisme révolutionnaire*. Paris, 1910.
Saint-Beuve, C. A. *Proudhon, sa vie et sa correspondance*. Paris, 1870.

Woodcock, G. *Pierre-Joseph Proudhon: A Biography*. London, 1956.
(Highly recommended.)

Chapters on Proudhon can be found in, for example, *The Anarchists*
by J. Joll (London, 1964), *A History of Socialist Thought*, Vol. 1
by G. D. H. Cole (London, 1953) and *Anarchism* by G. Woodcock
(London, 1963).

Chapter V

Comte

Texts

Cours de philosophie positive. 6 vols. Paris, 1830–42. There is a loose
English version (approved by Comte) by H. Martineau, *Cours,
The Positive Philosophy of Auguste Comte*. 2 vols, London 1853.

Discours sur l'esprit positif. Paris, 1849. (This was originally prefixed
to the *Traité philosophique d'astronomie populaire*.) Translated
by Fr. S. Beesly as *A Discourse on the Positive Spirit*. London,
1903.

Discours sur l'ensemble du positivisme. Paris, 1848.

Calendrier positiviste. Paris, 1849.

Système de politique positive. 4 vols. 1851–54. Translated by J. H.
Bridges and F. Harrison as *The System of Positive Polity*,
4 vols., London, 1857–77.

Catéchisme positiviste. Paris, 1852. Translated by R. Congreve as
The Catechism of Positive Religion. London, 1858.

Appel aux conservateurs. Paris, 1855.

*Synthèse subjective, ou Système universel des conceptions propres à
l'état normal de l'humanité*. Vol. 1, Paris, 1856.

Rather oddly, there is no complete and critical selection of Comte's
works. H. Gouhier however has published *Oeuvres choisies
d'Auguste Comte*, Paris, 1943, while C. Le Verrier has published
in two volumes the first two lectures of the *Cours de philosophie
positive* and the *Discours sur l'esprit positif*, Paris, 1943.

There are several collections of letters. *Lettres d'Auguste Comte à
John Stuart Mill*, 1841–6 (Paris 1877), *Lettres à des positivistes
anglais* (Paris, 1889), *Correspondance inédite d'Auguste Comte*
(4 vols., Paris, 1903–04), *Nouvelles lettres inédites* (Paris, 1939).

Studies

Arbousse-Bastide, P. *La doctrine de l'éducation universelle dans la
philosophie d'Auguste Comte*. 2 vols. Paris, 1957.
     Auguste Comte. Paris, 1968.

Caird, E. *The Social Philosophy and Religion of Comte*. Glasgow, 1885.

Cresson, A. *Auguste Comte, sa vie, son oeuvre*. Paris, 1941.

Defourny, G. *La sociologie positiviste d'Auguste Comte*. Louvain, 1902.

De Lubac, H. *Le drame de l'humanisme athée*. Paris, 1944. Translated by E. M. Riley as *The Drama of Atheist Humanism*. London, 1950. (Comte is one of the philosophers considered in this work.)

Devolvé, J. *Réflexions sur la pensée comtienne*. Paris, 1932.

Ducassé, P. *Méthode et intuition chez Auguste Comte*. Paris, 1939.

Dumas, G. *Psychologie de deux Messies positivistes: Saint-Simon et Auguste Comte*. Paris, 1905.

Gouhier, H. *La vie d'Auguste Comte*. Paris, 1931.
      La jeunesse d'Auguste Comte et la formation du positivisme. 3 vols. Paris, 1933–41. (Highly recommended.)

Gould, F. J. *Auguste Comte*. London, 1920.

Gruber, H. *Comte, der Begründer des Positivismus*. Freiburg i/B., 1889.

Hawkins, R. L. *Auguste Comte and the United States (1816–53)*. Cambridge (Mass.), 1936.

Lacroix, J. *La sociologie d'Auguste Comte*. Paris, 1956.

Lévy-Bruhl, L. *La philosophie d'Auguste Comte*. Paris, 1900. Translated by K. de Beaumont-Klein as *The Philosophy of Auguste Comte*. New York, 1903.

Littré, E. *Auguste Comte et la philosophie positive*. Paris, 1863.
      Auguste Comte et Stuart Mill. Paris, 1867.

Marvin, F. S. *Comte: The Founder of Sociology*. London, 1936.

Mill, J. S. *Auguste Comte and Positivism*. London, 1865.

Moschetti, A. M. *Auguste Comte e la pedagogia positiva*. Milan, 1953.

Negt, O. *Strukturbeziehungen zwischen den Gesellschaftslehren Comtes und Hegels*. Frankfort, 1964.

Peter, J. *Auguste Comte. Bild vom Menschen*. Stuttgart, 1936.

Whittaker, T. *Comte and Mill*. London, 1908.

Part II: Chapter VI

1. *Littré*

Texts

De la philosophie positive. Paris, 1845.

Application de la philosophie positive au gouvernement des sociétés. Paris, 1849.

Conservation, révolution et positivisme. Paris, 1852 (2nd edition, 1879).

Paroles de philosophie positive. Paris, 1859 (2nd edition, 1863).

Auguste Comte et la philosophie positive. Paris, 1863.

Auguste Comte et Stuart Mill. Paris, 1867.

Principes de philosophie positive. Paris, 1868.

La science au point de vue philosophique. Paris, 1873.

Fragments de philosophie positive et de sociologie contemporaine. Paris 1876. (The articles published in *De la philosophie positive* are reprinted in this work.)

Studies

Aquarone, S. *The Life and Works of Emile Littré*. Leyden, 1958.
Caro, E. *Littré et le positivisme*. Paris, 1883.
Charlton, D. G. See under General Works.
Six, L. *Littré devant Dieu*. Paris, 1962.

2. *Bernard*

Texts

Introduction à la médecine expérimentale. Paris, 1865. Translated by
   N. C. Green as *An Introduction to the Study of Experimental
   Medicine*. New York, 1927.
La science expérimentale. Paris, 1878.
Pensées. Notes détachées, edited by L. Delhoume. Paris, 1937.
Philosophie, edited by J. Chevalier. Paris, 1938.
*Leçons sur les phénomènes de la vie communs aux animaux et aux
   végétaux*. Paris, 1966.

Studies

Clarke, R. *Claude Bernard et la médecine expérimentale*. Paris, 1961.
Cotard, H. *La pensée de Claude Bernard*. Grenoble, 1945.
Foulquié, P. *Claude Bernard*. Paris (undated).
Lamy, P. *Claude Bernard et le matérialisme*. Paris, 1939.
Mauriac, P. *Claude Bernard*. Paris, 1941 (2nd edition 1954).
Olmsted, J. M. D. and E. H. *Claude Bernard and the Experimental
   Method in Medicine*. New York, 1952.
Sertillanges, A. D. *La philosophie de Claude Bernard*. Paris, 1944.
Virtanen, R. *Claude Bernard and his Place in the History of Ideas*.
   Lincoln (Nebraska), 1960.
Various Authors. *Philosophie et méthodologie scientifique de Claude
   Bernard*. Paris, 1966.

3. *Taine*

Texts

Les philosophes français du dix-neuvième siècle. Paris, 1857.
Essais de critique et d'histoire. Paris, 1858.
Histoire de la littérature anglaise. 4 vols. Paris, 1863–4. Translated by
   H. van Laun as *History of English Literature*, 2 vols, Edinburgh,
   1873.
Nouveaux essais de critique et d'histoire. Paris, 1865.
Philosophie de l'art. Paris, 1865. Translated by J. Durand as *The
   Philosophy of Art*. New York, 1865. (Second French edition
   1880.)
De l'intelligence. 2 vols. Paris, 1870. Translated by T. D. Hayes as
   Intelligence. London 1871.

Les origines de la France contemporaine. 5 vols. Paris, 1875–93.
Derniers essais de critique et d'histoire. Paris, 1894.

Studies

Aulard, A. *Taine, historien de la révolution française.* Paris, 1907.
Barzelotti, G. *Ippolito Taine.* Rome, 1896.
Boosten, J. P. *Taine et Renan et l'idée de Dieu.* Maastricht, 1936.
Castiglioni, G. *Taine.* Brescia. 1945.
Cresson, A. *Hippolyte Taine.* Paris, 1951.
Giraud, V. *Essai sur Taine: son œuvre et son influence.* Paris, 1901.
   Hippolyte Taine: Études et documents. Paris, 1928.
Ippolito, F. G. *Taine e la filosofia dell'arte.* Roma, 1911.
Kahn, S. J. *Science and Aesthetic Judgment: A Study in Taine's Critical Method.* New York, 1953.
Lacombe, P. *La Psychologie des individus et des sociétés chez Taine.* Paris, 1906.
   Taine, historien et sociologue. Paris, 1909.
La Ferla, G. *Ippolito Taine.* Rome, 1937.
Mongardini, C. *Storia e sociologia nell'opera di Hippolyte Taine.* Milan, 1965.
Relevant aspects of Taine's thought are discussed in such works as Benedetto Croce's *Estetica* and *Teoria e storia della storiografia* and H. Sée's *Science et philosophie de l'histoire* (2nd edition, Paris, 1933).

4. *Durkheim*

Texts

De la division du travail social. Paris, 1893. Translated by G. Simpson as *The Division of Labour in Society,* New York, 1952.
Les règles de la méthode sociologique. Paris, 1895. Translated by S. A. Solovay and J. H. Mueller as *The Rules of Sociological Method,* Chicago, 1938 (republished at Glencoe, Illinois, 1950).
Le suicide. Étude de sociologie. Paris, 1897. Translated by J. A. Spaulding and G. Simpson as *Suicide: A Study in Sociology,* Glencoe, Illinois, 1951).
Les formes élémentaires de la vie religieuse: le système totémique en Australie. Paris, 1912. Translated by J. W. Swain as *The Elementary Forms of the Religious Life: A Study in Religious Sociology,* London and New York, 1915.
Éducation et sociologie. Paris, 1922. Translated by J. D. Fox as *Education and Sociology,* Glencoe, Illinois, 1956.
Sociologie et philosophie. Paris, 1924. Translated by D. F. Pocock as *Sociology and Philosophy,* London and Glencoe, Illinois, 1953.

L'éducation morale. Paris, 1925, Translated by E. K. Wilson and H. Schnurer as *Moral Education: A Study in the Theory and Application of the Sociology of Education*, New York, 1961.

Le socialisme. Paris, 1928.

L'évolution pédagogique en France. France, 1938.

Leçons de sociologie: physique des mœurs et du droit. Paris, 1950. Translated by C. Brookfield as *Professional Ethics and Civic Morals*, London, 1957.

Montesquieu et Rousseau, précurseurs de la sociologie. Paris, 1953.

La science sociale et l'action. Introduction et présentation de J. C. Filloux. Paris, 1970.

There are various collections of articles by Durkheim, such as *Journal sociologique*, edited by J. Duvignaud, Paris, 1969. In English there is *Émile Durkheim, 1858–1917: A Collection of Essays, with Translations and a Bibliography*, edited by K. H. Wolff, Columbus, Ohio, 1960. This work also contains essays on Durkheim by various authors.

Studies

Aimard, G. *Durkheim et la science économique*. Paris, 1962.

Alpert, H. *Émile Durkheim and His Sociology*. New York, 1939.

Bierstedt, R. *Émile Durkheim*. New York and London, 1966.

Coser, L. A. *Masters of Sociological Thought*. New York, 1971. (Contains a chapter on Durkheim.)

Davy, G. *Durkheim, choix de textes avec étude du système sociologique*. Paris, 1911.

Duvignard, J. *Durkheim: sa vie, son œuvre, avec un exposé de sa philosophie*. Paris, 1965.

Fletcher, R. *The Making of Sociology*, Vol. 2. London, 1971.

Gehlke, C. E. *Émile Durkheim's Contributions to Sociological Theory*. New York, 1915.

La Capra, D. *Émile Durkheim: Sociologist and Philosopher*. Ithaca and London, 1972.

Lukes, S. *Émile Durkheim. His Life and Work. A Historical and Critical Study*. London, 1973. (Highly recommended. Includes a comprehensive bibliography.)

Nisbet, R. A. *Émile Durkheim*. Englewood Cliffs, N.J., 1965.

Parsons, T. *The Structure of Social Action*. New York, 1937, and Glencoe, Illinois, 1949.

Seger, I. *Durkheim and his Critics on the Sociology of Religion*. New York, 1957.

Vialatoux, J. *De Durkheim á Bergson*. Paris, 1939.

Wolff, K. H. (editor). See above under Texts.

5. *Lévy-Bruhl*

Texts

Histoire de la philosophie moderne en France. Paris. Translated by G. Coblence, London and Chicago, 1899.

La Philosophie de Jacobi. Paris, 1894.

La philosophie d' Auguste Comte. Paris, 1900. Translated by K. de Beaumont-Klein as *The Philosophy of Auguste Comte*, London, 1903.

Les fonctions fondamentales dans les sociétés inférieures. Paris, 1910. Translated by L. A. Clare as *How Natives Think*, London and New York, 1923.

La mentalité primitive. Paris, 1921. Translated by L. A. Clare as *Primitive Mentality*, London, 1928.

L'âme primitive. Paris, 1921. Translated by L. A. Clare as *The 'Soul' of the Primitive*, London, 1928.

Le surnaturel et la nature dans la mentalité primitive. Paris, 1931. Translated by L. A. Clare as *Primitives and the Supernatural*, London, 1936.

La mythologie primitive. Le monde mythique des Australiens et des Papous. Paris, 1935.

L'expérience mystique et les symboles chez les primitifs. Paris, 1938.

Les carnets de Lucien Lévy-Bruhl. Paris, 1949.

Studies

Cailliet, E. *Mysticisme et 'mentalité mystique'. Étude d'un problème posé par les travaux de M. Lévy-Bruhl sur la mentalité primitive*. Paris, 1938.

Cazeneuve, J. *Lévy-Bruhl. Sa vie, son œuvre, avec un exposé de sa philosophie*. Paris, 1963.

Evans-Pritchard, E. *Lévy-Bruhl's Theory of Primitive Mentality*. Oxford, 1934.

Leroy, O. *La raison primitive. Essai de réfutation de la théorie du prélogisme*. Paris, 1927.

Chapter VII

1. *Cournot*

Texts

Recherches sur les principes mathématiques de la théorie des richesses. Paris, 1938. Translated by N. I. Bacon as *Researches into the Mathematical Principles of the Theory of Wealth*, London, 1877.

Exposition de la théorie des chances et des probabilités, Paris, 1843.

Essai sur les fondements de nos connaissances et sur les caractères de la critique philosophique. 2 vols. Paris, 1851. Translated by M. H. Moore as *An Essay on the Foundations of all Knowledge*, New York, 1956.

Traité de l'enchaînement dans les idées fondamentales dans les sciences et dans l'histoire. 2 vols. Paris, 1861. (The 2nd and 3rd editions, 1911 and 1922, are each comprised in one volume.)

Principes de la théorie des richesses. Paris, 1863.

Des institutions d'instruction publique en France. Paris, 1864.

Considérations sur la marche des idées et des événements dans les temps modernes. 2 vols. Paris, 1872. (Reissued Paris, 1934).

Matérialisme, vitalisme, nationalisme: Études sur l'emploi des données de la science en philosophie. Paris, 1875.

Souvenirs: 1760 à 1860, edited by E. P. Bottinelli. Paris, 1913.

There are some other writings in the fields of mathematics and economics which are not mentioned above.

Studies

Bottinelli, E. P. *A. Cournot, métaphysicien de la connaissance.* Paris, 1913.

Caizzi, B. *La filosofia di A. Cournot.* Bari, 1942.

Callot, E. *La philosophie biologique de Cournot.* Paris, 1959.

Darbon, A. *Le concept du hasard dans la philosophie de Cournot.* Paris, 1911.

De la Harpe, J. *De l'ordre et du hasard. Le réalisme critique d'Antoine Augustin Cournot.* Neuchatel, 1936.

Mentré, F. *Cournot et la renaissance du probabilisme au XIXe siècle.* Paris, 1908.

Milhaud, G. *Études sur Cournot.* Paris, 1927.

Ruyer, R. *L'humanité de l'avenir d'après Cournot.* Paris, 1930.

Segond, J. *Cournot et la psychologie vitaliste.* Paris, 1911.

An issue of the *Revue de métaphysique et de morale* (1905, vol. 13, is devoted to articles on Cournot by various authors.

2. Renouvier

Texts

Manuel de philosophie moderne. Paris, 1842.

Manuel de philosophie ancienne. Paris, 1844.

Manuel républicain de l'homme et du citoyen. Paris, 1848.

Essais de critique générale. 4 vols. Paris, 1854–64. (The four volumes treat respectively of logic, national psychology, the principles of Nature, and philosophy of history.)

La science de la morale. 2 vols. Paris, 1869.

Uchronie, l'utopie dans l'histoire. Esquisse historique du développement de la civilisation européenne, tel qu'il n'a pas été, tel qu'il aurait pu être. Paris, 1876.

Esquisse d'une classification systématique des systèmes philosophiques. 2 vols. Paris, 1885–6.

La philosophie analytique de l'histoire,. 4 vols. Paris, 1896–7.

Les dilemmes de la métaphysique pure. Paris, 1901.
Histoire et solution des problèmes métaphysiques. Paris, 1901.
Le personnalisme. Paris, 1903.
Les derniers entretiens, edited by L. Prat. Paris, 1904.
La critique de la doctrine de Kant, edited by L. Prat. Paris, 1906.

Studies

Foucher, L. *La jeunesse de Renouvier et sa première philosophie.* Paris, 1927.
Galli, G. *Prime linee di un idealismo critico e due studi sul Renouvier.* Turin, 1943.
Hamelin, O. *Le système de Renouvier.* Paris, 1927.
Lombardi, V. *Lo sviluppo del pensiero di Charles Renouvier.* Naples, 1932.
Méry, M. *La critique du christianisme chez Renouvier.* 2 vols. Paris, 1953.
Milhaud, G. *La philosophie de Charles Renouvier.* Paris, 1972.
Mouy, P. *L'idée de progrès dans la philosophie de Renouvier.* Paris, 1972.
Prat, L. *Charles Renouvier, philosophe.* Ariège, 1973.
Séailles, G. *La philosophie de Charles Renouvier.* Paris, 1905.
Verneaux, R. *L'idéalisme de Renouvier.* Paris, 1945. *Esquisse d'une théorie de la connaissance. Critique du néocriticisme.* Paris, 1954.

3. *Hamelin*

Texts

Essai sur les éléments principaux de la représentation. Paris, 1907.
Le système de Descartes, edited by L. Robin. Paris, 1910.
Le système d'Aristote, edited by L. Robin. Paris, 1920.
Le système de Renouvier, edited by P. Mary. Paris, 1927.
La théorie de l'intellect d'après Aristote et ses commentateurs, edited by E. Barbotin. Paris, 1953.
Le système du savoir, selections edited by L. Millet. Paris, 1956.

Studies

Beck, L. J. *La méthode synthétique de Hamelin.* Paris, 1935.
Carbonara, C. *L'idealismo di Octave Hamelin.* Naples, 1927.
Deregibus, A. *La metafisica critica di Octave Hamelin.* Turin, 1968.
Sesmat, A. *Dialectique. Hamelin et la philosophie chrétienne.* Paris, 1955.

4. *Brunschvicg*

Texts

Spinoza. Paris, 1894. (Later edition, with additional material, *Spinoza et ses contemporains,* Paris, 1923.)

La modalité du jugement. Paris, 1897. (Third edition, with a French translation of Brunschvicg's 1897 Latin thesis, Paris, 1964.)
L'idéalisme contemporain. Paris, 1905.
Les étapes de la philosophie des mathématiques. Paris, 1912.
Introduction à la vie de l'esprit. Paris, 1920.
L'expérience humaine et la causalité physique. Paris, 1922.
Le progrès de la conscience dans la philosophie occidentale. 2 vols. Paris, 1927.
La raison et la religion. Paris, 1939.
Descartes et Pascal, lecteurs de Montaigne. Neuchâtel, 1942.
Héritage de mots, héritage d'idées. Paris, 1945.
Écrits philosophiques, edited by A. R. Weill-Brunschvicg and C. Lehec. 3 vols. Paris, 1951–8.

Studies

Boriel, R. *Brunschvicg.* Paris, 1964.
Carbonara, C. *Léon Brunschvicg.* Naples, 1931.
Centineo, E. *La filosofia dello spirito di Léon Brunschvicg.* Palermo, 1950.
Cochet, M. A. *Commentaire sur la conversion spirituelle dans la philosophie de Léon Brunschvicg.* Brussels, 1937.
Deschoux, M. *La philosophie de Léon Brunschvicg.* Paris, 1949. (includes a full bibliography.)
Mersaut, J. *La philosophie de Léon Brunschvicg.* Paris, 1938.

Chapter VIII

1. Ravaisson

Texts

Essai sur la métaphysique d'Aristote. 2 vols. Paris, 1837–46.
L'habitude. Paris, 1839. (With an introduction by J. Baruzi, Paris, 1957.)
Rapport sur la philosophie en France au XIXᵉ siècle. Paris, 1867.
Testament philosophique et fragments, edited by C. Devivaise, Paris, 1932.

Studies

Bergson, H. *Notice sur la vie et les œuvres de M. Félix Ravisson-Mollien.* Reprinted in Bergson's *La pensée et le mouvant* (Paris, 1934) from *Comptes-rendus de l'Académie des sciences morales et politiques* (Paris, 1904). Also contained in *Testament philosophique et fragments.*
Dopp, J. *Félix Ravaisson, la formation de sa pensée d'après des documents inédits.* Louvain, 1933.

Valerio, C. *Ravaisson et l'idealismo romantico in Francia*. Naples, 1936.

2. *Lachelier*

Texts

Oeuvres. 2 vols. Paris, 1933.
De nature syllogismi. Paris, 1871.
Du fondement de l'induction. Paris, 1871. (The second edition, 1896, includes *Psychologie et métaphysique*, while the 1901 *Notes sur le pari de Pascal* are added in the fifth edition.)
Études sur le syllogisme. Paris, 1907.
Lachelier, la nature, l'esprit, Dieu, edited by L. Millet. Paris, 1955.
The Philosophy of Jules Lachelier, edited by E. G. Ballard. The Hague, 1960. This work contains translations of *Du fondement de l'induction*, *Psychologie et métaphysique* and *Pari de Pascal*, with an introduction by the editor.

Studies

Agosti, V. *La filosofia di Jules Lachelier*. Turin 1952.
Giglio, P. *L'ideale della libertà nella filosofia di Lachelier*. Rome, 1946.
Jolivet, R. *De Rosmini à Lachelier*. Paris, 1953.
Mauchassat, G. *L'idéalisme de Lachelier*. Paris, 1961.
Millet, L. *Le symbolisme dans la philosophie de Jules Lachelier*. Paris, 1959.
Séailles, G. *La philosophie de Jules Lachelier*. Paris, 1921.
Mention can also be made of G. Devivaise's article *La philosophie religieuse de Jules Lachelier* in the *Revue des sciences philosophiques et théologiques* (139, pp. 435–64).

3. *Boutroux*

Texts

De la contingence des lois de la nature. Paris, 1874. Translated by F. Rothwell as *The Contingency of the Laws of Nature*, London and Chicago, 1916.
De l'idée de loi naturelle dans la science et la philosophie contemporaines. Paris, 1895. Translated by F. Rothwell as *Natural Law in Science and Philosophy*, London, 1914.
Études d'histoire de la philosophie. Paris, 1897. Translated by F. Rothwell as *Historical Studies in Philosophy*, London, 1912.
La science et la religion dans la philosophie contemporaine. Paris, 1908. Translated by J. Nield as *Science and Religion in Contemporary Philosophy*, London, 1909.
La nature et l'esprit. Paris, 1926. (This posthumous publication includes the programme for Boutroux's Gifford Lectures.)

Studies

Baillot, A. *Émile Boutroux et la pensée religieuse.* Paris, 1958.
Crawford, L. S. *The Philosophy of Émile Boutroux.* New York, 1929.
La Fontaine, A. P. *La philosophie d'Émile Boutroux.* Paris, 1921.
Ranzoli, C. *Boutroux. La vita, il pensiero filosofico.* Milan, 1924.
Schyns, M. *La philosophie d'Émile Boutroux.* Paris, 1924.

4. Fouillée

Texts

La philosophie de Platon. Paris, 1869.
La liberté et le déterminisme. Paris, 1872.
La philosophie de Socrate. Paris, 1874.
La science sociale contemporaine. Paris, 1880.
Critique des systèmes de morale contemporains. Paris, 1883.
L'avenir de la métaphysique. Paris, 1889
L'évolutionnisme des idées-forces. Paris, 1890.
Psychologie des idées-forces. 2 vols. Paris, 1893.
Le mouvement idéaliste et la réaction contre la science positive. Paris, 1896.
Les éléments sociologiques de la morale. Paris, 1905.
Morale des idées-forces. Paris, 1908.
La pensée et les nouvelles écoles anti-intellectualistes. Paris, 1911.
Esquisse d'une interprétation du monde. Paris, 1913.

Studies

Ganne de Beaucoudrey, E. *La psychologie et la métaphysique des idées-forces chez Alfred Fouillée.* Paris, 1936.
Guyau, A. *La philosophie et la sociologie d'Alfred Fouillée.* Paris, 1913.
Moretti Costanzi, T. *Il pensiero di Alfred Fouillée.* Naples, 1936.
Pawlicky, A. *Alfred Fouillée's neue Theorie der Ideenkräfte.* Vienna, 1893.

5. Guyau

Texts

La morale d'Épicure et ses rapports avec les doctrines contemporaines. Paris, 1878.
La morale anglaise contemporaine. Paris, 1879.
Les problèmes de l'esthétique contemporaine. Paris, 1884.
Esquisse d'une morale sans obligation ni sanction. Paris, 1885. Translated by G. Kapteyn as *A Sketch of Morality Independent of Obligation or Sanction,* London, 1898.
L'irréligion de l'avenir. Paris, 1887. Translated at *The Non-Religion of the Future,* London, 1897 (reprinted at New York, 1962).

L'art au point de vue sociologique. Paris, 1889.
Éducation et hérédité. Paris, 1889. Translated by W. J. Greenstreet
as *Education and Heredity*, London, 1891.
La genèse de l'idée de temps. Paris, 1890.

Studies

Aslan, G. *La morale selon Guyau.* Paris, 1906.
Fouillée, A. *La morale, l'art et la religion d'après Guyau.* Paris, 1889
(new edition 1901).
Royce, J. 'J. M. Guyau' in *Studies of Good and Evil.* New York,
1925.
Tisbe, A. *L'arte, la morale, la religione nel J.-M. Guyau.* Rome, 1938.

Chapters IX–X

Bergson

Texts

Oeuvres. Édition du centenaire. Paris, 1959. Introduction by H.
Gouhier, with notes by A. Robinet.
Quid Aristoteles de loco senserit. Paris, 1889. (Doctorate thesis,
translated by R. Mossé-Bastide as *L'Idée de lieu chez Aristote*
and published in *Les études Bergsoniennes*, Vol. 2, Paris, 1949.)
Essai sur les données immédiates de la conscience. Paris, 1889. Trans-
lated by F. L. Pogson as *Time and Free Will: an Essay on the
Immediate Data of Consciousness*, London and New York, 1910.
Matière et mémoire. Paris, 1896. Translated by N. M. Paul and W. S
Palmer as *Matter and Memory*, London and New York, 1911.
Le rire. Paris, 1900. Translated by G. C. Brereton and F. Rothwell
as *Laughter, An Essay on the Meaning of the Comic*, New York,
1910.
Introduction à la métaphysique. Paris, 1903 (in the *Revue de la méta-
physique. et de morale*, Vol. 11). Translated by T. E. Hulme as
An Introduction to Metaphysics, London and New York, 1912.
L'évolution créatrice. Paris, 1907. Translated by A. Mitchell as
Creative Evolution, London and New York, 1911.
L'énergie spirituelle. Paris, 1919. Translated by H. Wildon Carr as
Mind-Energy, London and New York, 1935.
Durée et simultanéité. Paris, 1922. (Second edition, with three
appendices, Paris, 1923.)
Les deux sources de la morale et de la religion. Paris, 1932. Translated
by R. A. Audra and C. Brereton, with the assistance of W.
Horsfall-Carter, as *The Two Sources of Morality and Religion*,
London and New York, 1935.

La pensée et le mouvant. Paris, 1934. Translated by M. L. Andison as
    The Creative Mind, New York, 1946.
Écrits et paroles, edited by R. M. Mossé-Bastide. 3 vols. Paris,
    1957–9.

Studies

Adolphe, L. *La philosophie religieuse de Bergson*. Paris, 1946.
          La dialectique des images chez Bergson. Paris, 1951.
Alexander, I. W. *Bergson: Philosopher of Reflection*. London, 1957.
Barthelemy-Madaule, M. *Bergson*. Paris, 1968.
Benda, J. *Le bergsonisme*. Paris, 1912.
          Sur le succès du bergsonisme. Paris, 1914.
Carr, H. W. *The Philosophy of Change*. London and New York, 1912.
Chevalier, A. *Bergson*. Paris, 1926. Translated by L. A. Clare as
    Henri Bergson, New York, 1928. (New French edition, revised
    by Bergson himself, Paris, 1948.)
          Entretiens avec Bergson. Paris, 1959.
Copleston, F. C. *Bergson and Morality*. London, 1955. (Proceedings
    of the British Academy, vol. 41.)
Cresson, A. *Bergson*. Paris, 1955.
Cunningham, G. W. *A Study in the Philosophy of Bergson*. New York,
    1916.
Delhomme, J. *Vie et conscience de la vie: Essai sur Bergson*. Paris,
    1954.
Fabris, M. *La filosofia sociale di Henri Bergson*. Bari, 1966.
Fressin, A. *La perception chez Bergson et chez Merleau-Ponty*. Paris,
    1967.
Giusso, L. *Bergson*. Milan, 1949.
Gouhier, H. *Bergson et le Christ des évangiles*. Paris, 1961.
Guitton, J. *La vocation de Bergson*. Paris, 1960.
Hanna, T. (editor). *The Bergsonian Heritage*. New York and London,
    1962. (Articles by various authors.)
Heidsieck, F. *Henri Bergson et la notion d'espace*. Paris, 1961.
Husson, L. *L'intellectualisme de Bergson*. Paris, 1947.
Jankélévitch, V. *Henri Bergson*. Paris, 1959.
Lacombe, R. E. *La psychologie Bergsonienne*. Paris, 1933.
Le Roy, E. *Une philosophie nouvelle: Henri Bergson*. Paris, 1912.
    Translated by V. Benson as *The New Philosophy of Henri
    Bergson*. New York, 1913.
Lindsay, A. D. *The Philosophy of Henri Bergson*. London, 1911.
McKellan Stewart, J. *A Critical Exposition of Bergson's Philosophy*.
    London, 1911.
Marietti, A. *Les formes du mouvement chez Bergson*. Paris, 1953.
Maritain, J. *La philosophie bergsonienne*. Paris, 1930.
Mathieu, V. *Bergson: 'Il profondo e la sua espressione.'* Turin, 1954.

Metz, A. *Bergson et le bergsonisme*. Paris, 1933.

Mossé-Bastide, R. M. *Bergson, éducateur*. Paris, 1955.

Moore, J. M. *Theories of Religious Experience, with special reference to James, Otto and Bergson*. New York, 1938.

Mousélos, G. *Bergson et les niveaux de réalité*. Paris, 1964.

Olgiate, F. *La filosofia di Enrico Bergson*. Turin, 1914. (second edition, 1922.)

Pflug, G. *Henri Bergson. Quellen und Konsequenzen einer induktiven Metaphysik*. Berlin, 1959.

Rideau, E. *Les rapports de la matière et de l'esprit dans le bergsonisme*. Paris, 1932.

Ruhe, A. *Henri Bergson*. London, 1914.

Russell, B. *The Philosophy of Bergson*. London, 1914.

Scharfstein, B. A. *Roots of Bergson's Philosophy*. New York, 1943.

Segond, J. *L'intuition bergsonienne*. Paris, 1913.

Sertillanges, A. D. *Henri Bergson et le Catholicisme*. Paris, 1941.

Stallknecht, N. P. *Studies in the Philosophy of Creation, with especial reference to Bergson and Whitehead*. Princeton, 1934.

Stephen, K. *The Misuse of Mind. A Study of Bergson's Attack on Intellectualism*. London, 1922.

Sundin, H. *La théorie bergsonienne de la religion*. Paris, 1948.

Thibaudet, A. *Le bergsonisme*. 2 vols. Paris, 1924.

Trotignon, P. *L'idée de vie chez Bergson et la critique de la métaphysique*. Paris, 1968.

There are several collections of articles by various authors. Mention should be made of *Etudes bergsoniennes*, 6 vols., Paris, 1948–61, which also contain some writings of Bergson himself. Another collection is *Pour le centenaire de Bergson*, Paris, 1959. Also *Bergson et nous*, 2 vols., Paris, 1959–60, and *Hommage à Henri Bergson*, Brussels, 1959.

Chapter XI

1. *Ollé-Laprune*

Texts

La philosophie de Malebranche. Paris, 1870.
De la certitude morale. Paris, 1880.
Essai sur la morale d'Aristote. Paris, 1881.
La philosophie et le temps présent. Paris, 1890.
Les sources de la paix intellectuelle. Paris, 1892.
Le Prix de la vie. Paris, 1894.
La vitalité chrétienne. Paris, 1901.
La raison et le rationalisme. Paris, 1906.
Croyance religieuse et croyance intellectuelle. Paris, 1908.

Studies

Acutis, G. *Un grande maestro: Ollé-Laprune.* Turin, 1947.
Blondel, M. *Ollé-Laprune.* Paris, 1925.
Crippa, R. *Il pensiero di Léon Ollé-Laprune.* Brescia, 1947.
Fonsegrive, G. *Léon Ollé-Laprune. L'homme et le penseur.* Paris, 1912.
There is an article on Ollé-Laprune by E. Boutroux in the *Revue philosophique* for 1903. See also G. Goyau's introduction (*Un philosophe chrétien*) to *La vitalité chrétienne.*

2. Blondel

Texts

L'Action. Essai d'une critique de la vie et d'une science de la pratique. Paris, 1893. (Revised edition, Paris, 1950, in *Premiers écrits.*)
De vinculo substantiali et de substantia composita apud Leibnitium. Paris, 1893. (A French version, *Une énigme historique: le 'Vinculum substantiale' d'après Leibniz,* was published at Paris in 1930.)
La pensée. 2 vols. Paris, 1934.
L'être et les êtres. Paris, 1935.
Action. 2 vols. Paris, 1936–7. (Not to be confused with the original *L'Action.*)
La philosophie et l'esprit chrétien. 2 vols. Paris, 1944–6.
Exigences philosophiques du christianisme. Paris, 1950.
Premiers écrits. Paris, 1956.
Carnets intimes. 2 vols. Paris, 1901–66.
Blondel published a considerable number of essays. His *Lettre sur les exigences de la pensée contemporaine en matière d'apologétique* (1896, and included in *Premiers écrits*) and his *Histoire et dogme* (1904, also in *Premiers écrits*) have been translated into English, with an introduction, by A. Dru and I. Trethowan as *Maurice Blondel: The Letter on Apologetics and History and Dogma.* London, 1914.
As for letters, *Lettres philosophiques* appeared at Paris in 1961, while Blondel's correspondence with Auguste Valensin was published in three volumes at Paris, 1957–65, and his *Correspondance philosophique avec Laberthonnière* appeared at Paris in 1962.
Études blondéliennes has been published from time to time, from 1951, by the *Société des amis de Maurice Blondel.*

Studies

Archambault, P. *Vers un réalisme intégral. L'œuvre philosophique de Maurice Blondel.* Paris, 1928.
    Initiation à la philosophie blondélienne, en forme de court traité de métaphysique. Paris, 1946.

(Archambault and Others). *Hommage à Maurice Blondel*. Paris, 1946.

Bouillard, H. *Bergson et le christianisme*. Paris, 1961.

Buonaiuti, E. *Blondel*. Milan, 1926.

Cartier, A. *Existence et vérité. Philosophie blondélienne de l'action et problématique existentielle*. Paris, 1955.

Cramer, T. *Le problème religieux dans la philosophie de l'Action*. Paris, 1912.

Crippa, R. *Il realismo integrale di Maurice Blondel*. Milan, 1954.

Duméry, H. *La philosophie de l'action. Essai sur l'intellectualisme blondélien*. Paris, 1948.

    Raison et religion dans la philosophie de l'action. Paris, 1963.

École, J. *La métaphysique dans la philosophie de Blondel*. Paris and Louvain, 1959.

Giordano, V. *La scienza della practica in Maurice Blondel*. Palermo, 1955.

Hayen, A. *Bibliographie blondélienne (1888–1951)*. Paris and Louvain, 1953.

Henrici, P. *Hegel und Blondel. Eine Untersuchung über Form und Sinn der Dialektik in der 'Phänomenologie des Geistes' und der ersten 'Action'* Pullach (Munich), 1958.

Lacroix, J. *Maurice Blondel. Sa vie, son oeuvre*. Paris, 1963.

La Via, V. *Blondel e la logica dell'azione*. Catania, 1964.

Lefèvre, F. *L'itinéraire philosophique de Maurice Blondel*. Paris, 1928.

McNeill, J. J. *The Blondelian Synthesis. A Study of the Influence of German Philosophical Sources on the Formation of Blondel's Method and Thought*. Leiden, 1966.

Paliard, J. *Maurice Blondel, ou le dépassement chrétien*. Paris, 1950.

Polato, F. *Blondel e il problema della filosofia come scienza*. Bologna, 1965.

Renault, M. *Déterminisme et liberté dans 'l'Action' de Maurice Blondel*. Lyons, 1965.

Romeyer, B. *La philosophie religieuse de Maurice Blondel. Origine, évolution, maturité et son achèvement*. Paris, 1943.

Saint-Jean, R. *Genèse de l'Action, 1882–93*. Paris, 1965.

Sartori, L. *Blondel e il cristianesimo*. Padua, 1953.

Sciacca, M. F. *Dialogo con Maurice Blondel*. Milan, 1962.

Somerville, J. M. *Total Commitment. Blondel's L'Action*. Washington, D.C., 1968.

Tayman's d'Eypermon, F. *Le blondélisme*. Louvain, 1935.

Tresmontant, C. *Introduction à la métaphysique de Maurice Blondel*. Paris, 1963.

Valensin, A. (with Y. de Montcheuil). *Maurice Blondel*. Paris, 1934.

Valori, P. *Maurice Blondel e il problema d'una filosofia cattolica*. Rome, 1950.

3. *Laberthonnière*

Texts

Oeuvres. 2 vols. Paris, 1948–55.
Essais de philosophie religieuse. Paris, 1903.
Le réalisme chrétien et l'idéalisme grec. Paris, 1904.
Positivisme et catholicisme. Paris, 1911.
Le témoignage des martyrs. Paris, 1912.
Sur le chemin du catholicisme. Paris, 1913.

As stated in the text, in 1913 Laberthonnière was prohibited from publishing. One or two works, pretty well written by him, were published by friends. But the bulk of his writings had to await posthumous publication, edited by L. Canet. Among these are:

Études sur Descartes. 2 vols. Paris, 1935.
Études de philosophie cartésienne et premiers écrits philosophiques. Paris, 1938.
Esquisse d'une philosophie personnaliste. Paris, 1942.

A volume of philosophical correspondence between Blondel and Laberthonnière appeared at Paris in 1961, edited by C. Tresmontant.

Studies

Abauzit, F. *La pensée du père Laberthonnière.* Paris, 1934.
Ballarò, R. *La filosofia di Lucien Laberthonnière.* Rome, 1927.
Bonafede, G. *Lucien Laberthonnière, studio critico con pagine scelte.* Palermo, 1958.
Castelli, F. *Laberthonnière.* Milan, 1927.
D'Hendercourt, M. M. *Essai sur la philosophie du père Laberthonnière.* Paris, 1948.
Golinas, J. P. *La restauration du Thomisme sous Léon XIII et les philosophies nouvelles. Études de la pensée de M. Blondel et du père Laberthonnière.* Washington, D.C., 1959.

Chapter XII

1. *Maritain*

Texts

La philosophie bergsonienne. Paris, 1914 (3rd edition 1948). Translated by M. L. and J. G. Andison as *Bergsonian Philosophy and Thomism,* New York, 1955.
Art et scolastique. Paris, 1920 (and subsequent editions). Translated by J. F. Scanlan as *Art and Scholasticism,* with Other Essays, London, 1930.
Éléments de philosophie. I, *Introduction générale à la philosophie.* Paris, 1920. II, *L'ordre des concepts.* Paris, 1923.

Théonas. Paris, 1921. Translated by F. J. Sheed as *Theonas: Conversations of a Sage*, London and New York, 1933.

Introduction à la philosophie. Paris, 1925. Translated as *Introduction to Philosophy*, London, 1930.

Trois réformateurs. Paris, 1925. Translated as *Three Reformers: Luther, Descartes, Rousseau*, London, 1928.

Réflexions sur l'intelligence et sur sa vie propre. Paris, 1924.

La primauté du spirituel. Paris, 1927. Translated by J. F. Scanlan as *The Things That are not Caesar's*, London, 1930.

Le Docteur angélique. Paris, 1929. Translated by J. F. Scanlan as *St Thomas Aquinas, Angel of the Schools*, London, 1942.

Distinguer pour unir, ou les degrés du savoir. Paris, 1932 (4th edition, Paris, 1946). Translated by G. B. Phelan as *The Degrees of Knowledge*, New York and London, 1959.

Le songe de Descartes. Paris, 1932. Translated by M. L. Andison as *The Dream of Descartes*, New York, 1944, and London, 1946.

De la philosophie chrétienne. Paris, 1933. Translated by E. H. Flannery as *An Essay on Christian Philosophy*, New York, 1955.

Du régime temporel et de la liberté. Paris, 1933. Translated by R. O'Sullivan as *Freedom in the Modern World*, London, 1935.

Sept leçons sur l'être et les premiers principes de la raison spéculative. Paris, 1934. Translated as *A Preface to Metaphysics: Seven Lectures on Being*, London and New York, 1939.

Frontières de la poésie et autres essais. Paris, 1935. Translated by J. W. Evans as *Art and Scholasticism and the Frontiers of Poetry*, New York, 1962. (The earlier translation, mentioned above, of *Art et scolastique* also contains a translation of the essay on the frontiers of poetry.)

Science et sagesse. Paris, 1935. Translated by B. Wall as *Science and Wisdom*, London and New York, 1940.

Humanisme intégral. Paris, 1936. Translated by M. R. Adamson as *True Humanism*, London and New York, 1938.

Situation de la poésie. Paris, 1938. Translated by M. Suther as *The Situation of Poetry*, New York, 1955.

Scholasticism and Politics, edited by M. J. Adler. London, 1940.

Les droits de l'homme et la loi naturelle. New York, 1942.

Christianisme et démocratie. New York, 1943.

Redeeming the Time. Various essays translated by H. L. Binsse. London, 1943.

Education at the Crossroads. New Haven, 1943.

De Bergson à Thomas d'Aquin. New York, 1944, and Paris, 1947.

Court traité de l'existence et de l'existant. Paris, 1947. Translated by L. Galantière and G. B. Phelan as *Existence and the Existent*, New York, 1948.

La personne et le bien commun. Paris, 1947. Translated by J. J. Fitzgerald as *The Person and the Common Good*, London, 1948.

Neuf leçons sur les notions premières de la philosophie morale. Paris, 1951.

Man and The State. Chicago, 1951.

The Range of Reason. New York, 1952.

Approches de Dieu. Paris, 1953. Translated by P. O'Reilly as *Approaches to God*, New York, 1954.

Creative Intuition in Art and Poetry. New York, 1953.

On the Philosophy of History. New York, 1957, London, 1959.

La philosophie morale: Vol. 1, Examen historique et critique des grands systèmes. Paris, 1960. Translated by M. Suther and Others as *Moral Philosophy: An Historical and Critical Survey of the Great Systems*, London, 1964.

The Responsibility of the Artist. New York, 1960.

Dieu et la permission du mal. Paris, 1963. Translated by J. W. Evans as *God and the Permission of Evil*, Milwaukee, 1966.

Carnet de Notes. Paris, 1964.

For a fuller bibliography see *The Achievement of Jacques and Raissa Maritain: A Bibliography, 1906–61* by D. and I. Gallagher. New York, 1962.

Studies

Bars, H. *Maritain en notre temps.* Paris, 1959.
              La politique selon Jacques Maritain. Paris, 1961.

Cassata, M. L. *La pedagogia di Jacques Maritain.* Palermo, 1953.

Croteau, J. *Les fondements thomistes du personnalisme de Maritain.* Ottawa, 1955.

Evans, J. W. (editor). *Jacques Maritain: The Man and his Achievement.* New York, 1965.

Fecher, C. A. *The Philosophy of Jacques Maritain.* Westminster, Maryland, 1953.

Forni, G. *La filosofia della storia nel pensiero politico di Jacques Maritain.* Bologna, 1965.

Lundgaard Simonsen, V. *L'esthétique de Jacques Maritain.* Paris, 1956.

Maritain, Raïssa. *Les grandes amitiés.* 2 vols. New York 1941. Translated by J. Kernan as (Vol. 1) *We have been Friends Together* and (Vol. 2) *Adventures in Grace*, New York, 1942 and 1945.

Michener, N. W. *Maritain on the Nature of Man in a Christian Democracy.* Hull (Canada), 1955.

Pavan, A. *La formazione del pensiero di Jacques Maritain.* Padua, 1967.

Phelan, G. B. *Jacques Maritain.* New York, 1937.

Timosaitis, A. *Church and State in Maritain's Thought.* Chicago, 1959.

Volume V of *The Thomist* (1943), devoted to the thought of Maritain, has been published separately as *The Maritain Volume of the Thomist*, New York, 1943.

2. *Gilson*

Texts

Index scolastico-cartésien. Paris, 1913.

La liberté chez Descartes et la théologie. Paris, 1913.

Le Thomisme. Introduction à l'étude de S. Thomas d'Aquin. Strasbourg, 1919. There have been a number of revised and enlarged editions. The English version, *The Christian Philosophy of St Thomas Aquinas* (New York, 1956) is really a work on its own.

La philosophie au moyen-âge. Paris, 1922. A revised and enlarged edition appeared at Paris in 1944.

La philosophie de S. Bonaventure. Paris, 1924. Translated by I. Trethowan as *The Philosophy of St Bonaventure*, London, 1938. Second French edition, Paris, 1943.

Introduction à l'étude de S. Augustin. Paris, 1929. Second edition, Paris, 1943. Translated by L. E. M. Lynch as *The Christian Philosophy of Saint Augustin*, New York, 1960; London, 1961.

Études sur le rôle de la pensée médiévale dans la formation du système cartésien. Paris, 1930.

L'esprit de la philosophie médiévale. 2 vols. Paris, 1932. Second edition, Paris, 1944: in one volume, 1948. Translated by A. H. C. Downes as *The Spirit of Medieval Philosophy*, London, 1950.

La théologie mystique de S. Bernard. Paris, 1934. Translated by A. H. C. Downes as *The Mystical Theology of St Bernard*, London, 1940. Second French edition, Paris, 1947.

Héloïse et Abélard. Paris, 1938 (new edition, 1964). Translated by L. K. Shook as *Heloïse and Abelard*, London, 1953.

Dante et la philosophie. Paris, 1939. Translated by D. Moore as *Dante the Philosopher*, New York, 1949. Second French edition, Paris, 1953.

The Unity of Philosophical Experience. New York, 1937; London, 1955.

Réalisme thomiste et critique de la connaissance. Paris, 1939.

L'être et l'essence. Paris, 1948. English revision, *Being and Some Philosophers*, Toronto, 1949. Second French edition, Paris, 1962.

Les métamorphoses de la Cité de Dieu. Louvain, 1952.

Jean Duns Scot. Introduction à ses positions fondamentales. Paris, 1952.
Christian Philosophy in the Middle Ages. London, 1955.
Peinture et réalité. Paris, 1958. English version, *Painting and Reality*, New York, 1958.
Éléments de philosophie chrétienne. Paris, 1960. English version, *Elements of Christian Philosophy*, New York, 1960.
Le philosophe et la théologie. Paris, 1960. Translated by E. Gilson as *The Philosopher and Theology*, New York, 1962.
Modern Philosophy, Descartes to Kant. New York, 1962. (In collaboration with T. Langan.)
Introduction aux arts de beau. Paris, 1963.
The Spirit of Thomism. New York, 1964.
Recent Philosophy, Hegel to the Present. New York, 1966. (In collaboration with A. Maurer.)

Studies

Edie, C. J. (editor). *Mélanges offerts à Étienne Gilson.* Paris and Toronto, 1959. (This volume includes a bibliography of books and articles by Gilson up to the date of printing.)
Quinn, J. M. *The Thomism of Étienne Gilson: A Critical Study*, Villanova, Pa., 1971.

3. Maréchal

Texts

Le point de départ de la métaphysique. Leçons sur le développement historique et théorique du problème de la connaissance. 5 vols. Vols. 1, 2 and 3, Bruges and Paris, 1922–3; Vol. 4, Brussels, 1947; Vol. 5, Louvain and Paris, 1926.
Études sur la psychologie des mystiques. 2 vols. Vol. 1, Bruges and Paris, 1924; Vol. 2, Brussels, 1937. Translated (in part) by A. Thorold as *Studies in the Psychology of the Mystics*, London, 1927.
Précis d'histoire de la philosophie moderne. Vol. 1, De la Renaissance à Kant. Louvain, 1933. (This is the only volume.)
Mélanges Maréchal. Vol. 1, Oeuvres. Brussels, 1950. (A collection of articles, with a bibliography.)

Studies

Casula, M. *Maréchal e Kant.* Rome, 1955.
Mélanges Maréchal, Vol. 2. Paris, 1950.
Muck, O. *Die transzendentale Methode in der scholastischen Philosophie der Gegenwart.* Innsbruck, 1964. Translated by W. J. Seidensticker as *The Transcendental Method*, New York, 1968.

Chapter XIII

1. *Poincaré*

Texts

Oeuvres de Jules Henri Poincaré. 11 vols. Paris, 1928–56. (Vol. 2 contains a biography by G. Darboux, while Vol. 11 contains centenary lectures on Poincaré.)

La science et l'hypothèse. Paris, 1902. Translated by W. J. Greenstreet as *Science and Hypothesis*, London, 1905; New York, Dover Publications, 1952.

La valeur de la science. Paris, 1905. Translated by G. B. Halsted as *The Value of Science*, London, 1907.

Science et méthode. Paris, 1908. Translated by F. Maitland as *Science and Method*, London, 1914.

Dernières Pensées. Paris, 1912. Translated by J. W. Bolduc as *Mathematics and Science: Last Essays*, New York, 1963.

Studies

Bellivier, A. *Henri Poincaré, ou la vocation souveraine.* Paris, 1956.

Frank, P. *Modern Science and Its Philosophy.* Cambridge, Mass., 1949.

Hadamard, J. S. *The Early Scientific Work of Henri Poincaré.* Houston, Texas, 1922.

   The Later Scientific Work of Henri Poincaré. Houston, Texas, 1933.

(Both of the above are Rice Institute Pamphlets.)

Popper, K. R. *The Logic of Scientific Discovery.* London, 1959.

Revue de métaphysique et de morale. Vol. 211 (1913), pp. 585–718.

2. *Duhem*

Texts

Le potentiel thermodynamique et ses applications à la mécanique chimique et à la théorie des phénomènes électriques. Paris, 1886.

Le mixte et la combination chimique. Essai sur l'évolution d'une idée. Paris, 1902.

Les théories électriques de J. Clerk Maxwell. Étude historique et critique. Paris, 1902.

L'évolution de la mécanique. Paris, 1903.

Les origines de la statique. 2 vols. Paris, 1905–06.

La théorie physique, son objet et sa structure. Paris, 1906. The second edition (1914) has been translated by P. P. Wiener as *The Aim and Structure of Physical Theory*, Princeton, 1954.

Études sur Léonard de Vinci; ceux qu'il a lus et ceux qui l'ont lu. 3 vols. Paris, 1906–13.

Essai sur la notion de théorie physique de Platon à Galilée. Paris, 1908.

Le système du monde. Histoire des doctrines cosmologiques de Platon à Copernic. 8 vols. Paris, 1913–58.

Studies

Duhem, H. P. *Un savant français: P. Duhem.* Paris, 1936.

Frank, P. *Modern Science and its Philosophy.* Cambridge, Mass., 1949.

Humbert, P. *Pierre Duhem.* Paris, 1923.

Mieli, A. *L'opera di Pierre Duhem come storico della scienza.* Grotta-ferrata, 1917.

Picard, E. *La vie et l'œuvre de Pierre Duhem.* Paris, 1922.

Popper, K. R. *The Logic of Scientific Discovery.* London, 1959.

There are several notable articles on Duhem, such as "La philosophie-scientifiquede M. Duhem" by A. Rey in the *Revue de méta-physiquede et morale* (vol. 12, 1904, pp. 699–744) and 'Duhem versus Galilée" in *The British Journal for the Philosophy of Science* (1957, pp. 237–248).

3. *Milhaud*

Texts

Leçons sur l'origine de la science grecque. Paris, 1893.

Essai sur les conditions et les limites de la certitude logique. Paris, 1894.

Le rationnel. Paris, 1898.

Les philosophes-géomètres de la Grèce. Platon et ses prédécesseurs. Paris, 1900.

Le positivisme et le progrès de l'esprit. Étude critique sur Auguste Comte. Paris, 1902.

Études sur la pensée scientifique chez les Grecs et chez les modernes. Paris, 1906.

Nouvelles études sur l'histoire de la pensée scientifique. Paris, 1911.

Descartes, savant. Paris, 1923.

Études sur Carnot. Paris, 1927.

La philosophie de Charles Renouvier. Paris, 1927.

(The last three works were published posthumously.)

Studies

Nadal, A. *Gaston Milhaud* in *Revue d'histoire des sciences* (Vol. 12, 1959, pp. 1–14).

See also the *Bulletin de la société française de philosophie* of 1961 for articles by various authors on *Emile Meyerson and Gaston Milhaud.*

4. *Meyerson*

Texts

Identité et réalité. Paris, 1908. Translated by K. Loewenberg as *Identity and Reality*, London and New York, 1930.
De l'explication dans les sciences. 2 vols. Paris, 1921.
La déduction relativiste. Paris, 1925.
Du cheminement de la pensée. 3 vols. Paris, 1931.
Réel et déterminisme dans la physique quantique. Paris, 1933.
Essais. (posthumous.) Paris, 1936.

Studies

Abbagnano, N. *La filosofia di Émile Meyerson e la logica dell'identità.* Naples, 1929.
Boas, G. *A Critical Analysis of the Philosophy of Émile Meyerson.* Baltimore, 1930.
Kelly, T. R. *Explanation and Reality in the Philosophy of Émile Meyerson.* Princeton, N.J., 1937.
La Lumia, J. *The Ways of Reason: A Critical Study of the Ideas of Émile Meyerson.* London, 1967.
Metz, A. *Meyerson, une nouvelle philosophie de la connaissance.* Paris, 1932; 2nd edition, 1934.
Stumpfer, S. *L'explication scientifique selon Émile Meyerson.* Luxembourg, 1929.
See also the essays by various authors under the general title *Émile Meyerson et Gaston Milhaud* in the *Bulletin de la société française de philosophie* for 1961.

5. *Lalande*

Texts

Lectures sur la philosophie des sciences. Paris ,1893.
L'idée directrice de la dissolution opposée à celle de l'évolution dans la méthode des sciences physiques et morales. Paris, 1898. A revised edition appeared in 1930 with the title *Les illusions évolutionistes.*
Quid de mathematica vel rationali vel naturali senserit Baconus Verulamius. Paris, 1899. (Lalande's Latin thesis.)
Précis raisonné de morale pratique. Paris, 1907.
Vocabulaire technique et critique de la philosophie. 2 vols. Paris, 1926. Publication of this work was begun in 1902 in the *Bulletin de la société française de la philosophie.* The work was published in one volume.
Précis raisonné de morale pratique. Paris, 1907.

Vocabulaire technique et critique de la philosophie. 2 vols. Paris, 1926. (This work, which originally appeared in fascicules of the *Bulletin de la société française de philosophie*, from 1902 onwards, was later published in one volume, as in the 8th edition, 1962.)

Les théories de l'induction et de l'expérimentation. Paris, 1929.

La psychologie des jugements de valeur. Cairo, 1929.

La raison et les normes. Essai sur le principe et sur la logique des jugements de valeur. Paris, 1948.

Studies

Bertoni, I. *Il neo-illuminismo etico di André Lalande.* Milan, 1965.

Lacroix, J. *L'épistémologie de l'identité d'André Lalande.* In *Panorama de la philosophie française contemporaine*, pp. 185–191. Paris, 1966.

Lalande, W. (editor). *André Lalande par lui-même.* Paris, 1967. (With a bibliography.)

6. *Bachelard*

Texts

Essai sur la connaissance approchée. Paris, 1928.

L'intuition de l'instant. Paris, 1932.

Le pluralisme cohérent de la chimie moderne. Paris, 1932.

Les intuitions atomistiques. Paris, 1933.

Le nouvel esprit scientifique. Paris, 1934.

La continuité et la multiplicité temporelles. Paris, 1937.

L'expérience de l'espace dans la physique contemporaine. Paris, 1973.

La formation de l'esprit scientifique. Paris, 1938.

Le psychanalyse du feu. Paris, 1938.

La philosophie du non. Essai d'une philosophie du nouvel esprit scientifique. Paris, 1940.

L'eau et les rêves. Essai sur l'imagination de la matière. Paris, 1942.

L'air et les songes. Paris, 1943.

La terre et les rêveries de la volonté. Paris, 1945.

La terre et les rêveries du repos. Paris, 1945.

Le rationalisme appliqué. Paris, 1949.

L'activité rationaliste de la physique contemporaine. Paris, 1951.

Le matérialisme rationnel. Paris, 1953.

La poétique de l'espace. Paris, 1957.

La poétique de la rêverie. Paris, 1960.

La flamme d'une chandelle. Paris, 1961.

Studies

Hommage à Gaston Bachelard. Paris, 1957.

Dagognet, F. *Gaston Bachelard. Sa vie, son œuvre, avec un exposé de sa philosophie.* Paris, 1965.

Quillet, P. *Gaston Bachelard.* Paris, 1964.

The *Revue internationale de philosophie* (Vol. 19, 1964) contains a bibliography of Bachelard's works and of articles on him.

Chapter XIV

1. *Polin*

Texts

> *La création des valeurs.* Paris, 1944.
> *La compréhension des valeurs.* Paris, 1945.
> *Du laid, du mal, du faux.* Paris, 1948.
> *Philosophie et politique chez Thomas Hobbes.* Paris, 1953.
> *La politique morale de John Locke.* Paris, 1960.
> *Le bonheur considéré comme l'un des beaux-arts.* Paris, 1965.
> *Éthique et politique.* Paris, 1968.

2. *Le Senne*

Texts

> *Introduction à la philosophie.* Paris, 1925 (revised editions, 1939 and 1947.)
> *Le devoir.* Paris, 1930.
> *Le mensonge et le caractère.* Paris, 1930.
> *Obstacle et valeur.* Paris, 1934.
> *Traité de morale générale.* Paris, 1942.
> *Traité de caractérologie.* Paris, 1945.
> *La destinée personnelle.* Paris, 1951.
> *La découverte de Dieu.* Paris, 1955.

Studies

> Berger, G. *Notice sur la vie et les travaux de René Le Senne.* Paris, 1956.
> Centineo, E. *René Le Senne.* Palermo, 1953.
>   *Caratterologia e vita morale. La caratterologia del Le Senne.* Bologna, 1955.
> Gutierrez, M. *Estudio del carácter según Le Senne.* Madrid, 1964.
> Guzzo, A. and Others. *René Le Senne.* Turin, 1951.
> Paumen, J. *Le spiritualisme existentiel de René Le Senne.* Paris, 1949.
> Pirlot, J. *Destinée et valeur. La philosophie de René Le Senne.* Namur, 1953.
> The third numbers of *Études philosophiques* and of the *Giornale di metafisica* for 1955 contain articles on Le Senne by various authors.

3. *Ruyer*

Texts

> *Esquisse d'une philosophie de la structure.* Paris, 1930.

La conscience et le corps. Paris, 1937.
Éléments de psycho-biologie. Paris, 1946.
Le monde de valeurs. Paris, 1948.
Néo-finalisme. Paris, 1952.
Philosophie de la valeur. Paris, 1952.
La cybernétique et l'origine de l'information. Paris, 1954.
La genèse des formes vivantes. Paris, 1958.

4. *Pucelle*

Texts

L'idéalisme en Angleterre. Neuchâtel, 1955.
Le Temps. Paris, 1955.
La source des valeurs. Paris, 1957.
Le règne des fins. Paris, 1959.
La nature et l'esprit dans la philosophie de T. H. Green. I, Méta-physique-Morale. Louvain, 1961.

5. *Lavelle*

Texts

La dialectique du monde sensible. Strasbourg, 1921.
La perception visuelle de la profondeur. Strasbourg, 1921.
La dialectique de l'éternel présent. 3 vols, Paris. Vol. 1, *De l'être,* 1928; Vol. 2, *De l'acte,* 1937; Vol. 3, *Du temps et de l'éternité,* 1945.
La conscience de soi. Paris, 1933.
La présence totale. Paris, 1934.
Le moi et son destin. Paris, 1936.
L'erreur de Narcisse. Paris, 1939. Translated by William Gairdner as *The Dilemma of Narcissus.* London, 1973.
Les puissances du moi. Paris, 1939.
Le mal et la souffrance. Paris, 1940.
La philosophie française entre les deux guerres. Paris, 1942.
La parole et l'écriture.
Introduction à l'ontologie. Paris, 1947.
Traité des valeurs. 2 vols., Paris. Vol. 1, *Théorie générale de la valeur,* 1951; Vol. 2, *Le système de différentes valeurs,* 1955.
L'intimité spirituelle. Paris, 1955.
Conduite à l'égard d'autrui. Paris, 1957.
Manuel de méthodologie dialectique. Paris, 1962.

Studies

Andrés, M. *El problema del assoluto-relativo en la filosofia de Louis Lavelle.* Buenos Aires, 1957.
Beschin, G. *Il tempo e la libertà in Louis Lavelle.* Milan, 1964.

Centineo, E. *Il. problema della persona nella filosofia di Lavelle.* Palermo, 1944.

D'Ainval, C. *Une doctrine de la présence spirituelle. La philosophie de Louis Lavelle.* Louvain and Paris, 1967.

Delfgaauw, B. M. I. *Het spiritualistiche Existentialisme van Louis Lavelle.* Amsterdam, 1947.

École, J. *La métaphysique de l'être dans la philosophie de Louis Lavelle.* Louvain and Paris, 1957.

Grasso, P. G. *Louis Lavelle.* Brescia. 1948.

Nobile, O. M. *La filosofia di Louis Lavelle.* Florence, 1943.

Sargi, B. *La participation à l'être dans la philosophie de Louis Lavelle.* Paris, 1957.

Truc, G. *De Jean-Paul Sartre à Louis Lavelle, ou désagrégation et réintégration.* Paris, 1946.

6. *Mounier*

Texts

Oeuvres, edited by P. Mounier, 4 vols. Paris, 1961–3.

La pensée de Charles Péguy. Paris, 1931. (Written in collaboration with M. Péguy and G. Izard.)

Révolution personnaliste et communautaire. Paris, 1935.

De la propriété capitaliste à la propriété humaine. Paris, 1936.

Manifesto au service du personnalisme. Paris, 1936.

L'affrontement chrétien. Paris, 1944.

Liberté sous conditions. Paris, 1946.

Traité du caractère. Paris, 1946. Translated by C. Rowland as *The Character of Man.* London, 1956.

Introduction aux existentialismes. Paris, 1946. Translated by E. Blow as *Existentalist Philosophies*, London, 1948.

Qu'est-ce que le personnalisme? Paris, 1947. Translated by C. Rowland in *Be Not Afraid*, London, 1951.

La petite peur du XXe siècle. Paris and Neuchâtel, 1948. Translated by C. Rowland in *Be Not Afraid*, London, 1951.

Le personnalisme. Paris, 1949. Translated by C. Mairet as *Personalism*, London, 1952.

Carnets de route. 3 vols. Paris, 1950–3.

Les certitudes difficiles. Paris, 1951.

Communisme, anarchie et personnalisme. Paris, 1966. (Published by the *Bulletin des amis d'Emmanuel Mounier.*)

Studies

Amato, C. *Il personalismo rivoluzionario di E. Mounier.* Messina, 1966.

Campanini, G. *La rivoluzione cristiana. Il pensiero politico di Emmanuel Mounier.* Brescia, 1967.

Carpentreau, J. and L. Rocher. *L'esthétique personnaliste d'Emmanuel Mounier*. Paris, 1966.

Conihl, J. *Emmanuel Mounier: sa vie, son œuvre, avec un exposé de sa philosophie*. Paris, 1966.

Guissard, L. *Mounier*. Paris, 1962.

Moix, C. *La pensée d'Emmanuel Mounier*. Paris, 1960.

Rigobello, A. *Il contributo filosofico di Emmanuel Mounier*. Rome, 1955.

Esprit for December 1950 is devoted to Mounier. See also the Bulletin published by the Association des amis d'Emmanuel Mounier.

Chapter XV

1. *Teilhard de Chardin*

Texts

Oeuvres, edited by C. Cuénot. 10 vols. (to date). Paris, 1955–

Le phénomène humain. Paris, 1955. Translated by B. Wall, with a preface by Sir Julian Huxley, as *The Phenomenon of Man*, London and New York, 1959.

L'apparition de l'homme. Paris, 1956. Translated by J. M. Cohen as *The Appearance of Man*, London, 1965.

Le groupe zoologique humain. *Paris*, 1956. Later editions entitled *La place de l'homme dans la nature*. Translated by R. Hague as *Man's Place in Nature. The Human Zoological Group*, London and New York, 1966.

Le milieu divin. Paris, 1957. Translated by B. Wall and Others as *Le Milieu Divin: An Essay on the Interior Life*, London, 1960.

La vision du passé. Paris, 1957. Translated by J. M. Cohen as *The Vision of the Past*, London, 1966.

L'avenir de l'homme. Paris, 1959. Translated by N. Denny as *The Future of Man*, London, 1964.

Hymne de l'univers. Paris, 1961. Translated by G. Vann as *Hymn of the Universe*, London, 1965.

L'énergie humaine. Paris, 1962. Translated by J. M. Cohen as *Human Energy*, London, 1969.

L'activation de l'énergie. Paris, 1963.

Science et Christ. Paris, 1965. Translated by R. Hague as *Science and Christ*, London, 1968.

Comment je crois. Paris, 1969. The essay with the title translated by R. Hague as *How I believe*, London and New York, 1969. The other essays translated as *Christianity and Evolution*, London, 1971.

Of the various volumes of correspondence which have been published some are available in English translations. For example, *Lettres de voyages* (Paris, 1956) has been translated by R. Hague and Others as *Letters from a Traveller* (London, 1962), while the correspondence with Blondel, with commentary by H. de Lubac (Paris, 1965) has been translated by W. Whitman (New York, 1967).

From 1958 the Fondation Teilhard de Chardin has published at Paris a number of Cahiers containing hitherto unpublished material.

For futher bibliographical material see C. Cuénot's *Teilhard de Chardin* (as mentioned below) and the *Internationale Teilhard-Bibliographie, 1955–1965* edited by L. Polgar (Munich, 1965). For an annual list of publications of more recent date see the *Archivum Historicum Societatis Jesu*, published at Rome.

Studies

Barjon, L. and Leroy, P. *La carrière scientifique de Pierre Teilhard de Chardin*. Monaco, 1964.

Barral, L. *Eléments du bâti scientifique teilhardien*. Monaco, 1964.

Barthélemy-Madaule, M. *Bergson et Teilhard de Chardin*. Paris, 1963. *La personne et le drame humain chez Teilhard de Chardin*. Paris, 1967.

Blanchard, J. P. *Méthode et principes du père Teilhard de Chardin*. Paris, 1961.

Chauchard, P. *Man and Cosmos. Scientific Phenomenology in Teilhard de Chardin*. New York, 1965.

Cognet, L. *Le père Teilhard de Chardin et la pensée contemporaine*. Paris, 1952.

Corbishley, T. *The Spirituality of Teilhard de Chardin*. London, 1971.

Corte, N. *La vie et l'âme de Teilhard de Chardin*. Paris, 1957. Translated by M. Jarrett-Kerr as *Pierre Teilhard de Chardin: his Life and Spirit*, London, 1960.

Crespy, C. *La pensée théologique de Teilhard de Chardin*. Paris, 1961.

Cuénot, C. *Pierre Teilhard de Chardin: les grandes étapes de son évolution*. Paris, 1958 (second edition, 1962). Translated by V. Colimore and edited by R. Hague as *Teilhard de Chardin: A Biographical Study*, Baltimore and London, 1965. (This work includes a complete bibliography of Teilhard's writings.)

Delfgaauw, B. *Teilhard de Chardin*, Baarn, 1961. Translated by H. Hoskins as *Evolution: The Theory of Teilhard de Chardin*, London and New York, 1969.

De Lubac, H. *La pensée religeuse du père Teilhard de Chardin*. Paris, 1962. Translated by R. Hague as *The Religion of Teilhard de Chardin*, London, 1967.

La prière du père Teilhard de Chardin. Paris, 1964. Translated by R. Hague as *The Faith of Teilhard de Chardin*, London, 1965.

Teilhard, missionnaire et apologiste. Toulouse, 1966. Translated by A. Buono as *Teilhard Explained*, New York, 1968.

L'éternel féminin. Paris, 1968. Translated by R. Hague as *The Eternal Feminine*, London, 1971.

De Terra, H. *Mein Weg mit Teilhard de Chardin.* Munich, 1962. Translated by J. Maxwell Brownjohn as *Memories of Teilhard de Chardin*, London and New York, 1969.

D'Ouince, R. *Un prophète en procès: Teilhard de Chardin dans l'église de son temps.* Paris, 1970.

Francoeur, R. T. (editor). *The World of Teilhard.* Baltimore, 1961.

Frenaud, G. and Others. *Gli errori di Teilhard de Chardin.* Turin, 1963.

Grenet, P. B. *Pierre Teilhard de Chardin, ou le philosophe malgré lui.* Paris, 1960.

Haguette, A. *Panthéisme, action, Oméga chez Teilhard de Chardin.* Paris, 1967.

Hanson, A. (editor). *Teilhard Reassessed.* London, 1970.

Monestier, A. *Teilhard ou Marx?* Paris, 1965.

Müller, A. *Das Naturphilosophische Werk Teilhard de Chardins. Seine naturwissenschaftlichen Grundlagen und seine Bedeutung für eine natürliche Offenbarung.* Munich, 1964.

North, R. *Teilhard de Chardin and the Creation of the Soul.* Milwaukee, 1967.

Philippe de la Trinité. *Teilhard et teilhardisme.* Rome, 1962.

Rabut, O. *Dialogue avec Teilhard de Chardin.* Translated as *Dialogue with Teilhard de Chardin.* London and New York, 1961.

Raven, C. E. *Teilhard de Chardin: Scientist and Seer.* London, 1962.

Rideau, E. *La pensée du père Teilhard de Chardin.* Paris, 1965. Translated by R. Hague as *Teilhard de Chardin: A Guide to His Thought*, London, 1967.

Smulders, P. *La vision de Teilhard de Chardin. Essai de réflexion théologique.* Paris, 1964.

Soucy, C. *Pensée logique et pensée politique chez Teilhard de Chardin.* Paris, 1967.

Speaight, R. *Teilhard de Chardin. A Biography.* London, 1967.

Thys, A. *Conscience, réflexion, collectivisation chez Teilhard.* Paris, 1964.

Towers, B. *Teilhard de Chardin.* London, 1966.

Tresmontant, C. *Introduction à la pensée de Teilhard de Chardin.* Paris, 1956.

Vernet, M. *La grande illusion de Teilhard de Chardin.* Paris, 1964.

Vigorelli, G. *Il gesuita proibito. Vita e opere del Padre Teilhard de Chardin*. Milan, 1963.

Wildiers, N. M. *Teilhard de Chardin*. Paris, 1960 (revised edition, 1964). Translated by H. Hoskins as *An Introduction to Teilhard de Chardin*, London and New York, 1968.

Zaehner, R. C. *Evolution in Religion. A Study in Sri Aurobindo and Pierre Teilhard de Chardin*. Oxford, 1971.

Of the books listed above some are concerned with showing the religious orthodoxy of Teilhard de Chardin, while a few (such as those listed under Frenaud, Philippe and Vernet) are frankly polemical. For a much more extensive bibliography of writing on Teilhard see the work by J. E. Jarque: *Bibliographie générale des œuvres et articles sur le père Teilhard de Chardin, parus jusqu'à fin décembre 1969*. Fribourg (Switzerland), 1970.

2. *Marcel*

Texts

Journal métaphysique. Paris, 1927. Translated by B. Wall as *Metaphysical Journal*, London and Chicago, 1952.

Être et avoir. Paris, 1935. Translated by K. Farrer as *Being and Having*, London, 1949.

Du refus à l'invocation. Paris, 1940. Translated by R. Rosthal as *Creative Fidelity*, New York, 1964.

Homo Viator. Paris, 1945. Translated by E. Craufurd, London and Chicago, 1951.

La métaphysique de Royce. Paris, 1945. Translated by V. and G. Ringer as *Royce's Metaphysics*, Chicago, 1956.

Positions et approches concrètes du mystère ontologique. Louvain and Paris, 1949 (with an introduction by M. De Corte). This essay was originally published with the play *Le Monde cassé* (Paris, 1933). An English translation by M. Harari is included in *Philosophy of Existence*, London, 1948; New York, 1949. This collection of essays was republished at New York in 1961 under the title *Philosophy of Existentialism*.

The Mystery of Being. 2 vols. I, *Reflection and Mystery*, translated by G. S. Fraser, London and Chicago, 1950; II, *Faith and Reality*, translated by R. Hague, London and Chicago, 1951. This work consists of Marcel's Gifford Lectures. The French version, *Le mystère de l'être*, was published in two volumes at Paris in 1951.

Les hommes contre l'humain. Paris, 1951. Translated by G. S. Fraser as *Man against Humanity*, London, 1952, and *Man against Mass Society*, Chicago, 1952. (This work consists of articles and lectures, 1945–50.)

Le déclin de la sagesse. Paris, 1954. Translated by M. Harari as *The Decline of Wisdom*, London, 1954; Chicago, 1955.

L'homme problématique. Paris, 1955. Translated by B. Thompson as *Problematic Man*, New York, 1967.

Présence et immortalité. Paris, 1959. Translated by M. A. Machado (and revised by A. J. Koren) as *Presence and Immortality*, Pittsburgh, 1967.

Fragments philosophiques, 1909–14. Louvain, 1962.

The Existential Background of Human Dignity. Cambridge, Mass., 1963. This volume contains Marcel's Williams James Lectures for 1961. The French version, *La dignité humaine et ses assises existentielles*, was published at Paris in 1964.

(Marcel's plays have not been listed above, exept for the incidental reference to *Le monde cassé*.)

Studies

Ariotti, A. M. *L'"homo viator" nel pensiero di Gabriel Marcel*. Turin, 1966.

Bagot, J. P. *Connaissance et amour: Essai sur la philosophie de Gabriel Marcel*. Paris, 1958.

Bernard, M. *La philosophie religieuse de Gabriel Marcel* (with an appendix by Marcel). Paris, 1952.

Cain, *Gabriel Marcel*. London and New York, 1963.

Chaigne, L. *Vies et œuvres d'écrivains. Tome 4*. Paris, 1954.

Chenu, J. *Le théâtre de Gabriel Marcel et sa signification métaphysique*. Paris, 1948.

Davy, M. M. *Un philosophie itinérant; Gabriel Marcel*. Paris, 1959.

De Corte, M. *La philosophie de Gabriel Marcel*. Paris, 1938. (Compare De Corte's introduction to *Positions et approches*, as mentioned above.)

Fessard, G. *Théâtre et mystère*. (Introduction to Marcel's play *La soif*, Paris, 1938.)

Gallagher, K. T. *The Philosophy of Gabriel Marcel* (with a Foreword by Marcel). New York, 1962.

Hoefeld, F. *Der christliche Existenzialismus Gabriel Marcels*. Zürich, 1956.

O'Malley, J. B. *The Fellowship of Being. An Essay on the Concept of Person in the Philosophy of Gabriel Marcel*. The Hague, 1966.

Parainvial, J. *Gabriel Marcel*. Paris, 1966.

Prini, P. *Gabriel Marcel et la méthodologie de l'invérifiable*. Paris, 1953.

Ralston, Z. T. *Gabriel Marcel's Paradoxical Expression of Mystery*. Washington, 1961.

Rebollo Pena, A. *Crítica de la objectividad en el existencialismo de Gabriel Marcel*. Burgos, 1954.

Ricoeur, P. *Gabriel Marcel et Karl Jaspers.* Paris, 1947.

Schaldenbrand, M. A. *Phenomenologies of Freedom. An Essay on the Philosophies of J. P. Sartre and Gabriel Marcel.* Washington, 1960.

Scivoletto, A. *L'esistenzialismo di Marcel.* Bologna, 1951.

Sottiaux, E. *Gabriel Marcel, philosophe et dramaturge.* Louvain, 1956.

Troisfontaines, R. *De l'existence à l'être.* 2 vols. Paris, 1953. (With a preface by Marcel. Contains a bibliography up to 1953.)

Widmer, C. *Gabriel Marcel et le théisme existentiel.* Paris, 1971.

Chapters XVI–XVII

Sartre

Texts

La transcendance de l'égo. Esquisse d'une description phénoménologique. Paris, *Recherches philosophiques*, (6, pp. 85–123), 1936–37. Translated by F. Williams and R. Kirkpatrick as *The Transcendence of the Ego*, New York, 1957.

L'imagination. Étude critique. Paris, 1936. Translated by F. Williams as *Imagination: A Psychological Critique*, Ann Arbor, Mich., 1962.

La Nausée. Paris, 1938. Translated by L. Alexander as *The Diary of Antoine Roquentin*, London, 1949, and as *Nausea*, New York, 1949. Translated by R. Baldick as *Nausea*, Harmondsworth, 1965.

Esquisse d'une théorie des émotions. Paris, 1939. Translated by B. Frechtman as *Outline of a theory of the Emotions*, New York, 1948, and by P. Mairet as *Sketch for a Theory of the Emotions*, London, 1962.

Le Mur. Paris, 1939. Translated by L. Alexander as *Intimacy*, London, 1949; New York, 1952. (Panther Books edition, London, 1960.)

L'imaginaire. Psychologie phénoménologique de l'imagination. Paris, 1940. Translated by B. Frechtman as *The Psychology of the Imagination*, London, 1949.

L'Être et le néant. Essai d'ontologie phénoménologique. Paris, 1943. Translated by H. Barnes as *Being and Nothingness*, New York, 1956; London, 1957.

Les Mouches. Paris, 1943. Translated by S. Gilbert as *The Flies* in *Two Plays*, London, 1946.

Les chemins de la liberté; I. *L'Âge de raison.* Paris, 1945. Translated by E. Sutton as *The Age of Reason*, London, 1947. The second volume, *Le Sursis* (Paris, 1945), was translated by E. Sutton as *The Reprieve*, London, 1947. And the third volume, *La mort dans l'âme* (Paris, 1949), was translated by G. Hopkins as *Iron in the Soul*, London, 1950.

Huis Clos. Paris, 1945. Translated by S. Gilbert as *In Camera* in *Two Plays*, London, 1946.

L'existentialisme est un humanisme. Paris, 1946. Translated by B. Frechtman as *Existentialism*, New York, 1947 and by P. Mairet as *Existentialism and Humanism*, London, 1948.

Réflexions sur la question juive. Paris, 1946 (reissued, Paris, 1954). Translated by E. de Mauny as *Portrait of the Anti-Semite*, London, 1948; and by J. Becker as *Anti-Semite and Jew*, New York, 1948.

Baudelaire. Paris, 1947. Translated by M. Turnell as *Baudelaire*, London, 1949.

Situations: 1, Paris, 1947; 2, Paris, 1948; 3, Paris, 1949; 4–5, Paris, 1964. These are collections of essays. Some of the essays contained in *Situations* 1–3 have been translated by A. Michelson as *Literary and Philosophical Essays*, London, 1955. An essay from *Situations* 2 has been translated by B. Frechtman as *What is Literature?* New York, 1949, and London, 1951.

Entretiens sur la politique (with D. Rousset and G. Rosenthal). Paris, 1949.

Saint Genet: comédien et martyr. (Vol. 1 of the *Oeuvres complètes* of Jean Genet.) Translated by B. Frechtman as *Saint Genet*, New York, 1963.

Critique de la raison dialectique. Tome 1: Théorie des ensembles pratiques. Paris, 1960. The *Question de méthode*, which forms the first part of this volume, has been translated by H. Barnes as *Search for a Method*, New York, 1963.

Les Mots. Paris, 1964. Translated by I. Clephane as *Words. Reminiscences* of Jean-Paul Sartre, London, 1964, and by B. Frechtman as *The Words: The Autobiography of Jean-Paul Sartre*, New York, 1964.

The Philosophy of Jean-Paul Sartre, edited by R. D. Cumming (London, 1968), contains extensive selections in English from Sartre's writings.

Only those plays and stories by Sartre which are mentioned in the text of this volume have been listed above. And no attempt has been made to list the multitudinous essays which Sartre has published, especially in *Les Temps Modernes*. For details of Sartre's life during the period not covered by *Words* see the three volumes of Simone de Beauvoir's memoirs which have been published at London in English translations in 1959, 1960 and 1965 (Deutsch, Weidenfeld and Nicolson).

Studies

Albérès, R. M. *Jean-Paul Sartre.* Paris, 1953.

Ayer, A. J. 'Novelist-Philosophers: J. P. Sartre' in *Horizon*, vol. 12 (1945).

Campbell, R. *Jean-Paul Sartre, ou une Littérature philosophique*, Paris, 1945.

Cera, G. *Sartre tra ideologia e storia*. Brescia, 1972.

Champigny, R. *Stages on Sartre's Way*. Bloomington, Indiana, 1959.

Chiodi, P. *Sartre e il marxismo*. Milan, 1965.

Contat, M. and Rybalka, M. *Les écrits de Sartre*. Paris, 1970.

Cranston, M. *Sartre*. London, 1962.

Dempsey, P. J. R. *The Psychology of Sartre*. Cork and Oxford, 1950.

Desan, W. *The Tragic Finale. An Essay on the Philosophy of Jean-Paul Sartre*. Cambridge, Mass., 1954.

    The Marxism of Jean-Paul Sartre. New York, 1965.

    (Both these books are careful and critical expositions.)

Fell, J. P. III. *Emotion in the Thought of Sartre*. New York and London, 1965.

Greene, N. N. *Jean-Paul Sartre: The Existentialist Ethic*. Ann Arbor, Mich., 1960.

Green, M. *Dreadful Freedom*. London and Chicago, 1948.

Hartman, K. *Grundzüge der Ontologie Sartre's*. Berlin, 1963.

Haug, W. F. *Jean-Paul Sartre und die Konstruktion des Absurden*. Frankfurt, 1967.

    Sartre's Sozialphilosophie. Eine Untersuchung zur 'Critique de la raison dialectique'. Berlin, 1966.

Holz, H. H. *Jean-Paul Sartre: Darstellung und Kritik seiner Philosophie*. Meisenheim, 1951.

Jameson, F. R. Sartre. *The Origins of a Style*. New Haven, 1961.

Jeanson, F. *Le problème morale et la pensée de Sartre*. Paris, 1947. (With a preface by Sartre.)

    Sartre par lui-même. Paris, 1958.

Jolivet, R. *Sartre ou la théologie de l'absurde*. Paris, 1965.

Kuhn, H. *Encounter with Nothingness*. Hinsdale, Illinois, 1949.

Lafarge, R. *La philosophie de Jean-Paul Sartre*. Toulouse, 1967.

Laing, R. D. and Cooper, D. G. *Reason and Violence: A Decade of Sartre's Philosophy, 1950–1960*. London, 1964. (This work includes a treatment of the *Critique de la raison dialectique*. There is a Foreword by Sartre.)

Manno, A. *L'esistenzialismo di Jean-Paul Sartre*. Naples, 1958.

Manser, A. *Sartre: A Philosophic Study*. London, 1966. (Examines Sartre's thought as expressed in his writings as a whole.)

Möller, J. *Absurdes Sein? Eine Auseinandersetzung mit der Ontologie Jean-Paul Sartres*. Stuttgart, 1959.

Murdoch, I. *Sartre: Romantic Rationalist*. Cambridge and New Haven, 1953.

Natanson, M. A. *A Critique of Jean-Paul Sartre's Ontology*. Lincoln, Nebraska, 1951.

Palumbo, G. *La filosofia existenziale di Jean-Paul Sartre.* Palermo, 1953.

Pressault, J. *L'être-pour-autrui dans la philosophie de Jean-Paul Sartre.* Rome, 1969. (Dissertation.)

Schaldenbrand, M. A. *Phenomenologies of Freedom. An Essay on the Philosophies of Jean-Paul Sartre and Gabriel Marcel.* Washington, 1960.

Spiegelberg, H. *The Phenomenological Movement.* 2 vols. The Hague, 1960. (Ch. 10 of Vol. 2 is devoted to Sartre.)

Stern, A. *Sartre: His Philosophy and Psychoanalysis.* New York, 1953.

Streller, J. *Jean-Paul Sartre: To Freedom Condemned.* New York, 1960.

Thody, P. *Jean-Paul Sartre: A Literary and Political Study.* London, 1960.

Troisfontaines, R. *Le choix de Jean-Paul Sartre.* Paris, 1945.

Truc, G. *De Jean-Paul Sartre à Louis Lavelle, ou désagrégation et réintégration.* Paris, 1946.

Varet, G. *L'ontologie de Sartre.* Paris, 1948.

Warnock, M. *The Philosophy of Sartre.* London, 1965.

All general studies of existentialism include a treatment of Sartre. Among such studies by French philosophers we can mention the following:

Jolivet, R. *Les doctrines existentialistes de Kierkegaard à Jean-Paul Sartre.* Paris, 1948.

Mounier, E. *Introduction aux existentialismes.* Paris, 1946.Translated by E. Blow as *Existentialist Philosophies.* London, 1948.

Wahl, J. *Les philosophies de l'existence.* Paris, 1959. Translated by F. M. Lory as *Philosophies of Existence. An Introduction to the Basic Thought of Kierkegaard, Heidegger, Jaspers, Marcel and Sartre,* London, 1969.

Chapter XVIII

1. *Camus*

Texts

Oeuvres Complètes. 6 vols. Paris, 1962.

L'étranger. Paris, 1942. Translated by S. Gilbert as *The Stranger,* New York, 1946; London, 1946, *The Outsider.*

Le Mythe de Sisyphe. Paris, 1942. Translated by J. O'Brien as *The Myth of Sisyphus and Other Essays,* New York and London, 1955.

Lettres à un ami allemand. Paris, 1945. Translated by J. O'Brien in *Resistance, Rebellion and Death,* New York and London, 1961.

La Peste. Paris, 1947. Translated by S. Gilbert as *The Plague*, London, 1948.

Actuelles. 3 vols. Paris, 1950–58. A selection of the articles collected in these volumes have been published in English translation in *Resistance, Rebellion and Death* (see above).

L'homme révolté. Paris, 1951. Translated by A. Bower as *The Rebel*, London, 1953. (Revised version, New York, 1956.)

La chute. Paris, 1956. Translated by J. O'Brien as *The Fall*, London and New York, 1957.

L'exil et le royaume. Paris, 1957. Translated by J. O'Brien as *Exile and the Kingdom*, London and New York, 1957.

Réflexions sur la peine capitale. Paris, 1960. Translated as 'Reflections on the Guillotine' in *Resistance, Rebellion and Death* (see above).

Carnets. Paris, 1962. Translated by P. Thody, as *Notebooks 1935–42* and by J. O'Brien as *Notebooks 1942–51*, New York and London, 1963 and 1965.

R. Ruillot has edited Camus' published writings in two volumes: *Théâtre, récits, nouvelles* (Paris, 1962) and *Essais* (Paris. 1965).

The Collected Fiction of Albert Camus (London, 1960) contains *The Outsider* (*L'Étranger*), *The Plague*, *The Fall*, and *Exile and the Kingdom.*

Caligula and Three Other Plays (New York, 1958) contains translations of Camus' plays translated by S. Gilbert.

Studies

Bonnier, H. *Albert Camus ou la force d'être.* Lyons, 1959.

Brée, G. *Camus.* New Brunswick, 1961.

⎯⎯⎯ (editor). *Camus: A Collection of Critical Essays.* Englewood Cliffs, N.J., 1962.

Brisville, J. C. *Camus.* Paris, 1959.

Cruickshank, J. *Albert Camus and the Literature of Revolt.* London, 1959.

Durand, A. *Le cas Albert Camus.* Paris, 1961.

Gélinas, G. P. *La liberté dans la pensée de Camus.* Fribourg, 1965.

Ginestier, P. *Pour connaître la pensée de Camus.* Paris, 1964.

Hanna, T. *The Thought and Art of Albert Camus.* Chicago, 1958.

Hourdin, G. *Camus le juste.* Paris, 1960.

Lebesque, M. *Camus par lui-même.* Paris, 1963.

Majault, J. *Camus.* Paris, 1965.

Nicolas, A. *Une philosophie de l'existence; Albert Camus.* Paris, 1964.

Onimus, J. *Camus.* Paris, 1965. Translated by E. Parker as *Albert Camus and Christianity*, Dublin and London, 1970.

Papamalamis, D. *Albert Camus et la pensée grecque.* Nancy, 1965.

Passeri Pignoni, V. *Albert Camus, uomo in rivolta.* Bologna, 1965.

Parker, E. *Albert Camus: The Artist in the Arena*. Madison, Wisc., 1965.

Quillot, R. *La mer et les prisons*. Paris, 1956 (revised edition, 1970.)

Rigobello, A. *Albert Camus*. Naples, 1963.

Roeming, R. F. *Camus: A Bibliography*. Madison, Wisc., 1968. (Complete bibliography of writings by and on Camus.)

Sarocchi, J. *Camus*. Paris, 1968.

Schaub, K. *Albert Camus und der Tod*. Zürich, 1968.

Simon, P. H. *Présence de Camus*. Paris, 1962.

Stuby, G. *Recht und Solidarität im Denken von Albert Camus*. Frankfurt, 1965.

Thody, P. *Albert Camus: A Study of His Work*. London, 1957.
　　　　　　　Albert Camus, 1913–1960. London and New York, 1961.

Van-Huy, N. P. *La métaphysique du bonheur chez Albert Camus*. Neuchâtel, 1964.

In 1960 special numbers of *La table ronde* (February), of *La nouvelle revue française* (March) and of *Yale French Studies* (Spring) were devoted to Camus.

2. *Merleau-Ponty*

Texts

La structure du comportement. Paris, 1942 (2nd edition, 1949). Translated by A. L. Fisher as *The Structure of Behaviour*, Boston, 1963; London, 1965.

Phénoménologie de la perception. Paris, 1945. Translated by C. Smith as *Phenomenology of Perception*, London and New York, 1962.

Humanisme et terreur. Paris, 1947. Translated in part by N. Metzel and J. Flodstrom in *The Primacy of Perception and Other Essays*, edited by J. M. Edie, Evanston, Illinois, 1964.

Sens et non-sens. Paris, 1948. Translated by H. L. and P. A. Dreyfus as *Sense and Nonsense*, Evanston, Illinois, 1964.

Les relations avec autrui chez l'enfant. Paris, 1951. Translated by W. Cobb in *The Primacy of Perception* (see above).

Les sciences de l'homme et la phénoménologie: Introduction. Paris, 1951. Translated by J. Wild in *The Primacy of Perception* (see above).

Éloge de la philosophie. Paris, 1953. Translated by J. M. Edie and J. Wild as *In Praise of Philosophy*, Evanston, Illinois, 1963.

Les aventures de la dialectique. Paris, 1955. Translated in part by N. Metzel and J. Flodstrom in *The Primacy of Perception* (see above).

Signes. Paris, 1960. Translated by R. C. McCleary as *Signs*, Evanston, Illinois, 1964.

L'œil et l'esprit. Paris, 1961. Translated by C. Dallery in *The Primacy of Perception* (see above).

Le visible et l'invisible suivi de notes de travail. Paris, 1964. This work, edited by C. Lefort, contains the part of a book which Merleau-Ponty had written before his death, together with notes for the projected parts.

For a list of the writings of Merleau-Ponty, including articles, see A. Rabil's work, listed below.

Studies

Barral, M. E. *Merleau-Ponty: The Role of the Body—Subject in Interpersonal Relations*. Pittsburgh and Louvain, 1965.

Centineo, E. *Una fenomenologia della storia. L'esistenzialismo di Merleau-Ponty*. Palermo, 1959.

Derossi, G. *Maurice Merleau-Ponty*. Turin, 1965.

De Waehlens, A. *Une philosophie de l'ambiguité: l'existentialisme de Maurice Merleau-Ponty*. Louvain, 1951 (2nd edition, 1967).

Fressin, A. *La perception chez Bergson et chez Merleau-Ponty*. Paris, 1969.

Halda, B. *Merleau-Ponty ou la philosophie de l'ambiguité*. Paris, 1966.

Heidsieck, F. *L'ontologie de Merleau-Ponty*. Paris, 1971.

Hyppolite, J. *Sens et existence. La philosophie de Maurice Merleau-Ponty*. Oxford, 1963 (Zaharoff Lecture).

Kaelin, E. *An Existentialist Aesthetic: The Theories of Sartre and Merleau-Ponty*. Madison, Wisc., 1962.

Kwant, R. C. *The Phenomenological Philosophy of Merleau-Ponty*. Pittsburgh and Louvain, 1963.

> *From Phenomenology to Metaphysics. An Inquiry into the Last Period of Merleau-Ponty's Philosophical Life.* Pittsburgh and Louvain, 1966.

Langan, T. *Merleau-Ponty's Critique of Reason*. New Haven and London, 1966.

Maier, W. *Das problem der Leiblichkeit bei Jean-Paul Sartre und Maurice Merleau-Ponty*. Tübingen, 1964.

Rabil, A., Jr. *Merleau-Ponty: Existentialist of the Social World*. New York and London, 1967. (With bibliographies.)

Robinet, A. *Merleau-Ponty: Sa vie, son œuvre, avec un exposé de sa philosophie*. Paris, 1963.

Semerari, G. *Da Schelling a Merleau-Ponty. Studi sulla filosofia contemporanea*. Bologna, 1962.

Speigelberg, H. *The Phenomenological Movement: A Historical Introduction*. 2 vols. The Hague, 1960. (Ch. 11 of Vol. 2 is devoted to Merleau-Ponty.)

Strasser ,S. *Phenomenology and the Human Sciences*. Translated by H. J. Koren, Pittsburgh, 1963.

Tilliette, X. *Philosophes contemporains* (pp. 49–86). Paris, 1962.
    Le corps et le temps dans la 'Phénoménologie de la perception'. Basle, 1964.
Touron del Pie, E. *El hombre, el mundo en la fenomenologia de Merleau-Ponty*. Madrid, 1961.
See also *Maurice Merleau-Ponty*, a volume of articles by various authors, Paris, 1961.

INDEX

(When there are several references, the principal ones are in heavy type. A small *n* indicates that the reference is to a note. There are entries for both Marx and Marxism. Otherwise references to theories, such as Cartesian, are generally included in the entries for the relevant philosophers. The Index does not include references to the Bibliography.)